HISTORY AND METHODS OF SCIENCE

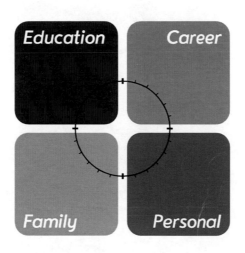

CUSTOM EDITION

The Sciences: An Integrated Approach
Fourth Edition
Trefil - Hazen

To order books or for customer service, please call 1(800)-CALL-WILEY (225-5945).

Printed in the United States of America.

ISBN-10   0-471-68267-5

10 9 8 7 6 5 4 3 2 1

THE SCIENCES

AN INTEGRATED APPROACH

THE SCIENCES

AN INTEGRATED APPROACH

FOURTH EDITION

JAMES TREFIL
ROBERT M. HAZEN

George Mason University

John Wiley & Sons, Inc.

SENIOR ACQUISITIONS EDITOR	Keri L. Witman
SENIOR MARKETING MANAGER	Clay Stone
SENIOR PRODUCTION EDITOR	Norine M. Pigliucci
SENIOR DESIGNER	Kevin Murphy
ILLUSTRATION EDITOR	Anna Melhorn
PHOTO EDITOR	Lisa Gee
PHOTO RESEARCHERS	Teresa Romito, Teri Stratford
PRODUCTION MANAGEMENT SERVICES	Suzanne Ingrao
EDITORIAL ASSISTANT	Maureen Powers
COVER PHOTO	© Michael P. Gadomski/Photo Researchers, Inc.

This book was set in Galliard by Progressive Information Technologies and printed and bound by Von Hoffmann Corp. The cover was printed by Von Hoffmann Corp.

This book is printed on acid free paper. ∞

To order books or for customer service please, call 1(800)-CALL-WILEY (225-5945).

Library of Congress Cataloging in Publication Data
Trefil, James S., 1938–
   The sciences : an integrated approach / James Trefil, Robert M. Hazen.—4th ed.
     p. cm.
   Includes bibliographical references and index.
   ISBN 0-471-21963-0 (acid-free paper)
     1. Science—Study and teaching (Higher)—United States. I. Hazen, Robert M., 1948.—II.
Title.

   Q161.2T74 2004
   500—dc21

                                 2003041129

ISBN 0-471-21963-0 (pbk.)

Printed in the United States of America

10 9 8 7 6

Scientific advances touch all our lives every day. We benefit from new materials in the form of cosmetics, appliances, clothing, and sports equipment. We rely on new sources of energy and more efficient ways to use that energy for transportation, communication, heating, and lighting. We call on science to find new ways to treat disease and allow people to lead longer, healthier lives. And science represents our best hope to solve pressing problems related to the growing global population, limited resources, and sometimes fragile environment.

In spite of the central role that science plays in modern life, most Americans are poorly equipped to deal with scientific principles and methods. A 1996 survey by the National Science Foundation found that fewer than half of all Americans know that the Earth orbits the Sun, or that humans evolved from earlier species of animals. At a time when molecular biology is making breakthrough discoveries almost daily, fewer than a quarter of Americans understand the term "DNA," and only about 10% understand the term "molecule." There can be little doubt that we are faced with a generation of students who complete their education without learning even the most basic concepts about science. They lack the critical knowledge to make informed personal and professional decisions regarding health, safety, resources, and the environment.

Science Education Today

This book attempts to address two problems that pervade the organization and presentation of science at many U.S. colleges and universities. First, many introductory science courses are geared toward science majors. Specialization is vital for these students, who must learn an appropriate vocabulary and develop skills in experimental method and mathematical manipulations to solve problems. Specialization, however, is not well suited for the majority of students—the nonscience majors, for whom experimental technique and mathematical rigor often divorce science from its familiar day-to-day context. Introductory science courses designed for science majors fail to foster scientific understanding among nonscience majors. Ultimately, this needlessly narrow approach to science education alienates most nonmajors, who graduate with the perception that science is difficult, boring, and irrelevant to their everyday interests.

The second problem with most introductory science courses at the college level, even among those science courses specifically designed for nonscientists, is that they rarely integrate physics, astronomy, chemistry, Earth science, and biology. Such departmentally based courses cannot produce graduates who are broadly literate in science. The students who take introductory geology learn nothing about lasers or nuclear reactions, while those who take courses such as "Physics for Poets" remain uninformed about the underlying causes of earthquakes and volcanoes. And neither physics nor geology classes touch on such vital modern fields as genetics, environmental chemistry, space exploration, or materials science. Therefore, students must take courses in at least four departments to gain a basic overview of the sciences.

Perhaps most disturbing, few students—science majors or nonmajors—ever learn how the often arbitrary divisions of specialized knowledge fit into the overall sweep of the sciences. In short, traditional science curricula of most colleges and universities fail to provide the basic science education that is necessary to understand the many scientific and technological issues facing our society.

This situation is slowly changing. Since the preliminary edition of *The Sciences: An Integrated Approach* appeared in 1993, hundreds of colleges and universities have begun the process of instituting new integrated science courses as an option for undergraduates. In the process, we have had the opportunity to interact with hundreds of our colleagues across the country, as well as more than 3000 of our students at George Mason University, and have received invaluable guidance in preparing this extensively revised edition.

The Need for a New Science Education

In the coming decades, the 1996 publication of the *National Science Education Standards* by the National Research Council may be seen as a pivotal event in American science education. The *Standards,* which represents the collective effort and consensus of more than 20,000 scientists, educators, administrators, and parents, offers a dramatically new vision of science education for all Americans.

The *National Science Education Standards* calls for reform in both the content and context of science education. The central goal of science education must be to give every student the ability to place important public issues such as the environment, energy, and medical advances in a scientific context.

A central emphasis throughout the *Standards* is development of student understanding of the scientific process, as opposed to accumulation of scientific facts. Emphasis is placed on the role of experiments in probing nature, and the importance of mathematics in describing its behavior. Rather than developing esoteric vocabulary and specialized knowledge, the *Standards* strives to empower students to read and appreciate popular accounts of major discoveries in physics, astronomy, chemistry, geology, and biology, as well as advances in medicine, information technology, and new materials. Students develop an understanding that a few universal laws describe the behavior of our physical surroundings—laws that operate every day, in every action of our lives.

Achieving this kind of scientific proficiency requires a curriculum quite different from the traditional, departmentally based requirements for majors. Most societal issues concerning science and technology draw on a broad range of knowledge. For example, to understand the debate over nuclear waste disposal, one needs to know how nuclei decay to produce radiation (physics), how radioactive atoms interact with their environment (chemistry), how radioactive elements from waste can enter the biosphere (Earth science), and how the radiation will affect living things (biology). These scientific aspects must be weighed with other societal issues—economics, energy demand, perceptions of risk, and demographics, for example. Other public issues, such as global warming, space research, alternative energy sources, and AIDS prevention, also depend on a spectrum of scientific concepts, as well as other social concerns.

The Goals of This Book

Interdisciplinary courses are not yet widely taught nor have other appropriate textbooks or support materials been available. This text, based on our course "Great Ideas in Science," which has been developed at George Mason University, is an attempt to fill those gaps. Our approach recognizes that science forms a seamless web of knowledge about the universe. Our integrated course encompasses physics, chemistry, astronomy, Earth sciences, and biology, and emphasizes general principles and their application to real-world situations rather than esoteric detail.

Many ways exist to achieve this synthesis, but any general treatment should take advantage of the fact that virtually everything in science is based on a few simple overarching principles. By returning to general science courses for all students, we have the means to achieve our goal—to produce college graduates who appreciate that scientific understanding is one of the crowning achievements of the human mind, that the universe is a place of magnificent order, and that science provides the most powerful means to discover knowledge that can help us understand and shape our world.

The Organization of *The Sciences*

As authors of substantial segments of the *Standards,* we have undertaken this revision of *The Sciences: An Integrated Approach* with the *Standards'* mandate in mind. We have increased the emphasis on the scientific process, reorganized and added text to elucidate the historical significance of key principles, and underscored the integrated nature of scientific knowledge and its application to everyday experience.

The text adopts a distinctive and innovative approach to science education, based on the principle that general science courses are a key to a balanced and effective college-level science education for nonmajors and future elementary and high school teachers, and a broadening experience for science majors. We organize the text around a series of 25 scientific concepts. The most basic principle, the starting point of all science, is the idea that the universe can be studied by observation and experiment (Chapter 1). A surprising number of students—even science majors—have no clear idea how this central concept sets science apart from religion, philosophy, and the arts as a way to understand our place in the cosmos.

Once students understand the nature of science and its practice, they can appreciate some of the basic principles shared by all sciences: Newton's laws governing force and motion (Chapter 2); the laws of thermodynamics that govern energy and entropy (Chapters 3 and 4); the equivalence of electricity and magnetism (Chapters 5 and 6); and the atomic structure of all matter (Chapters 8–11). These concepts apply to everyday life, explaining, for example, the compelling reasons for wearing seat belts, the circulation of the blood, the dynamics of a pot of soup, the regulation of public airwaves, and the rationale for dieting. In one form or another, all of these ideas appear in virtually every elementary science textbook, but often in abstract form. As educators, we must strive to make them part of every student's day-to-day experience. An optional chapter on the theory of relativity (Chapter 7) examines the consequences of a universe in which all observers discern the same laws of nature.

Having established these general principles, we go on to examine specific natural systems such as atoms, the Earth, or living things. The realm of the nucleus (Chapter 12) and subatomic particles (Chapter 13), for example, must follow the basic rules governing all matter and energy.

In sections on astronomy and cosmology (Chapters 14–16), students learn that stars and planets form and move as predicted by Newton's laws, that stars eventually burn up according to the laws of thermodynamics, that nuclear reactions fuel stars by the conversion of mass into energy, and that stars produce light as a consequence of electromagnetism.

Plate tectonics (Chapter 17), and the cycles of rocks, water, and the atmosphere (Chapter 18, substantially revised in this edition), unify the Earth sciences. The laws of thermodynamics, which decree that no feature on the Earth's surface is permanent, can be used to explain geological time, gradualism, and the causes of earthquakes and volcanoes. The fact that matter is composed of atoms tells us that individual atoms in the Earth—for example, in a grain of sand or a student's most recent breath—have been recycling for billions of years.

Living things (Chapters 19–25) are arguably the most complex systems that scientists attempt to understand. We identify seven basic principles that apply to all living systems: interdependent collections of living things (ecosystems) recycle matter while energy flows through them; living things use many strategies to maintain and reproduce life; all living things obey the laws of chemistry and physics; all living things incorporate a few simple molecular building blocks; all living things are made of cells; all living things use the same genetic code; and all living things evolved by natural selection.

The section covering living things has been extensively revised. Chapter 19 includes new information on ecosystems and their importance to the environment. One chapter (20) covers the organization and characteristics of living things. A revised chapter on biotechnology (24) explores several recent advances in our molecular understanding of life to cure diseases and better the human condition. We end the book with a discussion of evolution (25) that emphasizes observational evidence first. To improve the book's integration in this edition, we have also added more biological coverage to the early chapters on basic scientific principles.

The text has been designed so that four chapters—relativity (7), quantum mechanics (9), particle physics (13), and cosmology (15)—may be skipped without loss of continuity.

Special Features

In an effort to aid student learning and underscore the integration of the sciences, we have attempted to relate scientific principles to each student's everyday life. To this end, we have incorporated several distinctive features throughout the book.

Great Ideas Each chapter begins with a statement of a great unifying idea or theme in science, so that students immediately grasp the chief concept of that chapter. These statements are not intended to be recited or memorized, but rather to provide a framework for placing everyday experience in a broad context.

Great Ideas Across the Sciences Our theme of integration is reinforced with a tree diagram that appears at the beginning of every chapter. The diagram ties together some of the examples discussed and shows how the Great Idea has been applied in different branches of science and everyday life.

Science Through the Day Each chapter also begins with a "Science Through the Day" section, in which we tie the chapter's main theme to common experiences, such as eating, driving a car, or suntanning. These 25 vignettes, taken in sequence, tell the story of one student's day, from sunrise, through an excursion to the beach, to day's end. In this way we emphasize that all the great ideas of science are constantly part of our lives.

The Science of Life To help show the interdisciplinary nature of the many concepts we introduce, we have included sections on living things in most chapters. Thus, while chapters emphasizing principles specifically related to life are at the end of the book, biological examples appear throughout.

Science in the Making These historical episodes trace the process of scientific discovery and portray the lives of central figures in science. In these episodes we have tried to illustrate the process of science, examine the interplay of science and society, and reveal the role of serendipity in scientific discovery.

The Ongoing Process of Science Science is a never-ending process of asking questions and seeking answers. In these features we examine some of the most exciting questions currently being addressed by scientists.

Stop and Think! At various points in each chapter we ask students to pause and think about the implications of a scientific discovery or principle.

Technology The application of scientific ideas to commerce, industry, and other modern technological concerns is perhaps the most immediate way in which students encounter science. In most chapters we include examples of these technologies, such as petroleum refining, microwave ovens, and nuclear medicine.

Science News Scientific breakthroughs are happening every day. In many chapters we include summaries of recent articles from the weekly periodical *Science News*. These sections are intended to give students a better understanding of new discoveries that were reported in the popular press.

Mathematical Equations and Worked Examples Unlike the content of many science texts, formulas and mathematical derivations play a subsidiary role in our treatment. We rely much more on real-world experience and everyday vocabulary. We believe, however, that every student should understand the role of mathematics in science. Therefore, we have included a few key equations and appropriate worked examples in many chapters. *Whenever an equation is introduced, it is presented in three steps:* first as an English sentence, then as a word equation, and finally in its traditional symbolic form. In this way, students can focus on the meaning rather than the abstraction of the mathematics. We also include an appendix on English and SI units.

Science by the Numbers We also think that students should understand the importance of simple mathematical calculations in making estimates and determining orders of magnitude. Thus we have incorporated many nontraditional calculations of this kind: for example, how much solid waste is generated in the United States, how long it would take to erode a mountain, and how many people were required to build Stonehenge.

Web Links At the end of each chapter you will find a list of relevant websites. In addition, the www icon appears in the margin throughout the book to highlight links that amplify the text. These links have been well researched and provide additional content on many fascinating topics. You can also visit *The Sciences* home page at *http://www.wiley.com/college/thesciences*, to explore materials developed to support and enhance the study of science.

Thinking More About Each chapter ends with a section that addresses a social or philosophical issue tied to science, such as federal funding of science, nuclear waste disposal, the Human Genome Project, and priorities in medical research,

Key Words Most science texts suffer from too much complex vocabulary, and we have avoided unnecessary jargon. Nevertheless, the scientifically literate student must be familiar with many words and concepts that appear regularly in newspaper articles or other material for general readers. In each chapter a number of these words appear in **boldface** type, and they are listed at the end of the chapters. For example, in Chapter 12 on nuclear physics, key words include proton, neutron, isotope, radioactivity, half-life, radiometric dating, fission, fusion, and nuclear reactor—all terms likely to appear in the newspaper. In the back of the book is a glossary of all the key words.

Many other scientific terms are important, although more specialized; we have highlighted these terms in *italics*. We strongly recommend that students be expected to know the meaning and context of key words but not be expected to memorize these italicized words. We encourage all adopters of this text to provide their own lists of key words and other terms—both ones we have omitted and ones they would eliminate from our list.

Questions We feature four levels of end-of-chapter questions. "Review Questions" test important factual information covered in the text, and are provided to emphasize key points. Many of the Review Questions have been substantially rewritten for this edition. "Discussion Questions" are also based on material in the text, but they examine student comprehension and explore applications and analysis of the scientific concepts. "Problems" are quantitative questions that require students to use mathematical operations, typically those introduced in worked examples or "Science by the Numbers." Finally, "Investigations" require additional research outside the classroom. Each instructor should decide which levels of questions are most appropriate for his or her students. We welcome suggestions for additional questions, which will be added to the next edition of this text.

Illustrations Students come to any science class with years of experience dealing with the physical universe. Everyday life provides an invaluable science laboratory—the physics of sports, the chemistry of cooking, and the biology of being alive. This book has thus been extensively illustrated with familiar color images in an effort to amplify the key ideas and principles. All diagrams and graphs have been designed for maximum clarity and impact.

Supplements

The *Study Guide* contains many elements to help foster student success, including a chapter review, learning objectives, key chapter concepts, and key concept charts. Because science depends on the individuals who made important discoveries, also included is an exposition of key individuals linking scientists with their findings. Since many scientific concepts are linked to math, key formulas and equations are also provided. Self-tests and crossword quizzes allow students to test their knowledge.

The *Instructor Companion Website* located at www.wiley.com/college/trefil contains many resources for both new and experienced teachers. Download the *Instructor's Manual* for teaching suggestions, lecture notes, answers to problems from the textbook, and additional problems. Download and edit the *Test Bank* with multiple choice, short answer, and essay questions. All of the *Line Art* from the textbook will also be available on the website for use in Powerpoint presentations or handouts.

The *Student Companion Website* located at www.wiley.com/college/trefil includes web links related to the topics within the text chapters. There are also self-tests students can use to prepare for exams.

Acknowledgments

The development of this text has benefited immensely from the help and advice of numerous people.

Student Involvement

Students in our "Great Ideas in Science" course at George Mason University have played a central role in designing this text. Approximately 3000 students, the majority of whom were nonscience majors, have enrolled in the course over the past 15 years. They represent a diverse cross section of American students: more than half were women, and many minority, foreign-born, and adult learners were enrolled. Their candid assessments of course content and objectives, as well as their constructive suggestions for improvements, have helped shape our text.

Faculty Input

We are also grateful to members of the Core Science Course Committee at George Mason University, including Richard Diecchio (Earth Systems Science), Don Kelso and Harold Morowitz (Biology), Minos Kafatos and Jean Toth-Allen (Physics), and Suzanne Slayden (Chemistry), who helped design many aspects of this treatment.

We thank the many teachers across the country who are developing integrated science courses. Their letters to us and responses to our publisher's survey inspired us to write this text. In particular we would like to thank Michael Sable of The Massachusetts College for the Liberal Arts, whose long and thoughtful letter after the first edition was a tremendous help.

We especially thank the professors who used and class-tested the preliminary edition, sharing with us the responses of their students and their own analyses. Their classroom experience continues to help us shape the book.

Lauretta Bushar
Beaver College
Tim Champion
Johnson C. Smith University
Ben Chastain
Samford University
Marvin Goldberg
Syracuse University
James Grant and Michael Held
St. Peter's College
Jim Holler
University of Kentucky
Patricia Hughey
Lansing Community College

Joseph Ledbetter and Rick Saparano
Contra Costa College
Leigh Mazany
Dalhousie University
Donald Miller
University of Michigan at Dearborn
Lynn Narasimhan
DePaul University
Ervin Poduska
Kirkwood Community College
Gail Steehler
Roanoke College
Jim Yoder
Hesston College

We gratefully acknowledge the significant contributions of many reviewers who commented on early drafts of the first edition. Their insights and teaching experience have been invaluable to us.

Debra J. Barnes
Contra Costa College
Doug Bingham
West Texas State University
Larry Blair

Berea College
Virginia R. Bryan
Southern Illinois University
Joe C. Burnell
University of Indianapolis

W. Barkley Butler
Indiana University of Pennsylvania
Ben B. Chastain
Samford University
LuAnne Clark
Lansing Community College
John Cobley
University of San Francisco
Stan Cohn
DePaul University
Marjorie Collier
St. Peter's College
Rod Cranson
Lansing Community College
Phillip D. Creighton
Salisbury State University
Whitman Cross II
Southern Museum of Flight
John Cruzan
Geneva College
E. Alan Dean
University of Texas at El Paso
J.-Cl. De Bremaeker
Rice University
Normand A. Dion
Franklin Pierce College
William Faissler
Northeastern University
Paul Fishbane
University of Virginia
John Freeman
Rice University
William Fyfe
University of Western Ontario
Biswa Ghosh
Hudson County College
John Graham
Carnegie Institution of Washington
J. Howard Hargis
Auburn University
Dennis Hibbert
North Seattle Community College
David Hickey
Lansing Community College
Patricia M. Hughey
Lansing Community College
Gerry Karp, formerly of

University of Florida, Gainesville
Larry Kodosky
Oakland Community College
Roger Koeppe
Oklahoma State University
Diona Koerner
Marymount College
Hallie M. Krider
University of Connecticut
Charles J. Kunert
Concordia College
Kathleen H. Lavoie
University of Michigan—Flint
Joseph E. Ledbetter
Contra Costa College
Robert W. Lind
University of Wisconsin—Plattesville
Sam LittlePage
University of Findlay
Becky Lovato
Lansing Community College
Bruce MacLaren
Eastern Kentucky University
Donald Miller
University of Michigan at Dearborn
Harold Morowitz
George Mason University
Bjorn Mysen
Geophysical Laboratory
Michael J. Neilson
University of Alabama
Joseph Ruchlin
Lehman College of CUNY
Selwyn Sacks
Carnegie Institution of Washington
Frederick D. Shannon
Houghton College
Howard J. Stein
Grand Valley State University
Herbert H. Stewart
Florida Atlantic University
John S. Thompson
Texas A&M University at Kingsville
Barbara E. Warkentine
Lehman College of CUNY
Jim Yoder
Hesston College

The second edition has benefitted from detailed chapter reviews by experts in biology and chemistry: Anthony Gaudin of Ivy Tech State College, and Anthony Jacob of the University of Wisconsin, Madison.

We are also grateful to the professors who looked at the first edition and early drafts of the second edition. Their invaluable suggestions and comments helped us immensely in the preparation of this revision.

C. Brannon Andersen
Furman University
Maura Flannery
St. John's University
Ben Golden
Kennesaw State University
Robert Kearney
University of Idaho
William Keller
St. Petersburg Junior College
Albert Kudo
University of New Mexico

Joseph Ledbetter
Contra Costa College
Gary Lewis
Kennesaw State University
Scott Mohr
Boston University
Richard Petriello
St. Peter's College
Francis Tam
Frostburg State University
Andrew Wallace
Angelo State University

The third edition also benefitted greatly from professors who reviewed the second edition and drafts of the third edition manuscript. We are especially grateful to those who have been involved through successive revisions of the text.

Sheila K. Bennett
University of Maine at Augusta
Tarun Biswas
State University of New York at New Paltz
Richard Deslippe
Texas Tech University
Robert T. Downs
University of Arizona
Raymond L. Ethington
University of Missouri at Columbia
Michael F. Farona
University of North Carolina at Greensboro
Anthony J. Gaudin
Ivy Tech State College
Annette Halpern
California State University at Bakersfield
Louis Irwin
University of Texas at El Paso
Mary H. Korte
Concordia University Wisconsin
Jeffrey A. Lee
Texas Tech University

Robley J. Light
Florida State University
Jefferey J. Miller
Metropolitan State College of Denver
David E. Marx
University of Scranton
Charlotte Ovechka
University of St. Thomas
Reno Parker
Montana State University
Barry Perlmutter
New Jersey City University
Joaquin Ruiz
University of Arizona
Timothy D. Swindle
University of Arizona
John Truedson
Bemidji State University
David Wong
University of California at San Diego
David P. Wright
St. Edward's University

The third edition and early drafts of the fourth edition also benefitted from the reviews of the following people.

Felicia Barbieri
Gwynedd-Mercy College
Susan Bornstein-Forst
Marian College
Linda Brown
Gainesville College
George Cassiday
University of Utah
Kailash Chandra
Savannah State University
Randy Criss
University of Saint Leo
David Dimattio
St. Bonaventure University

Robert Downs
University of Arizona
David Emigh
Quinebaug Valley Community College
Robert Gannon
Dowling College
Benjamin Grinstein
University of California—San Diego
David Hedgepeth
Valdosta State University
Patricia Kenyon
City College of New York
Lynn Maelia
Mount Saint Mary College

Kingshuk Majumdar
Berea College
David Marx
University of Scranton
Kevin Morris
Carthage College
Charlotte Ovechka
University of St. Thomas
Patrick Pfaffle
Carthage College
Scott Pinkus
New Jersey City University

Harry Pylypiw
Quinnipiac University
Paul Simony
Jacksonville University
Neal Sumerlin
Lynchburg College
Timothy Swindle
University of Arizona
Steven Warren
Andrews University

Publisher Support

Finally, as in the previous editions, we gratefully acknowledge the dedicated people at John Wiley, who originally proposed this textbook and have helped us in developing every aspect of its planning and production. Editor Keri Witman managed the project, while Maureen Powers served with skill and professionalism as editorial assistant. David Chelton also provided invaluable editorial assistance. Geraldine Osnato oversaw the production of supplements to the text with care and dedication.

We also thank the production team of the fourth edition. The project was ably managed by Norine Pigliucci and meticulously produced by Suzanne Ingrao of Ingrao Associates, who dealt with the countless technical details associated with an integrated science book. Kevin Murphy designed the handsome text, and Lisa Gee researched the numerous new photos and illustrations for the fourth edition. Clay Stone supervised the effective marketing of *The Sciences*.

To all the staff at John Wiley, we owe a great debt for their enthusiastic support, constant encouragement, and sincere dedication to science education reform.

Contents

1
Science: A Way of Knowing:
How do you know what you know?
Great Idea: *Science is a way of asking and answering questions about the physical universe.*

Science Through the Day: Sunrise • 2

The Role of Science 2

Making Choices 2

Why Study Science? 3

The Scientific Method 4
Observation 4 / Identifying Patterns and Regularities 5 / Mathematics, the Language of Science 6 / Hypothesis and Theory 8 / Prediction and Testing 8 / The Scientific Method in Operation 9

THE ONGOING PROCESS OF SCIENCE • 11
Biodiversity 11

SCIENCE IN THE MAKING • 12
Dimitri Mendeleev and the Periodic Table 12

THE SCIENCE OF LIFE • 13
William Harvey and the Blood's Circulation 13

Other Ways of Knowing 14
Different Kinds of Questions 14 / Pseudoscience 15

SCIENCE BY THE NUMBERS • 17
Astrology 17

The Organization of Science 18 / The Divisions of Science 18 / The Branches of Science 20 / The Web of Knowledge 20 / Basic Research, Applied Research, and Technology 21

TECHNOLOGY • 22
SETI@Home 22

Funding for Science 23/ Communication Among Scientists 24

Thinking More About Research • 25
Stem Cells 25

2
The Ordered Universe:
Why do planets appear to wander slowly across the sky?
Great Idea: *Newton's laws of motion and gravity predict the behavior of objects on Earth and in space.*

Science Through the Day: Cause and Effect • 30

The Night Sky 30
Stonehenge 31

SCIENCE IN THE MAKING • 32
The Discovery of the Spread of Disease 32

SCIENCE BY THE NUMBERS • 33
Ancient Astronauts 33

The Birth of Modern Astronomy 34
The Historical Background: Ptolemy and Copernicus 35 / Observations: Tycho Brahe and Johannes Kepler 35

The Birth of Mechanics 37
Galileo Galilei 38

SCIENCE IN THE MAKING • 38
The Heresy Trial of Galileo 38

Speed, Velocity, and Acceleration 38 / The Father of Experimental Science 40

THE SCIENCE OF LIFE • 43
Experiencing Extreme Acceleration 43

Isaac Newton and the Universal Laws of Motion 45
The First Law 45 / The Second Law 46 / The Third Law 47 / Newton's Laws at Work 48

Momentum 49
Conservation of Linear Momentum 50 / Angular Momentum 50

Technology • 52
Inertial Guidance System 52

The Universal Force of Gravity 52
The Gravitational Constant, G 53 / Weight and Gravity 54 / Big G and Little g 54

Thinking More About Order • 57
Predictability 57

3
Energy:
Why must animals eat to stay alive?
Great Idea: *The many different forms of energy are interchangeable, and the total amount of energy in an isolated system is conserved.*

Science Through the Day: Morning Routine • 62

The Great Chain of Energy 62

Scientifically Speaking 62
Work 63 / Energy 65 / Power 65

SCIENCE IN THE MAKING • 67
James Watt and the Horsepower 67

Forms of Energy 67
Kinetic Energy 68 / Potential Energy 69 / Heat, or Thermal Energy 70

SCIENCE IN THE MAKING • 70
Discovering the Nature of Heat 70

Wave Energy 72 / Mass as Energy 73

The Interchangeability of Energy 74

THE ONGOING PROCESS OF SCIENCE • 74
New Sources of Energy 74

THE SCIENCE OF LIFE • 76
Energy for Life and Trophic Levels 76

The First Law of Thermodynamics: Energy Is Conserved 78

SCIENCE BY THE NUMBERS • 79
Diet and Calories 79

SCIENCE IN THE MAKING • 80
Lord Kelvin and the Age of the Earth 80

TECHNOLOGY • 81
The Economics of Alternative Energy 81

Thinking More About Energy • 81
Fossil Fuels 81

4
Heat and the Second Law of Thermodynamics:
How do humans control their body temperature?

Great Idea: *Heat is a form of energy that flows from warmer to cooler objects.*

Science Through the Day: A Hot Breakfast • 86

Nature's Direction 86

Coming to Terms with Heat 88
Heat and Temperature 88 / Temperature Conversions 89

TECHNOLOGY • 90
Thermometers 90

Specific Heat Capacity 91

Heat Transfer 91

TECHNOLOGY • 95
Home Insulation 95

THE SCIENCE OF LIFE • 95
Animal Insulation: Fur and Feathers 95

THE SCIENCE OF LIFE • 97
Temperature Regulation 97

The Second Law of Thermodynamics 98
1. Heat Will Not Flow Spontaneously from a Cold to a Hot Body 99 / 2. You Cannot Construct an Engine That Does Nothing but Convert Heat to Useful Work 99

SCIENCE BY THE NUMBERS • 101
Efficiency 101

3. Every Isolated System Becomes More Disordered with Time 102

SCIENCE IN THE MAKING • 105
The Heat Death of the Universe 105

Consequences of the Second Law 106
The Arrow of Time 106 / Built-in Limitations of the Universe 106

THE SCIENCE OF LIFE • 107
Does Evolution Violate the Second Law? 107

Thinking More About Entropy • 107
Aging 107

5
Electricity and Magnetism:
What is lightning?

Great Idea: *Electricity and magnetism are two different aspects of one force—the electromagnetic force.*

Science Through the Day: The Hidden Force • 111

Nature's Other Forces 111

Static Electricity 111

SCIENCE IN THE MAKING • 113
Benjamin Franklin and Electrical Charge 113

The Movement of Electrons 114 / Coulomb's Law 115

SCIENCE BY THE NUMBERS • 116
Two Forces Compared 116

The Electric Field 117

Magnetism 117

THE SCIENCE OF LIFE • 119
Magnetic Navigation 119

Pairs of Poles 120

Batteries and Electric Circuits 120

THE SCIENCE OF LIFE • 120
Luigi Galvani and Life's Electric Force 120

Batteries and Electrical Current 122

TECHNOLOGY • 123
Batteries and Electric Cars 123

Electric Circuits 124 / Ohm's Law 125

THE SCIENCE OF LIFE • 127
The Propagation of Nerve Signals 127

Two Kinds of Electric Circuits 129

Connections Between Electricity and Magnetism 129

Magnetic Effects from Electricity 130
The Electromagnet 130

TECHNOLOGY • 131
The Electric Motor 131

Why Magnetic Poles Don't Exist 132

THE SCIENCE OF LIFE • 132
Magnetic Resonance 132

Electrical Effects from Magnetism 133

TECHNOLOGY • 135
AC versus DC 135

SCIENCE IN THE MAKING • 135
Michael Faraday 135

Maxwell's Equations 135

Thinking More About Electromagnetism • 136
  Basic Research 136

6

Waves and Electromagnetic Radiation:
Why do we see in color?

Great Idea: *Whenever an electrically charged object is accelerated, it produces electromagnetic radiation—waves of energy that travel at the speed of light.*

Science Through the Day: The Radio • 141

The Nature of Waves 141
  Energy Transfer by Waves 141 / The Properties of Waves 142 / The Relationship Among Wavelength, Frequency, and Velocity 143 / The Two Kinds of Waves: Transverse and Longitudinal 144

SCIENCE BY THE NUMBERS • 145
  The Sound of Music 145

THE SCIENCE OF LIFE • 147
  Use of Sound by Animals 147

  Interference 148

The Electromagnetic Wave 149
  The Anatomy of the Electromagnetic Wave 150

SCIENCE IN THE MAKING • 150
  The Ether 150

  Light 151 / The Energy of Electromagnetic Waves 151 / The Doppler Effect 152 / Transmission, Absorption, and Scattering 154

The Electromagnetic Spectrum 157
  Radio Waves 158

TECHNOLOGY • 159
  AM and FM Radio Transmission 159

  Microwaves 160

TECHNOLOGY • 161
  Microwave Ovens 161

  Infrared Radiation 162 / Visible Light 163

THE SCIENCE OF LIFE • 163
  The Eye 163

  Ultraviolet Radiation 163 / X-rays 164

THE ONGOING PROCESS OF SCIENCE • 165
  Intense X-ray Sources 165

  Gamma Rays 166

Thinking More About Electromagnetic Radiation • 167
  Is ELF Radiation Dangerous? 167

7

Albert Einstein and the Theory of Relativity:
Can a human ever travel faster than the speed of light, at "warp speed"?

Great Idea: *All observers, no matter what their frame of reference, see the same laws of nature.*

Science Through the Day:
  Waiting at the Stoplight • 172

Frames of Reference 172
  Descriptions in Different Reference Frames 173 / The Principle of Relativity 173

Relativity and the Speed of Light 175

SCIENCE IN THE MAKING • 175
  Einstein and the Streetcar 175

Special Relativity 176
  Time Dilation 176 / The Size of Time Dilation 177

SCIENCE BY THE NUMBERS • 180
  How Important Is Relativity? 180

THE SCIENCE OF LIFE • 181
  Space Travel and Aging 181

  Distance and Relativity 181 / So What About the Train and the Flashlight? 183 / Mass and Relativity 183 / Mass and Energy 184

General Relativity 185
  The Nature of Forces 185 / Predictions of General Relativity 187 / Who Can Understand Relativity? 188

Thinking More About Relativity • 189
  Was Newton Wrong? 189

8

The Atom:
Why?

Great Idea: *All of the matter around us is made of atoms—the chemical building blocks of our world.*

Science Through the Day: A Deep Breath • 193

The Smallest Pieces 193
  The Greek Atom 193 / Elements 193 / Are Atoms Real? 195 / Discovering Chemical Elements 196

The Structure of the Atom 198
  The Atomic Nucleus 198 / Why the Rutherford Atom Couldn't Work 199

When Matter Meets Light 200
  The Bohr Atom 200 / Photons: Particles of Light 202 / An Intuitive Leap 204

Spectroscopy 205

THE SCIENCE OF LIFE • 207
  Spectra of Life's Chemical Reactions 207

SCIENCE IN THE MAKING • 207
  The Story of Helium 207

TECHNOLOGY • 207
  The Laser 207

The Periodic Table of the Elements 210
  Periodic Chemical Properties 210 / Why the Periodic Table Works: Electron Shells 211

Science News • 213
  Morphing Atoms 213

Thinking More About Atoms • 213
  What Do Atoms "Look Like"? 213

9
Quantum Mechanics:
How can the electron behave like both a particle and a wave?
Great Idea: *At the subatomic scale everything is quantized. Any measurement at that scale significantly alters the object being measured.*

Science Through the Day: **Digital Pictures** • 217

The World of the Very Small 217
Measurement and Observation in the Quantum World 218 / The Heisenberg Uncertainty Principle 219

SCIENCE BY THE NUMBERS • 220
Uncertainty in the Newtonian World 220

Probabilities 221

Wave-Particle Duality 222
The Double-Slit Test 223

TECHNOLOGY • 225
The Photoelectric Effect 225

THE SCIENCE OF LIFE • 226
The CAT Scan 226

Wave-Particle Duality and the Bohr Atom 226
Quantum Weirdness 228

Science News • 228
Quantum Mechanics Illuminates the Living Cell 228

SCIENCE IN THE MAKING • 228
A Famous Interchange 228

Thinking More About Quantum Mechanics • 229
Uncertainty and Human Beings 229

10
Atoms in Combination: The Chemical Bond:
How does blood clot?
Great Idea: *Atoms bind together in chemical reactions by the rearrangement of electrons.*

Science Through the Day: **Throwing Things Away** • 233

Our Material World 233

Electron Shells and the Chemical Bond 233

Types of Chemical Bonds 235
Ionic Bonds 235 / Metallic Bonds 236 / Covalent Bonds 238 / Polarization and Hydrogen Bonds 240 / Van der Waals Forces 241

States of Matter 242
Gases 243 / Plasma 243 / Liquids 244 / Solids 244

TECHNOLOGY • 247
Liquid Crystals and Your Hand Calculator 247

SCIENCE IN THE MAKING • 248
The Discovery of Nylon 248

Changes of State 248

Chemical Reactions and the Formation of Chemical Bonds 249

Chemical Reactions and Energy: Rolling Down the Chemical Hill 250 / Common Chemical Reactions 251

THE SCIENCE OF LIFE • 255
Antacids 255

Polymerization and Depolymerization 255

Building Molecules: The Hydrocarbons 257

TECHNOLOGY • 258
Refining Petroleum 258

THE SCIENCE OF LIFE • 259
The Clotting of Blood 259

Thinking More About Atoms in Combination • 260
Life Cycle Costs 260

11
Properties of Materials:
How have computers gotten so much faster?
Great Idea: *A material's properties result from its constituent atoms and the arrangements of chemical bonds that hold those atoms together.*

Science Through the Day: **Hauling Gear** • 264

Materials and the Modern World 264

The Strengths of Materials 266
Different Kinds of Strength 266 / Composite Materials 268

Electrical Properties of Materials 269
Conductors 269 / Insulators 270 / Semiconductors 270 / Superconductors 271

THE ONGOING PROCESS OF SCIENCE • 272
Searching for New Superconductors 272

Magnetic Properties of Materials 273

Microchips and the Information Revolution 274
Doped Semiconductors 275 / Diodes 275

TECHNOLOGY • 277
Photovoltaic Cells and Solar Energy 277

The Transistor 278 / Microchips 280 / Information 281

SCIENCE BY THE NUMBERS • 282
Is a Picture Really Worth a Thousand Words? 282

Computers 282

THE SCIENCE OF LIFE • 284
The Computer and the Brain 284

Science News • 284
Planet's Slim-Fast Plan 284

Thinking More About Properties of Materials • 285
Thinking Machines 285

12
The Nucleus of the Atom:
How do scientists determine the age of the oldest human fossils?
Great Idea: *Nuclear energy depends on the conversion of mass into energy.*

Science Through the Day:
Radioactivity Around Us • 289

Empty Space, Explosive Energy 289

SCIENCE BY THE NUMBERS • 290
Mass and Energy 290

The Organization of the Nucleus 291
Element Names and Atomic Numbers 292 / Isotopes and the Mass Number 292 / The Strong Force 294

Radioactivity 294
What's Radioactive? 295

SCIENCE IN THE MAKING • 295
Becquerel and Curie 295

The Kinds of Radioactive Decay 295 / Moving Down the Chart of the Isotopes 298 / Radiation and Health 299

THE SCIENCE OF LIFE • 300
Robert Hazen's Broken Wrist 300

Half-Life 301 / Radiometric Dating 302 / Decay Chains 303 / Indoor Radon 305

SCIENCE BY THE NUMBERS • 303
Dating a Frozen Mammoth 303

Energy from the Nucleus 305
Nuclear Fission 305 / Fusion 307

TECHNOLOGY • 309
Nuclear Weapons 309

SCIENCE IN THE MAKING • 310
Superheavy Elements 310

Science News • 310
Muon Manna 310

Thinking More About The Nucleus • 311
Nuclear Waste 311

13
The Ultimate Structure of Matter:
How can antimatter be used
to probe the human brain?
Great Idea: *All matter is made of quarks and leptons, which are the fundamental building blocks of the universe.*

Science Through the Day: **Looking at Sand** • 315

Of What Is the Universe Made? 315
The Library 315 / Reductionism 316 / The Building Blocks of Matter 317

Discovering Elementary Particles 318
Cosmic Rays 318

TECHNOLOGY • 319
Detecting Elementary Particles 319

Particle Accelerators: The Essential Tool 319

THE SCIENCE OF LIFE • 321
Accelerators in Medicine 321

The Elementary Particle Zoo 321
Leptons 322 / Hadrons 322 / Antimatter 322

SCIENCE IN THE MAKING • 322
The Discovery of Antimatter 322

THE ONGOING PROCESS OF SCIENCE • 323
How Does the Brain Work? 323

Quarks 324 / Quarks and Leptons 325 / Quark Confinement 326

The Four Fundamental Forces 326
Force as an Exchange 327 / Unified Field Theories 328

Science News • 329
Rare Events—Exotic Processes Probe the Heart of Matter 329

Thinking More About Particle Physics • 330
Searching for the Ultimate Theory • 330

14
The Stars:
How much longer can the Sun sustain life
on Earth?
Great Idea: *The Sun and other stars use nuclear fusion reactions to convert mass into energy. Eventually, when a star's nuclear fuel is depleted, the star must burn out.*

Science Through the Day: **Sunshine** • 334

The Nature of Stars 334

Measuring the Stars with Telescopes and Satellites 335
Telescopes 335 / Orbiting Observatories 336

The Anatomy of Stars 338
The Structure of the Sun 338

THE SCIENCE OF LIFE • 340
Why Is the Visible Spectrum Visible? 340

The Sun's Energy Source: Fusion 341

THE ONGOING PROCESS OF SCIENCE • 342
The Solar Neutrino Problem 342

TECHNOLOGY • 343
Dyson Spheres, an Ultimate Technology 343

The Variety of Stars 343
The Astronomical Distance Scale 344 / The Hertzsprung-Russell Diagram 345

The Life Cycles of Stars 346
The Birth of Stars 346 / The Main Sequence and Death of Stars 347 / Neutron Stars and Pulsars 351 / Black Holes 352

Science News • 353
Fiber Helper 353

Thinking More About Stars • 353
Generation of the Chemical Elements 353

15
Cosmology:
Will the universe ever end?
Great Idea: *The universe began billions of years ago in the big bang, and it has been expanding ever since.*

Science Through the Day:
A Glowing Charcoal Fire • 358

Galaxies 358
The Nebula Debate 358 / Edwin Hubble and the Discovery of Galaxies 359 / Kinds of Galaxies 359

The Redshift and Hubble's Law 362

SCIENCE BY THE NUMBERS • 364
Analyzing Hubble's Data 364

The Big Bang 365
The Large-Scale Structure of the Universe 366 / Some Useful Analogies 367 / Evidence for the Big Bang 369

The Evolution of the Universe 371
Some General Characteristics of an Expanding Universe 371 / 10^{-43} Second: The Freezing of All Forces 371 / 10^{-35} Second: The Freezing of the Electroweak and Strong Forces 372 / 10^{-10} Second: The Freezing of the Weak and Electromagnetic Forces 374 / 10^{-5} Second: The Freezing of Elementary Particles 374 / Three Minutes: The Freezing of Nuclei 375 / Before One Million Years: The Freezing of Atoms 375

Dark Matter and Ripples at the Beginning of Time 376

The End of the Universe 377

Science News • 378
In the Beginning 378

Thinking More About Cosmology • 378
The History of the Universe 378

16
The Earth and Other Planets:
Is Earth the only planet with life?
Great Idea: *The Earth, one of nine planets that orbit the Sun, formed 4.5 billion years ago from a great cloud of dust.*

Science Through the Day:
The Sun and the Moon • 382

The Sun and Its Planets 382
The Solar System 382 / The Distribution of Mass 384

The Nebular Hypothesis 385

THE SCIENCE OF LIFE • 388
Gravity and Bones 388

The Formation of Terrestrial Planets 389

SCIENCE BY THE NUMBERS • 390
The Growth of the Earth 390

Differentiation 391 / The Interior of the Earth 391 / The Formation of the Moon 393 / Formation of the Other Terrestrial Planets 394

TECHNOLOGY • 392
Producing World-Record High Pressures 392

THE SCIENCE OF LIFE • 394
When Could Life Begin? 394

The Evolution of Planetary Atmospheres 395 / Exploring Mars 396

The Outer Solar System 396
Moons and Rings of the Outer Planets 398 / Pluto 399

SCIENCE IN THE MAKING • 400
The Discovery of Pluto 400

SCIENCE IN THE MAKING • 401
The Voyager Satellites 401

Asteroids, Comets, and Meteors 401

THE SCIENCE OF LIFE • 403
Comets and Life on Earth 403

Meteoroids, Meteors, and Meteorites 403

SCIENCE IN THE MAKING • 403
Discovering New Planetary Systems 403

Science News • 405
Distant and Strange 405

Thinking More About Planets • 405
Human Space Exploration 405

17
Plate Tectonics:
Can we predict destructive earthquakes?
Great Idea: *The entire Earth is still changing, due to the slow convection of soft, hot rocks deep within the planet.*

Science Through the Day: **Windblown Sand • 410**

The Dynamic Earth 410

SCIENCE BY THE NUMBERS • 410
How Long Could a Mountain Last? 410

The Case of the Disappearing Mountains 412 / Volcanoes and Earthquakes—Evidence of Forces in the Earth 413 / The Movement of the Continents 415 / New Support for the Theory 419

SCIENCE BY THE NUMBERS • 419
The Age of the Atlantic Ocean 419

Plate Tectonics: A Unifying View of the Earth 420
The Convecting Mantle 421

THE ONGOING PROCESS OF SCIENCE • 422
A Competing Model 422

SCIENCE IN THE MAKING • 423
Reactions to Plate Tectonics 423

Plate Boundaries 424

THE SCIENCE OF LIFE • 427
Upright Posture 427

The Geological History of North America 427

Another Look at Volcanoes and Earthquakes 428
Plates and Volcanism 429 / Earthquakes 430 / Seismology: Exploring the Earth's Interior with Earthquakes 431

THE ONGOING PROCESS OF SCIENCE • 432
Seismic Tomography 432

TECHNOLOGY • 432
The Design of Earthquake-Resistant Buildings 432

Science News • 433
Mapping with Grace 433

Thinking More About Plate Tectonics • 433
Earthquake Prediction 433

18
Cycles of the Earth:
Will we ever run out of fresh water?

Great Idea: *All matter above and beneath the Earth's surface moves in cycles.*

Science Through the Day: **A Seaward Breeze** • 438

Cycles Small and Large 438
Recycling 439 / The Nature of Earth's Cycles 439

The Hydrologic Cycle 440
Reservoirs of Water 440 / Movements of Water Between Reservoirs 441 / Chemical Cycles in the Oceans 443

THE SCIENCE OF LIFE • 443
Sobering Facts About Water 443

THE SCIENCE OF LIFE • 444
Element Residence Times 444

SCIENCE BY THE NUMBERS • 445
The Ocean's Gold 445

Ice Ages 445 / Milankovitch Cycles 446

SCIENCE IN THE MAKING • 448
Milankovitch Decides on His Life's Work 448

The Atmospheric Cycle 448
Air Masses: Reservoirs of the Atmosphere 448 / Weather 449 / The General Circulation of the Atmosphere 451 / Common Storms and Weather Patterns 452 / Climate 453

THE ONGOING PROCESS OF SCIENCE • 453
How Steady Is Earth's Climate? 453

Understanding Climate 454

TECHNOLOGY • 455
Doppler Radar 455

The Rock Cycle 455
Igneous Rocks 456 / Sedimentary Rocks 457

THE SCIENCE OF LIFE • 459
Coral Reefs 459

Metamorphic Rocks 460 / The Story of Marble 460

SCIENCE IN THE MAKING • 461
Hutton and the Discovery of "Deep Time" 461

The Interdependence of Earth's Cycles 463

Science News • 463
Slippin' Slide 463

Thinking More About Cycles • 463
Beach Erosion 463

19
Ecology, Ecosystems and the Environment:
Are human activities affecting the global environment?

Great Idea: *Ecosystems are interdependent communities of living things that recycle matter while energy flows through.*

Science Through the Day:
Life Under the Sand • 468

Ecology and Ecosystems 468
Characteristics of Ecosystems 469

The Law of Unintended Consequences 472
The Lake Victoria Disaster 472

SCIENCE IN THE MAKING • 473
Island Biogeography 473

Threats to the Global Ecosystem and Environment 474
The Problem of Urban Landfills 474

SCIENCE BY THE NUMBERS • 475
Trash 475

TECHNOLOGY • 475
The Science in Recycling 475

The Ozone Problem 476 / Acid Rain and Urban Air Pollution 479 / The Greenhouse Effect 481 / Debates About Global Warming 483

THE ONGOING PROCESS OF SCIENCE • 485
Dealing with the Greenhouse Effect 485

Science News • 486
Hawaii's Hated Frogs 486

Thinking More About Global Warming • 486
How Certain Do You Have to Be? 486

20
Strategies of Life:
What is life?

Great Idea: *Living things use many strategies to deal with the problems of acquiring and using matter and energy.*

Science Through the Day:
The Diversity of Life • 490

The Organization of Living Things 490
Ways of Thinking About Living Things 490

What Is Life? 492
The Characteristics of Life 492

SCIENCE IN THE MAKING • 494
Measuring Plant Growth 494

Classifying Living Things 495
Cataloging Life 495

THE ONGOING PROCESS OF SCIENCE • 499
A Different Division of Kingdoms 499

SCIENCE BY THE NUMBERS • 499
How Many Species Are There? 499

Classifying Human Beings 501/ Implications of Linnaean Classification 501

Survival: A New Look at the Life Around You 503

Strategies of Fungi 503

SCIENCE IN THE MAKING • 505
The Discovery of Penicillin 505

Strategies of Plants 505
The Simplest Plants 506 / Vascular Plants 506

Strategies of Animals 508
Invertebrates 509 / Vertebrates 510

Science News • 513
Camelid Comeback 513

Thinking More About Life's Strategies • 513
Eating Through the Phyla 513

21
Molecules of Life:
What constitutes a healthy diet?
Great Idea: *A cell's major parts are constructed from a few simple molecular building blocks.*

Science Through the Day: **An Afternoon Snack** • 518

Organic Molecules 518
Four Basic Characteristics 518 / Chemical Shorthand 520

SCIENCE IN THE MAKING • 521
The Synthesis of Urea 521

Proteins: The Workhorses of Life 521
Amino Acids: The Building Blocks of Proteins 522 / The Structure of Proteins 523

SCIENCE BY THE NUMBERS • 525
How Many Proteins Can You Make? 525

Proteins as Enzymes 525

THE SCIENCE OF LIFE • 527
Proteins and Diet 527

How Drugs Work 528

Carbohydrates 529

Lipids 531
Saturated and Unsaturated Fats 531

TECHNOLOGY • 533
Nonfattening Fats 533

Cell Membranes 533

Minerals and Vitamins 534
Minerals 534 / Vitamins 536

Science News • 537
Unnatural Biochemistry 537

Thinking More About The Molecules of Life • 537
Dietary Fads 537

22
The Living Cell:
What is the smallest living thing?
Great Idea: *Life is based on chemistry, and chemistry takes place in cells.*

Science Through the Day: **Sunburn!** • 541
The Nature and Variety of Cells 541

SCIENCE IN THE MAKING • 542
The Discovery of Cells 542

The Cell Theory 542

How Does a Cell Work? 542
Observing Cells 543 / Cell Membranes 545 / Transporting Material Across a Cell Membrane 546 / The Nucleus 547 / The Energy Organelles: Chloroplasts and Mitochondria 549 / Cytoskeleton 550

Metabolism: Energy and Life 551
The Cell's Energy Currency 551 / Photosynthesis 552 / Glycolysis: The First Step in Energy Generation in the Cell 553 / Fermentation: A Way to Keep Glycolysis Going 554 / The Final Stages of Respiration 555

Cell Division 556
Mitosis 557 / Meiosis 559

Science News • 561
Teasing Out Tongue's Taste Receptors 561

Thinking More About Cells • 562
Biochemical Evidence for Evolution 562

23
Classical and Modern Genetics:
Why do offspring resemble their parents?
Great Idea: *All living things use the same genetic code to guide the chemical reactions in every cell.*

Science Through the Day:
A Family Resemblance • 566

Classical Genetics 566
The Rules of Classical Genetics 569 / Qualitative versus Quantitative Genetics 570

DNA and the Birth of Molecular Genetics 570
Nucleotides: The Building Blocks of Nucleic Acids 571 / DNA Structure 572 / RNA Structure 572 / The Replication of DNA 573

The Genetic Code 575
Transcription of DNA 575 / The Synthesis of Proteins 576 / Mutations and DNA Repair 580 / Why Are Genes Expressed? 580 / Viruses 581 / Viral Epidemics 582

THE SCIENCE OF LIFE • 583
The Human Genome Project 583

SCIENCE BY THE NUMBERS • 584
The Human Book of Life 584

TECHNOLOGY • 585
New Ways to Sequence 585

Science News • 586
Delivering the Goods 586

Thinking More About Genetics • 586
The Ethics of Genes 586

24

The New Science of Life:

Can we cure cancer?

Great Idea: *Our new understanding of genetic mechanisms is leading to enormous advances in medicine and other aspects of our lives.*

Science Through the Day: **A Break in the Case** • 591

The Technology of Genes 591
Genetic Engineering 591

TECHNOLOGY • 594
DNA Fingerprinting 594

Copying DNA—The PCR Process 595

Cloning 597
What Is a Clone? 597 / Stem Cells 598

Curing Disease 599
Gene Therapy 600 / Cancer—A Different kind of Genetic Disease 602

SCIENCE BY THE NUMBERS • 604
Double-Blind Clinical Trials 604

DNA Repair in the Cell 604

AIDS 607
Computer-Assisted Drug Design 608

Science News • 610
Losing Rhythm **610**

Thinking More About Drug Design • 610
The Evolving Resistance to Antibiotics 610

25

Evolution:

How did life arise?

Great Idea: *All life on Earth evolved from single-celled organisms by the process of natural selection.*

Science Through the Day: **Day's End** • 614

The Fact of Evolution 614
The Fossil Record 615 / The Biochemical Evidence 616 / Evidence from Anatomy: Vestigial Organs 617

Chemical Evolution 618
Black Smokers 620 / RNA Enzymes 620 / The Window of Opportunity 621 / The First Cell 621

SCIENCE BY THE NUMBERS • 622
Cell Division 622

THE ONGOING PROCESS OF SCIENCE • 623
Did Life Also Originate on Mars? 623

Natural Selection and the Development of Complex Life 624
Natural Selection 624

SCIENCE IN THE MAKING • 627
The Reception of Darwin's Theory 627

The Story of Life 628 / Geological Time 630 / Mass Extinctions and the Rate of Evolution 630

The Evolution of Human Beings 633

Science News • 636
Retaking Flight **636**

Thinking More About Evolution • 637
Young-Earth Creationism 637

Appendices

A. **Human Anatomy** A1

B. **Units and Numbers** A8

C. **The Geological Time Scale** A13

D. **Selected Physical Constants and Astronomical Data** A17

E. **Properties of the Planets** A17

F. **The Chemical Elements** A18

Glossary A20

Credits A47

Index I-1

1

Science: A Way of Knowing

How do you know what you know?

GREAT IDEA

Science is a way of asking and answering questions about the physical universe.

PHYSICS

What are the most fundamental building blocks of matter? (Ch. 8)

CHEMISTRY

How can we combine atoms to form new materials? (Ch. 11)

ENVIRONMENT

Do human activities affect the Earth's global climate? (Ch. 19)

GEOLOGY

What dynamic processes occur deep within the Earth? (Ch. 17)

HEALTH & SAFETY

What causes cancer? (Ch. 24)

ASTRONOMY

What will be ultimate fate of the universe? (Ch. 15)

TECHNOLOGY

How can we design power plants that generate electricity more efficiently? (Ch. 4)

BIOLOGY

How do complex organisms develop from a single cell? (Ch. 25)

Red = applications of the great idea discussed in this chapter

Orange = other applications, some of which are discussed in other chapters

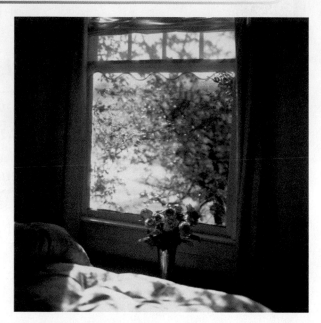

Sunlight streams through your East window. As you wake up, you remember it's Saturday. No classes! And you're headed to the beach with friends. It looks like it's going to be a beautiful day, just like the weather forecast promised.

We take so much about the natural world for granted. Every day the Sun rises at a precisely predictable time in the East. Every day the Sun sets in the West. So, too, the phases of the Moon and the seasons of the year follow their familiar repetitive cycles.

Ancient humans took note of these and many other predictable aspects of nature and they patterned their lives and cultures accordingly. Today, we formalize this search for regularities in nature and we call the process science.

The Role of Science

Our lives are filled with choices. What should I eat? Is it safe to cross the street? Should I bother to recycle an aluminum can, or just throw it in the trash? Every day we have to make dozens of decisions; each choice is based, in part, on the knowledge that actions in a physical world have predictable consequences. By what process do you make those decisions?

Making Choices

When you pull into a gas station you have to decide what sort of gasoline to buy for your car. Over a period of time you may try many different types, observing how your car responds to each. In the end, you may conclude that a particular brand and grade suits your car best, and decide to buy that one in the future. You engage in a similar process when you buy shampoo, pain relievers, athletic shoes, and scores of other products.

These simple examples illustrate one way we learn about the universe. First, we look at the world to see what is there and to learn how it works. Then we generalize, making rules that seem to fit what we see. And finally, we apply those general rules to new situations we've never encountered before. And we fully expect the rules to work.

There doesn't seem to be anything Earth shattering about choosing a brand of gasoline or shampoo. But the same basic procedure can be applied in a more formal and quantitative way when we want to understand the workings of a distant star or a living cell. In these cases, the enterprise is called science, and the people who study these questions for a living are called scientists.

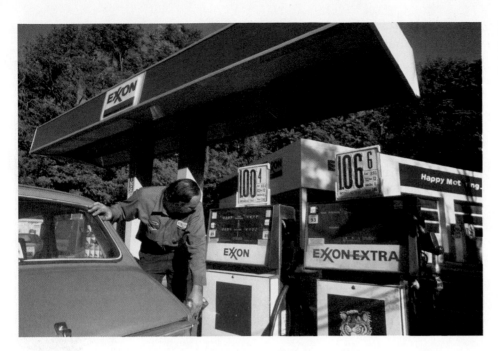

Even something simple like choosing a brand of gasoline can involve observation and experiment.

Why Study Science?

Pick up your local newspaper any morning of the week and glance at the headlines. On a typical day you'll see articles about the weather, environmental concerns, and long-range planning by one of your local utility companies. There might be news about a new treatment for AIDS, an earthquake in California, or new advances in biotechnology. The editorial pages might feature comments on cloning humans, arguments for a NASA planetary mission, or perhaps a trial involving DNA fingerprinting. What do all of these stories have in common? They all affect your life in one way or another, and they all depend to a significant degree on science.

We live in a world of matter and energy, forces and motions. Everything we experience in our lives takes place in an ordered universe with regular and predictable phenomena. You have learned to survive in this universe, so many of these scientific ideas are second nature to you. When you drive a car, cook a meal, or play a pickup game of basketball, you instinctively take advantage of a few simple physical laws. As you eat, sleep, work, or play, you experience the world as a biological system and must come to terms with the natural laws governing all living things.

Science gives us a powerful tool to understand how our world works and how we interact with our physical surroundings. Science not only incorporates basic ideas and theories about how our universe behaves, it also provides a framework for learning more and tackling new questions and concerns that come our way. Science represents our best hope for predicting and coping with natural disasters, curing diseases, and discovering new materials and new technologies with which to shape our world. Science also provides an unparalleled view of the magnificent order and symmetry of the universe and its workings—from the unseen world of the atomic nucleus to the inconceivable vastness of space.

So why should you study science? Chances are you aren't going to be a professional scientist. Even so, your job will probably depend on advances in science and technology. New technologies are a driving force in economics, business, and even many aspects of law: new semiconductor technology, agricultural methods, and information processing have altered our world. Biological research and drug development play crucial roles in the medical professions: genetic diseases, AIDS vaccines, and nutritional information appear in the news every day. Even professional athletes must constantly evaluate and use new and improved gear and rely on improved medical treatments and therapies. By studying science you will not only be better able to incorporate these advances into your professional life, but you will also better understand the process by which such advances were made.

Science is no less central to your everyday life away from school or work. As a consumer, you are besieged by new products and processes, not to mention a bewildering variety of warnings about health and safety. As a taxpayer, you must vote on issues that directly affect your community—energy taxes, recycling proposals, government spending on research, and more. As a living being, you must make informed decisions about diet and lifestyle. And as a parent, you will have to nurture and guide your children through an ever-more-complex world. A firm grasp of the principles and methods of science will help you make life's important decisions in a more informed way. As an extra bonus, you will be poised to share in the excitement of the scientific discoveries that, week-by-week, transform our understanding of the universe and our place in it. Science opens up astonishing, unimagined worlds—bizarre life forms in deep oceans, exploding stars in deep space, and aspects of the history of life and our world more wondrous than any fiction.

The Scientific Method

Science is a way of asking and answering questions about the physical universe. It is not simply a set of facts or a catalog of answers, but rather a process for conducting an ongoing dialogue with our physical surroundings. Like any human activity, science is enormously varied and rich in subtleties. Nevertheless, there are a few basic steps that, taken together, can be said to comprise the **scientific method**.

Observation

If our goal is to learn about the world, the first thing we have to do is look around us and see what's there. This statement seems obvious to us in our technological age, yet throughout much of history, learned men and women rejected the idea that you can understand the world simply by observing it.

Some Greek philosophers living during the Golden Age of Athens argued that one cannot deduce the true nature of the universe by trusting to the senses. The senses lie, they would have said. Only the use of reason and the insights of the human mind can lead us to true understanding. In his famous book *The Republic,* Plato compared human beings to people living in a cave, watching shadows on a wall but unable to see the objects causing the shadows. In just the same way, he argued, observing the physical world will never put us in contact with reality, but will doom us to a lifetime of wrestling with shadows. Only with the "eye of the mind" can we break free from illusion and arrive at the truth.

In the Middle Ages in Europe, a similar frame of mind was to be found, but with a devout trust in received wisdom replacing the use of human reason as the ultimate tool in the search for truth. There is a story about a debate in an Oxford college on the question of how many teeth a horse has. One learned scholar got up and quoted the Greek scientist Aristotle on the subject, and another quoted the theologian St. Augustine to put forward a different answer. Finally, a young monk at the back of the hall got up and noted that since there was a horse outside, they could settle the question by looking in its mouth. At this point, the manuscript states, the assembled scholars "fell upon him, smote him hip and thigh, and cast him from the company of educated men."

Plato argued that humans observing nature were like men watching shadows on the wall of a cave.

As these examples illustrate, many distinguished thinkers have attacked the problem of learning about the physical world without actually making observations and measurements. These approaches are perfectly self-consistent and were pursued by people every bit as intelligent as we are. They are not, however, the methods of science, nor did they produce the kinds of advanced technologies and knowledge that we associate with modern societies.

In the remainder of this book, we differentiate between **observations**, in which we observe nature without manipulating it, and **experiments**, in which we manipulate some aspect of nature and observe the outcome. An astronomer, for example, observes distant stars without changing them, while a chemist may experiment by mixing materials together and seeing what happens.

Identifying Patterns and Regularities

When we observe a particular phenomenon over and over again, we begin to get a sense of how nature behaves. We start to recognize patterns in nature. Eventually, we generalize our experience into a synthesis that summarizes what we have learned about the way the world works. We may, for example, notice that whenever we drop something, it falls. This statement represents a summary of the results of many observations.

Table 1-1 Measurements of Falling Objects

Time of Fall (seconds)	Distance of Fall (meters)
1	5
2	20
3	45
4	80
5	125

It often happens that at this stage scientists summarize the results of their observations in mathematical form, particularly if they have been making quantitative measurements. In the case of a falling object, for example, they might be measuring the time it takes an object to fall a certain distance, rather than just noticing that the object falls. The first step would be to collect data in the form of a table (see Table 1-1). These data could also be presented in the form of a graph, in which distance of the fall (in meters) is plotted against time of the fall (in seconds; Figure 1-1). This example also illustrates the importance of units in scientific measurements (distance in meters, time in seconds, etc.). Most scientific measurements require both a number and a unit of measurement, and we'll encounter many different units in the coming chapters.

After preparing tables and graphs of their data, scientists would notice that the longer something falls, the farther it travels. Furthermore, the distance isn't simply proportional to the time of fall. If one object falls for twice as long as another, it will travel four times as far; if it falls three times longer, it will travel nine times as far; and so on. This statement can be summarized in three ways (a format used throughout this book):

▶ **In words:** The distance traveled is proportional to the square of the time of travel.

▶ **In equation form:**

$$\text{distance} = \text{constant} \times (\text{time})^2$$

▶ **In symbols:**

$$d = k \times t^2$$

The constant, k, has to be determined from the measurements. We'll return to the subject of constants in the next chapter.

Mathematics: The Language of Science

To many people science brings to mind obscure equations written in strange, undecipherable symbols. Next time you're in the science area of your college or university, look into an advanced classroom. Chances are you'll see a confusing jumble of unintelligible formulas on the blackboard. Have you ever wondered why scientists need all those complex mathematical equations? Science is supposed to help us understand the physical world around us, so why can't scientists just use plain English?

Take a stroll outside and look carefully at a favorite tree. Think about how you might describe the tree in as much detail as possible so that a distant friend could envision exactly what you see and distinguish that tree from all others.

A cursory description would note the rough brown bark, branching limbs, and canopy of green leaves, but that description would do little to distinguish your tree from most others. You might use adjectives like lofty, graceful, or stately to convey an overall impression of the tree. Better yet, you could identify the exact kind of tree and specify its stage of growth—a sugar maple at the peak of autumn color, for example—but even then your friend has relatively little to go on.

Your description would be far more accurate by giving exact dimensions of the tree—its height, the distance spanned by its branches, or the diameter of the trunk. You could document the shape and size of leaves, the thickness and texture of the bark, the angles and spacing of the branching limbs, and the tree's approximate age. You could be even more exact and calculate the number of board feet of lumber the tree could produce. Finally, you could talk about the

• **Figure 1-1** Measurements of a falling object can be presented visually in the form of a graph. Time of fall in seconds (on the horizontal axis) is plotted versus distance of fall in meters (on the vertical axis).

There are many ways of describing a tree.

basic molecular processes that allow the tree to extract energy from sunlight and carry out the other chemical tasks we associate with life.

As we move through these descriptions of the tree, our language becomes more and more quantitative. In some cases, such as supplying a detailed description of the tree's shape or its chemistry, that description could become quite long and cumbersome. That's why scientists employ **mathematics**, which is a concise language that allows them to communicate their results in compact form and often, as an added benefit, allows them to make very precise predictions about expected outcomes of experiments or observations. But anything that can be said in an equation can also be said (albeit in a less concise way) in a plain English

One way of looking at a tree is to think about the lumber it might produce.

sentence. When you encounter equations in your science courses, you should always ask, "What English sentence does this equation represent?" Learning to "read" equations will keep the mathematics from obscuring the simple ideas that lie behind most equations.

Hypothesis and Theory

Once we have summarized experimental and observational results, we can form a **hypothesis**—a tentative educated guess—about how the world works. In the case of our everyday experience with falling objects, this hypothesis could be very simple. We could say, "When I drop something, it falls." In other cases, the formation of the hypothesis may be more complicated, and the hypothesis may be stated in the form of mathematical equations. When confronted with a new phenomenon, scientists often weigh several different hypotheses at once, much as a detective in a murder mystery may consider several different suspects.

A **theory** is a description of the world that covers a relatively large number of phenomena and has met many observational and experimental tests. After observing hundreds of dropped objects, for example, we could state a theory such as, "In the absence of wind resistance, all objects fall a distance proportional to the square of the time of the fall." Just as a detective announces a theory at the conclusion of a murder mystery, so, too, scientists reach a conclusion based on their observations of nature. Furthermore, as in real courtroom verdicts, scientific conclusions about complex issues such as those affecting the environment (see Chapter 19) may represent a best guess based on the preponderance of evidence, rather than incontrovertible proof.

Prediction and Testing

In science, every hypothesis and theory must be tested by using them to make **predictions** about how a particular system will behave, then observing nature to see if the system behaves as predicted. If we hypothesize that all objects fall when they are dropped, for example, then that idea can be tested by dropping all sorts of objects. Each drop constitutes a test of our prediction, and the more successful tests we perform, the more confidence we have that the hypothesis is correct.

As long as we restrict our tests to solids or liquids on the Earth's surface, the hypothesis is consistently confirmed. Test a helium-filled balloon, however, and we discover a clear exception to the rule. The balloon "falls" up. The original hypothesis, which worked so well for most objects, fails for certain gases. And more tests would show there are other limitations. If you were an astronaut in a space shuttle, every time you held something out and let it go, it would just float in space. Evidently our hypothesis is invalid in space, as well.

This example illustrates an important aspect about testing hypotheses and theories in science. Tests do not necessarily prove or disprove a theory; instead, they often serve to define the range of situations under which the theory is valid. We may, for example, observe that nature behaves in a certain way only at high temperatures or only at low velocities. In these sorts of situations, it usually happens that the original theory is seen to be a special case of a deeper, more general theory. In the case of the balloon, for example, the simple "things fall down" will be replaced by a much more general theory based on statements called Newton's laws of motion and the law of universal gravitation—laws we'll study in the next chapter.

When a theory or group of related theories has been tested extensively and seems to apply everywhere in the universe, when we have had enough experience

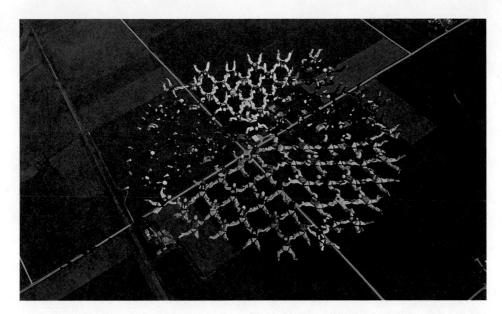

Equations allow us to describe with precision the behavior of objects in our physical world. One such equation predicts the behavior of falling objects.

with it to have a lot of confidence that it is true, we generally elevate the theory to a new status. We call it a law of nature—an overarching statement of how the universe works. In the example of falling objects, we shall see that the theory that "objects fall when dropped" has been replaced by Isaac Newton's more sophisticated and general laws of motion, and the law of universal gravitation. These laws of nature describe and predict the motion of dropped objects both on the Earth and in space and, therefore, are a more successful set of statements than the original hypothesis. We will discuss them in more detail in the next chapter.

We will encounter many such laws in this book, all backed by millions of observations and measurements. Remember, however, where these laws come from. They are not written on tablets of stone, nor are they simply good ideas that someone once had. They arise from repeated and rigorous observation and testing. They represent our best understanding of how nature works.

We never stop questioning the validity of our hypotheses, theories, or laws of nature. Scientists constantly think up new, more rigorous experiments to test the limits of our theories. In fact, one of the central tenets of science is this:

> **Every theory and law of nature is subject to change, based on new observations.**

This is an extremely important statement about science, and one that is often ignored in public debates. It means that it must be possible, in principle, that every statement in a scientific system *could* be false. You should, in other words, be able to imagine an experimental outcome that would prove the statement false, even if that outcome never happens in the real world. Philosophers have called this property of the scientific method *falsifiability*.

The Scientific Method in Operation

These elements—observation, hypothesis, prediction, and testing—together comprise the scientific method. In practice, you can think of the method as working

• **Figure 1-2** The scientific method can be illustrated as an endless cycle of collecting observations (data), identifying patterns, and regularities in the data, forming hypotheses, making predictions, and collecting more observations.

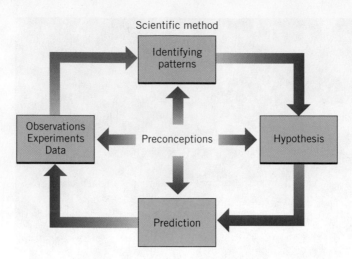

as shown in Figure 1-2. It is a never-ending cycle in which observations lead to hypotheses, which lead to more observations.

If observations confirm a hypothesis, then more tests may be devised. If the hypothesis fails, then the new observations are used to revise it, after which the revised hypothesis is tested again. Scientists continue this process until the limits of existing equipment are reached, in which case researchers often try to develop better instruments to do even more tests. If and when it appears that there's just no point to going further, the hypothesis may be elevated to a theory, or even a law of nature.

It is important to realize, however, that while the orderly cycle shown in Figure 1-2 provides a useful framework to help us think about science, it shouldn't be thought of as a rigid cookbook-style set of steps to follow. Science can be every bit as creative an endeavor as art or music. Because science is done by human beings, it involves occasional bursts of intuition, sudden leaps, a joyful breaking of the rules, and all the other characteristics we associate with other human activities.

Several other important points should be made about the scientific method.

1. Scientists are not required to observe nature with an "open mind," with no preconceptions about what they are going to find. Most experiments and observations are designed and undertaken with a specific hypothesis in mind, and most researchers have preconceptions about whether that hypothesis is right or wrong. Nevertheless, scientists have to believe the results of their experiments and observations, whether or not they fit preconceived notions. Science demands that whatever our preconceptions, we must be ready to change those ideas if the evidence forces us.

2. There is no "right" place to enter the cycle. Scientists can (and have) started their work by making extensive observations, but they can also start with a theory and test it. It makes no difference where you enter the cycle—eventually the scientific process takes you all the way around.

3. Observations and experiments must be reported in such a way that anyone with the proper equipment can verify the results. Scientific results, in other words, must be **reproducible**, and they must be reproducible by anyone, not just the original experimenters.

4. The cycle is continuous; it has no end. Science does not provide final answers, nor is it a search for ultimate truth. Instead, it is a way of producing

successively more detailed and exact descriptions of wider and wider areas of the physical world—descriptions that allow us to predict more of the behavior of that world with higher and higher levels of confidence.

THE ONGOING PROCESS OF SCIENCE •

Biodiversity

The dynamic process of scientific research is illustrated by a recent experiment in *ecology*—the study of communities of interdependent living things. Many current public debates focus on possible adverse effects of human activities on *biodiversity*, which is defined as the number of different species that coexist at a given place. Before we can identify human influences, however, we must first examine the role that biodiversity plays in nature. To answer this question, researchers apply the scientific method and design an experiment to study areas that differ only in the number of species.

Starting in 1982, ecologist David Tilman at the University of Minnesota carried out just such an experiment. He began by choosing four grassy fields in the Cedar Creek Natural History Area. These fields had either never been tilled, or had lain fallow for a minimum of 14 years. First Tilman fenced off the fields, then split them into plots about 12 feet on a side—207 plots in all. Different plots were treated in different ways.

1. Some plots, called controls, received no treatment.
2. Some plots were given a group of essential nutrients such as phosphorus and potassium, but no nitrogen.
3. Some plots were given the same set of nutrients, but different amounts of nitrogen.

These three photos illustrate a nitrogen addition experiment at Cedar Creek Natural History Area in St. Paul, Minnesota. The aerial photo, on the left, shows one of the four fields at Cedar Creek in 1983, the second year of the experiment. The different colors of the plots illustrate visually the changes in plant species composition caused by the different rates of nitrogen addition. The center photo shows a typical control plot at this same field. This plot has high plant diversity, is dominated by native plant species, and did not receive any added nitrogen. The photo on the right shows a plot that received the highest rate of N addition and has become almost totally dominated by the nonnative perennial weedy grass, *Agropyron repens* (quack grass).

Think for a moment about this experimental design. All of the plots start with the same soil and receive the same rainfall. The only difference between them is the amount of nitrogen and other nutrients. In the language of experimental science, we say that the amounts of nitrogen and other nutrients are the "independent variables," and results such as biodiversity or the amount of vegetation on each plot are "dependent variables." Thus whatever results we find can be attributed to the presence or absence of nitrogen and other nutrients.

During each of the 11 years that the experiment ran, the experimenters measured two things: (1) the amount of vegetation (or biomass) on each plot, and (2) the number of species (or biodiversity). In normal years, there was a clear result: the more nitrogen added, the more biomass produced, while the amounts of other nutrients had little effect. Furthermore, the plots with the highest biomass tended to have fewer species, and hence lower biodiversity, because when a few species flourished they crowded out the others.

By chance, however, the period of the experiment included the years 1987–88, which contained the third worst drought in the last 150 years. In this year, adding nitrogen made little difference—all the plots produced very low biomass. But the drought also highlighted the role of biodiversity, because, while the biomass in plots with low biodiversity dropped to as low as one-eighth of its non-drought levels, the biomass of plots with high biodiversity fell by only a half. (Although the percentage drop was bigger for plots with more nitrogen, in fact all plots produced roughly the same biomass in the drought years.)

Thus biodiversity appears to represent a kind of insurance policy for natural ecosystems; it's not too important in normal years, but it carries the system through periods of high stress (like droughts). By designing and performing carefully thought-out experiments, scientists are able to arrive at this kind of understanding. •

SCIENCE IN THE MAKING •

Dimitri Mendeleev and the Periodic Table

Discoveries of previously unrecognized patterns in nature, a key step in the scientific method, provide scientists with some of their most exhilarating moments. Dimitri Mendeleev (1834–1907), a popular chemistry professor at the Technological Institute of St. Petersburg in Russia, experienced such a breakthrough in 1869 as he was tabulating data for a new chemistry textbook.

The mid-nineteenth century was a time of great excitement in chemistry. Almost every year saw the discovery of one or two new chemical elements, and new apparatus and processes were greatly expanding the repertoire of laboratory and industrial chemists. In such a stimulating field, it was no easy job to keep up to date with all the developments and summarize them in a textbook. In an effort to consolidate the current state of knowledge about the most basic chemical building blocks, Mendeleev listed various properties of the 63 known chemical elements (substances that could not be divided by chemical means). He arranged his list in order of increasing atomic weight, then noted the distinctive chemical behavior of each element.

Examining his list, Mendeleev realized an extraordinary pattern: elements with similar chemical properties appeared at regular, or *periodic,* intervals. One group of elements, including lithium, sodium, potassium, and rubidium (he called them group-one elements), all were soft, silvery metals that formed compounds with chlorine in a one-to-one ratio. Immediately following the group-one elements in the list were beryllium, magnesium, calcium, and barium—group-two elements that form compounds with chlorine in a one-to-two ratio, and so on.

Dimitri Mendeleev recognized regular patterns in the properties of known chemical elements, and thereby devised the first periodic table of elements.

Figure 1-3 The periodic table systematizes all known chemical elements.

Periodic table (Figure 1-3). Legend: metal, metalloid, nonmetal. Each cell: atomic number (top), symbol, atomic mass (bottom).

IA (1)	IIA (2)	IIIB (3)	IVB (4)	VB (5)	VIB (6)	VIIB (7)	VIIIB (8)	VIIIB (9)	VIIIB (10)	IB (11)	IIB (12)	IIIA (13)	IVA (14)	VA (15)	VIA (16)	VIIA (17)	VIIIA (18)
1 H 1.00794																	2 He 4.00260
3 Li 6.941	4 Be 9.01218											5 B 10.811	6 C 12.011	7 N 14.00674	8 O 15.9994	9 F 18.99840	10 Ne 20.1797
11 Na 22.98977	12 Mg 24.3050											13 Al 26.98154	14 Si 28.0855	15 P 30.97376	16 S 32.066	17 Cl 35.4527	18 Ar 39.948
19 K 39.0983	20 Ca 40.078	21 Sc 44.95591	22 Ti 47.88	23 V 50.9415	24 Cr 51.9961	25 Mn 54.9380	26 Fe 55.847	27 Co 58.93320	28 Ni 58.69	29 Cu 63.546	30 Zn 65.39	31 Ga 69.723	32 Ge 72.61	33 As 74.92159	34 Se 78.96	35 Br 79.904	36 Kr 83.80
37 Rb 85.4678	38 Sr 87.62	39 Y 88.90585	40 Zr 91.224	41 Nb 92.90638	42 Mo 95.94	43 Tc 98.9072	44 Ru 101.07	45 Rh 102.90550	46 Pd 106.42	47 Ag 107.8682	48 Cd 112.411	49 In 114.82	50 Sn 118.710	51 Sb 121.75	52 Te 127.60	53 I 126.90447	54 Xe 131.29
55 Cs 132.90543	56 Ba 137.327	57 *La 138.9055	72 Hf 178.49	73 Ta 180.9479	74 W 183.85	75 Re 186.207	76 Os 190.2	77 Ir 192.22	78 Pt 195.08	79 Au 196.96654	80 Hg 200.59	81 Tl 204.3833	82 Pb 207.2	83 Bi 208.98037	84 Po 208.9824	85 At 209.9871	86 Rn 222.0176
87 Fr 223.0197	88 Ra 226.0254	89 †Ac 227.0278	104 Rf 261.11	105 Ha 262.114	106 Sg 263.118	107 Ns 262.12	108 Hs (265)	109 Mt (266)	110 Uun (269)	111 Uuu (272)	112 Uub (277)						

Alkali Metals — Alkaline Earth Metals. Halogens — Nobel or Inert Gases.

*Lanthanides:

58 Ce 140.115	59 Pr 140.90765	60 Nd 144.24	61 Pm 144.9127	62 Sm 150.36	63 Eu 151.965	64 Gd 157.25	65 Tb 158.92534	66 Dy 162.50	67 Ho 164.93032	68 Er 167.26	69 Tm 168.93421	70 Yb 173.04	71 Lu 174.967

†Actinides:

90 Th 232.0381	91 Pa 231.0359	92 U 238.0289	93 Np 237.0482	94 Pu 244.0642	95 Am 243.0614	96 Cm 247.0703	97 Bk 247.0703	98 Cf 242.0587	99 Es 252.083	100 Fm 257.0951	101 Md 258.10	102 No 259.1009	103 Lr 260.105

As other similar patterns emerged from his list, Mendeleev realized that the elements could be arranged in the form of a table (Figure 1-3). Not only did this so-called periodic table highlight previously unrecognized relationships among the elements, it also revealed obvious gaps where as-yet undiscovered elements must lie. The power of Mendeleev's periodic table of the elements was underscored when several new elements, with atomic weights and chemical properties just as he had predicted, were discovered in the following years.

The discovery of the periodic table ranks as one of the great achievements of science. It was so important, in fact, that Mendeleev's students carried a large poster of it behind his coffin in his funeral procession. •

THE SCIENCE OF LIFE •

William Harvey and the Blood's Circulation

It's common knowledge that blood circulates in your body, but stop and think for a moment. How do we know? One of the great puzzles faced by scientists who studied the human body was deducing the role played by the blood. English physician William Harvey (1578–1657) gave us our current picture of the pattern of circulation, in which blood is pumped from the heart to all parts of the body through arteries, and returned to the heart through veins. His experiments reveal the scientific method at work.

Prior to Harvey's work, several competing hypotheses had been proposed. Some scientists had taught that blood didn't move at all, but simply pulsed in response to pumping of the heart. Others taught that the arteries and veins constituted different systems, with blood in the veins flowing from the liver to the various parts of the body, where it was absorbed and its nutrients taken in. Harvey, on the other hand, adopted the hypothesis that blood circulates through a connected system of arteries and veins. When confronted with such conflicting hypotheses, a scientist must devise experiments that test the distinctive predictions of each competing idea.

• **Figure 1-4** One of William Harvey's famous experiments on the circulation of the blood tested the hypothesis that blood flows from veins to the heart. Harvey first applied a tourniquet to a subject's arm and had the subject squeeze something to raise the veins (*a*). Pressing down on the vein caused it to gradually subside (*b*), indicating that the blood was indeed flowing back to the heart.

Before

After

To establish the circulation of the blood, Harvey first performed careful dissections of animals to trace out the veins and arteries. Second, he undertook studies of live animals, often killing them so that he could observe the veins and arteries as the heart stopped beating. Then, as now, animals were sometimes sacrificed to advance medical science (see Investigation 7). Finally, Harvey performed a series of experiments to establish that blood in the veins did indeed flow back to the heart, rather than simply being absorbed in tissue like a stream of water in the desert. One of those experiments is shown in Figure 1-4. A tourniquet was applied to a subject's arm, and he was asked to squeeze something so that the veins filled with blood and "popped." (You have probably done the same thing when having blood drawn in a doctor's office.) Harvey would then press down on the vein and note that it would subside (indicating that the blood was leaving it) on the side toward the heart. This result is just the opposite of what would occur if blood were flowing from the liver to the extremities. Based on this experiment, and many others like it, Harvey eventually concluded that blood circulates continuously. •

Other Ways of Knowing

Scientists discover laws that describe how nature works by performing reproducible observations and measurements. Every idea in science is subject to test at any time—there are no absolute truths. If an idea cannot be tested in a manner that yields reproducible results then it simply isn't a part of science.

Different Kinds of Questions

The first step in any scientific investigation is to ask a question about the physical world. A scientist can ask, for example, whether a particular painting was executed in the seventeenth century. Various physical and chemical tests can be used to find the age of the paint, study the canvas, X-ray the painting, and so on. Whether the painting is old or a modern forgery, the question itself can be investigated by the scientific method.

But the methods of science cannot answer other equally valid questions. No physical or chemical test will tell us whether the painting is beautiful, or tell us how we are to respond to it. These questions are simply outside the realm of science.

The scientific method is not the only way to answer questions that matter in our lives. Science provides us with a powerful way of tackling questions about the physical world—how it works and how we can shape it to our needs. But many questions, some would say the most important questions, lie beyond the scope of science and scientific methods. Some of these questions are deeply philosophical: What is the meaning of life? Why does the world hold so much suffering? Is there a God? Other important questions are more personal: What career should I choose? Whom should I marry? Should I have children? We cannot answer these questions by the cycle of observation, hypothesis, and testing. For answers, we turn instead to religion, philosophy, and the arts.

A symphony, a poem, and a painting are not, in the end, objects to be studied scientifically. This is not a criticism; they are not supposed to be. These art forms address different human needs than science, and they use different methods. The same can be said about religious faith. Strictly speaking, there should be no conflict between the questions asked by science and religion, because they deal with different aspects of life. Conflicts arise only when zealots on either side try to apply their methods to questions where those methods aren't applicable.

Pseudoscience

Many kinds of inquiry, including creationism, extrasensory perception (ESP), unidentified flying objects (UFOs), astrology, crystal power, reincarnation, or many other notions you see in the tabloids at supermarket checkout counters, fail the elementary test that defines the sciences. None of these subjects, collectively labeled **pseudoscience**, can be tested in the sense that we are using the term. There is no reproducible test you can imagine that will convince people who believe in these notions that their ideas are wrong. Yet, as we have seen, the central property of scientific ideas is that they are testable and could be wrong, at

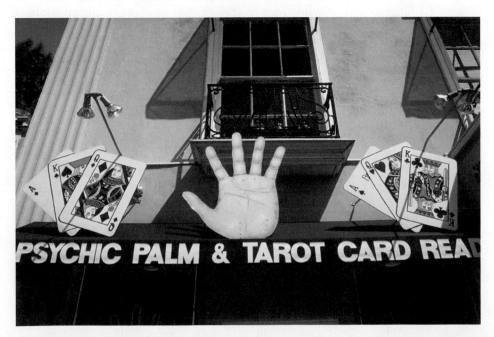

This psychic's shop in Hollywood is an example of pseudoscience.

least in principle. Pseudoscience lies outside the domain of science, and falls instead in the realm of belief or dogma.

In the following "Science by the Numbers" section we examine the nature of one pseudoscience, astrology. When confronted with other kinds of pseudo-science, you can ask a number of questions to come to your own conclusions:

1. Are the "facts" true as stated?

The first step is to be sure that the facts stated in support of a pseudo-scientific claim are actually true. For example, the Great Pyramids of Egypt are frequently the subject of these sorts of arguments. In one version, it is argued that the pyramids must have been built by extraterrestrials because, among other things, their bases are perfect squares and laying out a perfect square was beyond the capability of Egyptian engineers. In fact, according to modern surveys of the pyramids, the longest side of the Pyramid of Cheops is 8 feet longer than the shortest side—it's not a perfect square at all. Digging out the true facts can sometimes be tedious, but it's a necessary first step.

2. Is there an alternative explanation?

In dealing with UFO sightings, it often happens that you can't prove that the object seen wasn't a UFO, but there exists a "normal" explanation for the same event. For example, a light in the sky could be an extraterrestrial space-ship, but could also be the planet Venus (the most commonly reported "UFO"). In this case, it is necessary to invoke a doctrine called the "burden of proof." If someone makes a claim, it is up to that person to establish the claim: it is not up to you to disprove it. Furthermore, the more far-reaching the claim, the higher the standard of proof becomes. In the words of the late Carl Sagan, "Extraordinary claims require extraordinary proofs."

3. Is the claim falsifiable?

As we stated above, a central aspect of the scientific method is that every scientific statement is subject to experimental or observational test, so that it is possible to imagine an experimental result that would prove the statement wrong (although whether that result will ever actually be seen is a separate question). Such systems are said to be falsifiable. A system with statements that aren't falsifiable is simply not part of science. For example, some creationists talk about the doctrine of "created antiquity," by which they mean that the universe was created to look *exactly* as if it were billions of years old, even though it was created a few thousand years ago. This statement is not falsifi-able, and therefore this doctrine is not part of science.

🛑 **Stop and Think!** Can any experiment or observation (in principle) show created antiquity to be false?

4. Have the claims been rigorously tested?

Many pseudoscientific claims are based on anecdotes and stories. An example is provided by the practice known as "dowsing" or "water witching," in which someone walking on the surface (usually holding a forked stick) can detect the presence of underground water. Stories about this practice can be found in almost any rural area of the United States. Yet when the Committee for the Scientific Investigation of Claims for the Paranormal (CSICOP) con-ducted controlled tests in which water pipes were buried beneath a plowed surface, dowsers did no better than chance at locating the water. Tests like these are difficult to arrange, and often don't get much publicity, but they're worth looking for (http://www.csicop.com).

5. Do the claims require unreasonable changes in accepted ideas?

Often a pseudoscientific claim will seem to explain a small set of facts, but at the same time will require that a much wider assortment of facts be ignored. The psychiatrist Immanuel Velikosky, for example, looked at stories in ancient texts and tried to alter astronomy (violating most of the laws of physics in the process) in order to preserve the texts as literal statements of fact, rather than as allegory or metaphor. It's much more reasonable to accept the well-verified laws of physics and give up the literal reading of the text.

SCIENCE BY THE NUMBERS •

Astrology

Astrology is a very old system of beliefs that most modern scientists would call a pseudoscience. The central belief of astrology is that the positions of objects in the sky at a given time (a person's birth, for example) determine a person's future. Astrology was part of a complex set of omen systems developed by the Babylonians, and it was practiced by many famous astronomers well into modern times.

As the Earth travels around the Sun, the stars in the night sky change. This band of background stars through which the Sun appears to move is called the zodiac. The stars of the zodiac are customarily divided into 12 constellations, which are called "signs" or "houses."

At any time, the Sun, the Moon, and the planets all appear in one of these constellations, and a diagram showing these positions is called a horoscope. When this system was first introduced, the constellation in which the Sun appeared at the time of your birth is your "Sun sign," or, simply, your "sign." Today, the position of the Sun in the sky has shifted due to the motion of the Earth's axis, but the original dates for the "signs" are still used.

Astrology is a pseudoscience that is based on the belief that the positions of astronomical objects influence our personal lives.

Astrologers have a complex (and far from unified) system in which each combination of heavenly bodies and signs is believed to signify particular things. The Sun, for example, is thought to indicate the outgoing, expressive aspects of one's character, the Moon the inner-directed ones, and so on.

Scientists reject astrology for two reasons. First, there is no known way that planets and stars could exert a significant influence on a child at birth. It is true, as we shall learn in Chapter 2, that they exert a gravitational force on the infant, but the gravitational force exerted by the delivering physician (who is smaller but closer) is much greater than that exerted by any celestial object.

More importantly, scientists reject astrology because it just doesn't work. Over the millennia, there has been no evidence at all that the stars can predict the future.

You can test the ideas of astrology for yourself, if you like. Try this: Have a member of the class take the horoscopes from yesterday's newspaper and type them on a sheet of paper without indicating which horoscope goes with which sign. Then ask members of your class to indicate the horoscope that best matches the day they actually had. Have them write their birthday (or sign) on the paper as well.

If people just picked horoscopes at random, you would expect about 1 person in 12 to pick the horoscope corresponding to his or her sign. Are the results of your survey any better than that? What does this tell you about the predictive power of astrology? •

The Organization of Science

Scientists investigate all sorts of natural objects and phenomena: the tiniest elementary particles, microscopic living cells, the human body, forests, the Earth, stars, and the entire cosmos. Throughout this vast sweep, the same scientific method can be applied. Men and women have been carrying out this task for hundreds of years, and by now we have a pretty good idea about how the many parts of our universe work. In the process, scientists have also developed a social structure that provides unity to the pursuit of scientific knowledge, as well as recognition of important disciplinary differences within the larger scientific framework.

The Divisions of Science

Science is a human endeavor, and humans invariably form themselves into groups with shared interests. When modern science first started in the seventeenth century, it was possible for one person to know almost all there was to know about the physical world and the "three kingdoms" of animals, vegetables, and minerals. In the seventeenth century, Isaac Newton could do forefront research in astronomy, in the physics of moving objects, in the behavior of light, and in mathematics. Thus, for a time prior to the mid-nineteenth century, scholars who studied the workings of the physical universe formed a more-or-less cohesive group, who called themselves "natural philosophers." But, as human understanding expanded and knowledge of nature became more detailed and technical, science began to fragment into increasingly specialized disciplines and subdisciplines.

Today, our knowledge and understanding of the world is so much more sophisticated and complex that no one person could possibly be at the frontier in such a wide variety of fields. Scientists today must choose a field—biology, chemistry, physics, and so on—and study one small part of the subject at great length.

Within each of these broad disciplines there are hundreds of different subspecialties. In physics, for example, a student may elect to study the behavior of light, the properties of materials, the nucleus of the atom, elementary particles, or the origin of the universe. The amount of information and expertise required to get to the frontier in any of these fields is so large that most students have to ignore almost everything else to learn their specialty.

Science is further divided because scientists within each subspecialty approach problems in different ways. Some scientists are *field researchers,* who go into natural settings to observe nature at work. Other scientists are *experimentalists,* who manipulate nature with controlled experiments. Still other scientists, called *theorists,* spend their time imagining universes that might exist. These different kinds of scientists need to work together to make progress.

The fragmentation of science into disciplines was formalized by a peculiar aspect of the European university system. In Europe, each academic department can have only one "professor." All other teachers, no matter how famous and distinguished, have less prestigious titles. And so, as the number of outstanding scientists grew in the nineteenth century, universities were forced to create new departments to attract new professors. A number of German universities, for example, supported separate departments of theoretical and experimental physics. And Cambridge University in England at one point had seven different specialized departments of chemistry!

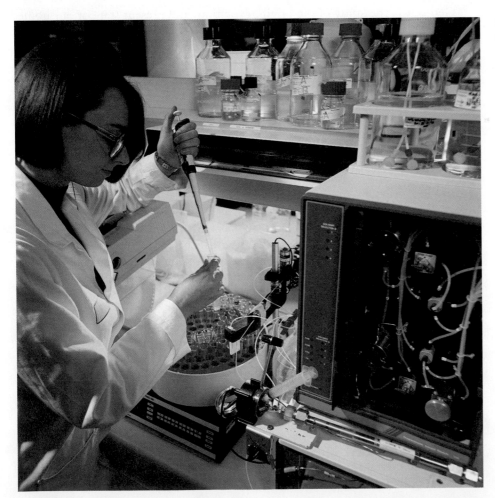

Scientists work at many different tasks.

In North America, each academic department generally has many professors. Nevertheless, American science faculties are often divided into several departments, including physics, chemistry, astronomy, geology, and biology—the so-called branches of science.

The Branches of Science

Several branches of science are distinguished by the scope and content of the questions they address:

Physics is the search for laws that describe the most fundamental aspects of nature: matter, energy, forces, motion, heat, light, and other phenomena. All natural systems, including planets, stars, cells, and people, display these basic phenomena, so physics is the starting point for almost any study of how nature works.

Chemistry is the study of atoms in combination. Chemicals form every material object of our world, while chemical reactions initiate vital changes in our environment and our bodies. Chemistry is thus an immensely practical (and profitable) science.

Astronomy is the study of stars, planets, and other objects in space. We are in an era of unprecedented astronomical discovery thanks to human and robotic space exploration.

Geology is the study of the origin, evolution, and present state of our home, planet Earth. Many geology departments also emphasize the study of other planets as a way to understand the unique character of our own world.

Biology is the study of living systems. Biologists document life at many scales, from individual microscopic molecules and cells to expansive ecosystems.

In spite of this division of science into separate disciplines, all branches of science are interconnected in a single web of knowledge.

The Web of Knowledge

The organization of science can be compared to an intricate spider web (Figure 1-5). Around the periphery of the web are all the objects and phenomena examined by scientists, from atoms to fish to comets. Moving toward the web's center, we find the cross-linking hypotheses that scientists have developed to explain how these phenomena work. The farther in we move, the more general these hypotheses become and the more they explain. Radiating out from the center of the web, connecting all the parts and holding the entire structure together, we find a small number of very general principles that have attained the rank of laws of nature.

No matter where you start on the web, no matter what part of nature you investigate, you will eventually come to one of the fundamental overarching ideas that intersect at the central core. Everything that happens in the universe happens because one or more of these physical laws is operating.

The hierarchical organization of scientific knowledge provides an ideal way to approach the study of science. At the center of any scientific question are a few laws of nature. We begin by looking at those laws that describe everyday forces and motions in the universe. These overarching principles of science are accepted and shared by all scientists, no matter what their field of research. These ideas recur over and over again as we study different parts of the world. You will find that many of these ideas and their consequences seem quite simple—perhaps even

• **Figure 1-5** The interconnected web of scientific knowledge.

Laws of Nature

obvious—because you are intimately familiar with the physical world in which these laws of nature constantly operate.

After introducing these general principles, we look at how the scientific method is applied to specific physical systems in nature. We examine the nature of materials and the atoms that make them, for example, and look at the chemical reactions that form them. We explore the planet on which we live and discover how mountains and oceans, rivers and plains are formed and evolve over time. And we examine living organisms at the scale of molecules, cells, organisms, and ecosystems.

By the time you have finished this journey, you will have touched on many of the great truths about the physical universe that scientists have deduced over the centuries. You will discover how the different parts of our universe operate and how all the parts fit together, and you will know that there are still great unanswered questions that drive scientists today. You will understand some of the great scientific and technological challenges that face our society and, more importantly, you will know enough about how the world works to deal with many of the new problems that will arise in the future.

Basic Research, Applied Research, and Technology

The physical universe can be studied in many ways, and many reasons exist for doing so. Many scientists are simply interested in finding out how the world

Table 1-2 **Major Research Laboratories**

Facility	Type	Location
Argonne National Laboratory	Govt/Univ	Near Chicago, IL
AT&T Bell Laboratories	Industrial	Murray Hill, NJ
Brookhaven National Laboratory	Government	Long Island, NY
Dupont R & D Center	Industrial	Wilmington, DE
Fermi National Accelerator Lab	Govt/Univ	Near Chicago, IL
IBM Watson Research Laboratory	Industrial	Yorktown Hts, NY
Keck Telescope	University	Mauna Kea, HI
Los Alamos National Laboratory	Government	Los Alamos, NM
National Institutes of Health	Government	Bethesda, MD
National Institutes of Standards and Technology	Government	Gaithersburg, MD
Oak Ridge National Laboratory	Government	Oak Ridge, TN
Stanford Linear Accelerator	Govt/Univ	Stanford, CA
Texas Center for Superconductivity	University	Houston, TX
United States Geological Survey	Government	Reston, VA
Upjohn Pharamaceuticals Laboratory	Industrial	Kalamazoo, MI
Woods Hole Oceanographic Institution	University	Woods Hole, MA

works—in knowledge for its own sake. They are engaged in **basic research**, and may be found studying the behavior of distant stars or of subatomic particles. Although discoveries made by basic researchers may have profound effects on society (see the discussion of the discovery of the electric generator in Chapter 5, for example), that is not the primary goal of these scientists.

Many other scientists approach their work with specific practical goals in mind. They wish to develop **technology**, in which they apply the results of science to specific commercial or industrial goals. These scientists are said to be doing **applied research**, and their ideas are often translated into practical systems by large-scale **research and development (R&D)** projects.

Government laboratories, colleges and universities, and private industries all support both basic and applied research; however, most large-scale R&D (as well as most applied research) is done in government laboratories and private industry (Table 1-2).

TECHNOLOGY •

SETI@HOME

The Search for Extraterrestrial Intelligence (SETI) has had a long and somewhat varied history. Scientists in the early 1960s realized that radio telescopes then in operation could detect signals from other civilizations (provided, of course, that the signals were being sent). Since that time, astronomers have looked for these signals without success. Nevertheless, the importance of finding even one extraterrestrial civilization is so great that the search goes on.

Hunting for a signal is a little like looking for a radio station in an unfamiliar city. You dial across the frequencies, listening for a moment to each station, until you find what you are looking for. In the same way, SETI astronomers point their

The radio telescope at Arecibo, in Puerto Rico, is one instrument used in SETI.

telescope at a small region of the sky, dial through the frequencies, then move on to the next region. Because there is a lot of sky and many frequencies, the sheer volume of data that have to be analyzed has been the primary roadblock in the search.

Recently, scientists at the University of California at Berkeley have harnessed the new technology of the Internet to attack this problem. Radio data from the Arecibo Observatory in Puerto Rico are sent to Berkeley, where they are sorted into small chunks. These data chunks are then sent out to participants in the *SETI@home* project—over a million participants in hundreds of countries worldwide. Typically, these participants use downloaded software to let their personal computers analyze the data when the machine isn't doing anything else (a typical setup uses the SETI program as a screen saver). When the chunk of data is analyzed it is sent back to Berkeley and new data are returned.

Several million computers connected in this way form the largest computing project on Earth. More importantly, they are probably a taste of things to come, when distributed computers, working part time, will help scientists analyze massive data sets that are being developed in all sorts of fields. If you want to join, the address is http://setiathome.ssl.berkeley.edu. •

Funding for Science

An overwhelming proportion of funding for American scientific research comes from various agencies of the federal government—your tax dollars at work (see Table 1-3). In 2002, the U.S. government's total research and development budget was about 100 billion dollars. The *National Science Foundation,* with an annual budget of about three billion dollars, supports research and education in all areas of science. Other agencies, including the National Institutes of Health, the Department of Energy, the Department of Defense, the Environmental Protection Agency, and the National Aeronautic and Space Administration, fund

Table 1-3 **Your Tax Dollars: 2001 Federal Science Funding**

Agency or Department	Funding (in millions of $)
Department of Agriculture	1,436
Department of Defense	35,870
Department of Energy	
General science and research	5,208
Environmental restoration; nuclear waste management	5,837
Environmental Protection Agency	350
National Aeronautics and Space Administration	
Research and development	5,891
Human space flight and mission support	8,129
National Institutes of Health	11,334
National Institutes of Standards and Technology	790
National Oceanographic and Atmospheric Administration	259
National Science Foundation	3,360

research and science education in their own particular areas of interest, while Congress may appropriate additional money for special projects.

An individual scientist seeking funding for research will usually submit a grant proposal to the appropriate federal agency. Such a proposal will include an outline of the planned research together with a statement about why the work is important. The agency evaluating the proposals asks panels of independent scientists to rank them in order of importance, and funds as many as it can. Depending on the field, a proposal has anywhere from about a 10% to a 40% chance of being successful. This money from federal grants buys experimental equipment and computer time, pays the salaries of researchers, and supports advanced graduate students. Without this support, science in the United States would all but come to a halt. The funding of science by the federal government is one place where the opinions and ideas of the citizen, through his or her elected representatives, have a direct effect on the development of science.

As you might expect, scientists and politicians engage in many debates about how this research money should be spent. One constant point of contention, for example, concerns the question of basic versus applied research. How much money should we put into the latter, which can be expected to show a quick payoff, as opposed to the former, which may not have a payoff for years (if at all)?

Communication Among Scientists

Sometimes it's easier to do your homework with other students than by yourself, and the same is true of the work that scientists do. Working in isolation can be very hard, and scientists often seek out other people with whom to converse and collaborate. The popular stereotype of the lonely genius changing the course of history just doesn't describe the world of the working scientist. The next time you walk down the hall of a science department at your university, you will probably see faculty and students deep in conversation, talking and scribbling on blackboards. This direct contact between colleagues is the simplest type of scientific communication.

Scientific meetings provide a more formal and structured forum for communication. Every week of the year, at conference retreats and convention centers across the country, groups of scientists gather to trade ideas. You may notice that science stories in your newspapers often originate in the largest of these meetings, where thousands of scientists converge at one time, and a cadre of science reporters with their own special briefing room is poised to publicize exciting results. Scientists often hold off announcing important discoveries until they can make a splash at such a well-attended meeting and press conference.

Finally, scientists communicate with each other in writing. In addition to rapid communications such as letters, fax, and electronic mail, almost all scientific fields have specialized journals to publish the results of research. The system works like this: When a group of scientists have finished a piece of research and want to communicate their results, they write a concise paper describing exactly what they've done, giving the technical details of their method so that others can reproduce the data, and stating their results and conclusions. The journal editor sends the submitted manuscript to one or more knowledgeable scientists who act as referees. These reviewers, whose identities are not usually revealed to the authors, read the paper carefully, checking for mistakes, misstatements, or shoddy procedures. If they tell the editor that the work passes muster, it will probably be published. Often, such a recommendation is accompanied by a list of necessary modifications and corrections. This system, called **peer review**, is one of the cornerstones of modern science.

Peer review provides a clear protocol for entering new results into the scientific literature. Little wonder, then, that scientists get so upset when one of their colleagues tries to bypass the system and announces results at a press conference. Such work has not been subject to the thorough review process, and no one can be sure that it meets established standards. When the results turn out to be irreproducible, overstated, or just plain wrong, it damages the credibility of the entire scientific community.

Thinking More About | Research

Stem Cells

When cells in your body divide, they make cells like themselves. Muscle cells produce more muscle cells, skin cells produce more skin cells, and so on. On the other hand, in the very early stages of development, cells in an embryo retain the ability to form into any kind of cell whatsoever. Cells that have this property are called "stem cells." Normally, stem cells lose their ability to develop freely after a few generations—in effect they "choose" one type of cell to produce.

In 1998, researchers at a number of institutions succeeded in keeping stem cells proliferating for long periods of time. The medical implications of this development are enormous. If we have cells that can develop into any kind of human tissue, you can imagine being able to treat degenerative diseases like Parkinson's and Alzheimer's, and perhaps even heal crippling spinal cord injuries.

On the other hand, the most reliable source of such stem cells is human embryos, either those grown specifically in the laboratory or harvested from abortions or miscarriages. In the United States, federal funds cannot be used to develop new cell lines from these sources.

How do you weigh the possible good that could come from research on stem cells against the moral objections to this type of use of human embryos? Should the moral standards of one segment of the population prevent research that would benefit those who do not share those standards? Who should make decisions like this?

Web Sites

http://www.nasa.gov
http://www.energy.gov
http://www.epa.gov
http://www.nih.gov

SUMMARY

Science is a way of learning about our physical universe. The *scientific method* relies on making *reproducible observations* and *experiments*, which may suggest general trends and *hypotheses*, or *theories*. Hypotheses, in turn, lead to *predictions* that can be tested with more observations and experiments. Theories, no matter how successful, are always subject to further testing. Experimental analyses and the development of theories are often guided by the language of *mathematics*. Science and the scientific method differ from other ways of knowing, including religion, philosophy, and the arts, and differ from *pseudosciences*.

Science is organized around a hierarchy of fundamental principles. Overarching concepts about forces, motion,

matter, and energy apply to all scientific disciplines, including *physics, chemistry, astronomy, geology,* and *biology.* Additional great ideas relate to specific systems—molecules, cells, planets, or stars. This body of scientific knowledge forms a seamless web, in which every detail fits into a larger, integrated picture of our universe.

Scientists engage in *basic research* to acquire fundamental knowledge, as well as *applied research* and *research and development (R&D)*, which are aimed at specific problems. *Technology* is developed by this process. Scientific results are communicated in *peer-reviewed* publications. The federal government plays the important role of funding most scientific research and advanced science education in the United States.

KEY TERMS

scientific method	theory	chemistry	technology
observation	prediction	astronomy	applied research
experiment	reproducible	geology	research and development (R&D)
mathematics	pseudoscience	biology	peer review
hypothesis	physics	basic research	

REVIEW QUESTIONS

1. What is science?

2. How might Plato, a medieval scholar at Oxford, and the Italian scientist Galileo have differed in the importance each placed on the role of rational processes, observations, and received wisdom in the study of nature?

3. Write an equation in words and then in symbols for the following sentence: The price of coffee beans is equal to the weight of the beans times the price of the beans per pound.

4. Write an equation in words and then in symbols for the following sentence: The change in the number of individuals in a population is equal to the difference between the number of births and deaths.

5. Describe the steps of the scientific method.

6. Describe the roles of hypotheses, theories, and predictions in the scientific method.

7. Describe the difference between an observation and an experiment.

8. Why might the term "scientific cycle" be a good substitute for "scientific method"?

9. By what criteria might you determine whether a question might be answered using the scientific method?

10. Describe the difference between basic and applied research. Give examples of basic and applied research that might be undertaken on transportation and on health.

11. In what ways do scientists communicate with their colleagues?

12. Describe the steps a scientist would take to obtain funding for a research project. What sources of funds might be available? What role would peer review play in the process?

DISCUSSION QUESTIONS

1. Why are studies of unidentified flying objects (UFOs) considered to be pseudoscience by most scientists? What kind of discovery might change scientists' minds?

2. Which of the following statements could be tested scientifically?

a. The Moon is made of green cheese.

b. Most of the Sun's energy is in the form of heat energy.

c. Unicorns are now extinct.

d. Beethoven wrote beautiful music.

e. The Earth was created over 4 billion years ago.

f. The Earth was created in a miraculous event.

g. Diamond is harder than steel.

h. Diamond is more beautiful than ruby.

3. What was the role of a control in David Tilman's experiments on biodiversity?

4. How do the studies of Harvey and Mendeleev illustrate the scientific method?

5. Scientists are currently investigating whether certain microscopic organisms can clean up toxic wastes. How might you set up an experiment to determine that you had found such an organism?

6. Categorize the following examples as basic research or applied research.

a. the discovery of a new species of bird

b. the development of better methods to make window glass

c. the breeding of a new variety of disease-resistant wheat

d. a study of the ecological role of fungus in tropical rain forests

e. the identification of a new chemical compound

f. an investigation of the solubility of gold in hot water

g. the improvement of a method to extract the element gold from stream gravels

7. The claim is sometimes made that the cycle of the scientific method produces closer and closer approximations to "reality." Is this a scientific statement? Why or why not?

8. A recent television commercial claimed that an antacid consumed "47 times its own weight in excess stomach acid." How might you test this statement in the laboratory? As a consumer, what additional questions would you ask before deciding to buy this product? Are all of these questions subject to the scientific method?

9. What are some of the criteria that scientists might use to select which one research grant proposal, among five finalists, to fund?

PROBLEMS

1. Pablo has kept careful records of driving speed versus fuel efficiency. He has noted that when traveling 20 miles per hour (mph) he averages 26 miles per gallon of gasoline (mpg). Similarly, he gets 29 mpg at 30 mph, 32 mpg at 40 mph, 31 mpg at 50 mph, 30 mpg at 50 mph, and 29 mpg at 55 mph. Describe and illustrate some of the ways you might present these data. What additional data would you like to obtain to improve your description?

2. Tabulate the age, gender, height, and weight of 12 friends. Present these data both in a table, and in one or more graphs. Do you observe any striking trends? Why might physicians find such a table useful?

3. Pick a favorite tree and write down at least 10 adjectives to describe the tree. Then cite at least five ways in which you might use numbers to describe a tree more precisely than using just words. Make one of these measurements on your chosen tree.

4. Someone says to you, "I was thinking about Aunt Maria the other day, and she called me on the phone. Doesn't that prove ESP exists?" How would you design an experiment to test this sort of claim?

INVESTIGATIONS

1. What is the closest major government research laboratory to your school? The closest industrial laboratory? Describe one research project that is now underway at one of these laboratories.

2. Describe a program of scientific research carried out by a member of your school's faculty. How is the scientific method employed in this research? Would you characterize the research as basic or applied?

3. Identify a current piece of legislation relating to science or technology (perhaps an environmental or energy bill). How did your representatives in Congress vote on this issue?

4. Look at a recent newspaper article about science funding. What is the funding agency? Is the proposed research basic or applied? Are the projects described big or little science?

5. Find a science story in a newspaper or popular magazine. Who were the scientists who conducted the research? Where did they do the work? How was the research funded?

6. How were scientists depicted in the novel and film versions of *Jurassic Park* by Michael Crichton? Were you convinced by these portrayals? Why? How do these portrayals compare with those in other popular movies and books?

7. Was Harvey justified in his use of animals in studies of the circulatory system? What limits should scientists accept in research using animals? What national organizations are involved in this debate?

8. Design an experiment to test the relative strengths of three different kinds of aluminum can. What data would you need to collect? How might you present these data in tables and graphically?

9. Malaria, the deadliest infectious disease in the world, kills more than 2 million people (mostly children in poor countries) every year. The annual malaria research budget in the United States is less than a million dollars, a minuscule fraction of spending on cancer, heart disease, and AIDS. Should the United States devote more research funds to this disease, which does not occur in North America? Why or why not?

10. Look at a carefully tended lawn at your school and compare it with a patch of wild ground. Do your observations match those of the Minnesota biodiversity experiment? Why or why not?

WWW Resources

See *The Sciences* homepage at: **http://www.wiley.com/college/trefil** for valuable web links.

1. http://www.sciam.com
Scientific American—for great links, click on *"Feature Articles"* for a comprehensive list of solid links.

2. http://www.sciencenews.org
Science News Online—see *"Table of Contents"* for quick updates on the current week's "Science News," and *"Science Safari"* for general-interest links.

3. http://www.particleadventure.org/particleadventure
The Particle Adventure Home Page, an excellent site from CERN.

4. http://www.sciencenetlinks.com
AAAS Science NetLinks, a dependable resource for science links that includes reviews of selected sites.

5. http://jersey.uoregon.edu/vlab
Virtual Laboratory, from the University of Oregon, a fascinating site. If you go here, be sure that you have some time to spend enjoying the interactive projects.

6. http://www.thetech.org/
The Tech Museum of Innovation—see *"Online Exhibits"*

7. http://www.pbs.org/science/
PBS Online Science, for popular science in the news.

2

The Ordered Universe

Why do planets appear to wander slowly across the sky?

GREAT IDEA

Newton's laws of motion and gravity predict the behavior of objects on Earth and in space.

PHYSICS

Collisions of atoms and automobiles illustrate the laws of motion.

CHEMISTRY

A force different from gravity must be responsible for the chemical bonding of atoms to each other. (Ch. 10)

ENVIRONMENT

Gravity may cause land to collapse in regions where too much groundwater is pumped out of the ground. (Ch. 18)

GEOLOGY

Gravity controls the flow of water through vast systems of streams and rivers.

HEALTH & SAFETY

Air bags reduce injuries from high-speed automobile collisions.

ASTRONOMY

The universal law of gravitation can tell you why the Moon orbits the Earth and the Earth orbits the Sun.

TECHNOLOGY

Lighter-than-air, helium-filled aircraft may provide a cheap and reliable method of transportation in the twenty-first century.

BIOLOGY

Land plants and animals must develop strong supportive structures to counteract the force of gravity.

Red = applications of the great idea discussed in this chapter.

Orange = other applications, some of which are explored in other chapters.

Y ou jump out of bed, eager to start the day. The air smells fresh and cool, but the Sun's rays already feel warm. It should be perfect beach weather.

When the Sun comes up in the morning you expect temperatures to become warmer; in the evening, as the Sun goes down, you expect temperatures to fall. When you turn the key in the ignition in your car you expect it to start. When you flip a light switch, you expect a light to go on.

Our world is filled with ordinary events like these—events we take so much for granted that we scarcely notice them. Yet they set the background for the way we think about the world. We believe in cause and effect because it's so much a part of our lives.

The regular passage of seasons, with the shortening and lengthening of days and gradual changes in temperature, provides a template for our lives. We plant and harvest crops, purchase wardrobes, and

even schedule vacations around this predictable cycle, in the sure knowledge that we must adapt and prepare for nature's cycles. Indeed, the predictability of our physical world has become the central principle of science—an idea so important that science could never have developed it had it not been true.

The Night Sky

Among the most predictable objects in the universe are the lights we see in the sky at night—the stars and planets. Modern men and women, living in large metropolitan areas, are no longer very conscious of the richness of the night sky's shifting patterns. But think about the last time you were out in the country on a clear moonless night, far from the lights of town. There, the stars seem very close, very real. Before the nineteenth-century development of artificial lighting, human beings often experienced jet-black skies filled with brilliant pinpoint stars.

The sky changes; it's never quite the same from one night to the next. Living with this display all the time, our ancestors noticed regularities in the arrangement and movements of stars and planets, and they wove these almost lifelike patterns into their religion and mythology. They learned that when the Sun rose in a certain place, it was time to plant crops because spring was on its way. They learned that at certain times of the month a full Moon would illuminate the ground, allowing them to continue harvesting and hunting after sunset. To these people, knowing the behavior of the sky was not an intellectual game or an educational frill, it was an essential part of their lives. It is no wonder, then, that astronomy, the study of the heavens, was one of the first sciences to develop.

By relying on their observations and records of the regular motions of the stars and planets, ancient observers of the sky were perhaps the first humans to accept the most basic tenet of science:

Physical events are predictable and quantifiable.

Without the predictability of physical events the scientific method could not proceed.

Stonehenge

No symbol of humankind's early preoccupation with astronomy is more dramatic than Stonehenge, the great prehistoric stone monument on Salisbury Plain in southern England. The structure consists of a large circular bank of earth surrounding a ring of single upright stones, which in turn encircle a horseshoe-shaped structure of five giant stone archways. Each arch is constructed from three massive blocks—two vertical supports several meters tall capped by a great stone lintel. The open end of the horseshoe aligns with an avenue that leads northeast to another large stone, called the "heel stone" (see Figure 2-1).

Stonehenge was built in spurts over a long period of time, starting in about 2800 B.C. Despite various legends assigning it to the Druids, Julius Caesar, the magician Merlin (who was supposed to have levitated the stones from Ireland), or other mysterious unknown races, archaeologists have shown that Stonehenge was built by several groups of people, none of whom had a written language and some of whom even lacked metal tools. Why would these people expend such a great effort to erect one of the world's great monuments?

Stonehenge, like many similar structures scattered around the world, was built to mark the passage of time. It served as a giant calendar based on the movement of objects in the sky. The most famous astronomical function of Stonehenge was to mark the passage of the seasons. In an agricultural society, after all, you have to know when it's time to plant the crops, and you can't always tell by looking at the weather. At Stonehenge, this job was done by sighting through the stones. On midsummer's morning, for example, someone standing in the center of the monument will see the Sun rising directly over the heel stone.

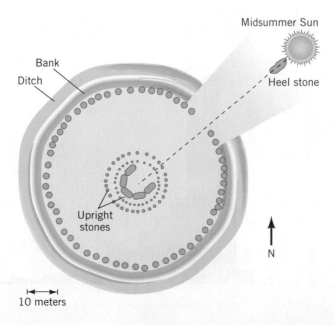

• **Figure 2-1** Stonehenge is built so that someone standing at the center will see the Sun rise over the heel stone on midsummer's morning.

Building a structure like Stonehenge required accumulation of a great deal of knowledge about the sky—knowledge that could have been gained only through many years of observation. Without a written language, people would have had to pass complex information about the movements of the Sun, the Moon, and the planets from one generation to the next. How else could they have aligned their stones so perfectly that modern-day Druids in England can still greet the midsummer sunrise over the heel stone?

If the universe was not regular and predictable, if repeated observation could not show us patterns that occur over and over again, the very concept of a monument like Stonehenge would be impossible. And yet, there it stands after almost 5000 years, a testament to human ingenuity and to the possibility of predicting the behavior of the universe we live in.

SCIENCE IN THE MAKING •
The Discovery of the Spread of Disease

Observing nature is a crucial part of the scientific method. During the nineteenth century, for example, Europe experienced an epidemic of cholera, a severe and often fatal intestinal disease. No one knew the cause of the disease (the discovery of the germ theory of disease was still decades in the future), but doctors could record their observations about the illness. A list of cholera outbreaks was chronicled in 1854 by John Snow (1823–1858), a distinguished London physician who pioneered the use of anesthetics and assisted at the birth of Queen Victoria's children. He noticed that in London the diseases seemed to be centered around certain public squares. At that time, most people in London got their drinking water from fountains and pumps in those squares. The Broad Street pump, located in a place called Golden Square, seemed to be the focus of a particularly large number of cases. Upon investigation, Snow found that the square was surrounded by a large number of homes where human waste was dumped into backyard pits. He argued that these findings suggested the disease was somehow related to contamination of the water supply (Figure 2-2).

Driven by Snow's findings, the city of London (and soon all major population centers) began to require that human waste be carried away from dwellings

• **Figure 2-2** John Snow plotted the number of cases of cholera versus the date for residents in the vicinity of the Broad Street pump. The number of cases declined in early September because most residents fled the area, but few new cases occured after the pump handle was removed on September 8.

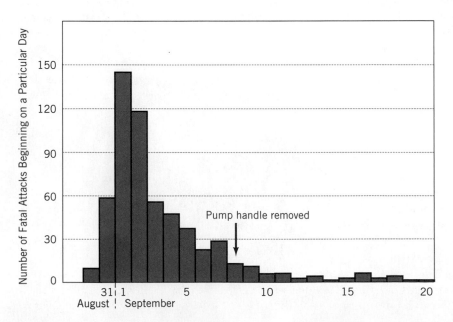

into sewers. Thus Snow's discovery of a regularity in nature (in this case between disease and polluted water) was the foundation on which modern sanitation and public health systems are based.

Just as the builders of Stonehenge had no idea of the structure of the solar system or why the heavens behave as they do, Snow had no idea why keeping human waste out of the drinking water supply should eliminate a disease such as cholera. It wasn't until the early 1890s, in fact, that the German scientist Robert Koch first suggested that the disease was caused by a particular bacterium, *Vibrio cholerae,* that is carried in human waste. •

SCIENCE BY THE NUMBERS •

Ancient Astronauts

Confronted by a monument such as Stonehenge, with its precise orientation and epic proportions, some people refuse to accept the notion that it could have been built by the ingenuity and hard work of ancient peoples. Instead, they evoke some outside intervention, frequently in the form of visitors from other planets whose handiwork survives in the monument today. Many ancient monuments, including the pyramids of Egypt, the Mayan temples of Central America, and the giant statues of Easter Island, have been ascribed to these mysterious aliens.

Such conjecture is unconvincing unless you first show that building the monument was beyond the capabilities of the indigenous people. Suppose, for example, that Columbus had found a glass-and-steel skyscraper when he landed in America. Both the ability to produce the materials (steel, glass, and plastic, for example) and the ability to construct a building dozens of stories tall were beyond the abilities of Native Americans at that time. A reasonable case could have been made for the intervention of ancient astronauts or some other advanced intelligence.

Is Stonehenge a similar case? The material, local stone, was certainly available to anyone who wanted to use it. Working and shaping stone was also a skill, albeit a laborious one, that was available to early civilizations. The key question, then, is whether people without steel tools or wheeled vehicles could have moved the stones from the quarry to the construction site (Figure 2-3).

The largest stone, about 10 meters (more than 30 feet) in length, weighs about 50 metric tons (50,000 kilograms, or about 100,000 pounds) and had to be moved overland some 30 kilometers (20 miles) from quarries to the north. Could this massive block have been moved by primitive people, equipped only with wood and ropes?

While Stonehenge was being built, it snowed frequently in southern England, so the stones could have been hauled on sleds. A single person can easily haul 100 kilograms on a sled (think of pulling a couple of your friends). How many people would it take to haul a 50,000-kilogram stone?

> 50,000 kilograms/100 kilograms pulled by each person
> = 500 people

Organizing 500 people for the job would have been a major social achievement, of course, but there's nothing physically impossible about it. So, while scientists cannot absolutely disprove the possibility that Stonehenge was constructed by some strange, forgotten technology, why should we evoke such alien intervention when the concerted actions of a dedicated, hard-working human society would have sufficed?

When confronted with phenomena in a physical world, we should accept the most straightforward and reasonable explanation as the most likely. This procedure is called *Ockham's razor,* after William of Ockham, a fourteenth-century English

• **Figure 2-3** One puzzling aspect of the construction of Stonehenge is the raising of the giant lintel stones. Three steps in the process were probably (*a*) to dig a pit for each of the upright stones; (*b*) to pile dirt into a long sloping ramp up to the level of the two uprights so that the lintel stones could be rolled into place; and (*c*) to cart away the dirt, thus leaving the stone archway.

philosopher who argued that "postulates must not be multiplied without necessity"—that is, given a choice, the simplest solution to a problem is most likely to be right. Scientists thus reject the notion of ancient astronauts building Stonehenge, and they relegate such speculation to the realm of pseudoscience. •

The Birth of Modern Astronomy

When you look up at the night sky you see a dazzling array of objects. Thousands of visible stars fill the heavens and appear to move each night in stately circular arcs centered on the North Pole star. The relative positions of these stars never seem to change, and closely spaced groups of stars called constellations have been given names such as the Big Dipper and Leo the Lion. Moving across this fixed starry background are the Earth's Moon, with its regular succession of phases, and half-a-dozen planets that wander through the zodiac. You might also see swift streaking meteors or long-tailed comets—transient objects that grace the night sky from time to time.

What causes these objects to move, and what do those motions tell us about the universe in which we live?

The Historical Background: Ptolemy and Copernicus

Since before recorded history people have observed the distinctive motions of objects in the sky and have tried to explain them. Most societies created legends and myths tied to these movements, and some (the Babylonians, for example) had long records of sophisticated astronomical observations. It was the Greeks, however, who devised the first astronomical explanations that incorporated elements of modern science.

Claudius Ptolemy, an Egyptian-born Greek astronomer and geographer who lived in Alexandria in the second century A.D., proposed the first plausible explanation for complex celestial motions. Working with the accumulated observations of earlier Babylonian and Greek astronomers, he put together a singularly successful model—a theory, to use the modern term, about how the heavens had to be arranged to produce the display we see every night. In the Ptolemaic description of the universe, the Earth sat unmoved at the center. Around it, on a concentric series of rotating spheres, moved the stars and planets. The model was carefully crafted to take account of observations. The planets, for example, were attached to small spheres rolling inside of the larger spheres so that their uneven motion across the sky could be understood.

This system remained the best explanation of the universe for almost 1500 years. It successfully predicted planetary motions, eclipses, and a host of other heavenly phenomena, and was one of the longest-lived scientific theories ever devised.

During the first decades of the sixteenth century, however, a Polish cleric by the name of Nicolas Copernicus (1473–1543) proposed a competing hypothesis that was to herald the end of Ptolemy's crystal spheres. His ideas were published in 1543 under the title *On the Revolutions of the Spheres.* Copernicus retained the notions of a spherical universe with circular orbits, and even kept the ideas of spheres rolling within a sphere, but he asked a simple and extraordinary question: "Is it possible to construct a model of the heavens whose predictions are as accurate as Ptolemy's, but in which the Sun, rather than the Earth, is at the center?" We do not know how Copernicus, a busy man of affairs in medieval Poland, conceived this question, nor do we know why he devoted his spare time for most of his adult life to answering it. We do know, however, that in 1543, for the first time in over a millennium, the Ptolemaic system was faced by a serious challenger (see Figure 2-4).

Observations: Tycho Brahe and Johannes Kepler

With the publication of the Copernican theory, astronomers were confronted by two competing models of the universe. The Ptolemaic and Copernican systems differed in a fundamental way that had far-reaching implications about the place of humanity in the universe. They both described possible universes, but in one the Earth, and by implication humankind, was no longer at the center. The astronomers' task was to decide which model best describes the universe we actually live in.

To resolve the question astronomers had to compare the predictions of the two competing hypotheses to the observations of what was actually seen in the sky.

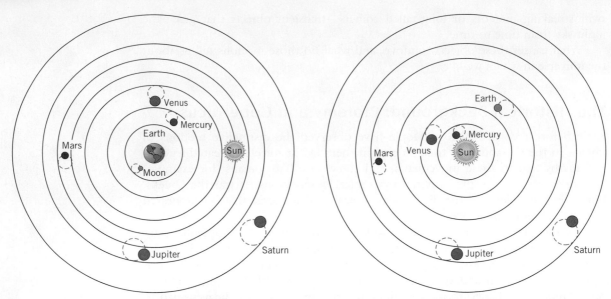

• **Figure 2-4** The Ptolemaic (*a*) and Copernican (*b*) systems both assumed that all orbits are circular. The fundamental difference is that Copernicus placed the Sun at the center.

When they performed these observations, a fundamental problem became apparent. Although the two models made different predictions about the position of a planet at midnight, for example, or the time of moonrise, the differences were too small to be measured with equipment available at the time. The telescope had not yet been invented, and astronomers had to record planetary positions by depending entirely on naked-eye measurements with awkward instruments. Until the accuracy of measurement was improved, the question of whether the Earth was at the center of the universe couldn't be decided.

The Danish nobleman Tycho Brahe (1546–1601) showed the way out of this impasse. Tycho, as he was known, is one of those people who, in addition to making important contributions to knowledge, led a truly bizarre life. He was, for example, abducted in infancy and raised by his uncle. As a young man he lost the end of his nose in a duel with a fellow student over who was the better mathematician; for the rest of his life he had to wear a silver and gold prosthesis.

Tycho's scientific reputation was firmly established at the age of 25, when he observed and described a new star in the sky (in fact, a supernova—see Chapter 14). Within the next five years, the Danish king had given him the island of Hveen off the coast of Denmark and funds to construct a royal observatory there.

Tycho built his career on the design and use of vastly improved observational instruments. He determined the position of each star or planet with a "quadrant," a large sloping device something like a gun sight, recording each position as two angles. If you were to do this today, you might, for example, measure one angle up from the horizon and a second angle around from due north. Tycho constructed his sighting device of carefully selected materials, and he learned to correct his measurements for thermal contraction—the slight shrinkage of brass and iron components that occurred during the cold Danish nights. Over a period of 25 years, he used these instruments to accumulate extremely accurate data on the positions of the planets.

When Tycho died in 1601, his data passed into the hands of his assistant, Johannes Kepler (1571–1630), a skilled German mathematician who had joined

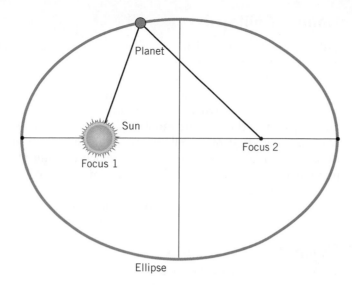

• **Figure 2-5** Kepler's first law, shown schematically, states that the orbit of every planet is an ellipse, a geometrical figure in which the sum of the distances to two fixed points (each of which is called a focus) is always the same. For planetary orbits in the solar system, the Sun is at one focus of the ellipse (greatly exaggerated in this figure).

Tycho two years before. Kepler analyzed Tycho Brahe's decades of planetary data in new ways, and he found that the data could be summarized in three mathematical statements about the solar system. Kepler's first and most important law (shown in Figure 2-5) states that all planets, including the Earth, orbit the Sun in elliptical, not circular, paths. In this picture, the spheres-within-spheres are gone, because ellipses fully account for the observed planetary motions. Not only do Kepler's laws give a better description of what is observed in the sky, but they present a simpler picture of the solar system as well.

Previous astronomers had assumed that planetary orbits must be perfect circles, and many believed on theological or philosophical grounds that the Earth had to be the center of a spherical universe. In science, such assumptions of ideality may guide thinking, but they must be replaced when observations prove them wrong.

The work of Tycho Brahe and Johannes Kepler firmly established that the Earth is not at the center of the universe, that planetary orbits are not circular, and that the answer to the contest between the Ptolemaic and Copernican universes is "neither of the above." This research also illustrates a recurrent point about scientific progress. The ability to answer scientific questions, even questions dealing with the most fundamental aspects of human existence, often depends on the kinds of instruments scientists have at their disposal, and the ability of scientists to apply advanced mathematical reasoning to their data.

At the end of this historical episode, astronomers had Kepler's laws that describe how the planets in the solar system move, but they had no idea *why* planets behave the way they do. The answer to that question was to come from an unexpected source.

The Birth of Mechanics

Mechanics is an old word for the branch of science that deals with the motions of material objects. A rock rolling down a hill, a ball thrown into the air, and a sailboat skimming over the waves are all fit subjects for this science. Since ancient times, philosophers had speculated on why things move the way they do, but it wasn't until the seventeenth century that our modern understanding of the subject began to emerge.

Galileo Galilei (1564–1642)

• **Figure 2-6** Telescopes used by Galileo Galilei in his astronomical studies.

Galileo Galilei

The Italian physicist and philosopher Galileo Galilei (1564–1642) was, in many ways, a forerunner of the modern scientist. A professor of mathematics at the University of Padua, he quickly became an advisor to the powerful court of the Medici at Florence as well as a consultant at the Arsenal of Venice, the most advanced naval construction center in the world. He invented many practical devices, such as the first thermometer, the pendulum clock, and the proportional compass that draftsmen still use today. Galileo is also famous as the first to observe the heavens with a telescope, which he built after hearing of the instrument from others (Figure 2-6). His astronomical writings, which supported the Sun-centered Copernican model of the universe, led to his trial, conviction, and eventual imprisonment by the Inquisition.

SCIENCE IN THE MAKING •

The Heresy Trial of Galileo

In spite of his great scientific advances, Galileo is remembered primarily because of his heresy trial in 1633. In 1610 Galileo had published a summary of his telescopic observations in *The Starry Messenger*, a book written in everyday Italian rather than scholarly Latin. Some readers complained that these ideas violated Catholic Church doctrine, and in 1616 Galileo was called before the College of Cardinals. The Catholic Church supposedly warned Galileo not to discuss Copernican ideas unless he treated them as an unproven hypothesis.

In spite of these instructions, in 1632 Galileo published *A Dialogue Concerning Two World Systems*, which was a long defense of the Copernican system. This action led to the famous trial, at which Galileo purged himself of suspicion of heresy by denying that he held the views in his book. He was already an old man by this time, and he spent his last few years under virtual house arrest in his villa near Florence.

The legend of Galileo's trial, in which an earnest seeker of truth is crushed by a rigid hierarchy, bears little resemblance to the historical events. The Catholic Church had not banned Copernican ideas. Copernicus, after all, was a savvy Church politician who knew how to get his ideas across without ruffling feathers. But Galileo's confrontational tactics—notably putting the Pope's favorite arguments into the mouth of a foolish character in the book—brought the predictable reaction.

A footnote: In 1992, the Catholic Church reopened the case of Galileo and, in effect, issued a retroactive "not guilty." The grounds for the reversal were that the original judges had not separated questions of faith from questions of scientific fact. •

Speed, Velocity, and Acceleration

To lay the groundwork for understanding Galileo's study of moving objects (and ultimately to understand the workings of the solar system), we have to begin with precise definitions of three familiar terms: speed, velocity, and acceleration.

Speed and Velocity

Speed and velocity are everyday words that have precise scientific meanings. **Speed** is the distance an object travels divided by the time it takes to travel that distance. **Velocity** has the same numerical value as speed, but it is a quantity that also includes information on the direction of travel. The speed of a car might be

40 miles per hour, for example, while the velocity is 40 miles per hour due west. Quantities like velocity that involve both a speed and a direction are called *vectors*. Velocity and speed are both measured in units of distance per time, such as meters per second, feet per second, or miles per hour.

▶ **In equation form:**

velocity (m/s) = distance traveled (m)/time of travel (s)

▶ **In symbols:**

$$v = d/t$$

Thus, if you know the distance traveled and the time elapsed during the travel, you can calculate the speed.

EXAMPLE 2-1

Driving

If your car travels 30 miles per hour, how many miles will you go in 15 minutes?

Reasoning and Solution: This question involves changing units, as well as applying the equation that relates time, velocity, and distance. First, we must know the travel time in hours:

$$\frac{15 \text{ minutes}}{(60 \text{ minutes/hour})} = 1/4 \text{ hour}$$

Then, rearranging the relationship between distance and time given above, we find:

distance = velocity × time
distance = 30 miles/hour × 1/4 hour
= 7.5 miles

It would take the average person about two hours to walk this far.

A word about units: You may have noticed that in the example we put 1/4 hour into the equation for the time instead of 15 minutes. The reason we did this was that we needed to be consistent with the units in which an automobile speedometer measures speed. Since the automobile dial reads in miles per hour, we also put the time in hours to make the equation balance. A useful way to deal with situations like this is to imagine that the units are quantities that can be canceled in fractions, just like numbers. In this case, we would have:

distance = (miles/hour) × hour
= miles

If, however, we put the time in minutes, we'd have:

distance = miles/hour × minutes

and there would be no cancellation.

Whenever you do a problem like this, it's a good idea to check to make sure the units come out correctly. This important process is known as *dimensional analysis*.

Acceleration

Acceleration is a measure of the rate of change of velocity. Whenever an object changes speed or direction, it accelerates. When you step on the gas pedal in your car, for example, the car accelerates forward. When you slam on the brakes, the car accelerates backward (what we usually call deceleration). When you go around a curve in your car, even if the car's speed stays exactly the same, the car is still accelerating because the direction of motion is changing. The most thrilling amusement park rides combine these different kinds of acceleration—speeding up, slowing down, and changing direction in bumps, tight turns, and rapid spins.

▶ **In words:** Acceleration is the amount of change in velocity divided by the time it takes that change to occur.

▶ **In equation form:**

acceleration (m/s^2) = [final velocity – initial velocity] (m/s)/time (s)

▶ **In symbols:**

$$a = \frac{(v_f - v_i)}{t}$$

Like velocity, acceleration requires information about the direction, and it is therefore a vector.

When velocity changes, it may be by a certain number of feet per second or meters per second in each second. Consequently, the units of acceleration are meters per second squared, usually described as "meters per second per second" (and abbreviated m/s^2), where the first "meters per second" refers to the velocity, and the last "per second" to the time it takes to change.

To understand the difference between acceleration and velocity, think about the last time you were behind the wheel of a car driving down a long straight road. You glance at your speedometer. If the needle is unmoving (at 30 miles per hour, for example), you are moving at a constant speed. Suppose, however, that the needle isn't stationary on the speedometer scale (perhaps because you have your foot on the gas or on the brake). Your speed is changing and, by the definition above, you are accelerating. The higher the acceleration, the faster the needle moves. If the needle doesn't move, however, *this doesn't mean you and the car aren't moving*. As we saw above, an unmoving needle simply means that you are traveling at a constant speed without acceleration. Motion at a constant speed in a single direction is called *uniform motion*.

The Father of Experimental Science

Galileo devised an ingenious experiment to determine the relationships among distance, time, velocity, and acceleration. Many scientists now view Galileo's greatest achievement as this experimental work on the behavior of objects thrown or dropped on the surface of the Earth. Greek philosophers, using pure reason, had taught that heavier objects must fall faster than light ones. In a series of classic experiments, Galileo showed that this was not the case—that at the surface of the Earth all objects accelerate at the same rate as they fall downward. Ironically, Galileo probably never performed the one experiment for which he is most famous—dropping two different weights from the Leaning Tower of Pisa to see which would land first.

To describe falling objects, it's necessary to make precise measurements of two variables: distance and time. Distance was easily measured by Galileo and his contemporaries using rulers, but their timepieces were not precise enough to measure the brief times it took objects to fall straight down. While previous workers had simply observed the behavior of falling objects, Galileo constructed a

Galileo's apparatus inclined plane

Time	Distance
0	0
1	1
2	4
3	9
4	16
5	25
6	36

• **Figure 2-7** Galileo's falling-ball apparatus with a table of measurements and a graph of distance versus time.

special apparatus designed purely to measure acceleration (see Figure 2-7). He slowed down the time of fall by rolling large balls down an inclined plane crafted of brass and hard wood, and measured the time of descent by listening to the "ping" as the ball rolled over wires stretched along its path. (The human ear is quite good at hearing equal time intervals). The balls accelerated as they moved down the plane, and by increasing the angle of elevation of the plane, he could increase that acceleration. At an elevation of 90 degrees, of course, the ball would fall freely.

Galileo's experiments convinced him that any object accelerating at the Earth's surface, no matter how heavy or light, falls with exactly the same constant acceleration. For balls on his plane, his results can be summarized in a simple equation:

▶ **In words:** The velocity of an accelerating object that starts from rest is proportional to the length of time that it has been falling.

▶ **In equation form:**

$$\text{velocity (m/s)} = \text{constant } a \text{ (m/s}^2\text{)} \times \text{time (s)}$$

▶ **In symbols:**

$$v = a \times t$$

The velocity of Galileo's objects, of course, was always directed downward.

This equation tells us that an object that falls two seconds achieves a velocity twice that of an object that falls only one second, one that falls three seconds will be moving three times as fast as one that falls one second, and so on. The exact value of the velocity depends on the acceleration, which, in Galileo's experiment, depended on the angle of elevation of the plane.

In the special case where the ball is falling freely (i.e., when the plane is at 90 degrees), the acceleration is such a important number that it is given a special letter of the alphabet, g. This is the acceleration that all objects experience at the Earth's surface. (Note that the Moon and other planets will have their own very different surface accelerations; g applies *only* to the Earth's surface.) The value of g can be determined by measuring the fall rate of objects in a laboratory (Figure 2-8), and turns out to be

$$g = 9.8 \text{ m/s}^2 = 32 \text{ feet/s}^2$$

• **Figure 2-8** The accelerated motion of a falling apple is captured by a multiple-exposure photograph. In each successive time interval the apple falls farther.

Table 2-1 Equations Relating d, v, a, and t

$$v = \frac{d}{t} \qquad d = v \times t$$

$$t = \frac{d}{v} \qquad a = \frac{(v_f - v_i)}{t}$$

$$v = a \times t \qquad d = \frac{1}{2}at^2$$

This equation tells us that in the first second a falling object accelerates from a stationary position to a velocity of 9.8 m/s (about 22 miles per hour), straight down. After two seconds the velocity doubles to 19.6 m/s, after three seconds it triples to 29.4 m/s, and so on.

Galileo's work also demonstrated that the distance covered by an accelerating object depends on the square of the travel time.

▶ **In equation form:**

distance traveled (m) = 1/2 × acceleration (m/s²) × time² (s²)

▶ **In symbols:**

$$d = \frac{1}{2}at^2$$

Armed with the several equations that relate distance, velocity, acceleration, and time (Table 2-1), scientists were poised to study motions throughout the cosmos.

EXAMPLE 2-2

Out of the Blocks

A sprinter accelerates from the starting blocks to a speed of 10 meters per second in one second. Answer the following questions about the sprinter's speed, acceleration, time, and distance run. In each case, answer the question by substituting into the appropriate motion equation.

1. What is his acceleration?

acceleration = (final velocity – initial velocity)/time

In this case, the sprinter starts at rest at the beginning of the race, so his initial velocity is 0.

$$\text{acceleration} = \frac{(10 \text{ m/s})}{(1 \text{ s})}$$
$$= 10 \text{ m/s}^2$$

2. How far does the sprinter travel during this 1 second of acceleration?

$$\text{distance} = 1/2 \text{ acceleration} \times \text{time}^2$$
$$= 1/2 \times (10 \text{ m/s}^2) \times (1 \text{ s})^2$$
$$= 5 \text{ meters}$$

3. Assuming the sprinter covers the remaining 95 meters at a speed of 10 m/s, what will be his time for the event? We have already calculated that the time to cover the first five meters is 1 s. The time required to cover the remaining 95 meters at a constant velocity of 10 m/s is:

$$\text{time} = \frac{\text{distance}}{\text{velocity}}$$
$$= 95 \text{ m}/(10 \text{ m/s})$$
$$= 9.5 \text{ s}$$

Thus,

total time = 1 + 9.5 = 10.5 seconds

For reference, the world's record for the 100-meter dash, set by Tim Montgomery of the United States in 1999, is 9.78 seconds.

EXAMPLE 2-3

Dropping a Penny from the Sears Tower

The tallest building in the United States is the Sears Tower in Chicago, with a height of 1454 feet. Ignoring wind resistance, how fast would a penny dropped from the top be moving when it hit the ground?

Reasoning: The penny is dropped with zero initial velocity. We first need to calculate the time it takes to fall 1454 feet. From this time we can calculate the velocity at impact.

Step 1—Time of fall: The distance traveled by an accelerating object is:

$$\text{distance} = 1/2 \times \text{acceleration} \times \text{time}^2$$
$$= 1/2 \times 32 \text{ ft/s}^2 \times t^2 = 16 \text{ ft/s}^2 \times t^2$$

Recall that distance equals 1454 feet, so rearranging gives:

$$t^2 = \frac{1454}{(16 \text{ ft/s}^2)}$$
$$= 90.88 \text{ s}^2$$

Taking the square root of both sides gives time:

$$t = 9.5 \text{ s}$$

Step 2—Velocity at impact: The velocity of an accelerating object is:

$$\text{velocity} = \text{acceleration} \times \text{time}$$
$$= 32 \text{ ft/s}^2 \times 9.5 \text{ s} = 304 \text{ ft/s}$$

This high velocity, about 200 miles per hour, could easily kill a person, so *don't* try this experiment! In fact, most objects dropped in air will not accelerate indefinitely. Because of air resistance an object will accelerate until it reaches its *terminal velocity;* and it will continue falling at a constant velocity after that point. Terminal velocity for a penny would be somewhat less than 200 miles an hour, though still fast enough to kill.

THE SCIENCE OF LIFE •

Experiencing Extreme Acceleration

You experience accelerations every day of your life. Just lying in bed you feel acceleration equal to *g,* due to the Earth's gravitational pull. When you travel in a car or plane, ride an elevator, and especially when you enjoy amusement park rides, your body is subjected to additional accelerations, though rarely exceeding 2*g*. But jet pilots and astronauts experience accelerations many times that caused by the Earth's gravitational pull during takeoffs, sharp turns, and emergency ejections. What happens to the human body under extreme acceleration, and how can equipment be designed to reduce the risk of injury? In the early days of rocket flights and high-speed-jet design, government scientists had to know.

Controlled laboratory accelerations were produced by rocket sleds (Figure 2-9) or centrifuges, which may reach accelerations exceeding 10*g*. Researchers quickly discovered that muscles and bones behave as an effectively rigid framework. Sudden extreme acceleration, such as that experienced in a car crash, may cause damage,

• **Figure 2-9** Colonel John Stapp experienced extreme acceleration in rocket sled experiments. The severe contortion of soft facial tissues was recorded by a movie camera.

but these parts can withstand the more gradual changes in acceleration associated with flight.

The body's fluids, on the other hand, shift and flow under sustained acceleration. A pilot in a sharp curve will be pushed down into the seat and experience something like the feeling you get when an elevator starts upward. The blood in the arteries leading up to the brain will also be pushed down, and, if the acceleration is big enough, the net effect will be to drain blood temporarily from the brain. The heart simply can't push the blood upward hard enough to overcome the downward pull. As a result, a pilot may experience a blackout, followed by unconsciousness. Greater accelerations could be tolerated in the prone position adopted by the first astronauts, who had to endure sustained $8g$ conditions during takeoffs.

One of the authors (J.T.) once rode in a centrifuge and experienced an $8g$ acceleration. The machine itself was a gray, egg-shaped capsule located at the end of a long steel arm. When in operation, the arm moved in a horizontal circle. Funny things happen at $8g$. For example, the skin of your face is pulled down, so that it's hard to keep your mouth open to breathe. The added weight feels like a very heavy person sitting on your chest.

There is, however, one advantage to having had this particular experience. Now, whenever he encounters the question, "What is the most you have ever weighed?" on a medical form, the author can write "1600 pounds." •

Isaac Newton and the Universal Laws of Motion

With Galileo's work, scientists began to isolate and observe the motion of material objects in nature, and to summarize their results into mathematical relationships. As to why bodies should behave this way, however, they had no suggestions. And there was certainly little reason to believe that the measurements of falling objects at the Earth's surface had anything at all to do with motions of planets and stars in the heavens.

Isaac Newton (1642–1727)

The English scientist Isaac Newton (1642–1727), one of history's most brilliant scientists, synthesized the work of Galileo and others into a statement of the basic principles that govern the motion of everything in the universe, from stars and planets to clouds, cannonballs, and the muscles in your body. These results, called **Newton's laws of motion**, sound so simple and obvious that it's hard to realize they represent the results of centuries of experiment and observation, and even harder to appreciate what an extraordinary effect they had on the development of science.

The young Newton was interested in mechanical devices and eventually enrolled as a student at Cambridge University. For most of the 1665–66 school year the University was closed due to the Great Plague that devastated much of Europe. Isaac Newton spent the time at a family farm in Lincolnshire, reading and thinking about the physical world. There he began thinking through his extraordinary discoveries in the nature of motion, as well as pivotal advances in optics and mathematics.

Three laws summarize Newton's description of motions.

The First Law

A moving object will continue moving in a straight line at a constant speed, and a stationary object will remain at rest, unless acted on by an unbalanced force.

Newton's first law seems to state the obvious: if you leave an object alone, it won't change its state of motion. In order to change it, you have to push it or pull it, thus applying a force. Yet virtually all scientists from the Greeks to Copernicus would have argued that the first law is wrong. They believed that because the circle is the most perfect geometrical shape, objects will move in circles unless something interferes. They believed that heavenly objects would keep turning without any outside force acting (indeed, they had to believe this or face the question of why the heavens didn't just run down).

Newton, basing his arguments on observations and the work of his predecessors, turned this notion around. An object left to itself will move in a straight line, and if you want to get it to move in a circle, you have to apply a force (Figure 2-10). You know this is true—if you swing something around your head, it will move in a circle only as long as you hold on to it. Let go, and off it goes in a straight line.

This simple observation led Newton to recognize two different kinds of motion. An object is in **uniform motion** if it travels in a straight line at constant speed. *All other motions are called acceleration.* Accelerations can involve changes of speed, changes of direction, or both.

Newton's first law tells us that when we see acceleration, something must have acted to produce that change. We define a **force** as something that produces a change in the state of motion of an object. In fact, we will use the first law of motion extensively in this book to tell us how to recognize when a force, particularly a new kind of force, is acting.

• **Figure 2-10** This hammer thrower is applying a force to keep the weight moving in a circle.

The tendency of an object to remain in uniform motion is called *inertia*. A body at rest tends to stay at rest because of its inertia, while a moving body tends to keep moving because of its inertia. We often use this idea in everyday speech; for example, we may talk about the inertia in a company or government organization that is resistant to change.

The Second Law

The acceleration produced on a body by a force is proportional to the magnitude of the force and inversely proportional to the mass of the object.

If Newton's first law of motion tells you when a force is acting, then the second law of motion tells you what the force does when it acts. This law conforms to our everyday experience: it is easier to move a bicycle than a car, easier to lift a child than an adult, easier to push a ballerina than a defensive tackle.

Newton's second law is often expressed as an equation.

▶ **In words:** The greater the force, the greater the acceleration; but the more massive the object being acted on by a given force, the smaller the acceleration.

▶ **In equation form:**

$$\text{force} = \text{mass (kg)} \times \text{acceleration (m/s}^2)$$

▶ **In symbols:**

$$F = m \times a$$

This equation, well known to generations of physics majors, tells us that if we know the forces acting on a system of known mass, we can predict its future motion. The equation conforms to our experience that an object's acceleration is a balance between two factors: force and **mass**, which is related to the amount of matter in an object.

A force causes the acceleration. The greater the force, the greater the acceleration. The harder you throw a ball, the faster it goes. Mass measures the amount of matter in any object. The greater the object's mass, the more "stuff" you have to accelerate, the less effect a given force is going to have. A given force will accelerate a golf ball more than a bowling ball, for example. Newton's second law of motion thus defines the balance between force and mass in producing an acceleration.

Newton's first law defines the concept of force as something that causes a mass to accelerate, but the second law goes much further. It tells us the exact magnitude of the force necessary to cause a given mass to achieve a given acceleration. Because force equals mass times acceleration, the units of force must be the same as mass times acceleration. Mass is measured in kilograms (kg) and acceleration in meters per second per second (m/s^2), so the unit of force is the "kilogram-meter-per-second-squared" ($kg\text{-}m/s^2$), which is called the newton. The symbol for the newton is N.

EXAMPLE 2-4

From Zero to Ten in Less Than a Second

What is the force needed to accelerate a 75-kilogram sprinter from rest to a speed of 10 meters per second (a very fast run) in a half second?

Reasoning and Solution: We must first find the acceleration, and then use Newton's second law to find the force.

$$\text{acceleration } (m/s^2) = \frac{[\text{final velocity} - \text{initial velocity } (m/s)]}{\text{time(s)}}$$
$$= \frac{(10\ m/s - 0\ m/s)}{0.5\ s}$$
$$= \frac{(10\ m/s)}{0.5\ s}$$
$$= 20\ m/s^2$$

What force is needed to produce this acceleration? From Newton's second law,

$$\text{force } (N) = \text{mass } (kg) \times \text{acceleration } (m/s^2)$$
$$= 75\ kg \times 20\ m/s^2$$
$$= 1500\ \text{newtons}$$

The second law of motion does not imply that every time a force acts, motion must result. A book placed on a table still feels the force of gravity, and you can push against a wall without moving it. In these situations, the atoms in the table or the wall shift around and exert their own force that balances the one that acts on them. It is only the net, or unbalanced, force that actually gives rise to acceleration.

The Third Law

For every action there is an equal and opposite reaction.

Newton's third law of motion tells us that whenever a force is applied to an object, that object simultaneously exerts an equal and opposite force (Figure 2-11). When you push on a wall, for example, it instantaneously pushes back on you; you can feel the force on the palm of your hand. In fact, the force the wall exerts on you is equal in magnitude (but opposite in direction) to the force you exert on it.

The third law of motion is perhaps the least intuitive of the three. We tend to think of our world in terms of causes and effects, in which big or fast objects exert forces on smaller, slower ones: a car slams into a tree, a batter drives the ball into deep left field, a boxer punches his opponent's eye. But in terms of Newton's third law it is equally valid to think of these events the "other way around."

• **Figure 2-11** Two automobiles in a collision exert equal and opposite forces on each other.

Newton's laws of motion can be seen in operation in many places, including this roller coaster.

The tree stops the car's motion, the baseball alters the swing of the bat, and the opponent's eye blocks the thrust of the boxer's glove, thus exerting a force and changing the direction and speed of the punch.

Forces always act simultaneously in pairs. You can convince yourself of this fact by thinking about any of your day's myriad activities. As you sit in a chair reading this book, your weight exerts a force on the chair, but the chair exerts an equal and opposite force (called a contact force) on you, preventing you from falling to the floor. The book feels heavy in your hands as it presses down, but your hands hold the book up, exerting an equal and opposite force. You may feel a slight draft from an open window or fan, but as the air exerts that gentle force on you, your skin just as surely exerts an equal and opposite force on the air, causing it to change its path.

Newton's Laws at Work

Every motion in your life, indeed, every motion in the universe, involves the constant interplay of all three of Newton's laws. The laws of motion never occur in isolation, but rather are interlocking aspects of every object's behavior. The interdependence of Newton's three laws of motion can be envisioned by a simple example. Imagine a boy standing on roller skates holding a stack of baseballs. He throws the balls, one by one. Each time he throws a baseball, the first law tells us that he has to exert a force so that the ball accelerates. The third law tells us that the baseball will exert an equal and opposite force on the boy. This force acting on the boy will, according to the second law, cause him to recoil backward.

The space shuttle *Discovery* rises from its launch pad at Cape Canaveral, Florida. As hot gases accelerate violently out the rocket's engine, the shuttle experiences an equal and opposite acceleration that lifts it into orbit.

While the example of the boy and the baseballs may seem a bit contrived, it exactly illustrates the principle by which fish swim and rockets fly. As a fish moves its tail, it applies a force against the water. The water, in turn, pushes back on the fish and propels it forward. In a rocket motor, forces are exerted on hot gases, accelerating them out the tail end. By the argument just presented, this means that an equal and opposite force must be exerted on the rocket, propelling it forward. Every rocket, from simple fireworks to a space shuttle, works this way.

Isaac Newton's three laws of motion form a comprehensive description of all possible motions, as well as the forces that lead to them. In and of themselves, however, Newton's laws do not say anything about the nature of those forces. In fact, much of the progress of science since Newton's time has been associated with the discovery and elucidation of the forces of nature.

Momentum

Newton's laws tell us that the only way to change the motion of an object is to apply a force. We all have an intuitive understanding of this tendency. We sense, for example, that a massive object like a large train, even if it is moving slowly, is very hard to stop. This knowledge is often used by people who make science fiction movies. It's almost a cliché now that when a spaceship is huge and bulky, the film-makers supply a deep, rumbling soundtrack that mimics a slowly moving train. (In this case artistic truth conflicts with the laws of nature, because in the vacuum of space there can be no sound waves.)

At the same time, a small object moving very fast—a rifle bullet, for example—is very hard to stop as well. Thus, our everyday experience tells us that the tendency of a moving object to remain in motion depends both on the mass of the object and on its speed. The higher the mass and the higher the speed, the more difficult it is to stop the object or change its direction of motion.

Physicists encapsulate these notions in a quantity called *linear momentum,* which equals the product of an object's mass times its velocity.

▶ **In equation form:**

$$\text{momentum (kg-m/s)} = \text{mass (kg)} \times \text{velocity (m/s)}$$

▶ **In symbols:**

$$p = mv$$

EXAMPLE 2-5

Play Ball

A baseball with mass 0.3 kg moves to the right with a velocity of 30 meters/sec (about the speed of a good fastball). What is its momentum?

Solution: The momentum is defined to be

$$p = mv$$

If we substitute the numbers for mass and velocity, we find that

$$p = 0.3 \text{ kg} \times 30 \text{ m/s} = 9 \text{ kg-m/s}$$

Conservation of Linear Momentum

We can derive a very important consequence from Newton's laws. If no external forces act on a system, then Newton's second law says that the change in the total momentum of a system is zero. When physicists find a quantity that does not change, they say that the quantity is *conserved*. The conclusion we have just reached, therefore, is called the *law of conservation of linear momentum*.

It's important to keep in mind that the law of conservation of momentum doesn't say that momentum can never change. It just says that it won't change unless an outside force is applied. If a soccer ball is rolling across a field and a player kicks it, a force is applied to the ball as soon as her foot touches it. At that moment, the momentum of the ball changes, and that change is reflected in its change of direction and speed.

You saw the consequences of the conservation of momentum the last time you watched a fireworks display. The rocket arches up and explodes just at the moment that the rocket is stationary at the top of its path, at the instant when its total momentum is zero. After the explosion, brightly colored burning bits of material fly out in all directions. Each of these pieces has a mass and a velocity, so each has some momentum. Conservation of momentum, however, tells us that when we add up all the momenta of the pieces, they should cancel each other out and give a total momentum of zero. Thus, for example, if there is a one-gram piece moving to the right at 10 meters per second, there has to be the equivalent of a one-gram piece moving to the left at the same velocity. Thus conservation of momentum gives fireworks their characteristic symmetric starburst pattern.

Angular Momentum

Just as an object moving in a straight line will keep moving unless a force acts, an object that is rotating will keep rotating unless a twisting force called a *torque* acts to make it stop. A spinning top will keep spinning until the friction between its point of contact and the floor slows it down. A wheel will keep turning until friction in its bearing stops it. This tendency to keep rotating is called angular momentum.

Think about some common experiences with spinning objects. Two factors increase an object's angular momentum, and thus make it more difficult to slow down and stop the rotating object. The first factor is simply the rate of spin; the

This symmetrical fireworks display illustrates the law of conservation of momentum.

faster an object spins, the harder it is to stop. The second, more subtle factor relates to the distribution of mass. Objects with more mass, or with mass located farther away from the central axis of rotation, have greater angular momentum. Thus, a solid metal wheel has more angular momentum than an air-filled tire of the same diameter and rate of spin.

The consequences of the conservation of angular momentum you're most likely to experience occur when something happens to change a spinning object's

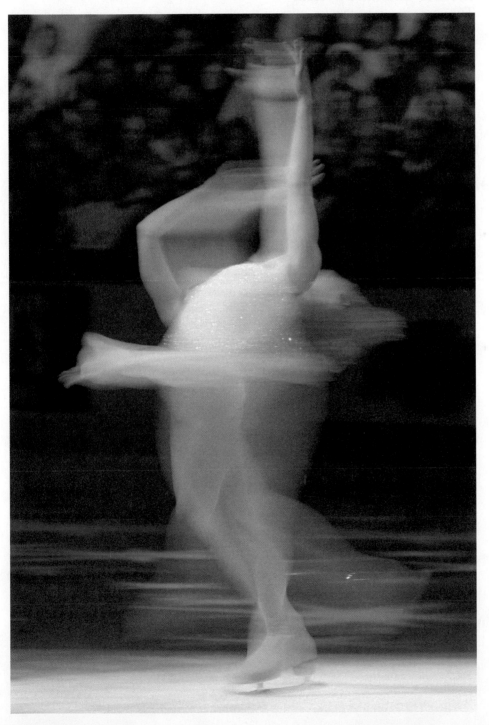

When the skater spins faster as she pulls in her arms, she is demonstrating the conservation of angular momentum.

distribution of mass. A striking illustration of this point can be seen in figure skating competitions. As a skater goes into a spin with her arms spread, she spins slowly. As she pulls her arms in tight to her body, her angular momentum must remain constant, since no outside force acts to affect the spin. Her rate of spin must increase.

TECHNOLOGY •
Inertial Guidance System

The conservation of angular momentum plays an important role in so-called "inertial guidance systems" for navigation in airplanes and satellites. The idea behind such systems is very simple. A massive object like a sphere or a flat circular disk is set into rotation inside a device in which very little resistance (that is, almost no torque) is exerted by the bearings. Once such an object is set into rotation, its angular momentum continues to point in the same direction, regardless of how the spaceship moves around it. By sensing the constant rotation and seeing how it is related to the orientation of the satellite, engineers can tell which way the satellite is pointed. •

The Universal Force of Gravity

Gravity is the most obvious force in our daily lives. It holds you down in your chair and keeps you from floating off into space. It guarantees that when you drop things they fall. The effects of what we call gravity were known to the ancients, and its quantitative properties were studied by Galileo and many of his contemporaries, but Isaac Newton revealed its universality.

By Newton's account, he experienced his great insight in an apple orchard. He saw an apple fall, and at the same time, saw the Moon in the sky behind it. He wondered whether the gravity that caused the apple to move downward could extend far outward to the Moon, supplying the force that kept it in its orbit.

Look at the problem this way: If the Moon goes around the Earth, then it isn't moving in a straight line. From the first law of motion it follows that a force must be acting on it. Newton hypothesized that this was the same force that made the apple fall—the familiar force of gravity (see Figure 2-12).

Eventually, he realized that the orbits of all the planets could be understood if gravity was not restricted to the surface of the Earth but was a force found throughout the universe. He formulated this insight (an insight that has been overwhelmingly confirmed by observations) in what is called **Newton's law of universal gravitation**.

▶ **In words:** Between any two objects in the universe there is an attractive force (gravity) that is proportional to the masses of the objects and inversely proportional to the square of the distance between them.

▶ **In equation form:**

$$\text{force of gravity (newtons)} = \frac{[G \times \text{mass}_1 \text{ (kg)} \times \text{mass}_2 \text{ (kg)}]}{[\text{distance (m)}]^2}$$

▶ **In symbols:**

$$F = \frac{(G \times m_1 \times m_2)}{d^2}$$

where G is a number known as the *gravitational constant* (see below).

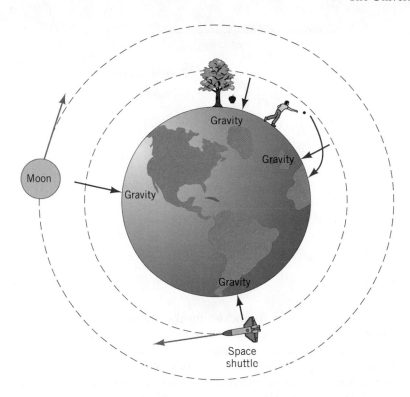

• **Figure 2-12** An apple falling, a ball being thrown, a space shuttle orbiting the Earth, and the orbiting Moon, all display the influence of the force of gravity.

In everyday words, this law tells us that the more massive two objects are, the greater the force between them will be; the farther apart they are, the less the force will be.

The Gravitational Constant, *G*

When we say that *A* is *directly proportional* to *B*, we mean that if *A* increases, *B* must increase by the same proportion. If *A* doubles then *B* must double as well. We can state this idea in mathematical form by writing

$$A = k \times B$$

where *k* is a number known as the constant of proportionality between *A* and *B*. This equation tells us that if we know the constant *k* and either *A* or *B*, then we can calculate the exact value of the other. Thus the constant of proportionality in a relationship is a useful thing to know.

The gravitational constant, *G*, is a constant of direct proportionality; it expresses the exact numerical relation between the masses of two objects and their separation, on the one hand, and the force between them on the other.

$$\text{force} = \frac{(G \times m_1 \times m_2)}{d^2}$$

Unlike *g*, however, which applies only to the Earth's surface, *G* is a universal constant that applies to any two masses anywhere in the universe.

Henry Cavendish (1731–1810), a scientist at Oxford University in England, first measured *G* in 1798 by using the experimental apparatus shown in Figure 2-13. Cavendish suspended a dumbbell made of two small lead balls by a stiff wire and fixed two larger lead spheres near the suspended balls. The gravitational attraction between the hanging lead balls and the fixed spheres caused the

• **Figure 2-13** The Cavendish balance measures the universal gravitational constant *G*. This experimental device balances the gravitational attractive force between the suspended balls and fixed spheres, against the force exerted by a twisted wire.

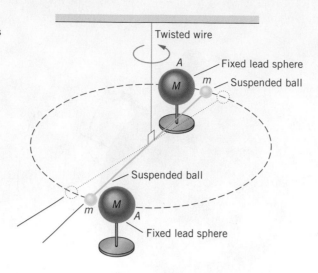

wire to twist slightly. By measuring the amount of twisting force, or torque, on the wire, Cavendish could calculate the gravitational force on the dumbbells. This force, together with a knowledge of the masses of the dumbbells (m_1 in the equation) and the heavy spheres (m_2), as well as their final separation (d), gave him the numerical value of everything in Newton's law of universal gravitation except *G*, which he then calculated using simple arithmetic. In metric units, the value of *G* is 6.67×10^{-11} m³/s²-kg, or 6.67×10^{-11} N-m²/kg² (recall that N is the symbol for a newton, the unit of force). This constant appears to be universal, holding true everywhere in our universe.

Weight and Gravity

The law of universal gravitation says that there is a force between any two objects in the universe: two dancers, two stars, this book and you—all exert forces on each other. The gravitational attraction between you and the Earth would pull you down if you weren't standing on the ground. As it is, the ground exerts a force equal and opposite to that of gravity, a force you can feel in the soles of your feet. If you were standing on a scale, the gravitational pull of the Earth would pull you down until a spring or other mechanism in the scale exerted the opposing force. In this case, the size of that counterbalancing force registers on a display and you call it your **weight**.

Weight, in fact, is just the force of gravity on an object located at a particular point. Weight depends on where you are; on the surface of the Earth you weigh one thing, on the surface of the Moon another, and in the depths of interstellar space you would weigh next to nothing. You even weigh a little less on a high mountaintop than you do at sea level, because you are farther from the Earth's center. Weight contrasts with your mass (the amount of matter), which stays the same no matter where you go.

Big *G* and Little *g*

The law of universal gravitation, coupled with the experimental results on bodies falling near the Earth, can be used to reveal a close relationship between the universal constant *G* and the Earth's gravitational acceleration *g*. According to the law of universal gravitation, the gravitational force on an object of any mass at the Earth's surface is

$$force = \frac{(G \times mass \times M_E)}{R_E^2}$$

where M_E and R_E are the mass and radius of the Earth, respectively. On the other hand, Newton's Second Law says that

$$force = mass \times g$$

Equating the right sides of these two equations,

$$mass \times g = \frac{(G \times mass \times M_E)}{R_E^2}$$

Dividing both sides by mass,

$$g = \frac{G \times M_E}{R_E^2}$$

But the values of G, M_E, and R_E have been measured:

$$g = \frac{(6.67 \times 10^{-11} \text{ N-m}^2/\text{kg}^2) \times (6.02 \times 10^{24} \text{ kg})}{(6.40 \times 10^6 \text{ m})^2}$$
$$= \frac{(4.015 \times 10^{14} \text{ N-m}^2/\text{kg})}{(4.10 \times 10^{13} \text{ m}^2)}$$
$$= 9.8 \text{ N-kg} = 9.8 \text{ m/s}^2$$

Thus the value of the Earth's gravitational acceleration, g, can be calculated from Newton's universal equation for gravity.

This result is extremely important. For Galileo, g was a number to be measured, but whose value he could not predict. For Newton, on the other hand, g was a number that could be calculated purely from the size and mass of the Earth. Because we understand where g comes from, we can now predict the appropriate value of gravitational acceleration not only for the Earth, but for any body in the universe, provided we know its mass and radius.

 Stop and Think! Can the gravitational force between two objects in the universe ever be equal to zero? Why or why not?

EXAMPLE 2-6

Weight on the Moon

The mass of the Moon is $M_M = 7.18 \times 10^{22}$ kg, and its radius R_M is 1738 km. If your mass is 100 kg, what would you weigh on the Moon?

Reasoning: We have to calculate the force exerted on an object at the surface of an astronomical body. This time both the mass and the radius of the body are different from that of the Earth, although G is the same.

Solution: From the equation that defines weight, we have

$$weight = \frac{(G \times mass_1 \times mass_2)}{distance^2}$$
$$= \frac{(G \times 100 \text{ kg} \times M_M)}{R_M^2}$$

$$= \frac{(6.67 \times 10^{-11} \text{ N-m}^2/\text{kg}^2) \times 100 \text{ kg} \times (7.18 \times 10^{22} \text{ kg})}{(1.738 \times 10^6 \text{m})^2}$$

$$= \frac{(6.67 \times 10^{-11} \text{ N-m}^2/\text{kg}^2) \times (7.18 \times 10^{24} \text{ kg})}{(3.02 \times 10^{12} \text{m}^2)}$$

$$= \frac{(4.79 \times 10^{14} \text{N-m}^2)}{(3.02 \times 10^{12} \text{m}^2)}$$

$$= 159 \text{ newtons}$$

This weight is about one-sixth of the weight that the same object would have on Earth, *even though its mass is the same in both places.*

Newton bequeathed a picture of the universe that is beautiful and ordered. The planets orbit the Sun in stately paths, forever trying to move off in straight lines, forever prevented from doing so by the inward tug of gravity. The same laws that operate in the cosmos operate on Earth, and these laws were discovered by the application of the scientific method. To a Newtonian observer, the universe was like a clock. It had been wound up and was ticking along according to God's laws. Newton and his followers were persuaded that in carrying out their work, they were discovering what was in the mind of God when the universe was created.

Of all celestial phenomena, none seemed more portentous and magical than comets, yet even these chance wanderers were subject to Newton's laws. In 1682, British astronomer Edmond Halley (1656–1742) used Newtonian logic to compute the orbit of the comet that bears his name, and he predicted its return in 1758. The "recovery" of Halley's Comet on Christmas Eve of that year was celebrated around the world as a triumph for the Newtonian system.

Halley's comet as it appeared on its last visit to Earth, in 1985.

Thinking More About | The Ordered Universe

Predictability

The Newtonian universe seemed regular and predictable in the extreme. Indeed, from the point of view of the Newtonians, if you knew the present state of a system and the forces acting on it, the laws of motion would allow you to predict its entire future. This notion was taken to the extreme by the French mathematician Pierre Simon Laplace (1749–1827), who proposed the notion of the *Divine Calculator*. His argument (in modern language) was this: If we knew the position and velocity of every atom in the universe and we had infinite computational power, then we could predict the position and velocity of every atom in the universe for all future times. There is no distinction in this argument between an atom in a rock and an atom in your hand. Thus Laplace would say that all of your movements are completely determined by the laws of physics to the end of time. You cannot choose your future. What is to be was determined from the very beginning.

This idea has been negated by two modern developments in science. One of these, the Heisenberg uncertainty principle (see Chapter 8), tells us that at the level of the atom it is impossible to know simultaneously and exactly both the position and velocity of any particle. Thus you can never get the information the Divine Calculator needs to begin working.

Furthermore, scientists working with computer models have recently discovered that many systems in nature can be described in simple Newtonian terms, but have futures that are, to all intents and purposes, unpredictable. These situations are called "chaotic systems," and their field of study is called chaos.

Whitewater in a mountain stream is a familiar chaotic system. If you put two chips of wood down on the upstream side of the rapids, those chips (and the water on which they ride) will be widely separated by the time they get to the end. This is true no matter how small you make the chips, or how close together they are at the beginning. If you know the exact initial position of a chip and every aspect of the waterway in such a system with complete mathematical precision, you can in principle predict where it will come out downstream. But if there is the slightest error in your initial description, no matter how small, the actual position of the chip and your prediction may differ significantly. Every measurement in the real world has some error associated with it, so it is never possible to determine the exact position of the chip at the start of its trip. You cannot predict exactly where it will come out *even if you know all the forces acting on it*.

The existence of chaos, then, tells us that the philosophical conclusions drawn from the Newtonian vision of the universe don't apply to some systems in nature. The flow of Earth's atmosphere and the long-term development of weather, for example, appear to be chaotic, and it may turn out that ecosystems (see Chapter 19) behave this way as well. If this is true, what implications might there be when governments have to deal with issues such as global warming (see Chapter 19) and the preservation of endangered species? How confident do you have to be that something bad is going to happen before you start taking steps to avoid it?

SUMMARY

Since before recorded history, people have observed regularities in the heavens, and have built monuments such as Stonehenge to help order their lives. Models, such as the Earth-centered system of Ptolemy and the Sun-centered system of Copernicus, attempted to explain these regular motions of stars and planets. New, more precise astronomical data by Tycho Brahe led mathematician Johannes Kepler to propose his laws of planetary motion, which state that planets orbit the Sun in elliptical orbits, not circular orbits as had been previously assumed.

Meanwhile, Galileo Galilei and other scientists investigated the science of *mechanics*—the way things move near the Earth's surface. These investigators recognized two fundamentally different kinds of motion: *uniform motion*, which is a constant *speed* and direction (*velocity*), and *acceleration*, which entails a change in either speed or direction of travel. Galileo's experiments revealed that all objects fall the same way, at the constant acceleration of 9.8 meters/second^2. Isaac Newton combined the work of Kepler, Galileo, and others in his sweeping *laws of motion* and the *universal law of gravitation*. Newton realized that nothing accelerates without a *force* acting on it, and that the amount of acceleration is proportional to the force applied, but inversely proportional to the *mass*. He also pointed out that forces always act in pairs.

This understanding of forces and motions led Newton to describe *gravity,* the most obvious force in our daily lives. An object's *weight* is the force it exerts due to gravity. He demonstrated that the same force that pulls a falling apple to the Earth causes the Moon to curve around the Earth in its elliptical orbit. Indeed, the force of gravity operates everywhere, with pairs of forces between every pair of masses in the universe.

KEY TERMS

mechanics   acceleration   force   Newton's law of universal gravitation
speed   Newton's laws of motion   mass   weight
velocity   uniform motion   gravity

KEY EQUATIONS AND THEIR UNITS

$$\text{speed(m/s)} = \frac{\text{distance (m)}}{\text{time (s)}}$$

$$\text{distance (m)} = \frac{\text{speed (m/s)}}{\text{time (s)}}$$

$$\text{time (s)} = \frac{\text{distance (m)}}{\text{speed (m/s)}}$$

$$\text{acceleration (m/s}^2) = \frac{[\text{final velocity} - \text{initial velocity (m/s)}]}{\text{time (s)}}$$

velocity of a falling object (m/s) = g (m/s^2) × time (s)

velocity (m/s) = acceleration (m/s^2) × time (s)

force (N) = mass (kg) × acceleration (m/s^2)

$$\text{force (N)} = \frac{G \times \text{first mass (kg)} \times \text{second mass (kg)}}{\text{distance}^2 \text{ (m}^2)}$$

force (N) = mass (kg) × g = weight

Constants

g = 9.8 m/s^2 = acceleration due to gravity on Earth

G = 6.67 × 10^{-11} N-m^2/kg^2 = universal gravitational constant

REVIEW QUESTIONS

1. In what ways did Stonehenge serve as a calendar? How did Stonehenge allow ancient people to make predictions?

2. Why do scientists argue that Stonehenge was not built by ancient astronauts?

3. What were Tycho Brahe's principal contributions to science? How did he try to resolve the question of the structure of the universe?

4. What was Kepler's role in interpreting Tycho Brahe's data?

5. How did Galileo apply the scientific method to his study of falling objects?

6. A hockey player hits a puck at one end of an empty skating rink. The puck travels across the ice in a straight line until it is stopped by the goal at the other end. Explain how each of Newton's laws of motion applies to this situation.

7. According to Newton, what are the two kinds of motion in the universe? How did this view differ from those of previous scholars?

8. Why is gravity called a universal force?

9. What is the difference between the constants g and G?

10. What similarities did Newton see between the Moon and an apple?

11. What is the difference between weight and mass?

DISCUSSION QUESTIONS

1. Can scientists prove that Stonehenge was not built by ancient astronauts?

2. Which of the following is in uniform motion, and which is in accelerated motion?

a. a car heading west at 35 mph on a level road

b. a car heading west at 35 mph on a hill

c. a car going around a curve at 35 mph

d. a dolphin leaping out of the water

e. an airplane sitting at the end of a runway

3. Which, if any, of the following objects does not exert a gravitational force on you?

a. this book

b. the Sun

c. the nearest star

d. a distant galaxy

4. What pairs of forces act in the following situations?

a. A batter hits a baseball.

b. A leaf falls to the ground.

c. The Moon orbits the Earth.

d. You sit in a chair.

5. What was the role of mathematics in the science of mechanics?

6. In what sense is the Newtonian universe simpler than Ptolemy's? Suppose observations had shown that the two did equally well at explaining the data. Construct an argument to say that Newton's universe should still be preferred.

7. Why don't the planets just fly off into space? What keeps them in their orbits?

8. How did Henry Cavendish's experiment fit into the scientific method?

PROBLEMS

1. What do you weigh in pounds? In newtons?

2. If a race car completes a 2-mile oval track in 58 seconds, what is its average speed? Did the car accelerate during the 58 seconds?

3. If your car goes from 0 to 55 miles per hour in 6 seconds, what is your acceleration?

4. What is your mass in kilograms?

5. Estimate the largest force that you can exert without mechanical aids. How would you exert this force?

6. What would you weigh on Mars? On Jupiter? (Data on the masses and radii of planets appear in Appendix E.)

7. How much force must be applied to accelerate a 10,000-kg space shuttle to counter the Earth's gravitational acceleration of 9.8 m/s^2?

8. In Chapter 1 we discussed why scientists consider astrology to be a pseudoscience. Calculate the gravitational forces on a 3-kg newborn infant exerted by the planets Venus, Mars, and Jupiter at their closest approach to Earth (see Appendix E for the relevant distances and masses). Compare these forces with the gravitational force exerted by a 100-kg physician 0.1 m away. [*Hint:* The closest approach of a planet equals the difference between the Earth's distance from the Sun and the other planet's distance from the Sun.]

INVESTIGATIONS

1. Read the Bertolt Brecht play *Galileo,* which dramatizes Galileo Galilei's heresy trial. Discuss the dilemma faced by scientists whose discoveries offend conventional ideas. What scientific research does today's society find offensive or immoral? Why?

2. The concept of predestination plays an important role in some kinds of theology. What is it? How does it relate to Laplace? To chaos?

3. What other kinds of models of the universe did old civilizations develop? Look up those of the Mayans, the Chinese, and the Indians of the American Southwest.

4. Investigate the scientific contributions of Galileo. What other experiments did he design? How was this research funded? Was he engaging in basic or applied research?

5. The gravitational constant is now known to one part in 10,000, yet physicists are still trying to measure this constant. Why?

6. People have claimed that the Great Pyramids of Egypt had to have been built by ancient astronauts because the Egyptians were too primitive to have built them. Look up the weight of the largest stones in the pyramids and estimate the number of people it would take to move them. Then comment on the ancient astronaut argument.

7. Galileo was one of the first people to look at the planets through a telescope. He discovered the four largest moons of Jupiter, which are still called the "Galilean" moons. Why did this discovery cast doubt on the Ptolemaic system? What else did Galileo see through his telescope?

8. In what ways does gravity affect the form and function of living things? (Think about both plants and animals.)

WWW RESOURCES

See *The Sciences* homepage at: **http://www.wiley.com/college/trefil** for valuable web links.

1. **http://www.kepler.arc.nasa.gov/johannes.html**
   Johannes Kepler: His Life, His Laws and Times, from NASA, an interesting and helpful site.

2. **http://www.wam.umd.edu/~tlaloc/archastro**
   Center for Archaeoastronomy—Click on "*What is archaeoastronomy?*" and be sure to browse their links.

3. **http://es.rice.edu/ES/humsoc/Galileo**
   The Galileo Project, from Rice University—a paradigm for effective and aesthetically pleasing educational websites.

3

Energy

Why must animals eat to stay alive?

GREAT IDEA

*The many different forms of energy are interchangeable,
and the total amount of energy in an isolated system is conserved.*

PHYSICS
When a bowler bowls a strike, some of the bowling ball's kinetic energy is transferred to scatter the pins.

CHEMISTRY
Stored chemical energy in fossil fuels (coal, gas, and oil) is converted to heat energy during the process of burning.

ENVIRONMENT
Wind and rain obtain their energy through the conservation of the Sun's radiant energy. (Ch. 18)

GEOLOGY
During an earthquake, elastic potential energy stored in rock is suddenly converted to kinetic energy as the rock breaks. (Ch. 17)

HEALTH & SAFETY
Vigorous exercise converts the body's stored chemical energy into kinetic energy.

ASTRONOMY
Stars convert the element hydrogen into helium, and radiate energy through the process of nuclear fusion. (Ch. 14)

TECHNOLOGY
A new generation of powerful and lightweight batteries that convert chemical potential energy into electricity is needed to power electric cars. (Ch. 15)

BIOLOGY
Plants convert the radiant energy of sunlight into the chemical energy neccesary to sustain life for organisms at every trophic level.

Red = applications of the great idea discussed in this chapter.

Orange = other applications, some of which are explored in other chapters.

The daily routine begins. You turn on the overhead light, squinting as your eyes adjust to the brightness. Then you take your morning shower; it feels great to just stand there and let the hot water wash over you. Soon you'll boil water for coffee, eat a hearty breakfast, and then drive to the beach.

During every one of these ordinary actions—indeed every moment of every day—you use energy in its many varied and interchangeable forms.

The Great Chain of Energy

Hundreds of millions of years ago, a bit of energy was generated in the core of the Sun. For thousands of years, that energy percolated outward to the Sun's surface; then, in a mere eight minutes, it made the trip through empty space to Earth in the form of sunlight. Unlike other bits of energy that were reflected back into space by clouds or simply served to warm the Earth's soil, this particular energy was absorbed by organisms known as algae floating on the warm ocean surface.

Through the process of photosynthesis (see Chapter 22), this algae transformed the Sun's energy into the chemical energy needed to hold together its complex molecules. Eventually these algae died and sank to the bottom of the ocean, where, over long eons, they were buried deeper and deeper. Under the influence of pressure and heat, the dead algae were eventually transformed into fossil fuel—petroleum.

Then, a short while ago, engineers pumped that petroleum with its stored energy up out of the ground. At a refinery, the large molecules were broken down into gasoline, and the gasoline was shipped to your town. A few days ago you put it into the tank of your car. The last time you drove you burned that gasoline, converting the stored energy into the engine's mechanical energy that moved your car. When you parked the car, the hot engine slowly cooled, and that bit of heat, after having been delayed for a few hundred million years, was radiated out into space to continue its voyage away from the solar system. As you read these words, the energy you freed yesterday has long since left the solar system and is out in the depths of interstellar space.

Scientifically Speaking

At this moment, trillions of cells in your body are hard at work turning the chemical energy of the food you ate yesterday into the chemical energy that will keep you alive today. Energy in the atmosphere generates sweeping winds and powerful storms, while the ocean's energy drives mighty currents and incessant tides. Meanwhile, deep within the Earth, energy in the form of heat is moving the continent on which you are standing.

This oil pump in Colorado is bringing up solar energy stored millions of years ago.

All situations where energy is expended have one thing in common. If you look at the event closely enough, you will find that, in accord with Newton's laws of motion (Chapter 2), a force is being exerted on an object to make it move. When your car burns gasoline, the fuel's energy ultimately turns the wheels of your car, which then exert a force on the road; the road exerts an equal and opposite force on the car, pushing it forward. When you climb the stairs, your muscles exert a force that lifts you upward against gravity. Even in your body's cells, a force is exerted on molecules in chemical reactions. Energy thus is intimately connected with the application of a force.

In everyday conversation we speak of someone having lots of energy, but in science the term *energy* has a precise definition that is somewhat different from the ordinary meaning. To see what scientists mean when they talk about energy, we must first introduce the familiar concept of work.

Work

Scientists say that **work** is done whenever a force is exerted over a distance. Pick up this book and raise it a foot. Your muscles applied a force equal to the weight of the book over a distance of a foot. You did work.

This definition of work differs considerably from everyday usage. From a physicist's point of view, if you accidentally drive into a tree and smash your fender, work has been done, because a force deformed the car's metal a measurable distance. On the other hand, a physicist would say that you haven't done any work if you spend an hour in a futile effort to move a large boulder, no matter how tired you get. Even though you have exerted a considerable force, the distance over which you exerted it is negligible.

Physicists provide an exact mathematical definition to their notion of work.

▶ **In words:** Work is equal to the force that is exerted times the distance over which it is exerted.

▶ **In equation form:**

$$\text{work (joules)} = \text{force (newtons)} \times \text{distance (meters)}$$

where a joule is the unit of work, as defined in the following paragraph.

Work is done when a force is exerted over a distance.

► **In symbols:**

$$W = F \times d$$

In practical terms, even a small force can do a lot of work if it is exerted over a long distance.

As you might expect from this equation, units of work are equal to a force unit times a distance unit (Figure 3-1). In the metric system of units, where force is measured in *newtons* (abbreviated N), work is measured in "newton-meters (N-m)." For reference, a Newton is roughly equal to the force exerted on your hand by a baseball (or by 7 Fig Newtons!).

This unit is given the special name "joule," after the English scientist James Prescott Joule (1818–1889), one of the first people to understand the properties of energy. One *joule* is defined as the amount of work done when a force of one newton is exerted through a distance of one meter.

1 joule of work = 1 N of force × 1 m of distance

In the English system of units (see Appendix B), where force is measured in pounds, work is measured in a unit called the foot-pound (usually abbreviated ft-lb).

EXAMPLE 3-1

Working Against Gravity

How much work do you do when you carry a 20-kilogram television set up a flight of stairs (about 4 meters)?

Reasoning: We must first calculate the force exerted by a 20-kg mass before we can determine work. From the previous chapter, we know that to lift a 20-kg mass against the acceleration of gravity (9.8 m/s^2) requires a force given by

$$\text{force} = \text{mass} \times g$$
$$= 20 \text{ kg} \times 9.8 \text{ m/s}^2$$
$$= 196 \text{ newtons}$$

Solution: Then, from the equation for work,

$$\text{work} = \text{force} \times \text{distance}$$
$$= 196 \text{ N} \times 4 \text{ m}$$
$$= 784 \text{ joules}$$

Energy

Energy is defined as the ability to do work. If a system is capable of exerting a force over a distance, then that system possesses energy. The amount of a system's energy, which can be recorded in joules or foot-pounds (the same units used for work), is a measure of how much work the system might do. When a system runs out of energy, it simply can't do any more work.

Power

Power provides a measure of both the amount of work done (or, equivalently, the amount of energy expended) and the time it takes to do that work. In order to complete a physical task quickly, you must generate more power than if you do the same task slowly. If you run up a flight of stairs, your muscles need to generate more power than they would if you walked up the same flight, even though you expend the same amount of energy in either case. A power hitter in baseball swings the bat faster, converting the chemical energy in his muscles to kinetic energy more quickly than most other players.

Scientists define power as the rate at which work is done, or the rate at which energy is expended.

▶ **In words:** Power is the amount of work done divided by the time it takes to do that work.

▶ **In equation form:**

$$\text{power (watts)} = \frac{\text{work (joules)}}{\text{time (seconds)}}$$

where the watt is the unit of power, as defined in the following paragraph.

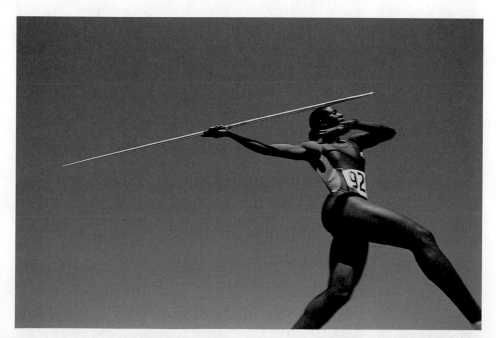

Athletes must release their energy quickly and with great power to succeed in events such as the javelin throw.

▶ **In symbols:**

$$P = W/t$$

If you do more work in a given span of time, or do a task in a shorter time, you use more power.

In the metric system, power is measured in **watts**, after James Watt (1736–1819), the Scottish inventor who developed the modern steam engine that powered the Industrial Revolution. The watt, a unit of measurement that you probably encounter every day, is defined as the expenditure of 1 joule of energy in 1 second:

$$1 \text{ watt of power} = \frac{(1 \text{ joule of energy})}{(1 \text{ second of time})}$$

The unit of 1000 watts (corresponding to an expenditure of 1000 joules per second) is called a **kilowatt**, and is a commonly used measurement of electrical power. The English system, on the other hand, uses the more colorful unit *horsepower*, which is defined as 550 foot-pounds per second.

The familiar rating of a lightbulb (60 watts or 100 watts, for example) is a measure of the rate of energy that the lightbulb consumes when it is operating. As another familiar example, most electric hand tools or appliances in your home will be labeled with a power rating in watts.

The equation we have introduced defining power as energy divided by time may be rewritten as follows:

$$\text{energy (joules)} = \text{power (watts)} \times \text{time (seconds)}$$

This important equation allows you (and the electric company) to calculate how much energy you consume (and how much you have to pay for). Note from this equation that, while the joule is the standard scientific unit for energy, energy can also be measured in units of power × time, such as the familiar kilowatt-hour (often abbreviated kwh) that appears on your electric bill. Table 3-1 summarizes the important terms we've used for force, work, energy, and power.

James Watt boiling water in his fireplace.

Table 3-1 **Important Terms**

Quantity	Definition	Units
Force	mass × acceleration	newtons
Work	force × distance	joules
Energy	ability to do work	joules
Energy	power × time	joules
Power	work/time = energy/time	watts

SCIENCE IN THE MAKING •

James Watt and the Horsepower

The horsepower, a unit of power with a colorful history, was devised by James Watt so that he could sell his steam engines. Watt knew that the main use of his engines would be in mines, where owners traditionally used horses to drive pumps that removed water. The easiest way to promote his new engines was to tell the mining engineers how many horses each engine would replace. Consequently, he did a series of experiments to determine how much energy a horse could generate over a given amount of time. Watt found that an average, healthy horse can do 550 ft-lbs of work every second over an average working day—a unit he defined to be the horsepower, and rated his engines accordingly. We still use this unit (the engines of virtually all cars and trucks are rated in horsepower), although we seldom build engines to replace horses these days. •

EXAMPLE 3-2

Paying the Piper

A typical CD system uses 250 watts of electrical power. If you play your system for three hours in an evening, how much energy do you use? If energy costs eight cents a kilo-watt-hour, how much do you owe the electrical company?

Reasoning and Solution: The total amount of energy you use will be given by

$$\text{energy} = \text{power} \times \text{time}$$
$$= 250\ \text{W} \times 3\ \text{h}$$
$$= 750\ \text{Wh}$$

Because 750 watts equals 0.75 kilowatt,

$$\text{energy} = 0.75\ \text{Kwh}$$

The cost will be as follows:

$$\text{cost} = 8\ \text{cents per Kwh} \times 0.75\ \text{Kwh}$$
$$= 6\ \text{cents}$$

Forms of Energy

Energy, the ability to do work, appears in all natural systems, and it comes in many forms. The identification of these forms posed a great challenge to scientists in the nineteenth century. Ultimately, they recognized two very broad categories. **Kinetic energy**, including heat and wave energy, is energy associated with moving objects, whereas stored or **potential energy** is energy waiting to be released.

Kinetic Energy

Think about a cannonball flying through the air. When it hits a wooden target, the ball exerts a force on the fibers in the wood, splintering and pushing them apart and creating a hole. Work has to be done to make that hole; fibers have to be moved aside, which means that a force must be exerted over the distance they move. When the cannonball hits the wood, it does work, and so a cannonball in flight clearly has the *ability* to do work—that is, it has energy—because of its motion. This energy of motion is what we call kinetic energy.

You can find countless examples of kinetic energy in nature. A fish moving through water, a bird flying, and a predator catching its prey all have kinetic energy. So do a speeding car, a flying Frisbee, a falling leaf, and anything else that is moving.

Our intuition tells us that two factors govern the amount of kinetic energy contained in any moving object. First, heavier objects that are moving have more kinetic energy than lighter ones: a bowling ball traveling 10 m/s (a very fast sprint) carries a lot more kinetic energy than a golf ball traveling at the same speed. In fact, kinetic energy is directly proportional to mass: double the mass, double the kinetic energy.

Second, the faster something is moving, the greater the force it is capable of exerting and the greater energy it possesses. A high-speed collision causes much more damage than a fender bender in a parking lot. It turns out that an object's kinetic energy increases as the square of its speed. A car moving 40 mph has four times as much kinetic energy as one moving 20 mph, while at 60 mph a car carries nine times as much kinetic energy as at 20 mph. Thus a modest increase in speed can cause a large increase in kinetic energy.

These ideas are combined in the equation for kinetic energy.

▶ **In words:** Kinetic energy equals the mass of the moving object times the square of that object's speed, times the constant $\frac{1}{2}$.

▶ **In equation form:**

$$\text{kinetic energy (joules)} = \tfrac{1}{2} \times [\text{mass (kg)}] \times [\text{speed (m/s)}]^2$$

This breaching humpback whale has kinetic energy because he is moving.

▶ In symbols:

$$E = \tfrac{1}{2} \, mv^2$$

EXAMPLE 3-3

Bowling Balls and Baseballs

What is the kinetic energy of a 4-kg (about 8-lb) bowling ball rolling down a bowling lane at 10 m/s (about 22 mph)? Compare this energy with that of a 250-gram (about half-a-pound) baseball traveling 50 m/s (almost 110 mph). Which object would hurt more if it hit you (i.e., which object has the greater kinetic energy)?

Reasoning: We have to substitute numbers into the equation for kinetic energy.

Solution: For the 4-kg bowling ball traveling at 10 m/s:

$$\begin{aligned}
\text{energy (joules)} &= 1/2 \times \text{mass (kg)} \times [\text{speed (m/s)}]^2 \\
&= 1/2 \times 4 \text{ kg} \times (10 \text{ m/s})^2 \\
&= 1/2 \times 4 \text{ kg} \times 100 \text{ m}^2/\text{s}^2 \\
&= 200 \text{ kg-m}^2/\text{s}^2
\end{aligned}$$

Note that

$$\begin{aligned}
200 \text{ kg-m}^2/\text{s}^2 &= 200 \ (\text{kg-m/s}^2 \times \text{m}) \\
&= 200 \text{ N} \times \text{m} \\
&= 200 \text{ joules}
\end{aligned}$$

For the 250 g baseball traveling at 50 m/s:

$$\begin{aligned}
\text{energy (joules)} &= 1/2 \times \text{mass (kg)} \times [\text{speed (m/s)}]^2 \\
&= 1/2 \times 250 \text{ g} \times (50 \text{ m/s})^2
\end{aligned}$$

A gram is a thousandth of a kilogram, so 250 g = 0.25 kg:

$$\begin{aligned}
\text{energy (joules)} &= 1/2 \times 0.25 \text{ kg} \times 2500 \text{ m}^2/\text{s}^2 \\
&= 312.5 \text{ kg-m}^2/\text{s}^2 \\
&= 312.5 \text{ joules}
\end{aligned}$$

Even though the bowling ball is much more massive than the baseball, a hard-hit baseball carries more kinetic energy than a typical bowling ball because of its high speed.

Potential Energy

Almost every mountain range in the country has a "balancing rock"—a boulder precariously perched on top of a hill so that it looks as if a little push would send it tumbling down the slope. If the balancing rock were to fall, it would clearly acquire kinetic energy, and it would do "work" on anything it smashed. The balancing rock has the ability to do work even though it's not doing work right now, and even though it's not necessarily going to be doing work any time in the near future. The boulder possesses energy just by virtue of its position.

This kind of energy, which could result in the exertion of a force over distance but is not doing so now, is called potential energy. In the case of the balancing rock, it is called *gravitational potential energy* because the force of gravity gives the rock the capability of exerting its own force. An object that has been lifted above the surface of the Earth possesses an amount of gravitational potential energy exactly equal to the total amount of work you would have to do to lift it from the ground to its present position.

▶ **In words:** The gravitational potential energy of any object equals its weight (the gravitational force exerted downward by the object) times its height above the ground.

▶ **In equation form:**

$$\text{gravitational potential energy (joules)} = \text{mass (kg)} \times g \ (\text{m/s}^2) \times \text{height (m)}$$

where g is the acceleration due to gravity at the Earth's surface (see Chapter 2).

▶ **In symbols:**

$$E = mgh$$

In Example 3-1 we saw that it requires 784 joules of energy to carry a 20-kg television set 4 meters distance up the stairs. Thus 784 joules is the amount of work that would be done if the television set were allowed to fall, and it is the amount of gravitational potential energy stored in the elevated television set.

We encounter many other kinds of potential energy besides the gravitational kind in our daily lives. *Chemical potential energy* is stored in the gasoline that moves your car, the batteries that power your radio, and the food you eat. All animals depend on the chemical potential energy of food, and all living things rely on molecules that store chemical energy for future use. In each of these situations, potential energy is stored in the chemical bonds between atoms (see Chapter 9).

Wall outlets in your home and at work provide a means to tap into *electrical potential energy,* waiting to turn a fan or drive a vacuum cleaner. A tightly coiled spring, a flexed muscle, and a stretched rubber band contain *elastic potential energy,* while a refrigerator magnet carries *magnetic potential energy.* In every case, energy is stored, ready to do work (Figure 3-2).

Heat, or Thermal Energy

Two centuries ago, scientists understood the basic behavior of kinetic and potential energy, but the nature of heat was far more mysterious. We now know that atoms and molecules, the minute particles that make up all matter, move around and vibrate, and therefore these particles possess kinetic energy. The tiny forces that they exert are experienced only by other atoms and molecules, but the small scale doesn't make the forces any less real. If molecules in a material begin to move more rapidly, they have more kinetic energy and are capable of exerting greater forces on each other in collisions. If you touch an object whose molecules are moving fast, the collisions of those molecules with molecules in your hand will exert greater force, and you will perceive the object to be hot. What we normally call **heat**, therefore, is simply **thermal energy**—the kinetic energy of atoms and molecules.

SCIENCE IN THE MAKING •

Discovering the Nature of Heat

What is heat? How would you apply the scientific method to determine its origins? That was the problem facing scientists 200 years ago.

In many respects, they realized, heat behaves like a fluid. It flows from place to place, and it seems to spread out evenly like water that has been spilled on the floor. Some objects soak up heat faster than others, and many materials seem to swell up when heated, just like waterlogged wood. Thus, in 1800, after years of observations and experiments, many physicists mistakenly accepted the theory

• **Figure 3-2** Potential energy comes in many forms.

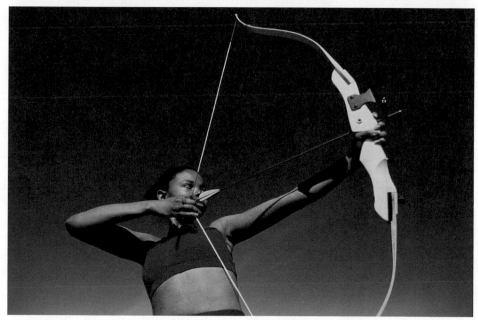

that heat is an invisible fluid—they called it "caloric." According to the caloric theory of heat, the best fuels, such as coal, are saturated with caloric, while ice is virtually devoid of the substance.

One of the most influential investigators of heat was the Massachusetts-born Benjamin Thompson (1752–1814), who led a remarkably adventurous life. At the age of 19 he married an extremely wealthy widow, 14 years his senior. He sided with the British during the Revolutionary War, first working as a spy, then as an officer in the British Army of Occupation in New York. After the Americans won the war, Thompson abandoned his wife and infant daughter and fled to Europe, where he was knighted by King George III. Later in his turbulent life he was forced to flee England on suspicion of spying for the French, and he eventually

Benjamin Thompson, Count Rumford, in a Bavarian cannon foundry in 1798, calling attention to the transformation of mechanical energy into heat.

wound up in the employ of the Elector of Bavaria, where his duties included the manufacture and machining of cannons.

If heat is a fluid, then each object must contain a fixed quantity of that substance. But Thompson noted that the increase in temperature that accompanies boring a cannon had nothing at all to do with the quantity of brass to be drilled. Sharp tools, he found, cut brass quickly with minimum heat generation, while dull tools made slow progress and produced prodigious amounts of heat.

Thompson proposed an alternative hypothesis. He suggested that the increase in temperature in his brass was a consequence of the mechanical energy of friction, not some theoretical, invisible fluid. He proved his point by immersing an entire cannon-boring machine in water, turning it on, and watching the heat that was generated turn the water to steam. British chemist and popular science lecturer Sir Humphry Davy (1778–1829) further dramatized Thompson's point when he generated heat by rubbing pieces of ice together on a cold London day.

The work of Thompson, Davy, and others inspired English researcher James Prescott Joule to devise a special experiment to test the predictions of the rival theories. As shown in Figure 3-3, Joule's apparatus employed a weight that was lifted up and attached to a rope. The rope turned a paddle wheel immersed in a tub of water. The weight had gravitational potential energy and, as it fell, that energy was converted into kinetic energy of the rotating paddle. The paddle wheel's kinetic energy, in turn, was transferred to kinetic energy of water molecules. As Joule suspected, the water heated up. Heat, he declared, is just another form of energy. •

Wave Energy

Anyone who has watched surf battering a seashore has first-hand knowledge of **wave energy**. In the case of water waves, the type of energy involved is obvious. Large amounts of water are in rapid motion and therefore possess kinetic energy. It is this energy that we see released when waves hit the shore.

Other kinds of waves possess energy, as well. For example, when a *sound wave* is generated, molecules in the air are set in motion and the energy of the sound wave is associated with the kinetic energy of those molecules. Similar sound waves traveling through the solid earth, called *seismic waves,* can carry the potentially destructive energy that is unleashed in earthquakes (see Chapter 17).

• **Figure 3-3** Joule's experiment demonstrated that heat is another form of energy by showing that the kinetic energy of a paddle wheel is transferred to thermal energy of the agitated water.

In Chapter 6 we will meet another important kind of wave, the kind associated with electromagnetic radiation, such as the radiant energy (light) that streams from the Sun. This sort of wave stores its energy in changing electrical and magnetic fields.

Mass as Energy

The discovery that certain atoms, such as uranium, spontaneously release energy as they disintegrate—the phenomenon of radioactivity—led to the realization in the early twentieth century that mass is a form of energy. This principle is the focus of Chapter 11, but the main idea is summarized in Albert Einstein's most famous equation.

▶ **In words:** Every object at rest contains potential energy equivalent to the product of its mass times a constant, which is the speed of light squared.

▶ **In equation form:**

$$\text{energy (joules)} = \text{mass (kg)} \times [\text{speed of light (m/s)}]^2$$

▶ **In symbols:**

$$E = mc^2$$

where c is the symbol for the speed of light, a constant equal to 300,000,000 meters per second (3×10^8 m/s).

This equation, which has achieved the rank of a cultural icon, tells us that it is possible to create energy from mass and to use energy to create mass. (*Note:* This equation does not mean the mass has to be traveling at the speed of light; the mass is assumed to be at rest.) Furthermore, because the speed of light is so great, the energy stored in even a tiny amount of mass is enormous.

EXAMPLE 3-4

Lots of Potential

According to Einstein's equation, how much potential energy is contained in the mass of a grain of sand with a mass of 0.001 gram?

Reasoning and Solution: Substitute the mass, 0.001 gram, into Einstein's famous equation. Remember that 1 gram is a thousandth of a kilogram, so a thousandth of a gram equals a millionth of a kilogram (10^{-6} kg). Also, the speed of light is a constant, 3×10^8 m/s.

$$\begin{aligned}
\text{energy (joules)} &= \text{mass (kg)} \times [\text{speed of light (m/s)}]^2 \\
&= 10^{-6} \text{ kg} \times (3 \times 10^8 \text{ m/s})^2 \\
&= 10^{-6} \times 9 \times (10^{16} \text{ kg-m}^2/\text{s}^2) \\
&= 9 \times 10^{10} \text{ joules}
\end{aligned}$$

The energy contained in the mass of a single grain of sand is prodigious: almost 100 billion joules, which is 25,000 kilowatt-hours. The average American family uses about 1000 kilowatt-hours of electricity per month, so a sand grain—if we had the means to convert its mass entirely to electrical energy (which we don't)—could satisfy your home's energy needs for the next two years!

In practical terms, Einstein's equation showed that mass could be used to generate electricity in nuclear power plants, in which a few pounds of nuclear fuel is enough to power an entire city.

The Interchangeability of Energy

You know from everyday experience that energy can be changed from one form to another (Table 3-2). Plants absorb light streaming from the Sun and convert that radiant energy into the stored chemical energy of cells and plant tissues. You eat plants and convert the chemical energy into the kinetic energy of your muscles—energy of motion that in turn can be converted into gravitational potential energy when you climb a flight of stairs, elastic potential energy when you stretch a rubber band, or heat when you rub your hands together. The lesson from these examples is clear.

> **The many different forms of energy are interchangeable.**

Energy in one form can be converted into others.

Bungee jumping provides a dramatic illustration of this rule (Figure 3-4). Bungee jumpers climb to a high bridge or platform, where elastic cords are attached to their ankles. Then they launch themselves into space and fall toward the ground until the cords stretch, slow them down, and stop their fall.

From an energy point of view, a bungee jumper uses the chemical potential energy generated from food to walk up to the launching platform. The work that had been done against gravity provides the jumper with gravitational potential energy. During the long descent, the gravitational potential energy diminishes, while the jumper's kinetic energy simultaneously increases. As the cords begin to stretch, the jumper slows down and kinetic energy gradually is converted to stored elastic potential energy in the cords. Eventually, the gravitational potential energy that the jumper had at the beginning is completely transferred to the stretched elastic cords, which then rebound, converting some of the stored elastic energy back into kinetic energy and gravitational potential energy. All the time, some of the energy is also converted to thermal energy: increased temperature in the stressed cord, on the jumper's ankles, and the air as it is pushed aside.

One of the most fundamental properties of the universe in which we live is that every form of energy on our list can be converted to every other form of energy.

THE ONGOING PROCESS OF SCIENCE •

New Sources of Energy

The realization that energy can shift from one form to another drives many scientists to search for new energy-gathering technologies. For thousands of years, humans have used sunlight to grow crops, wind to propel their ships, and waterfalls to turn their millstones. Energy in the form of blowing wind, falling water, and brilliant sunlight is still all around us, just waiting to be used, if only we had the means to convert it cheaply and efficiently into electricity. Given society's incessant and growing demand for energy, research on new sources of energy continues to be

Table 3-2 Some Forms of Energy

Potential Energy	Kinetic Energy	Other
Gravitational	Moving objects	Mass
Chemical	Heat	
Elastic	Sound and other waves	
Electromagnetic		

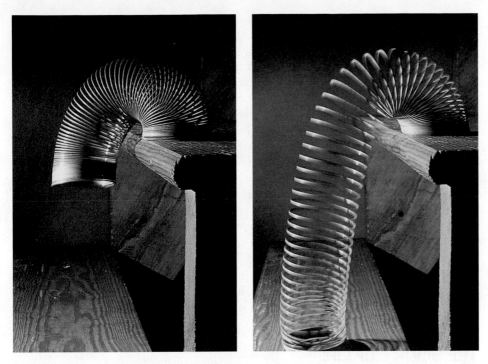

A Slinky provides a dramatic example of energy changing from one form to another. Can you identify some of the kinds of energy changes involved?

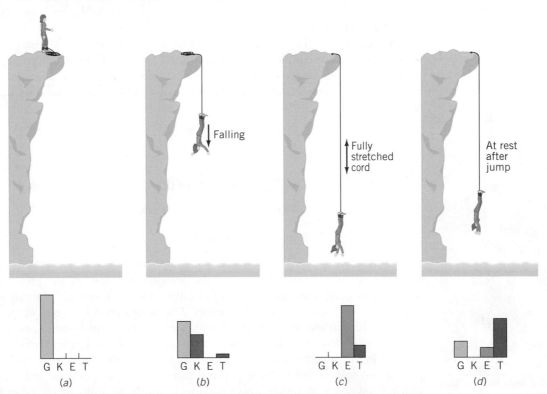

• **Figure 3-4** "Energy changes form during a bungee jump, though the total energy is constant. Histograms display the distribution of energy among gravitational potential (G), kinetic (K), elastic potential (E) and heat (H). Initially (a), all of the energy to be used in the jump is stored as gravitational potential energy. During the descent (b), the gravitational potential energy is converted to kinetic energy. At the bottom of the jump, the bungee cord stretches (c), so that most energy is in the form of elastic potential. At the end of the jump (d) most of the energy winds up as heat."

a major scientific enterprise. At the moment, the most important areas of development are in the use of solar and wind energy to generate electricity.

The most promising use of solar energy is in a field called photovoltaics. In a solar photovoltaic installation, sunlight falls on panels of specially engineered material, called semiconductors. These special materials have the ability to convert light directly into an electric current. (The exact means by which this conversion is accomplished will be discussed in Chapter 10.) While the Sun is shining, electrical current flows into the power grid from the installation.

Electrical energy can also be generated by modern versions of the traditional windmill. High-tech propeller-like blades perched on a high tower turn in the wind, thus running an electric generator. The wind resource in the United States is immense. Indeed, the "wind belt" stretching from the Dakotas to New Mexico could easily generate a significant fraction of American electrical power. In addition, the cost of generating electricity with wind has dropped dramatically in recent years, and is now comparable to the cost of conventional generators.

At the moment, wind and solar energy account for less than 2% of American energy consumption, but that percentage is growing. As research improves the efficiency and lowers the cost of these alternative energy sources, we can expect to see them come into more widespread use. •

THE SCIENCE OF LIFE •

Energy for Life and Trophic Levels

All of Earth's systems, both living and nonliving, transform the Sun's radiant energy into other forms. Just how much energy is available, and how is it used by living organisms?

At the top of the Earth's atmosphere, the Sun's incoming energy is 1400 watts per square meter. To calculate the total energy of this solar power, we first need to calculate the cross-sectional area of the Earth in square meters. The radius of the Earth is 6375 kilometers (6,375,000 meters), and so the cross-sectional area is

$$\text{area of a circle} = \text{pi} \times (\text{radius})^2$$
$$= 3.14 \times (6,375,000 \text{ m})^2$$
$$= 1.28 \times 10^{14} \text{ m}^2$$

Thus the total power received at the top of the Earth's atmosphere is

$$\text{power} = \text{solar energy per m}^2 \times \text{Earth's cross-sectional area}$$
$$= 1400 \text{ watts/m}^2 \times 1.28 \times 10^{14} \text{ m}^2$$
$$= 1.79 \times 10^{17} \text{ watts}$$

Solar photovoltaic cells, like this array in Albuquerque, New Mexico, convert the energy in sunlight directly into electrical current.

Each second, the top of the Earth's atmosphere receives 1.79×10^{17} joules of energy, but that is more than twice the amount that reaches the ground. When solar radiation encounters the top of the atmosphere, about 25% of it is immediately reflected back into space. Another 25% is absorbed by gases in the atmosphere, and Earth's surface reflects an additional 5% back into space. These processes leave about 45% of the initial amount to be absorbed at the Earth's surface.

All living systems take their energy from this 45%, but absorb only a small portion of this amount—only about 4% to run photosynthesis and supply the entire food chain. A much larger portion heats the ground or air, or evaporates water from lakes, rivers, and oceans.

The concept of the food chain and its trophic levels is particularly useful when tracking the many changes of energy as it flows through living systems of Earth. A **trophic level** consists of all organisms that get their energy from the same source

Big Carnivores	Fourth trophic level
Carnivores	Third trophic level
Herbivores	Second trophic level
Producers – Photosynthetic Organisms	First trophic level

Mass of living materials per unit of area

• **Figure 3-5** The food chain. Living organisms are arranged in trophic levels according to how they obtain energy. The first trophic level consists of plants that produce energy from photosynthesis. In the higher trophic levels, animals get their energy by feeding on organisms from the next lowest level.

(Figure 3-5). In this ranking scheme, all plants that produce energy from photosynthesis are in the *first trophic level*. These plants all absorb energy from sunlight and use it to drive chemical reactions that make plant tissues and other complex molecules subsequently used as energy sources by organisms in higher trophic levels.

The *second trophic level* includes all *herbivores*—animals that get their energy by eating plants of the first trophic level. Cows, rabbits, and many insects occupy this level. The *third trophic level,* as you might expect, consists of *carnivores*—animals that get their energy by eating organisms in the second trophic level. This third level includes such familiar animals as wolves, eagles, and lions, as well as insect-eating birds, blood-sucking ticks and mosquitoes, and many other organisms.

A few more groups of organisms fill out the scheme of trophic levels on the Earth. Carnivores that eat other carnivores, such as killer whales, occupy the fourth trophic level. Termites, vultures, and a host of bacteria and fungi get their energy from feeding on dead organisms and are generally placed in a trophic level separate from the four we've just described. (The usual convention is that this trophic level is not given a number because the dead organisms can come from any of the other trophic levels.)

A number of animals and plants span the trophic levels. Human beings, raccoons, and bears, for example, are *omnivores* that gain energy from plants and from organisms in other trophic levels, while the Venus flytrap supplements its diet with trapped insects. •

 Stop and Think! From which trophic levels did you obtain energy during the past 24 hours?

Although you might expect it to be otherwise, the efficiency with which solar energy is used by Earth's organisms is very low, despite the struggle by all these organisms to use energy efficiently. When sunlight falls, for example, on a cornfield in the middle of Iowa in August—arguably one of the best situations in the world for plant growth—only a small percentage of the solar energy striking the field is actually transformed as chemical energy in the plants. All the rest of the energy is reflected, heats up the soil, evaporates water, or performs some other function. It is a general rule that no plants anywhere transform as much as 10% of solar energy available to them.

The same situation applies to trophic levels above the first. Typically, less than 10% of a plant's chemical potential energy winds up as tissue in the animal of the second trophic level that eats the plants. That is, less than about 1% (10% of 10%) of the original energy in sunlight is transformed into chemical energy of the second trophic level. Continuing with the same pattern, animals in the third trophic level also use less than 10% of the energy available from the second level.

You can do a rough verification of this statement in your supermarket. Whole grains (those that have not been processed heavily) typically cost about one-tenth as much as fresh meat. Examined from an energy point of view, this cost differential is not surprising. It takes 10 times as much energy to make a pound of beef as it does to make a pound of wheat or rice, and this fact is reflected in the price.

One of the most interesting examples of energy flow through trophic levels can be seen in the fossils of dinosaurs. In many museum exhibits, the most dramatic and memorable specimen is a giant carnivore—a *Tyrannosaurus* or *Allosaurus* with six-inch dagger teeth and powerful claws. So often are these impressive skeletons illustrated that you might get the impression that these finds are common. In fact, fossil carnivores are extremely rare and represent only a small fraction of known dinosaur specimens. Our knowledge of the fearsome *Tyrannosaurus,* for example, is based on only about a dozen skeletons, and most of those are quite fragmentary. By contrast, paleontologists have found hundreds of skeletons of plant-eating dinosaurs. This distribution is hardly chance. Carnivorous dinosaurs, like modern lions and tigers, were relatively scarce compared to their herbivorous victims. In fact, statistical studies of all dinosaur skeletons reveal a roughly 10:1 herbivore-to-carnivore ratio, a value approaching what we find today for the ratio of warm-blooded herbivores to warm-blooded carnivores, and much higher than the herbivore-to-carnivore ratio observed in modern cold-blooded reptiles. This pattern is cited by many paleontologists as evidence that dinosaurs were warm-blooded.

The First Law of Thermodynamics: Energy Is Conserved

Scientists are always on the lookout for attributes of the ever-changing universe that are constant and unchanging. If the total number of atoms, electrons, or electrical charges is constant, then that attribute is said to be conserved. Any statement that an attribute is *conserved* is called a **conservation law**. (Note that these meanings of "conserved" and "conservation" are different from the more common uses of the words associated with modest consumption and recycling.)

Before describing the conservation law that relates to energy, we must first introduce the idea of a system. You can think of a **system** as an imaginary box into which you put some matter and some energy that you'd like to study. Scientists might want to study a system containing only a pan of water, or one consisting of a forest, or even the entire planet Earth. Doctors examine your nervous system, astronomers explore the solar system, and biologists observe a variety of ecosystems. In each case, the investigation of nature is simplified by focusing on one small part of the universe.

If the system under study can exchange matter and energy with its surroundings—a pan full of water that is heated on a stove and gradually evaporates, for example—then it is an *open system*. An open system is like an open box where you can take things out and put things back in. Alternatively, if matter and energy in a system do not freely exchange with their surroundings, as in a tightly shut box, then the system is said to be *closed* or isolated. Earth and its primary source of energy, the Sun, together make a system that may be thought of for most purposes as closed, because there are no significant amounts of matter or energy being added from outside sources.

The most important conservation law in the sciences is the law of *conservation of energy*. This law is also called the **first law of thermodynamics**. (*Thermodynamics*—literally the study of the movement of heat—is a term used for the science of heat, energy, and work.) The law can be stated as follows:

In an isolated system the total amount of energy, including heat, is conserved.

This law tells us that, although the kind of energy in a given system can change, the total amount cannot. For example, when a bungee jumper hurls herself into space, the gravitational potential energy she had at the beginning of the fall is converted to an equal amount of other kinds of energy. When she's moving, some of the gravitational potential energy changes into kinetic energy, some into elastic potential energy, and some into the increased temperature of the surroundings. At each point during the fall, however, the sum of kinetic, elastic potential, gravitational potential, and heat energies has to be the same as the gravitational energy at the beginning.

Energy is something like an economy with an absolutely fixed amount of money. You can earn it, store it in a bank or under your pillow, and spend it here and there when you want to. But the total amount of money doesn't change just because it passes through your hands. Likewise, in any physical situation you can shuffle energy from one place to another. You could take it out of the account labeled "kinetic" and put it into the account labeled "potential"; you could spread it around into accounts labeled "chemical potential," "elastic potential," "heat," and so on; but the first law of thermodynamics tells us that, in a closed system, you can never have more or less energy than you started with.

To many scientists of the nineteenth century the first law of thermodynamics represented more than just a useful statement about energy. For them it carried a profound significance about the underlying symmetry—even beauty—of the natural order. Joule described the first law in the following poetic way: "Nothing is destroyed, nothing is ever lost, but the entire machinery, complicated as it is, works smoothly and harmoniously. . . . Everything may appear complicated in the apparent confusion and intricacy of an almost endless variety of causes, effects, conversions, and arrangements, yet is the most perfect regularity preserved—the whole being governed by the sovereign will of God." To Joule, the first law was nothing less than proof of the beneficence of the Creator—a natural law analogous to the immortality of the soul.

SCIENCE BY THE NUMBERS •

Diet and Calories

The first law of thermodynamics has a great deal to say about the American obsession with weight and diet. Human beings take in energy with their food, energy we usually measure in *calories*. (Note that the calorie we talk about in foods is defined as the amount of energy needed to raise the temperature of a kilogram of water 1° Celsius, a unit we will later call a kilocalorie.) When a certain amount of energy is taken in, the first law says that only one of two things can happen to it: it can be converted into work and increased temperature of the surroundings, or it can be stored. If we take in more energy than we expend, the excess is stored in fat. If, on the other hand, we take in less than we expend, energy must be removed from storage to meet the deficit, and the amount of body fat decreases.

Here are a couple of rough rules you can use to calculate calories in your diet:

1. Under most circumstances, normal body maintenance uses up about 15 calories per day for each pound of body weight.

2. You must consume about 3500 calories to gain a pound of fat.

William Thomson, Lord
Kelvin (1824–1907)

Suppose you weigh 150 pounds. To keep your weight constant, you have to take in

$$150 \text{ pounds} \times 15 \text{ calories/pound} = 2250 \text{ calories per day}$$

If you wanted to lose one pound (3500 calories) a week (7 days), you would have to reduce your daily calorie intake by

$$\frac{3500 \text{ calories}}{7 \text{ days}} = 500 \text{ calories per day}$$

Another way of saying this is that you would have to reduce your calorie intake to 1750 calories—the equivalent of skipping dessert every day.

Alternatively, the first law says you can increase your energy use through exercise. Roughly speaking, to burn off 500 calories you'd have to run 5 miles, bike 15 miles, or swim for an hour.

It's a whole lot easier to refrain from eating than to burn off the weight by exercise. In fact, most researchers now say that the main benefit of exercise in weight control has to do with its ability to help people control their appetites. •

SCIENCE IN THE MAKING •

Lord Kelvin and the Age of the Earth

The first law of thermodynamics provided physicists with a powerful tool for describing and analyzing their universe. Every isolated system, the law tells us, has a fixed amount of energy. Naturally, one of the first systems that scientists considered was the Earth and Sun.

British physicist William Thomson (1824–1907), knighted as Lord Kelvin, asked a simple question: How much energy could be stored in the Earth? And, given the present rate at which energy radiates out into space, how old might the Earth be? Though simple, these questions had profound implications for philosophers and theologians who had their own ideas about the Earth's relative antiquity. Some Biblical scholars believed that the Earth could be no more than a few thousand years old. Most geologists, on the other hand, saw evidence in layered rocks to suggest an Earth at least hundreds of millions of years old. Biologists also required vast amounts of time to account for the gradual evolution of life on Earth. Who was correct?

Kelvin assumed, as did most of his contemporaries, that the Earth had formed from a contracting cloud of interstellar dust (see Chapter 16). He thought that the Earth began as a hot body because impacts of large objects on it early in its history must have converted huge amounts of gravitational potential energy into thermal energy. He used new developments in mathematics to calculate how long it took for the hot Earth to cool to its present temperature. He assumed that there were no sources of energy inside the Earth, and found that the age of the Earth had to be less than about 100 million years. He soundly rejected the geologists' and biologists' claims of an older Earth because these claims seemed to violate the first law of thermodynamics.

Seldom have scientists come to such a bitter impasse. Two competing theories about the age of the Earth, each supported by seemingly sound observations, were at odds. The calculations of the physicist seemed unassailable, yet the observations of biologists and geologists in the field were equally meticulous. What could possibly resolve the dilemma? Had the scientific method failed? The solution came from a totally unexpected source when scientists discovered in the 1890s that rocks hold a previously unknown source of energy, radioactivity (see Chapter 11), in which thermal energy is generated by the conversion of mass. Lord Kelvin's rigorous age calculations were in error only because he and his contemporaries were unaware of this critical component of the Earth's energy budget. The Earth's deep interior, we now know, gains approximately half of its thermal energy from radioactive decay. Revised calculations suggest an Earth several billions of years old, in conformity with geological and biological observations. •

TECHNOLOGY •

The Economics of Alternative Energy Sources

Throughout history, society has been shaped in part by its favored sources of energy. The character of nineteenth-century America, for example, changed dramatically as people gradually shifted from wood, which an individual could gather, to coal and oil, which required an extensive transportation and marketing infrastructure. Thus, while the development of new technology for energy production is important, it is not the whole story about alternative energy. In order for new technology to have an impact, people must choose to use it, and this choice, in turn, depends on a variety of factors such as convenience and cost.

Take solar energy as an example. It now costs about two to three times as much to generate a kilowatt-hour of electrical energy from solar photovoltaic cells as it does to generate that same energy from fossil fuels (the exact number depends on how you calculate costs). As the technology improves, this cost will come down—solar electricity was over eight times as expensive as conventional electricity when the first edition of this book was published in 1994, for example.

To understand how solar energy will enter the mass market in electricity, we have to understand that engineers customarily divide electrical demand into two categories—*base load* and *peak load*. Base load refers to that part of the demand that is pretty steady from day to day. Peak load refers to the extra demand that comes under special circumstances, such as a hot August afternoon when everyone turns on his or her air conditioner. Generating base load requires large coal or nuclear plants, and achieving the lowest cost of production is very important. Peak load, on the other hand, is usually generated by gas turbines that run only a fraction of the year, and hence peak load electricity is very expensive. The first major breakthrough for solar energy will probably come when companies use solar plants to generate peak load electricity. Solar energy doesn't have to compete with cheap coal, in other words, but rather with the much more expensive peak load generators. •

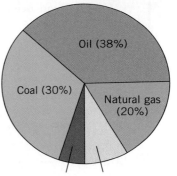

• **Figure 3-6** Sources of energy for the United States and other industrial nations. Note that most of our energy comes from fossil fuels.

Thinking More About | Energy

Fossil Fuels

All life is rich in the element carbon, which plays a key role in virtually all the chemicals that make up our cells. Life uses the Sun's energy, directly through photosynthesis or indirectly through food, to form these carbon-based substances that store chemical potential energy. When living things die, they may collect in layers at the bottoms of ponds, lakes, or oceans. Over time, as the layers become buried, the Earth's temperature and pressure may alter the chemicals of life into deposits of fossil fuels.

Fossil fuels, carbon-rich deposits of ancient life that burn with a hot flame, have been the most important energy source during the past century and a half. *Coal, oil (petroleum),* and *natural gas,* the most common fossil fuels, are consumed in prodigious quantities around the

world (Figure 3-6). They now account for approximately 90% of all energy consumed by industrial nations. In the United States alone, approximately 1 billion tons of coal and 2.5 billion barrels of petroleum are used every year.

Geologists estimate that it takes tens of millions of years of gradual burial under layers of sediments, combined with the transforming effects of temperature and pressure, to form a coal seam or petroleum deposit. Coal forms from layer upon layer of plants that thrived in vast ancient swamps, while petroleum represents primarily the organic matter once contained in plankton, microscopic organisms that float near the ocean's surface. While these natural processes continue today, the rate of coal and petroleum formation in the Earth is only a small fraction of the fossil fuels being consumed. For this reason, fossil fuels are classified as *nonrenewable resources.*

One consequence of this situation is clear. Humans cannot continue to rely on fossil fuels forever. Reserves of high-grade crude oil and the cleanest-burning varieties of coal may last less than 100 more years. Less efficient forms of fossil fuels, including lower grades of coal and oil shales in which petroleum is dispersed through solid rock, could be depleted within a few centuries. All the energy now locked up in those valuable energy reserves will still exist, but in the form of unusable heat radiating far into space.

Given the irreversibility of burning up our fossil fuel reserves, what steps should we take to promote energy conservation? Should energy be taxed at a higher rate? Should we assume that new energy sources will become available as they are needed?

SUMMARY

Work, measured in *joules* (or foot-pounds), is defined as a force applied over a distance. You do work every time you move an object. Every action of our lives requires *energy* (also measured in joules), which is the ability to do work. *Power*, measured in *watts* or *kilowatts*, indicates the rate at which energy is expended.

Energy comes in several forms. *Kinetic energy* is the energy associated with moving objects such as cars or cannonballs. *Potential energy*, on the other hand, is stored, ready-to-use energy, such as the chemical energy of coal, the elastic energy of a coiled spring, the gravitational energy of dammed-up water, or the electrical energy in your wall socket. *Thermal energy* or *heat* is the form of kinetic energy associated with vibrating atoms and molecules. Energy can also take the form of *wave energy*, such as sound waves or light waves. And early in the twentieth century it was discovered that mass is also a form of energy. All around us energy constantly shifts from one form to another, and all of these kinds of energy are interchangeable.

Energy from the Sun is used by photosynthetic plants in the first *trophic level*; these plants provide the energy for animals in higher trophic levels. Roughly speaking, only about 10 percent of the energy available at one trophic level finds its way to the next.

The most fundamental idea about energy, expressed in the *first law of thermodynamics*, is that it is *conserved*: the total amount of energy in an isolated *system* never changes. Energy can shift back and forth between the different kinds, but the sum of all energy is constant.

KEY TERMS ABOUT ENERGY

work (measured in joules)
energy (measured in joules)
power (measured in watts or kilowatts)
kinetic energy

potential energy
thermal energy (heat)
wave energy
trophic level

conservation law
system
first law of thermodynamics

KEY EQUATIONS

work (joules) = force (newtons) × distance (meters)

$$\text{power (watts)} = \frac{\text{energy (joules)}}{\text{time (seconds)}}$$

energy (joules) = power (watts) × time (seconds)

kinetic energy (joules) = $\frac{1}{2}$ × [mass (kg)] × [speed (m/s)]^2

gravitational potential energy (joules) = g × mass (kg) × height (m)

energy associated with mass at rest (joules) = mass (kg) × [speed of light (m/s)]^2

Constant
$c = 3 \times 10^8$ m/s = speed of light

REVIEW QUESTIONS

1. What is the scientific definition of work? How does it differ from ordinary English usage?
2. What is the difference between the watt and the horsepower?

3. What is the difference between energy and power?
4. List some different kinds of energy. Explain how they differ from each other.

5. What is the relationship between heat, energy, and motion?

6. Explain why waves carry energy.

7. What does it mean to say that different forms of energy are interchangeable?

8. Give an example of change of energy from potential to kinetic; from kinetic to potential.

9. What is a trophic level? Give some examples.

10. What does it mean to say that energy is conserved?

11. How did the discovery that mass is a form of energy resolve the debate over the age of the Earth?

12. Explain what it means to say, "Energy flows through the Earth."

DISCUSSION QUESTIONS

1. Identify at least five key words in this and previous chapters for which the scientific meaning differs from the everyday colloquial meaning.

2. If plants use only a small percentage of the Sun's radiant energy, where does the rest of the energy go?

3. You use energy to heat your home. What ultimately happens to the energy that you pay for in your heating bill?

4. Think about your activities today. Pick one of them and identify the chain of energy that led to it. Where will the energy in that chain eventually wind up?

5. Many technological devices are designed to convert one kind of energy into another as efficiently as possible. An electric motor, for example, converts electrical potential energy into kinetic energy. Identify household devices that do the following:

a. converts gravitational potential energy into kinetic energy

b. converts electrical potential energy into heat

c. converts chemical potential energy into light

d. converts elastic potential energy into kinetic energy

e. converts sound into electrical potential energy

6. Describe how you might convert the elastic potential energy of a coiled spring into heat energy. How might you convert heat energy into gravitational potential energy?

7. Identify four sources of energy around us that are constantly being renewed. What sources of energy do we use that are not constantly renewed?

8. Plants and animals are still dying and falling to the ocean bottom today. Why, then, do we not classify fossil fuels as renewable resources?

9. Some people say that you lose more calories by eating celery than you gain. How could that be?

10. Ancient human societies are described as *labor intensive* while modern society is said to be *energy intensive*. What is meant by these terms?

PROBLEMS

1. How much work against gravity do you do when you bench press a 50-kg mass (a distance of about 1 meter)? Compare this work to that done by a 100-watt lightbulb in an hour. How many times would you have to press the 50-kg mass to equal the work of the lightbulb in one hour?

2. Would you rather be hit by a 5-kilogram mass traveling 10 meters per second, or a 10-kilogram mass traveling 5 meters per second? Why?

3. Compared to a car moving at 40 miles per hour, how much kinetic energy does that same car have when it moves at 50 miles per hour? 60? 70? What do these numbers suggest to you about the difficulty of stopping a car as its speed increases?

4. According to Einstein's famous equation, $E = mc^2$, how much energy would be released if a pound of feathers was converted entirely into energy? A pound of lead? (*Note*: You will first need to convert pounds into kilograms.)

5. A small air conditioner operates on a 2.0-horsepower electric motor for 12 hours a day. How much energy is consumed by the air conditioner daily? If electricity costs 10 cents a kilowatt-hour, how much does it cost to run the air conditioner each day? (*Note*: 1 horsepower equals about 750 watts.)

6. Joules and kilowatt-hours are both units of energy. How many joules are equal to 1 kilowatt-hour?

7. Estimate what the price of lion meat might be, and give reasons for your prediction.

INVESTIGATIONS

1. Look at your most recent electric bill and find the cost of one kilowatt-hour in your area. Then,

a. Look at the back of your CD player or an appliance and find the power rating in watts. How much does it cost for you to operate the device for one hour?

b. If you leave a 100-watt lightbulb on all the time, how much will you pay in a year of electric bills?

c. If you had to pay $10.00 for a high-efficiency bulb that provided the same light as the 100-watt bulb with only 10 watts of power, how much would you save per year of electric bills, assuming you use the light five hours per day? Would it be worth your while to buy the energy-efficient bulb if the ordinary bulb cost $1.00?

2. In this chapter we introduced several energy units: the joule, the foot-pound, the kilowatt-hour, and the calorie. There are other energy units as well, including the BTU, the erg, the electron-volt, and many more. Look in a science reference book for conversion factors between different pairs of energy units; you may find more than a dozen different units. Who uses each of these different units? Why are there so many different units for the same phenomenon—energy?

3. What kind of fuel is used at your local power plant? What are the implications of the first law of thermodynamics regarding our use of fossil fuels? Our use of solar energy?

4. Keep a record of the calorie content of the food you eat and the amount of exercise you do for a few days.

If you wanted to gain a pound per month for the next year, how might you change your current habits?

5. Check your household's electric bills for the past year and calculate your total electric consumption for the year.

a. How many 50-kilogram weights would you have to bench press 1 meter to produce a gravitational potential energy equal to this consumption?

b. How much mass is equal to this consumption ($E = mc^2$)?

c. Identify five ways that you might reduce your energy consumption without drastically changing your life-style.

d. Draft a plan by which you reduce your energy consumption by 10%. About how much money might this save you per year?

6. Investigate the history of the controversy between Lord Kelvin and his contemporaries regarding the age of the Earth. When did the debate begin? How long did it last? What kinds of evidence did biologists, geologists, and physicists use to support their differing calculations of the Earth's age?

7. At one point the Clinton-Gore administration advocated the imposition of a BTU tax on energy. What is this tax? How might it be implemented? What are the pros and cons? If new revenues were essential to prevent the budget deficit from growing, how would you vote on legislation to impose a BTU tax? Why?

WWW RESOURCES

See *The Sciences* homepage at: **http://www.wiley.com/college/trefil** for valuable web links.

1. http://www.unidata.ucar.edu/staff/blynds/tmp.html
About Temperature—not flashy, but thorough and concise.

2. http://www.energyquest.ca.gov/story/index.html
The Energy Story, a comprehensive survey of energy technology, from the California Energy Dept.

4

Heat and the Second Law of Thermodynamics

How do humans control their body temperature?

GREAT IDEA

Heat is a form of energy that flows from warmer to cooler objects.

PHYSICS

A pot of boiling water gradually cools as heat energy dissipates into the surroundings.

CHEMISTRY

The chemical energy of gasoline, once released by burning, cannot be reused.

ENVIRONMENT

Violent weather, including thunderstorms and tornadoes, occurs when warmer and cooler air masses collide.

GEOLOGY

Volcanoes transfer heat energy from the Earth's interior. (Ch. 17)

HEALTH & SAFETY

Arthritis is a disease of the joints that results from the gradual deterioration of smooth joint surfaces.

ASTRONOMY

Heat energy from the Sun flows outward from its core, first by conduction, then convection, then radiation. (Ch. 14)

TECHNOLOGY

Modern high-efficiency appliances are designed to minimize the production of waste heat.

BIOLOGY

All living things grow old and die, as molecular defects in cells increase.

Red = applications of the great idea discussed in this chapter.

Orange = other applications, some of which are explored in other chapters.

Time for a hearty breakfast. You scramble eggs, squeeze some fresh juice, toast a muffin, and brew a pot of coffee. As you prepare the meal you notice an obvious but extraordinary fact: nature seems to have a direction. Many events in daily life progress only one way in time. It's easy to scramble eggs, but impossible to unscramble them. You can squeeze juice from a piece of fruit, but never un-squeeze it. Toast can't be untoasted and coffee can't be unbrewed.

But why should this be? Nothing in Newton's laws of motion or the law of gravity suggests that events work only in one way. Nothing that we have learned about energy explains the directionality of nature.

As you drink your cold juice and hot coffee you realize that food and drinks that are very hot or very cold display a similar kind of direction. A glass of ice-cold juice gradually gets warmer, while a cup of steaming hot coffee cools. Heat spreads out uniformly.

These everyday events are so familiar that we take them for granted, yet underlying the scrambling of an egg and the cooling of a hot drink is one of nature's most subtle and fascinating laws: the second law of thermodynamics.

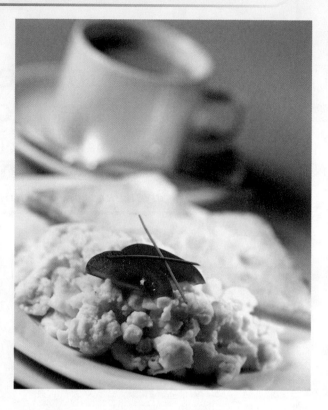

Nature's Direction

Think about the dozens of directional events that happen every day. A drop of perfume quickly pervades an entire room with scent, but you'd be hard pressed to collect all those perfume molecules into a single drop again. Your dorm room seems to get messy in the course of the week all by itself, but it takes time and effort to clean it up. And you constantly experience the inevitable, irreversible process of aging.

The first law of thermodynamics, conservation of energy, in no way forbids events to progress in the "wrong" direction. In fact, it would take exactly as much energy to unscramble an egg, if we could do it, as it takes to scramble it. The energy of a room with perfume molecules dispersed throughout is the same as the energy of the room with those molecules tightly bottled. And the energy that went into strewing things about your room is exactly the same energy it takes to put everything back again. Yet there seems to be some natural tendency for things to become less orderly with time.

This directionality in nature can be traced, ultimately, to the behavior of atoms and molecules in materials. If you hold an object in your hand, for example, its atoms are moving at more or less the same average speed. If you introduce one more atom into this collection, an atom that is moving much faster than any of its neighbors, you will have a situation in which many atoms move slowly and one atom moves fast.

Over the course of time, the fast atom will collide again and again with the others. In each collision it will probably lose some of its energy, much as a fast-moving billiard ball slows down after it collides with a couple of other billiard balls. If you wait long enough, the fast-moving atom will share its energy with all the other atoms. Consequently, every atom in the collection will be moving slightly faster than those in the original collection, and there will be no single fast atom.

If you watch this collection of atoms for a long period of time, it's extremely unlikely that the collisions will ever arrange themselves in such a way that one atom moves very fast in a collection of very slow ones. In the language of the physicists, the original state with only one fast atom is highly improbable. Over the course of time, any unlikely initial state will evolve into a more probable state—a situation like the one in which all the atoms have approximately the same energy.

The tendency of all systems to evolve from improbable to more probable states accounts for the directionality that we see in the universe around us (Figure 4-1). There is no reason from the point of view of energy alone that improbable situations can't occur. Fifteen slow-moving billiard balls have enough energy to produce one fast-moving ball. The fact that this situation doesn't occur in nature is an important clue as to how things work at the atomic level.

Nineteenth-century scientists discovered the underlying reasons for nature's directionality by studying heat, the motion of atoms and molecules. Before dealing with the details of these discoveries, as summarized in the second law of thermodynamics, let's consider some properties of heat.

• **Figure 4-1** The second law of thermodynamics tells us that it is easier to tear something down than to build it. This law is shown dramatically in this sequence of photos showing the demolition of an apartment building.

Coming to Terms with Heat

Atoms never sit still. They are always moving, and in the process they distribute their kinetic energy—what we called *thermal energy,* or *internal energy.* If you have ever tried to warm a house during a cold winter day, you have practical experience of this fact. If you turn off the furnace, the energy in the house gradually leaks away to the outside, and the house begins to get cold. The only way you can keep things warm is to keep adding more thermal energy. Similarly, our bodies constantly produce energy to maintain our core body temperature close to 98.6 degrees Fahrenheit (37°C). Both your furnace and your body produce energy on the inside—energy that will inevitably flow to the outside as heat. You use that heat on the fly, as it were.

In order to understand the nature of heat and its movement, we need to define three closely related terms: heat, temperature, and specific heat capacity.

Heat and Temperature

In everyday conversation we often use the words temperature and heat interchangeably, but to scientists the words have different meanings. Heat is a form of energy that moves from a warmer object to a cooler object; heat is thus energy in motion. Any object that is hot can transfer its internal energy to the surroundings as heat. A gallon of boiling water contains more internal energy than a pint of boiling water, and it can thus transfer more heat to its surroundings.

Heat is often measured in calories, a common unit of energy defined as the amount of heat required to raise one gram of room-temperature water by one degree Celsius in temperature. (Don't confuse this calorie, abbreviated cal, with the calorie unit commonly used in nutrition discussions. The dietary calorie, abbreviated Cal, equals 1000 calories. See Appendix B.)

Temperature, on the other hand, is a relative term and reflects how vigorously atoms in a substance are moving and colliding. Two objects are defined to be at the same temperature if no heat flows spontaneously from one to the other. A gallon of boiling water, therefore, is at the same temperature as a pint of boiling water. The difference in temperature between two objects is one of the factors that determine how quickly heat is transferred between those two objects: the larger the temperature difference, the more rapidly heat is transferred. You may have seen this phenomenon at work in the summertime when violent winds, often accompanied by a line of thunderstorms, precede a cold front. The strong winds are a consequence of rapid heat transfer between two air masses at very different temperatures.

Temperature scales provide a convenient way to compare the temperatures of two objects. Many different temperature scales have been proposed; all scales and temperature units are arbitrary, but every scale requires two easily reproduced temperatures for calibration. The freezing and boiling points of pure water are commonly used standards today in the *Fahrenheit scale* (32 and 212 degrees for freezing and boiling, respectively) and the *Celsius scale* (where 0 and 100 degrees correspond to freezing and boiling water, respectively). The Kelvin temperature scale uses the same degree as the Celsius scale, with 100 increments between the freezing and boiling points of water. This scale defines 0 kelvin (abbreviated K) as **absolute zero**, which is the coldest attainable temperature—the temperature at which it is impossible to extract any heat at all from atoms or molecules. The temperature of absolute zero is approximately –273°C, or –460°F. It turns out, therefore, that freezing and boiling occur at about 273 and 373 kelvins, respectively (Figure 4-2).

• **Figure 4-2** The Fahrenheit, Celsius, and Kelvin temperature scales compared.

Temperature Conversions

It's often necessary to convert from one temperature scale to another. American travelers, for example, often have to convert from degrees Celsius (used in most of the rest of the world) to degrees Fahrenheit. This conversion requires the following formula:

$$°F = (1.8 × °C) + 32$$

The "1.8" in this formula reflects the fact that the Fahrenheit degree is smaller than the Celsius degree, while the "32" reflects the fact that water freezes at 32°F but 0°C. To convert the opposite way, from Fahrenheit to Celsius, the formula is:

$$°C = \frac{(°F - 32)}{1.8}$$

Remember, all temperature scales measure the exact same phenomenon. They just use a different number scale to do so.

EXAMPLE 4-1

What to Wear?

You awake in Paris to a forecast high temperature of 32°C. Should you wear gloves and an overcoat?

Reasoning and Solution: Apply the equation to convert temperature from Celsius to Fahrenheit:

$$°F = (1.8 × °C) + 32$$
$$= (1.8 × 32) + 32$$
$$= 89.6°F$$

Looks like you won't be needing your overcoat today!

TECHNOLOGY •

Thermometers

A *thermometer* is a device used to measure temperature. Most thermometers display temperature either digitally or on a numbered scale. Thermometers work by incorporating a material whose properties change significantly with temperature. Many materials expand when heated and contract when cooled, and this behavior can be used to gauge temperature. In the old-style mercury thermometer, for

One of the most visually intriguing types of thermometers, invented by Galileo Galilei in the early 1600s, employs changes in liquid density as a function of temperature. The "Galilean thermometer" consists of a large sealed flask with a liquid that changes density as it is heated. Suspended in this liquid are dozens of small numbered weights, each of a slightly different density. At low temperature, most of the weights rise to the top of the flask. As temperature increases, the denser weights sink one-by-one to the bottom. The temperature is read simply as the lowest number on the weights that remain floating at the top of the thermometer.

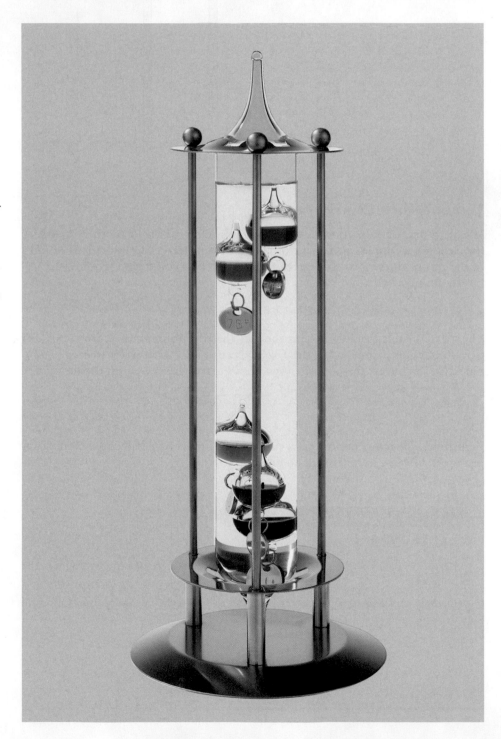

example, a bead of mercury expands into a thin glass column with increasing temperature; you read the height of the mercury against a scale marked in degrees. Many other (much safer) thermometers rely on changes in the electrical properties of a temperature sensor. •

 Stop and Think! Why are the freezing and boiling points of pure water commonly used as standards for temperature scales? Can you think of other standards that would be useful for everyday measurements?

Specific Heat Capacity

Specific heat capacity is a measure of the ability of a material to absorb heat, and is defined as the quantity of heat required to raise the temperature of one gram of that material by 1°C. Water displays the largest heat capacity of any common substance; by definition, one calorie is required to raise the temperature of a gram of water by 1°C. By contrast, you know that metals heat up quickly in a fire, so a small amount of absorbed heat can cause a significant increase in the metal's temperature.

Think about the last time you boiled water in a copper-bottomed pot. It doesn't take long to raise the temperature of a copper pot to above the boiling point of water because copper, like most other metals, can't absorb much heat. In fact, one calorie will raise the temperature of a gram of copper by about 10°C. But water is a different matter; it must absorb 10 times more heat per gram than copper to raise its temperature. Thus, even at the highest stove setting, it can take several minutes to boil a pot of water. This ability of water to store thermal energy plays a critical role in the Earth's climate, which is moderated by the relatively steady temperatures of the oceans.

Heat Transfer

You can't prevent heat from moving from an object at high temperature to its cooler surroundings, you can only slow the rate of movement. In fact, scientists and engineers have spent many decades studying the phenomenon known as **heat transfer**—the process by which heat moves from one place to another. Heat transfers by three basic mechanisms, conduction, convection, and radiation, each of which is important to different aspects of everyday experience.

1. Conduction. Have you ever reached for a pan on a hot stove, only to have your fingers scorched when you grasped the metal handle? If so, you have had firsthand experience of conduction, the movement of heat by atomic-scale collisions.

As shown in Figure 4-3, conduction works through the action of individual atoms or molecules that are linked together by chemical bonds. If a piece of metal is heated at one end, the atoms and their electrons at that end begin to move faster. When they vibrate and collide with atoms farther away from the heat source, they are likely to transfer energy to those atoms, so that the farther molecules will begin to move faster as well. A chain of collisions occurs, with atoms progressively farther and farther away from the heat source moving faster and faster as time goes by.

Conduction of heat is responsible for a large part of the heating bills in homes and office buildings. The process works like this: The air inside a house in winter is kept warmer than the air outside, so that the molecules of the air inside are moving faster than the molecules in the air outside. When the molecules inside collide with materials in the wall (a windowpane, for example), they impart some of their

• **Figure 4-3** Heat energy moves by conduction through the action of atoms or molecules that jostles their neighbors.

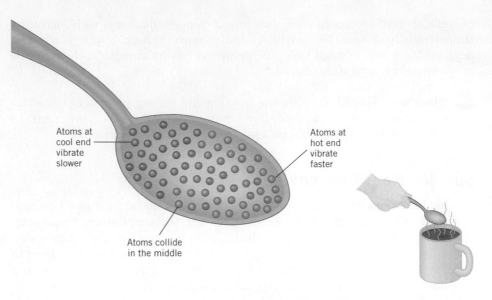

Atoms at cool end vibrate slower

Atoms at hot end vibrate faster

Atoms collide in the middle

heat to the molecules in those materials. At that point, conduction takes over and heat is transferred to the outside of the wall. There the heat is transferred to the outdoors by convection and radiation, processes that we will describe in a moment. The key point, however, is that you can think about every part of your house as being a kind of conduit carrying heat from the interior to the outside.

One way of slowing down the flow of heat out of a house is to add insulation to the walls or to use special kinds of glass for the windows. These processes work because materials differ in their **thermal conductivity**—their ability to transfer heat from one molecule to the next by conduction. Have you ever noticed that a piece of wood at room temperature feels "normal," while a piece of metal at the same temperature feels cold to the touch? The wood and metal are at exactly the same temperature, but the metal feels cold because it is a good *heat conductor*—it

Steelworkers test a molten sample from the furnace. Why does the worker at the left use thick insulated gloves to hold the cool end of the rod? Heat transfers from the hot end to the cool end by the process of conduction.

Even an unexpected material like ice can provide insulation.

moves heat rapidly away from your skin, which is generally warmer than air temperature. The wood, on the other hand, is a good *heat insulator*—it impedes the flow of heat and so it feels comparatively warm. The insulation in your home is designed to have especially low thermal conductivity, so that heat transfer is slowed down (but never completely stopped). Thus when you use special insulated windowpanes or put certain kinds of insulation in your walls, you make it more difficult for heat to flow outside, and thereby allow yourself to use the heat longer before it ultimately leaks away.

2. Convection.   Let's look carefully at a pot of boiling water on a stove. On the surface of the water you will see a rolling, churning motion as the water moves and mixes. If you put your hand above the water, you feel heat. Heat has been transferred from the water at the bottom of the pot to the top by convection, the transfer of heat by the bulk motion of the water itself, as shown in Figure 4-4.

Water near the bottom of the pan expands as it is heated by the flames. Therefore, it weighs less per unit volume than the colder water immediately above it. A situation like this, with colder, denser water above and warmer, less dense water below, is unstable. The denser fluid tends to descend and displace the less dense fluid, which in turn begins to rise. Consequently, the warm water from the bottom rises to the top, while the cool water from the top sinks to the bottom (Figure 4-4). In convection, masses of water move in bulk and carry the fast-moving molecules with them.

Convection is a continuous, cyclic process as long as heat is added to the water. As cool water from the top of a pot arrives at the bottom, it begins to be heated by the burner. As hot water gets to the top, its heat is sent off into the air. The water on the top cools and contracts, while the water on the bottom heats and expands. The original situation is repeated continuously, with the less dense fluid on the bottom always rising and the more dense fluid on the top always sinking. This transfer of fluids results in a kind of a rolling motion, which you see when you look at the surface of boiling water. Each of these regions of rising and sinking water is called a **convection cell**.

• **Figure 4-4** Convection. Heat is transferred by the bulk motion of water. As hot water rises, cooler water sinks.

The areas of clear water, which seem to be bubbling up, are the places where warm water is rising. The places where bubbles and scum tend to collect—the places that look rather stagnant—are where the cool water is sinking, leaving behind whatever passengers (such as minerals) it happened to be carrying at the surface. Heat is carried from the burner through the convection of the water, and is eventually transferred to the atmosphere. Convection is thus a very efficient way of transferring heat.

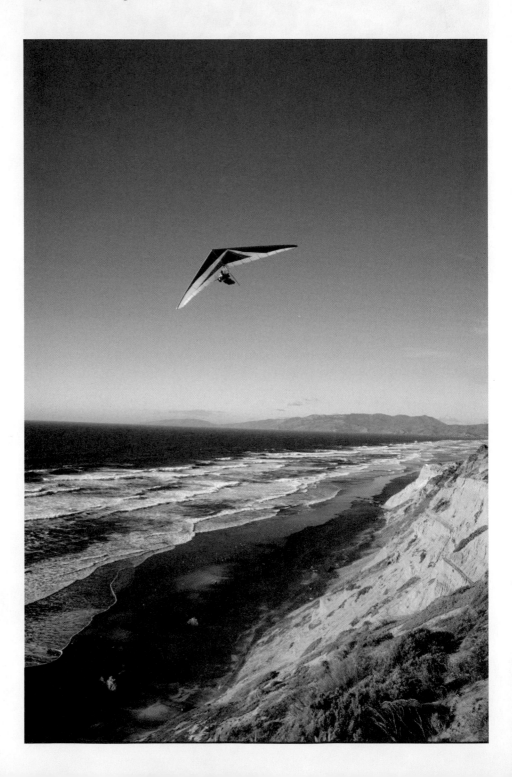

Convection cells in the air keep this hang glider in California aloft.

You experience many examples of the convection process, from the small-scale circulation of cold water in a glass of iced tea, to air rising above a radiator or toaster, to large-scale motions of the earth's atmosphere. You may even have seen convection cells in operation in large urban areas. When you're in the parking lot of a large shopping mall on a hot summer day, you can probably see the air shimmer. What you are seeing is air, heated by the hot asphalt, rising upward. Some place farther away, perhaps out in the countryside, cooler air is falling. The shopping center is called a "heat island" and is the hot part of a convection cell.

You may also have noticed that the temperature in big cities is usually a few degrees warmer than in outlying suburbs. Cities help create their own weather because they are heat islands where convection cells develop. Rainfall is typically higher in cities than in the surrounding atmosphere because cities set up convection cells that draw in cool moist air from surrounding areas.

TECHNOLOGY •

Home Insulation

Today's homebuilders take heat convection and conduction very seriously. An energy-efficient dwelling has to hold onto its heat in the winter and remain cool in the summer. A variety of materials provide effective solutions to this insulation problem.

Fiberglass, the most widely used insulation, is made of loosely intertwined strands of glass. It works by minimizing the opportunities for conduction and convection of heat out of your home. Solid glass is a rather poor heat insulator, but it takes a long time for heat to move along a thin, twisted glass fiber, and even longer for heat to transfer across the occasional contact points between pairs of crossed fibers. A cloth-like mat of fiberglass, furthermore, disrupts airflow and prevents heat transfer by convection. A thick, continuous layer of fiberglass in your walls and ceiling thus acts as an ideal barrier to the flow of heat.

Windows pose a special insulation problem. Old-style single-pane windows conduct heat rapidly, so how do we let light in without letting heat out? One solution is double-pane windows with sealed, airtight spaces between the panes that greatly restrict heat conduction. In addition, builders employ a variety of caulking and foam insulation to seal any possible leaks around windows and doors.

Recent high-tech materials are providing new types of insulation. Like fiberglass, most of these new materials depend on the insulating properties of trapped air for their effectiveness. Older homes are now routinely insulated by injecting liquid foams between exterior and interior walls, for example. When the foam hardens, tiny bubbles of trapped air slow down the transfer of heat. In new construction, sheets of solid Styrofoam, which contains the same kind of trapped air bubbles, are often used instead of fiberglass, and foams are sprayed onto the inner surface of concrete to increase its insulating power.

Even windows can be made into good insulators by using new experimental window glasses in which microscopic air bubbles are trapped. Although this distorts the incoming light a bit—the effect is roughly like looking through a dirty window—a glass pane made from this material has an insulating power equivalent to 6 inches of fiberglass. •

THE SCIENCE OF LIFE •

Animal Insulation: Fur and Feathers

Houses aren't the only place where insulation can be seen in our world. Two kinds of animals—birds and mammals—maintain a constant body temperature despite the temperature of their surroundings, and both have evolved methods

Feathers, fur, and fat help animals by providing insulation to keep body heat in.

to control the flow of heat into and out of their bodies. Part of these strategies involves the use of insulating materials—furs, feathers, and fat—that serve to slow down the heat flow. Because most of the time an animal's body is warmer than the environment, the most common situation is one in which the insulation works to keep heat in.

Whales, walruses, and seals are example of animals that have thick layers of fat to insulate them from the cold arctic waters in which they swim. Fat is a poor conductor of heat and plays much the same role in their bodies as the fiberglass insulation in your attic.

Feathers are another kind of insulation; in fact, most biologists believe that feathers evolved first as a kind of insulation to help birds maintain their body temperature, and only later were adapted for flight. Feathers are made of light, hollow tubes connected to each other by an array of small interlocking spikes. They have some insulating properties themselves, but their main effect comes from the fact that they trap air next to the body, and, as we have pointed out, stationary air is a rather good insulator.

Birds often react to extreme cold by contracting muscles in their skin so that the feathers fluff out. This has the effect of increasing the thickness (and hence the insulating power) of the layer of trapped air. (Incidentally, birds need insulation more than we do because their normal body temperature is 41°C or 106°F.)

Hair (or fur) is actually made up of dead cells similar to those in the outer layer of the skin. Like feathers, hair serves as an insulator in its own right and traps a layer of air near the body. In some animals (for example, polar bears) the insulating power of the hair is increased because each hair contains tiny bubbles of trapped air. The reflection of light from these bubbles makes polar bear fur appear white—the strands of hair are actually translucent.

Hair grows from follicles in the skin, and small muscles allow animals to make their hair stand up to increase its insulating power. Human beings, who evolved in a warm climate, have lost much of their body hair as well as the ability to make most of it stand up. There is a reminder of our mammalian nature, however, in the phenomenon of "goose bumps," which is the attempt by muscles in the skin to make the nonexistent hair stand up. •

3. Radiation.   Everyone has had the experience of coming inside on a cold day and finding a fire in the fireplace or an electric heater glowing red hot. The normal reaction is to walk up to the source of heat, hold out your hands, and feel the warmth moving into your skin.

How did the heat get from the fire to your hands? It couldn't have done so by conduction; it's too hard to carry heat through the air that way. It couldn't have been convection, either, because you don't feel a hot breeze.

What you experience is the third kind of heat transfer—radiation, or the transfer of heat by electromagnetic radiation, which is a form of wave energy that we will discuss in Chapter 6. A fire or an electric heater radiates energy in the form of *infrared radiation*. This radiation travels like light from the source of heat to your hand, where it is absorbed and converted into kinetic energy of molecules. You perceive heat because of the energy that the infrared radiation carries to your hand.

Every object in the universe radiates energy. Under normal circumstances, as an object gives off radiation to its surroundings, it also receives radiation from those surroundings. Thus a kind of equilibrium is set up, and there is no net loss of energy because the object is at the same temperature as its surroundings. If, however, the object is at a higher temperature than its surroundings, it will radiate more energy than it receives. Your body, for example, constantly radiates energy into its cooler surroundings. You will continue to radiate this energy as long as your body processes the food that keeps you alive (see Chapter 20).

Radiation is the only kind of energy that can travel through the emptiness of space. Conduction requires atoms or molecules that can vibrate and collide with each other. Convection requires atoms or molecules of liquid or gas in bulk, so that they can move. But radiation, remarkably, doesn't require any medium to move heat; radiation can even travel through a vacuum. The energy that falls on Earth in the form of sunlight, which is almost all of the energy that sustains life on Earth, travels through 93 million miles (150 million km) of intervening empty space in the form of radiation.

In the real world all three types of heat transfer—conduction, convection, and radiation—occur all the time. Any one can occur by itself or in combination with another, or all three can occur simultaneously. At this moment, heat is being generated in your body. It travels by conduction through tissues, by convection through blood circulation, and by radiation from the surface of your skin. In fact, everywhere in the natural world heat is constantly being transferred by these three mechanisms.

THE SCIENCE OF LIFE •

Temperature Regulation

Animals get the energy they need to run their metabolism by "burning" fuels they take in as food, and the laws of thermodynamics tell us that this process must generate waste heat. For small animals, this heat can be dumped into the environment by simple conduction, but the larger an animal is, the more complex the system for disposing waste heat has to be.

By the same token, animals must be able to absorb heat from their environment to maintain their internal temperature. Some animals (reptiles, for example) absorb energy directly from radiation. This is why you often see snakes and lizards "sunning" themselves on warm days, and why they are so sluggish on cold mornings. Other animals, such as mammals (a group that includes human beings) and birds, have intricate mechanisms for maintaining a constant body temperature.

Human beings have complex ways of raising and lowering the body's temperature in response to changes in the temperature of the environment. If your body temperature starts to rise, blood vessels near the surface of your skin dilate so that the blood can carry more heat to the surface by convection. There, the excess heat can be radiated away. This response is why you often appear flushed after being in the sun for a while. In addition, you start to sweat. The purpose of sweating is to put water on your skin, then use body heat to evaporate that water.

When the temperature falls, the blood vessels near the surface contract, lowering the ability of the blood to carry heat to the surface. In extreme cases, this situation can lead to frostbite, in which cells die because they are denied oxygen and other substances normally carried to them by the blood. Cold also causes the metabolism of the body to increase, generating more heat. Shivering, for example, is a response in which the heat generated by involuntary contractions of the muscles is used to counterbalance the falling temperature.

Incidentally, you may recall that you often start shivering at the onset of a fever. This seemingly paradoxical response occurs because, in response to the disease, the body's internal "thermostat" is adjusted to a higher than normal setting. You shiver and feel cold because, when this happens, normal body temperature is below the new setting of the "thermostat" and more heat is needed to raise the body's temperature. •

 Stop and Think! The ears of an elephant are believed to function partly to keep the animal from overheating. What properties of the ears would make them well-suited to this function? What types of heat transfer would be involved?

The Second Law of Thermodynamics

Throughout the universe the behavior of energy is regular and predictable. According to the first law of thermodynamics, the total amount of energy is constant, though energy may change from one form to another over and over again. Energy in the form of heat can flow from one place to another by conduction, convection, and radiation. But everyday experience tells us that there is more to the behavior of energy—that there is a direction to energy's flow. Hot things tend to cool off, cold things tend to warm up, and an egg, once broken, can never be reassembled. These commonsense ideas are the domain of the **second law of thermodynamics**, which is one of the most fascinating and powerful ideas in science.

The second law of thermodynamics places restrictions on the way heat and other forms of energy can be transferred and used to do work. We will explore three different statements of this law:

1. Heat will not flow spontaneously from a cold to a hot body.
2. You cannot construct an engine that does nothing but convert heat to useful work.
3. Every isolated system becomes more disordered with time.

Although these three statements appear very different, they are actually logically equivalent—given any one statement, you can derive any of the others as a consequence. Given the statement that heat flows from hot to cold objects, for example, a physicist could produce a set of mathematical steps that would show that no engine can convert heat to work with 100% efficiency. In this sense, the three statements of the law all say the same thing.

1. Heat Will Not Flow Spontaneously from a Cold to a Hot Body

The first statement of the second law of thermodynamics describes the behavior of two objects at different temperatures. If you take an ice cream cone outside on a hot summer afternoon, it will melt. In the language of energy, heat will flow from the warm atmosphere to the cold ice cream cone and cause its temperature to rise above the melting point. By the same token, if you take a cup of hot chocolate outside on a cold day, it will cool as heat flows from the cup into the surroundings.

From the point of view of energy alone, there is no reason why things should work this way. Energy would be conserved if heat stayed put, or even if heat flowed from an ice cream cone into the warm atmosphere, making the ice cream cone grow colder. Our everyday experience (and many experiments) convinces us that our universe does not work this way. In our universe heat flows in only one direction, from hot to cold. This everyday observation may seem trivial, but in this statement is hidden all the mystery of those changes that make the future different from the past.

This version of the second law is easy to explain at the molecular level. If two objects collide and one of them is moving faster than the other, chances are that the slower object will be speeded up and the faster object slowed down by the collision. It's unlikely that events will go the other way. Thus, as we saw in the discussion of heat conduction, faster-moving molecules tend to share their energy with slower-moving ones. On the macroscopic scale, this process is seen as heat flowing from warm regions to cold ones by conduction. For the second law to be violated, the molecules in a substance would have to conspire so that collisions would cause slower-moving molecules to slow down even more, giving up their energy to faster molecules so they could go even faster. Experience tells us that this doesn't happen.

The second law does not state that it is impossible for heat to flow from a cold to a hot body. When a refrigerator is operating, heat is removed from the colder interior to the warmer exterior, a fact that you can verify by putting your hand under the refrigerator and feeling the warm air coming off it. The second law merely says that this action cannot take place spontaneously, of its own accord. If you wish to cool something in this way, you must supply energy. In fact, an alternative statement of the second law of thermodynamics could be: A refrigerator won't work unless it's plugged in.

The second law doesn't tell you that you can't make ice cubes, only that you can't make ice cubes without expending energy. Paying the electric bill, of course, is another part of our everyday experience.

2. You Cannot Construct an Engine That Does Nothing but Convert Heat to Useful Work

The second statement of the second law of thermodynamics places a severe restriction on the way we can use energy. At first glance, this statement about heat and work seems to have very little to do with the idea that heat never flows spontaneously from a cold object to a hot object. Yet the two statements are logically equivalent—given the one, the other must follow.

Energy is defined as the ability to do work. This second statement of the second law tells us that whenever energy is transformed from heat to another type—from heat to an electrical current, for example—some of that heat must be dumped into the environment and is unavailable to do work. This energy is neither lost nor destroyed, but it can't be used to make electricity to play your radio or gasoline to drive your car.

Scientists and engineers have defined a special term, efficiency, to quantify the loss of useful energy. **Efficiency** is the amount of work you get from an engine, divided by the amount of energy you put into it.

In Chapter 3 we discovered that heat and other forms of energy are interchangeable, and the total amount of energy is conserved. From the point of view of the first law of thermodynamics, there is no reason why energy in the form of heat could not be converted to electrical energy with 100% efficiency. But the second law of thermodynamics tells us that such a process is not possible. The flow of energy, like time, has a direction. Another way of stating this law is to say that energy always goes from a more useful to a less useful form.

Your car engine provides a familiar example of this everyday rule of nature. When you turn on the ignition, an exploding mixture of gasoline and air creates a high-temperature, high-pressure gas that pushes down on a piston. The piston's motion is converted into rotational motion of a series of machine parts that eventually turn the car's wheels. Some of the energy is lost because of friction, but the second law of thermodynamics would restrict our use of the energy even if friction did not exist, and even if every machine in the world was perfectly designed.

Look at the various stages of an engine's operation (Figure 4-5). There seems to be no obvious reason why energy in the form of heat in the explod-

Gasoline–air mixture enters cylinder through open intake port

Cylinder sealed as both intake valve and exhaust valve are closed

Spark plug fires, igniting the compressed mixture of gasoline and air and begins the power stroke

Combustion products are swept out of the cylinder through the open exhaust port

(a)　　　(b)　　　(c)　　　(d)　　　(e)

• **Figure 4-5** The cycle of an engine's piston. (*a*) The beginning of the intake stroke. (*b*) The middle of the intake stroke as a gasoline-air mixture enters the cylinder. (*c*) The beginning of the compression stroke. (*d*) At the beginning of the power stroke the spark plug fires, igniting the compressed mixture of gasoline and air. (*e*) At the beginning of the exhaust stroke combustion products are swept out. Note that each cycle involves two complete rotations of the crankshaft.

ing air-gas mixture could not be converted with 100% efficiency into energy of motion of the engine's piston, which is translated into the motion of the car. But you can't just think about the downward motion of a piston, what engineers call the *power stroke,* in the operation of your car's engine. If that was all the engine did, then the engine in every car could turn over only once. The problem is that once you have the piston pushed all the way down—once you have extracted useful work from the air-gas mixture—you have to return the piston to the top of the cylinder so that the cycle can be repeated. In other words, in order to reset the engine to its original position so that more useful work can be done, some energy has to be expended to lift the piston back up.

Ignore for a moment the fact that a real engine is more complicated than the one we are discussing. Suppose that all you had to do was to lift the piston up after you had gotten the work from it. The cylinder is full of air, and consequently when you lift the piston up the air will be compressed and heated. In order to return the engine to the precise state it was in before the explosion, the heat from this compressed air has to be taken away. In practice, it is dumped into the atmosphere.

In the language of physics, the exploding hot gas-air mixture is called a *high-temperature reservoir,* and the atmosphere into which the heat of compression is dumped is called a *low-temperature reservoir.* The second law of thermodynamics says that any engine operating between two temperatures must dump some energy in the form of heat into the low-temperature reservoir. In your car's engine, for example, heat produced by moving the piston back up has to be dumped. A similar argument can be made for any conceivable engine you could build.

Some of the chemical potential energy stored in gasoline can be used to run your car, but most of the energy must be dumped into the low-temperature reservoir of the atmosphere. Once that heat has gone into the atmosphere, it can no longer be used to run the engine. Thus this version of the second law tells us that any real engine operating in the world, even an engine in which there is no friction, must waste some of the energy that goes into it.

This version of the second law explains why petroleum reserves and coal deposits play such an important role in the world economy. They are high-grade and nonrenewable sources of energy that can be used to produce high-temperature reservoirs. They are also sources of energy that can be used only once. When fossil fuels are burned to produce a high-temperature reservoir and generate electricity, for example, a large portion of energy must simply be thrown away.

Although the second law sets rather stringent limits on engines that work in cycles, it does not apply to many other uses of energy. No engine is involved if you burn natural gas to heat your home or use solar energy to heat water, for example. Consequently these limits needn't apply. Thus burning fossil fuels or employing solar energy to supply heat directly can be considerably more efficient than using it to generate electricity.

SCIENCE BY THE NUMBERS •

Efficiency

The second law of thermodynamics can be used to calculate the maximum possible efficiency of an engine. Let's say that the high-temperature reservoir is at a temperature T_{hot} and the low-temperature reservoir is at a temperature T_{cold} (temperatures are measured in the Kelvin scale). The maximum theoretical efficiency—the percentage of energy available to do useful work—of any engine in the real world can be calculated as follows:

▶ **In words:** Efficiency is obtained by comparing the temperature difference between the high-temperature and low-temperature reservoirs, with the temperature of the high-temperature reservoir.

▶ **In equation form:**

$$\text{efficiency (percent)} = \frac{(\text{temperature}_{\text{hot}} - \text{temperature}_{\text{cold}})}{\text{temperature}_{\text{hot}}} \times 100$$

▶ **In symbols:**

$$\text{efficiency} = \frac{(T_{\text{hot}} - T_{\text{cold}})}{T_{\text{hot}}} \times 100$$

Any loss of energy due to friction in pulleys or gears or wheels in a real machine will make the actual efficiency less than this theoretical maximum. This maximum is actually a very stringent constraint on real engines.

Consider the efficiency of a normal coal-fired electrical generating plant. The temperature of the high-energy steam (the hot reservoir) is about 500 K, while the temperature of the air into which waste heat must be dumped (the "cold" reservoir) is around room temperature, or 300 K. The maximum possible efficiency of such a plant is given by the second law to be:

$$\begin{aligned}
\text{efficiency (percent)} &= \frac{(T_{\text{hot}} - T_{\text{cold}})}{T_{\text{hot}}} \times 100 \\
&= \frac{(500 - 300)}{500} \times 100 \\
&= 40.0\%
\end{aligned}$$

In other words, more than half of the energy produced in a typical coal-burning power plant must be dumped into the atmosphere as waste heat. This fundamental limit is independent of the engineers' ability to make the plant operate efficiently. In fact, engineers do very well in this regard—most generating plants operate within a few percent of the maximum efficiency allowed by the second law of thermodynamics.

This result has important implications for energy policy. It tells us that there are fundamental limits to the efficiency with which we can convert heat generated by coal or nuclear reactors to electricity. An important question we will have to debate in the future is whether it is better to use our stocks of coal and petroleum to generate electricity, thereby converting most of them to waste heat, or retain them for use in the production of synthetic materials such as plastic (see Chapter 10). •

3. Every Isolated System Becomes More Disordered with Time

The third statement of the second law of thermodynamics, in many ways the most profound, describes the familiar tendency of systems all around us to become increasingly disordered. Your carefully cleaned room gets messy, your brand new car becomes dirty and scratched, and we all age as our bodies gradually wear out. For physicists, however, this statement of the second law has a very precise and special meaning.

• **Figure 4-6** Highly ordered, regular patterns of objects are less likely to occur than disordered, irregular patterns.

To understand this statement of the second law, you need to know what a physicist means by "order" and "disorder" (Figure 4-6). An ordered system is one in which a number of objects, be they atoms or automobiles, are positioned in a completely regular and predictable pattern. Atoms in a perfect crystal or automobiles in a perfect line, for example, form highly ordered systems. A disordered system, on the other hand, contains objects that are randomly situated, without any obvious pattern. Atoms in a gas or automobiles after a multicar pileup on a freeway are examples of disordered systems.

A mathematical definition of order and disorder requires considering the number of different ways a system can be arranged. To get a feel for this idea, consider three orange balls numbered 1, 2, and 3, and three green balls numbered 4, 5 and 6. Ask yourself, how many different ways are there to arrange these six balls in a row (Figure 4-7)? There are six different possibilities for the first ball, then five possibilities for the second, four for the third, and so on. So if you multiply that out:

$$6 \times 5 \times 4 \times 3 \times 2 \times 1 = 720$$

It turns out that there are 720 ways to arrange these six numbered balls in a row—720 different possible configurations.

• **Figure 4-7** There are 720 different ways to arrange six numbered balls. If three balls are orange and three are green, then only a small fraction of these arrangements are ordered by color.

But how many of those arrangements have the ordered state with three orange balls followed by three green balls? There are exactly six different ways to arrange three orange balls ($3 \times 2 \times 1$), and then six different ways to arrange the three green balls. Altogether, that's 6×6, or 36 different configurations with three orange balls followed by three green balls out of 720 total configurations. Only 5% of all possible arrangements (36/720) are ordered in this way. All of the remaining 684 configurations are different. So, by a 19:1 margin, these other arrangements are much more probable, because there are many more ways to achieve a disordered state than an ordered one.

You can repeat this exercise for other numbers of balls (see Problems 4 and 5). For a sequence of 10 balls (5 orange and 5 green), it turns out that there are more than 3.6 million different configurations, but only 120 of those sequences have five orange followed by five green balls. That's only 0.003% of all possible arrangements!

As the number of objects increases from 6, to 10, to trillions of trillions (as we find in even a very small collection of atoms), the fraction of arrangements that is highly ordered becomes infinitesimally small. In other words, highly ordered configurations are improbable because almost every possible configuration is disordered.

This concept of a system's state of disorder is described by the term **entropy**. The second law of thermodynamics can be restated as:

> **The entropy of an isolated system remains constant or increases.**

The word *entropy* was proposed by the German engineer Rudolf Clausius (1822–1888), who played a central role in the formulation of the second law of thermodynamics. In his own words: "I propose to name the [quantity] entropy, . . . from the Greek word for a transformation. I have intentionally formed the word entropy so as to be as similar as possible to the word energy, since both these quantities . . . are so nearly related to each other."

The definition of entropy, as a measure of disorder, may seem a bit fuzzy, but it was placed on a firm quantitative footing in the late nineteenth century by the German physicist, Ludwig Boltzmann (1844–1906). Boltzmann used probability theory to demonstrate that the entropy of any arrangement of atoms is related to the number of possible ways that you can achieve that arrangement. The numerical value of entropy is thus related to the number of ways a system like the numbered balls in a row can be rearranged. If you have a collection of sodium and chlorine atoms, for example, there are many more ways to mix those atoms randomly in a liquid than there are to have them strictly alternating, as they do in a salt crystal. That's why the entropy of sodium and chlorine atoms dissolved in water is much greater than the entropy of those atoms in a salt crystal.

According to the second law of thermodynamics, any system left to itself will evolve toward the most disordered state, the state with the maximum uncertainty in the arrangement of its parts. Without careful chemical and physical controls, atoms and molecules will tend to become more intermixed; without careful driving, collections of automobiles will also tend to become more disordered.

The example we gave at the beginning of the chapter, with the one fast atom in a collection of slow atoms, shows very clearly how such a process works. In the most likely situation, when all of the atoms are in the same low-energy state, the entropy is maximized. A much less probable situation occurs when one of the atoms is in a high-velocity state. Another way of saying this is that systems tend to avoid states of high improbability.

While systems tend to become more disordered, the second law does not require every system to approach a state of lower order. Think about water, a substance of high disorder because water molecules are arranged at random. If you put water into a freezer you get an ice cube, a much more ordered state in which water molecules have formed a regular crystal structure. You have caused a system to evolve to a state of higher order. How can this be reconciled with our statement of the second law?

The answer to this seeming paradox lies in the simple word "isolated." The refrigerator in which you make the ice cubes is not an isolated system, because it has a power cord plugged into the wall, and ultimately connected to the generating plant. The isolated system in this case is the refrigerator plus the generating plant. The second law of thermodynamics says that the system's total entropy must increase. It does not say that the entropy has to increase in all the different parts of the system.

In this example, one part of the system (the ice cube) becomes more ordered, while another part of the system (the generating plant, its burning fuel, and the surrounding air) becomes more disordered. All that the second law requires is that the increase of disorder at the generating plant be greater than the increase of order at the ice cube. As long as this requirement is met, the second law is not violated. In fact, in this particular example, the disorder at the generating plant greatly exceeds any possible order that could take place inside your refrigerator.

SCIENCE IN THE MAKING •

The Heat Death of the Universe

The nineteenth-century discovery of the second law of thermodynamics was a gloomy event. The prevailing philosophy of the time was that life, society, and the universe in general were on a never-ending upward spiral of progress. In this optimistic climate, the discovery that the energy in the universe was being steadily and irrevocably degraded was very hard for nineteenth-century scientists and philosophers to accept. The second law seemed to imply that all the energy in the universe would eventually be degraded into waste heat, and that everything in the universe would eventually come to the same temperature. This outcome was called the "heat death" of the universe, and some scholars saw it as the ultimate end of the laws of thermodynamics.

This notion even affected the literature and music of the time. For example, here is an excerpt from Algernon Swinburne's "The Garden of Proserpine":

> *From too much love of living*
> *From hope and death set free*
> *We thank with weak thanksgiving*
> *Whatever gods there be*
> *That no man lives forever*
> *That dead men rise up never*
> *That even the weariest river*
> *Flows somewhere safe to sea.*

Today, we have a rather different view of how the universe will end, a view that will be discussed in detail in Chapter 15. Suffice to say, however, that

Swinburne and his colleagues may have been premature in their gloom (although one could argue that poets of that period seemed to grab at any excuse for being gloomy). •

Consequences of the Second Law

The Arrow of Time

We live in a world of four dimensions. Three of these—the dimensions of space—have no obvious directionality. You can go east or west, north or south, and up or down in our universe. But time, the fourth dimension, has direction.

Take one of your favorite home movies or just about any videotape and play it in reverse. Chances are that before too long you'll see something silly—something that couldn't possibly happen, that will make you laugh. Spring-board divers fly out of the water and land completely dry on the diving board. From a complete stop golf balls fly off toward the tee. Ocean spray coalesces into smooth waves that recede from shore. Most physical laws, such as Newton's laws of motion or the first law of thermodynamics, say nothing about time. The motions predicted by Newton and the conservation of energy are independent of time. They work just as well if you play a video forward or backward.

The second law of thermodynamics is different. By defining a sequence of events—heat flows from hot to cold; concentrated fuels burn to produce waste heat; the disorder of isolated systems never spontaneously decreases; you get older—we have established a direction to time. We experience the passage of events as dictated by the second law. Scientists cannot answer the deeper philosophical question of why we perceive the arrow of time in only one direction, but through the second law they can describe the effects of that directionality.

Built-in Limitations of the Universe

The second law of thermodynamics has both practical and philosophical consequences. It poses severe limits on the way that human beings can manipulate nature, and on the way that nature itself operates. It tells us that some things cannot happen in our universe.

At the practical level, the second law tells us that if we continue to generate electricity by burning fossil fuels or by nuclear fission, we are using up energy that is locked in those concentrated nonrenewable resources. These limitations are not a question of sloppy engineering or poor design; they're simply built into the laws of nature. If you could design an engine or other device that would extract energy from coal and oil with higher efficiency than the second law limits, then you could also design a refrigerator that would work when it wasn't plugged in.

At the philosophical level, the second law tells us that nature has a built-in hierarchy of more useful and less useful forms of energy. The lowest or least useful state of energy is the low-temperature reservoir into which all energy eventually gets dumped. Once the energy is in that lowest-energy reservoir, it can no longer be used to do work. For the Earth, energy passes through the region that supports life, the biosphere, but is eventually lost as it is radiated into the black void of space.

THE SCIENCE OF LIFE •

Does Evolution Violate the Second Law?

Creationists, who argue that life on Earth was created in a single miraculous event, often use the second law of thermodynamics to argue against theories of life's gradual evolution. These arguments reflect a common misunderstanding of the second law.

Creationists point out that because life is a highly ordered system, in which trillions of atoms and molecules must occur in exactly the right sequence, it could not possibly have arisen spontaneously without violating the second law. What they neglect to consider, however, is that the energy that drives living systems is sunlight, so that the "isolated system" that the second law speaks of is the Earth's biosphere plus the Sun. All that you need to make the evolution of life consistent with the second law is that the order observed in living things must be offset by a greater amount of disorder in the Sun. Once again, as with the earlier example of the ice cube, this requirement is easily met by the Sun and the biosphere taken together. Science cannot yet give a complete, detailed description of how life arose on our planet, but it can show that this development is in no way inconsistent with the universal laws of thermodynamics. •

Thinking More About | Entropy

Aging

Nothing in our experience better illustrates the directionality of nature than human aging. It's all very well to talk about collisions of atoms and the making of ice cubes, but when we see the inevitable effects of aging in ourselves and those around us, we come to realize that the second law of thermodynamics has a very real meaning for each of us. In fact, there is probably no older dream in human history than that somehow, someday, someone will find out how to reverse the aging process.

Modern biologists approach the problem of aging by noting that the process of evolution (see Chapter 25) acts to preserve those traits that help an organism survive until it has offspring to which those traits can be transmitted. After that, no particular reason exists from the point of view of a species' survival for an individual to live any longer. Indeed, throughout most of the history of the human race, few individuals lived past the age of 40, so aging was not perceived to be a significant problem until recently.

Two general types of theory attempt to explain why aging occurs. The first we can call "planned obsolescence." It suggests that the human body is actually designed to self-destruct after a certain time, perhaps to insure that more food and other resources are available for children. The second, which we can call the "accumulated accident" school, holds that the general wear and tear of existence eventually overcomes the

body's ability to make repairs, and the system just runs down. In modern language, scientists talk of accumulated damage to DNA (see Chapter 23), the molecule that contains the cell's operating instructions.

At the moment, the evidence seems to support the second of these alternatives. Scientists are starting to identify specific processes that damage DNA, and to document the precise sort of damage that occurs. As always, the research must be done on animals before it can be applied to humans. One group at the University of California at Irvine, for example, has produced a strain of fruit fly that lives twice as long as normal, and has identified a substance produced in their cells that seems to explain their enhanced lifetime. Another group at McGill University in Montreal has identified specific changes in the DNA of a microscopic worm that can increase the life expectancy from 9 days to 2 months (although in this case, the changes also cause the worm to move and feed more slowly). It is, of course, a long way from fruit flies to human beings, but it's not too much of a stretch to say that sometime we will understand why our bodies age; and from that point, it is probably only a small step to being able to do something about it.

What sort of problems do you think society would have to face if life expectancy increased to 120 years? What kinds of changes in education, work habits, and government might you expect to see? Do you think this sort of research should be pursued?

SUMMARY

All objects in the universe are at a *temperature* above *absolute zero,* and thus they hold some internal energy—the kinetic energy of moving atoms. *Heat* is energy that moves spontaneously from a warmer to a cooler object. *Specific heat capacity* defines how much energy is required to raise 1 gram of a substance by 1°C.

Heat transfer between two objects that are at different temperatures may occur in three ways. *Conduction* involves the transfer of heat through collisions at the scale of atoms and electrons. *Thermal conductivity* is a measure of how easily this energy transfer occurs. *Convection* involves the motion of a mass of fluid in a *convection cell,* in which warmer atoms are physically transported from one place to another. Heat can also be transferred by *radiation*—infrared energy and other forms of light that travel across a room or across the vastness of space until they are absorbed.

The first law of thermodynamics promises that the amount of energy never changes, no matter how it shifts from one form to another, but the *second law of thermodynamics* restricts how you can shift energy. Three different but equivalent statements of the second law underscore these restrictions.

1. Heat will not flow spontaneously from a colder to a hotter body. This first statement places a restriction on the transfer of heat; for example, you have to supply an external source of energy to a refrigerator before it will work.

2. It is impossible to construct a machine that does nothing but convert heat into useful work. This different but equivalent statement of the second law precludes the construction of an engine that operates with 100% *efficiency.* All engines operate on a cycle, and every engine must expend some of its energy returning to its initial state.

3. The *entropy* of an isolated system always increases. The third statement of the second law of thermodynamics introduces the concept of entropy—the tendency of isolated systems to become more disordered with time. This directionality of energy flow in the universe defines our sense of the direction of time.

KEY TERMS ABOUT HEAT AND THE SECOND LAW OF THEROMODYNAMICS

temperature	heat transfer	convection	second law of thermodynamics
absolute zero	conduction	convection cell	efficiency
specific heat capacity	thermal conductivity	radiation	entropy

KEY EQUATION

$$\text{efficiency (percent)} = \frac{(T_{hot} - T_{cold})}{T_{hot}} \times 100$$

REVIEW QUESTIONS

1. What are the three different ways by which heat is transferred? How are these three phenomena occurring while you are reading this book?

2. What is the difference between temperature and heat?

3. Why does it take longer to heat a kilogram of water to a given temperature than to heat a kilogram of copper to the same temperature?

4. Describe three common temperature scales. What fixed points are used to calibrate them?

5. State the second law of thermodynamics in three different ways. In what ways are these three statements equivalent?

6. What is the high-temperature reservoir in your car's engine? What is the low-temperature reservoir?

7. What is entropy? Give an example of a situation in which entropy increases.

8. In what way is aging an example of the second law of thermodynamics?

9. What is meant by the "heat death" of the universe?

DISCUSSION QUESTIONS

1. Why don't all the atoms in the room you're sitting in move to one side, leaving you in a vacuum? [*Hint*: Think about probabilities.]

2. Generally the first thing you see when you approach an electrical generating plant is the big cooling stacks. Given what you know about efficiency, what do you think the function of these stacks might be?

3. Identify three examples of the second law of thermodynamics in action that have occurred since you woke up this morning.

4. Imagine lying on a hot beach on a sunny summer day. In what different ways is heat transferred to your body? In each case what was the original source of the energy?

5. "Cogeneration" is a term used to describe systems in which waste heat from electrical generating plants is used to heat nearby homes and businesses with efficiencies much greater than 50%. Does cogeneration violate the second law? Why or why not?

6. Why is it not possible to construct a perpetual-motion machine—a machine that runs forever without any energy input?

7. Sea water is full of moving molecules that possess kinetic energy. Could we extract this energy from sea water? Why or why not?

8. Describe at least five examples of heat transfer that occur while you drive an automobile on a cold day. In each instance, state whether the heat transfer is by conduction, convection, or radiation. Where does the energy come from? Where does it end up?

9. What are some of the ways that animals (including humans) keep warm in cold climates?

10. Under what circumstances might the universe not end by the "heat death" scenario?

PROBLEMS

1. Calculate the maximum possible efficiency of a power plant that burns natural gas at a temperature of 600 K, with low-temperature surroundings at 300 K. How much more efficient would the plant be if it were built in the Arctic where the low-temperature reservoir is at 250 K? Why don't we build all power plants in the Arctic?

2. The Ocean Thermal Electric Conversion system (OTEC) is a kind of a high-tech electric generator. It takes advantage of the fact that in the tropics, deep ocean water is at a temperature of 4°C, while the surface is at a temperature around 25°C. The idea is to find a material that boils between these temperatures. The material in fluid form is brought up through a large pipe from the depths, and the expansion associated with its boiling is used to drive an electric turbine. The gas is then pumped back to the depths, where it condenses back to a liquid and the whole process repeats.

a. What is the maximum efficiency with which OTEC can produce electricity? [*Hint*: Remember to convert all temperatures to the Kelvin scale.]

b. Why do you suppose engineers are willing to pursue the scheme, given your answer in part a?

c. What is the ultimate source of the energy generated by OTEC?

3. Some experimental nuclear reactors use materials kept at a temperature of 700 K to transfer energy from the hot core to steam, which drives an electricity-generating turbine.

a. What is the maximum possible efficiency of such a reactor in your neighborhood? In the Arctic?

b. What kinds of problems do you suppose might arise from using such a high temperature in the reactor design? [*Hint*: Look up the melting points of common substances. How hot is 700 K in more familiar units?]

4. You have a collection of 8 numbered balls; 1 through 4 are orange and 5 through 8 are green. How many different arrangements of these balls in a line are possible? What percentage of those arrangements have 4 orange balls followed by 4 green balls?

5. Repeat Problem 4 for a collection of 12 numbered balls (6 orange and 6 green). What happens to the probability of an ordered configuration as the total number of balls increases?

INVESTIGATIONS

1. Investigate the daily high and low temperatures for the past week in a nearby city and one of its surrounding towns. On average, what is the difference in temperature? What causes this difference?

2. How are your home's walls, windows, and doors insulated? What could you do to improve your home's insulation? (If your doors or windows are not well sealed, you might save considerably on heating and cooling bills by using inexpensive caulking and weatherstripping.)

3. Get a glass, an aluminum cup, a coffee mug, and a plastic drinking cup. Simply by feeling these objects, can you guess their relative thermal conductivities? Their heat capacities? What experiment might you perform to test your guess?

4. Propose an experiment that you could perform at home to measure the relative heat capacities of different substances such as soap, wood, and glass.

5. Visit a building supply store and look at the doors and windows they sell. What steps have manufacturers taken to reduce heat flow from homes?

6. Play a videotape of a favorite movie backward. How many violations of the second law of thermodynamics can you spot?

7. Boil a pan of water on your stove. Can you identify the convection cells in the pan? How hot does the water have to be before convection starts?

[*Hint*: A small amount of food coloring can reveal the formation of convection cells.]

WWW Resources

See *The Sciences* homepage at: **http://www.wiley.com/college/trefil** for valuable web links.

1. http://jersey.uoregon.edu/vlab
Virtual Laboratory, from the University of Oregon. Click on "Thermodynamics." Worth the wait to download.

2. http://www.temperatureworld.com/
Temperature World, a good site for temperature news, resources, and links.

3. http://www.nhm.org/research/mammals/jj/index.html
Cold Tongues, Warm Hearts: Temperature Regulation in Baleen Whales, from the Los Angeles Museum of Natural History—a little off-beat, but interesting.

5

Electricity and Magnetism

What is lightning?

GREAT IDEA

Electricity and magnetism are two different aspects of one force—the electromagnetic force.

PHYSICS

Electricity can be generated by rotating coils of wire in the vicinity of a magnet.

CHEMISTRY

Chemical energy stored in batteries can be used to supply electrical energy.

ENVIRONMENT

Power lines and electric appliances have increased the intensity of electromagnetic fields in which we live; scientists are studying the possible long-term effects of such exposure. (Ch. 6)

GEOLOGY

Lightning conducts electricity between negative charges in a cloud and positive charges on the ground.

HEALTH & SAFETY

Doctors use magnetic resonance imaging (MRI) machines, which employ strong magnetic fields, to probe the body's internal structures without potentially dangerous radiation.

ASTRONOMY

The Earth and other planets behave like giant magnets.

TECHNOLOGY

Photocopiers rely on static electricity to transfer black particles to white paper.

BIOLOGY

Nerve impulses are electrical signals that travel along conducting fibers (nerves) to and from the brain.

Red = applications of the great idea discussed in this chapter.

Orange = other applications, some of which are explored in other chapters.

Time to clean up from breakfast. You rinse off your dishes and turn on the garbage disposal; the powerful motor whirs into action. As you open the refrigerator to put away the milk and butter; the light comes on and the refrigerator's compressor hums. On the refrigerator door you see the magnet that holds the note reminding you to renew your driver's license. Then your digital watch beeps the hour; 8 A.M.—better get moving.

All of these familiar objects—lights, motors, magnets, beepers, and dozens of other essential technologies—owe their existence to the pervasive, invisible force called electromagnetism.

Nature's Other Forces

According to Newton's laws of motion, nothing happens without a force, but the law of gravity that Newton discussed cannot explain many everyday events. How does a refrigerator magnet cling to metal, defying gravity? How does a compass needle swing around to the north? How can static cling wrinkle your shirt, or lightning shatter an old tree? These phenomena point to the existence of some underlying force that is different from gravity.

Newton may not have known about these forces, but he did give us a method for studying them. First observe natural phenomena and learn how they behave, then organize those observations into a series of natural laws, and finally use those laws to predict future behavior of the physical world. This is the process we have called the scientific method.

In particular, we will find Newton's first law of motion (see Chapter 2) to be very useful in our investigation of nature's other forces. According to this law, whenever we see a change in the state of motion of any material object, we know that a force has acted to produce that change. Thus whenever we see such a change and can rule out the action of known forces such as gravity, we can conclude that the change must have been caused by a hitherto unknown force. We shall use this line of reasoning to show that electrical and magnetic forces exist in the natural world.

Our understanding of the phenomena associated with static electricity and magnetism began in the eighteenth century with a group of scientists in Europe and North America who called themselves "electricians." These researchers were fascinated by the many curious phenomena associated with nature's unseen forces. Their thoughts were not focused on practical applications, nor could they have imagined how their work would transform the world.

Static Electricity

Various phenomena related to electricity have been known since ancient times. The Greeks knew that if you rub a piece of amber with cat's fur and then touch other objects with the amber, those other objects are repelled from each other.

The same thing happens, they found, if you rub a piece of glass with silk: objects touched with the glass are repelled from each other. On the other hand, if you bring objects that have been touched with the amber near objects touched with the glass, they are attracted toward each other. Objects that behave in this way are said to possess **electrical charge**, or to be "charged."

The force that moves objects toward and away from each other in these simple demonstrations was named **electricity** (from *electro,* the Greek word for amber). In these simple experiments, the electrical charge doesn't move once it has been placed on an object, so the force is also called **static electricity**.

The electrical force is clearly different from gravity. Unlike the electrical force, gravity can never be repulsive: when a gravitational force acts between two objects, it always pulls them together. The electrical force, on the other hand, can attract some objects toward each other and push other objects apart. The electrical force, furthermore, is vastly more powerful than gravity. A pocket comb charged with static electricity easily lifts a piece of paper against the gravitational pull of the entire Earth.

Today, we understand that the properties of the electrical force arise from the existence of two kinds of electrical charge (Figure 5-1). We say that objects touched with the same source, be it amber or glass, have the same electrical charge and are repelled from each other. On the other hand, one object touched with amber will have a different electrical charge than a second object touched with glass. This difference is reflected in their behavior—they attract each other.

When the girl touched the electrically charged sphere, her hair became electrically charged as well. Individual hairs repel each other and thus "stand on end."

SCIENCE IN THE MAKING •

Benjamin Franklin and Electrical Charge

The most famous North American "electrician" was Benjamin Franklin (1706–1790), one of the pioneers of electrical science as well as a central figure in the founding of the United States of America. Franklin began his electrical experiments in 1746 with a study of electricity generated by friction. Most scientists of the time thought that electrical effects resulted from the interaction of two different "electrical fluids." Franklin, however, became convinced that all electrical phenomena could be explained by the transfer of a single electrical fluid from one object to another. He realized that objects could have an excess or a deficiency of this fluid, and he applied the names "negative" and "positive" to these two situations.

Following this work, Franklin is said to have demonstrated the electrical nature of lightning in June 1752 with his famous (and extremely dangerous) kite experiment. A mild lightning stroke hit his kite and passed along the wet string to produce sparks and an electrical shock. Not content with acquiring theoretical knowledge, Franklin followed his discovery of the electrical nature of lightning

Metal spheres with opposite charges are attracted to each other.

Metal spheres with the same charge are repelled from each other.

• **Figure 5-1** The two kinds of electrical charges. Opposite charges attract, while like charges repel.

Benjamin Franklin engaged in his famous (and potentially lethal) kite experiment.

with the invention of the lightning rod, a metal rod with one end in the ground and the other end sticking up above the roof of a building. It carries the electrical charge of lightning into the earth, diverting it away from the building. Lightning rods caught on quickly in the wooden cities of North America and Europe, preventing countless deadly fires. They are still widely used. •

The Movement of Electrons

We now understand that there are two kinds of electrical charge, so observations of both attractive and repulsive behavior of charged objects are easy to understand. In modern language, we say that all objects are made up of minute building blocks called atoms, and all atoms are made up of still smaller particles that have electrical charge. As we shall see in Chapter 7, negatively charged electrons move around a heavy, positively charged nucleus near the center of every atom. Electrons and the nucleus have opposite electrical charges, so an attractive force exists between them. This force in atoms plays a role similar to that played by gravity in keeping the solar system together. Most atoms are electrically neutral, because the positive charge of the nucleus cancels the negative charge of the electrons.

Electrons, particularly those in outer orbits, tend to be rather loosely bound to their parent nucleus. These electrons can be removed from the atom and, once removed, can move freely in metals or can react with other elements.

When electrons are pulled out of a material, they no longer cancel the positive charges in the nucleus. The result is a net excess of positive charge in the object, and we say that the object as a whole has acquired a **positive electrical charge**. Similarly, an object acquires a **negative electrical charge** when extra electrons are pushed into it. This happens when you run a comb through your hair on a dry day; electrons are pushed into the comb from your hair, so the comb acquires a negative charge. Simultaneously, your hair loses electrons, so individual strands become positively charged.

Lightning will be attracted to this metal rod and allowed to run harmlessly into the ground. Lightning rods like this were first introduced by Benjamin Franklin.

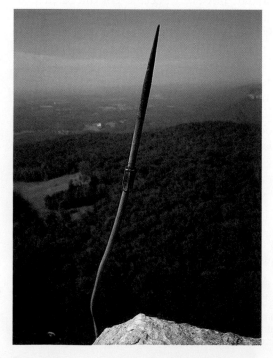

During a thunderstorm, the same phenomenon occurs on a much larger scale, as wind and rain disrupt the normal distribution of electrons in clouds. When a charged cloud passes over a tall tree or tower, the violent electrical discharge called lightning may result from the attraction of the positive charges on the ground and negative charges in the cloud (although in the case of lightning, both the positive and negative charges move).

Although historical investigations of electrical charge tended to concentrate on somewhat artificial experiments, we have come to know that electrically charged particles play important roles in many natural systems. Virtually all of the atoms in the Sun, for example, have lost electrons and thus are positively charged. In all advanced life forms (including human beings), charged atoms are routinely moved into and out of cells to maintain the processes of life. As you read these words, for example, positively charged potassium and sodium atoms are moving across the membranes of cells in your optic nerve to carry signals to your brain.

Coulomb's Law

The phenomenon of electricity remained something of a mild curiosity until the mid-eighteenth century, when scientists began applying the scientific method to investigate it. One of the first tasks was to develop a precise statement about the nature of the electrical force. The French scientist Charles Augustin de Coulomb (1736–1806) was most responsible for this work. During the 1780s, at the same time the United States Constitution was being written by Benjamin Franklin and others, Coulomb devised a series of experiments in which he passed different amounts of electrical charge onto objects and then measured the force between them.

After repeated measurements he discovered that the electrical force was in some ways very similar to the gravitational force that Isaac Newton had discovered a century earlier. Coulomb summarized his discoveries in a simple relationship known as **Coulomb's law**:

▶ **In words:** The force between any two electrically charged objects is proportional to the product of their charges divided by the square of the distance between them.

▶ **In equation form:**

$$\text{force (newtons)} = k \times \frac{\text{1st charge} \times \text{2nd charge}}{\text{distance}^2}$$

▶ **In symbols:**

$$F = k \times \frac{q_1 \times q_2}{d^2}$$

where distance d is measured in meters, charge q is measured in a unit called the coulomb (see the following explanation), and k is the coulomb constant, a number that plays the same role in electricity that the gravitational constant G plays in gravity.

Like G, k is a number (9.00×10^9 newton-meter^2/coulomb^2 in one common system of units) that can be determined experimentally, and which turns out to be the same for all charges and all separations of those charges anywhere in the universe.

Coulomb observed that if two electrically charged objects are moved farther away from each other, the force between them gets smaller, just like gravity. In fact, if the distance between two objects is doubled, the force decreases by a factor of four—the familiar 1/distance^2, or inverse-square relationship, that we saw in the law of universal gravitation in Chapter 2. Coulomb also discovered that the size of the force depends on the product of the charges of the two objects—double the charge on one object and the force doubles; double the charge on both objects and the force increases by a factor of four.

Coulomb's law is a summary of a large number of experiments done on stationary electrical charges, or static electricity. In order to come to a result like this, scientists had to define a unit of electrical charge, called the *coulomb* (abbreviated C) after the scientist who did so much of this important work. A coulomb equals the charge on 6.3×10^{18} electrons, a very large number. When this many electrons have been added to or subtracted from an object, that object will have one coulomb of electrical charge.

SCIENCE BY THE NUMBERS •

Two Forces Compared

In Chapter 7 we will examine compelling evidence that the atoms that compose all the materials in our physical surroundings have a definite internal structure. Tiny negatively charged particles called electrons circle in orbits around a positively charged nucleus. Thus, inside an atom, two forces act between the nucleus and an electron: the force of gravity and the electrical force. We can use this fact to get a sense of the relative strength of the two forces.

The simplest atom is hydrogen, in which a single electron circles a single positively charged particle known as a proton (see Chapter 7). The masses of the electron and proton are 9×10^{-31} kg and 1.7×10^{-27} kg, respectively. The charge on the proton is 1.6×10^{-19} C, and the charge on the electron has the same magnitude but is negative. A typical separation of these two particles in an atom is 10^{-10} m.

Given these numbers, what are the values of the electrical and gravitational attractions between these two particles?

▶ **Gravity.** The force of gravity between the two particles is given by Newton's law of gravity:

$$\text{force of gravity (in newtons)}$$
$$= G \times \frac{\text{mass}_1 \text{ (kg)} \times \text{mass}_2 \text{ (kg)}}{\text{distance}^2 \text{ (m)}}$$
$$= (6.7 \times 10^{-11} \text{ m}^3/\text{kg-s}^2) \times \frac{(1.7 \times 10^{-27} \text{ kg}) \times (9 \times 10^{-31} \text{ kg})}{(10^{-10} \text{ m})^2}$$
$$= 1.0 \times 10^{-47} \text{ N}$$

▶ **Electricity.** The electrical force, on the other hand, is given by Coulomb's law:

$$\text{force of static electricity (in newtons)}$$
$$= k \times \frac{\text{charge}_1 \text{ (C)} \times \text{change}_2 \text{ (C)}}{\text{distance}^2 \text{ (m)}}$$
$$= (9 \times 10^9 \text{ N-m}^2/\text{C}^2) \times \frac{(1.6 \times 10^{-19} \text{ C}) \times (1.6 \times 10^{-19} \text{ C})}{(10^{-10} \text{ m})^2}$$
$$= 2.6 \times 10^{-8} \text{ N}$$

From this simple calculation we can see that, in the atom, the electrical force (2.6×10^{-8} N) is many orders of magnitude (factors of 10) larger than the gravitational force (1.0×10^{-47} N). This is why, in our discussion of the atom in subsequent chapters, we ignore the effects of gravity completely. •

The Electrical Field

Imagine that you have an electrical charge sitting at a point (Figure 5-2). The charged object could be a piece of lint, an electron, or one of your hairs. If you brought a second charged object to a spot near the first, the second object would feel a force. If you then moved the second object to another spot near the lint, it would still feel a force, but the force would, in general, be a different magnitude and point in a different direction than at the first spot. In fact, the second charged object would feel a force at every point in space around the first.

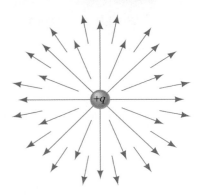

You can make a picture that represents this fact as in Figure 5-2. The arrows at various points around the original charged object represent the forces that would be felt by other charged objects if they were brought to the point in space where the arrow originates. The collection of all the arrows that represent these forces is called the **electrical field** of the original charged object. We can think of every charged object as being surrounded by such a field, as shown in the figure. Notice that the electrical field is defined as the force that would be felt by another charge if that charge were located at a particular point, so that the field is present even if no other charge is in the region.

• **Figure 5-2** An electrical field surrounding a positive charge, $+q$, may be represented by lines of force radiating outward. Any charged object that approaches $+q$ experiences a greater and greater electrical force the closer it gets. Positively charged objects will be repelled, while negatively charged objects will be attracted.

Technically, the electric field at a point is defined to be the force that would be felt by a positive 1-coulomb charge if it were brought to that point. The field is usually drawn so that the direction of the arrow corresponds to the direction of that force, and the length of the arrow corresponds to its magnitude.

Magnetism

Just as electrical phenomena were known to the ancient philosophers, so too were the phenomena we place under the title of magnetism. The first known **magnets** were naturally occurring iron minerals. If you bring one of these minerals (a common one is magnetite or "lodestone") near a piece of iron, the iron will be attracted to it. You have undoubtedly seen experiments in which magnets were placed near nails, which jumped up and hung from them.

The fact that the nails behave in this way tells you that there must be yet another force in nature, a force seemingly different from both electricity and gravity. Electrical attraction doesn't make the nails move, nor is it gravity that causes the nails to jump up. The simple experiment of picking up a nail with a magnet illustrates beyond a shadow of a doubt that there is a **magnetic force** in the universe—a force that can be identified and described by the same methods we used to investigate gravity and electricity.

Whereas electricity remained a curiosity until well into modern times, magnetism was put to practical use very early. The compass, invented in China and used by Europeans to navigate the oceans during the age of exploration, is the first magnetic device on record. A sliver of lodestone, left free to rotate, will align itself in a north–south direction. We use compasses so often these days that it's easy to forget how important it was for early travelers to know directions, particularly travelers who ventured out of sight of land in sailing ships.

In the late sixteenth century the English scientist William Gilbert (1544–1603) conducted the first serious study of magnets. Though revered in his day as a doctor (he was physician to both Queen Elizabeth I and King James I), his most lasting fame came from his discovery that every magnet can be characterized by what he called **poles**. If you take a piece of naturally occurring magnet and let it rotate, one end of the magnet points north and the other end points south. These two ends of

• **Figure 5-3** A compass needle and the Earth. Any magnet will twist because of the forces between its poles and those of the Earth. Note that Earth's north and south magnetic poles don't quite line up with the Earth's axis of rotation.

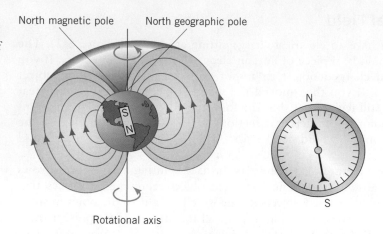

the magnet are called poles. The two poles of a magnet are given the labels **north** and **south**, and the resulting magnet is called a *dipole magnet.*

In the course of his research, Gilbert discovered many important properties of magnets. He learned to magnetize iron and steel rods by stroking them with a lodestone. He discovered that hammered iron becomes magnetic and found that iron's magnetism can be destroyed by heating. He realized that the Earth itself is a giant dipole magnet, a fact that, as we shall see, explains the operation of the compass. Gilbert found that if two magnets are brought near each other so that the north poles are close together, a repulsive force develops between the magnets and they are forced apart. The same thing happens if two south poles are brought together. If, however, the north pole of one magnet is brought near the south pole of another magnet, the resulting force is attractive. In this respect, magnetism seems to mimic the eighteenth-century studies of static electricity. William Gilbert's results can be summarized in two simple statements.

1. **Every magnet has at least two poles.**
2. **Like magnetic poles repel each other, while unlike poles attract.**

Once you know that a magnet has two poles, you can understand how a compass behaves. The Earth itself is a giant dipole magnet, with one pole in Canada and the other pole in Antarctica. If a piece of magnetized iron (for example, a compass needle) is allowed to rotate freely, one of its poles will be attracted to and twist around toward Canada in the north, and the other end will point to Antarctica in the south (see Figure 5-3).

Recall that an electrical force can be represented by an electric field, with arrows that represent the direction and strength of the field at every point (Figure 5-2). So too can the magnetic force be represented in terms of a **magnetic field**. Any dipole magnet displays a curving field pattern characteristic of any magnet with two poles. If many small compass needles are brought near the magnet, as shown in Figure 5-4, the forces exerted by the magnet will twist the needles around parallel to the magnetic field at each point. The compass needles' directions will, in general, be different at different locations around the magnet.

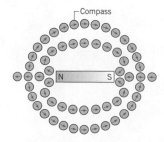

• **Figure 5-4** The curving lines of a magnetic field are revealed by an array of small compass needles that surround a bar magnet.

Just as we can imagine any collection of electrical charges as being surrounded by the imaginary lines of force of an electric field, we can imagine every magnet as being surrounded by an imaginary set of lines of the magnetic field (Figure 5-5). These lines are drawn so that if a compass were brought to a point in space, the

Magnetic field lines

(a)   (b)

• **Figure 5-5** (*a*) A bar magnet and its magnetic dipole field. (*b*) Iron filings placed near a bar magnet align themselves along the field.

A spectacular example of the aurora borealis, caused by particles from the Sun interacting with the Earth's magnetic field.

needle would turn and point along the line. The number of lines in a given area is a measure of the strength of the forces exerted on the compass. You can see one consequence of this effect in the northern lights, or aurora borealis. Charged particles streaming from the Sun can emit light when they interact with a magnetic field. The convergence of magnetic field lines near the Earth's North and South Poles enhances this effect and produces the colorful display.

THE SCIENCE OF LIFE •

Magnetic Navigation

Many living things in addition to humans use the Earth's magnetic field for navigation. This ability was demonstrated by scientists at the Massachusetts Institute of Technology in 1975, when they were studying a single-celled bacterium that lived in the ooze at the bottom of nearby swamps. They found that the bacteria incorporate about 20 microscopic crystals of the mineral magnetite into their bodies. These minute crystals are strung out in a line, in effect forming a microscopic compass needle.

Because the Earth's magnetic field dips into the surface in the Northern Hemisphere and rises up out of it in the Southern, the Massachusetts bacteria

Grains of iron minerals in this bacterium allow it to tell up from down.

• **Figure 5-6** Cut magnets. If you break a dipole magnet in two, you get two smaller dipole magnets, not an isolated north or south pole.

have a built-in "up" and "down" indicator. This internal magnet allows the bacteria to navigate down into the nutrient-rich ooze at the bottom of the pond. Interestingly enough, related bacteria in the Southern Hemisphere follow the field lines in the opposite direction to get to the bottom of their ponds.

Since 1975, similar internal magnets have been discovered in many animals. Some migratory birds, for example, use internal magnets as one of several cues to guide them on flights thousands of miles in length. In the case of the Australian silvereye, evidence suggests that the bird can "see" the magnetic field of the Earth, through a process involving modification of molecules normally involved in color vision. •

Pairs of Poles

The dipole magnetic field shown in Figure 5-5 plays a very important role in nature. All magnets found in nature have both north and south poles—you never find one without the other. Even if you take an ordinary bar magnet and cut it in two, you don't get a north and a south pole in isolation, but rather two small magnets each with a north and a south pole (Figure 5-6). If you took each of those halves and cut them in half, you would continue to get smaller and smaller dipole magnets. In fact, it seems to be a general rule of nature that

> **There are no isolated magnetic poles in nature.**

In the language of physicists, a single isolated north or south magnetic pole is called a *magnetic monopole*. Although physicists have conducted extensive searches for monopoles, no experiment has yet found unequivocal evidence for their existence.

● Batteries and Electric Circuits

Discovery of the surprising connection between electricity and magnetism had to await the invention of two familiar devices—the battery and the electric circuit. Remarkably, these commonplace technologies were inspired by the study of frogs.

THE SCIENCE OF LIFE •
Luigi Galvani and Life's Electrical Force
Scientists of the eighteenth century discovered unexpected links between life and electricity. Of all the phenomena in nature, none fascinated these scientists more than the mysterious "life force," which seemed to allow animals to move and

grow. An old doctrine called *vitalism* held that this force was found only in living organisms, and not found in the rest of nature. Luigi Galvani (1737–1798), an Italian physician and anatomist, added fuel to the debate about the nature of life with a series of classic experiments demonstrating the effects of electricity on living things.

Galvani's most famous investigations employed an electric spark to induce convulsive twitching in amputated frogs' legs—a phenomenon not unlike a person's involuntary reaction to a jolt of electricity. Later he was able to produce a similar effect simply by poking a frog's leg simultaneously with one fork of copper and one of iron. In modern language, we would say that the electrical charge and the presence of the two metals in the salty fluid in the frog's leg led to a flow of electrical charge in the frog's nerves, a process that caused contractions of the muscles (Figure 5-7). Galvani, however, argued that his experiments showed that

• **Figure 5-7** Luigi Galvani showed that the frog's legs would twitch when stimulated by electrical current, a phenomenon that eventually led to the invention of the battery (as well as the novel *Frankenstein*).

The idea behind the legend of Frankenstein may have been suggested by early experiments on animal electricity.

there was a vital force in living systems, something he called "animal electricity," that made them different from inanimate matter. This idea gained some acceptance among the scientific community, but provoked a long debate between Galvani and the Italian physicist Alessandro Volta (1745–1827). Volta argued that Galvani's effects were caused by chemical reactions between the metals and the salty fluids of the frogs' legs. In retrospect, both of these scientists had part of the truth. Muscle contractions are indeed initiated by electrical signals, even if there is no such thing as animal electricity, and electrical charges can be induced to flow by chemical reactions.

The controversy that surrounded Galvani's experiments had many surprising effects. On the practical side, as we discuss in the text, Volta's work on chemical reactions led to the development of the battery, and, indirectly, to our modern understanding of electricity. The notion of animal electricity proved a great boon to medical quacks and con men, and for centuries various kinds of electrical devices were palmed off on the public as cures for almost every known disease. Some of these devices can be seen on sale today, in the form of magnets that, when strapped to the body, are supposed to cure various illnesses.

Finally, in a bizarre epilogue to Galvani's research, other researchers used batteries to study the effects of electrical currents on human cadavers. In one famous public demonstration, a corpse was made to sit up and kick its legs by electrical stimulation. Such unorthodox experiments helped inspire Mary Shelley's famous novel, *Frankenstein*. •

Batteries and Electrical Current

Although we encounter static electricity in our everyday lives, most of our contact with electricity comes from moving charges. In your home, for example, negatively charged electrons move through wires to run all of your electric appliances. A flow of charged particles is called an **electrical current**.

Until the work of Alessandro Volta, scientists could not produce persistent electrical currents in their laboratories, and therefore knew little about them. As a result of his investigations into Galvani's work, Volta developed the first **battery**, a device that converts stored chemical energy in the battery materials into kinetic energy of electrons running through an outside wire.

The first battery was a crude affair, but we now use its descendants to start our cars and run all sorts of portable electrical equipment. Your car battery, a reliable and beautifully engineered device, routinely performs for years before it needs replacing. It is made of alternating plates of two kinds of material, lead and lead oxide, immersed in a bath of dilute sulfuric acid. When the battery is being discharged, the lead plate interacts with the acid, producing lead sulphate (the white crud that collects around the posts of old batteries) and some free electrons. These electrons run through an external wire to the other plates, where they interact with the lead oxide and sulfuric acid to form lead sulphate. The electrons running through the outside wire are what start your car.

When the battery is completely discharged, it consists of plates of lead sulphate immersed in water, a configuration from which no energy can be obtained. Running a current backward through the battery, however, runs all the chemical reactions in reverse and restores the original configuration. We say that the battery has been recharged. Once recharged, the whole cycle can proceed again. In your car, the generator constantly recharges the battery whenever the engine is running, so that it's always ready to use.

Technology •

Batteries and Electric Cars

Modern urban areas are troubled by pollutants introduced into the air by the burning of gasoline in cars and trucks (see Chapter 19). A possible solution to this

Electric cars can run on the stored chemical energy in batteries.

problem is the introduction of battery-powered electric cars. In these cars, chemical energy stored in batteries rather than in gasoline provides the motive power.

Many electric vehicles, such as golf carts, are already in use, but much more powerful batteries are needed for cars on the highway. The most difficult technical problem standing in the way of development of practical electric cars is the fact that batteries actually store rather small amounts of energy for their weight. It would take about 800 pounds of the kind of lead-acid battery that you use to start your car, for example, to supply as much energy as a gallon of gasoline. Because the car has to move the batteries as well as its normal load, this heavy weight leads to problems.

Perhaps the most severe problem is the comparatively short distance an electric car can go before the batteries need to be recharged, a distance called the car's "range." Many of the first-generation purely electric cars have effective ranges of only 40 to 50 miles (65–80 kilometers), though engineers are steadily improving the performance of these cars. Two types of advanced batteries—nickel-cadmium (the type you probably use in your laptop computer) and designs using nickel and other metals—deliver about twice the power of lead-acid batteries.

A new generation of hybrid cars, which incorporate both gasoline engines and electric motors with batteries, represents an effective compromise. These cars can build up electrical energy in their batteries while coasting, braking, or descending a hill. Hybrid cars thus feature the range of conventional automobiles, but boast fuel economies that typically exceed 50 miles per gallon. For example, in 2001 Honda introduced the Insight, the first commercial hybrid car on the American market. The car gets about 70 miles per gallon on the highway.

 Stop and Think! You often hear that electric cars are pollution free. Is this really true? Where does the energy to recharge the car's batteries come from?

Electric Circuits

Most people come into contact with electrical phenomena through electric circuits in their homes and cars. An **electric circuit** is an unbroken path of material that carries electricity—an *electrical conductor* like copper wire. The electric light that you are using to read this book, for example, is part of an electric circuit that begins at a power plant that generates electricity many miles away. That electricity continues through power lines into your town and is distributed on overhead or underground wires until it finally gets to where you live. There, the circuit of which the light is a part is made up of wires that run through the walls of your home. One set of these wires goes first to a circuit breaker (to break the circuit in case of a dangerous overload of too much current), then to a switch, and finally to the lightbulb. When you turn on the switch, you complete an unbroken path that runs all the way from the generating plant to the lightbulb. When electricity flows through the bulb, the electrical current must pass through a very narrow wire called a *filament*, in which electrons are crowded and jostled together to heat up the wire until it glows. When you put the switch in the "off" position, it's like raising a drawbridge: the current is blocked from flowing into this part of the circuit and none reaches the light. The room becomes dark.

Every circuit consists of three parts: a source of energy like a battery, a closed path usually made of metal wire through which the current can flow, and a device such as a motor or a lightbulb that uses the electrical energy (Figure 5-8).

Ohm's Law

One way to think about electric circuits is to draw an analogy between electrons flowing through a wire and water flowing through a pipe. In the case of water, we use two quantities to characterize the flow: the amount of water that passes a point each second, and the pressure behind that water. The numbers we use to describe the flow of electrons in an electric circuit are exactly the same.

The amount of current (the number of electrons) that actually flows in a wire is measured in a unit called the **ampere** or **amp**, named after French physicist Andre-Marie Ampere (1775–1836). One amp corresponds to a flow of one coulomb (the unit of electrical charge) per second past a point in the wire:

$$1 \text{ amp of current} = 1 \text{ coulomb of charge per second}$$

Electrical current, therefore, is analogous to the current of a river or stream. Typical household appliances use anywhere from about 1 amp (100-watt bulb) to 40 amps (an electric range with all burners and the oven blazing away).

We call the pressure produced by the energy source in a circuit the **voltage**, measured in **volts** (abbreviated V) and named after Alessandro Volta, the Italian scientist who invented the chemical battery. You can think of voltage in circuits much the same way you think of water pressure in your plumbing system. More volts in a circuit mean more "oomph" to the current, just as more water pressure makes the water flow faster. Typically, a new flashlight battery produces 1.5 volts, a fully charged car battery produces about 15 volts (even though they are called "12-volt" batteries), and ordinary household circuits operate on either 115 or 230 volts.

Wires through which the current (electrons) flows are analogous to pipes carrying water: the smaller the pipe, the harder it is to push water through it. Similarly, it is harder to push electrons through some wires than others. The quantity that measures how hard it is to push electrons through wires is called **electrical resistance**, and it is measured in a unit called the **ohm**. The higher the resistance (i.e., the lower the efficiency), the more electron energy that is converted into heat. Ordinary copper wire, for example, has a low resistance, which explains why we use it to carry electricity around our homes. Toasters and space heaters, on the other hand, employ high-resistance wires so that they will produce large amounts of heat when current flows through them. In transmission lines, it is important that as much energy as possible gets from one end of the line to the other; thus we use very thick low-resistance (high-efficiency) wires.

You can understand the behavior of lightning in terms of electric circuits. In a thunderstorm, collisions between particles in the clouds produce a buildup of

These lightning strikes over Seattle are examples of electrical currents in nature.

negative charge at the bottom of the cloud and a corresponding buildup of positive charge in objects on the ground underneath the cloud. This buildup creates a voltage between cloud and ground, and the lightning stroke is the electrical current that runs between the two when the voltage is high enough. Lightning, like any other electrical current, will flow along the path of least resistance. Lightning normally strikes tall objects like buildings and trees, because the resistance of the building is lower than the resistance of the air. As we mentioned earlier, the lightning rod, invented by Benjamin Franklin, uses this principle by allowing the lightning to flow through a low-resistance bar of metal instead of the building.

 Stop and Think! In Franklin's time, some people believed that one way to prevent lightning damage was to climb into church steeples and ring the bells. Was this a good idea?

The *load* in any electric circuit is the "business end"—the place where useful work gets done. The filament of a lightbulb, the heating element in your hair dryer, or an electromagnetic coil of wire in an electric motor are typical loads in household circuits. The power used by the load depends both upon how much current flows through it and the size of the voltage. The greater the current or voltage, the more power is used. A simple equation allows us to calculate the amount of electrical power used.

▶ **In words:** The power consumed by an electric appliance is equal to the product of the current and the voltage.
▶ **In equation form:**

$$\text{power (watts)} = \text{current (amps)} \times \text{voltage (volts)}$$

▶ **In symbols:**

$$P = I \times V$$

This equation, known as *Ohm's law*, tells us that both the current and the voltage have to be high for a device to consume high levels of electrical power. Table 5-1 summarizes some key terms about electric circuits.

Table 5-1 Terms Related to Electric Circuits

Term	Definition	Unit	Plumbing Analog
Voltage	Electrical pressure	volt	Water pressure
Resistance	Resistance to electron flow	ohm	Pipe diameter
Current	Flow rate of electrons	amp	Flow rate
Power	Current × voltage	watt	Rate of work done by moving water

EXAMPLE 5-1

Starting Your Car

When you turn on the ignition of your automobile, your 15-volt car battery must turn a 400-amp starter motor. How much power is required to start your car?

Reasoning and Solution: In order to calculate electrical power, we need to multiply current times voltage. We apply the equation for electrical power:

$$\text{power (watts)} = \text{current (amps)} \times \text{voltage (volts)}$$
$$= 400 \text{ amps} \times 15 \text{ volts}$$
$$= 6000 \text{ watts} = 6 \text{ kilowatts}$$

Most early automobiles were started by a hand crank, which might have required 100 watts of power, a reasonable amount for an adult. Modern, high-compression automobile engines require much more starting power than could be generated by one person.

EXAMPLE 5-2

The Power of Sound

In Example 3-2, we talked about a 250-watt compact disc system. Assuming that this system is plugged into a normal household outlet rated at 115 volts, how much current will flow through the stereo at full power?

Reasoning: The current used at full power can be calculated by rearranging the equation that relates power, current, and voltage:

$$\text{power (watts)} = \text{current (amps)} \times \text{voltage (volts)}$$

Solution: We can manipulate this equation to find the current:

$$\text{current} = \frac{\text{power}}{\text{voltage}}$$
$$= \frac{250 \text{ watts}}{115 \text{ volts}}$$
$$= 2.17 \text{ amps}$$

This amount is slightly more current than flows through two 100-watt lightbulbs.

THE SCIENCE OF LIFE •

The Propagation of Nerve Signals

All of your body's movements, from the beating of your heart to the blinking of your eyes, are controlled by nerve impulses. Although nerve signals in the human body are electrical in nature, they bear little resemblance to the movement of electrons through a wire. Nerve cells of the type illustrated in Figure 5-9 form the fundamental element of the nervous system. A nerve cell consists of a central body with a large number of filaments going out from it. These filaments connect one nerve cell to others. The branched filament that carries signals away from the central nerve body and delivers those signals to other cells is called the *axon*.

The membrane surrounding the axon is a complex structure, full of channels through which atoms and molecules can move. When the nerve cell is resting, positively charged objects tend to be outside the membrane, negatively charged

• **Figure 5-9** A nerve cell consists of a central body and a number of filaments. The dendrites receive incoming signals, and the axon conducts outgoing signals away from the cell body. The myelin sheath helps insulate the axon from neighboring electrical interference.

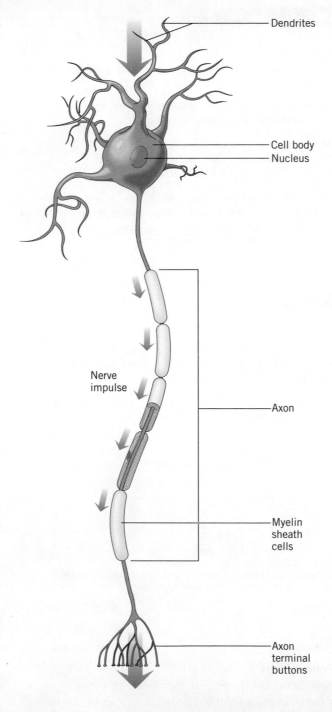

Dendrites

Cell body

Nucleus

Nerve impulse

Axon

Myelin sheath cells

Axon terminal buttons

(a) Series Circuit

(b) Parallel Circuit

ones inside. When an electrical signal triggers the axon, however, the membrane is distorted and, for a short time, positive charges (mainly sodium atoms) pour into the cell. When the inside becomes more positively charged, the membrane changes again and positive charges (this time mainly potassium) move back outside to restore the original charge. This charge disturbance moves down the filament as a nerve signal. When the signal reaches the end of one of the filaments, it is transferred to the next cell by a group of molecules called *neurotransmitters* that are sprayed out from the end of the "upstream" cell, and received by special structures on the "downstream" cell. The reception of neurotransmitters initiates a complex and poorly understood process by which the nerve cell decides whether to send a signal down its axon to other cells. Thus, although the human nervous system is not an ordinary electric circuit, it does operate by electrical signals. •

Two Kinds of Electric Circuits

Common household circuits come in two different types, depending on the arrangement of wires and loads. In *series circuits* (Figure 5-10*a*), two or more loads are linked along a single loop of wire. In *parallel circuits* (Figure 5-10*b*), by contrast, different loads are situated on different wire loops.

The differences between these two types of circuits can become obvious around Christmas time. Many older strands of Christmas lights were linked by a single series circuit. If any one light burned out, the entire strand went dark because the electric circuit was broken (and it could be a frustrating experience trying to find the one bad bulb). Most modern light strands, on the other hand, feature several parallel loops, each with just a few lights. So today, if one light burns out, only a few bulbs along the strand will go dark.

Connections Between Electricity and Magnetism

In our everyday experience, static electricity and magnetism seem to be two unrelated phenomena. Yet scientists in the nineteenth century, probing deeper into the electrical and magnetic forces, discovered remarkable connections between the two—a discovery that transformed every aspect of technology.

Electromagnets, which can be turned on and off, are ideal for moving scrap iron at a junkyard.

Magnetic Effects from Electricity

In the spring of 1820, a strange thing happened during a physics lecture in Denmark. The lecturer, Professor Hans Christian Oersted (1777–1851), was using a battery to demonstrate some properties of electricity. By chance he noticed that whenever he connected the battery (so that an electrical current began to flow through a circuit), a compass needle on a nearby table began to twitch and move. When he disconnected the battery, the needle went back to pointing north. This accidental discovery led the way to one of the most profound insights in the history of science. Oersted had discovered that electricity and magnetism—two forces that seem as different from each other as night and day—are in fact intimately related to each other. They are two sides of the same coin.

In subsequent studies, Oersted and his colleagues established that whenever electrical charge flows through a wire, a magnetic field will appear around that wire. A compass brought near the wire will twist around until it points along the direction of that field. This leads to an important experimental finding in electricity and magnetism.

> **Magnetic fields can be created by motions of electrical charges.**

Like all fundamental discoveries, the discovery of this law of nature has important practical consequences. Perhaps most importantly, it led to the development of the **electromagnet**, a device composed of a coil of wire that produces a magnetic field whenever an electrical charge runs through the wire. Almost every electric appliance in modern technology uses this device.

• **Figure 5-11** A schematic drawing of an electromagnet reveals the principal components—a loop of wire and a source of electrical current. When a current flows through the wire loop, a magnetic field is created around it.

The Electromagnet

Electromagnets work on a simple principle, as illustrated in Figure 5-11. If an electrical current flows in a loop of wire, then a magnetic field will be created around the wire, just as Oersted discovered in 1820. That magnetic field will have the shape sketched in the figure, a shape familiar to you as the dipole magnetic field shown in Figure 5-5.

In other words, we can create the equivalent of a magnetized piece of iron simply by running electrical current around a loop of wire. The stronger the current (i.e., the more electrical charge we push through the wire), the stronger the magnetic field will be. But unlike a bar magnet, an electromagnet can be turned on and off. To differentiate between these two sorts of magnets, we often refer to magnets made from materials such as iron as permanent magnets.

The electromagnet can be used in all sorts of practical ways, including buzzers, switches, and electric motors. In each of these devices a piece of iron is placed near the magnet. When a current flows in the loops of wire, the iron is pulled toward the magnet. In some cases, the electromagnet can be used to complete an electrical circuit by pulling a switch closed. As soon as the current is turned off in the electromagnet, a spring pushes the iron back, and the current in the larger circuit also shuts off.

You use electromagnetic switches in many household appliances. For example, your home is probably heated by a furnace that is linked to a thermostat on the wall in your living room or hallway. You set the thermostat to a specific temperature. If the temperature in the room falls below the desired temperature, the thermostat responds by using an electromagnet to close a switch, allowing a small current to flow. While the current flows, the switch is closed and the furnace operates, heating the rooms in your house. When the temperature reaches the level you have set, the thermostat stops the current that flows to the electromagnet, the switch opens, and the furnace shuts off. In this way, you can adjust the temperature of your house without having to run to the basement every time you need to turn on the furnace.

TECHNOLOGY •

The Electric Motor

Look around your room and try to count the number of electric motors that you use every day. They are in fans, clocks, disk drives, VCRs, CD players, hair dryers, electric razors, and dozens of other familiar objects. Electromagnets are crucial components in every one of those **electric motors**.

The simplest electric motors, as shown in Figure 5-12, employ a pair of permanent magnets and a rotating loop of wire inside the poles of the magnets. The current in the rotating loop adjusts so that when it is oriented as shown in Figure 5-12*a*, the south pole of the electromagnet lies near the north pole of the permanent magnet, and the north pole of the electromagnet lies near the south pole of the permanent magnet. The attractive forces between north and south poles cause the wire loop to spin. As soon as the loop gets to the position shown in Figure 5-12*b*, the current reverses so that the south pole of the electromagnet lies just past the south pole of the permanent magnet, and the north pole of the electromagnet lies just past the north pole of the permanent magnet. The repulsive forces between like magnetic poles act to continue the rotation. By alternating the current in the loop, a continuous rotational force is kept on the wire, and thus the wire keeps turning.

This simple diagram contains all the essential features of an electric motor, but most electric motors are much more complex. Typically, they have three or more different electromagnets and at least three permanent magnets, and the alternation of the current direction is somewhat more complicated than we have

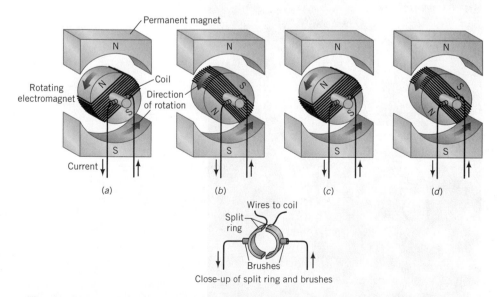

• **Figure 5-12** An electric motor. The simplest motors work by placing an electromagnet that can rotate between two permanent magnets. (*a*) When the current is turned on, the north and south poles of the electromagnet are attracted to the south and north poles of the permanent magnets. (*b*)–(*d*) As the electromagnet rotates, the current direction is switched, causing the electromagnet to continue rotating.

indicated. By artfully juxtaposing electromagnets and permanent magnets, inventors have produced an astonishing variety of electric motors: fixed-speed for your CD player, variable-speed for your food processor, reversible motors for power screwdrivers and drills, and specialized motors for many industrial uses. •

Why Magnetic Monopoles Don't Exist

Earlier we stated that isolated north or south magnetic poles don't exist in nature. Electromagnets provide a basis for understanding where this law comes from. At the atomic scale, an electron in motion around an atom constitutes a "current," analogous to the circle of wire in an electromagnet. As we shall see in Chapter 10, the magnetism in permanent magnets can be traced ultimately to the summation of the behavior of countless electrons, each in motion about an atom's nucleus. This fact explains why ordinary magnets can never be broken down into magnetic monopoles. If you break a magnet down to one last individual atom, you still have a dipole field because of the atomic-scale current loop. If you try to break the atom down further, the dipole field will disappear and there will be no magnetism except that associated with the particles themselves. Thus magnetism in nature is ultimately related to the arrangement of electrical charges, rather than to anything intrinsic to matter itself.

SCIENCE OF LIFE •

Magnetic Resonance

Just as the motion of electrons in atoms creates a current that produces a magnetic field, so too does the rotation of the nucleus of the atom. In fact, the nucleus of most atoms can be pictured as a microscopic dipole magnet. This fact

Magnetic resonance image (MRI) of the human head and shoulders, showing the ability of this technique to produce visualizations of soft tissue.

gives rise to one of the most useful tools in modern medicine, magnetic resonance imaging (MRI).

In this technique, the patient is placed between the poles of a strong magnet. The magnetic field that permeates the patient's tissue causes the tiny nucleus-scale magnets in those tissues to rotate. Because of this effect, the nuclei absorb radio waves whose frequency is timed to coincide with the rotation. By sending radio waves into the patient's tissue and seeing which frequencies are absorbed by rotating nuclei, doctors can determine what sorts of atoms are present at each place in the body, and hence form detailed images of the body's tissues. Unlike X-rays, which have difficulty distinguishing between different kinds of soft tissue, MRI can provide detailed cross-sectional images of any part of the body. •

Electrical Effects from Magnetism

Once Oersted and others demonstrated that magnetic effects arise from electricity, it did not take long for scientists to realize that electrical effects arise from magnetism. British physicist Michael Faraday (1791–1867) is the person who is usually associated with this discovery.

Faraday's key experiment took place on August 29, 1831, when he placed two coils of wire—in effect, two electromagnets—side by side in his laboratory. He used a battery to pass an electrical current through one of the coils of wire, and he watched what happened to the other coil. Astonishingly, even though the second coil of wire was not connected to a battery, a strong electrical current developed. We now know what happened in Faraday's experiment: the loop of wire through which current was running produced a magnetic field in the neighborhood of the second loop. This changing magnetic field, in turn, produced a current in the second loop by means of a process called *electromagnetic induction* (see Figure 5-13).

• **Figure 5-13** Electromagnetic induction. (*a*) When a current flows in the circuit on the left, a current is observed to flow in the circuit on the right, *even though there is no battery or power source in that circuit*. (*b*) Moving a magnet into the region of a coil of wire causes a current to flow in the circuit, even in the absence of a battery or other source of power.

An identical effect was observed when Faraday waved a permanent magnet in the vicinity of his wire coil. He produced an electrical current without a battery.

Michael Faraday's research can be summarized by a simple law:

> **Electrical fields and electrical currents can be produced by changing magnetic fields.**

Figure 5-14 illustrates the **electric generator**, or *dynamo,* a vital tool of modern technology that demonstrates this effect. Place a loop of electrical wire with no batteries or other power source between the north and south poles of a strong horseshoe magnet. As long as the loop of wire stands still, no current flows in the wire, but as soon as we begin to rotate the loop, a current flows in the wire. This current flows in spite of the fact that there is no battery or other power source in the wire.

From the point of view of the electrons in the wire, any rotation changes the orientation of the magnetic field. The electrons sense a changing magnetic field and hence, by Faraday's findings, a current flows in the loop. If we spin the loop continuously, a continuous current flows in it. The current flows in one direction for half of the rotation, then flows in the opposite direction for the other half of the rotation. This vitally important device, the electric generator, followed immediately from Faraday's discovery of electromagnetic induction.

In an electric generator, some source of energy, such as water passing over a dam, steam produced by a nuclear reactor or coal-burning furnace, or wind-driven propeller blades, turns a shaft. In your car, the energy to turn the coils in a magnetic field comes from the gasoline that is burned in the motor. In every

• **Figure 5-14** An electric generator. As long as the loop of wire rotates, there is a changing magnetic field near the loop and a current flows in the wire.

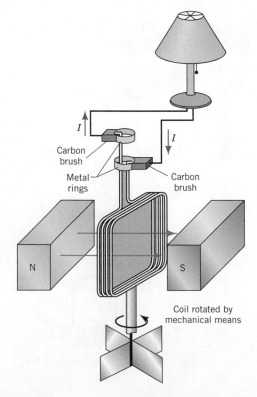

Carbon brush

Metal rings

Carbon brush

N

S

Coil rotated by mechanical means

generator the rotating shaft links to coils of wire that spin in a magnetic field. Because of the rotation, electrical current flows in the wire and that electricity can be tapped off onto external lines. Almost all the electricity used in the United States is generated in this way.

You may have noticed a curious fact about electric motors and generators. In an electric motor, electrical energy is converted into the kinetic energy of the spinning shaft, while in a generator, the kinetic energy of the spinning shaft is converted into electrical energy. Thus motors and generators are, in a sense, exact opposites in the world of electromagnetism.

TECHNOLOGY •

AC versus DC

Because the current in the generating coils flows first one way and then the other, it will do the same thing in the wires in your home. This kind of current, the kind used in household appliances and cars, is called **alternating current**, or **AC**, because the direction keeps alternating. In contrast, chemical reactions in a battery cause electrons to flow in one direction only and produce what is called **direct current**, or **DC**.

On a historical note, a major debate raged in the United States in the late nineteenth century about whether to use AC or DC as the commercial standard. Some very famous people—Thomas Edison, for example—were on the losing side. •

SCIENCE IN THE MAKING •

Michael Faraday

Michael Faraday, one of the most honored scientists of the nineteenth century, did not come easily to his profession. The son of a blacksmith, he received only a rudimentary education as a member of a small Christian sect. Faraday was apprenticed at the age of 14 to a London book merchant, and he became a voracious reader as well as a skilled bookbinder. Chancing upon the *Encyclopedia Britannica,* he was fascinated by scientific articles, and he determined then and there to make science his life.

The young Faraday pursued his scientific career in style. He attended a series of public lectures at the Royal Institution by London's most famous scientist, Sir Humphry Davy, a world leader in physical and chemical research. Then, in a bold and flamboyant move, Faraday transcribed his lecture notes into beautiful script, bound the manuscript in the finest tooled leather, and presented the volume to Davy as his calling card. Michael Faraday soon found himself working as Davy's laboratory assistant.

After a decade of work with Davy, Faraday had developed into a creative scientist in his own right. He discovered many new chemical compounds, including liquid benzene, and enjoyed great success with his lectures for the general London public at the Royal Institution. But his most lasting claim to fame was a series of classic experiments through which he discovered a central idea that helped link electricity and magnetism. •

Maxwell's Equations

Electricity and magnetism are not distinct phenomena at all, but are simply different manifestations of one underlying fundamental entity—the **electromagnetic force**. In the 1860s, Scottish physicist James Clerk Maxwell (1831–1879) realized

Michael Faraday
(1791–1867)

that the four very different statements about electricity and magnetism that we have talked about constitute a single coherent description of electricity and magnetism.

The four mathematical statements that he wrote down have come to be known as *Maxwell's equations,* because he was the first to realize their true import. Maxwell manipulated the mathematics to make important predictions, which we will discuss in detail in the next chapter. For reference, the four fundamental laws of electricity and magnetism known as Maxwell's equations (even though we present them here in statement form) are:

1. Coulomb's law: like charges repel, unlike attract.
2. There are no magnetic monopoles in nature.
3. Magnetic phenomena can be produced by electrical effects.
4. Electrical phenomena can be produced by magnetic effects.

Thinking More About | Electromagnetism

Basic Research

It's hard to imagine modern American society without electricity. We use it for transportation, communication, heat, light, and many other necessities and amenities of life. Yet the men who gave us this marvelous gift were not primarily concerned with developing better lamps or modes of transportation. In terms of the categories we introduced in Chapter 1, they were doing basic research. Galvani and Volta, for example, were drawn to the study of electricity by their research on frog muscles that contracted by jolts of electrical charge. Volta's first battery was built to duplicate the organs found in electric fish. Scientific discoveries, even those that bring enormous practical benefit to humanity, can come from unexpected sources.

What does this tell you about the problem of allocating government research funding? Can you imagine trying to justify funding Galvani's experiments on frogs' legs to a government panel on the grounds that it would lead to something useful? Would a federal research grant designed to produce better lighting systems have produced the battery (and, eventually, the electric light), or would it more likely have led to an improvement in the oil lamp? How much funding do you think should go to offbeat areas (on the chance that they may produce a large payoff) as compared to projects that have a good chance of producing small but immediate improvements in the quality of life?

While you're thinking about these issues, you might want to keep in mind Michael Faraday's response to a question. When asked by a political leader what good his electric motor was, he is supposed to have answered, "What good is it? Why, Mr. Prime Minister, someday you will be able to tax it!"

SUMMARY

The forces of *electricity* and *magnetism* are quite different from the universal gravitational force that Newton described in the seventeenth century. Nevertheless, Newton's laws of motion provided eighteenth- and nineteenth-century scientists with a way to describe and quantify a range of intriguing electromagnetic behavior.

The phenomena of *static electricity,* including lightning and static cling, are caused by *electrical charges,* which arise from the transfer of electrons between objects. An excess of electrons imparts a *negative charge,* while a deficiency causes an object to have a *positive charge.* Objects with like charge experience a repulsive force, while oppositely charged objects attract each other. These observations were quantified in *Coulomb's law,* which states that the magnitude of electrostatic force between any two objects is proportional to the charges of the two objects,

and inversely proportional to the square of the distance between them.

Scientists investigating the very different phenomenon of magnetism observed that every *magnet* has a *north* and *south pole* and that magnets exert forces on each other. No matter how many times a magnet is divided, each of its pieces will have two poles—there are no isolated magnetic poles. Like magnetic poles repel each other, while opposite poles attract. A compass is a needle-shaped magnet that is designed to point at the poles of the Earth's dipole magnetic field. Both *electrical* and *magnetic forces* can be described in terms of force *fields*—imaginary lines that reveal directions of forces that would be experienced in the vicinity of electrically charged or magnetic objects.

Batteries provide a continuous source of electricity. All electrical currents (measured in *amperes* or *amps*) are characterized by an electric "push" or *voltage* (measured in *volts*) and *electrical resistance* (measured in *ohms*). An *electric circuit* is a closed loop of material that carries electricity.

Nineteenth-century scientists discovered that the seemingly unrelated phenomena of electricity and magnetism are actually two aspects of one *electromagnetic force.* Hans Oersted found that an electrical current passing through a coil of wire produces a magnetic field. The *elec-* *tromagnet* and *electric motor* were direct results of his work. Michael Faraday discovered the opposite effect when he induced an electrical current by placing a wire coil near a magnetic field, thus designing the first *electric generator,* which produced an *alternating current (AC).* Batteries, on the other hand, develop a *direct current (DC).*

James Clerk Maxwell realized that the many independent observations about electricity and magnetism constitute a complete description of electromagnetism.

KEY TERMS ABOUT ELECTRICITY AND MAGNETISM

electrical charge
electricity
static electricity
positive charge
negative charge
Coulomb's law
electrical field
magnet

magnetic force
poles (north and south)
magnetic field
electrical current (measured in amperes or amps)
battery
electric circuit
voltage (measured in volts)
electrical resistance (measured in ohms)

electromagnet
electric motor
electric generator
alternating current (AC)
direct current (DC)
electromagnetic force

KEY EQUATIONS ABOUT ELECTRICITY AND MAGNETISM

$$\text{electrostatic force (newtons)} = k \times \frac{\text{1st charge} \times \text{2nd charge (coulombs)}}{\text{distance}^2}$$

1 coulomb = the charge on 6.3×10^{18} electrons

electric power (watts) = current (amps) × voltage (volts)

1 ampere of current = 1 coulomb of charge per second

Universal Electrostatic Constant

$$k = 9.00 \times 10^9 \text{newton-meter}^2/\text{coulomb}^2$$

REVIEW QUESTIONS

1. How might you demonstrate the existence of an electrical force?

2. Compare and contrast the behavior of an electrical force and gravity.

3. How can the movement of negative charges such as the electron produce a material that has a positive charge?

4. How might you demonstrate the existence of a magnetic force?

5. Why do magnets have dipole fields and not monopole fields?

6. Under what circumstances can electrical charges produce a magnetic field?

7. Describe the working and function of an electromagnet.

8. How does an electromagnet differ from a permanent magnet?

9. Explain how electromagnets can be used in the design of an electric motor.

10. Identify two different ways that a single atom might produce a magnetic field.

11. Under what circumstances can a magnetic field produce an electrical current?

12. Explain why electric motors and electric generators are opposites. Under what conditions is each type of device useful?

13. Which of Maxwell's four equations was derived from observations of each the following:

a. bar magnets

b. wire loops carrying electrical current

c. two different materials being rubbed together

d. the effects of a current-carrying wire coil on a nearby coil

14. What properties of electrical currents are measured by amperes, volts, and ohms? Where do you run across each of these terms in your everyday experience?

15. Identify differences between the diagnostic benefits of medical X-rays and medical magnetic resonance imaging.

16. What is the relation between the power an appliance consumes, the voltage across it, and the current through it?

DISCUSSION QUESTIONS

1. Your car uses a 15-volt battery, but do you need all of its energy to start the car? [*Hint*: What happens if you leave the lights on for half an hour; can you still start it?]

2. If you took an electric motor and turned it by hand, what do you think would happen in the coils of wire?

3. What motivated the research of Volta? Of Galvani? Of Faraday?

4. How did Benjamin Franklin discover that lightning had an electrical nature? How did he apply this understanding?

5. Identify five objects in your room that would not be possible without discoveries in electromagnetism.

At least two of these objects should not be, themselves, electric or magnetic devices. [*Hint*: How are everyday objects manufactured?]

6. How does the first law of thermodynamics apply to electric circuits?

7. How does the second law of thermodynamics apply to electric circuits?

8. There is an old saying that lightning never strikes the same place twice. Given what you know about electrical charge, is this statement likely to be true? Why or why not?

9. Why should you never seek the shelter of a tree if you get caught out in a thunderstorm?

PROBLEMS

1. Many bonds between atoms result from the attraction of positively and negatively charged atoms. Based on electrical charges and separations, which of the following atomic bonds is strongest? [*Hint*: You are interested only in the relative strengths, which depend only on the relative charges and distances.]

a. a +1 sodium atom separated by 2.0 distance units from a −1 chlorine atom in table salt

b. a +1 hydrogen atom separated by 1.0 distance unit from a −2 oxygen atom in water

c. a +4 silicon atom separated by 1.5 distance units from a −2 oxygen atom in glass

2. When a car battery runs down, it is recharged by running current through it backward. Typically, you might run 5 amps at 12 volts for an hour. How much energy does it take to recharge a battery?

3. Most household circuits have fuses or circuit breakers that open a switch when the current in the circuit exceeds 15 amps. Would the lights go off when you plug in an air-conditioner (1 kilowatt), a TV (250 watts), and four 100-watt lightbulbs? Why?

4. Energy-efficient appliances are important in today's economy. Suppose that a 20-watt lightbulb gives as much light as a 100-watt bulb, while costing $4.00 more. If electricity costs 8 cents per kilowatt-hour, how long will the bulb have to operate to make up the difference in price?

5. An energy-efficient air-conditioner draws 7 amps in a standard 115-volt circuit. It costs $55 more than a standard air-conditioner that draws 12 amps. If electricity costs 8 cents per kilowatt-hour, how long would you have to run the efficient air-conditioner to recoup the difference in price?

INVESTIGATIONS

1. Make an inventory of all your electric appliances. How many watts does each use?

2. Most household circuits have fuses or circuit breakers that open a switch when the current in the circuit exceeds 15 amps. How many of the appliances in (1) could you run on the same circuit without overloading it?

3. Read a biography of Luigi Galvani, Alessandro Volta, Michael Faraday, or Hans Oersted. Why did they become scientists? How did they support their research? What personal philosophical viewpoints guided their investigations?

4. Imagine that you were stranded on a mineral-rich island. What steps would you take to develop basic electrical devices? What reference books would you want to have with you on the island?

5. Examine carefully your most recent electric bill. How much power did you use? How much did it cost? Is there a discount for electricity used at off-peak hours? Examine your use of electricity and plan a strategy for reducing your electric bill by 10% next month. You can reduce consumption by turning off lights and appliances when not in use, installing lower-wattage bulbs, or using electricity during low-rate times.

6. Find out where your electrical power is generated. Does your local utility buy additional power from some other place? What kind of fuel or energy is used to drive the turbines? Are there pollution controls that restrict the use of certain kinds of fuels at your local power plant? See if you can arrange a tour of the power plant.

7. How many kilowatts of electrical power does a typical commercial power plant generate? How much electricity does the United States use each year? Is this amount going up or down?

8. Take an old appliance with a small electric motor (a razor, coffee grinder, or fan, for example) and dissect the motor. How many permanent magnets are inside? How many electromagnets (i.e., separate coils of wire)?

9. Identify the major electric-circuit components in your automobile. Which require the greatest power?

10. Investigate how electric eels generate electrical shocks. Do any other living things create electrical currents?

11. How does an electroencephalogram (EEG) work? How does it differ from an electrocardiogram (EKG)?

12. Many kinds of living things, from bacteria to vertebrates, incorporate small magnetic particles. Investigate the ways in which living things use magnetism.

13. Read the novel *Frankenstein* (or see the classic 1931 movie with Boris Karloff and Colin Clive, which is admittedly only loosely based on the novel). Discuss the ideas about the nature of life that are implicit in the story. Does it represent a realistic picture of scientific research? Why or why not?

14. How long is the average commute between home and work for people in your area? Might electric cars be of use in the future?

WWW RESOURCES

See *The Sciences* homepage at: **http://www.wiley.com/college/trefil** for valuable web links.

1. http://www.usbr.gov/lc/hooverdam/
Hoover Dam's Home Page—let your Dam Guide take you on a virtual tour of the dam that tamed the Colorado River. Great site!

2. http://www.energyquest.ca.gov/story/chapter02.html
"What Is Electricity?" from the California Dept. of Energy's *The Energy Story*.

3. http://jersey.uoregon.edu/vlab
Virtual Laboratory, from the University of Oregon. Click on "Energy and the Environment." Worth the wait to download.

6

Waves and Electromagnetic Radiation

Why do we see in color?

GREAT IDEA

Whenever an electrically charged object is accelerated, it produces electromagnetic radiation—waves of energy that travel at the speed of light.

PHYSICS

Radio and television signals are transmitted by electromagnetic waves.

CHEMISTRY

X-rays are used to determine the atomic structure of minerals.

ENVIRONMENT

A trace amount of the gas ozone in the Earth's upper atmosphere protects life by absorbing much of the Sun's harmful ultraviolet radiation. (Ch. 19)

GEOLOGY

Doppler radar units track the movement of dangerous storms by measuring the frequency of electromagnetic waves. (Ch. 18)

HEALTH & SAFETY

Laser scalpels have created opportunities for precise microscopic eye surgery. (Ch. 8)

ASTRONOMY

Stars give off all wavelengths of electromagnetic radiation, from radio waves to gamma rays, which can be detected by orbiting telescopes. (Ch. 14)

TECHNOLOGY

Microwave ovens rely on the fact that foods absorb microwave energy, while the walls of the oven reflect it.

BIOLOGY

Through a series of processes, the eye converts electromagnetic radiation into images and colors.

Red = applications of the great idea discussed in this chapter.

Orange = other applications, some of which are explored in other chapters.

The car is packed and ready to go. As you begin the 90-minute drive to the beach, you tune the radio to a favorite FM music station and turn up the volume to feel the beat. From time to time, though, you check an AM station that features traffic and weather reports, just to avoid any problems.

The radio is so familiar and essential, yet still it's somewhat magical. How can music and news travel invisibly through air from the radio station? How can so many different stations broadcast at the same time without interfering with each other? The answers, surprisingly, are intimately tied to the behavior of waves and the electromagnetic force.

The Nature of Waves

Waves are all around us. Waves of water travel across the surface of the ocean and crash against the land. Waves of sound travel through the air when we listen to music. Some parts of the United States suffer from mighty waves of rock and soil called earthquakes. All of these waves must move through matter.

But the most remarkable waves of all can travel through an absolute vacuum at the speed of light. The sunlight that warms you at the beach and provides virtually all of the energy necessary for life on Earth is transmitted through space by just such a wave. The radio waves that carry your favorite music, the microwaves that heat your dinner, and the X-rays your dentist uses to check for cavities are also types of electromagnetic waves—invisible waves that carry energy and travel at light speed. In this chapter, we will look at waves in general, then focus on electromagnetic waves, which play an enormous role in our everyday life.

Waves are fascinating, at once familiar and yet somewhat odd. Scientists study waves by observing their distinctive behavior, particularly their unique ability to transfer energy without transferring mass.

Energy Transfer by Waves

Energy can be transferred in two forms in our everyday world: the particle and the wave. Suppose you have a domino sitting on a table and you want to knock it over, a process that requires transferring energy from you to the domino. One way to proceed would be to take another domino and throw it. From the standpoint of energy, you would say that the muscles in your arms impart kinetic energy to the moving domino, which, in turn, would impart enough of that energy to the standing domino to knock it over (Figure 6-1a). We say that the energy transfers by the motion of a solid piece of matter.

Alternatively, you could line up a row of standing dominoes, knock over the first, which would then knock over the second, which in turn would knock over the third, and so on (Figure 6-1b). Eventually the falling chain of dominoes would hit the last one and you would have achieved the same goal. In the case of

• **Figure 6-1** You can use a domino to knock over other dominoes in two different ways: (*a*) you can throw a domino, or (*b*) you can trigger a wave of dominoes.

the lined-up dominoes, however, no single object traveled from you to the most distant domino. In the language of physics we say that you started a wave of falling dominoes and the wave is what knocked over the final domino. A **wave**, then, is a traveling disturbance; it carries energy from place to place without requiring matter to travel across the intervening distance.

The Properties of Waves

Think about a familiar example of waves. You are standing on the banks of a quiet pond on a crisp autumn afternoon. There's no breeze and the pond in front of you is still and smooth. You pick up a rock and toss it into the middle of the pond. As soon as the rock hits the water a series of ripples moves outward from the point of impact. In cross section, the ripples have the familiar wave shape shown in Figure 6-2. You can use four measurements to characterize the ripples.

1. **Wavelength** is the distance between crests, or the highest points of adjacent waves. On a pond the wavelength might be only a centimeter or two, while ocean waves may be tens or hundreds of meters between crests.
2. **Frequency** is the number of wave crests that go by a given point every second. A wave that sends one crest by every second (completing one cycle) is said to have a frequency of one cycle per second or one **hertz** (abbreviated 1 Hz). Small ripples on a pond might have a frequency of several Hz, while large ocean waves might arrive only once every few seconds.
3. *Velocity* is the speed and direction of the wave crest itself. Water waves typically travel a few meters per second, about the speed of walking or jogging, whereas sound waves in air travel about 340 meters (1100 feet) per second.

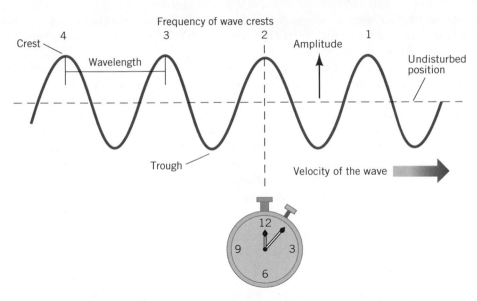

• **Figure 6-2** A cross section of a wave reveals the characteristics of wavelength, velocity, and amplitude. Successive wave crests are numbered 1, 2, 3, and 4. An observer at the position of the clock records the number of crests that pass by in a second. This is the frequency, which is measured in cycles per second, or hertz.

4. *Amplitude* is the height of the wave crest above the undisturbed position, for example, the undisturbed water level.

The Relationship Among Wavelength, Frequency, and Velocity

A simple relationship exists among wavelength, frequency, and velocity. In fact, if we know any two of the three, we can calculate the third from a simple equation.

To understand why this is so, think about waves on water. Suppose you are sitting on a sailboat, watching a series of wave crests passing by. You can count

Waves passing a sailboat reveal how wavelength, velocity, and frequency are related. If you know the distance between wave crests (the wavelength) and the number of crests that pass each second (the frequency), then you can calculate the wave's velocity.

the number of wave crests going by every second (the frequency) and measure the distance between the crests (the wavelength). From these two numbers, the speed of the wave can be calculated.

If, for example, one wave arrives every two seconds and the wave crests are six meters apart, then the waves must be traveling six meters every two seconds—a velocity of three meters per second. You might look out across the water and see a particularly large wave crest that will arrive at the boat after four intervening smaller waves. You would predict that the big wave is 30 meters away (five times the wavelength), and that it will arrive in 10 seconds. That kind of information can be very helpful if you are plotting the best course for an America's Cup yacht race or estimating the path of potentially destructive ocean waves.

This relationship among wavelength, velocity, and frequency can be written in equation form:

▶ **In words:** The velocity of a wave is equal to the length of each wave times the number of waves that pass by each second.

▶ **In equation form:**

$$\text{wave velocity (m/s)} = \text{wavelength (m)} \times \text{frequency (Hz)}$$

▶ **In symbols:**

$$v = \lambda \times \omega$$

where λ and ω are common symbols for wavelength and frequency. This simple equation holds for all kinds of waves.

EXAMPLE 6-1

At the Beach

On a relatively calm day at the beach ocean waves traveling 2 meters per second hit the shore once every 5 seconds. What is the wavelength of these ocean waves?

Reasoning: We can solve for wavelength, given the wave's velocity (2 meters per second) and frequency (1 wave per 5 seconds, or 1/5 Hz):

$$\text{wave velocity (m/s)} = \text{wavelength (m)} \times \text{frequency (Hz)}$$

Solution: We can rearrange the equation to solve for wavelength.

$$\begin{aligned} \text{wavelength (m)} &= \frac{\text{velocity (m/s)}}{\text{frequency (Hz)}} \\ &= \frac{(2 \text{ m/s})}{(\frac{1}{5}\text{ Hz})} \\ &= 10 \text{ m} \end{aligned}$$

The Two Kinds of Waves: Transverse and Longitudinal

Imagine that a chip of bark or a piece of grass is lying on the surface of a pond when you throw a rock into the water. When the ripples go by, the floating object and the water around it move up and down; they do not move to a different spot. At the same time, however, the wave crest moves in a direction parallel to the surface of the water. This means that *the motion of the wave is different from the motion of the medium on which the wave moves.* This kind of wave, where the motion is perpendicular to the direction of the wave, is called a *transverse wave* (Figure 6-3*a*).

Transverse

(*a*)

Longitudinal

(*b*)

You can observe (and participate in) this phenomenon if you ever go to a sporting event in a crowded stadium where fans "do the wave." Each individual simply stands up and sits down, but the visual effect is of a giant sweeping motion around the entire stadium. In this way waves can move great distances, even though individual pieces of the transmitting medium hardly move at all.

Not all waves are transverse waves like those on the surface of water—we used the example of a pond simply because it is so familiar and can be visualized. Sound is a form of wave that moves through the air. When you talk, for example, your vocal cords move air molecules back and forth. The vibrations of these air molecules set the adjacent molecules in motion, which sets the next set of molecules in motion and so forth. A circular wave moves out from your mouth, and that wave looks similar to ripples on a pond. Sound waves differ, however, because in the air the wave crest that is moving out is not a raised portion of a water surface, but a denser region of air molecules. In the language of physics, sound is a *pressure wave* or *longitudinal wave*. As a longitudinal wave of sound moves through the air, gas molecules vibrate forward and back *in the same direction as the wave*. This motion is very different from the *transverse wave* of a ripple in water, where the water molecules move *perpendicular to the direction of the waves* (see Figure 6-3). Note that in both longitudinal and transverse waves, the energy always moves in the direction of the wave.

 Stop and Think! How would you do a transverse wave in a stadium?

SCIENCE BY THE NUMBERS •

The Sound of Music

The speed of sound in air is more or less constant for all kinds of sound. The way we perceive a sound wave, therefore, depends on its other properties: wavelength, frequency, and amplitude. For example, we sense the amplitude of a sound wave as loudness—the greater the amplitude, the louder the sound. Similarly, we hear high-frequency sound waves (sound with short wavelengths) as high pitches, while we perceive low-frequency sound waves (with long wavelengths) as low-pitched sounds.

You can experience one consequence of this contrast when you listen to a symphony orchestra. The highest notes are played by small instruments, such as the piccolo and violins, while the lowest notes are the domain of the massive tuba and double basses. Similarly, the size of each of a pipe organ's thousands of pipes determines which single note it will produce. An organ pipe encloses a column of air in which a sound wave can travel back and forth, down

Different-sized instruments in a New Orleans jazz ensemble play in different ranges. The larger trombone on the left plays low notes, and the smaller trumpet at center plays in a higher range.

• **Figure 6-4** An organ pipe produces a single note. Air in the pipe vibrates and produces a sound wave with a wavelength related to the length of the pipe.

the length of the pipe over and over again. The number of waves completing this circuit every second—the frequency—defines the pitch that you hear (see Figure 6-4).

We can calculate the necessary length of an organ pipe from the desired frequency and the known speed of sound. The note that we hear as "middle A," the pitch to which most orchestras tune, has a frequency of 440 Hz. Sound travels through air at about 340 meters per second. An organ pipe that is open at both ends produces a note with a wavelength twice as long as the pipe. The length of an organ pipe air column that plays middle A, therefore, is given by half the wavelength in the equation:

$$\text{wavelength (m)} = \frac{\text{velocity (m/s)}}{\text{frequency (Hz)}}$$
$$= \frac{(340 \text{ m/s})}{(440 \text{ Hz})}$$
$$= 0.773 \text{ m (about 2 ft)}$$

The length of the organ pipe is half the wavelength:

$$\text{organ pipe length (m)} = \frac{\text{wavelength (m)}}{2}$$
$$= \frac{0.773 \text{ m}}{2}$$
$$= 0.387 \text{ m (about 15 in.)}$$

Notes in the middle range on the pipe organ are thus produced by pipes that are about one-half-meter long. •

 Stop and Think! At which end of a clarinet would you expect to find the keys for playing low notes? Why?

EXAMPLE 6-2

The Limits of Human Hearing

The human ear can hear sounds at frequencies from about 20 to 20,000 Hz. What are the longest and shortest wavelengths you can hear? What are the longest or shortest organ pipes you are likely to see?

Reasoning: Each organ pipe has a fixed length and produces just one note. We have to calculate the wavelength needed for both the lowest and highest frequency.

Solution: The lowest audible note, at 20 Hz, would require a wavelength as follows:

$$\text{wavelength (m)} = \frac{\text{velocity (m/s)}}{\text{frequency (Hz)}}$$
$$= \frac{(340 \text{ m/s})}{(20 \text{ Hz})}$$
$$= 17 \text{ m (about 50 ft)}$$

Similarly, the highest audible note, at 20,000 Hz, is produced by

$$\text{wavelength (m)} = \frac{\text{velocity (m/s)}}{\text{frequency (Hz)}}$$
$$= \frac{(340 \text{ m/s})}{(20,000 \text{ Hz})}$$
$$= 0.017 \text{ m (about two-thirds of an inch)}$$

Organ pipes producing these notes would be about half the wavelengths of approximately 8.5 and 0.009 meters, respectively. Most large pipe organs have pipes ranging from about 8 meters to less than 0.05 meter in length. Next time you have the chance, visit a church or auditorium with a large pipe organ and look at the variety of pipes. Not only are there many different lengths, but there are also many distinctive shapes, each sounding like a different instrument.

THE SCIENCE OF LIFE •

Use of Sound by Animals

Humans use sound to communicate, of course, as do many other animals. But some animals have refined the use of sound to a much higher level. In 1793, Italian physiologist Lazzaro Spallanzani did some experiments with bats that established that they use sound to locate their prey. He took bats that lived in the cathedral tower in Pavia, blinded them, and then turned them loose. Weeks later, those bats had fresh insects in their stomachs, proving that they didn't locate food by sight. Similar experiments with bats that were made deaf, however, showed that they could neither fly nor locate insects.

Today, we understand that bats navigate by emitting high-pitched sound waves and then listening for the reflection of those waves off of other objects. By measuring the time it takes for a pulse of sound waves to go out, be reflected, and come back, the bat can determine the distance to surrounding objects, particularly the flying insects that make up its diet. Typically, a bat can detect the presence of an insect up to 10 meters away. In addition, bats use the Doppler effect (see explanation later in this chapter) to tell whether the target is moving.

In an interesting application of the principle of natural selection (see Chapter 25), some species of moths have developed sophisticated sense organs to hear the sound emitted by bats. Using ears on their thorax or abdomen, these moths can hear the high-pitched sounds emitted by bats, and thus can tell when they are being "seen." When they hear the sound, the moths take immediate evasive action. In a few cases, moths have developed an even more sophisticated defense. When a bat approaches, they emit a series of high-pitched clicks that "jam" the bat's detection system.

At the opposite end of the sound spectrum, when confronted by very low-frequency sounds, we often don't so much hear sound waves as feel them. We sense the vibrations in our bodies. You may have experienced this sensation when hearing very low notes on an organ. Some animals (elephants, for example) routinely use sound in the 20–40 Hz range to communicate with each other over

A bat navigates by emitting high-pitched sounds and listening for their echoes.

• **Figure 6-5** Two waves originating from different points create an interference pattern. Bright regions correspond to constructive interference, while dark regions correspond to destructive interference.

(a)

(b)

• **Figure 6-6** Cross sections of interfering waves illustrate the phenomena of constructive (a) and destructive (b) interference.

long distances. The mating call of the female elephant, for example, is experienced as a vibration by humans, but attracts bull elephants from many miles away.

Whales, dolphins, and porpoises use low-frequency sound echoes as a navigation tool in the ocean, much as bats do in air. Sometimes, however, the sounds that they emit are in the audible range for humans. Perhaps the most famous examples of sophisticated use of sound by animals are the songs of humpback whales, which have appeared on a number of commercial recordings. The functions of these songs are not clear. It appears, however, that all of the whales in a wide area of ocean (the South Atlantic, for example) sing the same song, although some individuals may leave out parts. The songs change every year, but the whales in a given area change their songs together. •

Interference

Waves from different sources may overlap and affect each other in the phenomenon called interference. **Interference** describes what happens when waves from two different sources come together at a single point—each wave interferes with the other, and the observed wave amplitude is the sum of the amplitudes of the interfering waves. Consider the common situation shown in Figure 6-5. Suppose you and a friend each throw rocks into a pond at two separate points as in the figure. The waves from each of these two points travel outward and eventually will meet. What will happen when the two waves come together?

One easy way to think about what happens is to imagine that each part of each wave carries with it a set of instructions for the water surface—"move down two feet," or "move up one foot." When two waves arrive simultaneously at a point, the surface responds to both sets of instructions. If one wave says to move down three feet and the other to move up one foot, the result will be that the water surface will move down two feet. Thus each point on the surface of the water moves a different distance up or down depending on the instructions that are brought to it by the two waves.

One possible situation is shown in Figure 6-6*a*. Two waves, each carrying the command "go up one foot" arrive at a point together. The two waves act together to lift the water surface to the highest possible height it can have. This effect is called *constructive interference* or reinforcement. On the other hand, you could have a situation like the one shown in Figure 6-6*b*, where the two waves arrive at a point such that one is giving an instruction to go up one foot and the other to go down one foot. In this case, the water surface will not move up or down at all. This situation is called *destructive interference* or cancellation. And, of course, waves can interfere anywhere between these two extremes.

The most familiar example of destructive interference does not take place with water waves, but with sound waves. Occasionally an auditorium may be designed in such a way that almost no sound can be heard in certain seats. This unfortunate situation results when two waves—for example, one directly from the stage and one bouncing off the ceiling—arrive at those seats in just such a way as to cause partial or total destructive interference. One of the main goals of acoustical design of auditoriums, a field that relies on complex computer modeling of sound interference patterns, is to avoid such problems.

The Electromagnetic Wave

Have you ever had your teeth X-rayed? Cooked a meal in a microwave oven? Watched television or listened to radio? If so, then you have firsthand experience with the phenomenon of electromagnetic waves.

Physicists characterize waves by a mathematical expression called a "wave equation," which describes the movement of the medium for every wave, whether it's a water wave moving through a liquid, a sound wave in air, or a seismic wave causing an earthquake. Physicists have learned that whenever an equation of this or some closely related form appears, a corresponding wave should be seen in nature.

Soon after Maxwell wrote down the four equations that describe electricity and magnetism (see Chapter 5), he realized that some rather straightforward mathematical manipulation led to yet another equation, one that describes waves. The waves that Maxwell predicted are rather strange sorts of things, and we'll describe their anatomy in more detail later. The important point, however, is that these are waves in which energy is transferred not through matter, but through electrical and magnetic fields. It appears from the equations that whenever an electrical charge is accelerated, for example, one of these waves is emitted. Maxwell called this phenomenon **electromagnetic waves** or **electromagnetic radiation**. An electromagnetic wave is a wave that is made up of electrical and magnetic fields that fluctuate together; once it starts, the wave keeps itself going, even in a vacuum.

Maxwell's equations also predicted exactly how fast the waves could move—the wave velocity depends only on known constants such as the universal electrostatic constant in Coulomb's equation (see Chapter 5). These numbers are known from experiment, and when Maxwell put the numbers into his expression for the velocity of his new waves, he found a very surprising answer. The predicted velocity of the wave turned out to be 300,000 kilometers per second (186,000 miles per second).

If you just had an "aha!" moment, you can imagine how Maxwell felt. The number that he calculated is the speed of light, which means that the waves described by his equation are actually the familiar (but mysterious) waves of light.

This result was astonishing. For centuries scientists had puzzled over the origin and nature of light. Newton and others had discovered natural laws that describe the connections between forces and motion, as well as the behavior of

James Clerk Maxwell
(1831–1879)

• **Figure 6-7** A diagram of an electromagnetic wave shows the relationship of the electrical field, the magnetic field, and the direction that the wave is moving. A and B indicate points of maximum and minimum field strength.

matter and energy. But light remained an enigma. How did radiation from the Sun travel to the Earth? What caused the light produced by a candle?

There is no obvious reason why static cling, refrigerator magnets, or the workings of an electric generator should be connected in any way to the behavior of visible light. Yet Maxwell discovered that **light** and other kinds of radiation are a type of wave that is generated whenever electrical charges are accelerated.

The Anatomy of the Electromagnetic Wave

A typical electromagnetic wave, shown in Figure 6-7, consists of electrical and magnetic fields arranged at right angles to each other and perpendicular to the direction the wave is moving. To understand how the waves work, go back to Maxwell's equations that describe how a changing magnetic field produces an electrical field, and vice versa (Chapter 5). At the point labeled A in Figure 6-7, the electrical and magnetic fields associated with the wave are at maximum strength, but these fields are changing slowly, so both decrease in strength. At point B, the fields are at minimum strength, but they are changing rapidly and so begin to increase. Thus at point A, the magnetic and electrical fields begin to die out, while at point B just the reverse happens. In this way the electromagnetic wave leapfrogs through space, bouncing its energy back and forth between electrical and magnetic fields as it goes.

Once you understand that the electromagnetic wave has this kind of ping-pong arrangement between electricity and magnetism, you can understand one of the most puzzling aspects of it—the fact that it can travel through a vacuum. Every other wave we talked about is easy to visualize because the wave moves through a medium. We know that the motion of the wave is not the same as the motion of the medium, but in every other way the medium is there to give the wave material support. The electromagnetic wave is, in a sense, the logical extension of this idea. It is a wave that has no medium whatsoever, but simply keeps itself going through its own internal mechanisms.

Electromagnetic waves, then, carry radiant energy, or radiation, created when electrical charges accelerate. Once they start moving, however, they no longer depend on the source that emitted them.

SCIENCE IN THE MAKING •

The Ether

When Maxwell first proposed his idea of electromagnetic radiation, he was not prepared to deal with a wave that required no medium whatsoever. Previous scientists who had studied light, including such luminaries as Isaac Newton, assumed that light must travel through a hypothetical substance called "ether" that permeates all space. Ether, they thought, served as the medium for light, and so Maxwell assumed that ether provided the medium for his electromagnetic waves. In Maxwell's picture, the ether was a tenuous transparent substance, perhaps like Jell-O, that filled all of space. An accelerating charge shook the Jell-O at one point, and after that the electromagnetic waves moved outward at the speed of light.

The idea of an ether goes back to the ancient Greeks, and for most of recorded history scholars imagined that the vacuum of space was filled with this imaginary substance. It wasn't until 1887 that two U.S. physicists, Albert A. Michelson (1852–1931) and Edward W. Morley (1838–1923), working at what is now Case Western Reserve University in Cleveland, performed experiments that demonstrated that the ether could not be detected. This failure was interpreted to mean that the ether did not exist.

The concept of the experiments was very simple. Michelson and Morley reasoned that if an ether really existed, then the motion of the Earth around the Sun and the Sun around the center of our galaxy would produce an apparent ether "wind" at the surface of the Earth, much as someone riding in a car on a still day feels a wind. They used very sensitive instruments to search for interference effects in light waves, effects that would result from the deflection of light by the ether wind. When their experiment turned up no such deflection, they concluded that ether does not exist.

In 1907 Albert Michelson became the first U.S. scientist to win a Nobel Prize, an honor that recognized his pioneering experimental studies of light. •

Light

Once Maxwell understood the connection between electromagnetism and light, his equations allowed him to draw several important conclusions. For one thing, because the velocity of the electromagnetic waves depends entirely on the nature of interactions between electrical charges and magnets, it cannot depend on the properties of the wave itself. Thus, all electromagnetic waves, regardless of their wavelength or frequency, have to move at exactly the same velocity. This velocity—the **speed of light**—turns out to be so important in science that we give it a special letter, c. The speed of electromagnetic waves in a vacuum is one of the fundamental constants of nature.

For electromagnetic waves, the relation among velocity, wavelength, and frequency takes on a particularly simple form:

$$\text{wavelength} \times \text{frequency} = c$$
$$= 300{,}000 \text{ km/s} \ (= 186{,}000 \text{ mi/s})$$

In other words, if you know the wavelength of an electromagnetic wave, you can calculate its frequency and vice versa.

The Energy of Electromagnetic Waves

Think about how you might produce an electromagnetic wave with a simple comb. Electromagnetic waves are generated any time a charged object is accelerated, so imagine combing your hair on a dry winter day when the comb picks up a static charge. Each time you move the comb back and forth, an electromagnetic wave traveling 300,000 kilometers per second is sent out from the comb.

If you wave the electrically charged comb up and down slowly, once every second, you create electromagnetic radiation, but you're not putting much

186,000 Miles Per Second Is Not Just A Good Idea It's The Law energy into it. You produce a low-frequency, low-energy wave with a wavelength of about 300,000 kilometers. (Remember, each wave moves outward 300,000 kilometers in a second, which is the separation between wave crests.)

If, on the other hand, you could vibrate the comb vigorously—say at 300,000 times per second—you would produce a higher-energy, high-frequency wave with a 1-kilometer wavelength. By putting more energy into accelerating the electrical charge, you have more energy in the electromagnetic wave.

Visible light, the first example of an electromagnetic wave known to humans, bears out this kind of reasoning. A glowing ember has a dull red color, corresponding to relatively low energy. Hotter, more energetic fires show a progression of more energetic colors, from the yellow of a candle flame to the blue-white flame of a blowtorch. These colors are merely different frequencies, and therefore different energies, of light; high-frequency light corresponds to a blue color, low-frequency to red.

Red light has a wavelength corresponding to the distance across about 7000 atoms or about 700 nanometers (a nanometer is 10^{-9} meter, about 40 billionths of an inch). Red light is the longest wavelength that the eye can see, and is the least energetic of the visible electromagnetic waves. Violet light, on the other hand, has a shorter wavelength corresponding to the distance across about 4000 atoms, or about 400 nanometers, and is the most energetic of the visible electromagnetic waves. All of the other colors have wavelengths and energies between those of red and violet.

EXAMPLE 6-3

Figuring Frequency

The wavelength of yellow light is about 580 nanometers, or 5.8×10^{-7} m. What is the frequency of a yellow light wave?

Reasoning: We know that for all electromagnetic waves,

$$\text{wavelength} \times \text{frequency} = 300,000 \text{ km/s}$$
$$= 3 \times 10^8 \text{ m/s}$$

We want to determine frequency, so rearrange this equation:

$$\text{frequency} = \frac{(3 \times 10^8 \text{ m/s})}{\text{wavelength}}$$

Solution: This means that for yellow light with a wavelength of 5.8×10^{-7} m,

$$\text{frequency} = \frac{(3 \times 10^8 \text{ m/s})}{(5.8 \times 10^{-7} \text{m})}$$
$$= 0.52 \times 10^{15} \text{ Hz}$$
$$= 5.2 \times 10^{14} \text{ Hz}$$

(Remember, a hertz equals one cycle per second.) In order to generate yellow light by vibrating a charged comb you would have to wiggle it more than 500 trillion (520,000,000,000,000) times per second.

The Doppler Effect

Once waves have been generated, their motion is independent of the source. It doesn't matter what kind of charged object accelerates to produce an electromagnetic wave; once produced, all such waves behave exactly the same way. This statement has an important consequence that was discovered in 1842 by Austrian physicist Christian Johann Doppler (1803–1853). This consequence is called the **Doppler effect** in his honor. The Doppler effect describes the way the frequency of a wave appears to change if there is relative motion between the wave source and the observer.

Let's take sound as an example. Figure 6-8a shows the way a sound wave looks when the source is stationary relative to a listener—when you listen to your radio, for example. In this case everything sounds "normal."

(a)

Sound

Emitter motion

Lower frequency   Higher frequency

(b)

Light

Redshift   Blueshift

Emitter motion

(c)

• **Figure 6-8** The Doppler effect occurs whenever a source of waves is moving relative to the observer of the waves. (*a*) Sound waves spread out from a source in all directions; stationary listeners hear the same pitch. (*b*) Sound waves from a moving source seem to increase or decrease in pitch, depending on whether the sound is approaching or receding. (*c*) The Doppler shift for light waves causes a blueshift for approaching sources, and a redshift for receding sources.

If the source of sound—a racing ambulance, for example—is moving relative to the listener, however, a different situation occurs (Figure 6-8b). Periodically, a pulse of high pressure moves away from the source of the sound wave and travels out in a sphere *centered on the spot where the source was located when that particular crest was emitted*. By the time the source is ready to emit other crests, it will have moved, and the second sound-wave sphere emitted will be centered at the new location. As the source continues to move, it will emit sound waves centered farther and farther to the right in the figure, producing a characteristic pattern as shown.

To an observer standing in front of the source, the crests appear to be bunched up. To this observer, the frequency of the wave appears to be higher than it would normally be. In the case of a sound wave, this means that the sound will be higher-pitched than it would have been had the source been stationary. On the other hand, if the observer is standing in back of the source, the distance between crests will be stretched out, and the frequency and pitch of the resulting sound will be lower.

You probably have heard the Doppler effect. Think of standing on a highway while cars go by at high speeds. The engine noise appears to be very high-pitched as a car approaches you and then suddenly drops in pitch as the car passes you. This effect is particularly striking at automobile races where cars are moving at very high velocity.

This sort of change in pitch provided the first example of the Doppler effect to be studied. Scientists hired a band of trumpeters to sit on an open railroad car and blast a single long, loud note as the train whizzed by at a carefully controlled speed. Musicians on the ground determined the pitches they heard as the train approached and as it receded, and they compared those pitches to the actual note the musicians were playing.

The same sort of bunching up and stretching out of crests can happen for any wave, including light. If you are standing in the path of a source of light that is moving toward you, the light you see will be of higher frequency, and hence will look bluer than it would ordinarily. (Remember, blue light has a higher frequency than red light.) We say the light is *blueshifted* (Figure 6-8c).

If, on the other hand, you are standing in back of the moving source, the distance between crests will be stretched out and it will look to you as if the light had a lower frequency. We say that it is *redshifted*. In Chapter 15 we will see that the redshifting of light from distant moving sources is one of the main clues that we have about the structure of the universe.

The Doppler effect also has practical applications much closer to your home. Police radar units send out a pulse of electromagnetic waves that is absorbed by the metal in your car, then reemitted. The waves that come back will be Doppler shifted, and by comparing the frequency of the wave that went out and the wave that comes back, the speed of your car can be deduced. A similar technique is used by meteorologists, who employ Doppler radar to measure wind speed and direction during the approach of potentially damaging storms (see Chapter 18).

Transmission, Absorption, and Scattering

The only way we can know about electromagnetic radiation is to observe its interaction with matter. Our eyes, for example, interact with visible light and send nerve impulses to our brain—impulses that are interpreted as what we "see." When an electromagnetic wave hits matter, one of three processes takes place:

1. *Transmission*. The wave will often pass right through matter, as light passes through your window. This process is called **transmission**. Transparent

materials do not affect the wave other than slowing it down a bit while it is in transit, or perhaps changing its direction slightly as in eyeglasses, a process called **refraction** (Figure 6-9).

2. *Absorption*. Other matter may soak up the wave and its energy, like an asphalt driveway on a summer day—the process of **absorption**. The energy of absorbed electromagnetic radiation is converted into some other form of energy, usually heat. Black and dark colors, for example, absorb visible

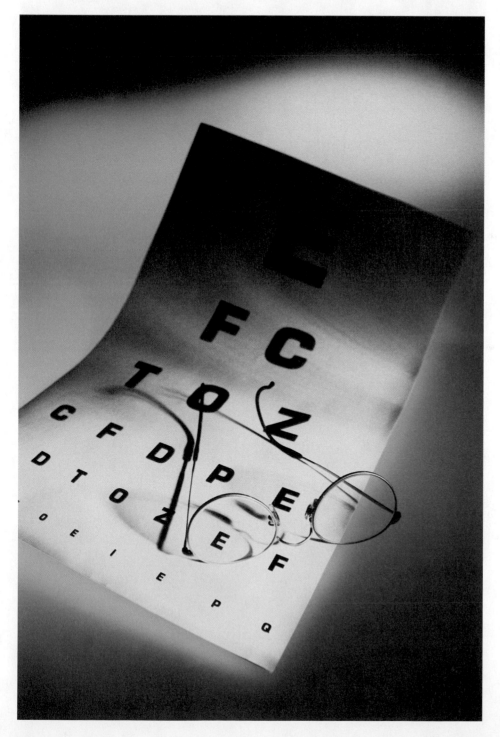

• **Figure 6-9** The lenses in eyeglasses use the phenomenon of refraction to focus light.

The asphalt on this highway absorbs sunlight and heats up on warm days.

light: you've probably noticed how hot black pavement can become on a sunny day.

3. *Scattering.* Alternatively, electromagnetic waves may be absorbed and rapidly reemitted in the process of **diffuse scattering** (Figure 6-10). Most white materials, such as a wall or piece of paper, scatter light in all directions. White objects such as clouds and snow, which scatter light from the Sun back into space, play a major role in controlling the Earth's climate (see Chapter 18). Mirrors, on the other hand, scatter light at the same angle as the original wave, a process called **reflection** (Figure 6-11).

• **Figure 6-10** Clouds appear white because of diffuse scattering of sunlight.

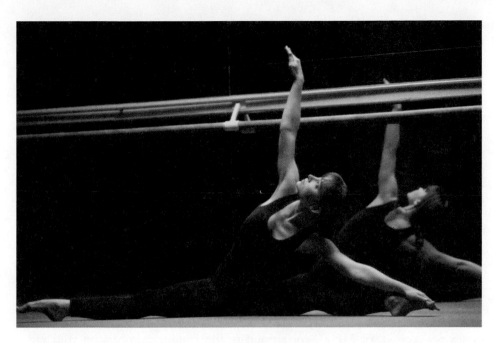

• **Figure 6-11** Mirrors scatter light through the process of reflection.

All electromagnetic waves are detectable in some way. For each of them to be useful, researchers must find appropriate materials to transmit, absorb, and scatter the waves. For each wavelength there must be instruments that produce the waves and others that detect their presence. While only a very narrow range of electromagnetic waves can be detected by the human eye, scientists have devised an extraordinary range of transmitters and detectors to produce and measure electromagnetic radiation that we can't see.

The Electromagnetic Spectrum

A profound puzzle accompanied Maxwell's original discovery that light is an electromagnetic wave. Waves can be of almost any length. Water waves on the ocean, for example, range from tiny ripples to globe-spanning tides. Yet visible light spans an extremely narrow range of wavelengths, only about 390 to 710 nanometers. According to the equations that Maxwell derived, electromagnetic waves could exist at any wavelength (and, consequently, any frequency) whatsoever. The only constraint is that the wavelength times the frequency must be equal to the speed of light. Yet when Maxwell looked into the universe, he saw visible light as the only example of electromagnetic waves. It was as if a splendid symphony, ranging from the deep bass of the tuba to the sharp shrill of the piccolo, was playing, but you could hear only a couple of notes.

In such a situation it would be natural to wonder what had happened to the rest of the waves. Scientists looked at Maxwell's equations, looked at nature, and realized that something was missing. The equations predicted that there ought to be more kinds of electromagnetic waves than light; waves that no one had seen up to that time; waves performing the waltz between electricity and magnetism, but with frequencies and wavelengths different from those of visible light. These as-yet unseen waves would have exactly the same structure as the one shown in Figure 6-7, but they could have either longer or shorter wavelengths than visible light depending on the acceleration of the electrical charge that created them. These waves would move at the speed of light, and would be exactly the same as visible light except for the differences in the wavelength and frequency.

Between 1885 and 1889, German physicist Heinrich Rudolf Hertz (1857–1894), after whom the unit of frequency is named, performed the first experiments that confirmed these predictions. He discovered the waves that we now know as radio. Since that time, all manner of electromagnetic waves have been discovered, from those with wavelengths longer than the radius of the Earth to those with wavelengths shorter than the size of the nucleus of the atom. They include radio waves, microwaves, infrared, visible light, ultraviolet, X-rays, and gamma rays. This entire symphony of waves is called the **electromagnetic spectrum** (see Figure 6-12). Remember that every one of these waves, no matter what its wavelength or frequency, is the result of an accelerating electrical charge.

Radio Waves

The **radio wave** part of the electromagnetic spectrum ranges from the longest waves, those whose wavelength is longer than the size of the Earth, to waves a few meters long. The corresponding frequencies, from roughly a kilohertz (a thousand cycles per second, or kHz) to several hundred megahertz (a million cycles per second, or MHz), correspond to the familiar numbers on your radio dial. There are various subdivisions of radio waves, but the most important fact about them is that, like light, they can penetrate long distances through the atmosphere. This makes radio waves very useful in communication systems.

Have you ever been driving at night and picked up a radio signal from a station a thousand miles away? If so, you have had firsthand experience of the

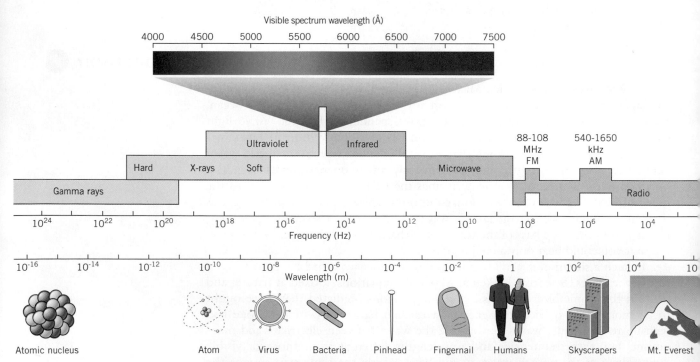

• **Figure 6-12** The electromagnetic spectrum includes all kinds of waves that travel at the speed of light, including radio, microwave, infrared, visible light, ultraviolet, X-rays, and gamma rays. Note that sound waves, water waves, seismic waves, and other kinds of waves that require matter in order to move travel much slower than light speed.

ability of radio waves to travel long distances through the atmosphere. In Chapter 14, we will see how important this fact is for astronomy, where scientists speak of the "radio window" in the atmosphere, which allows Earth-based telescopes to monitor radio waves emitted by objects in the sky.

A typical radio wave used for communication can be produced by pushing electrons back and forth rapidly in a tall metal antenna. This acceleration of electrons produces outgoing radio waves, just as throwing a rock in a pond produces outgoing ripples. When these waves encounter another piece of metal (for example, the antenna in your radio or TV set) the electrical fields in the waves accelerate electrons in that metal, so that its electrons move back and forth. This electron motion constitutes an electrical current that electronics in your receiver turn into a sound or a picture.

Most construction materials are at least partially transparent to radio waves. Thus you can listen to the radio even in the basement of most buildings. In long tunnels or deep valleys, however, absorption of radio waves by many feet of rock and soil may limit reception.

In the United States, the Federal Communications Commission (FCC) assigns frequencies in the electromagnetic spectrum for various uses. Each commercial radio station is assigned a frequency (which they use in association with their call letters), as is each television station. All manner of private communication—ship-to-shore radio, civilian band (CB) radio, emergency police and fire channels, and so on—need their share of the spectrum as well. In fact, the right to use a part of the electromagnetic spectrum for communications is very highly prized because only a limited number of frequency slices or "bands" exist, and many more people want to use those frequencies than can do so.

TECHNOLOGY •

AM and FM Radio Transmission

Radio waves carry signals in two ways: AM and FM. Broadcasters can send out their programs at only one narrow range of frequencies, a situation very different from music or speech, which use a wide range of frequencies. Thus radio stations cannot simply transform a range of sound-wave frequencies into a similar range of radio-wave frequencies. Instead, the information to be transmitted must be impressed in some way on the narrow frequency range of your station's radio waves.

This problem is similar to one you might experience if you had to send a message across a lake with a flashlight at night. You could adopt two strategies. You could send a coded message by turning the flashlight on and off, thus varying the brightness (the amplitude) of the light. Alternatively, you could change the color (the frequency) of the light by passing blue or red filters in front of the beam.

Radio stations also adopt these two strategies (see Figure 6-13). All stations begin with a carrier wave of fixed frequency. AM radio stations typically broadcast at frequencies between about 530 and 1600 kHz (thousands of hertz), whereas the carrier frequencies of FM radio stations range from about 88 to 110 MHz (millions of hertz).

The process called *amplitude modulation*, or *AM*, depends on varying the strength (or amplitude) of the radio's carrier wave according to the sound signal to be transmitted (Figure 6-13*a*). Thus the shape of the sound wave is impressed on the radio's carrier wave signal. When this signal is taken into your radio, the electronics are designed so that the original sound signal is recovered and used to run the speakers. The original sound signal is what you hear when you turn on your radio. Because AM frequencies easily scatter off the layers of the atmosphere, they can be heard over great distances.

• **Figure 6-13** AM (amplitude modulation) and FM (frequency modulation) transmission differ in the way that a sound wave (A) is superimposed on a carrier wave of constant amplitude and frequency (B). The carrier wave can be varied, or modulated, to carry information (C) by altering its amplitude or its frequency.

(a) Amplitude modulation

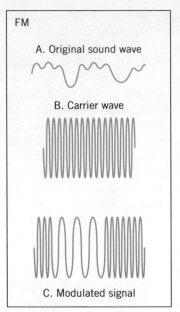

(b) Frequency modulation

Alternatively, you can slightly vary the frequency of the radio's wave according to the signal you want to transmit, a process called *frequency modulation,* or *FM,* as shown in Figure 6-13*b.* A radio that receives this particular signal will unscramble the changes in frequency and convert them into electrical signals that run the speakers so that you can hear the original signal. TV broadcasts, which use carrier frequencies about a thousand times higher than FM radio, typically send the picture on an AM signal, and the sound on an FM signal at a slightly different frequency. •

Microwaves

Microwaves include electromagnetic waves whose wavelengths range from about 1 meter (a few feet) to 1 millimeter (a thousandth of a meter, or about 0.04 inch). The longer wavelengths of microwaves travel easily through the atmosphere, like their cousins in the radio part of the spectrum, though most microwaves are absorbed by rock and building materials. Therefore, microwaves are used extensively for line-of-sight communications. Most satellites broadcast signals to the Earth in microwave channels, and these waves also commonly carry long-distance telephone calls and TV broadcasts. The satellite antennas that you see on private homes and businesses are designed primarily to receive microwave transmissions, as are the large cone-shaped receivers attached to the microwave relay towers found on many hills or tall buildings.

The distinctive transmission and absorption properties of microwaves make them ideal for use in aircraft radar. Solid objects, especially those made of metal, reflect most of the microwaves that hit them. By sending out timed pulses of microwaves and listening for the echo, you can judge the direction, distance (from the time it takes the wave to travel out and back), and speed (from the Doppler effect) of a flying object. Modern military radar is so sensitive that it can detect a single fly at a distance of a mile. To counteract this sensitivity, aircraft designers have developed planes with "stealth" technology—combinations of

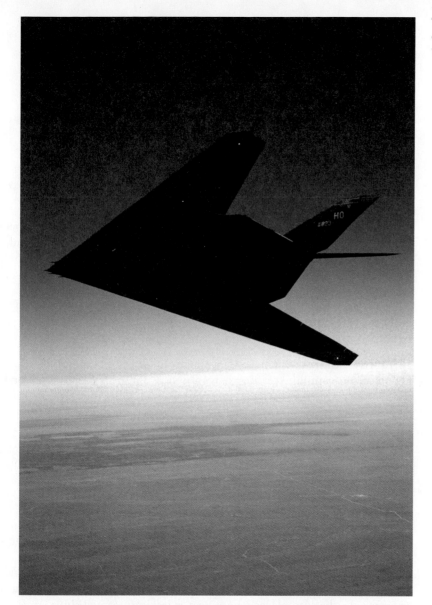

The Stealth fighter has been engineered to avoid detection by radar.

microwave-absorbing materials, angled shapes that reduce the apparent cross-section of the plane, and electronic jamming to avoid detection.

TECHNOLOGY •

Microwave Ovens

The same kind of waves used for phone calls, television broadcasts, and radar can be used to cook your dinner in an ordinary microwave oven. In this type of oven (Figure 6-14) a special electronic device accelerates electrons rapidly and produces the microwave radiation, which carries energy. These microwaves are guided into the main cavity of the oven, which is composed of material that scatters microwaves. Thus the wave energy remains inside the box until it is absorbed by something.

It turns out that microwaves are absorbed quickly by water molecules. This means that the energy used to create microwaves is carried by those waves to food inside the oven, where it is absorbed by water and converted into heat. This

• **Figure 6-14** Every microwave oven contains a device that generates microwaves by accelerating electrons, and walls that scatter the microwaves until they are absorbed, usually by water molecules that get hot from the absorbed energy.

absorption of microwave energy results in a very rapid rise in temperature, and rapid cooking. Paper and glass, which don't contain water molecules, are not heated by microwaves. Despite the different applications, from the point of view of the electromagnetic spectrum there is no fundamental difference between the microwaves used for cooking and those used for communication. •

Infrared Radiation

Infrared radiation includes wavelengths of electromagnetic radiation that extend from a millimeter down to about a micron (10^{-6} meter, or less than a ten-thousandth of an inch). Our skin, which absorbs infrared radiation, provides a crude kind of detector. You feel infrared radiation when you put your hands out to a warm fire or the cooking element of an electric stove. Infrared waves are what we feel as heat radiation.

Warm objects emit infrared radiation, and this fact has been used extensively in both civilian and military technology. Infrared detectors are used to guide air-to-air missiles to the exhaust of jet engines in enemy aircraft, and infrared detectors are often used to "see" human beings and warm engines at night. Similarly, many insects (such as mosquitoes and moths) and other nocturnal animals (including opossums and some snakes) have developed sensitivity to infrared radiation; thus they can "see" in the dark.

Infrared detection is also used to find heat leaks in homes and buildings (Figure 6-15). If you take a picture of a house at night using film that is sensitive to infrared radiation, places where heat is leaking out will show up as bright spots

• **Figure 6-15** A photograph using infrared film reveals heat energy escaping from houses. This "false-color" image is coded so that white is hottest, followed by red, pink, blue, and black.

on the film. This information can be used to correct the loss and thus conserve energy. In a similar way, Earth scientists often monitor volcanoes with infrared detectors. The appearance of a new "hot spot" may signal an impending eruption.

Stop and Think! We often say that we get heat from the Sun. What actually travels between the Sun and the Earth?

Visible Light

All of the colors of the rainbow are contained in **visible light**, whose wavelengths range from red light at about 700 nanometers down to violet light at about 400 nanometers (Figure 6-16). From the point of view of the larger universe, the visible world in which we live is a very small part of the total picture (see Figure 6-12).

Our eyes distinguish several different *colors*, but these portions of the electromagnetic spectrum have no special significance except in our perceptions. In fact, the distinct colors that we see—red, orange, yellow, green, blue, and violet— represent very different-sized slices of the electromagnetic spectrum. The red and green portions of the spectrum are rather broad, spanning more than 50 nanometers of frequencies; we thus perceive many different wavelengths as red or blue. In contrast, the yellow part of the spectrum is quite narrow, encompassing wavelengths from only about 570 to 590 nanometers.

Why should our eyes be so sensitive to such a restricted range of the spectrum? The Sun's light is especially intense in this part of the spectrum, so some biologists suggest that our eyes evolved to be especially sensitive to these wavelengths, in order to take maximum advantage of the Sun's light (Figure 6-16). Our eyes are ideally adapted for the light produced by our Sun during daylight hours. Animals that hunt at night, such as owls and cats, have eyes that are more sensitive to infrared wavelengths, radiation that makes warm living things stand out against the cooler background.

THE SCIENCE OF LIFE •

The Eye

The light detector with which we are most familiar is one we carry around with us all the time—the human eye. Eyes are marvelously complex organs, turning incoming electromagnetic radiation into images through the use of a combination of physical and chemical processes (Figure 6-17).

Light waves enter the eye through a clear lens whose thickness can be changed by a sheath of muscles around it. The direction of the waves is changed by refraction in the lens so that they are focused at receptor cells located in the retina at the back of the eye. There the light is absorbed by two different kinds of cells, called rods and cones (the names come from their shape, not their function). The rods are sensitive to light and dark, including low levels of light; they give us night vision. Three kinds of cones, sensitive to red, blue, and green light, allow us to see colors.

The energy of incoming light triggers complex changes in molecules in the rods and cones, initiating a series of reactions that eventually leads to a nerve signal that travels along the optic nerve to the brain (see Chapter 5). •

Ultraviolet Radiation

At wavelengths shorter than visible light, we begin to find waves of high frequency and therefore high energy and potential danger. The wavelengths of

• **Figure 6-16** Humans perceive the visible light spectrum as a sequence of color bands. The relative sensitivity of the human eye differs for different wavelengths. Our perception peaks near wavelengths that we perceive as yellow, though the colors we see have no special physical significance.

A glass prism separates white light into the visible spectrum.

• **Figure 6-17** A cross-section of the human eye reveals the path of light, which enters through the protective cornea and travels through the colored iris. The pupil changes the size of the aperture through which light passes, thus controlling the amount of light entering the eye. Muscles move the eye and change the shape of the lens, which focuses light onto the retina, where the light's energy is converted into nerve impulses. These signals are carried to the brain along the optic nerve.

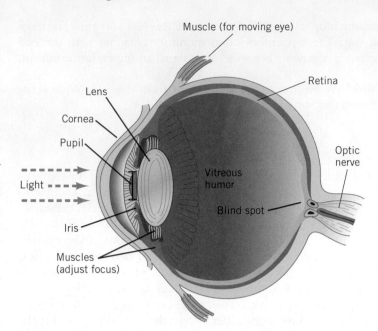

ultraviolet radiation range from 400 nanometers down to about 100 nanometers (the size of a hundred atoms placed end-to-end) in length. The energy contained in longer ultraviolet waves can cause a chemical change in skin pigments, a phenomenon known as tanning. This lower-energy portion of the ultraviolet is not particularly harmful by itself.

Shorter-wavelength (higher-energy) ultraviolet radiation, on the other hand, carries more energy—enough that this radiation can damage skin cells, causing sunburn and skin cancer in human beings. The wave's energy is absorbed by cells and can cause extensive damage to DNA (see Chapter 23). The ability of ultraviolet radiation to kill living cells is used by hospitals to sterilize equipment and kill unwanted bacteria.

The Sun produces intense ultraviolet radiation in both longer and shorter wavelengths. Fortunately, our atmosphere absorbs much of the harmful short wavelengths and thus shields living things. Nevertheless, if you spend much time outdoors under a bright Sun, you should protect exposed skin with a sunblocking chemical, which is transparent (colorless) to visible light, but reflects harmful ultraviolet rays.

The energy contained in both long and short ultraviolet wavelengths can be absorbed by atoms, which in special materials may subsequently emit a portion of that absorbed energy as visible light. (Remember, both visible light and ultraviolet light are forms of electromagnetic radiation, but visible light has longer wavelengths, and therefore less energy, than ultraviolet radiation.) This phenomenon, called *fluorescence,* provides the so-called "black light" effects so popular in stage shows and nightclubs. We'll examine the origins of fluorescence in more detail in Chapter 8.

X-rays

X-rays are electromagnetic waves that range in wavelength from about 100 nanometers down to 0.1 nanometer, smaller than a single atom. These high-frequency (and thus high-energy) waves can penetrate several centimeters into most solid matter, but are absorbed to different degrees by all kinds of materials.

A physician examines medical X-rays. Internal structures are revealed because bones and different tissues absorb X-rays to different degrees.

This fact allows X-rays to be used extensively in medicine to form visual images of bones and organs inside the body. Bones and teeth absorb X-rays much more efficiently than skin or muscle, so a detailed picture of inner structures emerges. X-rays are also used extensively in industry to inspect for defects in welds and manufactured parts.

The X-ray machine in your doctor's or dentist's office is something like a giant lightbulb with a glass vacuum tube. At one end of the tube is a tungsten filament that is heated to a very high temperature by an electrical current, just like in an incandescent lightbulb. At the other end is a polished metal plate. X-rays are produced by applying an extremely high voltage—negative on the filament and positive on the metal plate—so electrons stream off the filament and smash into the metal plate at high velocity. The sudden deceleration of the negatively charged electrons releases a flood of high-energy electromagnetic radiation—the X-rays that travel from the machine to you at light speed.

THE ONGOING PROCESS OF SCIENCE •

Intense X-ray Sources

X-rays have become supremely important in many facets of science and industry. X-ray crystallographers use beams of X-rays to determine the spacing and positions of atoms in a crystal (see Chapter 10), physicians use X-rays to reveal bone fractures and other internal injuries, and many industries use X-rays to scan for defects in manufactured products. However, many potential applications, such as structural studies of very small crystals or scans of unusually large manufactured products, are unrealized because of the relatively low intensity of conventional X-ray sources.

(*a*) A variety of chemical reactions, including fire, produces light energy. (*b*) One way of producing light is to convert stored chemical energy, as is done in this emergency flare. (*c*) Chemcial reactions also produce the light given off by a firefly.

A major effort is now underway to develop new, more powerful X-ray sources. One such facility, the Advanced Photon Source (APS) near Chicago, Illinois, generates intense X-ray beams a billion times stronger than conventional sources by accelerating electrons in a circular path (remember, electromagnetic radiation is emitted when charged particles are accelerated). Scientists converge on the APS from around the world to study the properties of matter. Eventually, even more powerful X-ray beams might be produced by an X-ray laser (see Chapter 8), though such a technology is now only a dream. •

Gamma Rays

The highest energies in the electromagnetic spectrum are called **gamma rays**. Their wavelengths range from slightly less than the size of an atom (about 0.1 nanometer, or 10^{-10} meter) to the size of a nucleus (less than a trillionth of a meter, or 10^{-12} meter). Gamma rays are normally emitted only in very high-energy nuclear and particle reactions (see Chapters 12 and 13), and they are not as common in nature as the other kinds of electromagnetic radiation that we have talked about.

Gamma rays have many uses in medicine. Some types of medical diagnosis involve giving a patient a radioactive chemical that emits gamma rays. If that chemical concentrates at places where bone is actively healing, for example, then doctors can monitor the healing by locating the places where gamma rays are emitted. The gamma ray detectors used in this specialized form of nuclear medicine are both large (to capture the energetic waves) and expensive. Doctors also use gamma rays for the treatment of cancer in humans. In these treatments, high-energy gamma rays are directed at tumors or malignancies that cannot be removed surgically. If the gamma ray energy is absorbed in those tissues, the tissues will die and the patient has a better chance to live.

Gamma rays are also used extensively in astronomy because many of the interesting processes going on in our universe involve bursts of very high energy and, hence, the emission of gamma rays.

Thinking More About | Electromagnetic Radiation

Is ELF Radiation Dangerous?

Maxwell's equations tell us that any accelerated charge will emit waves of electromagnetic radiation, not just those that are frequencies of millions or billions of hertz. In particular, the electrons that move back and forth in wires to produce the alternating current in household wiring generate electromagnetic radiation. Every object in which electrical power flows, from power lines to toasters, is a source of this weak, *extremely low-frequency (ELF) radiation.*

For more than a century, human beings in industrialized countries have lived in a sea of weak ELF radiation, but until recently no questions were raised about whether that radiation might have an effect on human health. In the late 1980s, however, a series of books and magazine articles created a minor sensation by claiming that exposure to ELF radiation might cause some forms of cancer, most notably childhood leukemia.

Scientists tended to downplay these claims, because the electrical fields most residents experience due to power lines are a thousand times smaller than those due to natural causes (such as electrical activity in nerve and brain cells). They also pointed out that age-corrected cancer rates in the United States (with the exception of lung cancer, which is caused primarily by smoking) have remained constant or dropped over the last 50 years, though exposure to ELF radiation has increased enormously. They also questioned the statistical validity of some studies: more detailed analysis of results did not demonstrate the connection between ELF radiation and disease. In 1995, the prestigious American Institute of Physics reviewed the scientific literature on this subject and concluded that there is no reliable evidence that ELF radiation causes any form of cancer and most funding for research in this area was cut off.

This situation is typical of encounters at the border between science and public health. Preliminary data indicate a possible health risk but do not prove that the risk is real. Settling the issue by further study takes years, while researchers carefully collect data and weigh the evidence. In the meantime, people have to make decisions about what to do. In addition, as in the case of ELF radiation, the cost of removing the risk is often very high.

Suppose you were a scientist who had shaky evidence that some common food—bread, for example, or a familiar kind of fruit—could be harmful. What responsibility would you have to make your results known to the general public? If you stress the uncertainty of your results and no one listens, should you make sensational (perhaps unsupported) claims to get people's attention?

Summary

Waves provide a way to transfer energy from one place to another through a medium without matter actually traveling across the intervening distance. Every wave can be characterized by a *wavelength,* a velocity, an amplitude, and a *frequency* (measured in cycles per second, or *hertz*). Transverse waves, such as swells on the ocean, occur when the medium moves perpendicular to the direction of the waves. Longitudinal waves, such as sound, occur when the medium moves in the same direction as the wave.

Two waves can interact with each other, causing constructive or destructive *interference.* The observed frequency of a wave depends on the relative motion of the wave's source and the observer—a phenomenon known as the *Doppler effect.* Waves encounting a surface can be reflected, or they may enter the medium moving in a different direction, a process called *refraction.*

The motion of every wave can be described by a characteristic wave equation. James Clerk Maxwell recognized that simple manipulation of his equations that describe electricity and magnetism pointed to the existence of *electromagnetic waves* or *electromagnetic radiation,* alternating electrical and magnetic fields that can travel through a vacuum at the *speed of light.* This discovery solved one of the oldest mysteries of science, the nature of *light.* While visible light was the only kind of electromagnetic radiation known to Maxwell, he predicted the existence of other kinds with longer and shorter wavelengths. Soon thereafter a complete *electromagnetic spectrum* of waves, including *radio waves, microwaves, infrared radiation, visible light, ultraviolet radiation, X-rays,* and *gamma rays,* was recognized.

Electromagnetic radiation can interact with matter in three ways: it can be *transmitted, absorbed,* or *scattered.* We use these properties in countless ways every day—radio and TV, heating and lighting, microwave ovens, tanning salons, medical X-rays, and more. Much of science and technology during the past 100 years has been an effort to find new and better ways to produce, manipulate, and detect electromagnetic radiation.

KEY TERMS ABOUT ELECTROMAGNETIC RADIATION

wave
wavelength
frequency (measured in hertz)
interference
electromagnetic wave, or
  electromagnetic radiation

light
speed of light, *c*
Doppler effect
transmission
refraction
absorption

diffuse scattering
reflection
electromagnetic spectrum
radio waves
microwaves
infrared radiation

visible light
ultraviolet radiation
X-rays
gamma rays

KEY EQUATIONS ABOUT WAVES

wave velocity (m/s) = wavelength (m) × frequency (Hz)

$$\text{wavelength (m)} = \frac{\text{velocity (m/s)}}{\text{frequency (Hz)}}$$

1 hertz = 1 cycle/second

For light: wavelength (m) × frequency (Hz) = *c*

Constant: Speed of Light

$$c = 300{,}000 \text{ km/s} = 3 \times 10^8 \text{ m/s}$$

REVIEW QUESTIONS

1. Which form of energy transfer occurs when sunlight heats beach sand? When microwaves are used to detect the flight path of an airplane? When radio waves transmit music?

2. Identify three characteristics that can be used to describe a wave. How are these three related?

3. Identify everyday examples of waves that travel through solids, liquids, and gases.

4. Use a Slinky™ toy to illustrate the difference between a longitudinal wave and a transverse wave.

5. What happens when two different waves overlap?

6. Under what circumstances will an electromagnetic wave form? Under what circumstances will no electromagnetic waves be produced?

7. What features are shared by all electromagnetic waves? In what ways might two electromagnetic waves differ?

8. Why did Maxwell think there were kinds of electromagnetic radiation other than visible light?

9. What was meant by "the ether"? What prompted the assumption that it existed? What proof destroyed the idea of its existence?

10. A vat of molten iron is heated until white hot, then poured into a mold. As it cools, its color changes to yellow and then red. Explain why this occurs.

11. Identify three common uses of microwaves.

12. Why is short-wave ultraviolet light more damaging to the skin than long-wave ultraviolet light?

13. What are some uses of gamma rays?

14. What kinds of electromagnetic radiation can you detect with your body?

15. What are some of the similarities and differences between water waves and light waves?

16. Describe the Doppler effect. Give an example of how you experience this effect.

17. Identify a substance that:

a. absorbs radio waves

b. scatters microwaves

c. transmits visible light

d. absorbs X-rays

e. scatters infrared radiation

DISCUSSION QUESTIONS

1. In what ways do sound waves differ from radio waves? In what ways are they similar?

2. If a tree falls in a forest, what kinds of waves are created? Where did the energy that produced those waves come from?

3. Propose an experiment to test whether lead is transparent to radio waves.

4. Fill a drinking glass with water and look through the water. Describe the different ways that light is interacting with matter.

5. How did Michelson and Morley demonstrate that ether does not exist? What was their hypothesis?

6. Why do people wear light-colored clothing in summer and dark-colored clothing in winter?

7. Why are X-rays used for medical diagnosis? What other wavelengths of electromagnetic radiation are used in medicine?

PROBLEMS

1. An organ pipe is 1.8 meters long. What is the frequency of the sound it produces? *Extra credit:* To what pitch does that frequency correspond?

2. An ocean liner experiences broad waves, called swells, with a frequency of one every 10 seconds (0.1 Hz) and a wavelength of 220 feet. Assume the waves are moving due east. If the liner maintains a speed of 15 miles per hour, will it have a smoother trip going east or west? Why?

3. Radio and TV transmissions are being emitted into space, so *Star Trek* episodes are streaming out into the universe. The nearest star is 9.5×10^{17} meters away. If civilized life exists on a planet near this star, how long will they have to wait for the next episode?

4. What is the wavelength of the carrier wave used by your favorite radio station?

5. The FM radio band in most places goes from frequencies of about 88 to 108 MHz. How long are the wavelengths of the radiation at the extreme ends of this range?

6. The AM radio band in most places goes from frequencies of about 535 to 1610 kHz. How long are the wavelengths of the radiation at the extreme ends of this range?

INVESTIGATIONS

1. Visit a local hospital and see how many types of electromagnetic radiation are used on a regular basis. From radio waves to gamma waves, how are the distinctive characteristics of absorption and transmission for each segment of the spectrum used at the facility?

2. What frequencies of electromagnetic radiation are used for emergency communications by police, fire, and medivac in your community? What are the corresponding wavelengths of these signals? What organizations allocate and monitor these frequencies?

3. Examine a microwave oven or, better yet, obtain an old broken oven that you can dissect. Locate the source of microwaves. Which materials in the oven transmit microwaves? Which ones scatter microwaves? Do you think any of the components absorb microwaves? Why?

4. In large metropolitan areas, a license to broadcast electromagnetic waves at an AM frequency may change hands for millions of dollars.

a. Why is electromagnetic "real estate" so valuable? Investigate how frequencies are divided up and who regulates the process. Should individuals or corporations be allowed to "own" portions of the spectrum, or to buy and sell pieces of it?

b. Currently the only portions of the electromagnetic spectrum that are regulated by national and international law are the longer wavelengths, including radio and microwave. Why are the shorter wavelengths, including infrared, visible light, ultraviolet, and X-ray wavelengths, not similarly regulated?

5. Different colors represent different wavelengths of electromagnetic radiation. Investigate the process by which the human eye detects color, as well as the means by which the brain interprets color. Do all mammals see in color? How do we know?

6. Find out how sonar works. Compare it to the use of sound by bats and the use of radar by police. Discuss the similarities and differences among the defenses of submarines against sonar, moths against bats, and motorists against police radar.

WWW Resources

See *The Sciences* homepage at: **http://www.wiley.com/college/trefil** for valuable web links.

1. **http://imagine.gsfc.nasa.gov/docs/science/know_l1/emspectrum.html**
   Electromagnetic Spectrum, from NASA—not flashy, but thorough.

2. **http://www.xray.hmc.psu.edu/rci/centennial.html**
   A Century of Radiology, from Penn State's Department of Radiology—an extensive and thoughtful history of radiology.

7

Albert Einstein and the Theory of Relativity

Can a human ever travel faster than the speed of light, at "warp speed?"

GREAT IDEA

All observers, no matter what their frame of reference, see the same laws of nature.

PHYSICS

Particle accelerators that control relativistic charged particles in a closed loop must be designed to correct for distortion of mass and time experienced by the speeding particles. (Ch. 13)

TECHNOLOGY

Atomic clocks have been shown to tick slightly slower when strapped aboard a high-speed plane, compared to a stationary clock.

ASTRONOMY

Stars are so massive that they can bend light coming from more distant objects to create a gravitational lens.

Red = applications of the great idea discussed in this chapter.

Orange = other applications, some of which are explored in other chapters.

Waiting in your car at a long stoplight, you daydream about the friends you're going to meet. You don't even notice the large bus in the lane next to you.

Suddenly you have the strange sensation that your car is moving backward. But your foot is on the brake—how can that be? You quickly realize that it's the bus that's moving forward, not you moving backward. It was just a brief optical illusion.

For that brief moment you saw the world through eyes unaffected by years of experience. You realized that there is always more than one way to view any kind of motion. One way, of course, is to say that you are stationary and the bus is moving with respect to you. But you could also say that the bus is stationary and you are moving backward relative to it. Which point of view is right?

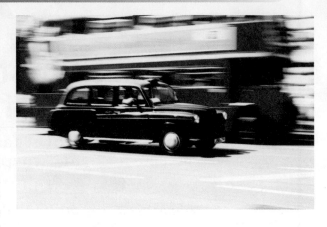

Almost 100 years ago, Albert Einstein made one of the greatest discoveries of the twentieth century thinking about situations just like this.

● Frames of Reference

A **frame of reference** is the physical surroundings from which you observe and measure the world around you. If you read this book at your desk or in an easy chair, you experience the world from the frame of reference of your room, which seems firmly rooted to the solid Earth. If you read on a train or in a plane, your frame of reference is the vehicle that moves with respect to the Earth's surface. And you could imagine yourself in an accelerating spaceship in deep space, where your frame of reference would be different still. In each of these reference frames you are what scientists call an "observer." An observer looks at the world from a particular frame of reference with anything from casual interest to a full-fledged laboratory investigation of phenomena that leads to a determination of natural laws.

For human beings who grow up on the Earth's surface, it is natural to think of the ground as a fixed, immovable frame of reference, and to refer all motion to it. After all, train or plane passengers don't think of themselves as stationary while the countryside zooms by. But, as we saw in the opening example, there are indeed times when we lose this prejudice and see that the question of who is moving and who is standing still is largely one of definition.

From the point of view of an observer in a spaceship above the solar system, there is nothing "solid" about the ground you're standing on. The Earth is rotating on its axis and moving in an orbit around the Sun, while the Sun itself is performing a stately rotation around the galaxy. Thus, even though a reference frame fixed in the Earth may seem "right" to us, there is nothing special about it.

Descriptions in Different Reference Frames

Different observers in different reference frames may provide very different accounts of the same event. To convince yourself of this idea, think about a simple experiment. While riding on a train, take a coin out of your pocket and flip it. You know what will happen—the coin will go up in the air and fall straight back into your hand, just as it would if you flipped it while sitting in a chair in your room (Figure 7-1a). But now ask yourself this question: How would a friend standing near the tracks, watching your train go by, describe the flip of the coin?

To that person it would appear that the coin went up into the air, of course, but by the time it came down the car would have traveled some distance down the tracks. As far as your friend on the ground is concerned, the coin traveled in an arc (Figure 7-1b).

So you, sitting in the train, say the coin went straight up and down, while someone on the ground says it traveled in an arc. You and the ground-based observer would describe the path of the coin quite differently, and you'd both be correct in your respective frames of reference. The universe we live in possesses this general feature—different observers will describe the same event in different terms, depending on their frames of reference.

Does this mean that we are doomed to live in a world where nothing is fixed, where everything depends on the frame of reference of the observer? Not necessarily. The possibility exists that even though different observers give different descriptions of the same event, they will agree on the underlying laws that govern it. Even though the observers disagree on the path followed by the flipped coin, they may very well agree that motion in their frame is governed by Newton's laws of motion and the law of universal gravitation.

The Principle of Relativity

Albert Einstein came to his theories of relativity by thinking about a fundamental contradiction between Newton's laws and Maxwell's equations. You can see the problem by thinking about a simple example. Imagine you're on a moving railroad car and you throw a baseball. What speed will the baseball have according to an observer on the ground?

Direction of train movement

Apparent direction of coin fall

(a) Frame of reference: inside the train   (b) Frame of reference: outside the train

• **Figure 7-1** The path of a coin flipped in the air depends on the observer's frame of reference. (a) A rider in the car sees the coin go up and fall straight down. (b) An observer on the street sees the coin follow an arching path.

Albert Einstein
(1879–1955)

If you throw the ball forward at 40 kilometers per hour while on a train traveling 100 kilometers per hour, the ball will appear to a ground-based observer to travel 140 km/h—40 km/h from the ball plus 100 km/h from the train. If, on the other hand, you throw the ball backward, the ground-based observer will see the ball moving at only 60 km/h—the train's 100 km/h minus the ball's 40 km/h. In our everyday world, we just add the two speeds to get the answer, and this notion is reflected in Newton's laws.

Suppose, however, that instead of throwing a ball you turned on a flashlight and measured the speed of the light coming from it. In Chapter 6 we saw that the speed of light is built into Maxwell's equations. If every observer is to see the same laws of nature, they all have to see the same speed of light. In other words, the ground observer would have to see light from the flashlight moving at 300,000 km/s, and *not* 300,000 km/s plus 100 km/h. In this case, velocities wouldn't add, as our intuition tells us they must.

Albert Einstein thought long and hard about this paradox, and he realized that it could be resolved in only three ways:

1. The laws of nature are not the same in all frames of reference (an idea Einstein was reluctant to accept on philosophical grounds); or,
2. Maxwell's equations could be wrong and the speed of light depends on the speed of the source emitting the light (in spite of abundant experimental support for the equations); or,
3. Our intuitions about the addition of velocities could be wrong, in which case the universe might be a very strange place indeed.

Einstein focused on the third of these possibilities.

The idea that the laws of nature are the same in all frames of reference is called the *principle of relativity*, and can be stated as follows:

> **Every observer must experience the same natural laws.**

This statement is the central assumption of Einstein's **theory of relativity**. Hidden beneath this seemingly simple statement lies a view of the universe that is both strange and wonderful. The extraordinary theoretical effort required to understand the consequences of this one simple assumption occupied Einstein during much of the first decades of the twentieth century.

 Stop and Think! It may seem obvious that the laws of nature are the same everywhere in the universe, but how can we know for sure? How might you test this statement?

We can begin to understand Einstein's work by recalling what Isaac Newton had demonstrated three centuries earlier, that all motions fall into one of two categories: uniform motion or acceleration (Chapter 2). Einstein therefore divided his theory of relativity into two parts—one dealing with each of these kinds of motion. The easier part, first published by Einstein in 1905, is called **special relativity** and deals with all frames of reference in uniform motion relative to one another—reference frames that do not accelerate. It took Einstein another decade to complete his treatment of **general relativity**, mathematically a much more complex theory, which applies to any reference frame whether or not it is accelerating relative to another.

At first glance, the underlying principle of relativity seems obvious, perhaps almost too simple. Of course the laws of nature are the same everywhere—that's the only way that scientists can explain how the universe behaves in an ordered way. But once you accept that central assumption of relativity be prepared for some surprises. Relativity forces us to accept the fact that nature doesn't always behave as our intuition says it must. You may find it disturbing that nature sometimes violates our sense of the "way things should be." But you'll have little problem with relativity if you just accept the idea that the universe is what it is, and not necessarily what we think it should be.

Another way of saying this is to note that our intuitions about how the world works are built up from experience with things that are moving at modest speeds—a few hundred, or at most a few thousand, miles per hour. None of us has any experience with things moving near the speed of light, so when we start examining phenomena in that range our intuitions won't necessarily apply. Strictly speaking, we shouldn't be surprised by anything we find.

Relativity and the Speed of Light

As the example of the train and the flashlight shows, one of the most disturbing aspects of the principle of relativity has to do with our everyday notions of speed. According to the principle, any observer, no matter what his or her reference frame, should be able to confirm Maxwell's description of electricity and magnetism. Because the speed of light is built into these equations, it follows that:

> **The speed of light, c, is the same in all reference frames.**

Strictly speaking, this statement is only one of many consequences of the principle of relativity. However, so many of the surprising results of relativity follow from it that it is often accorded special status and given special attention in discussions of those theories.

SCIENCE IN THE MAKING •

Einstein and the Streetcar

Newton and his apple have entered modern folklore as a paradigm of unexpected discovery. A less-well-known incident led Albert Einstein, then an obscure patent clerk in Bern, Switzerland, to relativity.

One day, while riding home in a streetcar, he happened to glance up at a clock on a church steeple (Figure 7-2). In his mind he imagined the streetcar speeding up, moving faster and faster, until it was going at almost the speed of light. Einstein realized that if the streetcar were to travel at the speed of light, it would appear to someone on the streetcar that the clock had stopped. The passenger would be like a surfer on a light-wave crest—a crest that originated at 12 noon, for example—and the same image of the clock would stay with him.

On the other hand, a clock moving with him—his pocket watch, for example—would still tick away the seconds in its usual way. Perhaps, Einstein thought, *time as measured on a clock, just like motion, is relative to one's frame of reference.* •

• **Figure 7-2** Albert Einstein, moving away from a clock tower, imagined how different observers might view the passage of time. If Einstein were traveling at the speed of light, for example, the clock would appear to him to have stopped, even though his own pocket watch would still be ticking.

Special Relativity

Time Dilation

Think about how you measure time. The passage of time can be measured by any kind of regularly repeating phenomenon—a swinging pendulum, a beating heart, or an alternating electrical current. To get at the theory of relativity, though, it's easiest to think of a rather unusual kind of clock. Suppose, as in Figure 7-3, we had a flashbulb, a mirror, and a photon detector. A "tick-tock" of this clock would consist of the flashbulb going off, the light traveling to the mirror, bouncing down to the detector, and then triggering the next flash. By adjusting the distance, *d*, between the light source and mirror, these pulses could correspond to any desired time interval. This unusual "light clock," therefore, serves the same function as any other clock—in fact, you could adjust it to be synchronized with anything from a grandfather's clock to a wristwatch.

Now imagine two identical light clocks: one next to you on the ground (Figure 7-3*a*), and the other whizzing by in a spaceship (Figure 7-3*b*). Imagine further that the mirrors are adjusted so that both clocks would tick at the same rate if they were standing next to each other. How would the moving clock look to you?

Standing on the ground, you would see the ground-based clock ticking along as the light pulses bounce back and forth between the mirror and detector. When you looked at the moving clock, though, you would see the light following a longer, zig-zag path. If the speed of light is indeed the same in both frames of reference, it should appear to you that the light in the moving frame takes longer to travel the zig-zag path from light to detector than the light on the ground-based clock. Consequently, from your point of view on the ground, the moving clock must tick more slowly. The two clocks are identical, but the moving clock runs slower. This surprising phenomenon is known as **time dilation**, and it is an essential consequence of relativity.

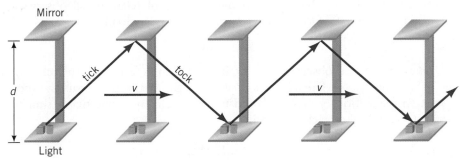

(a) Stationary light clock

(b) Moving light clock

• **Figure 7-3** A light clock incorporates a flashing light and a mirror. A light pulse bounces off the mirror and returns to trigger the next pulse. Two light clocks, one stationary (*a*) and one moving (*b*), illustrate the phenomenon of time dilation. Light from the moving clock must travel farther, and so it appears to the stationary observer to tick more slowly.

Remember that each observer regards the clocks in his or her own reference frame as completely normal, while all other clocks appear to be running slower. Thus, paradoxically, while we observe the spaceship clock as slow, observers in the speeding spaceship see the Earth-based clock moving and believe that the Earth-based clock is running more slowly than theirs.

Relativity's prediction of time dilation can be tested in a number of ways. Scientists have actually documented relativistic time dilation by comparing two extremely accurate atomic clocks, one on the ground and one strapped into a jet aircraft. Even though jets travel at a paltry hundred-thousandth of the speed of light, the difference in the time recorded by the two clocks can be measured.

Time dilation can also be observed with high-energy particle accelerators that routinely produce unstable subatomic particles (see Chapter 12). The normal half-life of these particles is well known. When accelerated to near the speed of light, however, these particles last much longer because of the relativistic slowdown in their decay rates.

Thus, although the notion that moving clocks run slower than stationary ones violates our intuition, it seems to be well documented by experiment. Why, then, aren't we aware of this effect in everyday life? To answer that question, we have to ask how big an effect time dilation is. How much do moving clocks slow down?

The Size of Time Dilation

We have tried, in general, to talk about science in everyday terms and stay away from formulas in this book. But we have now run into a rather fundamental question that requires some simple mathematics to answer. In this section, you'll be able to follow the kind of thought process used by Einstein when he first formulated his revolutionary theory.

Consider the two identical light clocks in Figure 7-3, one moving at a velocity, v, and one stationary on the ground. Each clock has a light-to-mirror separation distance of d. (The various symbols we are using are summarized in Table 7-1.)

The notation for the time it takes for light to travel the distance d from the light to its opposite mirror—that is, one "tick" of the stationary clock—is a little trickier, because we have to keep track of which clock we're looking at and from which reference frame we're looking. We will use two subscripts—the first subscript to tell us if the clock is on the ground (G) or moving (M), and the second subscript to indicate if the observer is on the ground or moving. Thus, t_{GG} is the time for one tick of the ground-based clock as observed by an observer on the ground. On the other hand, t_{MG} is the time for one tick of the moving clock from the point of view of this ground-based observer. According to the principle of relativity, all observers see clocks in their own reference frames as normal. Or, in equation form,

$$t_{GG} = t_{MM}$$

As ground-based observers, we are interested in determining the relative values of t_{GG} and t_{MG}—what we see as "ticks" of the stationary versus the moving clocks. In the stationary ground-based frame of reference, one tick is simply the time it takes light to travel the distance d:

$$\text{time} = \frac{\text{distance}}{\text{speed}}$$

Substituting values for the light clock into this equation,

$$\text{time for one tick} = \frac{\text{light-to-mirror distance}}{\text{speed of light}}$$

or,

$$t_{GG} = \frac{d}{c}$$

where c is the standard symbol for the speed of light.

We argued that to the observer on the ground, it appears that the light beam in the moving clock travels on a zig-zag path as shown in Figure 7-3, and that this made the moving clock appear to run more slowly. In what follows, we will show how to take an intuitive statement like this one and convert it into a precise mathematical equation. We begin by labeling the dimensions of our two clocks.

The moving clock travels a horizontal distance of $v \times t_{MG}$ during each of its ticks. In order to determine the value of t_{MG}, we must first determine how far light must travel in the moving clock as seen by the observer on the ground. As

Table 7-1 Symbols for Deriving Time Dilation

Symbol	Description
v	Velocity of the moving light clock relative to the ground
d	Distance between the clock's light and mirror
t_{GG}	Time for one tick (ground clock, ground observer)
t_{MG}	Time for one tick (moving clock, ground observer)
t_{GM}	Time for one tick (ground clock, moving observer)
t_{MM}	Time for one tick (moving clock, moving observer)
c	Speed of light, a constant

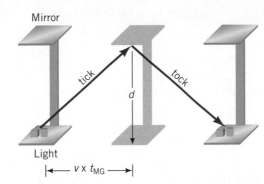

(a) Stationary light clock (b) Moving light clock

• **Figure 7-4** Light clocks with dimensions labeled. Both the stationary clock (*a*) and the moving clock (*b*) have light-to-mirror distance *d*. During one tick the moving clock must travel a horizontal distance $v \times t_{MG}$.

illustrated in Figure 7-4, we know the lengths of the two shortest sides of a right triangle. One side has length d, representing the vertical distance between light and mirror (a distance, remember, that is the same in both frames of reference). The other side is $v \times t_{MG}$, which corresponds to the distance traveled by the moving clock as observed in the stationary frame of reference. The distance traveled by the moving light beam in one tick is represented by the hypotenuse of this right triangle, and is given by the Pythagorean theorem.

▶ **In words:** The square of the length of a right triangle's long side equals the sum of the squares of the lengths of the other two sides.

▶ **In words (applied to our light clock):** The square of the distance light travels during one tick equals the sum of the squares of the light-to-mirror distance and the horizontal distance the clock moves during one tick.

▶ **In symbols:**

$$(\text{distance light travels})^2 = d^2 + (v \times t_{MG})^2$$

We can begin to simplify this equation by taking the square roots of both sides.

$$\text{distance light travels} = \sqrt{d^2 + (v \times t_{MG})^2}$$

Remember, time equals distance divided by velocity. So the time it takes light to travel this distance, t_{MG}, is given by the distance $\sqrt{d^2 + (v \times t_{MG})^2}$ divided by the velocity of light, c:

$$t_{MG} = \frac{\sqrt{d^2 + (v \times t_{MG})^2}}{c}$$

We now must engage in a bit of algebraic manipulation. First, square both sides of this equation.

$$t_{MG}^2 = \frac{d^2}{c^2} + \frac{v^2 t_{MG}^2}{c^2}$$

But we saw previously that $t_{GG} = d/c$, so, substituting,

$$t_{MG}^2 = t_{GG}^2 + \frac{v^2 t_{MG}^2}{c^2}$$

Dividing both sides by t_{MG}^2 gives

$$\frac{t_{MG}^2}{t_{MG}^2} = \frac{t_{GG}^2}{t_{MG}^2} + \frac{[v^2 t_{MG}^2/c^2]}{t_{MG}^2}$$

or,

$$1 = \left(\frac{t_{GG}}{t_{MG}}\right)^2 + (vc)^2$$

Finally, regrouping yields

$$t_{MG} = \frac{t_{GG}}{\sqrt{[1 - (v/c)^2]}}$$

This equation expresses in mathematical form what we said earlier in words—that moving clocks appear to run slower. It tells us that t_{MG}, the time it takes for one tick of the moving clock as seen by an observer on the ground, is equal to the time it takes for one tick of an identical clock on the ground *divided by a number less than one*. Thus the time required for a tick of the moving clock will always be greater than that for a stationary one.

The expression $\sqrt{1 - (v/c)^2}$ is a number, called the *Lorentz factor*, that appears over and over again in relativistic calculations. In the case of time dilation, the Lorentz factor arises from an application of the Pythagorean theorem.

One important point to notice is that if the velocity of the moving clock is very small compared to the speed of light, the quantity $(v/c)^2$ becomes very small and the Lorentz factor is almost equal to one. In this case, the time on the moving clock is equal to the time on the stationary one, as our intuition demands that it should be. Only when speeds get very high do the effects of relativity become important.

SCIENCE BY THE NUMBERS •

How Important Is Relativity?

To understand why we aren't aware of relativity in our everyday life, let's calculate the size of the time dilation for a clock in a car moving at 70 km/h (about 50 miles per hour).

The first problem is to convert the familiar speed in km/h to a speed in meters per second so we can compare it to the speed of light. There are 60×60 = 3600 seconds in an hour, so a car traveling 70 km/h is moving at a speed of

$$70 \text{ km/h} = \frac{70,000 \text{ m}}{3600 \text{ s}}$$
$$= 19.4 \text{ m/s}$$

For this speed, the Lorentz factor is

$$\sqrt{[1 - (19.4/300,000,000)^2]} = 0.9999999999999999$$

Thus the passage of time for a stationary and speeding car differs by only one part in the sixteenth decimal place.

To get an idea of how small the difference is between the ground clock and the moving one in this case, we can note that if you watched the moving car for a time equal to the age of the universe, you would observe it running *10 seconds slow* compared to your ground clock.

For an object traveling at 99% of the speed of light, however, the Lorentz factor is

$$\sqrt{[1 - (v/c)^2]} = \sqrt{[1 - (0.99)^2]}$$
$$= \sqrt{(0.0199)}$$
$$= 0.1411$$

In this case, you would observe the stationary clock to be ticking about seven times as fast as the moving one—that is, the ground clock would tick about seven times while the moving clock ticked just once.

This numerical example illustrates a very important point about relativity. Our intuition and experience tell us that the exterior clock on our local bank doesn't suddenly slow down when we view it from a moving car. Consequently, we find the prediction of time dilation to be strange and paradoxical. But all of our intuition is built up from experiences at very low velocities—none of us has ever moved at an appreciable fraction of the speed of light. For the everyday world, the predictions of relativity coincide precisely with our experience. It is only when we get into regions near the speed of light, where that experience isn't relevant, that the "paradoxes" arise. •

THE SCIENCE OF LIFE •

Space Travel and Aging

While humans presently do not experience the direct effects of time dilation in their day-to-day lives, at some future time they might. If we ever develop inter-stellar space travel with near-light speed, then time dilation may wreak havoc with family lives (and genealogists' records).

Imagine a spaceship that accelerates to 99% of the speed of light and goes on a long journey. While 15 years seem to pass for the crew of the ship, more than a century goes by on Earth. The space explorers return almost 15 years older than when they left, but biologically younger than their great-grandchildren! Friends and family all would be long-since dead.

If we ever enter an era of extensive high-speed interstellar travel, people may drift in and out of other people's lives in ways we can't easily imagine. Parents and children could repeatedly leapfrog each other in age, and the notion of relat-edness could take on complex twists in a society with widespread relativistic travel. •

Distance and Relativity

Many results from relativity run counter to our intuition. They can be derived by procedures similar to (but more complicated than) the one we just gave for work-ing out time dilation. In fact, using arguments like those we have presented, Ein-stein showed that *moving yardsticks must appear to be shorter than stationary ones in the direction of motion* (see Figure 7-5).

The equation that relates the ground-based observer's measurement of a sta-tionary object's length, L_{GG}, to that observer's measurement of the length of an identical moving object, L_{MG}, is

$$L_{MG} = L_{GG} \times \sqrt{[1 - (v/c)^2]}$$

The term on the right side of this equation is the familiar Lorentz factor that we derived from our study of light clocks. The equation tells us that the length of the moving ruler can be obtained by multiplying the length of the stationary ruler by a number less than one, and thus must appear shorter. This phenomenon is known as **length contraction**.

Note that the height and width of the moving object do not appear to change—only the length along the direction of motion. A moving basketball, then, takes on the appearance of a pancake at speeds near those of light.

• **Figure 7-5** A spaceship in motion appears to contract in length, *L*, along the direction of motion. However, the height, *H*, and width of the ship do not appear to change.

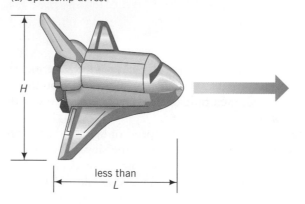

(*a*) Spaceship at rest

(*b*) Spaceship at high speed

Length contraction is not just an optical illusion. While relativistic shortening doesn't affect most of our daily lives, the effect is real. Physicists who work at particle accelerators inject "bunches" of particles into their machines. As these particles approach light speed, the bunches are observed to contract according to the Lorentz factor, an effect that must be compensated for.

This series of four computer-generated images shows the changing appearance of a network of balls and rods as it moves toward you at different speeds. (*a*) At rest the normal view. (*b*) At 50% of light speed, the array appears to contract. (*c*) At 95% of light speed, the lattice has curved rods. (*d*) At 99% of light speed, the network is severely distorted.

(*a*)

(*b*)

Stop and Think! What does the "spaceship at rest" in Figure 7-5 look like to an observer in the "spaceship at high speed?" Does it appear to be normal length, shorter, or longer?

So What About the Train and the Flashlight?

Now that we understand a little about how relativity works, we can go back and unravel the paradox we discussed earlier in this chapter—the problem of how both an observer on the ground and an observer on the train could see light from a flashlight moving at the same speed.

Velocity is defined to be distance traveled divided by the time required for the travel to take place. Since both length and time appear to be different for different observers, it should come as no surprise that the rule that tells us how to add velocities (such as the velocity of the light and the train) might be more complicated than we would expect. The simple intuition that tells us that we should add the velocity of the train to the velocity of the ball, like our notions of time and space, is valid at small velocities but breaks down for objects moving near the speed of light. For those objects, a more complex addition has to be done, and when it is, we find that both observers see the light moving at a velocity of c.

Mass and Relativity

Perhaps the most far-reaching consequence of Einstein's theory of relativity was the discovery that mass, like time and distance, is relative to one's frame of reference. So far we have been faced with two strange ideas:

1. Clocks run fastest for stationary objects; moving clocks slow down. As the speed of light is approached, time slows down and approaches zero.
2. Distances are greatest for stationary objects; moving objects shrink in the direction of motion. As the speed of light is approached, distances shrink and approach zero.

(c)

(d)

Einstein showed that a third consequence followed from his principle:

3. Mass is lowest for stationary objects; moving objects become more massive. As an object's velocity approaches the speed of light, its mass approaches infinity.

Einstein showed that if the speed of light is a constant in all reference frames—which must follow from the central assumption of the theory of relativity—then an object's mass depends on its velocity. The faster an object travels, the greater its mass and the harder it is to deflect from its course. If a ground-based observer measures an object's stationary or "rest" mass, m_{GG}, then the apparent mass, m_{MG}, of that object moving at velocity v is

$$m_{MG} = \frac{m_{GG}}{\sqrt{[1 - (v/c)^2]}}$$

Once again the Lorentz factor comes into play. As we observe an object approach the speed of light, its mass appears to us to approach infinity.

This property of mass leads to the common misperception that relativity predicts that nothing can travel faster than the speed of light. In fact, the only thing we can conclude is that nothing that is now moving at less than the speed of light can be accelerated to or past that speed. It also says that, should there exist objects already moving faster than light, they could not be decelerated to speeds of less than c, and that the only objects that travel at the speed of light (such as photons) are those that have zero rest mass.

Mass and Energy

Time, distance, and mass—all quantities that we can easily measure in our homes or laboratories—actually depend on our frame of reference. But not everything in nature is so variable. The central tenet of relativity is that natural laws must apply to every frame of reference. Light speed is constant in all reference frames in accord with Maxwell's equations. Similarly, the first law of thermodynamics—the idea that total amount of energy in any closed system is constant—must hold, no matter what the frame of reference. Yet here, Einstein's description of the universe seems to run into a problem. He claims that the observed mass depends on your frame of reference. But, in that case, kinetic energy—defined as mass times velocity squared—could not follow the conservation of energy law. In Einstein's treatment, faster frames of reference seem to possess more energy than slower ones. Where does the extra energy come from?

Conservation of energy appeared to be violated because we missed one key form of energy in our equations: mass itself. In fact, Einstein was able to show that the amount of energy contained in any mass turns out to be the mass times a constant.

▶ **In words:** All objects contain a rest energy (in addition to any kinetic or potential energy), which is equal to the object's rest mass times the speed of light squared.

▶ **In equation form:**

$$\text{rest energy} = \text{rest mass} \times (\text{speed of light})^2$$

▶ **In symbols:**

$$E = mc^2$$

This familiar equation has become an icon of our nuclear age, for it defines a new form of energy. It says that mass can be converted to energy, and vice versa.

Furthermore, the amounts of energy involved are prodigious (because the constant, the speed of light squared, is so large). A handful of nuclear fuel can power a city; a fist-sized chunk of nuclear explosive can destroy it.

Until Einstein traced the implications of special relativity, the nature of mass and its vast potential for producing energy was hidden from us. Now nearly a quarter of all electrical power in the United States is produced in nuclear reactors that confirm the predictions of Einstein's theory every day of our lives (see Chapter 12).

General Relativity

Special relativity is a fascinating and fairly accessible intellectual exercise, requiring little more than an open mind and a lot of basic algebra. General relativity, which deals with all reference frames including accelerating ones, is much more challenging in its full rigor. While the details are tricky, you can get a pretty good feeling for Einstein's general theory by thinking about the nature of forces.

The Nature of Forces

Begin by imagining yourself in a completely sealed room that is accelerating at exactly one "g"—the Earth's gravitational acceleration. Could you devise any experiment that would reveal one way or the other if you were on Earth or accelerating in deep space?

If you dropped this book on Earth, the force of gravity would cause it to fall to your feet (Figure 7-6a). If you dropped the book in the accelerating spaceship, however, Newton's first law tells us that it will keep moving with whatever speed it had when it was released. The floor of the ship, still accelerating, will therefore come up to meet it (Figure 7-6b). To you, standing in the ship, it appears that the book falls, just as it does if you are standing on Earth.

From an external frame of reference, of course, these two situations would involve very different descriptions. In the one case the book falls due to the force of gravity; in the other the spaceship accelerates up to meet the free-floating book. But no experiment you could devise *in your reference frame* could distinguish between acceleration in deep space and the force of the Earth's gravitational field.

(a) On Earth

(b) In an accelerating spaceship

• **Figure 7-6** (*a*) If you drop a book on Earth, the force of gravity causes it to accelerate downward and fall at your feet. (*b*) If you dropped the same book in an accelerating spaceship, the floor of the ship will accelerate upward: the book will appear to fall at your feet.

In some deep and profound way, therefore, gravitational forces and acceleration are equivalent. Newton saw this connection in a way, for his laws of motion equate force with an accelerating mass. But Einstein went a step further by recognizing that what we call gravity versus what we call acceleration is a purely arbitrary decision, based on our choice of reference frame. Whether we think of ourselves as stationary on a planet with gravity, or accelerating on spaceship Earth, makes no difference in the passage of events.

Although this connection between gravity and acceleration may seem a bit abstract, you already have had experiences that should tell you it is true. Have you ever been in an elevator and felt momentarily heavier when it starts up or momentarily lighter when it starts down? If so, you know that the feeling we call "weight" can indeed be affected by acceleration.

The actual working out of the consequences of this notion of the equivalence of acceleration and gravity is complicated, but a simple analogy can help you visualize the difference between Einstein's and Newton's views of the universe. In the Newtonian universe, forces and motions can be described by a ball rolling on a perfectly flat surface with neatly inscribed grid lines (Figure 7-7a). The ball rolls on and on, following a line exactly, unless an external force is applied. If, for example, a large mass rests on the surface, the rolling ball will change its direction

• **Figure 7-7** Newtonian and Einsteinian universes treat the motion of rolling balls in different ways. In the Newtonian scheme (*a*), a ball travels in uniform motion unless acted upon by a force; motion occurs along curved paths in a flat universe. In the Einsteinian universe (*b*), a ball's mass distorts the universe; it moves in a straight line across a curved surface.

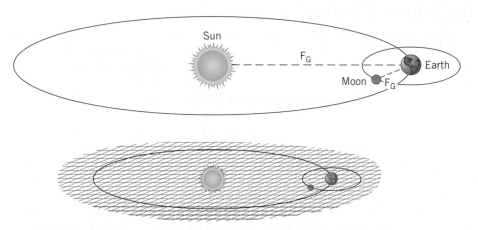

(*a*) Newtonian universe: gravitational forces in a "flat" universe

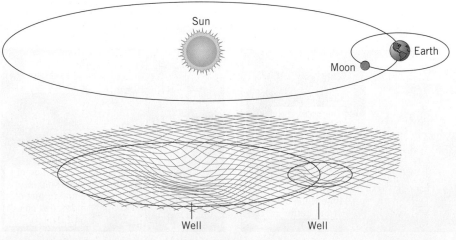

(*b*) Einstein's universe: motion in a curved universe.

and speed—it will accelerate in response to the force of gravity. Thus, for Newton, motion occurs along curving paths in a flat universe.

The description of that same event in general relativity is very different. In this case, as shown in Figure 7-7b, we would say that the heavy object distorts the surface. Peaks and depressions on the surface influence the ball's path, deflecting it as it rolls across the surface. For Einstein, the ball moves in a straight line across a curved universe.

Given these differing views, Newton and Einstein would give very different descriptions of physical events. Newton would say, for example, that the Moon orbits the Earth because of an attractive gravitational force between the two bodies (Figure 7-6a). Einstein, on the other hand, would say that space has been warped in the vicinity of the Earth–Moon system, and this warping of space governs the Moon's motion (Figure 7-6b). In the relativistic view, space deforms around the Sun, and planets follow the curvature of space like marbles rolling around in the bottom of a curved bowl.

We now have two very different ways of thinking about the universe. In the Newtonian universe, forces cause objects to accelerate. Space and time are separate dimensions that are experienced in very different ways. This view more closely matches our everyday experience of how the world seems to be. In Einstein's universe, objects move according to distortions in space, while the distinction between space and time depends on your frame of reference.

A computer-generated image of a gravity field reveals mass as gravity wells on an otherwise flat grid.

Predictions of General Relativity

The mathematical models of Newton and Einstein are not just two equivalent descriptions of the universe. They lead to slightly different quantitative predictions of events. In three specific instances, the predictions of general relativity have been confirmed.

1. The Gravitational Bending of Light
One consequence of Einstein's theory is that light can be bent as it travels along the warped space near strong gravitational centers such as the Sun. Einstein

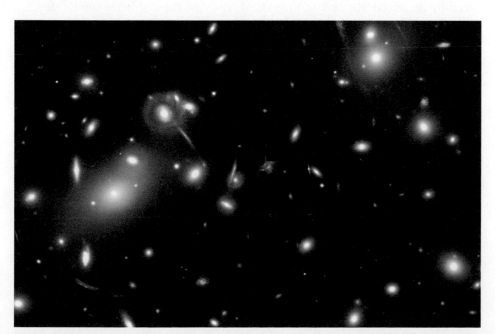

A gravitational lens. A distant massive object bends the light from even more distant objects beyond, causing multiple images.

predicted the exact amount of deflection that would occur near the Sun, and his prediction was confirmed by precise measurements of star positions during a solar eclipse in 1919. Today these measurements are made with much more precision by measuring the deflection of radio waves emitted by distant galaxies called quasars (see Chapter 18).

 Stop and Think! Given what you know about electromagnetic waves, do you think general relativity should predict that other waves—radio, for example—should be bent as they come around the Sun?

2. Planetary Orbits

In Newton's solar system, the planets adopt elliptical orbits, with long and short axes that rotate slightly because of the perturbing influence of other planets. Einstein's calculations make nearly the same prediction, but his axes advance slightly more than Newton's from orbit to orbit. In Einstein's theory, for example, the innermost planet, Mercury, was predicted to advance by 43 seconds of arc per century due to relativistic effects—a small perturbation superimposed on much larger effects due to the other planets. Einstein's prediction almost exactly matches the observed shift in Mercury's orbit.

3. The Gravitational Redshift

The theory of relativity predicts that as a photon (a particle of electromagnetic radiation) moves up in a gravitational field, it must lose energy in the process. The speed of light is constant, so this energy loss is manifest as a slight decrease in frequency (a slight increase in wavelength). Thus lights on the Earth's surface will appear slightly redder than they do on Earth if they are observed from space. By the same token, a light shining from space to the Earth will be slightly shifted to the blue end of the spectrum. Careful measurements of laser light frequencies have amply confirmed this prediction of relativity.

Recent advances in highly sensitive electronics are now providing more opportunities for researchers to measure the predictions of general relativity. One of the most intriguing tests will be conducted as part of a satellite mission in the late 1990s. Meticulously machined quartz spheres will be set into rotation and carefully measured. According to general relativity, these spheres should develop a small wobble as they rotate in the Earth's gravitational field. Sensitive electronics will detect any perturbations of this sort.

As scientists get better and better at making precision measurements, more and more tests of the extremely small differences between Newtonian and relativistic predictions of physical events can be made. A few years ago, for example, a group of scientists at institutions in the Washington, DC, area proposed an experiment in which light from a laser would be sent out over the city from the University of Maryland, reflected from a mirror on top of the National Cathedral, and received by detectors at the Naval Research Laboratory. Because of the rotation of the Earth, there should be a tiny difference in travel time between light traveling east and light traveling west. The theory of relativity predicts an additional, tinier difference as well. With good enough clocks and short enough laser pulses, these sorts of differences can be measured, and they provide just as good a check on general relativity as instruments in a satellite.

Who Can Understand Relativity?

Einstein's theory of relativity was extraordinary, but when first introduced was difficult to grasp in part because it relied on some complex mathematics that were unfamiliar to many scientists at the time. Furthermore, while the theory made specific predictions about the physical world, most of those predictions were exceedingly difficult to test. Soon after the theory's publication it became conventional wisdom that only a handful of geniuses in the world could understand it.

Einstein did make one very specific prediction, however, that could be tested. His proposal that the strong gravitational field of the Sun would bend the light coming from a distant star was different from other theories. The total eclipse of the Sun in 1919 gave scientists the chance to test Einstein's prediction. Sure enough, the apparent position of stars near the Sun's disk was shifted by exactly the predicted amount.

Around the world, front-page newspaper headlines trumpeted Einstein's success. He became an instant international celebrity and his theory of relativity became a part of scientific folklore. Attempts to explain the revolutionary theory to a wide audience began almost immediately.

Few scientists may have grasped the main ideas of general relativity in 1915, when the full theory was first unveiled, but that certainly is not true today. The basics of special relativity are taught to tens of thousands of college freshmen every year, while hundreds of students in astronomy and physics explore general relativity in its full mathematical splendor.

If this subject intrigues you, you might want to read some more, watch TV specials or videos about relativity, or even sign up for one of those courses!

Thinking More About | Relativity

Was Newton Wrong?

The theory of relativity describes a universe about which Isaac Newton never dreamed. Time dilation, contraction of moving objects, and mass as energy play no role in his laws of motion. Curved space–time is alien to the Newtonian view. Does that mean that Newton was wrong? Not at all.

In fact, all of Einstein's equations reduce exactly to Newton's laws of motion, at speeds significantly less than the speed of light. This feature was shown specifically for time dilation in the "Science by the Numbers" section in this chapter. Newton's laws, which have worked so well in describing our everyday world, fail only when dealing with extremely high velocities or extremely large masses. Thus Newton's laws represent an extremely important special case of Einstein's more general theory.

Science often progresses in this way, with one theory encompassing previous valid ideas. Newton, for example, merged discoveries by Galileo of Earth-based motions and Kepler's laws of planetary motion into his unified theory of gravity. And some day Einstein's theory of relativity may be incorporated into an even grander view of the universe.

SUMMARY

Every observer sees the world from a different *frame of reference*. Descriptions of actual physical events are different for different observers, but the *theory of relativity* states that all observers must see the universe operating according to the same laws. Because the speed of light is built into Maxwell's equations, this principle requires that all observers must see the same speed of light in their frames of reference.

Special relativity deals with observers who are not accelerating with respect to each other, while general relativity deals with observers in any frame of reference whatsoever. In special relativity, simple arguments lead to the conclusion that moving clocks appear to tick more slowly than stationary ones—a phenomenon known as *time dilation*. Furthermore, moving objects appear to get shorter in the direction of motion—the phenomenon of *length contraction*. Finally, moving objects become more massive than stationary ones, and an equivalence exists between mass and energy, as expressed by the famous equation, $E = mc^2$.

General relativity begins with the observation that the force of gravity is connected to acceleration, and describes a universe in which heavy masses warp the fabric of space–time and affect the motion of other objects. There are three classic tests of general relativity—the bending of light rays passing near the Sun, the changing orientation of the orbit of Mercury, and the redshift of light passing through a gravitational field.

KEY TERMS ABOUT RELATIVITY

frame of reference	special relativity	time dilation
theory of relativity	general relativity	length contraction

KEY EQUATIONS

Time dilation: $t_{MG} = \dfrac{t_{GG}}{\sqrt{[1 - (v/c)^2]}}$

Length contraction: $L_{MG} = L_{GG} \times \sqrt{[1 - (v/c)^2]}$

Mass effect: $m_{MG} = \dfrac{m_{GG}}{\sqrt{[1 - (v/c)^2]}}$

Rest mass: $E = mc^2$

REVIEW QUESTIONS

1. What is a frame of reference? Give examples of frames of reference you have been in today.

2. What is the central idea of Einstein's theory of relativity?

3. What is the difference between special and general relativity?

4. What is time dilation? How fast does something have to be moving for time dilation to be appreciable?

5. What is the Lorentz factor?

6. According to an observer on the ground, how does the length of a moving object compare to the length of an identical object on the ground? How does the mass compare?

7. What is the relation between the mass of an object and its energy?

8. How can we say that gravitational forces and acceleration are equivalent?

9. Explain three tests of general relativity. Are these the only tests possible?

10. According to Einstein's theory, which of the following factors depend on the frame of reference and which are constant? mass, distance, velocity of light, time, length.

DISCUSSION QUESTIONS

1. Imagine arriving by spaceship at the solar system for the first time. Identify three different frames of reference that you might choose to describe the Earth.

2. Did Einstein disprove Newton's laws of motion? Explain your answer.

3. In Chapter 2 we talked about the idea that Newton's work was profoundly in tune with the time in which he lived. In what sense might you say that relativity is in tune with the twentieth century?

4. The twentieth century has been called the age of relativism, where each person has his or her own ethical system and no set of values is absolute. Do you agree? Does the theory of relativity imply that no values are absolute?

PROBLEMS

1. You are traveling 80 km/h in your car when you throw a ball 50 km/h. What is the ball's apparent speed to a person standing by the road when the ball is thrown (a) straight ahead, (b) sideways, and (c) backward?

2. Calculate the Lorentz factor for objects traveling at 1%, 50%, and 99.9% of the speed of light.

3. What is the apparent mass of a 1-kg object that has been accelerated to 99% of light speed?

4. If a moving clock appears to be ticking half as fast as normal, at what percent of light speed is it traveling?

5. Draw a picture illustrating how a spaceship passing the Earth might look at 1%, 90%, and 99.9% of light speed.

INVESTIGATIONS

1. Read a biography of Albert Einstein. What were his major scientific contributions? For what work did he receive a Nobel prize?

2. Take a bathroom scale into an elevator in a tall building, stand on it, and record your weight under acceleration and deceleration. Why does the scale reading change?

3. Read the novel *Einstein's Dreams* by Alan Lightman. Each of the chapters explores different time–space relationships. Which chapters teach you something about Einstein's theory of relativity?

4. Investigate the influence of Einstein's theory of relativity on twentieth-century art and philosophy.

WWW RESOURCES

See *The Sciences* homepage at: **http://www.wiley.com/college/trefil** for valuable web links.

1. **http://www.westegg.com/einstein/**
   Albert Einstein Online—extensive links to pictures, quotes, letters, papers, physics, biography, and related sites.

2. **http://math.ucr.edu/home/baez/physics/**
   Usenet Relativity FAQs.

3. **http://www.pbs.org/wgbh/pages/nova/einstein/**
   Einstein Revealed, a comprehensive look at Einstein and his work from PBS.

8

The Atom

Why?

GREAT IDEA

All of the matter around us is made of atoms, the chemical building blocks of our world.

PHYSICS
Experiments reveal that atoms themselves are made of smaller particles.

CHEMISTRY
Elements in the periodic table are arranged according to the structure of their atoms.

GEOLOGY
Deep within the Earth, the element carbon is compressed into its densest form, the diamond. (Ch. 16)

ENVIRONMENT
Burning fossil fuels may release compounds of the element sulfur into the atmosphere, which leads to the formation of acid rain. (Ch. 19)

HEALTH & SAFETY
Atoms of heavy metal elements such as lead and mercury, when present in contaminated food and water, can build up gradually in the human body and produce toxic effects. (Ch. 18)

ASTRONOMY
The element helium was first discovered when its spectrum was seen in light from the Sun.

TECHNOLOGY
Laser beams are created when a collection of excited atoms releases photons.

BIOLOGY
Carbon, the sixth element of the periodic table, forms the backbone of most biological molecules. (Ch. 21)

Red = applications of the great idea discussed in this chapter.

Orange = other applications, some of which are explored in other chapters.

It's a beautiful day. As you drive down the road, into the open countryside, you open the window and take a deep breath of air. It's so relaxing to get away from school and work.

Breathing is so instinctive that we seldom stop to think about why we need oxygen. Oxygen is a chemical element, one of about a hundred basic building blocks that make up all the objects around us. With every breath you take, oxygen enters your body and sustains life by participating in chemical reactions that release the energy you use to grow, move, and think. Without an extremely active element like oxygen, these reactions couldn't take place. So our lives depend on oxygen, as well as many other kinds of atoms.

The Smallest Pieces

Imagine that you took a page from this book and cut it in half, then cut the half in half, cut half of the half in half, and so on. If paper is smooth and continuous, there would be no end to this process, no smallest piece of paper that couldn't be cut further. How could you tell if paper has a smallest piece?

The Greek Atom

In about 530 B.C., a group of Greek philosophers, the most famous of whom was a man named Democritus, gave this question some serious thought. Democritus argued (purely on philosophical grounds) that if you took the world's sharpest knife and started slicing chunks of matter, you would eventually come to a smallest piece—a piece that could not be divided further (Figure 8-1). He called this smallest piece the "atom," which translates roughly as "uncuttable." He argued that all material was formed from these atoms, and that the atoms are eternal and unchanging, but that the relationship between the atoms is constantly shifting.

 Stop and Think! What would happen to Democritus's argument if the dividing process never reached a smallest unit? Is such an outcome logically possible?

Elements

Modern atomic theory is generally attributed to an English meteorologist, John Dalton (1766–1844). In 1808, Dalton published a book called *New System of Chemical Philosophy,* in which he argued that the new knowledge being gained by

• **Figure 8-1** Repeatedly dividing a bar of gold, just like cutting paper repeatedly, produces smaller and smaller groups of atoms, until you come to a single gold atom. Dividing that atom into two parts produces fragments that no longer have the properties of gold.

Gold ingot   Gold nuggets   Gold dust

Ancient: All matter can be subdivided into atoms which cannot be subdivided further.

Modern: Further subdivision is possible, but the identity of the original element is lost.

Gold atom   Atomic fragments are not gold

chemists about materials provided evidence, in and of itself, that matter was composed of atoms. Chemists knew that most materials can be broken down into simpler chemicals. If you burn wood, for example, you get carbon dioxide, water, and all sorts of materials in the ash. If you use an electrical current to break down water, you get two gases, hydrogen and oxygen. Dalton and his contemporaries also recognized that a few materials, called **elements**, could not be broken down into other substances. Wood can be heated to get charcoal (essentially pure carbon), for example; but, try as you might, you can't break the carbon down any further.

The hypothesis that we now call *atomism* was very simple. Dalton suggested that for each chemical element there was a corresponding species of indivisible objects called **atoms**. He borrowed the name from the Greeks, but very little else. Two or more atoms stuck together form a **molecule**—the same term applies to any cluster of atoms that can be isolated, whether it contains two atoms or a thousand. Molecules make up most of the different kinds of material we see around us. Water, for example, forms from one oxygen atom and two hydrogen atoms (thus, the familiar H_2O). In Dalton's view, atoms were truly indivisible—he thought of them as little bowling balls (Figure 8-2). In Dalton's world, then, indivisible atoms provide the fundamental building blocks of all matter.

• **Figure 8-2** Atoms may be envisioned as solid balls that stack together to form crystals, like fruit at the supermarket. Atomic models are often drawn with spheres, though we now know that atoms are not solid objects.

Are Atoms Real?

Democritus and other Greek philosophers did not really engage in science—their reasoning lacked the interplay between observation and hypothesis that characterizes the scientific method. In fact, it wasn't until the beginning of the twentieth century that most scientists became convinced that atoms are real.

No matter how persuasively argued, philosophical speculations on the nature of matter and the existence of atoms were just that—speculations. Over the past three centuries, increasingly convincing evidence has mounted for the reality of atoms. Here are some examples of this growing body of evidence.

1. *The behavior of gas:* The Swiss physicist Daniel Bernoulli (1700–1782) realized that if atoms are real, they must have mass and velocity, and thus kinetic energy. He successfully applied Newton's second law of motion to atoms to explain the behavior of gases under pressure. Doubling the number of gas particles, or halving the volume, doubles the number of collisions between the gas and the confining walls. This increase also doubles the pressure, the force per unit area. Increasing temperature increases the average velocity of the gas particles, also increasing pressure.

2. *Chemical combinations:* English scientist John Dalton advanced the atomic theory based on the law of definite proportions—an empirical law that states that for any given compound, elements combine in a specific ratio of weights: water is always 8 parts oxygen to 1 part hydrogen. Furthermore, when two elements combine in more than one way, the ratios of weights for the two compounds will be a small whole number: 12 pounds of carbon can thus combine with either 32 pounds of oxygen or 64 pounds of oxygen. Dalton realized, therefore, that compounds don't generally have arbitrary fractional ratios of elements. The implication is that some units of elements are fundamentally indivisible.

3. *Radioactivity:* The discovery in 1896 of radioactivity, by which individual atoms emit radiation, provided a compelling piece of evidence for the atomic theory (see Chapter 12). Certain phosphors flash when hit by this radiation. In 1903, upon seeing the irregular twinkling caused by this effect, even the most vocal skeptics of the atomic theory had to take pause.

4. *Brownian motion:* Brownian motion is an erratic, jiggling motion observed in tiny dust particles of pollen grains suspended in water. In 1905 Albert Einstein (1879–1955) demonstrated mathematically that such motions must result from a force—the force of random collisions of atoms. Einstein realized that any small object suspended in liquid would be constantly bombarded by moving atoms. At any given moment, there will, purely by chance, be more atoms hitting on one side than the other. The object will be pushed toward the side with fewer collisions. A moment later, however, more atoms will be hitting another surface, and the object will change direction. Over time, Einstein argued, atomic collisions would produce precisely the sort of erratic motion that you see through a microscope.

   Einstein used the mathematics of statistics to make a number of predictions about how fast and how far the suspended grains would move, based on the hypothesis that the motion was due to collisions with real atoms. These were predictions that other scientists could test in a laboratory. French physicist Jean Baptiste Perrin (1870–1942) published the results of his careful experiments on Brownian motion in 1909. His results agreed with Einstein's calculations, and thus convinced many scientists of the reality of atoms.

   Note that, in spite of the variety of evidence for atoms, to this point all of this evidence was indirect. Matter was observed to behave *as if* it was made of atoms, but atoms, themselves, had not been directly observed.

5. *X-ray crystallography:* X-ray crystallography, developed in 1912, convinced any remaining skeptics by demonstrating the sizes and regular arrangements of atoms in crystals. X-rays can't bounce off of hypothetical ideas, so these images were further proof that atoms are real physical objects.

6. *Atomic-scale microscopy:* In 1980 the first photograph of an individual atom was taken at the University of Heidelberg in Germany. This image was produced by an instrument called a scanning tunneling microscope, which detects tiny flows of electrons in a microscopic needle placed next to a solid surface. Now, observational studies of individual atoms are undertaken around the world (Figure 8-3).

 Stop and Think! When in the chain of historical events would you have been willing to believe that atoms are real? When Dalton explained the existence of elements? When Einstein explained Brownian motion? When you were shown a picture like the one in Figure 8-3? Never? What does it take to make something "real"? And, finally, does it make a difference to science whether atoms are real?

Discovering Chemical Elements

Describing and isolating chemical elements provided a major challenge for chemists of the nineteenth century. In 1800, fewer than 30 elements had been isolated—not enough to establish any systematic trends in their chemical behavior. In the early 1800s, a new process that broke molecules down into atoms was developed. Called *electrolysis* ("splitting by electricity"), it was facilitated by Volta's invention of the battery (see Chapter 5) and allowed many new elements to be separated by means of electrical current. More than two dozen more elements thus were discovered in the first half of the nineteenth century.

Dimitri Mendeleev's invention of the first periodic table of the elements in 1869 (see Chapter 1) capitalized on these discoveries, and it became a powerful tool for predicting more new elements. The original table listed several dozen elements on the basis of their atomic weights (in rows from the upper left) and by groups with distinctive chemical properties (in columns). What Mendeleev could not know was that his table revealed much about the underlying structure of atoms and their electrons.

In the early 1800s, the list of known chemical elements was rapidly expanding, but contained only a few dozen entries. Today, the periodic table lists 112 elements, of which 92 appear in nature and the rest have been produced artificially. Most of the materials we encounter in everyday life are not elements, but

• **Figure 8-3** This electronic image representing individual atoms was taken with an instrument called a scanning probe microscope. The "mountains" correspond to individual atoms in a crystal.

compounds of two or more elements bound together. Table salt, plastics, stainless steel, paint, window glass, and soap are all made from a combination of elements.

Nevertheless, we do have experience with a few chemical elements in our everyday lives.

- *Helium:* A light gas that has many uses besides filling party balloons and blimps. In liquid form, helium is used to maintain superconductors at low temperatures (see Chapter 11).
- *Carbon:* Pencil lead, charcoal, and diamonds are all examples of pure carbon. The differences between these materials have to do with the way the atoms of carbon are linked together, as we discuss in Chapter 11.
- *Aluminum:* A lightweight metal used for many purposes. The dull white surface of the metal is actually a combination of aluminum and oxygen, but if you scratch the surface, the shiny material underneath is pure elemental aluminum.
- *Copper:* The reddish metal of pennies and pots. Copper wire provides a cheap and efficient conductor of electricity.
- *Gold:* A soft, yellow, dense, and highly valued metal. For thousands of years the element gold has been coveted as a symbol of wealth. Today it coats critical electrical contacts in spacecraft and other sophisticated electronics.

Although we know of more than 90 different elements in nature, many natural systems are constructed from just a few. Six elements—oxygen, silicon, magnesium, iron, aluminum, and calcium—account for almost 99% of the solid

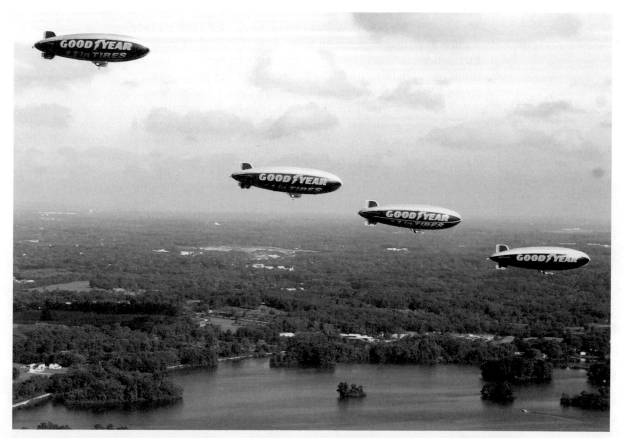

Helium-filled blimps.

Earth's mass. Most of the atoms in your body are hydrogen, carbon, oxygen, or nitrogen, with smaller but important roles played by phosphorus and sulfur. And most stars are formed almost entirely from the lightest element, hydrogen.

 Stop and Think! Look around you. How many different elements do you see? How many different compounds? Is it reasonable that there should be so many more compounds than elements? Why or why not?

The Structure of the Atom

Dalton's idea of the atom as a single indivisible entity was not destined to last. In 1897, English physicist Joseph John Thomson (1856–1940) unambiguously identified a particle called the **electron**, an object that has a negative electrical charge and is much smaller and lighter than even the smallest atom known. Because there was no place from which a particle such as the electron could come, other than inside the atom, Thomson's discovery provided incontrovertible evidence for what people had suspected for a long time. Atoms are not the fundamental building blocks of matter, but rather are made up of things that are smaller and more fundamental still. Table 8-1 summarizes some of the important terms related to atoms.

The Atomic Nucleus

The most important discovery about the structure of the atom was made by New Zealand–born physicist Ernest Rutherford (1871–1937) and his coworkers in Manchester, England, in 1911. The basic idea of the experiment is sketched in Figure 8-4. The experiment started with a piece of radioactive material—matter that sends out energetic particles (see Chapter 12). For our purposes, you can think of radioactive materials as sources of tiny subatomic "bullets." The particular material that Rutherford used produced bullets that scientists had named *alpha particles,* which are thousands of times heavier than electrons. By arranging the apparatus as shown, Rutherford produced a stream of these subatomic bullets moving toward the right in the figure. In front of this stream, he placed a thin foil of gold.

The experiment was designed to measure something about the way atoms were put together. At the time, people believed that the small, negatively charged electrons were scattered around the entire atom, more or less like raisins in a bun. Rutherford was trying to shoot bullets into the "bun" and see what happened.

What the experiment revealed was little short of astonishing. Almost all the subatomic bullets either passed right through the gold foil unaffected or were

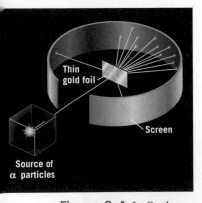

• **Figure 8-4** In Rutherford's experiment, a beam of radioactive particles was scattered by atomic nuclei in a piece of gold foil. A lead shield protected researchers from the radiation.

Table 8-1 Important Terms Related to Atoms

Element	A chemical substance that cannot be broken down further
Atom	The smallest particle that retains its chemical identity
Molecule	Any collection of two or more atoms bound together
Electron	An atomic particle with negative charge and low mass
Nucleus	The small, massive central part of an atom
Proton	Positively charged nuclear particle
Neutron	Electrically neutral nuclear particle
Ion	An electrically charged atom

scattered through very small angles. This result is easy to interpret: it means that most of the heavy alpha particles passed through spaces in between gold atoms, and that those that hit the gold atoms were only moderately deflected by the relatively low-density material in them.

One alpha particle in a thousand, however, was scattered through a large angle; some even bounced straight back. After almost two years of puzzling over these extraordinary results, Rutherford concluded that a large part of each atom's mass is located in a very small, compact object at the center—what he called the **nucleus**. About 999 times out of 1000 the alpha particles either missed the atom completely or went through the low-density material in the outer reaches of the atom. About 1 time out of 1000, however, the alpha particle hit the nucleus and was bounced through a large angle.

You can think of the Rutherford experiment in this way. If the atom were a large ball of mist or vapor with a diameter greater than a skyscraper, and the nucleus was a bowling ball at the center of that sphere of mist, then most bullets shot at the atom would go right through. Only those that hit the bowling ball would be bounced through large angles. In this analogy, of course, the bowling ball plays the part of the nucleus, while the mist is the domain of the electrons.

As a result of Rutherford's work, a new picture of the atom emerged, one that is very familiar to us. Rutherford described a small, dense, positively charged nucleus sitting at the atom's center, with light, negatively charged electrons circling it, like planets orbiting the Sun. Indeed, Rutherford's discovery has become an icon of the modern age, adorning everyday objects from postage stamps to bathroom cleaners (Figure 8-5).

Later on, physicists discovered that the nucleus itself is made up primarily of two different kinds of particles (see Chapter 11). One of these carries a positive charge and is called a *proton*. The other, whose existence was not confirmed until 1932, carries no electrical charge and is called a *neutron*.

For each positively charged proton in the nucleus of the atom, there is normally one negatively charged electron "in orbit." Thus the electrical charges of the electrons and the protons cancel out, and every atom is electrically neutral. In some cases, atoms either lose or gain electrons. In this case, they acquire an electrical charge and are called *ions*.

• **Figure 8-5** The Nuclear Regulatory Commission uses a highly stylized atomic model as its logo.

Why the Rutherford Atom Couldn't Work

The picture of the atom that Rutherford developed is intellectually appealing, particularly because it recalls to us the familiar orbits of planets in our solar system. We have already learned enough about the behavior of nature, however, to know that the atom that is described in the text could not possibly exist in nature. Why do we say this?

We learned in Chapter 2 that an object traveling in a circular orbit is constantly being accelerated—it is not in uniform motion because it is continually changing direction. Furthermore, we learned in Chapter 5 that any accelerated electrical charge must give off electromagnetic radiation, as a consequence of Maxwell's equations. Thus, if an atom was of the Rutherford type, the electrons moving in their orbits would constantly be giving off energy in the form of electromagnetic radiation. This energy, according to the first law of thermodynamics, would have to come from somewhere (remember conservation of energy!), so the electrons would gradually spiral in toward the nucleus as they gave up their energy to electromagnetic radiation. Eventually, the electrons would have to fall into the nucleus and the atom would cease to exist in the form we know.

In fact, if you put in the numbers, the life expectancy of the Rutherford atom turns out to be less than a second. Given the fact that many atoms have survived billions of years, since almost the beginning of the universe, this calculation poses a serious problem for the simple orbital model of the atom.

When Matter Meets Light

Almost from its inception, the Rutherford model of the atom encountered difficulties. Some of the problems involved its violations of fundamental physical laws as we have described, whereas others were more mundane—the Rutherford atom simply did not explain all the behavior of atoms that scientists knew about. The first decades of the twentieth century was a period of tremendous ferment in the sciences as people scrambled to find a new way of describing the nature of atoms.

The Bohr Atom

In 1913, Niels Bohr (1885–1962), a young Danish physicist working in England, produced the first model of the atom that avoided the kinds of objections encountered by Rutherford's model. The **Bohr atom** is very strange: it does not match well with our intuition about the way things "ought to be" in the real world. The only thing in the Bohr atom's favor was that it worked.

Bohr's insight began with an educated guess about the distinctive way in which hot hydrogen atoms give off light. Hydrogen gas glows by giving off light in several separate wavelengths, rather than in a continuous range of wavelengths.

Niels Bohr (1885–1962) with Aage Bohr, one of his five sons. Both won Nobel prizes in physics.

The young Bohr was deeply immersed in studying this emission of light and the way that atoms interact with light and other forms of electromagnetic radiation. He realized that one way of explaining what he saw in the laboratory was that electrons circling the nucleus, unlike planets circling the Sun, could not maintain their orbits at just any distance from the center. He suggested that there were only certain orbits—he called them "allowed orbits"—located at specified distances from the center of the atom in which an electron could exist for long periods of time *without giving off radiation*. (We prefer to use "electron energy levels" or "electron shells," rather than "allowed orbits," when describing the distribution of electrons in atoms, because the idea of electron orbits of any kind is conceptually misleading.) Bohr's picture of the atom is shown in Figure 8-6. The idea is that the electron can exist at a specific distance r_1 from the nucleus, or at a distance r_2 or r_3, and so on, each distance corresponding to a different electron energy level. As long as the electron remains at one of those distances, its energy is fixed. In the Bohr atomic model, the electron cannot ever, at any time, exist at any place between these allowed distances.

One way to think about the Bohr atom is to imagine what happens when you climb a flight of steps. You can stand on the first step or you can stand on the second step. It's very hard, however, to imagine what it would be like to stand somewhere between two steps. In just the same way, an electron can be in the first energy level, or in the second allowed energy level, and so on, but it can't be in between these allowed energy levels. In terms of energy, both the steps and the electrons in an atom may be represented by a simple pictorial description (Figure 8-7). Each time you change steps in your home, your gravitational potential energy changes. Similarly, each time an electron changes levels, its energy changes.

An electron in an atom can be in any one of a number of allowed energy levels, each corresponding to a different distance from the nucleus. You would have to exert a force over a distance to move an electron from one allowed energy level to another, just as your muscles have to exert a force to get you up a flight of stairs. Thus, the allowed energy levels of an atom occur as a series of steps as shown in the figure. An electron in the lowest energy level is said to be in the *ground state*, while all energy levels above the ground state are called *excited states*.

• **Figure 8-6** A schematic diagram of the Bohr atom showing the first three energy levels and respective distances (r_1, r_2, and r_3) from the nucleus.

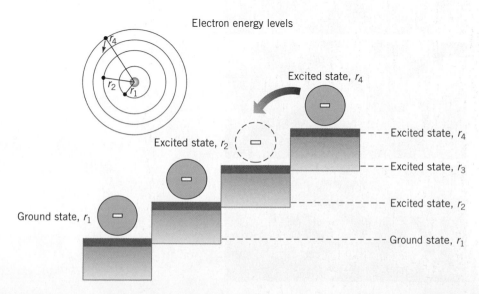

Electron energy levels

Excited state, r_4

Excited state, r_2

Ground state, r_1

Excited state, r_4

Excited state, r_3

Excited state, r_2

Ground state, r_1

• **Figure 8-7** Stairs provide an analogy to energy changes associated with electrons in the Bohr atom.

Photons: Particles of Light

One major feature of the Bohr atom is that an electron in a higher energy level can move down into an available lower energy level. This process is analogous to that by which a ball at the top of a flight of stairs can bounce down the stairs under the influence of gravity.

Assume that an electron is in an excited state, as shown in Figure 8-8. The electron can move to the lowest state, but if it does, something must happen to the extra energy. Energy can't just disappear. This realization was Bohr's great insight. The energy that's left over when the electrically charged electron moves from a higher state to a lower state is emitted by the atom in the form of a single packet of electromagnetic radiation—a particle-like bundle of light called a **photon**. Every time an electron jumps from a higher to a lower energy level, a photon moves away at the speed of light.

The concept of a photon raises a perplexing question: Is light—Maxwell's electromagnetic radiation—a wave or a particle? We will explore this puzzle at some length in Chapter 9, once we have learned more about the behavior of atoms.

The interaction of atoms and electromagnetic radiation provides the most compelling evidence for the Bohr atom. If electrons are in excited states, and if they make transitions to lower states, then photons are emitted. If we look at a group of atoms in which these transitions are occurring, we will see light or other electromagnetic radiation. Thus when you look at the flame of a fire or the glowing heating coil of an electric stove in your kitchen, you are actually seeing photons that were emitted by electrons jumping between allowed states in that material's atoms.

Not only does the Bohr atom give us a picture of how matter emits radiation, it provides an explanation for how matter absorbs radiation. Start with an electron in a low-energy state, perhaps its ground state. If a photon arrives that has

• **Figure 8-8** Electrons may jump between the energy levels shown in (*a*) and, in the process, (*b*) absorb or (*c*) emit energy in the form of a photon.

just the right amount of energy so that it can raise the electron to a higher energy (the next step up), the photon can be absorbed and the electron will be pushed up to an excited state. Absorption of light is something like a mirror image of light emission.

Our picture of the interaction of matter and radiation is exceedingly simple, but two key ideas are embedded in it. For one thing, when an electron moves from one allowed state to another, it cannot ever, at any time, be at any place in between. This rule is built into the definition of an allowed energy level. This means that the electron must somehow disappear from its original location and reappear in its final location *without ever having to traverse any of the positions in between*. This process, called a **quantum leap** or **quantum jump**, cannot be visualized, but it is something that seems to be fundamental in nature—an example of the "quantum weirdness" of nature at the atomic scale that we'll discuss in Chapter 9.

The second key idea is that if an electron is in an excited state, it can, in principle, get back down to the ground state in a number of different ways. Look at Figure 8-9. An electron in the upper energy level can move to the ground state by making one large jump and emitting a single photon with large energy. Alternatively, it can move to the ground state by making two smaller jumps, as shown. Each of these jumps emits a photon of somewhat less energy. The energies emitted in the two different jumps will generally be different from each other, but the sum of the two energies will equal that of the single large jump. If we had a large collection of atoms of this kind, we would expect that some electrons would make the large leap while others would make the two smaller ones. Thus, when we look at a collection of these atoms, we would measure three different energies of photons.

This curious behavior of electron energy levels helps to explain the familiar phenomenon of fluorescence that we introduced in Chapter 6. Recall that the energy of electromagnetic radiation is related to its frequency. In fluorescence, the atom in Figure 8-9 absorbs a higher-energy photon of ultraviolet radiation (which our eyes can't detect). The atom then emits two lower-energy photons, at least one of which is in the visible range. Consequently, by shining ultraviolet "black light" on the fluorescent material, it glows with a bright color.

• **Figure 8-9** An electron can jump from a higher to lower energy level in a single quantum leap (*a*), or by multiple quantum leaps (*b*).

A key point about the Bohr atom is that energy is required to lift an electron from the ground state to any excited state. This energy has to come from somewhere. We have already mentioned one possibility: that the atom will absorb a photon of just the right frequency to raise the electron to a higher energy level. There are other possibilities, however. If the material is heated, for example, atoms will move fast, gain kinetic energy, and undergo energetic collisions. In these collisions, an atom can absorb energy, and then use that energy to move electrons to a higher state. This explains why materials often glow when they are heated.

An Intuitive Leap

Bohr first proposed his model of the atom based on an intuition guided by experiments and ideas about the behavior of things in the subatomic world. In some ways the Bohr model was completely unlike anything we experience in the macroscopic world; indeed, the model seemed to some a little bit "crazy." It took two decades for scientists to develop a theory called *quantum mechanics* that showed why electrons can exist only in Bohr's "allowed orbits" and not in between. We will discuss this justification for the Bohr atom in Chapter 9, but it should be remembered that the justification occurred long after the initial hypothesis. The Bohr atom was accepted by physicists because it worked—it explained what they saw in nature and allowed them to make predictions about the behavior of real matter.

How could Bohr have come up with such a strange picture of the atom? He was undoubtedly guided by some of the early work that would lead to the theory of quantum mechanics (see Chapter 9). In the end, however, this explanation is unsatisfactory. Many people at the time studied the interactions of atoms and light, but only Bohr was able to make the leap of intuition to his description of the atom. This insight, like Newton's realization that gravity might extend to the orbit of the Moon, remains one of the great intuitive achievements of the human mind.

The elements (*a*) sodium, (*b*) potassium, and (*c*) lithium impart distinctive colors to a flame.

(*a*)   (*b*)   (*c*)

Stop and Think! How are intuitive leaps, such as the one made by Bohr, consistent or not consistent with the scientific method as described in Chapter 1?

Spectroscopy

Whenever energy is added to a system with many atoms in it, electrons in some atoms jump to excited states. As time goes by, these electrons will make quantum leaps down to the ground state, giving off photons or heat energy as they do. If some of those photons are in the range of visible light, the source will appear to glow.

You may not realize it, but you have looked at such collections of atoms all your life. Common mercury vapor street lamps contain bulbs filled with mercury gas. When the gas is heated, electrons are moved up to excited states. When they jump down, they emit photons that give the lamp a bluish-white color. Other types of streetlights, often used at freeway interchanges, use bulbs filled with sodium atoms. When sodium is excited, the most frequently emitted photons lie in the yellow range, so the lamps look yellow.

Yet another place where you can see photons emitted directly by quantum leaps is in Day-Glo colors, the vivid colors often used in sports clothing and advertising. From these examples, you can draw two conclusions: (1) quantum leaps are very much in evidence in your everyday life, and (2) different atoms give off different characteristic photons.

The second of these two facts is extremely important for scientists. If you think about the structure of an atom, the idea that different atoms emit and absorb different characteristic photons shouldn't be too surprising. Electron energy levels depend on the electrical attraction between the nucleus and the electrons, just as the orbits of the planets depend on the gravitational attraction between the planets and the Sun. Different nuclei have different numbers of protons, so electrons circling them are in different energy levels. In fact, the energy between the allowed energy levels within the atom is different in each of the hundred or so different chemical elements. Because the energy and frequency of photons emitted by an atom depend on the differences in energy between these levels, each chemical element emits a distinct set of characteristic photons.

You can think of the collection of characteristic photons emitted by each chemical element as a kind of "fingerprint"—something that is distinctive for that chemical element and none other. This feature opens up a very interesting possibility. The total collection of photons emitted by a given atom is called its **spectrum**, a characteristic fingerprint that can be used to identify chemical elements even when they are very difficult to identify by any other means.

In practice, the identification process works like this: Light from the gaseous atoms is spread out by being passed through a prism (Figure 8-10). Each possible quantum jump corresponds to light at a specific wavelength, so each type of atom produces a set of lines, as shown in Figure 8-11. This spectrum is the atomic fingerprint.

The Bohr picture suggests that if an atom gives off light of a specific wavelength and energy, then it will also *absorb* light at that wavelength. The emission and absorption processes, after all, may involve quantum jumps between the same two energy levels but in different directions. Thus if white light shines through a material containing a particular kind of atom, certain wavelengths of light will be absorbed. Observing that light on the other side of the material, you will see

• **Figure 8-10** A glass prism spreads out the colors of the visible spectrum.

certain colors missing. The dark areas corresponding to the absorbed wavelengths are called *absorption lines.* This set of lines is as much an atomic fingerprint as the set of colors that the atoms emit. And, although the use of visible light is very common, these arguments hold for radiation in any part of the electromagnetic spectrum.

Spectroscopy has become a standard tool that is used in almost every branch of science. Astronomers use emission spectra to find the chemical composition of

Atomic hydrogen (H)

Sodium (Na)

Neon (Ne)

• **Figure 8-11** Line spectra, shown here for hydrogen, sodium, and neon, provide distinctive fingerprints for elements and compounds.

distant stars, and they study absorption lines to determine the chemical composition of interstellar dust and the atmospheres of the outer planets. Spectroscopic analysis is also used in manufacturing to search for impurities on production lines, and by police departments to identify small traces of unknown materials when conducting investigations.

THE SCIENCE OF LIFE •

Spectra of Life's Chemical Reactions

In a classic set of experiments in the early 1940s, scientists used spectroscopy to work out in detail how chemical reactions governed by large molecules called enzymes (see Chapter 21) proceed in cells. In these experiments, a fluid containing the materials undergoing the chemical reactions was allowed to flow down a tube. The farther down the tube the fluid was, the farther along the reaction was. By measuring spectra at different points along the tube, scientists were able to follow the change in the behavior of electrons as the chemical reactions went along. In this way, part of the enormously complex problem of understanding the chemistry of life was unraveled.

More recently, scientists have begun to develop instruments that can use the principles of spectroscopy to identify pollutants emitted by automobile tailpipes as the cars drive by. If they are successful, we will have a major new tool in our battle against air pollution and acid rain (see Chapter 19). •

SCIENCE IN THE MAKING •

The Story of Helium

You have probably experienced helium, perhaps to inflate party balloons. Helium gas turns out to be a very interesting material, not only for its properties (it's less dense than air, so it floats up), but because of the history of its discovery.

The word helium refers to *helios*, the Greek word for Sun, because helium was first discovered in spectral lines in the Sun in 1868 by English scientist Joseph Norman Lockyer (1836–1920). Helium is very rare in Earth's atmosphere, and before Lockyer's discovery scientists were not even aware of its existence. Following the discovery, there was a period of about 30 years when astronomers accepted the fact that the element helium existed in the Sun, but were unable to find it on the Earth.

This supposition led to a very interesting problem. Could it be that there were chemical elements on the Sun that simply did not exist on our own planet? If so, it would call into question our ability to understand the rest of the universe, for the simple reason that if we don't know what an element is and can't isolate it in our laboratories, then we can never really be sure that we understand its properties. In fact, the existence of helium on Earth wasn't confirmed until 1895, when Lockyer identified its spectrum in a sample of radioactive material. •

TECHNOLOGY •

The Laser

The Bohr atom provides an excellent way of understanding the workings of one of the most important devices in modern science and industry—the laser. The word *laser* is an acronym for *light amplification by stimulated emission of radiation*. At the core of every laser is a collection of atoms—a crystal of ruby, perhaps,

• **Figure 8-12** Lasers produce a beam of light when one photon stimulates the emission of other photons.

or a gas enclosed in a glass tube. The term "stimulated emission" refers to a process that goes on when light and these atoms interact. If an electron is in an excited state, as shown in Figure 8-12, and one photon of just the right energy passes nearby, the electron may be stimulated to make the jump to a lower energy state, thus releasing a second photon. By "just the right energy" for the first photon, we mean a photon whose energy corresponds to the energy gap between two electron energy levels in the atom.

Furthermore, the stimulated atom emits photons in a special way. Remember that light is a form of electromagnetic radiation that can be described as a wave. In a laser, the crests of all the emitted photon waves line up exactly with the crests of the first photon, and the signal is enhanced by constructive interference. In the language of the physicists, we say that the photons are "coherent." Thus in stimulated emission, you have one photon at the beginning of the process and two coherent photons at the end.

Now suppose that you have a collection of atoms where most of the electrons are in the excited state, as shown in Figure 8-13. If a single photon of the correct frequency enters this system from the left and moves to the right, it will pass the first atom and stimulate the emission of a second photon. You will then have two photons moving to the right. As these photons encounter other atoms, they, too, stimulate emission so that you have four photons. It's not hard to see that light amplification in a laser will happen very quickly, cascading so that soon there is

• **Figure 8-13** The action of a laser. Electrons in the laser's atoms are continuously "pumped" into an excited state by an outside energy source, and the beam of photons is released when the electrons return to their ground state.

a flood of photons moving to the right through the collection of atoms. Energy added to the system from outside continuously returns atoms to their excited state—a process called *pumping*—so that more and more coherent photons can be produced.

In a laser, the collection of excited atoms is bounded on two sides by mirrors so that photons moving to the right hit the mirror, are reflected, and make another pass through the material, stimulating even more emission of photons as they go. If a photon happens to be lined up exactly perpendicular to the mirrors at the end of the laser, it will continue bouncing back and forth. If its direction is off by even a small angle, however, it will eventually bounce out through the sides of the laser and be lost. Thus only those photons that are exactly aligned will wind up bouncing back and forth between the mirrors, constantly amplifying the signal. Aligned photons will traverse the laser millions of times, building up an enormous cascade of coherent photons in the system.

The mirrors are designed to be partially reflective—perhaps 95% of the photons that hit the mirror are reflected back into the laser. The remaining 5% of photons that leak out form the familiar laser beam, which is made of intense, coherent light.

Laser beams have been applied in thousands of uses in science and industry since their development in the 1960s. Low-power lasers are ideal for optical scanners, such as the ones in supermarket checkout lines, and they make ideal light pointers for lectures and slide shows. The fact that the beam of light travels in a straight line makes the laser invaluable in surveying over long distances—for example, modern subway tunnels are routinely surveyed by using lasers to provide a straight line underground. Lasers are also used to detect movement of seismic faults in order to predict earthquakes (see Chapter 17). In this case, a laser is directed across the fault, so that small motions of the ground are easily measured. Finely focused laser beams have revolutionized delicate procedures such as eye surgery. Much more powerful lasers can transfer large amounts of energy. They are often used as cutting tools in factories, as well as implements for performing some kinds of surgery. The military has also adopted laser technology, in targeting and range finders, and in designs for futuristic energy beam weapons.

From the point of view of science, however, lasers are important because they enable us to make extremely precise measurements of atomic structures and properties. Almost all modern studies of the atom depend in some way on the laser. •

Lasers such as this argon laser have many uses. Light generated in the laser is carried by fiber optic cable for use in surgery on the human ear.

Lasers are used by astronomers to align and focus telescopes.

The Periodic Table of the Elements

The **periodic table of the elements**, which systematizes all known chemical elements, provides a powerful conceptual framework for understanding the structure and interaction of atoms. Dmitri Mendeleev, the Russian scientist who studied the regularity or periodicity in the known chemical elements (see Chapter 1), related that periodicity to each element's atomic properties. Today, each element is assigned an integer, called the *atomic number,* which defines the sequence of elements in the table. The atomic number corresponds to the number of protons in the atom, or, equivalently, if the atom is not charged, to the number of electrons surrounding the nucleus. If you arrange the elements as shown in Figure 8-14, with elements getting progressively heavier as you read from left to right and top to bottom as in a book, then elements in the same vertical column have very similar chemical properties.

Periodic Chemical Properties

The most striking characteristic of the periodic table is the similarity of elements in any given column. In the far left-hand column of the table, for example, are highly reactive elements called *alkali metals* (lithium, sodium, potassium, etc.). Each of these soft, silvery elements forms compounds (called *salts*) by combining in a one-to-one ratio with any of the elements in the seventh column (fluorine, chlorine, bromine, etc.). Water dissolves these compounds, which include sodium chloride, or table salt.

The elements in the second column, including beryllium, magnesium, and calcium, are metallic elements called the *alkaline earths,* and they too display

• **Figure 8-14** The periodic table of the elements. The weights of the elements increase from left to right. Each vertical column groups elements with similar chemical properties.

similar chemical properties among themselves. These elements, for example, combine with oxygen in a one-to-one ratio to form colorless compounds with very high melting temperatures.

Elements in the far right-hand column (helium, neon, argon, and so on), by contrast, are all colorless, odorless gases that are almost impossible to coax into any kind of chemical reaction. These so-called *noble gases* find applications when ordinary gases are too reactive. Helium lifts blimps, because the only other lighter-than-air gas is the dangerous, explosive element hydrogen. Argon fills incandescent lightbulbs, because nitrogen or oxygen would react with the hot filament.

In the late nineteenth century, scientists knew that the periodic table "worked"—it organized the 63 elements known at that time and implied the existence of others—but they had no idea *why* it worked. Their faith in the periodic table was buttressed by the fact that, when Mendeleev first wrote it down, there were holes in the table—places where he predicted elements should go, but for which no element was known. The ensuing search for the missing kinds of atoms produced the elements we now call scandium (in 1876) and germanium (in 1886).

Why the Periodic Table Works: Electron Shells

With the advent of Bohr's atomic model and its modern descendants, we finally have some understanding of why the periodic table works. We now realize that the pattern of elements in the periodic table mirrors the spatial arrangement of electrons around the atom's nucleus—a concentric arrangement of electrons into *shells*.

The atom is largely empty space. When two atoms come near enough to each other to undergo a chemical reaction—a carbon atom and an oxygen atom in a burning piece of coal, for example—electrons in the outermost shells meet each other first. We will see in Chapter 10 that these outermost electrons govern the chemical properties of materials. We have to understand the behavior of these electrons if we want to understand the periodic table.

To do this, we need to know one more curious fact about electrons. Electrons are particles that obey what is called the *Pauli exclusion principle*, which says that no two electrons can occupy the same energy state at the same time. One analogy is to compare electrons to cars in a parking lot. Each car takes up one space, and once a space is filled, no other car can go there. Electrons behave just the same way. Once an electron fills a particular niche in the atom, no other electron can occupy the same niche. A parking lot can be full long before all the actual space in the lot is taken up with cars, because the driveways and spaces between cars must remain empty. So, too, a given electron shell can be filled with electrons long before all the available space is filled.

In fact, it turns out that there are only two spaces that an electron can fill in the innermost electron shell, which corresponds to the lowest Bohr energy level. One of these spaces corresponds to a situation in which the electron "spins" clockwise on its axis, the other to a situation in which it "spins" counterclockwise on its axis. When we start to catalog all possible chemical elements in the periodic table, we have element one (hydrogen) with a single electron in the innermost shell, and element two (helium) with two electrons in that same shell. After this, if we want to add one more electron, it has to go into the second electron shell because the first electron shell is completely filled. This situation explains why only hydrogen and helium appear in the first row in the periodic table.

Adding a third electron yields lithium, an atom with two electrons in the first shell, and a single electron in the second electron shell. Lithium is the element just below hydrogen in the first column of the periodic table, because both hydrogen and lithium have a lone electron in their outermost shell.

The second electron shell has room for eight electrons, a fact reflected in the eight elements of the periodic table's second row, from lithium with three electrons to neon with 10. Neon appears directly under helium, and we expect these two gases to have similar chemical properties because both have a completely filled outer electron shell.

Thus, a simple counting of the positions available to electrons in the first two electron shells explains why the first row in the periodic table has two elements in it and the second row eight. By similar (but somewhat more complicated) arguments, you can show that the Pauli exclusion principle requires that the next row of the periodic table have 8 elements, the next 18, and so on (Figure 8-15). Thus, with an understanding of the shell-like structure of the atom's electrons, the mysterious regularity that Mendeleev found among the chemical elements becomes an example of nature's laws at work.

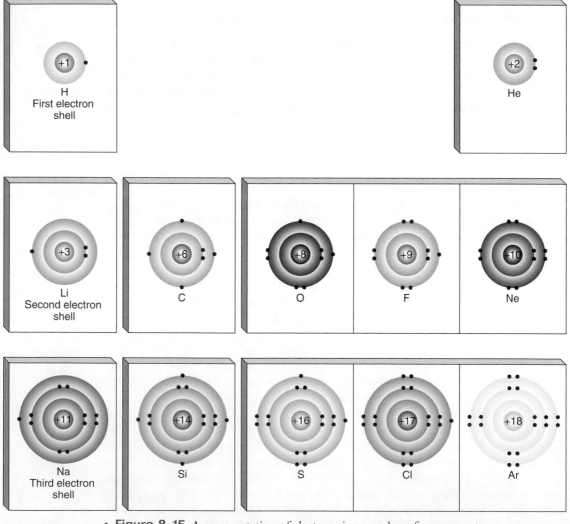

• **Figure 8-15** A representation of electrons in a number of common atoms.

Science News | Morphing Atoms
(SCIENCE NEWS, VOL. 163, MARCH 15, 2003, P. 174)

We are used to solid bodies holding their shape because of the strong bonds that form between atoms. As the number of atoms in a material becomes smaller and smaller, however, there comes a point intermediate between a solid, which contains many atoms, and a single atom in isolation. Scientists have been studying these so-called clusters, containing a few atoms each, in an attempt to learn more about how materials are put together. As the size of machines and electronic circuits becomes smaller and smaller, this sort of work becomes more and more important.

Recently scientists at the University of Virginia used fast lasers to investigate the process by which clusters form. They took a gas called cesium iodide and cooled it in helium so that seven atom clusters formed. These clusters could come in three shapes—a cube, a ring, or a ladder. They illuminated a stream of newly formed clusters with a laser with just enough energy to break up the cubic variety, but not the others. They then looked farther downstream to see if any of the intact clusters changed their shape to cubes. Surprisingly, they found that this kind of re-arrangement occurred in a very short time—as short as ten trillionths of a second.

The hope is that work like this will not only illuminate the forces that operate as atoms come together, but will lead to an understanding of how to produce stable clusters for use in the emerging field of nanotechnology.

Thinking More About | Atoms

What Do Atoms "Look Like"?

Throughout this book you will find drawings of atoms. In this chapter we drew atoms as electrons in circular shells around a central nucleus. In Chapter 10, atoms appear as little spheres in pictures of molecules like H_2O (water) and crystals like NaCl (table salt). In other chapters atoms are portrayed as fuzzy clouds, or waves, or even collections of dozens of smaller sphere-like particles. So, what do atoms really "look like"?

Strictly speaking, we only "see" something when electromagnetic waves from the visible part of the spectrum enter our eyes. We are accustomed, however, to talking about other ways of "seeing." You cannot see X-rays being absorbed by your teeth, for example, unless some intermediary system—film or electronic—converts the X-rays into a pattern that can be detected in the visible region of the electromagnetic spectrum. Similarly, astronomers often convert radio waves, infrared radiation, and other wavelength data into false-color images of distant objects. Scanning tunneling microscope "pictures" of atoms come from another such transformation. The amount of electrical charge at a particular point on a material's surface is converted into the height of the peak you see in the picture.

Is an X-ray picture of your teeth more real than the microscope picture of the atom? Why or why not?

SUMMARY

All the solids, liquids, and gases around us are composed of about 100 different *elements*. *Atoms*, the building blocks of our chemical world, combine into groups of two or more; these groups are called *molecules*. For thousands of years atoms were discussed purely as hypothetical objects, but studies of Brownian motion early in the twentieth century and recent imaging of individual atoms in new kinds of microscopes have confirmed the existence of these tiny particles.

Each atom contains a massive central *nucleus* made from positively charged protons and electrically neutral neutrons. Surrounding the nucleus are *electrons*, which are nega- tively charged particles that have only a small fraction of the mass of protons and neutrons. Early models of this kind of atom treated electrons like planets orbiting around the Sun. Those models were flawed, however, because each electron, constantly accelerating, would have to emit electromagnetic radiation continuously. Niels Bohr proposed an alternative model in which electrons exist in various energy levels, much as you can stand on different levels of a flight of stairs.

Electrons in the *Bohr atom* can shift to a higher energy level by absorbing the energy of heat or light. Electrons can also drop into a lower energy level, and in the process re- lease heat or a *photon*, an individual electromagnetic wave.

These changes in electron energy level are called *quantum leaps* or *quantum jumps*. *Spectroscopic* studies of the light emitted or absorbed by atoms—the atom's *spectrum*—reveal the nature of each atom's electron energy levels.

Each atom's electrons are arranged in concentric shells. When two atoms interact, electrons in the outermost shell come into contact. This shell-like electronic structure is reflected in the organization of the *periodic table of elements,* which lists all the elements in rows corresponding to increasing numbers of electrons in each shell, and in columns corresponding to elements with similar numbers of outer shell electrons and thus similar chemical behavior.

Key Terms About Atoms

element
atom
molecule

electron
nucleus
Bohr atom

photon
quantum leap, or quantum jump
spectrum

spectroscopy
periodic table of the elements

Review Questions

1. Did Democritus use the scientific method to study the existence of atoms?

2. Did Dalton use the scientific method in his studies of the existence of atoms?

3. Review six kinds of observational evidence that were used to support the atomic theory.

4. What three particles make up every atom? What are the major differences among these particles?

5. How does the nucleus differ from electrons?

6. Why is the smallest unit of an element an atom, but the smallest unit of a compound is a molecule?

7. Review the basic elements of Rutherford's experiment. What evidence did Rutherford use to justify his discovery of the nucleus?

8. How does Bohr's model of the atom differ from Rutherford's?

9. What is the relationship between a photon and a quantum leap?

10. How might an emission spectrum and an absorption spectrum of a given element differ in appearance?

11. Cite three examples of everyday objects with vivid emission spectra.

12. How might astronomers on Earth use spectroscopy to determine chemical elements that occur in stars?

13. Describe the basic components of a laser. How does a laser work?

14. In what ways are all the elements in a given column of the periodic table similar? In what ways are they different?

Discussion Questions

1. In what ways is the structure of an atom like the solar system of planets orbiting around the Sun? In what ways is it different?

2. Draw three different emission spectra that would appear red. [*Hint:* Think about different kinds of red objects, including a red laser, a red-hot coal, and a red sweater.]

3. Rutherford's experiment involved firing nucleus-sized "bullets" at atoms of gold. He found that one atom in a thousand bounced backward. What might Rutherford have seen if atoms were completely uniform in mass? What if electrons were the more massive particle? [*Hint:* What happens when a bowling ball collides with a Ping-Pong ball?]

4. Advertisers often describe improvements in their products as a "quantum leap." Is this an appropriate use of the term? How big is a quantum leap?

5. Based on your knowledge of Newton's laws of motion, the laws of thermodynamics, and the nature of electromagnetic radiation, explain why the Rutherford model of the atom couldn't work.

6. When you shine invisible ultraviolet light (black light) on certain objects, they glow with brilliant colors. How might this behavior be explained in terms of the Bohr atom?

7. Why do different lasers have different-colored beams?

8. What does it mean to say the periodic table was useful because it "worked"? How does this relate to the scientific method? Describe an imaginary discovery that might have invalidated the periodic table.

9. If you were told that fluorine is an extremely reactive element (that is, it combines readily with other elements), what other elements could you guess were also extremely reactive? Why?

10. Space probes often carry compact spectrometers among their scientific hardware. What kind of spectroscopy might scientists use to determine the surface composition of cold, outer planets that orbit the Sun? How might they use spectroscopy to determine the atmospheric composition of these planets?

11. In the science fiction series *Star Trek,* there is a weapon called the "photon torpedo." Given what you now know about photons, speculate about how such a weapon might work.

PROBLEMS

1. If the electrons in an atom can occupy any of four different energy levels, how many lines might appear in that atom's spectrum? What if the atom has five different energy levels?

2. Imagine that you have 5 different chemical elements in your chemical laboratory. What is the maximum number of 1:1 chemical compounds that you could form? What if you had 10 different chemical elements?

3. Imagine that you have six different chemical elements. What is the maximum number of 1:1:1 chemical compounds that you could form? What about 1:1:2 compounds? What about 1:2:3 compounds? How do these numbers compare with the number of known chemical elements?

INVESTIGATIONS

1. Investigate the history of the discovery of chemical elements. What technological innovations led to the discovery of several new elements? What was the most recent element to be discovered and how was it found?

2. Simple handheld spectroscopes are available in many science labs. Look at the spectra of different kinds of lightbulbs: an incandescent bulb, a fluorescent bulb, a halogen bulb, and any other kinds available to you. What differences do you observe in their spectra? Why?

3. Place pieces of transparent materials between a strong light source and the spectrometer described in Investigation 1. Does the spectrum change? Why?

4. Why do colors look different when viewed indoors under fluorescent light, and outdoors in sunlight? How might you devise an experiment to quantify these differences?

5. Investigate the variety of lasers that are currently available. What is the range of wavelengths available? How are different lasers used in medicine? In industry? In science?

WWW RESOURCES

See *The Sciences* homepage at: **http://www.wiley.com/college/trefil** for valuable web links.

1. http://www.thetech.org/exhibits/online/lasers
   Lasers: From Science Fiction to Everyday Life—click on "*Next*" to find out how lasers are used today and how they work.

2. http://library.thinkquest.org/17940/texts/atom/atom.html
   The Atom—an introduction to structure, nomenclature, fission, fusion, and the history of atomic research.

3. http://www.spectroscopynow.com/Spy/basehtml/SpyH/
   Extensive portal covering mass spectrometry, nuclear magnetic resonance, x-ray, atomic absorption, Raman, IR, UV/VIS, chemometrics, and other spectroscopic techniques.

9

Quantum Mechanics

How can the electron behave like both a particle and a wave?

GREAT IDEA

At the subatomic scale, everything is quantized. Any measurement at that scale significantly alters the object being measured.

PHYSICS

Quantum mechanics requires an entirely new way of describing the state of a system at the level of the atom.

CHEMISTRY

Wave-particle duality explains the position of allowed electron orbits, and therefore the chemical reactions of atoms.

GEOLOGY

The way that atoms combine to form minerals is governed by the laws of quantum mechanics.

HEALTH & SAFETY

In CAT scans, photoelectric devices convert X-ray photons into electrical currents, whose strength can be used to produce a picture of a patient's internal organs.

ASTRONOMY

The nuclear reactions that power the Sun are governed by the laws of quantum mechanics. (Ch. 14)

TECHNOLOGY

Sensitive electronic detectors can detect the emission of a single photon from an excited atom.

BIOLOGY

Some scientists think that quantum mechanics is intimately involved in the phenomenon of consciousness.

Red = applications of the great idea discussed in this chapter.

Orange = other applications, some of which are explored in other chapters.

It's 9:30 A.M. as you pull into the ocean-side parking lot. You've made great time and are eager to hit the beach. You see your friends waiting near the entrance. As you shout and wave, a classmate snaps your picture on her new digital camera. Everyone crowds around to see the crisp image on the camera's video monitor.

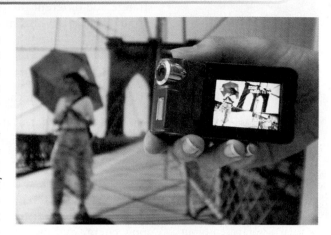

But how can a little box almost instantaneously capture and display a picture? At the heart of every digital camera is a plate of light-sensitive material called a *photoelectric device*—the same kind of material that converts the Sun's energy into electricity in a solar cell and measures brightness in a light meter. These everyday objects are practical consequences of one of the strangest discoveries in science—the discovery of the quantum world.

The World of the Very Small

In Chapter 8 we saw that when an electron moves between energy levels and emits a photon, it is said to make a *quantum leap*. The term **quantum mechanics** refers to the theory that describes this event and other events at the scale of the atom. The word *quantum* comes from the Latin word for "bundle," and mechanics, as we saw in Chapter 2, is the study of the motion of material objects. Quantum mechanics, then, is the branch of science that is devoted to the study of the motion of objects that come in small bundles, or quanta. We have already seen that material inside the atom comes in little bundles—tiny pieces of matter we call electrons travel in orbits around another little bundle of matter we call the nucleus. In the language of physicists, the atom's matter is said to be *quantized*.

Electrical charge is also quantized—every electron has a charge of exactly −1, while every proton has a +1 charge. We have seen that photons emitted by an atom can have only certain values of energy, so that energy levels in the atom and emitted energy are quantized. In fact, inside the atom, in the world of the submicroscopically small, *everything* comes in quantized bundles.

Our everyday world isn't like this at all. Although we have been told since childhood that the objects around us are made up of atoms, for all intents and purposes we experience matter as if it were smooth, continuous, and infinitely divisible. Indeed, for almost any phenomenon in the physical world, the idea of matter existing in continuous form works as well as anyone would want.

The quantum world is foreign to our senses. All of the intuition that we have built up about the way the world operates—all of the "gut feelings" we have about the universe—comes from our experiences with large-scale objects made up of apparently continuous material. If it should turn out (as it does) that the world of the quantum does not match our intuition, we should not be surprised. We have never dealt with this kind of world, so we have no particular reason, based on observations or experience, to believe that it should behave one way or the other.

This warning may not make you feel much better as you learn just how strange and different the quantum world really is, but it might help you come to intellectual grips with a most fascinating part of our physical universe.

Measurement and Observation in the Quantum World

Every measurement in the physical world incorporates three essential components:

1. A sample—a piece of matter to study
2. A source of energy—light or heat or kinetic energy that interacts with the sample
3. A detector to observe and measure that interaction

When you look at a piece of matter such as this book, you can see it because light bounces off the book and comes to your eye, a very sophisticated detector (see Chapter 6). When you examine a piece of fruit at the grocery store, you apply energy by squeezing it to detect if it feels too ripe.

Many professions employ sophisticated devices to make their measurements. Air traffic controllers reflect radio waves off airplanes to determine their positions, oceanographers bounce sound waves off deep-ocean sediments to map the seafloor, and dentists pass X-rays through your teeth and gums to look for cavities. In our everyday world we assume that such interactions of matter and energy do not change the objects being measured in any appreciable way. Microwaves don't alter an airplane's flight path, nor do sound waves disturb the topography of the ocean's bottom. And while prolonged exposure to X-rays can be harmful, the dentist's brief exploratory X-ray photograph has no obvious immediate effects on the tooth. Our experience tells us that a measurement can usually be made on a macroscopic object—something large enough to be seen without a microscope—without altering that object, because the energy of the probe is much less than the energy of the object.

The situation is rather different in the quantum world. If you want to "see" an electron, you have to bounce energy off it so that the information can be carried to your detectors. But nothing at your disposal can interact with the electron without simultaneously affecting it. You can bounce a photon off it, but in the process the electron's energy will change. You can bounce another particle off it, but the electron will recoil like a billiard ball. No matter what you try, the energy of the probe is too close to the energy of the thing being measured. The electron cannot fail to be altered by the interaction.

Many everyday analogies illustrate the process of measurement in the quantum world. It's like trying to detect bowling balls by bouncing other bowling balls off them. The act of measurement in the quantum world poses a dilemma analogous to trying to discover if there is a car in a tunnel when the only means of finding out is to send another car into the tunnel and listen for a crash. With this technique you can certainly discover whether the first car is there. You can probably even find out where it is by measuring the time it takes the probe car to crash. What you *cannot* do, however, is assume that the first car is the same after the interaction as it was before. In the same way, nothing in the quantum world can be the same after the interaction associated with a measurement as it was before.

In principle, this argument would apply to any interaction, whether it involves photons and electrons or photons and bowling balls. As we demonstrate in the "Science by the Numbers" section in this chapter, however, the effects of the interaction for large-scale objects are so tiny that they can simply be ignored, while in the case of interactions at the atomic level, they cannot. This fundamental difference between the quantum and macroscopic worlds is what makes quantum

A radar antenna sends out microwaves that interact with flying airplanes, are reflected, and detected on their return. This allows air traffic controllers to keep track of where airplanes are in the sky.

mechanics quite different from the classical mechanics of Isaac Newton. Remember that every experiment, be it on planets or fruit or quantum objects, involves interactions of one sort or another. The consequences of small-scale interactions make the quantum world different, not the fact that a measurement is being made.

The Heisenberg Uncertainty Principle

In 1927, a young German physicist, Werner Heisenberg (1901–1976), put the idea of limitations on quantum-scale measurements into precise mathematical form. His work, which was one of the first results to come from the new science of quantum mechanics, is called the *Heisenberg uncertainty principle* in his honor. The central concept of the uncertainty principle is simple:

> **At the quantum scale, any measurement significantly alters the object being measured.**

Suppose, for example, you have a particle such as an electron in an atom and want to know where it is *and* how fast it's moving. The uncertainty principle tells us that it is impossible to measure both the position and the velocity with infinite accuracy at the same time.

The reason for this state of affairs, of course, is that every measurement changes the object being measured. Just as the car in the tunnel could not be the same after the first measurement was made on it, so too will the quantum object change. The result is that as you measure one property such as position more and more exactly, your knowledge of a property such as velocity gets fuzzier and fuzzier.

The uncertainty principle doesn't say that we cannot know a particle's location with great precision. It is possible, at least in principle, for the uncertainty in position to be zero, which would mean that we know the exact location of a quantum particle. In this case, however, the uncertainty in the velocity has to be infinite. Thus, at the point in time when we know exactly where the particle is, we have no idea whatsoever how fast it is moving. By the same token, if we know exactly how fast the quantum particle is moving, we cannot know where it is. It could, quite literally, be in the room with us or in China.

In practice, every quantum measurement involves trade-offs. We accept some fuzziness in the location of the particle and some fuzziness in the knowledge of the velocity, playing the two off against each other to get the best solution to whatever problem it is we're working on. We cannot have precise knowledge of both at the same time, but we can know either one as accurately as we like at any time.

Let's look a little more closely at the differences between the world of our intuition and the quantum world. In the former, we assume that measurement doesn't affect the thing being measured, so that we can have exact, simultaneous knowledge of both the position and velocity of an object such as a car or a baseball. In the quantum world, as Heisenberg taught us, we cannot.

Heisenberg put his notion into a simple mathematical relationship, which is a complete and exact statement of the **uncertainty principle**.

▶ **In words:** The error or uncertainty in the measurement of an object's position, times the error or uncertainty in that object's velocity, must be greater than a constant (Planck's constant) divided by the object's mass.

▶ **In equation form:**

$$(\text{uncertainty in position}) \times (\text{uncertainty in velocity}) > \frac{h}{\text{mass}}$$

where h is a number known as Planck's constant (see below).

▶ **In symbols:**

$$\Delta x \times \Delta v > \frac{h}{m}$$

This equation is a precise, shorthand way of saying that you can never know both the position and velocity of an object with perfect accuracy. The difference between our everyday world and the world inside the atom hangs on the question of the numerical value of h/m, the numbers on the right side of Heisenberg's equation. In SI units (see Appendix A), Planck's constant, h, has a value of 6.63×10^{-34} joule-seconds.

The important point about the Heisenberg relationship is not the exact value of the number, h/m, but the fact that the number is greater than zero. Look at it this way. If you make more and more precise measurements about the location of a particle, you determine its position more and more exactly, and the uncertainty in position, Δx, must get smaller and smaller. In this situation, it follows that the uncertainty in velocity, Δv, has to get bigger and bigger. In fact, we can use the uncertainty principle to calculate exactly our uncertainty in velocity for a given uncertainty in position, and vice versa.

SCIENCE BY THE NUMBERS •

Uncertainty in the Newtonian World

The best way to understand why we do not have to worry about the uncertainty principle in our everyday life is to calculate the uncertainty in measurements in two separate situations: large objects and very small objects.

1. **Small Uncertainties with Large Objects.** A moving automobile with a mass of 1000 kilograms is located in an intersection that is 5 meters across. How precisely can you know how fast the car is traveling?

   We can solve this problem by noting that if the car is somewhere in an intersection 5 m across, then the uncertainty in position of the car is about equal to 5 m. Thus we know the car's mass and uncertainty in position, so we can calculate the uncertainty in velocity:

$$\text{uncertainty in position} \times \text{uncertainty in velocity} > \frac{h}{\text{mass}}$$

First, we must rearrange this equation to solve for uncertainty of velocity:

$$(\text{uncertainty in velocity}) > \frac{(h/\text{mass})}{\text{uncertainty in position}}$$

$$> \frac{[(6.63 \times 10^{-34}\,\text{J-s})/1000\,\text{kg}]}{5\,\text{m}}$$

$$> \frac{[(6.63 \times 10^{-37})\,\text{J-s/kg}]}{5\,\text{m}}$$

$$> 1.33 \times 10^{-37}\,\text{m/s}$$

Thus the uncertainty in the velocity of the automobile is greater than 1.33×10^{-37} m/s (note that the unit J-s/kg-m is equivalent to m/s; see Problem 2 at the end of the chapter). This uncertainty is extremely small. Theoretically, we could know the velocity of the car to an accuracy of 37 decimal places! In practice, however, we have no method of measuring velocities with present or foreseeable human technology to an accuracy remotely approaching this. The uncertainty is, for all practical purposes, indistinguishable from zero. Therefore, for objects with significant mass such as automobiles, the effects of the uncertainty principle are totally negligible. The equation confirms our experience that Newtonian mechanics works perfectly well in dealing with everyday objects.

2. **Large Uncertainty with a Small Object.** Contrast the preceding example with the uncertainty in velocity of an electron in an atom, located within an area about 10^{-10} meters on a side. To what accuracy can we measure the velocity of that electron?

   The mass of an electron is 9.11×10^{-31} kg. If we take the uncertainty in position to be 10^{-10} m, then according to the uncertainty principle,

$$\text{uncertainty in velocity} > \frac{(h/\text{mass})}{\text{uncertainty in position}}$$
$$> \frac{[(6.63 \times 10^{-34}\,\text{J-s})/(9.11 \times 10^{-31}\,\text{kg})]}{10^{-10}\,\text{m}}$$
$$> 7.3 \times 10^{6}\,\text{m/s}$$

This uncertainty is very large indeed. The mere fact that we know that an electron is somewhere in an atom means that we cannot know its velocity to within a million meters per second.

For ordinary-sized objects such as cars and bowling balls, whose mass is measured in kilograms, the number on the right side of the uncertainty relation is so small that we can treat it as being zero. Only when the masses get very small, as they do for particles such as the electron, does the number on the right get big enough to make a practical difference. •

Stop and Think! How big do you suppose something has to be before we can forget about the effects of the uncertainty principle? As big as a speck of dust? A baseball? A car?

Probabilities

The uncertainty principle has consequences that go far beyond simple statements about measurement. In the quantum world we must radically change the way that we describe events. Consider an everyday example in which the uncertainties are much larger (but easier to picture) than those associated with Heisenberg's equation. Think of a batter hitting a ball during a nighttime baseball game.

Imagine yourself at a big-league ball game under the lights of a great stadium. Cheering fans fill the stands, roving vendors sell their food and drink, and the pitcher and batter play out their classic duel. The pitcher stares the batter down, winds up, and hurls a fastball. But the batter is ready and pounces on the pitch. The ball leaps off the bat with a sharp crack. And then all the lights go out.

Where will the ball be in five seconds? If you were an outfielder, this would be more than a philosophical question. You would need to know where to go to make your catch, even in the dark. In a Newtonian world, you would have no problem in doing this. If you knew the position and velocity of the ball at the instant the lights went out, some simple calculations would tell you exactly where the ball would be at any time in the future.

If you were a quantum outfielder in an atom-sized ball field, on the other hand, you would have a much harder time of it. You couldn't know both the position and velocity of the quantum ball when the lights go out; at best you

• **Figure 9-1** The position of a "quantum baseball" cannot be precisely determined. Instead, you can predict only the probabilities of the ball being at various distances from home plate, as discussed in the text. The most likely location is at the peak of the curve, but the ball could be anywhere else.

Homeplate

could put some bounds on them. You might, for example, be able to say something like "It's somewhere inside this three-foot circle and traveling between 30 and 70 feet per second." This means that when you have to guess where it would be in five seconds, you wouldn't be able to do so with any accuracy. If you were thinking in Newtonian terms, you would have to say that the ball could be 147 feet from the plate (if it were traveling 30 feet per second and located at the back of the three-foot circle), 353 feet from the plate (if it were traveling 70 feet per second and located at the front of the circle), or anyplace in between. The best you could do would be to predict the likelihood, or **probability**, that the ball would be anywhere in the outfield, and you could present these probabilities on a graph like the one shown in Figure 9-1.

This example shows that the uncertainty principle requires a description of quantum-scale events in terms of probabilities. Just like the baseball in our example of the darkened stadium, there must be uncertainties in the position and velocity for every quantum object when we first start observing it, and hence there will be uncertainties at the end—uncertainties that can be dealt with by reporting probabilities.

This result is extremely important. It tells us that we cannot think of quantum events in the same way that we think of normal events in our everyday world. In particular, we have to rethink what it means to talk about concepts such as regularity, predictability, and causality at the quantum level.

Wave-Particle Duality

Quantum mechanics is sometimes called *wave mechanics* because it turns out that quantum objects sometimes act like particles, and sometimes like waves. This dichotomy is known as the problem of "wave-particle duality," and it has puzzled some of the best minds in science. To understand it, think about how particles and waves behave in our macroscopic world.

The Double-Slit Test

Energy travels either as a wave or as a particle in our everyday world (see Chapter 6). Particles transfer energy through collisions, while waves transfer energy through collective motion of the media or electromagnetic fields. Every aspect of the everyday world can be neatly divided into particles or waves, and many experiments can be used to determine whether something is a particle or wave. The most famous of these experiments uses a double-slit apparatus, which consists of a barrier that has two slits in it (Figure 9-2). If particles such as baseballs are thrown from the left side, a few will make it through the slits, but most will bounce off. If you were standing on the other side of the barrier you would expect to see the baseballs coming through more or less in the two places shown, accumulating in two piles behind the barrier. You wouldn't expect to see many particles (baseballs) at the spots between the slits.

If, however, waves of water were coming from the left side, you would expect to see the results of constructive and destructive interference (see Chapter 6).

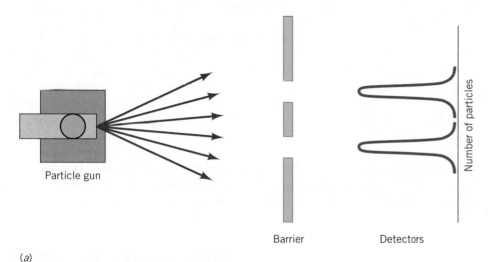

Particle gun

Barrier   Detectors

(a)

• **Figure 9-2** The two-slit experiment may be used to determine whether something is a wave or a particle. (*a*) A stream of particles striking the barrier will accumulate in the two regions directly behind the slits. (*b*) When waves converge on two narrow slits, however, constructive and destructive interference results in a series of peaks.

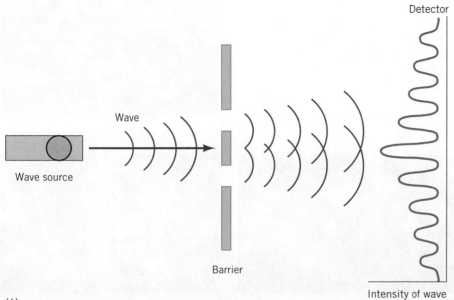

Detector

Wave

Wave source

Barrier

Intensity of wave

(b)

Rather than the two piles of baseballs, we would see perhaps half a dozen regions of high waves beyond the barrier, interspersed with regions of still water.

Now, let's use the same arrangement to see whether light behaves as a particle or a wave. In Chapter 8 we learned that light is emitted in discrete bundles of energy called *photons*. On the one hand, photons behave like particles in the sense that they can be localized in space. You can set up experiments in which a photon is emitted at one point, then received somewhere else after an appropriate lapse of time, just as a baseball is "emitted" by a pitcher and "received" later by a catcher (Figure 9-2*a*). If, on the other hand, you shine light—a flood of photons—on the two-slit apparatus, you will definitely get an interference pattern on the right (Figure 9-2*b*). In that experiment, photons act like waves. The big question: How can photons sometimes act like waves and sometimes act like particles?

You can make the problem even more puzzling by setting up the apparatus so that only one photon at a time comes through the slits. If you do this, you find that each photon arrives at a specific point at the screen—behavior you would expect of a particle. If you allow photons to accumulate over long periods of time, however, they will arrange themselves into an interference pattern characteristic of a wave (Figure 9-3).

You could do a similar series of experiments with any quantum object—electrons, for example, or even atoms. They all exhibit the properties of both particles and waves, depending on what sort of experiment is done. If you perform an experiment that tests the particle properties of these things, they look like particles. If you perform an experiment to test their wave properties, they look like waves. Whether you see quantum objects as particles or waves seems to depend on the experiment that you do.

Some experimenters have gone so far as to try to "trick" quantum particles such as electrons into revealing their true identity by using modern fast electronics to decide whether a particle- or wave-type experiment is being done *after* the quantum object is already on its way into the apparatus. Scientists who do these

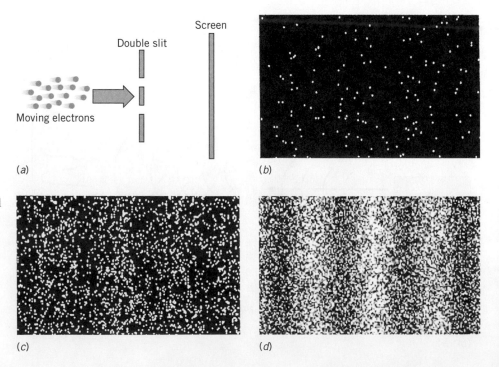

• **Figure 9-3** When electrons or photons (light particles) pass through a two-slit apparatus one at a time (*a*), they cause 100 single spots on a photographic film (*b*). As the number of electrons increases to 3000 (*c*), and then to 70,000 (*d*), a wavelike interference pattern emerges. The bright areas are places where constructive interference occurs, and the dark areas correspond to destructive interference.

Double slit

Screen

Moving electrons

(a)

(b)

(c)

(d)

experiments find that the quantum object seems to "know" what experiment is being done, because the particle experiments always turn up particle properties, while the wave experiments always turn up wave properties.

At the quantum level, the objects that we talk about are neither particles nor waves in the classical sense. In fact, we can't really visualize them at all, because we have never encountered anything like them in our everyday experience. They are a third kind of object, neither particle nor wave, but exhibiting the properties of both. If you persist in thinking about them as if they were baseballs or surf coming onto a beach, you will quickly lose yourself in confusion.

It's a little bit like finding someone who has seen only the colors red and green in her entire life. If she has decided that everything in the world has to be either red or green, she will be totally confused by seeing the color blue. What she has to realize is that the problem is not in nature, but in her assumption that everything has to be either red or green.

In the same way, the problem of wave-particle duality arises from our assumption that everything has to be either a wave or a particle. If we allow ourselves the possibility that quantum objects are things that we have never encountered before, and that they therefore might have unencountered properties, the puzzle vanishes. However, it vanishes only if we agree that we won't try to draw a picture of these objects or pretend that we can actually visualize what they are.

TECHNOLOGY •

The Photoelectric Effect

When photons of sufficient energy strike some materials, their energy can be absorbed by electrons, which are shaken loose from their home atoms. If the material in question is in the form of a thin sheet, then when light strikes one side, electrons are observed coming out of the other. This phenomenon is called the *photoelectric effect,* and it finds applications in numerous everyday devices.

One aspect of the photoelectric effect played a major role in the history of quantum mechanics. The time between the arrival of the light and the appearance of the electrons is extremely short—far too short to be explained by the relatively gentle action of a wave nudging the electrons loose. In fact, it was Albert Einstein who pointed out that the explanation of this rapid response depended on the particle-like nature of the photon. He argued that the interaction between the light and the electron is something like the collision between two billiard balls, with one ball shooting out instantly after the collision. It was this work, which led to our modern concept of the photon, that was the basis of Einstein's Nobel Prize in 1921.

The conversion of light energy into electrical current is used in many familiar devices. In a digital camera, for example, one photoelectric device measures the amount of light available to determine how wide to open the lens and what the shutter speed should be. Then a photoelectric plate collects the photographic image. In telephone systems that use fiber optics—glass fibers that act like pipes for visible light—light signals strike sophisticated semiconductor devices (see Chapter 11) and shake loose electrons. These electrons form a current that ultimately drives the diaphragm in your telephone and produces the sound that you hear. In CAT scans (see "The Science of Life" section that follows), photoelectric devices convert X-ray photons into electrical currents whose strength can be used to produce a picture of a patient's internal organs. As all of these examples show, an understanding of the way that objects interact in the quantum world can have enormous practical consequences. •

A boy having a CAT scan; a video monitor is in the foreground. A CAT scan of a human skull and brain is shown on the right.

THE SCIENCE OF LIFE •

The CAT Scan

Photoelectric detectors play a crucial role in a modern medical technique called the CAT scan. Ordinary X-ray photographs depend on the differences in density (and therefore in the ability to absorb X-rays) of the various materials in the body. In these photographs, the X-rays make one pass through, in one direction only, to produce pictures. They cannot produce a three-dimensional image of the interior of the body, nor can they produce sharp images of organs whose densities are not significantly different from the densities of their surroundings. These shortcomings are overcome by a different X-ray technique known as *computerized axial tomography (CAT)*.

The easiest way to visualize a CAT scan is to imagine dividing the body into slices perpendicular to the backbone, with each slice being a millimeter or so in width. The material in each slice is probed by successive short bursts of X-rays, lasting only a few milliseconds each, that cross the slice in different directions. Each part of the slice is thus traversed by many different X-ray bursts. Each burst of X-rays contains the same number of photons when it starts, and the ones that go all the way through the body (i.e., those not absorbed by material along their path) are measured by a photoelectric device (see the preceding "Technology" section).

Once all the data on a given slice have been obtained, a computer works out the density of each point of the body and produces a detailed cross-section along that particular slice. A complete picture of the body (or a specific part of it) can then be built up by combining successive slices. •

● Wave-Particle Duality and the Bohr Atom

Treating electrons as waves helps explain why only certain orbits are allowed in atoms (see Chapter 8). Every quantum object displays a simple relationship between its speed (when we think of it as a particle) and its wavelength (when we think of it as a wave). It turns out that for electrons, protons, and other quantum objects, a faster speed always corresponds to a shorter, more energetic wavelength (or a higher frequency).

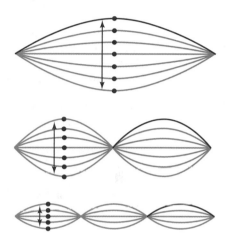

• **Figure 9-4** A vibrating string adopts a regular pattern, known as a standing wave. These photos and diagrams illustrate fixed patterns with $\frac{1}{2}$, 1, and $\frac{3}{2}$ wavelengths.

If you think of an electron as a particle, then you can treat its motion around an atom's nucleus in the same Newtonian way you treat the motion of the Earth in orbit around the Sun. That is, for any given distance from the nucleus, the electron must have a precise velocity to stay in a stable orbit. Provided it is moving at such a velocity, it will stay in that orbit just as the Earth stays in a stable orbit around the Sun. Any faster and it must adopt a higher orbit; any slower and it will move closer to the nucleus.

If we choose to think about the electron as a wave, however, a different set of criteria can be used to decide how to put the electron into its orbit. A wave on a straight string (on a guitar, for example) vibrates only at certain frequencies that depend on the length of the string (Figure 9-4). These frequencies correspond to fitting $\frac{1}{2}$, 1, and $\frac{3}{2}$ wavelengths on the string in the figure. Now imagine bending the guitar string around into a circular orbit. In this case, you will be able to fit only certain standing waves in the orbit, as shown in Figure 9-5.

You can now ask a simple question: Are there any orbits for which the wave and particle descriptions are consistent? In other words, are there orbits for which the velocity of the electron (when we think of it as a particle) is appropriate to the orbit, while at the same time the electron wave (when we think of it as a wave) fits onto the orbit, given the relation between wavelength and velocity?

When you do the mathematics, you find that the only orbits that satisfy these twin conditions are the Bohr orbits. That is to say, *the only orbits allowed in the atom are those for which it makes no difference whether we think of the electron as a particle or a wave.* In a sense, then, the wave-particle duality exists in our minds, and not in nature—nature has arranged things so that what we think doesn't matter.

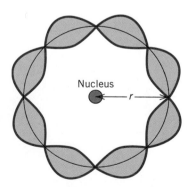

• **Figure 9-5** An electron in orbit about an atom adopts a standing wave like a vibrating string. This illustration shows a standing wave with four wavelengths fitting into the orbit's circumference.

Science News | Quantum Mechanics Illuminates the Living Cell
(SCIENCE NEWS, VOL. 163, FEB. 15, 2003, P. 106)

Ever since the living cell was discovered, scientists have tried to peer inside of it and watch its machinery in action. Starting with the use of dyes in the 19th century, they have progressed to the point where they can use fluorescence to see individual protein molecules in action, at least for short periods of time. Now, a material known as a quantum dot promises to allow them to watch the working of a single cell over a period of months or even years.

A quantum dot is a small sphere, perhaps a few nanometers across, made of a material that will, when hit with light, emit its own particular color of light in response. The color the dot gives off depends on its size—smaller dots glow blue, while larger ones glow red. The idea is to attach different sized dots to different protein molecules, then watch the complex interactions between the molecules themselves.

The advantage of the dots over the fluorescent dyes that have been the main research tool in this area up to now is that researchers can make all of the dots light up at the same time, so that they can watch all the molecules interact. Up to now, they have had to watch one molecule at a time, then try to piece the interactions together. One researcher likened this process to watching a game of monopoly in which you were allowed to see only one player's moves throughout the game, then the next player's, and so on. It would be possible to reconstruct the game, but it would be a lot easier if you could see all the moves at once. That's what quantum dots allow researchers to do in the cell.

The hope is that by watching individual proteins, scientists will learn how to create new and more effective medicines to combat disease.

Quantum Weirdness

The fact that quantum objects behave so differently from objects in our everyday experience causes many people to worry that nature has somehow become "weird" at the subatomic level. The description of particles in terms of a wave defies our common sense. Situations in which a photon or electron seems to "know" how an apparatus will be arranged before the arranging is done seem wrong and unnatural. Many people, scientists and nonscientists alike, find the conclusions of quantum mechanics to be quite unsettling. The American physicist Richard Feynmann stressed this point when he said, "I can safely say that nobody understands quantum mechanics. . . . Do not keep saying to yourself, 'But how can it be like that?' . . . Nobody knows how it can be like that."

In spite of this rather disturbing situation, the success of quantum mechanics provides ample evidence that there is a correct way to describe an atomic-scale system. If you ignore this fact you can get into a lot of trouble. Newtonian notions like position and velocity just aren't appropriate for the quantum world, which must be described from the beginning in terms of waves and probabilities. Quantum mechanics thus becomes a way of predicting how subatomic objects change in time. If you know the state of an electron now, you can use quantum mechanics to predict the state of that electron in the future. This process is identical to the application of Newton's laws of motion in the macroscopic world. The only difference is that in the quantum world, the "state" of the system is a probability.

In the view of most working scientists, quantum mechanics is a marvelous tool that allows us to do all sorts of experiments and build all manner of new and important pieces of equipment. The fact that we can't visualize the quantum world in familiar terms seems a small price to pay for all the benefits we receive.

SCIENCE IN THE MAKING •

A Famous Interchange

Many people are disturbed by the fact that nature must be described in terms of probabilities at the subatomic level. Many scientists were also disturbed when quantum mechanics was first developed in the early twentieth century. Even Albert Einstein, one of the founders of quantum mechanics, could not accept what it was telling us about the world. He spent a good part of the last half of his life trying to refute it. His most famous statement from this period was, "I cannot believe that God plays dice with the universe."

Confronted one too many times with this aphorism, Einstein's lifelong friend and colleague Neils Bohr is supposed to have replied, "Albert, stop telling God what to do." •

Thinking More About | Quantum Mechanics

Uncertainty and Human Beings

The ultimate Newtonian view of the universe was the concept of the Divine Calculator (see Chapter 2). This mythical being, given the position and velocity of every particle in the universe, could predict every future state of those particles. The difficulty with this concept, of course, is that if the future of the universe is laid out with clockwork precision, it allows no room for human action. No one can make a choice about what he or she will do, because that choice is already determined and exists (in the mind of God or the Divine Calculator) before it is made.

Quantum mechanics gives us one way to get out of this particular bind. Heisenberg tells us that, although we might be able to predict the future if we knew the position and velocity of every particle exactly, we can never actually get those two numbers. The Divine Calculator in a quantum world is doomed to wait forever for the input data with which to start the calculation.

One area where the uncertainty principle is starting to play a somewhat unexpected role is in the old philosophical argument about the connection between the mind and the brain. The brain is a physical object, an incredibly complex organ that processes information in the form of nerve impulses. (A more detailed description of the workings of the brain is given in Chapter 11.) The problem: What is the connection between the physical reality of the brain—the atoms and structures that compose it—and the consciousness that we all experience?

Many scientists and philosophers have argued that the brain is no more than a physical structure. These thinkers have run into a problem, however, because if the brain is purely a physical object, its future states should be predictable. Recently, scientists (most notably Roger Penrose of Cambridge University) have argued that quantum mechanics can introduce a kind of unpredictability that squares better with our perceptions of our own minds.

Think about how the workings of the brain might be unpredictable at the quantum level. Why might that uncertainty make it difficult (or even impossible) to make precise predictions of the future state of the brain?

SUMMARY

Matter and energy at the atomic scale come in discrete packets called quanta. The rules of *quantum mechanics,* the laws that allow us to describe and predict events in the quantum world, are disturbingly different from Newton's laws of motion.

At the quantum scale, unlike our everyday experience, any measurement of the position or velocity of a particle causes the particle to change in unpredictable ways. The mere act of measurement alters the thing being measured. Werner Heisenberg quantified this situation in the Heisenberg *uncertainty principle,* which states that the uncertainty in the position of a particle multiplied by the uncertainty in its velocity must be greater than a small positive number. Unlike the Newtonian world, you can never know the exact position and velocity of a quantum particle.

These uncertainties preclude us from describing atomic-scale particles in the classical way. Instead, quantum descriptions are given in terms of *probabilities* that an object will be in one state or another. Furthermore, quantum objects are not simply particles or waves, a dichotomy familiar to us in the macroscopic world. They represent something completely different from our experience, incorporating properties of both particles and waves.

KEY TERMS ABOUT QUANTUM MECHANICS

quantum mechanics   uncertainty principle   probability

KEY EQUATION

(uncertainty in position) × (uncertainty in velocity) > $\dfrac{h}{\text{mass}}$

REVIEW QUESTIONS

1. What does "quantum mechanics" mean?
2. Give three examples of properties that are quantized at the scale of an electron.
3. What are the three essential parts of every physical measurement?
4. In what way is a measurement at the quantum scale of an electron different from a measurement at large scales of everyday objects?
5. There was once a humorous poster showing a picture of a bed with the caption, "Heisenberg may have slept here." In what way is this an inaccurate representation of Heisenberg's uncertainty principle?
6. Under what circumstances can you know the position of an electron with great accuracy?
7. Why is quantum mechanics sometimes called "wave mechanics"?
8. Give an everyday example of "wave-particle duality."
9. Explain how the photoelectric effect works. Does it depend on the wave or the particle nature of light?
10. How does wave-particle duality explain the Bohr orbits of electrons in atoms?
11. Why did Albert Einstein use playing dice as an analogy for quantum mechanics?

DISCUSSION QUESTIONS

1. Identify the sample, the source of energy, and the detector in the following "experiments":
a. measuring the color of a distant star
b. determining the hardness of a piece of steel with an indentor
c. testing the electrical resistance of a piece of wire
d. determining the length of an iron bar
2. Which properties of electrons are particle-like? Which are wave-like?
3. What role does probability play in describing subatomic events?
4. Sketch a possible probability diagram for the final resting position of a golf ball on a driving range. Assume that the golf tee is the starting point and that an average drive is 250 feet.
5. In Chapter 2 we discussed the fact that chaotic systems are, for all practical purposes, unpredictable. How does this sort of unpredictability differ from that associated with quantum mechanics?
6. Present an argument in terms of the wave nature of the electron that shows that electrons in Bohr orbits cannot emit radiation and spiral in toward the nucleus, as they might be expected to do on the basis of Maxwell's equations. [*Hint:* See "Why the Rutherford Atom Couldn't Work" in Chapter 8.]
7. How does light behave like a particle? How does it behave like a wave?
8. If you threw baseballs through a large two-slit apparatus, would you produce a diffraction pattern? Why or why not?

PROBLEMS

1. A ball (mass 0.1 kg) is thrown with a speed between 20.0 and 20.1 m/s. How accurately can we determine its position?
2. In the "Science by the Numbers" section in this chapter, we converted the unit J-s/kg-m to the unit of velocity (m/s) without comment. Demonstrate the equivalence of these two units.
3. An atom of iron (mass 10^{-25} kg) travels at a speed between 20.0 and 20.1 m/s. How accurately can we determine its position? Is this accuracy in position attainable? How does it compare to the size of an atom? Of a nucleus?

INVESTIGATIONS

1. Look up the doctrine of predestination in an encyclopedia. Does it have a logical connection to the notion of the Divine Calculator? Which came first historically?

2. Werner Heisenberg was a central, and ultimately controversial, figure in German science of the 1930s and 1940s. Read a biography of Heisenberg. Discuss how his early work in quantum mechanics influenced his prominent scientific role in Nazi Germany.

3. What changes in artistic movements were taking place during the period around 1900 (just before the discoveries of quantum mechanics) and in the mid-twentieth century? Are there any connections between the artistic and scientific movements of those times?

4. Some people interpret the Heisenberg uncertainty principle to mean that you can never really know anything for certain. Would you agree or disagree?

WWW RESOURCES

See *The Sciences* homepage at: **http://www.wiley.com/college/trefil** for valuable web links.

1. **http://pdg.web.cern.ch/pdg/cpep/adventure_home.html**
Particle Adventure Home Page, an excellent site from CERN that includes a tour of the Standard Model.

2. **http://www.fnal.gov/pub/inquiring/more/more.html**
The Science of Particle Physics, from Fermilab, a government institution with an unusually high commitment to education. Choose the topic that you would like to know more about.

3. **http://particleadventure.org/particleadventure/other/othersites.html**
Particle Physics Education Sites, from CERN—visit this site to find more interactive sites.

4. **http://www.physics.purdue.edu/nanophys**
Great pictures of really small things.

10

Atoms in Combination: The Chemical Bond

How does blood clot?

GREAT IDEA

Atoms bind together in chemical reactions by the rearrangement of electrons.

PHYSICS

Atoms bond to each other by the action of electromagnetic forces.

CHEMISTRY

Inert gas elements, including helium and neon, have completely filled electron shells and thus rarely take part in chemical reactions.

GEOLOGY

The ionic bonding of most common minerals makes rocks hard and brittle.

ENVIRONMENT

The national recycling effort involves hundreds of different processes, each one designed for the chemical bonds in specific materials. (Ch. 19)

HEALTH & SAFETY

Many types of fire extinguishers blanket flames with a chemical that robs the fire of oxygen, and thus stops the violent flaming reaction.

ASTRONOMY

The predominant state of matter in the Sun and other stars is plasma.

TECHNOLOGY

Many modern high-strength glues, including epoxy resins and superglue, are liquids that undergo polymerization reactions to produce a solid.

BIOLOGY

Living cells break down the chemical bonds in energy-rich molecules such as glucose (a sugar) into water, carbon dioxide, and energy. (Ch. 22)

Red = applications of the great idea discussed in this chapter.

Orange = other applications, some of which are explored in other chapters.

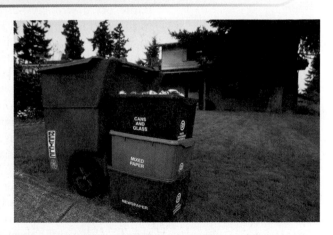

O n your way to pick the perfect spot on the beach, you and your friends divide up a heavy load of food and drinks. Your backpack is too full already, so you decide to discard a couple of old empty soft drink bottles, plastic wrappers, and an old newspaper to make more room. You walk over to the beach house where there are separate receptacles for glass, plastic, paper, and other trash.

It seems like a lot of extra work to sort out trash at the beach. Is it really worth the bother? But you dutifully follow the instructions, separate the different materials, and are soon on your way.

Our Material World

Think about all the things you've thrown away during the past month. Every day you toss out aluminum cans, plastic wrappers, glass jars, food scraps, and lots of paper. From time to time you also discard used batteries, disposable razors, dirty motor oil, worn-out shoes and clothes, even old tires or broken furniture. What happens to all that stuff after it becomes trash?

Many communities try to recycle much of their waste. Plastic, glass, aluminum, and newspaper, for example, can be reprocessed and turned into new products and packaging. Old oil can be refined and tires retreaded. But most trash ends up in landfills, where, we hope, it will eventually break down into soil.

The situation that faces our society is more than a little ironic. Everything you use and then throw away is made from collections of atoms bonded together. While they are in the store and for as long as we use them, we want these products and their packaging to last and keep looking new. But as soon as we throw them out, we'd like our disposable materials to fall apart and disappear. One way to achieve this end is to engineer biodegradable materials—paper, plastics, fabrics, and other goods designed to break apart when thrown away.

But what holds materials together in the first place? Why do certain atoms, when brought close together, develop an affinity and stick to each other? How do the molecules that play such an important role in our lives retain their identity? And how can we design new materials that will fall apart when their useful lives are over? The answers lie in the nature of the chemical bond.

Electron Shells and the Chemical Bond

Think about how two atoms might interact. You know that the atom is mostly empty space, with a tiny, dense nucleus surrounded by swift electrons. If two atoms approach each other, their outer electrons—the "border guards," if you will—encounter each other first. Whatever holds two atoms together thus involves primarily those outer electrons. In fact, the outer electrons play such an important role in determining how atoms combine that they are given the special name of *valence electrons* (see Chapter 8). Chemical bonding often involves an exchange or sharing of valence electrons, and the number of electrons in an atom's outermost shell is called its *valence*. Chemists often express the importance of the number of outer electrons by saying that valence represents the combining power of a given atom.

It turns out that by far the most stable arrangement of electrons—the electron configuration of lowest energy—is a completely filled outer shell. It is a fact of chemical life that different electron shells hold different numbers of electrons, which gives rise to the structure of the periodic table of the elements (Figure 10-1). A glance at the periodic table tells us that atoms with a total of 2, 10, 18, or 36 electrons (the atoms that appear in the extreme right-hand column) have filled shells and very stable configurations. Atoms with this many electrons in their outermost shells are *inert gases* (also called *noble gases*), which do not combine readily with other materials. Indeed, helium, neon, and argon, with atomic numbers 2, 10, and 18, and thus completely filled electron shells, are the only common elements that do not ordinarily react with other elements.

Every object in nature tries to reach a state of lowest energy, and atoms are no exception. Atoms that do not have the magic number of electrons (2, 10, 18, etc.) are more likely to react with other atoms to produce a state of lower energy. You are familiar with this kind of process in many other natural systems. If you put a ball on top of a hill, for example, it will tend to roll down to the bottom, creating a system of lower gravitational potential energy. Similarly, a compass needle tends to align itself spontaneously with the Earth's magnetic field, thereby lowering its magnetic potential energy. In exactly the same way, when two or more atoms come together the electrons tend to rearrange themselves to minimize the chemical potential energy of the entire system. This situation may require that they exchange or share electrons. As often as not, that process involves rearrangements with a total of 2, 10, 18, or 36 electrons.

Chemical bonds result from any redistribution of electrons that leads to a more stable configuration between two or more atoms, especially that of a filled electron shell.

> Most atoms adopt one of three simple strategies to achieve a filled shell: they give away electrons, accept electrons, or share electrons.

If the bond formation takes place spontaneously, without outside intervention, energy will be released in the reaction. The burning of wood or paper (once their temperature has been raised high enough) is a good example of this sort of

• **Figure 10-1** The first three rows (elements 1 to 18) of the periodic table showing element names, atomic numbers, and principal valences.

process, and the heat you feel when you put your hands toward a fire derives ultimately from the chemical potential energy that is given off as electrons and atoms are reshuffled. Alternatively, atoms may be pushed into new configurations by adding energy to systems. Much of industrial chemistry, from the smelting of iron to the synthesis of plastics, operates on this principle.

Types of Chemical Bonds

Atoms link together by three principal kinds of chemical bonds—ionic, metallic, and covalent—all of which involve redistributing electrons between atoms. In addition, three types of attractions—polarization, van der Waals interactions, and hydrogen bonding—result from shifts of electrons within their atoms or groups of atoms. Each type of bonding or attraction corresponds to a different way of rearranging electrons, and each produces distinctive properties in the materials it forms.

Ionic Bonds

We have seen that atoms with 2, 10, 18, or 36 electrons are particularly stable. By the same token, atoms that differ from these magic numbers by only one electron in their outer orbits are particularly reactive—in effect, they are "anxious" to fill or empty their outer orbits. Such atoms tend to form **ionic bonds**, chemical bonds in which the electrical force between two oppositely charged ions holds the atoms together.

Ionic bonds often form as one atom gives up an electron while another receives it. Sodium (a soft, silvery white metal), for example, has 11 electrons in an electrically neutral atom—2 in the lowest orbit, 8 in the next, and a single electron in its outer shell. Sodium's best bonding strategy, therefore, is to lose one electron. The 17th element, chlorine (a yellow-green toxic gas), on the other hand, is one electron shy of a filled shell. Highly corrosive chlorine gas will react with almost anything that can give it an extra electron. When you place sodium in contact with chlorine gas, the result is predictable: in a fiery reaction, each sodium atom donates its extra electron to a chlorine atom (Figure 10-2).

In the process of this vigorous electron exchange, atoms of sodium and chlorine become electrically charged—they become ions. Neutral sodium has 11 positive protons in its nucleus, balanced by 11 negative electrons in orbit. By losing an electron, sodium becomes an ion with one unit of positive charge, shown as Na^+ in Figure 10-2. Similarly, neutral chlorine has 17 protons and 17

A sodium atom		A chloride atom		A sodium cation		A chloride anion
Na	**+**	**Cl**		**Na⁺**	**+**	**Cl⁻**

• **Figure 10-2** Sodium, a highly reactive element, readily transfers its single valence electron to chlorine, which is one electron shy of the "magic" number 18. The result is the ionic compound sodium chloride—ordinary table salt. In these diagrams, electrons are represented as dots in shells around a nucleus.

Sodium ion (Na^+)

Chloride ion (Cl^-)

• **Figure 10-3** The atomic structure of a sodium chloride crystal consists of a regular pattern of alternating sodium and chloride ions.

electrons. The addition of an extra negative electron creates a chloride ion with one unit of negative charge, shown as Cl^- in the figure. The mutual electrical attraction of positive sodium and negative chloride ions is what forms the ionic bonds between sodium and chlorine. The resulting compound, sodium chloride or common table salt, has properties totally different from either sodium or chlorine.

Under normal circumstances sodium and chlorine ions will lock together into a crystal, a regular arrangement of atoms such as the one shown in Figure 10-3. Alternating sodium and chloride ions form an elegant repeating structure in which each Na^+ is surrounded by six Cl^-, and vice versa.

Ionic bonds may involve more than a single electron transfer. The 12th element, magnesium, for example, donates two electrons to oxygen, which has eight electrons. In the resulting compound, MgO (magnesium oxide), both atoms have stable filled shells of 10 electrons, and the ions, Mg^{2+} and O^{2-}, form a strong ionic bond. Ionic bonds involving the negative oxygen ion O^{2-} and positive ions, such as aluminum (Al^{3+}), magnesium (Mg^{2+}), silicon (Si^{4+}), and iron (Fe^{2+} or Fe^{3+}), are found in many everyday objects: in most rocks and minerals, in china and glass, and in bones and egg shells.

Ionic bonds in these compounds can be very strong, but only in certain ways. You can picture how this works by thinking about Tinkertoys.™ Tinkertoy structures can be quite strong; when assembled, it is difficult to break one apart by just pushing in the directions of the sticks. But Tinkertoy bonds break easily by twisting or snapping the sticks. In the same way, ionic bonds hold atoms together, but if the atoms should for some reason become displaced, the bond can't hold them very well. As a consequence, ionic-bonded materials such as rock, glass, or egg shells are usually quite brittle. These materials are strong in the sense that you can pile lots of weight on them. But once they shatter and ionic bonds are broken, they can't be put back together again.

EXAMPLE 10-1

Ionic Bonding of Three Atoms

Magnesium chloride, which plays an important role in some batteries, is an ionic-bonded compound with one part magnesium to two parts chlorine ($MgCl_2$). How are the electrons arranged in this compound?

Reasoning: From the periodic table (see Figure 10-1), magnesium and chlorine are elements 12 and 17, respectively. Magnesium, therefore, has 10 electrons ($2 + 8$) in inner shells and 2 valence electrons. Chlorine has 10 electrons ($2 + 8$) in its inner shells and 7 electrons in the outer one, meaning that it is 1 electron short of a filled outer shell (Figure 10-4).

Solution: Magnesium has two electrons to give, and chlorine seeks one electron, to achieve stable filled outer orbits. Thus magnesium gives one electron to each of two chlorine atoms, and the resulting Mg^{2+} ion attracts two Cl^- ions to form $MgCl_2$.

Metallic Bonds

Atoms in an ionic bond transfer electrons directly—electrons are on "permanent loan" from one atom to another. Atoms in a metal also give up electrons, but they use a very different bonding strategy. In a **metallic bond**, electrons are redistributed so that they are shared by many atoms.

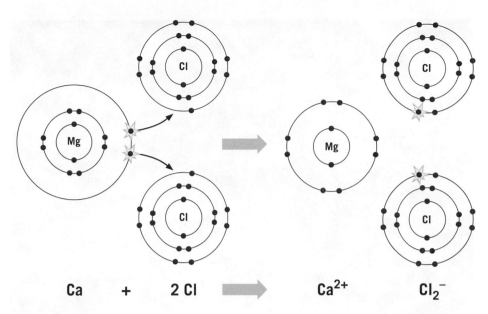

• **Figure 10-4** Magnesium and chlorine neutral-atom electron configurations (left), and their configurations after electrons have been transferred from the magnesium to the chlorine atoms (right).

$$Ca \quad + \quad 2\,Cl \quad \Longrightarrow \quad Ca^{2+} \quad Cl_2^{-}$$

Sodium metal, for example, is made up entirely of individual sodium atoms. All of these atoms begin with 11 electrons, but they release 1 to achieve the more stable 10-electron configuration. The extra electrons move away from their parent atoms to float around the metal, forming a kind of sea of negative charge. In this negative electron sea, the positive sodium ions adopt a regular crystal structure, as shown in Figure 10-5.

You can think of the metallic bond as one in which each atom shares its outer electron with all the other atoms in the system. Picture the free electrons as a kind of loose glue in which the metal atoms are placed. In fact, the idea of a metal as being a collection of marbles (the ions) in a sea of stiff, glue-like liquid provides a useful analogy.

Metals, characterized by their shiny luster and ability to conduct electricity, are formed by almost any element or combination of elements in which large numbers of atoms share electrons to achieve a more stable electron arrangement. Some metals, such as aluminum, iron, and copper, are familiar from everyday experience. But many elements can form into a metallic state when the conditions are right, including some that we normally think of as gases, such as hydrogen or oxygen at very high pressure. In fact, the great majority of chemical elements are known to occur in the metallic state. In

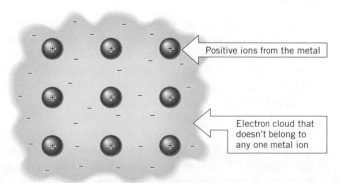

Positive ions from the metal

Electron cloud that doesn't belong to any one metal ion

• **Figure 10-5** Metallic bonding, in which a bond is created by the sharing of electrons among several metal atoms.

Gold metal is so soft and malleable that it can be hammered paper thin and applied to surfaces—an art known as *gilding*. The Invalides Dome in Paris, France is gilded in this manner.

addition, two or more elements can combine to form a metal *alloy*, such as brass (a mixture of copper and zinc) or bronze (an alloy of copper and tin). Modern specialty-steel alloys often contain more than half a dozen different elements in carefully controlled proportions.

The special nature of the metallic bond explains many of the distinctive properties we observe in metals. If you attempt to deform a metal by pushing on the marble-and-glue bonding system, atoms will gradually rearrange themselves and come to some new configuration—the metal is malleable. It's hard to break a metallic bond just by pushing or twisting, because the atoms are able to rearrange themselves. Thus when you hammer on a piece of metal, you leave indentations but do not break it, in sharp contrast to what happens when you hammer on a ceramic plate.

In Chapter 11, we will examine more closely the electrical properties of materials held together by the metallic bond. We will see that this particular kind of bond produces materials through which electrons—electrical current—can flow.

Covalent Bonds

In the ionic bond, one atom donates electrons to another on more-or-less permanent loan. In the metallic bond, on the other hand, atoms share some electrons throughout the material. In between these two types of bond is the extremely important **covalent bond**, in which well-defined clusters of neighboring atoms, called *molecules*, share electrons. These strongly bonded groups may consist of anywhere from two to many millions of atoms.

The simplest covalently bonded molecules contain two atoms of the same element, such as the diatomic gases hydrogen (H_2), nitrogen (N_2), and oxygen (O_2). In the case of hydrogen, for example, each atom has a relatively unstable single electron. Two hydrogen atoms can pool their electrons, however, to create a more stable two-electron arrangement. The two hydrogen atoms must remain close to each other for this sharing to continue, so a chemical bond is formed, as

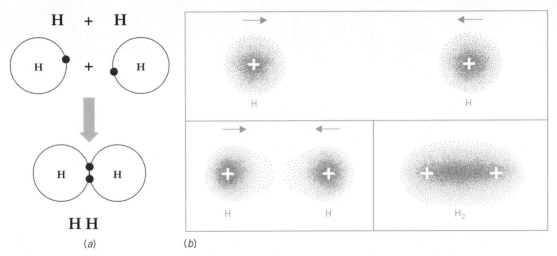

• **Figure 10-6** Two hydrogen atoms become an H_2 molecule by sharing each of their electrons in a covalent bond. This bonding may be represented schematically in a dot diagram (*a*), or by the merging of two atoms with their electron clouds (*b*).

shown in Figure 10-6. Similarly, two oxygen atoms, each with eight electrons, share two pairs of electrons.

Hydrogen, oxygen, nitrogen, and other covalently bonded molecules have lower chemical potential energy than isolated atoms because electrons are shared. These molecules are less likely to react chemically than the isolated atoms.

The most fascinating of all covalently bonded elements is carbon, which forms the backbone of all life's essential molecules. Carbon, with two electrons in its inner shell and four in its outer shell, presents a classic case of a half-filled shell. When carbon atoms approach each other, therefore, a real question arises as to whether they ought to accept or donate four electrons to achieve a more stable arrangement. You could imagine, for example, a situation where some carbon atoms give four electrons to their neighbors, while other carbon atoms accept four electrons, to create a compound with strong ionic bonds between C^{4+} and C^{4-}. Alternatively, carbon might become a metal in which every atom releases four electrons into an extremely dense electron sea. But neither of these things happens.

In fact, the strategy that lowers the energy of the carbon–carbon system the most is for the carbon atoms to share their outer electrons. Once bonds between carbon atoms have formed, the atoms have to stay close to each other for the sharing to continue. Thus the bonds generated are just like the bond in the case of hydrogen. The case of carbon is unusual, however, because the shape of its electron orbits allows a single carbon atom to form covalent bonds with up to four other atoms by sharing one of its four valence electrons with each. A *single bond* (shown as H—H) forms when one electron from each atom is shared, while a *double bond* (shown as O=O) results when two electrons from each atom are shared between one another.

By forming bonds among several adjacent carbon atoms, you can make rings, long chains, branching structures, planes, and three-dimensional frameworks of carbon in almost any imaginable shape. There is virtually no limit to the complexity of molecules you can build from such carbon–carbon bonding (Figure 10-7). So important is the study of carbon-based molecules that chemists have given it a special name: *organic chemistry*.

(a)

(b)

• **Figure 10-7** Carbon-based molecules may adopt almost any shape. The molecules may consist of long, straight chains of carbon atoms that form fibrous materials such as nylon (*a*), or they may incorporate complex rings and branching arrangements that form lumpy molecules such as cholesterol (*b*).

In fact, all the molecules in your body and in every other living thing are held together at least in part by covalent bonds in carbon chains (see Chapter 21). Covalent bonds also drive much of the chemistry in the cells of your body and play a role in holding together the DNA molecules that carry your genetic code. It would not be too much of an exaggeration to say that the covalent bond is the bond of life. Covalent bonds also play a critical role in the silicon-based integrated circuits that run your computer. The element silicon, like carbon, has four electrons in its outer shell.

(STOP) Stop and Think! Life on Earth is based on the properties of the element carbon. Looking at the first three rows of the periodic table in Figure 10-1, are there any other candidate elements that might form the basis of life elsewhere?

• **Figure 10-8** The water molecule and its polarity.

Polarization and Hydrogen Bonds

Ionic, metallic, and covalent bonds form strong links between individual atoms, but molecules also experience forces that hold one to another. In many molecules, the electrical forces are such that, although the molecule by itself is electrically neutral, one part of the molecule has more positive or negative charge than another. In water, for example, the electrons tend to spend more time around the oxygen atoms than around the hydrogen atoms. This uneven electron distribution has the effect of making the oxygen side of the water molecule more negatively charged, and the two "Mickey Mouse ears" of the hydrogen atom more positively charged (Figure 10-8). Atom clusters of this type, with a positive and negative end, are called *polar molecules*.

The electrons of an atom or molecule brought near a polar molecule such as water will tend to be pushed away from the negative side and shifted toward the positive side. Consequently, the side of an atom facing the negative end of a polar molecule will become slightly positive. This subtle electron shift, called *polarization,* in turn will give rise to an electrical attraction between the negative end of the polar molecule and the positive side of the other molecule. The electron movement thus creates an attraction between the atom and the molecule, even though the atoms and molecules in this scheme all may be electrically neutral. One of the most important consequences of forces due to polarization is the ability of water to dissolve many materials. Water, made up of strongly polar molecules, exerts forces that make it easier for ions such as Na^+ and Cl^- to dissolve.

A process related to the forces of polarization leads to the **hydrogen bond**, a weak bond that may form after a hydrogen atom links to an atom of certain other elements (oxygen or nitrogen, for example) by a covalent bond. Because of the kind of rearrangement of electrical charge described above, hydrogen may become polarized and develop a slight positive charge, which attracts another atom to it. You can think of the hydrogen atom as a kind of bridge in this situation, causing a redistribution of electrons that, in turn, holds the larger atoms or molecules together. Individual hydrogen bonds are weak, but in many molecules they occur repeatedly and therefore play a major role in determining the molecule's shape and function. Note that while all hydrogen bonds require hydrogen atoms, not all hydrogen atoms are involved in hydrogen bonds.

Hydrogen bonds are common in virtually all biological substances, from everyday materials such as wood, plastics, silk, and candle wax, to the complex structures of every cell in your body. As we shall see in Chapter 23, hydrogen bonds in every living thing link the two sides of the DNA double helix together, although the sides themselves are held together by covalent bonds. Ordinary egg white is made from molecules whose shape is determined by hydrogen bonds, and when you heat the material—when you fry an egg, for example—hydrogen bonds are broken and the molecules rearrange themselves so that instead of a clear liquid you have a white gelatinous solid.

Van der Waals Forces

The hydrogen bond exists because atoms or molecules can become polarized as their electrons shift to one side or another and thus create local electrical charges. In the molecules we've discussed so far, that electrical charge is more or less permanently locked into polar molecules in a fixed or static arrangement. Another force between molecules, called the van der Waals force, results from the polarization of electrically neutral atoms or molecules that are not themselves polar.

When two atoms or molecules are brought near each other, every part of one atom or molecule feels an electrical force exerted on it by all parts of the other. For example, an electron in one atom will be repelled by the electrons, but attracted to the nucleus, of an adjacent atom. The net result of these forces exerted on the electron may be a temporary shift of the electron. The same thing happens to every electron in any nearby atom or molecule, and the net result is that every electron is constantly shifting because of the presence of others.

What is remarkable is that this mutual, dynamic deformation gives rise to a net attractive force. In these van der Waals compounds, even if all the molecules

• **Figure 10-9** Graphite, a form of carbon that serves as the "lead" in your pencil, contains layers of carbon atoms strongly linked to each other by covalent bonds (represented by solid lines). These layers are held to each other by much weaker van der Waals bonds (represented by dashed lines).

are neutral and nonpolar, the sum of attractive forces wins out over repulsive forces and weak bonds are formed. This weak force that binds two atoms or molecules together is called the **van der Waals force**.

If you take a piece of clay and rub it between your fingers, your fingers pick up a slick coating of the material, even though the clay crumbles easily. The reason for this behavior is that the clay is made up of sheets of atoms. Within each sheet, atoms are held together by strong ionic and covalent bonds. One sheet is held to another, however, by comparatively weak van der Waals forces. This situation is not unlike the way a stack of photocopying paper will stick together on a dry day. Each sheet of paper is strong, but the stack of paper is stuck together by much weaker electrostatic forces. It is easy to pull the stack apart, but very difficult to rip the stack in two. When you crumble clay in your fingers, therefore, you are breaking weak van der Waals forces between layers, but preserving the stronger bonds that hold each layer together. The clay stains on your hands are thin sheets of atoms, held together by ionic and covalent bonds, and the crumbling you feel is the breaking of the van der Waals bonds.

Many other examples of van der Waals forces can be seen in everyday life. If you rub talcum powder on your body, for example, you use a layered material not unlike the clay just discussed. Similarly, when you write with a "lead" pencil, van der Waals–bonded layers of graphite (a form of carbon) are transferred from pencil to paper (Figure 10-9). As you draw the pencil across the paper, you break the van der Waals forces and leave behind dark graphite sheets on the paper. Van der Waals forces also link molecules in many everyday liquids and soft solids, from candle wax to Vaseline™ and other petroleum products.

States of Matter

So far, we have been talking about the ways in which the limited number of chemical elements in the periodic table can be locked together to give materials with many different properties. But chemical bonds alone cannot explain everything about the variety of materials in our world. All of our experience comes from interactions with large groups of atoms. Depending on how these groups of

Solid, molecules stay rigidly in place

(a)

Gas, molecules widely spaced apart

(c)

(b)

Liquid, molecules slide past one another

Three phases of water

• **Figure 10-10** The different states of matter are distinguished by the arrangements of their atoms (clockwise). In a gas (*a*) atoms or molecules are not bonded to each other, so they expand to fill any available volume. In a liquid (*b*) molecules are bound to each other but they are free to move relative to each other, yielding a material that can change shape but holds its volume. In a solid (*c*) atoms are locked into a rigid pattern that retains its shape and volume.

atoms are organized, they may take on many different forms. These different modes of organization, called the **states of matter**, include gases, plasmas, liquids, and solids (Figure 10-10).

Gases

A **gas** is any collection of atoms or molecules that expands to take the shape of and fill the volume available in its container (Figure 10-10*a*). Most common gases, including those that form our atmosphere, are invisible, but the force of a gust of wind is proof that matter is involved. The individual particles that comprise a gas may be isolated atoms such as helium or neon, or small molecules such as nitrogen (N_2) or carbon dioxide (CO_2). If we could magnify an ordinary gas a billion times, we would see these particles randomly flying about, bouncing off each other and anything else they contact. The gas pressure that inflates a basketball or tire is a consequence of these countless collisions.

Plasma

At extreme temperatures like those of the Sun, high-energy collisions between atoms may strip off electrons, creating a **plasma**, in which positive nuclei move about in a sea of electrons. Such a collection of electrically charged objects is something like a gas, but it displays unusual properties not seen in other states of matter. Plasmas, for example, are efficient conductors of electricity and, because they are gas-like, can be confined in a strong magnetic field or "magnetic bottle."

Plasmas are the least familiar state of matter to us, yet more than 99.9% of all the visible mass in the universe exists in this form. Not only are most stars composed of a dense hydrogen- and helium-rich plasma mixture, but several planets, including the Earth, have regions of thin plasma in their outer atmospheres. Some gradations exist between gas and plasma. Partially ionized gases in neon lights or fluorescent lightbulbs, for example, have a small fraction of their electrons in a free state. While not a complete plasma, these ionized gases do conduct electricity.

Liquids

Any collection of atoms or molecules that has no fixed shape but maintains its volume is called a **liquid** (Figure 10-10b). Other than water and biological fluids, few liquids occur naturally on Earth. Water, by far the most abundant liquid on the Earth's surface, is a dynamic force for geological change (see Chapter 18), and water-based solutions are essential to all life.

At the molecular level, liquids behave something like a container full of sand grains. The grains fill whatever volume they are poured into, freely flowing over each other without ever taking on a fixed shape. Attractive forces between individual atoms or molecules hold the liquid together. At the surface of the liquid, these attractive forces act to prevent atoms or molecules from escaping. In effect, they pull the surface in, giving rise to *surface tension*, the property that causes small quantities of the liquid to form beads or droplets.

Solids

Solids include all materials that possess a more or less fixed shape and volume (Figure 10-10c). In all solid materials the chemical bonds are both strong and directional. In detail, however, solids adopt several quite different kinds of atomic structures.

In **crystals**, groups of atoms occur in a regularly repeating sequence, the same atom or atoms appearing over and over again in a predictable way (Figure 10-11a). A crystal structure can be described by first determining the size and shape of the tiny box-like unit that repeats, then recording the exact type and posi-

○ Silicon atom
◉ Oxygen atom

(a)　　　　　　　　　　　　　　　(b)

• **Figure 10-11** The arrangement of atoms in a crystal (a) is regular and predictable over distances of thousands of atoms. The arrangement of atoms in a glass (b) is regular on a local scale, but irregular over a distance of three or four atoms.

Crystals of the mineral quartz, SiO_2, display faceted surfaces that result from the regular repetition of atoms.

tion of every atom that appears in the box. In common salt (see Figure 10-3), for example, the box is a tiny cube less than a billionth of a meter on an edge, and each box contains sodium atoms at the cube center and corners, and chlorine atoms at the center of every face. The regular atomic structure of crystals often leads to large single crystals with beautiful flat faces.

Common crystals include grains of sand and salt, computer chips, and gemstones. Most crystalline solids, however, are composed of numerous interlocking crystal grains. The two most important groups of these types of materials in our everyday life are metals and alloys that are characterized by metallic bonds, and most *ceramics,* a broad class of hard, durable solids that includes bricks, concrete, pottery, porcelain, and numerous synthetic abrasives, as well as teeth and bones and most rocks and minerals.

Glasses, in contrast to crystals, are solids with predictable local environments for most atoms, but no long-range order to the atomic structure (Figure 10-11b). In most common window and bottle glasses, for example, silicon and oxygen atoms form a strong three-dimensional framework. Most silicon atoms are surrounded by four oxygen atoms, and most oxygen atoms are linked to two silicon atoms. If you were placed on any atom in a glass, chances are you could predict the next-door atoms. Nevertheless, glasses have no regularly stacked boxes of structure. Travel more than two or three atom diameters from any starting point, and there is no way that you could predict whether you'd find a silicon or an oxygen atom.

🛑 **Stop and Think!** Glass window panes appear solid but after many, many years some glass begins to droop. How would you explain this behavior in terms of the structure of glass?

Polymers are extremely long and large molecules that are formed from numerous smaller molecules, like links forming a chain. The atomic structure of these materials is often one-dimensional, with predictable repeating sequences of atoms along the polymer chain (Figure 10-12). Common polymers include numerous biological materials, such as animal hair, plant cellulose, cotton, and spider's webs.

Polymers include all **plastics**, which are synthetic materials formed primarily from petroleum. They consist of intertwined polymer strands, much like the strands

• **Figure 10-12** Branched and unbranched polymers form from small molecules, just as long chains can form from individual links.

An unbranched polymeric chain

$CH_2 - CH_2 - CH_2 - CH_2 - CH_2 - CH_2 - CH_2 - CH_2 - CH_2 - CH_2 - CH_2 - CH_2$

A branched polymeric chain

Table 10-1 **Recycling Plastic**

#	Name	Principal Uses
1	PET	the most common recycled plastic, used for food and beverage containers
2	HDPE	rigid, narrow-neck containers for detergent and milk; grocery bags
3	PVC	plastic pipe, outdoor furniture, sturdy containers
4	LDPE	trash and produce bags, food storage containers
5	PP	aerosol caps, drinking straws
6	PS	packing peanuts, cups and plastic tableware

of fiberglass insulation. When heated, these strands slide across each other to adopt new shapes. When cooled, the plastic fiber mass solidifies into whatever shape is available. Though almost unknown a few decades ago, plastics have become our most versatile commercial materials, providing an extraordinary range of uses: films for lightweight packaging, dense castings for durable machine parts, thin strong fibers for clothing, colorful moldings for toys, and many others. (You've probably noticed the small triangular recycling symbol with a number inside on plastic containers. The numbers refer to common types of plastics, which are separated before reprocessing. Table 10.1 lists the most common varieties and their uses.) Plastics serve as paints, inks, glues, sealants, foam products, and insulation. New tough, resilient plastics have revolutionized many sports with products such as high-quality bowling and golf balls, and durable football and ice hockey helmets, not to mention a host of completely new products from Frisbees™ to roller blades.

TECHNOLOGY •

Liquid Crystals and Your Hand Calculator

Almost every material on Earth is easily classified as a solid, a liquid, or a gas, but scientists have synthesized an odd intermediate state of matter called *liquid crystals*. These materials have quickly found their way into many kinds of electronic devices, including the digital display of your pocket calculator. The distinction between a liquid and a crystal is one of atomic-scale order: atoms are disordered in a liquid, and ordered in a crystal. But what happens in the case of a liquid formed from very long or very flat molecules? Like a box of uncooked spaghetti or a plate of pancakes, in which the individual pieces may shift around but are well-oriented, these molecules may adopt ordered arrangements even in the liquid form.

(a)

(b)

• **Figure 10-13** Schematic diagram of a liquid crystal. Under normal circumstances, the elongated molecules are randomly oriented (*a*), but in an electric field the molecules align in an orderly pattern (*b*).

Liquid crystal displays are used in most pocket calculators.

If the molecules are polar, they may behave like tiny compass needles. Under ordinary circumstances these molecules will occur in random orientations, as in a normal liquid (Figure 10-13a). Under the influence of an electrical field, however, the molecules may adopt a partially ordered structure in which the molecules line up side-by-side (Figure 10-13b). This change in structure may even change some of the liquid's physical properties—its color or light-reflecting ability, for example. This phenomenon is now widely used in liquid crystal displays in watches and computers, in which electrical impulses align molecules in selected regions of the screen to provide a rapidly changing visual display.

Are liquid crystals found in nature? Every cell membrane is composed of a double layer of elongated molecules, called *lipids* (see Chapter 22). Many scientists now suspect that these "lipid bilayers" originated in the primitive ocean as molecules similar to today's liquid crystals. •

SCIENCE IN THE MAKING •

The Discovery of Nylon

Nature's success in making strong, flexible fibers inspired scientists to try the same thing. American chemist Wallace Carothers (1896–1937) began thinking about polymer formation while a graduate student in the 1920s. At the time, no one was sure how natural fibers formed, or what kinds of chemical bonds were involved. Carothers wanted to find out.

The chemical company Du Pont took a gamble by naming Carothers head of its new "fundamental research" group in 1928. No pressure was placed on him to produce commercial results, but within a few years his team had developed the synthetic rubber neoprene, and by the mid-1930s they had devised a variety of extraordinary polymers, including nylon, the first human-made fiber. Carothers also demonstrated conclusively that polymers in nylon are covalently bonded chains of small molecules, each with six carbon atoms.

Du Pont made a fortune out of nylon and related synthetic fibers. Nylon was inexpensive to manufacture and had many advantages over natural fibers. It could be melted and squeezed out of spinnerets to form strands of almost any desired size: threads, rope, surgical sutures, tennis racket strings, and paintbrush bristles, for example. These fibers could be made smooth and straight like fishing line, or rough and wrinkled like wool, to vary the texture of fabrics. Nylon fibers could also be kinked with heat, to provide permanent folds and pleats in clothing. The melted polymer could even be injected into molds to form durable parts such as tubing or zipper teeth.

Sadly, Wallace Carothers did not live to see the impact of his extraordinary discoveries. Suffering from increasingly severe bouts of depression and convinced that he was a failure as a scientist, Carothers took his own life in 1937, just a year before the commercial introduction of nylon. •

Changes of State

Place a tray of liquid water in the freezer and it will turn to solid ice. Heat a pot of water on the stove and it will boil away to a gas. These everyday phenomena are examples of **changes of state**, which are transitions among the solid, liquid, and gas states. *Freezing* and *melting* involve changes between liquids and solids, while *boiling* and *condensation* are changes between liquids and gases. In addition, some solids may transform directly to the gaseous state by *sublimation*.

Temperature induces these transitions by changing the speed at which molecules vibrate. An increase in the temperature of ice to above 0°C (32°F), for example, causes molecular vibrations to increase to the point that individual molecules jiggle loose and the crystal structure starts to break apart. A liquid forms. Then, above 100°C (212°F), individual water molecules move fast enough to break free of the liquid surface and form a gas. These changes require a great deal of energy, because a great many chemical attractions must be broken to change from a solid to a liquid, or from a liquid to a gas. Thus a pot of water may reach boiling temperature fairly quickly, but it takes a long time to break all the attractions between water molecules and boil the water away. By the same token, a glass of ice water will remain at 0°C for a long time, even on a warm day, until enough energy has been absorbed to break all the ice attractions. Only after the last bit of ice is gone can the water temperature begin to rise.

Chemical Reactions and the Formation of Chemical Bonds

Atoms, as well as smaller molecules, come together to form larger molecules, and larger molecules break up, in processes that we call **chemical reactions**. When we take a bite of food, light a match, wash our hands, or drive a car, we initiate chemical reactions. The Earth's chemical reactions include rock formation and rock weathering. Every moment of every day, countless chemical reactions in every cell of our bodies sustain life.

All chemical reactions involve rearrangement of the atoms in elements and compounds, as well as rearrangement of electrons to form chemical bonds. Such reactions can be expressed as a simple equation:

$$reactants \rightarrow products$$

All such reactions must balance, so that the total number and kinds of atoms are the same on both sides. For example, oxygen and hydrogen can form water by the reaction:

$$2H_2 + O_2 \rightarrow 2H_2O$$

This reaction is balanced because each side has four hydrogen atoms and two oxygen atoms. In the process of this reaction we can observe both chemical changes (the rearrangement of atoms) and physical changes (the gases hydrogen and oxygen transform into liquid water with different properties).

EXAMPLE 10-2

Balancing Chemical Equations

Your car battery contains plates of lead (Pb) and lead dioxide (PbO_2) immersed in a solution of sulfuric acid (H_2SO_4). After the battery has been discharged, both the lead and the lead dioxide have been converted into lead sulfate ($PbSO_4$), and the sulfuric acid has been converted into water (H_2O). Write a balanced reaction that models this process.

Reasoning and Solution: The reactants in this process are Pb, PbO_2 and H_2SO_4, while the products are $PbSO_4$ and H_2O. First write the equation in the simplest form, with one of each reactant and product molecule:

$$Pb + PbO_2 + H_2SO_4 \rightarrow PbSO_4 + H_2O$$

This equation, however, is not balanced. Two lead atoms appear on the left side, for example, while only one lead atom is on the right. The only way to make sure that there are as many atoms at the end as at the beginning is to write:

$$Pb + PbO_2 + 2H_2SO_4 \rightarrow 2PbSO_4 + 2H_2O$$

As you can see, on each side of the equation there are now two atoms of lead, two SO_4 groups, four hydrogen atoms, and two oxygen atoms. This balanced equation represents the reshuffling of atoms that goes on when your battery discharges. It tells us that two molecules of sulfuric acid will be used for each atom of lead, and that two molecules of water and two of lead sulfate will be produced at the end.

Every chemical reaction, no matter how complex, must balance: you must end with the same number of atoms with which you began.

Chemical Reactions and Energy: Rolling Down the Chemical Hill

Before considering the ways that atoms can combine to form molecules, pause for a moment to think about why these reactions take place at all. The fundamental reason, as so often happens with natural phenomena, has to do with energy, as described by the laws of thermodynamics (see Chapters 3 and 4).

Consider, for example, one of the electrons in the neutral sodium atom shown in Figure 10-2. This electron is moving in orbit around the nucleus, so it has kinetic energy. In addition, the electron possesses potential energy because it is a certain distance from the positively charged nucleus. Thus, just by virtue of its position, the electron is capable of doing work (this is the way potential energy was defined in Chapter 3). Finally, the electron has an additional component of potential energy because of the electrical repulsion between it and all of the other electrons in the atom. This is analogous to the small contribution to the Earth's potential energy from the other planets. The sum of these three energies—the kinetic energy associated with orbital motion, the potential energy associated with the nucleus, and the potential energy associated with the other electrons—is the total energy of the single electron in its orbit.

The atom's total energy is the sum of the energies of all of the electrons. For the isolated sodium atom in Figure 10-2, the total energy is the sum of the energy of the 11 electrons; for the chlorine atom, it is the sum of the energies of the 17 electrons. The total energy of the sodium–chlorine system is the sum of the individual energies of the two atoms.

Think about what happens to the energy of the sodium–chlorine system after the ionic bond has formed. The force on each electron is now different than it was before. For one thing, the number of electrons in each atom has changed; for another, the atoms are no longer isolated, so electrons in the sodium can exert forces on electrons in the chlorine and vice versa. Consequently, the orbits of all the electrons will shift a little due to the formation of the bond. This means that each electron will find itself in a slightly different position with regard to the nucleus, will be moving at a slightly different speed, and will experience a slightly different set of forces than it did before. The total energy of each electron will be different after the bond forms, the total energy of each atom will be different, and the total energy of the system will be different.

Whenever two or more atoms come together to form chemical bonds, the total energy of the system will be different after the bonds form than it was before.

Two possibilities exist: either the final energy of the two atoms is less than the initial energy, or the final energy is greater than the initial energy.

The reaction that produces sodium chloride from sodium and chlorine is an example of the first kind of reaction, in which the total energy of the electrons in the system is lower after the two atoms have come together. According to the first law of thermodynamics, the total energy must be conserved, and that difference is given off during the reaction in the form of heat, light, and sound (there is an explosion). A chemical reaction that gives off energy in some form is said to be *exothermic*.

Many examples of exothermic reactions occur in everyday life. The energy that moves your car is given off by the explosive chemical combination of gasoline and oxygen in the car's engine. The chemical reactions in the battery that runs your Walkman™ also produce energy, although in this case some of the energy is in the form of kinetic energy of electrons in a wire. At this moment, cells in your body are breaking down molecules of a sugar known as glucose to supply the energy you need to live.

If the final energy of the electrons in a reaction is greater than the initial energy, then you have to supply energy to make the chemical reaction proceed. Such reactions are said to be *endothermic*. The chemical reactions that go on when you are cooking (frying an egg, for example, or baking a cake) are of this type. You can put the ingredients of a cake together and let them sit for as long as you like, but nothing will happen until you turn on the oven and supply energy in the form of heat. When the energy is available, electrons can move around and rearrange their chemical bonds. The result: a cake where before there was only a mixture of flour, sugar, and other materials.

As we saw earlier, you can think of chemical reactions as being analogous to a ball lying on the ground. If the ball happens to be at the top of a hill, it will lower its potential energy by rolling down the hill, giving up the excess energy in the form of frictional heat. If the ball is at the bottom of the hill, you have to do work on it to get it to the top. In the same way, exothermic reactions correspond to systems that "roll down the hill," going to a state of lower energy and giving off excess energy in some form. Endothermic reactions, on the other hand, have to be "pushed up the hill," and hence absorb energy from their surroundings.

Common Chemical Reactions

Many millions of chemical reactions take place in the world around us. Some occur naturally, and some occur as the result of human design or intervention. In your everyday world, however, you are likely to see a few types of chemical reactions over and over again. Let's examine a few of these common reactions in more detail.

Oxidation and Reduction

Perhaps the most distinctive chemical feature of our planet is the abundance of a highly reactive gas, oxygen, in our atmosphere. This trait leads to many of the most familiar chemical reactions in our lives. **Oxidation** includes any chemical reaction in which an atom (such as oxygen or any other atom that will accept electrons) accepts electrons while combining with other elements. The atom that transfers the electrons is said to be *oxidized*. Rusting is a common gradual oxidation reaction in which iron metal combines with oxygen to form a reddish iron oxide, as given by the equation

$$4Fe + 3O_2 \rightarrow 2Fe_2O_3$$

Burning or *combustion* is a much more rapid oxidation, in which oxygen combines with carbon-rich materials to produce carbon dioxide and other byproducts that often pollute.

Hydrocarbons—chemical compounds of carbon and hydrogen—provide the most efficient fuels for combustion, with only carbon dioxide and water (hydrogen oxide) as products. This reaction is

▶ **In words**: Hydrocarbon plus oxygen reacts to form carbon dioxide plus water plus energy.

▶ **In chemical notation**:

$$C_nH_{2n+2} + \left[\frac{(3n+1)}{2}\right]O_2 \rightarrow nCO_2 + (n+1)H_2O + \text{energy}$$

If you heat or cook with natural gas, then you are using an oxidation reaction to generate energy in your home. The term "natural gas" refers to a compound that chemists call *methane*. A methane molecule consists of a single carbon atom covalently bonded to four hydrogen atoms, as shown in the drawing in Figure 10-14. The oxidation reaction involved in the burning of methane is written

$$CH_4 + 2O_2 \rightarrow CO_2 + 2H_2O$$

The opposite of oxidation is **reduction**, a chemical reaction in which electrons are transferred to an atom from other elements. The atom that receives the electrons is said to be *reduced*. Thousands of years before scientists discovered oxygen, primitive metalworkers had learned how to reduce metal ores by smelting. In the iron-smelting process (typical of the industry carried out at hundreds of North American furnaces 250 years ago), iron makers heated a mixture of ore (iron oxide) and lime (calcium oxide) in an extremely hot charcoal fire. The lime lowered the melting temperature of the entire mixture, which then reacted to produce iron metal and carbon dioxide.

A material that has been oxidized has lost electrons to oxygen or some other atom. A material that has been reduced, on the other hand, has gained electrons. You may find the mnemonic OIL RIG ("oxidation is loss, reduction is gain") useful in keeping the two straight.

Oxidation and reduction are essential to life, and they define the principal difference between plants and animals. As we shall see in Chapter 21, animals take in carbon-based molecules in their food and allow it to be oxidized in

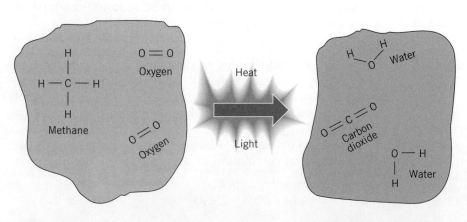

• **Figure 10-14** In pictorial form, an oxidation reaction involves the transfer of electrons to oxygen atoms. When natural gas (CH_4) burns, it combines with two oxygen molecules (O_2) to form a molecule of carbon dioxide (CO_2) and two molecules of water (H_2O).

their cells. Carbon dioxide is released as a byproduct. Plants take in carbon dioxide and use the energy in sunlight to reduce it, releasing oxygen as a byproduct.

Precipitation–Solution Reactions

Water and many other liquids have the ability to dissolve solids. You can observe such *solution reactions* when you put salt or sugar into water. You can also watch the opposite process—*precipitation reactions*—occur if you allow ocean water to evaporate. Ocean water contains a rich mixture of elements in solution that precipitate as the water evaporates. The complex sequence of precipitation includes calcium carbonate ($CaCO_3$), calcium sulfate ($CaSO_4$), sodium chloride (NaCl), and dozens of other more exotic compounds. In many locations around the world, including the area around Death Valley in California and the Great Salt Lake in Utah, thick deposits of these so-called "evaporite" chemicals are mined for sodium, potassium, boron, chlorine, and other elements. The next time you're at the ocean, scoop up a handful of salt water and, as the water evaporates, watch as tiny salt crystals precipitate on your palm.

Acid–Base Reactions

Acids are common substances, used by people for thousands of years. The word has even entered our everyday vocabulary; we may refer to someone with an "acid" wit when we mean a sense of humor that is sharp and corrosive. Acids corrode metals and have a sour taste. For our purposes, we can make a technical definition of an acid as follows: An *acid* is any material that, when put into water, produces positively charged hydrogen ions (i.e., protons) in the solution. Lemon juice, orange juice, and vinegar are examples of common weak acids, while sulfuric acid (used in car batteries) and hydrochloric acid (used in industrial cleaning) are strong acids.

Bases are another class of corrosive materials. They taste bitter and generally feel slippery between your fingers. For our purposes, we can define a *base* as any material that, when put into water, produces negatively charged OH^- ions. This ion, consisting of an oxygen–hydrogen system that has an extra electron, is called the hydroxide ion. Most antacids (e.g., milk of magnesia) are weak bases. Cleaning fluids containing ammonia are the strongest of bases we most often encounter, although still relatively weak. Most common drain cleaners are examples of strong bases.

Although the common definitions of acids and bases involve taste and feel, you shouldn't try these tests yourself. Many acids and bases are extremely dangerous and corrosive—for example, battery acid (H_2SO_4) and lye (NaOH).

When acids and bases are brought together in the same solution, the H^+ and the OH^- ions react together to form water, and we say that the substances neutralize each other. For instance, if we mix hydrochloric acid and lye, we will see the following reaction:

$$HCl + NaOH \rightarrow H_2O + NaCl$$

From this equation it appears that the formation of water removes both the positively charged hydrogen ion and the negatively charged hydroxide ion from solution, and the other parts of the original molecules come together to form a new material. Molecules formed by the neutralization of an acid and a base are called salts.

The definition of acids and bases in terms of whether they add positively charged protons or negatively charged hydroxide groups to water leads to a simple way of measuring the strength of a solution. Although you might not think so at first glance, pure distilled water always contains some protons and hydroxide groups. A small number of water molecules are always being broken up, and at the same time elsewhere in the liquid, protons and hydroxide groups come together to form new molecules of water. In fact, in pure water there are almost exactly 10^{-7} moles of positively charged particles per liter. Acids contain more positive charges than this, while bases contain fewer.

This fact is used to set the scale for measuring acids and bases. Pure water has a *pH* ("*power of Hydrogen*") of 7. An acid solution that has a larger number of positive charges—a concentration of 10^{-6} moles per liter, for example—will have a lower pH (a pH of 6 in this example). A base that has a lower concentration of positive charges—10^{-10} moles per liter, for example—will have a higher pH (a pH of 10 in this example). Here are some common pH values:

Stomach acid	1.0–3.0
Mean of Adirondack lakes, 1975	4.8
Normal rainwater	5.6
Mean of Adirondack lakes, 1930	6.5
Pure water	7.0
Human blood	7.3–7.5
Household ammonia	11.0

Note in particular the dramatic change in the acidity of lakes in New York's Adirondack Mountains between 1930 and 1975. The cause of this change is acid rain—a phenomenon we will examine in more detail in Chapter 19.

(a)

THE SCIENCE OF LIFE •

Antacids

The first step of digestion, once food is swallowed, takes place when acids in the stomach begin to break up the molecules that you have eaten. Occasionally, the stomach's acidity becomes too high, and we take antacids to feel better.

When you take an antacid, you are running a neutralization reaction in your body. Ordinary over-the-counter antacids contain bases such as aluminum hydroxide [$Al(OH)_3$] or sodium bicarbonate ($NaHCO_3$), which react with some of the acid in the stomach. These products do not neutralize all the stomach's hydrochloric acid, only enough of it to alleviate the symptoms. •

Polymerization and Depolymerization

The molecular building blocks of most common biological structures are small (see Chapter 21), consisting of a few dozen atoms at most. Yet most biological molecules are huge, with up to millions of atoms in a single unit. How can small building blocks yield large structures characteristic of living things? The answer lies in the process of polymerization.

A polymer is a large molecule that is made by linking smaller, simpler molecules together repeatedly to build up a complex structure (Figure 10-15). The word comes from the Greek *poly* (many) and *meros* (parts). In spider's webs, clotting blood, and a thousand other processes, living systems have mastered the art of combining small molecules into long chains.

(b)

• **Figure 10-15** Polymers may form by condensation (*a*) or addition polymerization reactions (*b*), with electrons represented as dots.

Polymerization reactions include all chemical reactions that form very large molecules from small molecules. Synthetic polymers usually begin in liquid form, with small molecules that move freely past their neighbors. Polyethylene, for example, begins as a gas with molecules containing just 6 atoms (2 carbon atoms and 4 hydrogen atoms), while the liquid that makes a common nylon contains molecules with 6 atoms of carbon, 11 of hydrogen, 1 of nitrogen, and 1 of oxygen—a combination that chemists write as $C_6H_{11}NO$. Polymers form from the liquid when the ends of these molecules begin to link up. In the case of nylon, the polymer forms by a *condensation reaction* in which each new polymer bond forms by the release of a water molecule (Figure 10-15*a*). Polyethylene, on the other hand, forms by *addition polymerization*, in which the basic building blocks are simply joined end to end (Figure 10-15*b*).

Polymers play an enormous role in our lives. The useful properties of these varied materials are related to the shapes of molecules and the way they come together to form materials (Figure 10-16). In polyethylene, for example, long-chain molecules wrap themselves together into something like a plate of hairy spaghetti. It's hard for water molecules to penetrate into this material, so it is widely used in packaging. The "plastic" on prepackaged fruit or meat at your supermarket may be made from polyethylene. A closely related polymer is polyvinyl chloride, whose basic building block, vinyl chloride, is just an ethylene molecule in which one of the four hydrogen atoms has been replaced by a chlorine atom. Because the chlorine atom is bigger than hydrogen, the molecules of the polymer are lumpy and cannot pack too closely together. Commercial PVC, widely used in water and sewer pipes, contains other kinds of molecules that move between the polymers, lubricating the system and making the resulting material highly flexible. Credit cards are also made from this material. Other common polymers include polypropylene (artificial turf), polystyrene ("foam" cups and packaging), and Teflon™ (nonstick cookware).

Many polymers are extremely long lasting, a situation that presents a growing problem in an age of diminishing landfills. Nevertheless, most polymers are not permanently stable. Given time, they will decompose into smaller molecules. This breakdown of a polymer into short segments is called *depolymerization*.

Perhaps the most familiar depolymerization reactions occur in your kitchen. Polymers cause the toughness of uncooked meat and the stringiness of many raw vegetables. We cook our food, in part, to break down these polymers. Chemicals

(*a*) Linear polymer   (*b*) Branched polymer   (*c*) Cross-linked polymer

• **Figure 10-16** Polymers can come in many forms: (*a*) a twisted chain, (*b*) a branched chain, and (*c*) chains that are linked together.

such as meat tenderizers and marinades can also contribute to depolymerization and can improve the texture of some foods.

Not all depolymerization is desirable. Museum curators are painfully aware of the breakdown process, which affects leather, paper, textiles, and other historic artifacts made of organic materials. Storage in an environment of low temperature, low humidity, and an inert atmosphere (preferably without oxygen) may slow the depolymerization process, but there is no known way to repolymerize old brittle objects.

Building Molecules: The Hydrocarbons

As an example of how a wide variety of materials can be made by assembling the same molecular building blocks in different ways, let's start with the methane molecule shown in Figure 10-14 and build a family of molecules known to chemists as *alkanes*. Alkanes are flammable materials (either gases or liquids) that burn readily and are often used as fuels. Most of the components of the gasoline in your car, for example, are members of this family. Alkanes are one example of **hydrocarbons**, molecules made completely from hydrogen and carbon atoms.

You can think of methane as being composed of a carbon atom and three hydrogen atoms (what chemists call the methyl group) plus a fourth hydrogen. We begin by noticing that we can replace the hydrogen in the methane by another methyl group to form a molecule with two carbons in it. This larger molecule is ethane, a volatile, flammable gas (Figure 10-17).

You can keep going. Adding a third methyl group produces propane, a three-carbon chain. Propane is widely used as a fuel for portable stoves; you may have used it on your last camping trip. The next step is to add another methyl group to form a four-carbon chain, a molecule called butane. But there is an ambiguity here. We could, as shown, add the new group at the end of the chain so that all four carbon atoms form a straight line. This process would give us a form of butane known as n-butane (or "normal" butane). However, we could just as well add the methyl group to the interior carbon atom. In this case, the molecule would be known as isobutane. Isobutane and n-butane have exactly the same numbers of carbon and hydrogen atoms, but are actually quite different materials. (To give just one example, the former boils at −11.6°C while the latter boils

Methane   Ethane   Propane   n-Butane

Isobutane

• **Figure 10-17** The alkane series may be built up by adding methyl groups to methane. The first three members of the group are methane (with one carbon atom), ethane (with two carbon atoms), and propane (with three carbon atoms). The next two members are isomers of butane (n-butane and isobutane, each with four carbons).

at −0.5°C.) Molecules that contain the same atoms but have different structures are called *isomers*.

As we continue the building process, moving to molecules with five carbons (pentane), six carbons (hexane), seven carbons (heptane), eight carbons (octane), and beyond, the number of different ways to assemble the atoms grows very fast. Octane, for example, has 18 different isomers; some have long chains, others are branched. As we shall see, these structural differences play an important role in a molecule's usefulness as an automotive fuel.

All other things being equal, the carbon chain length affects whether the alkane is a solid or liquid: the longer the chain, the higher the temperature at which that material can remain a solid. If carbon chains are straight, then alkanes with a half-dozen or so carbons are liquid, but those with more than 10 are soft solids. Good-quality paraffin candle wax, for example, which melts only near a hot flame of a wick, is composed primarily of chains with 20 to 30 carbon atoms. The presence of branches in the chain, however, makes it more difficult for the molecules to pack together efficiently. One consequence of branching is that the melting points are generally lowered compared to those of straight alkanes.

TECHNOLOGY •

Refining Petroleum

Deep underground are vast lakes of a thick, black liquid called petroleum, derived from many kinds of transformed molecules of former life forms. *Petroleum* is an extremely complex mixture of organic chemicals, as much as 98% molecules of hydrogen and carbon (mostly in the form of hydrocarbons), with about 2% of other elements. Engineers must separate this mixture into much purer fractions through the process of *distillation*.

• **Figure 10-18** A distillation column in a chemical plant separates hydrocarbons into fractions useful as gases, gasoline, kerosene, heating oil, lubricating oils and paraffin, asphalt, and tar.

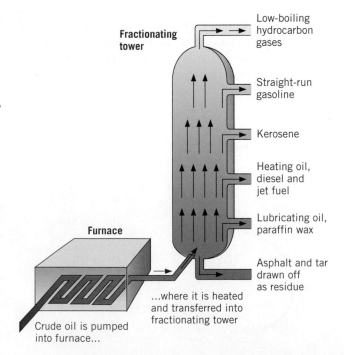

Hydrocarbons with different numbers and arrangements of carbon atoms have very different boiling temperatures. The key to distillation, then, is to boil off and collect different kinds of molecules successively, according to their boiling points. The most *volatile* hydrocarbon—the one with the lowest boiling point—is simple methane (CH_4), or natural gas. At the opposite extreme are very-long-chain hydrocarbons with dozens of carbon atoms, as in the molecules that comprise hard waxes, asphalt, and tar.

Modern chemical plants bristle with tall cylindrical towers that distill petroleum. Engineers pump crude oil into a tower, which is heated from below to create a temperature gradient up the tower (see Figure 10-18). At various levels of the tower, useful petroleum products such as gasoline or heating oil are recovered and sent to other parts of the plant for further processing.

Modern chemical plants bristle with tall distillation columns, in which petroleum products are purified.

The gasoline you buy at a service station is usually rated in "octanes." The octane rating of a gasoline is based on its ability to stand high compression in a cylinder without igniting. A fuel mixture that ignites while the piston is still moving up and compressing the gas in the cylinder will cause the engine to knock—a highly undesirable quality. In general, the more highly branched a molecule is, the better it will perform without knocking.

A particular isomer of octane that has five carbons in a row and the others on the sides turns out to have very good antiknock properties. This isomer is called isooctane, and an octane rating of 100 for any fuel mixture means that it is as good as pure isooctane. At the opposite extreme, n-heptane is an isomer with seven carbons in a straight chain that produces knocking all the time. An octane rating of zero means the fuel mixture is as bad as pure n-heptane. Thus the octane rating of a fuel is simply a statement that it performs as well as a particular mixture of isooctane and n-heptane. A fuel rated at 95 octane, for example, performs as well as a mixture of 95% isooctane and 5% n-heptane. •

THE SCIENCE OF LIFE •

The Clotting of Blood

Whenever you get a cut that bleeds, your blood begins a remarkable and complex sequence of chemical reactions called *clotting*. Normal blood, a liquid crowded with cells and chemicals that distribute nutrients and energy throughout your body, flows freely through the circulatory system. When that system is breached and blood escapes, however, the damaged cells release a molecule called *prothrombin*.

Prothrombin itself is inactive, but other blood chemicals convert it into the active chemical *thrombin*. The thrombin reacts to break apart other normally stable chemicals that are always present in blood, and thus produces small molecules that immediately begin to polymerize. The new polymer, called *fibrin*, congeals quickly and forms a tough fiber net that traps blood cells and seals the break in minutes.

Clotting chemical reactions differ depending on the nature of the injury and the presence of foreign matter in the wound. Biologists have discovered more than a dozen separate chemical reactions that may occur during the process. A number of diseases and afflictions may occur if some part of this complex chemical system is not functioning properly. Hemophiliacs lack one of the key clotting chemicals and so may bleed continuously from small cuts. Some lethal snake venoms, on the other hand, work by inducing clotting in a closed circulatory system. •

Thinking More About | Atoms in Combination

Life Cycle Costs

Every month chemists around the world develop thousands of new materials and bring them to market. Some of these materials do a particular job better than those they replace, some do jobs that have never been done before, and some do jobs more cheaply. All of them, however, share one property—when the useful life of the product of which they are a part is over, they will have to be disposed of in a way that is not harmful to the environment. Until very recently, engineers and planners had given little thought to this problem.

Think about the battery in your car, for example. The purchase price covered the cost of mining and processing the lead in its plates, pumping and refining the oil that was made into its plastic case, assembling the final product, and so on. When that battery reaches the end of its useful life, all of these materials have to be dealt with responsibly. For example, if you throw the battery into a ditch somewhere, the lead may wind up in nearby streams and wells.

One way of dealing with this sort of problem, of course, is to recycle materials—pull the lead plates out of the battery, process them, and then use them again. But even in the best system, some materials can't be recycled, either because they have become contaminated with other materials through use, or because we don't have technologies capable of doing the recycling. These materials have to be disposed of in a way that isolates them from the environment. The question becomes, "Who pays?"

Traditionally, in the United States, the person who does the dumping—in effect, the last user—must see to the disposal. In some European countries, however, a new approach is being introduced. Called "life cycle costing," this concept is built around the proposition that once a manufacturer uses a material, he or she owns it forever and is responsible for its disposal. The cost of a product such as a new car, then, has to reflect the fact that someday that car may be abandoned and the manufacturer will have to pay for its disposal.

Life cycle costing increases the price of commodities, contributing to inflation in the process. What do you think the proper trade-off is in this situation? How much extra cost should be imposed up front compared to eventual costs of disposal?

SUMMARY

Atoms link together by *chemical bonds,* which form when a rearrangement of electrons lowers the potential energy of the electron system, particularly by the filling of outer electron shells. *Ionic bonds* lower chemical potential energy by the transfer of one or more electrons to create atoms with filled shells. The positive and negative ions created in the process bond together through electrostatic forces. In *metals,* on the other hand, isolated electrons in the outermost shell wander freely throughout the material and create *metallic bonds.* *Covalent bonds* occur when adjacent atoms, or groups of atoms called molecules, share bonding electrons. *Hydrogen bonding* and *van der Waals forces* are special cases involving distortion of electron distributions to create electrical polarity—regions of slightly positive and negative charge that can bind together.

Atoms combine to form several different *states of matter. Gases* are composed of atoms or molecules that can expand to fill any available volume. *Plasmas* are ionized gases in which electrons have been stripped from the atoms. *Liquids* have a fixed volume but no fixed shape. *Solids* have fixed volume and shape. Solids include *crystals,* with a regular and repeating atomic structure; *glasses,* with a non-repeating structure; and *plastics,* which are composed of intertwined chains of molecules called *polymers.* The various states of matter can undergo *changes of state,* such as freezing, melting, or boiling, with changes in temperature or pressure.

Chemical bonds break and form during *chemical reactions,* which may involve the synthesis or decomposition of chemical elements or compounds. Reactions in which materials lose electrons to atoms such as oxygen are called *oxidation* reactions. In the opposite reaction, called *reduction,* electrons are moved onto atoms.

All life depends on *polymerization* reactions, in which small molecules link together to form long polymer fibers such as natural hair, silk, plant fiber, and skin, and synthetic materials such as polyesters, vinyl, cellophane, and other plastics. *Hydrocarbons,* widely used as fuels, are chainlike molecules made of carbon and hydrogen atoms. High temperatures and certain chemicals can cause the breakdown of polymers, or depolymerization, which is often a key objective in cooking.

KEY TERMS ABOUT CHEMICAL BONDING

chemical bond	metallic bond	covalent bond	van der Waals forces
ionic bond	metal	hydrogen bond	states of matter

gas	crystal	changes of state	polymerization
plasma	glass	chemical reaction	hydrocarbon
liquid	polymer	oxidation	
solid	plastic	reduction	

REVIEW QUESTIONS

1. When is an electron a valence electron? Why are valence electrons especially important in chemical reactions?

2. Describe the ionic bond. Give an example of a material that uses it.

3. Describe the metallic bond. What properties of metal follow from the properties of the bond?

4. Which type of chemical bond is found in an alloy? Give an example of an alloy.

5. Describe the covalent bond. Give an example of a material that uses it.

6. Describe the hydrogen bond. Explain how it affects the properties of water.

7. Describe the van der Waals force. Give an example of a material with van der Waals interactions. What distinctive properties does that material display?

8. Describe three everyday states of matter, including differences among them in volume and shape. In which states do the atoms or molecules have the greatest kinetic energy? The least?

9. How is a plasma like a gas? How is it like a metal? Where are plasmas found in the solar system? Where are they found in modern technologies?

10. How is a glass constructed from its atoms? A plastic? A cystalline solid?

11. Identify common changes of state and give examples of each.

12. In what sense are oxidation and reduction reactions opposites?

13. Are the following substances acid, base, or neutral: sodium bicarbonate (pH = 8.3); sugar solution (pH = 7.0); milk (pH = 6.7); orange juice (pH = 3.6); milk of magnesia (pH = 10.5)?

14. What is polymerization? Give an example.

15. What are the characteristics of alkanes? What are the names and properties of the first five alkanes?

16. How many isomers of hexane are there? Draw them.

DISCUSSION QUESTIONS

1. Identify objects around you that use the three kinds of chemical bonding or the three kinds of attraction. Which combine two or more kinds?

2. Why do most molecules have covalent bonds?

3. Classify the solid objects around you as ceramics, metals, glasses, and plastics.

4. Based on your experience today, list as many everyday chemical reactions as you can. Try to classify these reactions according to their type (i.e., polymerization, oxidation, etc.).

5. The chemistry of the planet Mars is quite similar to Earth except that there is almost no water. Which common chemical reactions that occur on Earth would you not expect to see on Mars?

6. Cooks often tenderize meat by soaking it in a liquid such as lemon juice or vinegar for several hours. What chemical reaction do you think is taking place in the meat? How is this reaction analogous to heating in an oven?

7. During icy winter conditions we often throw salt on sidewalks and streets. What occurs when salt comes in contact with ice? What reaction is involved? How do you think the melting point of salt water compares to that of pure water?

8. Explain why melting ice is considered an endothermic process.

PROBLEMS

1. When you burn natural gas (CH_4) it unites with oxygen (O_2) to form carbon dioxide (CO_2) and water (H_2O). Write an equation to balance the reactants and products of this reaction.

2. Use some other examples of the burning of hydrocarbons (e.g., ethane-C_2H_6 or propane-C_3H_8) to balance reaction equations.

INVESTIGATIONS

1. Look around your home and school and list the variety of plastic objects. What strategy might you develop to recycle plastics? Note the numbers surrounded by a triangle on many disposable plastics. What do the numbers mean?

2. What materials were used for the construction of buildings, furniture, and transportation devices in the United States 200 years ago? What modern technologies would be difficult or impossible with just those materials?

3. Why is it that some materials in landfills don't break down into their constituent chemical parts?

4. Dissect a disposable diaper. How many kinds of materials can you identify? What are the key properties of each? What kind of chemical bonding might contribute to the distinctive properties of these materials? Investigate the arguments for and against using disposable diapers.

5. We often refer to drinking water as being "soft" or "hard," based on the kind of impurities present in the water. Which kind do you have in your community? What kind of chemical reaction can take place if water is too hard? How can you prevent that reaction from occurring?

WWW RESOURCES

See *The Sciences* homepage at: **http://www.wiley.com/college/trefil** for valuable web links.

1. **http://www.chem.ox.ac.uk/mom/default.html**
Molecules of the Month includes 3D models of cholesterol, Viagra, and Molecules in the Bathroom.

2. **http://www.pc.chemie.tu-darmstadt.de/research/molcad/java/**
Learn about the chemistry of cocoa and chocolate.

11

Properties of Materials

How have computers gotten so much faster?

GREAT IDEA

A material's properties result from its constituent atoms and the arrangements of chemical bonds that hold those atoms together.

PHYSICS

Semiconductor diodes control the flow of electrons in modern electronic devices.

CHEMISTRY

Metals in which bonding electrons are shared among many atoms, make the best electrical conductors.

ENVIRONMENT

Photovoltaic cells will be used increasingly to convert environmentally safe solar energy into electricity.

GEOLOGY

Rocks tend to be tough and brittle because their atoms are held together primarily by strong ionic bonds.

HEALTH & SAFETY

Flexible synthetic fibers with high tensile strength are used in automobile seat belts.

ASTRONOMY

Modern telescopes rely on electronic light detectors that use photoelectronic material. (Ch. 14)

TECHNOLOGY

High-temperature superconductors, which operate at the temperature of liquid nitrogen, may soon find many applications in high-efficiency magnets and motors.

BIOLOGY

The human brain is made up of interconnectred nerve cells, which are arranged in a complex system that cannot be reproduced artificially.

Red = applications of the great idea discussed in this chapter.

Orange = other applications, some of which are explored in other chapters.

It's only 10 A. M. but the beach is already starting to get crowded. You and your friends decide to walk a few hundred meters down the beach to a more open stretch.

There's a surprising amount of gear to haul across the beach. You carry a Styrofoam cooler filled with aluminum soda cans, while your backpack holds a pile of sandwiches, SPF30 sunblock, a cotton towel, a Frisbee, and your Diskman with a stack of your favorite music.

Without even thinking about it you've loaded up with dozens of amazing high-tech materials, each with its own distinctive and valuable properties: insulating lightweight Styrofoam, shiny strong aluminum, creamy protective lotion, tasty layered sandwiches, soft cool cotton, durable hard plastic, and astonishingly versatile semiconductor devices in your electronic gear. Even your backpack features a score of different sophisticated polymer fibers, plastic zippers, synthetic dyes, and metal alloys. Every one of these distinctive materials has been designed to serve our needs, and every one is crafted from atoms.

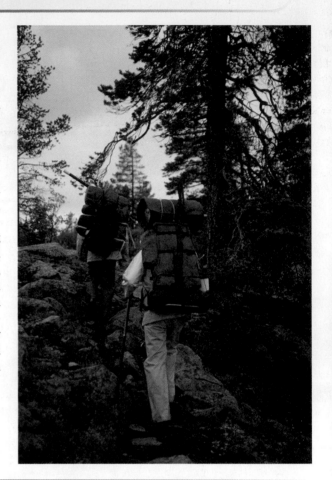

Materials and the Modern World

The materials people use, perhaps more than any other facet of a culture, define the technical sophistication of a society. We speak of the most primitive human cultures as Stone Age societies, and recognize Iron Age and Bronze Age peoples as progressively more advanced.

Stop and Think! Given that perspective, in what age are we now living?

Take a moment and look around your room. How many different kinds of materials do you see? The lights and windows employ glass—a brittle, transparent material. The walls may be made out of gypsum, a chalk-like mineral that has been compressed in a machine and placed between sheets of heavy paper. Your chair probably incorporates several materials, including metal, wood, woven fabric, and glues.

A typical room is filled with high-tech materials: synthetic fibers, specialized glass, colorful plastics, metal alloys, and cosmetics.

Many of these materials would have been familiar to Americans 200 years ago, when almost everything was made from less than a dozen common substances: wood, stone, pottery, glass, animal skin, natural fibers, and a few basic metals such as iron and copper. But, thanks to the discoveries of chemists, the number of everyday materials has increased by a thousandfold in the past two centuries. Cheap and abundant steel transformed the nineteenth-century world with railroads and skyscrapers, while aluminum provided a lightweight metal for hundreds of applications. The development of rubber, synthetic fibers, and a vast array of other plastics affected every kind of human activity from industry to sports. Brilliant new pigments enlivened art and fashion, while new medications cured many ailments and prolonged lives. And in our electronic age, the discovery of semiconductor and superconductor materials has changed life in the United States in ways that our eighteenth-century ancestors could not have imagined.

Chemists take natural elements and compounds that form earth, air, and water and devise thousands of useful materials. They succeed in part because materials display so many different properties: color, smell, hardness, luster, flexibility, density, solubility in water, texture, melting point, strength—the list goes on and on. Each new material holds the promise of doing some job cheaper or safer or otherwise better than any other.

Based on our understanding of atoms and their chemical bonding (see Chapter 10), we now realize that the properties of every material depend on three essential features:

1. The kind of atoms of which it is made
2. The way those atoms are arranged
3. The way the atoms are bonded to each other

In this chapter, we look at different properties of materials and see how they relate to their atomic architecture. We examine the strength of materials—how well they resist outside forces. We look at the ability of materials to conduct electricity, and whether they are magnetic. And, finally, we describe what are perhaps the most important new materials in modern society, the semiconductor and the microchip.

The Strengths of Materials

Have you ever carried a heavy load of groceries in a thin plastic grocery bag? You can cram a bag full of heavy bottles and cans and lift it by its thin handles without fear of breakage. How can something as light, flexible, and inexpensive as a piece of plastic be so strong?

Strength is the ability of a solid to resist changes in shape. Strength is one of the most immediately obvious material properties, and it bears a direct relationship to chemical bonding. A strong material must be made with strong chemical bonds. By the same token, a weak material, like a defective chain, must have weak links between some of its atoms. While no type of bond or attraction is universally stronger than the other kinds, van der Waals forces are generally the weakest. Any material with van der Waals forces will have one or more particularly soft directions of bonding, and you will probably be able to pull the material apart with your hands. You experience this softness whenever you use baby powder, graphite lubricant, or soap.

By contrast, many strong materials, such as rocks, glass, and ceramics, are held together primarily by ionic bonds. Next time you see a building under construction, look at the way beams and girders link diagonally to form a rigid framework. Chemical bonds in strong materials do the same thing. A three-dimensional network of ionic bonds in these materials holds them together like a framework of steel girders.

The strongest materials we know, however, incorporate long chains and clusters of carbon atoms held together by covalent bonds. The extraordinary strength of natural spider webs, synthetic Kevlar (used to make bulletproof vests), diamonds, and your plastic shopping bag all stem from the strength of covalent bonds to carbon atoms.

Different Kinds of Strength

Every material is held together by the bonds between its atoms. When an outside force is applied to a material, the atoms must shift their positions in response. The bonds stretch and compress, and an equal and opposite force is generated inside the material to oppose the force that is imposed from the outside, in accordance with Newton's third law of motion. The strength of a material is thus related to the size of the force it can withstand when it is pushed or pulled.

Material strength is not a single property, because there are different ways of placing an object under stress. Scientists and engineers recognize three very different kinds of strength when characterizing materials:

1. Its ability to withstand crushing (*compressive strength*)
2. Its ability to withstand pulling apart (*tensile strength*)
3. Its ability to withstand twisting (*shear strength*)

Your everyday experience will convince you that these three properties are often quite independent. A loose stack of bricks, for example, can withstand crushing pressures—you can pile tons of weight on it without having the stack collapse.

The strength of materials is vital to many activities. Bones and muscles provide a weightlifter's strength.

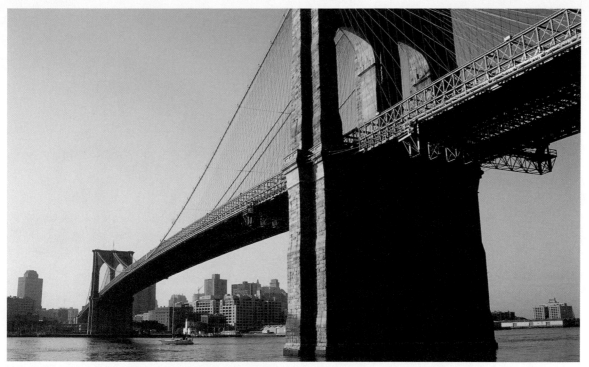

Suspension bridges feature vertical supports that are extremely strong under compression, and massive steel cables that are extremely strong under tension.

But the stack of bricks has little resistance against twisting. Indeed, it can be toppled by a child. A rope, on the other hand, is extremely strong when pulled, but has little strength under twisting or crushing.

The point at which a material stops resisting external forces and begins to bend, break, or tear is called its *elastic limit*. We see examples of this phenomenon every day. When you break an egg, crush an aluminum can, snap a rubber band, or fold a piece of paper, you exceed an elastic limit and permanently change the object. When the materials in your body exceed their elastic limit, the consequences can be catastrophic. Our bones may break if put under too much stress, while arteries under pressure that is too high may rupture in an aneurysm.

A material's strength is a result of the type and arrangements of chemical bonds. Think about how you might design a structure using Tinkertoys that would be strong under crushing, pulling apart, or twisting. The strongest arrangement would have lots of short sticks with triangular patterns. Nature's strongest structure, diamond, adopts this strategy; it is exceptionally strong under all three kinds of stress because of its three-dimensional framework of strong carbon–carbon bonds (see Figure 11-1). Glass, ceramics, and most rocks, which also feature rigid frameworks of chemical bonds, are relatively strong. Many plastics like the one in your shopping bag, however, have strong bonds in only one direction and thus are strong when stretched, but have little strength when twisted or crushed. Materials with layered atomic structures, in which planes of atoms are arranged like a stack of paper, are generally strong when squeezed, but quite weak under other stresses. Thus the strength of a material depends on the kind of atoms in it, the way they are arranged, and the kind of chemical bonds that hold the atoms together.

(a)

(b)

• **Figure 11-1** The girder framework of a skyscraper (*a*) and a diamond's crystal structure (*b*) are both strong because of numerous very strong connections. In a building the connections are steel girders; in diamond they are carbon–carbon covalent bonds.

Composite Materials

Composite materials combine the properties of two or more materials. The strength of one of the constituents is used to offset the weakness of another, resulting in a material whose strengths are greater than any of its components. Plywood, one of the most common composite materials, consists of thin wood layers glued together with alternating grain direction. The weakness of a single thin sheet of wood is compensated by the strength of the neighboring sheets. Not only is ply-

In composite materials, such as plywood and reinforced concrete, one material's weakness is compensated by the other's strength.

wood much stronger than a solid board of the same dimension, but it can also be produced from much smaller trees by slicing thin layers of wood off a rotating log, like removing paper from a roll.

Reinforced concrete is a common composite material in which steel rods (with great tensile strength) are embedded in a concrete mass (with great compressive strength). A similar strategy is used in fiberglass, formed from a cemented mat of glass fibers, and new carbon-fiber composites that are providing extraordinarily strong and lightweight materials for industry and sports applications.

The modern automobile features a wide variety of composite materials. Windshields of safety glass are layered to resist shattering and reduce sharp edges in a collision. Tires are intricately formed from rubber and steel belting for strength and durability. Car upholstery commonly mingles natural and artificial fibers, and dashboards often employ complexly laminated surfaces. The bodies of many cars are formed from a fiberglass or other molded lightweight composite. And, as we shall see, all of a modern automobile's electronics, from radio to ignition, depend on semiconductor composites of extraordinary complexity.

Electrical Properties of Materials

Of all the properties of materials, none are more critical to our world than those that control the flow of electricity. Glance around you and tally up the number of electrical devices nearby. Chances are your list will quickly grow to several dozen. Almost every aspect of our technological civilization depends on electricity, so scientists have devoted a good deal of attention to materials that are useful in electrical systems. (See Chapter 5 for a review of electricity and magnetism.) If the job at hand is to send electrical energy from a power plant to a distant city, for example, we need a material that will carry the electrical energy without much loss. If, on the other hand, the job is to put a covering over a wall switch so that we will not be endangered by electricity when we turn on a light, we want a material that will not conduct electricity at all. In other words, a large number of different kinds of materials contribute to any electrical device.

Conductors

Any material capable of carrying electrical current—that is, any material through which electrons can flow freely—is called an **electrical conductor**. Metals, such as the copper that carries electricity through the building in which you are now sitting, are the most common conductors, but many other materials also conduct electricity. Salt water, for example, contains ions of sodium (Na^+) and chlorine (Cl^-), which are free to move if they become part of an electric circuit. We can find out if a material will conduct electricity by making it part of an electric circuit and seeing if current will flow through it.

The arrangement of a material's electrons determines its ability to conduct electricity. In the case of metals, you will recall, some electrons are bonded fairly loosely and shared by many atoms. If you connect a copper wire across the poles of a battery, those electrons are free to move in response to the battery's potential. They flow from the negative pole toward the positive pole of the battery.

As we saw in Chapter 5, the motion of electrons in electrical currents is seldom smooth. Under normal circumstances, electrons moving through a metal will collide continuously with the much heavier ions in that metal. In each of those collisions, electrons lose some of the energy they have gotten from the battery, and that energy is converted to the faster vibration of ions—what we perceive as heat. The property by which materials drain the energy away from a current is called **electrical resistance**. Even very good conductors have some electrical resistance. (The inverse of electrical resistance is *electrical conductance,* or the ease with which electrons flow in a material. Resistance and conductance are thus different ways of describing the same property.)

Insulators

Many materials incorporate chemical bonds in which few electrons are free to move in response to the "push" of an electric field. In rocks, ceramics, and many biological materials such as wood and hair, for example, the electrons are bound tightly to one or more atoms by ionic or covalent bonds (see Chapter 10). It takes considerable energy to pry electrons loose from those atoms—energy that is normally much greater than the energy supplied by a battery or an electrical outlet. These materials will not conduct electricity unless they are subjected to an extremely high voltage, which can pull the electrons loose. If they are made part of an electric circuit, no electricity will flow through them. We call these materials **electrical insulators**.

The primary use of insulators in electric circuits is to channel the flow of electrons and to keep people from touching wires that are carrying current. The shields on your light switches and household power outlets and the casings for most car batteries, for example, are made from plastic, a reasonably good insulating material that has the added advantages of low cost and flexibility. Similarly, electrical workers use protective rubber boots and gloves when working on dangerous power lines. In the case of high-power lines, glass or ceramic components are used to isolate the current because of their superior insulating ability.

Semiconductors

Many materials in nature are neither good conductors nor perfect insulators. We call such materials **semiconductors**. As the name implies, a semiconductor will carry electricity but will not carry it very well. Typically, the resistance of silicon is a million times higher than the resistance of a conductor such as copper. Nevertheless, silicon is not an insulator, because some of its electrons do flow in an electric circuit. Why should this be?

In a silicon crystal (Figure 11-2), all the electrons are taken up in the covalent bonds that hold each silicon atom to its neighbors. At room temperature, the silicon atoms vibrate and a few of the covalent bonding electrons are shaken loose—think of them as picking up a little of the vibrational energy of the atoms. These *conduction electrons* are free to move around the crystal. If the silicon is made part of an electric circuit, a modest number of conduction electrons are free to move through the solid.

When a conduction electron is shaken loose, it leaves behind a defect in the silicon crystal—the absence of an electron. This missing electron is called a *hole*. Just as electrons move in response to electrical charges, so too can holes (see Figure 11-3).

The motion of holes in semiconductors is something like what you see in a traffic jam on a crowded expressway. A space will open up between two cars, after which one car moves up to fill the space, then another car moves up to fill that space, and so on. You could describe this sequence of events as the successive motion of cars. But you could just as easily (in fact, from a mathematical point of view *more* easily) say that the space between cars—the hole—moves backward down the line. In the same way, you can either describe the effects of the successive jumping of electrons from one atom to another, or talk about the hole moving through the material.

Electrical wiring consists of a conducting metal core surrounded by an insulating layer of plastic.

Silicon atom

Outer-shell electron

Pure material

• **Figure 11-2** A normal silicon crystal displays a regular pattern of silicon atoms. Some of its electrons are shaken loose by atomic vibrations, and these electrons are free to move around and conduct electricity.

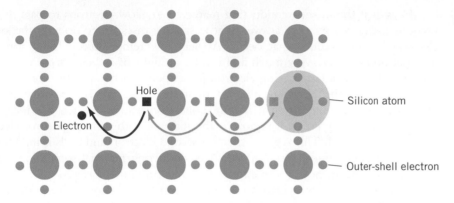

• Figure 11-3 A hole in a semiconductor is produced when an electron is missing. Holes can move, just like electrons. As an electron moves to fill a hole, it creates another hole where it used to be.

Although there are relatively few semiconducting materials in nature, they have played an enormous role in the microelectronics industry, as we shall see later.

Superconductors

Some materials cooled to within a few degrees of absolute zero exhibit a property known as **superconductivity**—the complete absence of any electrical resistance. Below some very cold critical temperature, electrons in these materials are able to move without surrendering any of their energy to the atoms. This phenomenon, discovered in Holland in 1911, was not understood until the 1950s. Today, superconducting technologies provide the basis for a billion-dollar-a-year industry worldwide. The principal reason for this success is that once a material becomes superconducting and is kept cool, current will flow in it forever. This behavior means that if you take a loop of superconducting wire and hook it up to a battery to get the current flowing, the current will continue to flow even if you take the battery away.

In Chapter 5, we learned that current flowing in a loop creates a magnetic field. If we make an electromagnet out of superconducting material and keep it cold, the magnetic field will be maintained at no energy cost except for the refrigeration. Indeed, superconductors provide strong magnetic fields much more cheaply than any conventional copper-wire electromagnet because they don't heat up from electrical resistance. Superconducting magnets are used extensively in many applications where very high magnetic fields are essential—for example, in particle accelerators (see Chapter 12), and in magnetic resonance imaging systems for medical diagnosis. Perhaps they will eventually be used in everyday transportation.

As cars in a traffic jam move slowly forward, "holes" in the traffic can be described as moving backward.

How is it that a superconducting material can allow electrons to pass through without losing energy? The answer in at least some cases has to do with the kind of electron–ion interactions that occur. At very low temperatures, heavy ions in a material don't vibrate very much and can be thought of as being fixed in more or less one place. As a fast-moving electron passes between two positive ions, the ions are attracted to the electron and start to move toward it. By the time the ions respond, however, the electron is long gone. Nevertheless, when the ions move close together, they create a region in the material with a more positive electrical charge than normal. This region attracts a second electron and pulls it in. Thus the two electrons can move through the superconducting material something like the way two bike racers move down a track, with one running interference for the other.

At the very low temperatures at which a material becomes superconducting, electrons hook up in pairs, and the pairs start to interlock like links of a complex, tangled matrix. While individual electrons are very light, the whole collection of interlocked electrons in a superconductor is quite massive. If one electron encounters an ion, the electron can't be easily deflected. In fact, to change the velocity of any electron, something you would have to do to get energy from it, you would have to change the velocity of *all* the electrons. Because this can't be done, no energy is given up in such collisions, and electrons simply move through the material together. If the temperature is raised, though, the ions vibrate more vigorously and are no longer able to perform the delicate minuet required to produce the electron pairs. Thus above the critical temperature, superconductivity breaks down.

THE ONGOING PROCESS OF SCIENCE •

Searching for New Superconductors

Until the mid-1980s, all superconducting materials had to be cooled in liquid helium, an expensive and cumbersome refrigerant that boils at a few degrees above absolute zero, because none of these materials was capable of sustaining superconductivity above about 20 kelvins. Acting on a hunch, scientists Karl Alex Müller and George Bednorz of IBM's Zurich, Switzerland, research laboratory began a search for new superconductors. Traditional superconductors are metallic, but Bednorz and Müller decided instead to focus on oxides—chemical compounds, such as most rocks and ceramics, in which oxygen participates in ionic bonds. It was an odd choice, for oxides make the best electrical insulators, although a few unusual oxides do conduct electricity.

Working with little encouragement from their peers and no formal authorization from their employers, the scientists spent many months mixing chemicals, baking them in an oven, and testing for superconductivity. The breakthrough came on January 27, 1986, when a small black wafer of baked chemicals was found to become superconducting at greater than 30 degrees above absolute zero—a temperature that shattered the old record and ushered in the era of "high-temperature" (though still extremely cold) superconductors. Their compound of copper, oxygen, and other elements seemed to defy all conventional wisdom, and it began a frantic race to study and improve the novel material.

Today, many scientists are attempting to synthesize new oxides closely related to those first described by Bednorz and Müller, while others struggle to devise practical applications for these new materials. Some recently developed compounds superconduct at temperatures as high as 160 degrees above absolute zero (see Figure 11-4). It may soon be possible to make commercially useful electrical devices out of these materials.

Perhaps equally important, high-temperature superconductors have taken superconductivity from the domain of a few specialists and brought it into class-

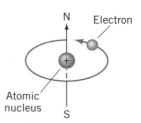

(a)   (b)

• **Figure 11-4** (*a*) A magnet floats "magically" above a black disk made from a new "high-temperature" superconductor. The clouds in the background form above the cold liquid-nitrogen refrigerant. (*b*) This technology has been used in Japan to float high-speed trains above their tracks.

rooms around the world. As a new generation of scientists grows up with these new superconductors, new questions will be asked and exciting new ideas and inventions are sure to be found. Within the next generation we may have electric motors that rotate a million revolutions per minute on superconducting bearings, superconducting electrical storage facilities that reduce our energy bills, and magnetically levitated trains that travel at jet speeds between cities. •

Magnetic Properties of Materials

The magnets that lie at the heart of most electric motors and generators, though critical to almost everything we do, are not much evident in our everyday lives. Similarly, we are usually unaware of the magnets that drive our stereo speakers, telephones, and other audio systems. Even refrigerator magnets and compass needles are so common that we take them for granted. But why do some common materials such as iron display strong magnetism, while other substances seem to be unaffected by magnetic fields?

In Chapter 5, we learned that one of the fundamental laws of nature is that every magnetic field is due, ultimately, to the presence of electrical currents. In particular, electrons spinning around an atom can be thought of as a small electrical current, so each electron in an atom acts like a little electromagnet. An atom can be thought of as being composed of many small electromagnets, each with different strength and pointing in a different direction. The total magnetic field of the atom arises by adding together the magnetic fields of all the tiny electron electromagnets.

It turns out that many atoms have magnetic fields that closely approximate the dipole type (originally shown in Figure 5-4); thus each atom in the material can be thought of as a tiny dipole magnet (Figure 11-5). The magnetic field of a solid material like a piece of lodestone arises from the combination of all these tiny magnetic fields.

It's somewhat harder to understand why most materials do not have magnetic fields. In Figure 11-6*a*, we show the orientation of atomic magnets in a typical material. They point in random directions, so at a place outside the material their effects tend to cancel. An observer looking at the material will measure no magnetic field, and a compass placed outside the material will not be deflected.

• **Figure 11-5** The dipole magnetic field of atoms takes the same form as that of larger magnets.

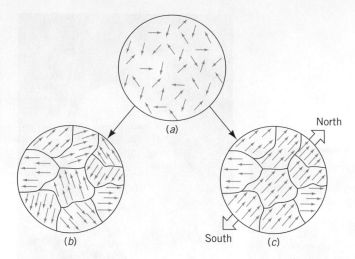

• **Figure 11-6** Different magnetic behavior in materials. (*a*) Nonmagnetic materials have random orientations of atomic spins. (*b*) Ferromagnetic materials with randomly oriented domains are not magnetic. (*c*) A permanent magnet has more uniformly oriented atomic spins.

This ordinary situation explains how materials made up of tiny magnets can, as a whole, be nonmagnetic.

In a few materials, including iron, cobalt, and nickel metals, the atomic magnets line up—an effect called *ferromagnetism* (Figure 11-6*b*). In a normal piece of iron, atoms within a specific domain will all be lined up pointing in the same direction, but the orientation of domains is random. Someone standing outside this material will not measure a magnetic field, because the magnetic fields due to different domains cancel each other. In special cases, as when iron cools from very high temperature in the presence of a strong magnetic field, all of the neighboring domains may line up and thus reinforce each other. Only when most of the magnetic domains line up (as shown in Figure 11-6*c*) do you get a material that exhibits an external magnet field—the arrangement that occurs in permanent magnets.

Microchips and the Information Revolution

Every material has hundreds of different physical properties. We have already seen how strength, electrical conductivity, and magnetism all result from the properties of individual atoms and how those atoms bond together. We could continue in this vein for many more chapters, examining optical properties, elastic properties, thermal properties, and so on. But such a treatment would miss another key idea about materials:

> **New materials often lead to new technologies that change society.**

Of all the countless new materials discovered in the last century, none has transformed our lives more than silicon-based semiconductors. From personal computers to auto ignitions, portable radios to sophisticated military weaponry, microelectronics are a hallmark of our age. Indeed, semiconductors have fundamentally changed the way we manipulate a society's most precious resource—information. The key to this revolution is our ability to fashion complex crystals atom-by-atom from silicon, a material that is produced from ordinary beach sand.

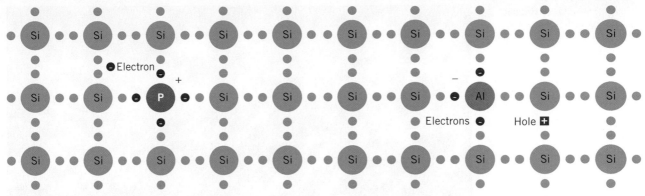

(a) Phosphorus-doped silicon n-type semiconductor   (b) Aluminum-doped silicon p-type semiconductor

• **Figure 11-7** (*a*) Phosphorus-doped silicon *n*-type semiconductors and (*b*) aluminum-doped silicon *p*-type semiconductors are formed from silicon crystals with a few impurity atoms.

Doped Semiconductors

The element silicon by itself is not a very useful substance in electric circuits. What makes silicon useful, and what has driven our modern microelectronic technology, is a process known as doping. **Doping** is the addition of a minor impurity to an element or compound. The idea behind silicon doping is simple. When silicon is melted before being made into circuit elements, a small amount of some other material is added to it. One common additive is phosphorus, an element that has five valence (bonding) electrons, as opposed to the four valence electrons of silicon.

When the silicon crystallizes to form the structure shown in Figure 11-7*a*, the phosphorus is taken into the crystalline structure. Of the five valence electrons in each phosphorus atom, however, only four are needed to make bonds to silicon atoms in the crystal. The fifth electron is not locked in at all. In this situation, it does not take long for the extra electron to be shaken loose and wander off into the body of the crystal. This action has two important consequences: (1) there are conduction electrons in the material, and (2) the phosphorus ion that has been left behind has a positive charge. A semiconductor doped with phosphorus is said to be an *n-type semiconductor*, because the moving charge is a negative electron.

Alternatively, silicon can be doped with an element such as aluminum, which has only three valence electrons (Figure 11-7*b*). In this case, when the aluminum is doped into the crystal structure, there will be one less valence electron compared to the silicon atoms it replaced in the crystal. This "missing" electron—a hole—creates a material that can now more easily carry an electrical current. The hole need not stay with the aluminum, of course, but is free to move around within the semiconductor as described earlier. Once it does so, the aluminum atom, which has now acquired an extra electron, will have a negative charge. This type of material is called a *p-type semiconductor*, because a hole—a missing negative electron—acts as a positive charge.

Diodes

You can understand the basic workings of a microchip by conducting an experiment in your mind. Imagine taking a piece of *n*-type semiconductor and placing it against a piece of *p*-type semiconductor. As soon as the two types of material are in contact, how will electrons move?

Semiconductors are used extensively in electronic devices, such as a photovoltaic array (top), the transitor (lower left), and the microchip.

Charge layers

p-type   *n*-type

• **Figure 11-8** The semiconductor diode consists of an *n*-type region and a *p*-type region. Electrons in this diode can flow easily from the negative to the positive region. The built-in electrical field, labeled *E*, blocks electrons from flowing the opposite way. The result is a one-way valve for electrons.

Near the contact, negatively charged electrons will diffuse from the *n*-type semiconductor over into the *p*-type, while positively charged holes will diffuse back the other way. Thus, on one side of the boundary there will be a region where negative aluminum ions—ions locked into the crystal structure by the doping process—acquire an extra electron. Conversely, on the other side of the boundary is an array of positive phosphorus ions, each of which has lost an electron, but which are nonetheless locked into the crystal.

A semiconducting device like this—formed from one *p* and one *n* region—is called a **diode** (see Figure 11-8). Once a diode is constructed, a permanent electrical field tends to push electrons across the boundary in only one direction, from the *n*-type side to the *p*-type side. As electrons are pushed "with the grain" in the diode, from negative to positive, the current flows through normally. When the current is reversed, however, the electrons are blocked from going through by the presence of the built-in electrical field. Thus the diode acts as a one-way gate, allowing the electrical current through in only one direction.

The semiconductor diode has many uses in technology. One use, for example, can be found in almost any electronic device that is plugged into a wall out-

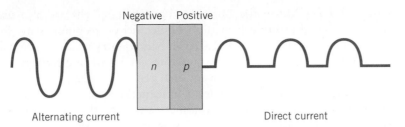

Negative   Positive

Alternating current   Direct current

• **Figure 11-9** A diode converts alternating current to direct current in most electronic devices. Half of the alternating current passes through the diode, but the other half is blocked.

let. As we saw in Chapter 5, electricity is sent to homes in the form of alternating current, or AC. It turns out, however, that most home electronics such as televisions and stereos require direct current, or DC. A semiconductor diode can be used to convert the alternating current into direct current by blocking off half of it. In fact, if you examine the insides of almost any electronic gear, the power cord leads directly to a diode and other components that convert pulsing AC into steady DC, as shown in Figure 11-9.

TECHNOLOGY •

Photovoltaic Cells and Solar Energy

Semiconducting diodes may play an important role in the energy future of the United States, through the use of a device called the photovoltaic cell. A *photovoltaic cell* is nothing more than a large semiconductor diode. A thin layer of *n*-type material overlays a thicker layer of *p*-type. Sunlight striking the top *n*-type layer shakes electrons loose from the crystal structure. These electrons are then accelerated through the *n-p* boundary and pushed out into an external circuit. Thus, while the Sun is shining, the photovoltaic cell acts in the same way as a battery. It provides a constant push for electrons and moves them through an external circuit. If large numbers of photovoltaic cells are put together, they can generate enormous amounts of current.

Photovoltaic cells enjoy many uses today. Your hand calculator, for example, may very well contain a photovoltaic cell that recharges the batteries (it's the small

The Sun's energy is converted to electricity by photovoltaic panels at a southern California generating plant.

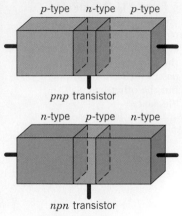

p-type   n-type   p-type

pnp transistor

n-type   p-type   n-type

npn transistor

• **Figure 11-10** A *pnp* and an *npn* transistor.

dark band just above the buttons). Photovoltaic cells are also used in regions where it is hard to bring in traditional electricity—to pump water in remote sites, for example, or to provide electricity in backcountry areas of national parks. At the moment, it costs several times as much to get a watt of electricity from a solar cell as from the most expensive conventional generating plants.

Another use of photovoltaics is in cameras. In products from TV cameras to the sensitive detectors that astronomers attach to their telescopes, light strikes a semiconductor rather than film. Using processes slightly more complex than those described for a photovoltaic cell, light striking each part of the semiconductor is converted into an electrical current, with the strengths of the currents from each part depending on the amount of light that falls there. The strength of those currents is then used to reconstruct the visual image. •

The Transistor

The device that drives the entire information age, and perhaps more than any other has been responsible for the transformation of our modern society, is the **transistor**. Invented just two days before Christmas, 1947, by Bell Laboratory scientists John Bardeen, Walter Brattain, and William Shockley, the early transistor was simply a sandwich of *n*- and *p*-type semiconductors.

In one kind of transistor, two *p*-type semiconductors form the "bread" of a sandwich, while the *n*-type semiconductor is the "meat." Another kind of transistor uses the *npn* configuration. Both kinds of transistors (Figure 11-10) control the flow of electrons. Electrical leads connect to each of the three semiconductor regions of the transistor. An electrical current goes into the region called the *emitter*; the thin slice of semiconductor in the middle is called the *base*; and the third semiconductor section is the *collector*.

Thus, the transistor has two built-in electrical fields, one at each *p-n* junction. The idea of the transistor is that a small amount of electrical charge run into or out of the base can change these electrical fields—in effect, opening and closing the gates of the transistor. The best way to think of the transistor is to make an analogy to a pipe that carries water. The electrical current that flows from emitter to collector is like water that flows through the pipe, and the base is like a valve in the pipe. A small amount of energy applied to turning the valve can have an enormous effect on the flow of water. In just the same way, a small amount of charge run onto the base can have an enormous effect on the current that runs through the transistor.

In your tape deck, for example, small electrical currents are created when the magnetized tape is run past the tape heads. This small current can be fed into the base of a transistor, and can thus be impressed on the much larger current that is flowing from the emitter to the collector. A device that takes a small current and converts it into a large one is called an *amplifier* (see Figure 11-11). The amplifier in your tape deck takes the small signal created by the tape and converts it into the much larger current that runs the speakers.

As important as the transistor's amplifying properties are, probably its most important use has been as a switch. If you run enough negative charge onto the base, it can repel any electrons that are trying to get through. Thus moving an electrical charge onto the base will shut off the flow of current through the transistor, whereas running the electrical charge off the base will turn the current back on. In this manner the transistor acts as an electron switch, and it can be used to process information in computers—arguably the most important device developed in the twentieth century (see Figure 11-12).

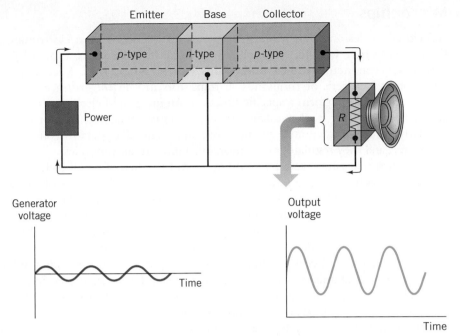

Emitter   Base   Collector

p-type   n-type   p-type

Power

R

• **Figure 11-11** A transistor acting as an amplifier. A small amount of energy, supplied by a power source such as a wall outlet to one region of a transistor, can be amplified because electrons flow easily between charged regions.

Generator voltage

Time

Output voltage

Time

Current onto base

Collector

Base

No current through the transistor, switch is off

Emitter

(a)

• **Figure 11-12** A transistor acting as a switch. A small current causes the transistor to switch from off to on.

Current off of base

Current through transistor

Current through the transistor, switch is open

(b)

Microchips

Individual diodes and transistors still play a vital role in modern electronics, but these devices have been largely replaced by much more complex arrays of *p*- and *n*-type semiconductors, called **microchips** (see Figure 11-13). Microchips may incorporate hundreds or thousands of transistors in one *integrated circuit*, specially designed to perform a specific function. An integrated circuit microchip lies at the heart of your pocket calculator or microwave oven control, for example. Similarly, arrays of integrated circuits store and manipulate data in your personal computer, and they regulate the ignition in all modern automobiles.

The first transistors were bulky things, about the size of a golf ball, but today a single microchip the size of a grain of rice can integrate hundreds of thousands of these devices. California's Silicon Valley has become a well-known center for the design and manufacture of these tiny integrated circuits. Production of thousands of transistors on a single silicon chip requires exquisite control of atoms. One technique is to put a thin wafer of silicon into a large heated vacuum chamber. Around the edges of the chamber is an array of small ovens, each of which holds a different element, such as aluminum or phosphorus. The side ovens are heated in carefully controlled sequence and opened to allow small amounts of other elements—the dopants—to be vaporized and enter the chamber along with silicon.

If you want to make a *p*-type semiconductor, for example, you could mix a small amount of phosphorus with the silicon in the chamber and let it deposit onto the silicon plate at the bottom. Typically, a device called a *mask* is put over the silicon chip so that the *p*-type semiconductor is deposited only in designated parts of the chip. Then the vapor is cleared from the chamber, a new mask is put on, and another layer of material is laid down. In this way, a complex three-dimensional structure can be built up at a microscopic scale. In the end, each microchip has many different transistors in it, connected exactly as designed by engineers.

• **Figure 11-13** A microchip incorporates many complex circuits built into a single piece of silicon. For comparison, the eye of an ordinary sewing needle is shown in the background.

TECHNOLOGY •

Jim Trefil Gives His Car a Tune-Up

As a student, I acquired the first of a long string of Volkswagen Beetles. Now let me tell you, my friends, *that* was a sweet car! There were never any problems with the cooling system, for the simple reason that there wasn't any—the engine was cooled by the air flowing by. And almost any repair could be made by someone with reasonable mechanical ability and a set of tools. While in graduate school, I spent many happy hours under my car, adjusting this or that.

But I never work on my cars any more. When I look under the hood, all I see is a complex array of computers and microchips—nothing a person can get a wrench around. Yet the car I drive today, provided everything is working, is much more user friendly than my old Volkswagen. The flow of gasoline to the cylinders, for example, is regulated by a small onboard computer, rather than by a clumsy mechanical carburetor.

This personal story about cars turns out to be a pretty good allegory for the way in which the science of materials has developed in the twentieth century. In the beginning, industry turned out big, relatively simple things that were easy to understand and work with—iron wheels for railroads, steel springs for car suspensions, wooden chairs and tables for the home. Today, industry turns out items that perform the same jobs better, but that are made from new kinds of materials such as plastics, composites, and semiconductors. Instead of manipulating large chunks of material, we now control the way atoms fit together. Like modern cars, modern materials do their job well, but they cannot be made (or, usually, repaired) by a simple craftsperson working with simple tools.

So while the materials we use are becoming better at what they do and easier for us to use, it becomes harder and harder for us to understand what those materials are. I might have been able to fix my Volkswagen myself, but there is no way I can look under the hood and shift atoms around in my modern car's microchip. In a sense, the improved performance of modern materials has been bought at the price of our ability to understand them. To a large extent, the emphasis of modern materials science has shifted away from manipulating large blocks of stuff, which are readily available to our senses, to manipulating atoms in ever-more-complex ways. And, of course, we can't see or taste or feel atoms. •

Information

The single most important use of semiconducting devices is in the storage and manipulation of information. In fact, the modern revolution in information technology—the development of arrays of interconnected computers, global telecommunications networks, vast data banks of personal statistics, digital recording, and the credit card—is a direct consequence of materials science.

While it may appear strange to say so, almost all the things we normally consider as conveying information—the printed or spoken word, pictures, or music, for example—can be analyzed in terms of their information content and manipulated by the microchips we've just discussed. The term "information," like many words, has a precise meaning when it is used in the sciences, a meaning that is somewhat different from colloquial usage. In its scientific context, information is measured in a unit that is called the *binary digit*, or **bit**.

You can think of the bit as the two possible answers to any simple question: yes or no, on or off, up or down. A single transistor being used as a switch, for example, can convey one bit of information—it is either on or off. Any form of communication contains a certain number of bits of information. As we shall see shortly, the computer is simply a device that stores and manipulates this kind of information.

What is the information content of a single letter of the alphabet? From the point of view of an information theorist, the answer is simply the minimum number of questions with yes-or-no answers that are required to identify a letter of the alphabet unambiguously. Let's see how you might go about asking such questions. Following are five questions you might ask to specify the letter *E*.

1. Is it in the first half of the alphabet? (yes)
2. Is it in the first six letters of the alphabet? (yes)
3. Is it in the first three letters of the alphabet? (no)
4. Is it *D*? (no)
5. Is it *E*? (yes)

From this simple example, you can see that you need the answers to five questions—five bits of information—to specify unambiguously a single letter of the alphabet. (You might be lucky and guess the answer in fewer questions, but five questions are always enough to pinpoint any one of the 26 letters.) We would say, then, that the information content of a single letter of the alphabet is five bits.

As a matter of fact, there are $2 \times 2 \times 2 \times 2 \times 2 = 32$ different things that can be specified using five bits of information. Thirty-two items is not enough, however, to handle all the numbers, capitalization, punctuation marks, and other symbols. Six bits of information are capable of specifying $2 \times 2 \times 2 \times 2 \times 2 \times 2 = 64$ different things, and you could argue that all the things you'd need to specify on a printed page could be included in those 64. Thus the information content of a single ordinary printed symbol is six bits. If you were using switches to store the information on a normal printed page, you would need six of them lined up in a row to specify each symbol.

 Stop and Think! There are many alphabets in the world besides the Latin alphabet used to write English. How does the number of bits required to designate a letter depend on the number of letters in the alphabet?

The average word is 6 letters long, so the information content of a typical word is 36 bits. The average printed page of a novel contains about 500 words, corresponding to an information content of almost 20,000 bits. A 200-page book in this scheme thus contains about 4 million bits, or 4 megabits, of information.

Historically, switches in computers were lumped together in groups of 8. Such a group is capable of storing 8 bits of information, or one **byte**. In terms of this unit, a 200-page book would contain 500,000 bytes, or half a megabyte.

SCIENCE BY THE NUMBERS •

Is a Picture Really Worth a Thousand Words?

Pictures and sounds can be analyzed in terms of information content, just like words. Your television screen, for example, works by splitting the picture into small units called pixels. In North America, the picture is split up into 525 segments on the horizontal and vertical axes, giving a total of about 275,000 pixels (in rounded numbers) for one picture on the TV screen. Your eye integrates these dots into a smooth picture. Every color can be thought of as a combination of the three colors red, green, and blue, and it is usual to specify the intensity of each of these three colors by a number that requires 10 bits of information to be recorded. (In practice, this means that the intensity of each color is specified on a scale of about 1 to 1000.) Thus each pixel requires 30 bits to define its color. Thus the total information content of a picture on a TV screen is

$$275,000 \text{ pixels} \times 30 \text{ bits} = \text{about 8 million bits}$$

Thus it requires about 8 megabits, or 1 megabyte, to specify a single frame on a TV picture. We should note that a TV picture typically changes 30 times a second, so the total flow of information on a TV screen may exceed 200 million bits per second.

It thus would appear that a picture is worth not only a thousand words, but much more. In fact, if a word contains 36 bits of information, then the picture will be worth 8 million bits per picture divided by 36 bits per word, which equals about 220,000 words per picture.

The old saying, if anything, underestimates the truth! •

Computers

A **computer** is a machine that stores and manipulates information. The information is stored in the computer in microchips, each of which incorporates many thousands of interconnected transistors that act as switches and carry information. In principle, a machine with a few million transistors could store the text for this entire book. In practice, however, computers do not normally work in this way. They have a *central processing unit (CPU)* in which transistors store and manipulate relatively small amounts of information at any one time. When the information is ready to be stored—for example, when you have finished working on

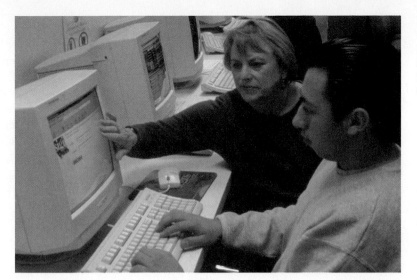

In less than a quarter of a century, the computer has evolved from a specialized research aid to an essential tool for business and education.

a text in a word processor, or writing a program to perform a calculation—it is removed from the CPU and stored elsewhere. It might, for example, be stored in the form of magnetically oriented particles on a floppy disk or a hard drive. In these cases, a bit of information is no longer a switch that is on or off, but a bit of magnetic material that has been oriented either "north pole up" or "north pole down."

The ability to store information in this way is extremely important in modern society. As just one example, think about the last time you made an airline reservation. You called in, and your travel agent got into communication with the airline's computer. Stored in strings of bits within that computer are the flights, the seating assignments, the ticket arrangements, and often the address and phone number of every passenger who will be flying on the particular day when you want to fly. When you change your reservation, make a new one, or perform some other manipulation, the information is taken out of storage, brought to the central processing unit, manipulated by changing the exact sequence of bits, and then put back into storage. This process—the storage and manipulation of vast amounts of data—forms the very fabric of our modern society.

You've probably noticed that the speed and information capacity of computers has increased astonishingly over the past few decades. Just look at the improvements in the images and action of video games. This tendency for ever-faster computers was first noted in 1965 by Gordon Moore, the founder of Intel. He pointed to a trend that the number of transistors that can be packed into every square inch of a microchip (a measure of computing power) tends to double about every two years. "Moore's Law" has held up remarkably for more than 30 years, though it can't continue indefinitely. The average size of a single transistor is now only a few thousand atoms across, and a semiconductor device can't be much smaller than that!

These advances are primarily the result of many improvements in materials and their processing at the atomic scale—a field called *nanotechnology*. New fine-grained magnetic materials have greatly increased the capacity of information storage devices such as hard disks, while improved semiconductor processing techniques continue to reduce the size of individual *n*- and *p*-type semiconductor domains. The result is smaller, more powerful computers—one of many ways that advances in material science play a direct role in our lives.

THE SCIENCE OF LIFE •

The Computer and the Brain

When computers first came into public awareness, there was a general sense that we were building a machine that would in some way duplicate the human brain. Concepts such as *artificial intelligence* were sold (some would say oversold) on the basis of the idea that they would soon be able to perform all those functions that we normally think of as being distinctly human. In fact, this scenario has not come to pass. The reason has to do with the difference between the basic unit of the computer, which is the transistor, and the basic unit of the brain, which is the nerve cell.

The transmission of electrical signals between the brain's neurons is fundamentally different from that between elements in ordinary electric circuits (see Chapter 5). This difference in signal transmission alone, however, does not make a brain so different from a computer. A computer normally performs a sequential series of operations—that is, a group of transistors takes two numbers, adds them together, feeds that answer to another group of transistors that performs another manipulation, and so on. Some computers are now being designed and built that have some parallel capacity at the same time—machines in which, for example, addition and other manipulations are done in parallel rather than one after the other. Nevertheless, the natural configuration of computers is to have each transistor hooked to, at most, a couple of others.

A nerve cell in the brain, however, operates in quite a different manner. Each of the brain's trillions of nerve cells connects to a thousand or more different neighboring nerve cells. Whether a nerve cell decides to fire—whether the signal moves out along the axon—depends in an unknown way on a complex integration of all the signals that come into that cell from thousands of other cells.

This complex arrangement means that the brain is a system that is highly interconnected, more interconnected than any other system known in nature. In fact, if the brain has trillions of cells and each cell has a thousand connections, there will be on the order of 1,000,000,000,000,000 connections among brain cells. Building a computer of this size and level of connectedness is at present totally beyond the capability of technology. •

Data, from *Star Trek: The Next Generation*, is an android. Computers that think like people have been a staple of science fiction stories, but could they really be built?

Science News | Planet's Slim-Fast Plan
(SCIENCE NEWS, VOL. 162, MARCH 15, 2003, P. 163)

With over a hundred so-called planetary systems known around other stars, we are finding some pretty strange beasts out there. One of the strangest, located about 150 light years from Earth, carries the innocuous name of HD209458b. It is a planet about 70% as big as Jupiter, but it orbits its star at a distance only one eighth of that between Mercury and our own sun. At this distance, the intense heat and gravitational pull of the star is expected to strip away the planet's outer coating, eventually destroying it completely. Recent results have given us some in-sight into this process, and suggest that the demolition process may be more intense than we thought.

The orbit of HD209458b happens to lie in a plane that brings the planet between its star and the Earth on each orbit. Thus, scientists on Earth can see a slight dimming of the star—about 1.5% of its total light—every time the planet passes between us. More recently, however, they have noted that light from hydrogen atoms is dimmed by as much as 15%. This means that hydrogen is being stripped from the planet at a prodigious rate, and trails behind it like the tail of a comet, absorbing light from the star as it does so. This finding is, by far, the most detailed look we've ever had at an extrasolar planet.

Thinking More About | Properties of Materials

Thinking Machines

One of the most intriguing questions about the ever-increasing abilities of complex computers is whether a computer can be built that would in some way mimic, or even replace, the human brain. Computers have been built that can add faster or remember more than any single human being, but these specific abilities by themselves do not seem to be crucial in developing a machine that thinks. The real question is whether a machine will be designed that is, by general consensus, regarded as "alive" or "conscious."

British mathematician Alan Turing proposed a test to address this question. The so-called "Turing test" operates this way: A group of human beings sit in a room and interact with something through some kind of computer terminal. They might, for example, type questions into a keyboard and read answers on a screen. Alternatively, they could talk into a microphone and hear answers played back to them by some kind of voice synthesizer. These people are allowed to ask the hidden "thing" any questions they like. At the end of the experiment, they have to decide whether they are talking to a machine or to a human being. If they can't tell the difference, the machine is said to have passed the Turing test.

As of this date, no machine has passed the test (there have been occasional contests in Silicon Valley in which machines were put through their paces).

But what if a machine did actually pass? Would that mean we have invented a truly intelligent machine? John Searle, a philosopher at the University of California at Berkeley, has recently challenged the whole idea of the Turing test as a way of telling if a machine can think by proposing a paradox he calls the "Chinese room."

The Chinese room works like this: An English-speaking person sits in a room and receives typed questions from a Chinese-speaking person in the adjacent room. The English-speaking person does not understand Chinese, but has a large manual of instructions. The manual might say, for example, that if a certain group of Chinese characters are received, then a second group of Chinese characters should be sent out. The English-speaking person could, at least in principle, pass the Turing test if the instructions were sufficiently detailed and complex. Obviously, however, the English speaker has no idea of what he or she is doing with the information that comes in or goes out. Thus, argues Searle, the mere fact that a machine passes the Turing test tells you nothing about whether it is aware of what it is doing.

Do you think a machine that can pass the Turing test must be aware of itself? Do you see any way around Searle's argument for the Chinese room? What moral and ethical problems might arise if human beings could indeed make a machine that everyone agreed has consciousness?

SUMMARY

All materials, from building supplies and fabrics to electronic components and food, have properties that arise from the kinds of constituent atoms and the ways those atoms are bonded together. The high *strength* of materials such as stone and synthetic fibers relies on interconnected networks of ionic or covalent bonds, while many soft and pliable materials such as wax and graphite incorporate weak van der Waals forces. *Composite materials,* such as plywood, fiberglass, and reinforced concrete, merge the special strengths of two or more materials.

The electrical properties of materials also depend on the kinds of constituent atoms and the bonds they form. For example, *electrical resistance*—a material's resistance to the flow of an electrical current—depends on the mobility of bonding electrons. Metals, which are characterized by loosely bonded outer electrons, make excellent *electrical conductors,* while most materials with tightly held electrons in ionic and covalent bonds are good *electrical insulators.* Materials such as silicon that conduct electricity, but not very well, are called *semiconductors.* At very low temperatures, some compounds lose all resistance to electron flow and become *superconductors.*

Magnetic properties also arise from the collective behavior of atoms. While most materials are nonmagnetic, ferromagnets have domains in which electron spins are aligned to each other.

New materials play important roles in modern technology. Semiconductors, in particular, are vital to the modern electronics industry. Semiconductor material, usually silicon, is modified by *doping* with small amounts of another element. Phosphorous doping adds a few mobile electrons to produce an *n*-type semiconductor, while aluminum doping provides positive holes in *p*-type semiconductors. Devices formed by juxtaposing *n*- and *p*-type semiconductors act as switches and valves for electricity. A *diode* joins single pieces of *n*- and *p*-type material, for example, to act as a one-way valve for current flow. *Transistors,* which incorporate a *pnp* or *npn* semiconductor sandwich, act as amplifiers or switches for current. *Microchips* can combine up to thousands of *n* and *p* regions in a single integrated circuit.

Semiconductor technology has revolutionized the storage and use of information. Any information can be reduced to a series of simple "yes–no" questions, or *bits*.

Eight-bit words, called *bytes,* are the basic information unit of most modern *computers.*

KEY TERMS ABOUT MATERIAL PROPERTIES

strength
composite materials
electrical conductor

electrical resistance
electrical insulator
semiconductor

superconductivity
doping
diode

transistor
microchip
bit

byte
computer

REVIEW QUESTIONS

1. What factors determine the strength of a material?

2. What kinds of chemical bonds are strongest? Why are these bonds so strong?

3. Define three different kinds of strengths. Give examples of materials that are strong in each of these modes. What kind of chemical bonding occurs in each of these materials?

4. Diamonds and graphite are both made from carbon atoms. Why is graphite so much weaker?

5. What is the difference between a composite material and a compound? Give an example of each.

6. Identify the materials that serve as an electrical insulator and an electrical conductor in an electrical device that you use every day.

7. What is unusual about superconductors? Under what conditions do materials exhibit superconductivity?

8. What is a semiconductor? Give an example.

9. Explain how holes can move in a semiconductor.

10. If all atoms have electrons that are in motion about an atom, why aren't all materials magnetic?

11. What is a ferromagnet?

12. What is a semiconductor diode? How do diodes convert AC into DC?

13. What is a transistor? What are the base, emitter, and collector, respectively?

14. How are diodes and transistors similar and how are they different?

15. What is an integrated circuit? How might one be made?

16. Give an example of a bit of information. What is the difference between a bit and a byte?

DISCUSSION QUESTIONS

1. How do the principles of physics and chemistry both come into play when developing new materials?

2. From the point of view of atomic architecture, how would you design a material that has great strength when pulled apart? How would you design a material that is strong when twisted?

3. How can you explain electrical resistance in terms of the second law of thermodynamics?

4. Identify five different materials that were invented in the twentieth century and that you use in your daily life.

5. Identify 10 objects in your home that use semiconductors. What other kinds of materials with spe-

cial electrical properties are found in all of these 10 objects?

6. If water in a pipe is analogous to electricity in a wire, what is analogous to a diode? A transistor? What electrical device is analogous to a water storage tank?

7. How would your life change if you had none of your electrical appliances?

8. Identify a material in the room you're sitting in that serves as an electrical insulator. What is it made of? What kind of chemical bonds does it have?

9. Would a silicon semiconductor doped with boron be *n* or *p* type? How about one doped with arsenic? [*Hint*: Look at the periodic table.]

PROBLEMS

1. There is an effort in the world today to convert television into so-called high-definition TV (HDTV). In HDTV, the picture is split up into as many as 1100 by 1100 (as opposed to 525 by 525) pixels.

What is the information content of an HDTV picture? What is the information content that must be transmitted each second in an HDTV broadcast?

2. Construct a set of yes-or-no questions to specify any letter of the alphabet, both upper- and lowercase, and all digits from zero to nine.

3. Construct a set of yes-or-no questions to specify any state in the United States.

4. Estimate the total amount of information contained in the printed words in this book. Estimate the information content of the illustrations in this book.

5. The Cyrillic alphabet (used to write Russian and some other Eastern European languages) was devised in the ninth century and had 43 letters, whereas modern Russian has 30. How many bits would it take to specify a single letter in each of these alphabets?

6. The version of modern written Japanese called *kanji* has 1945 different characters. How many bits would it take to specify a specific *kanji* character? Compare this to the number required in languages that have alphabets.

INVESTIGATIONS

1. Why does a magnet become demagnetized when you repeatedly hit it with a hammer? In what other ways can you destroy a permanent magnet? Why aren't "permanent magnets" permanent?

2. Shortly after the discovery of high-temperature superconductivity, many newspapers and TV shows ran features on how these new materials would change society. In what ways might superconductivity change society? Historically, what other new materials have caused significant changes in human societies?

3. Every year, one or two promising new materials capture public attention. Scan recent issues of *Science News* and identify one such material. Who made it? How might it be used?

4. Imagine that you are a science fiction writer. Concoct a description of a new material with unique (but plausible) properties and describe how that material might change a society.

5. Research the status of magnetically levitated trains, like the one now operating in Japan. How does it operate? How fast might it go? How soon might such a train operate in North America?

6. Read the book or watch the 1951 movie *The Man in the White Suit*. What unique material properties are described, and how is the new technology received by society?

7. A class of new materials called fullerenes, including the substance known as "buckyballs," were invented in 1990. Investigate these materials and their possible uses.

8. Visit a sports equipment store. Learn about the new materials that are used in tennis rackets, football helmets, and sports clothing.

9. Write a short story in which a new material with unique properties plays a central role.

10. What kinds of materials do surgeons use to replace broken hip bones? What are the advantages of this material?

11. Until recently, plastic surgeons used silicone-filled implants for breast enlargement and other cosmetic procedures. Intensive research is now underway to understand effects of silicone on the human body, due to claims of adverse reactions to these implants. Investigate the nature of silicone and summarize some of the contradictory results of recent research. Based on your investigation, do you think such implants should be banned?

WWW RESOURCES

See *The Sciences* homepage at: **http://www.wiley.com/college/trefil** for valuable web links.

1. **http://publicold.web.cern.ch/PublicOld/Science/whatismatter.html**
What Is Matter Made Of? from CERN.

2. **http://www.lbl.gov/MicroWorlds/Contents/**
Exploring the Material World, form Lawrence Berkeley National Laboratory, on using the advanced light source to study properties of materials—interesting.

3. **http://www.lucent.com/minds/transistor/pdf/trans-history.pdf**
50 Years of the Transistor, from Lucent Technologies.

4. **http://www.history.rochester.edu/class/PV/home.html**
Photovoltaic Energy, for a straightforward discussion of solar photovoltaic energy.

12

The Nucleus of the Atom

How do scientists determine the age of the oldest human fossils?

GREAT IDEA

Nuclear energy depends on the conversion of mass into energy.

PHYSICS
The nucleus is held together by the strong force.

CHEMISTRY
The chemical bonding of an atom's electrons has virtually no effect on what happens in the nucleus.

ENVIRONMENT
The storage of nuclear waste has become a significant environmental problem.

GEOLOGY
All rocks contain a trace of radioactive isotopes, notably those of uranium.

HEALTH & SAFETY
Doctors sometimes rely on radioactive tracers to diagnose injuries and disease.

ASTRONOMY
Fusion reactions that combine hydrogen to produce helium plus energy occur in the Sun and other stars. (Ch. 14)

TECHNOLOGY
Nuclear reactors produce energy by controlling nuclear fission reactions.

BIOLOGY
All life on earth evolved in a radioactive environment.(Ch. 25)

Red = applications of the great idea discussed in this chapter.

Orange = other applications, some of which are explored in other chapters.

It's great to be lying on the beach, lulled by the sound of the surf, soaking up the sun. Away from the pressures of school and work, time seems to stand still.

In such a relaxing setting it's hard to imagine that hundreds of energetic radioactive particles are tearing through your body every minute. Some of those speeding particles will damage your cells, breaking apart bonds in the molecules that control critical functions of metabolism and cell division.

But don't lose a moment worrying about this ubiquitous background radioactivity. Since the dawn of life, low levels of radioactivity in rocks, sand, soils, and the oceans have bathed every living thing. This radioactivity, a natural part of every environment on Earth, reveals much about the inner structure of the atom.

Empty Space, Explosive Energy

Imagine that you are holding a basketball, while 25 kilometers (about 15 miles) away a few grains of sand whiz around. And imagine that all of the vast intervening space—enough to house a fair-sized city—is absolutely empty. In some respects, that's what an atom is like, though on a much smaller scale, of course. The basketball is the nucleus, and the grains of sand represent the electrons (remember, though, that electrons display characteristics of both particles and waves). The atom, with a diameter 100,000 times that of its nucleus, is almost all empty space.

Previous chapters explored the properties of atoms in terms of their electrons. Chemical reactions, the way a material handles electricity, and even the very shape and strength of objects depend on the way that electrons in different atoms interact with each other. In terms of our analogy, all of the properties of the atoms that we have studied so far result from things that are taking place 25 kilometers from where the basketball-sized nucleus is sitting. The incredible emptiness of the atom is a key to understanding two important facts about the relation of the atom to its nucleus.

1. *What goes on in the nucleus of an atom has almost nothing to do with the atom's chemistry, and vice versa.* The chemical bonding of an atom's electrons has virtually no effect on what happens to the nucleus. In most situations you can regard the orbiting electrons and the central nucleus as two separate and independent systems.

2. *The energies available in the nucleus are much greater than those available among electrons.* The particles inside the nucleus are tightly locked in. It takes a great deal more energy to pull them out than it does to remove an electron from an atom.

When a bow is drawn, its mass has increased by a tiny amount.

The enormous energy we can get from the nucleus follows from the equivalence of mass and energy (which we will discuss in more detail in Chapter 13). This relationship is defined in Einstein's most famous equation.

▶ **In words:** Mass is a form of energy. When mass is converted into energy, the amount of energy produced is enormous—equal to the mass of the object multiplied by the speed of light squared.

▶ **In equation form:**

$$\text{energy} = \text{mass} \times (\text{speed of light})^2$$

▶ **In symbols:**

$$E = mc^2$$

Remember that the constant c, the speed of light, is a very large number (3×10^8 meters per second), and that this large number is squared in Einstein's equation to give an even larger number. Thus even a very small mass is equivalent to a very large energy, as shown in the following "Science by the Numbers" section.

Einstein's equation tells us that a given amount of mass can be converted into a specific amount of energy in any form, and vice versa. This statement is true for any process involving energy. When hydrogen and oxygen combine to form water, for example, the mass of the water molecule is a tiny bit less than the sum of the masses of the original atoms. This missing mass has been converted to binding energy in the molecule. Similarly, when an archer draws a bow, the mass of the bow increases by a tiny amount because of the increased elastic potential energy in the bent material.

The change in mass of objects in everyday events such as these is so small that it is customarily ignored, and we speak of the various forms of energy without thinking about their mass equivalents. In nuclear reactions, however, we cannot ignore the mass effects. A nuclear reactor, for example, can transform fully 20% of the mass of a proton into energy in each reaction by a process we will soon discuss. Thus nuclear reactions can convert significant amounts of mass into energy, while chemical reactions, which involve only relatively small changes in electrical potential energy, involve only infinitesimal changes in mass. This difference explains why an atomic bomb, which derives its destructive force from nuclear reactions, is so much more powerful than conventional explosives, such as dynamite, and conventional weapons, which depend on chemical reactions in materials such as TNT.

SCIENCE BY THE NUMBERS •

Mass and Energy

On the average, each person in the United States uses about 10,000 kilowatt-hours (kwh) of energy each year, a rate of about one kilowatt-hour each hour. In effect, each individual uses the energy equivalent of a toaster going full blast all the time. How much mass would have to be converted completely to energy to produce your year's supply of energy?

In Appendix A, we find that one kilowatt-hour of energy is the same as 3.6 million joules, so every year each of us uses:

$$\begin{aligned}
\text{annual energy use} &= (10{,}000 \text{ kwh}) \times (3.6 \times 10^6 \text{ joule/kwh}) \\
&= 36{,}000 \times 10^6 \text{ joule} \\
&= 3.6 \times 10^{10} \text{ joule}
\end{aligned}$$

In order to calculate the mass that is equivalent to this large amount of energy, we need to put this energy into the Einstein equation, which we can rewrite as

$$\text{mass} = \frac{\text{energy}}{(\text{speed of light})^2}$$

Written in this form, the number we seek (the mass) is expressed in terms of two numbers we already know. The speed of light, c, is 3×10^8 m/s, so we find that

$$\begin{aligned}
\text{mass} &= \frac{(3.6 \times 10^{10} \text{ joule})}{(3 \times 10^8 \text{ m/s})^2} \\
&= \frac{(3.6 \times 10^{10})}{(9 \times 10^{16} \text{ m}^2/\text{s}^2)} \\
&= 4.0 \times 10^{-7} \text{ joule-second}^2/\text{meter}^2 \\
&= 4.0 \times 10^{-7} \text{ kilograms}
\end{aligned}$$

In the last step we have to remember that a joule is defined as a kilogram-meter^2/second^2, so the units "joule-second^2/meter^2" in this answer are exactly the same as kilograms (see Appendix B). Our year's energy budget could be satisfied by a mass that weighs less than a millionth of a kilogram, or about the mass of a small sand grain, if you could unlock that energy!

The Organization of the Nucleus

As we saw in Chapter 10, Ernest Rutherford discovered the atomic nucleus by observing how fast-moving particles scatter off gold atoms. In later experiments with even faster atomic "bullets," scientists found that atomic nuclei sometimes break into smaller fragments. Thus, like the atom itself, the nucleus is made up of smaller pieces, most importantly the proton and the neutron. Approximately equal in mass, the proton and neutron can be thought of as the primary building blocks of the nucleus.

The **proton** (from Latin for "the first one") has a positive electrical charge of +1 and was the first of the nuclear constituents to be discovered and identified.

Stop and Think! Why might electrically charged particles be easier to identify than electrically neutral ones?

The number of protons determines the electrical charge of the nucleus. An atom in its electrically neutral state will have as many negative electrons in orbit as protons in the nucleus. Thus the number of protons in the nucleus determines the chemical identity of an atom.

When people began studying nuclei, however, they quickly found that the mass of a nucleus is significantly greater than the sum of the mass of its protons. In fact, for most atoms the nucleus is more than twice as heavy as its protons. What does this observation imply? Scientists concluded that the additional mass had to be in the nucleus, and we now realize that this extra mass is supplied by a particle with no electrical charge called the **neutron** (for "the neutral one"). The neutron has approximately the same mass as the proton. Thus a nucleus with equal numbers of protons and neutrons will have twice the mass of the protons alone.

The mass of a proton or a neutron is about 2000 times the mass of the electron. Therefore, almost all of the mass of the atom is contained within the protons and neutrons in its nucleus. You can think of things this way: electrons give an atom its size, but the nucleus gives an atom its mass.

Element Names and Atomic Numbers

The most important fact in describing any atom is the number of protons in the nucleus—the **atomic number**. This number defines which *element* you are dealing with. All atoms of gold (atomic number 79) have exactly 79 protons, for example. In fact, the name gold is simply a convenient shorthand for "atoms with 79 protons." Every element has its own atomic number: all hydrogen atoms have just 1 proton, carbon atoms must have 6 protons, and so on. The periodic table of the elements that we discussed in Chapter 7 can be thought of as a chart in which the number of protons in the atomic nucleus increases as we read from left to right.

Protons define the chemical behavior of an atom. The fixed number of positively charged protons dictates the arrangement of the atom's electrons, and thus its chemical properties.

Isotopes and the Mass Number

Each element has a fixed number of protons, but the number of neutrons may vary from atom to atom. In other words, two atoms with the same number of protons may have different numbers of neutrons. Such atoms are said to be **isotopes** of each other, and they have different masses. The total number of protons and neutrons is called the **mass number**.

Every element exists in several different isotopes, each with a different number of neutrons. The most common isotope of carbon, for example, has 6 neutrons, so it has a mass number of 12 (6 protons + 6 neutrons); it is usually written ^{12}C or carbon-12, and is called "carbon twelve." Other isotopes of the carbon nucleus, such as carbon-13 with 7 neutrons, and carbon-14 with 8 neutrons, are heavier than carbon-12, but they have the same electron arrangements and, therefore, the same chemical behavior. A neutral carbon atom, whether carbon-12, carbon-13, or carbon-14, must have 6 electrons in orbit to balance the required 6 protons.

The complete set of all the isotopes—every known combination of protons and neutrons—is often illustrated on a graph that plots number of protons versus number of neutrons (see Figure 12-1). Several features are evident from this

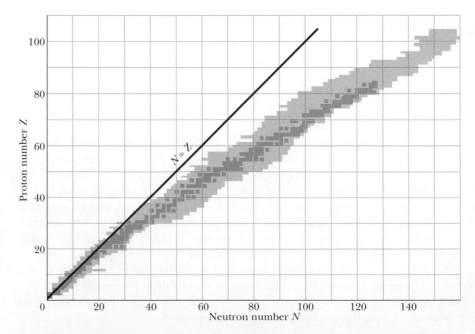

• **Figure 12-1** A chart of the isotopes. Stable isotopes appear in green, and radioactive isotopes are in beige. Each of the approximately 2000 known isotopes has a different combination of protons (Z on the vertical scale) and neutrons (N on the horizontal scale). Isotopes of the light elements (toward the bottom left of the chart) have similar numbers of protons and neutrons and thus lie close to the diagonal $N = Z$ line at 45 degrees. Heavier isotopes (on the upper right part of the chart) tend to have more neutrons than protons and thus lie well below this line.

graph. First, every chemical element has many known isotopes, in some cases, dozens of them. Close to 2000 isotopes have been documented, compared to the hundred or so different elements. This plot also reveals that the number of protons is not generally the same as the number of neutrons. While many light elements, up to about calcium (with 20 protons), often have nearly equal numbers of protons and neutrons, heavier elements tend to have more neutrons than protons. This fact plays a key role in the phenomenon of radioactivity, as we shall see.

EXAMPLE 12-1

Inside the Atom

We find an atom with 9 protons and 8 neutrons in its nucleus and 10 electrons in orbit.

1. What element is it?
2. What is its mass number?
3. What is its electrical charge?
4. How is it possible that the numbers of protons and electrons are different?

Reasoning: We can find the first three answers by looking at the periodic table, but we will refer back to Chapter 10 and the discussion of stable electron states for the last answer.

Solution:

1. The element name depends on the number of protons, which is 9. A glance at the periodic table reveals that element number 9 is fluorine.
2. Next, we calculate the mass number, which is the sum of protons and neutrons: $9 + 8 = 17$. This isotope is fluorine-17.
3. The electrical charge equals the number of protons (positive charges) in the nucleus minus the number of electrons (negative charges) surrounding the nucleus: $9 - 10 = -1$. The ion is thus F^{-1}.
4. The number of positive charges (9 protons) differs from the number of negative charges (10 electrons) because this atom is an ion. Atoms with 10 electrons are particularly stable (see Chapter 11), so fluorine usually occurs as a −1 ion in nature.

EXAMPLE 12-2

A Heavy Element

How many protons, neutrons, and electrons are contained in the atom ^{56}Fe when it has a charge of +2?

Reasoning: Once again we can look at the periodic table for the first two answers, but we will have to do a simple calculation for the last answer. Remember, the number of protons is the same as the atomic number; the number of neutrons is the mass number minus the number of protons; and we compare the number of protons and the +2 charge to determine the number of electrons.

Solution: From the periodic table, the element Fe (iron) is element number 26, so it has 26 protons.

The number of neutrons is the mass number, 56, minus the number of protons: $56 - 26 = 30$ neutrons.

The number of electrons surrounding the nucleus is equal to the number of protons minus the charge on the ion, which in this case is +2. Thus there are $26 - 2 = 24$ electrons in orbit.

The Strong Force

In Chapter 5 we learned that one of the fundamental laws of electricity is that like charges repel each other. If you think about the structure of the nucleus for a moment, you will realize that the nucleus is made up of a large number of positively charged objects (the protons) in close proximity to each other. Why doesn't the electrical repulsion between the protons push them apart and disrupt the nucleus completely?

The nucleus can be stable only if there is an attractive force capable of balancing or overcoming the electrical repulsion at the incredibly small scale of the nucleus. Much of the effort of physicists in the twentieth century has gone into understanding the nature of this force that holds the nucleus together. Whatever the force is, it must be vastly stronger than gravity or electromagnetism, the only two forces we've encountered up to this point. For this reason it is called the **strong force**. The strong force must operate only over very short distances, distances characteristic of the size of the nucleus, because our everyday experience tells us that the strong force doesn't act on large objects. Both with respect to its magnitude and its range, the strong force is somehow confined to the nucleus. In this respect, the strong force is unlike electricity or magnetism.

The strong force has another distinctive feature. If you weigh a dozen apples and a dozen oranges, their total weight is simply the sum of the individual pieces of fruit. But this is not true of protons and neutrons in the nucleus. The mass of the nucleus is always slightly less than the sum of the masses of the protons and neutrons. When protons and neutrons come together, some of their mass is converted into the energy that binds them together. We know this must be true, because it requires energy to pull most nuclei apart. This so-called "binding energy" varies from one nucleus to another. The iron nucleus is the most tightly bound of all the nuclei. This fact will become important in Chapter 14, when we discuss the death of stars.

Radioactivity

The vast majority of atomic nuclei in objects around you—more than 99.999% of the atoms in our everyday surroundings—are stable. In all probability, the nuclei in those atoms will never change to the end of time. But some kinds of atomic nuclei are not stable. Uranium-238, for example, which is the most common isotope of the rather common element uranium, has 92 protons and 146 neutrons in its nucleus. If you put a block of uranium-238 on a table in front of you and watched for a while, you would find that a few of the uranium nuclei in that block would disintegrate spontaneously. One moment there would be a normal uranium atom in the block, and the next moment there would be fragments of smaller atoms and no uranium. At the same time, fast-moving particles would speed away from the uranium block into the surrounding environment. This spontaneous release of energetic particles is called **radioactivity** or **radioactive decay**. The emitted particles themselves are referred to as radiation. The term *radiation* used in this sense is somewhat different from the electromagnetic radiation that we introduced in Chapter 6. In this case, radiation refers to whatever comes out from the spontaneous decay of nuclei, be it electromagnetic waves or actual particles with mass.

(STOP) **Stop and Think!** What might the world be like if most atoms were radioactive?

What's Radioactive?

Almost all of the atoms around you are stable, but most everyday elements have at least a few isotopes that are radioactive. Carbon, for example, is stable in its most common isotopes, carbon-12 and carbon-13; but carbon-14, which constitutes about a millionth of the carbon atoms in living things, is radioactive. A few elements such as uranium, radium, and thorium have no stable isotopes at all. Even though most of our surroundings are composed of stable isotopes, a quick glance at the chart of isotopes (Figure 12-1) reveals that most of the 2000 or so known natural and laboratory-produced isotopes are unstable and undergo radioactive decay of one kind or another.

SCIENCE IN THE MAKING •

Becquerel and Curie

The nature of radioactivity was discovered in 1896 by Antoine Henri Becquerel (1852–1908), who studied chemicals that incorporate uranium and other radioactive elements. He placed some of these samples in a drawer of his desk along with an unexposed photographic plate and a metal coin. When he developed the photographic plate sometime later, the silhouette of the coin was clearly visible. From this photograph he concluded that some as-yet-unknown form of radiation had traveled from the sample to the plate. The coin seemed to have absorbed the radiation and blocked it off, but the radiation that got through delivered enough energy to the plate to cause the chemical reactions that normally go into photographic development. Becquerel knew that whatever had exposed the plate must have originated in the minerals and traveled at least as far as the plate.

Becquerel's discovery was followed by an extraordinarily exciting time for chemists, who began an intensive effort to isolate and study the elements from which the radiation originated. The leader in the field we now call radiochemistry was also one of the best known scientists of the modern era, Marie Sklodowska Curie (1867–1934). Born in Poland and married to Pierre Curie, a distinguished French scientist, she conducted her pioneering research in France, often under extremely difficult conditions because of the unwillingness of her colleagues to accept her. She worked with tons of exotic uranium-bearing minerals from mines in Bohemia, and she isolated minute quantities of previously unknown elements such as radium and polonium. One of her crowning achievements was the isolation of 22 milligrams of pure radium chloride, which became an international standard for measuring radiation levels. She also pioneered the use of X-rays for medical diagnosis during World War I. For her work she became the first scientist to be awarded two Nobel prizes, one in physics and one in chemistry. She also was one of the first scientists to die from prolonged exposure to radiation, whose harmful effects were not known at that time. Her fate, unfortunately, was shared by many of the pioneers in nuclear physics. •

The Kinds of Radioactive Decay

Physicists who studied radioactive rocks and minerals soon discovered three different kinds of radioactive decay, each of which changes the nucleus in its own characteristic way, and each of which plays an important role in modern science and technology. These three kinds of radioactivity were dubbed alpha, beta, and gamma radiation to emphasize that they were unknown and mysterious when first discovered.

A safety officer in protective clothing uses a Geiger counter to examine waste for radioactivity.

The Curie family, with Marie Sklodowska, Pierre, and their daughter, Irene. Both parents received the Nobel prize in chemistry in 1911 for isolating radium and polonium. Their daughter received the 1935 prize with her husband, Frederic Joliot-Curie.

1. Alpha Decay

Some radioactive decays involve the emission of a relatively large and massive particle composed of two protons and two neutrons. Such a particle is exactly the same as the nucleus of a helium-4 atom. It is called an alpha particle, and the process by which it is emitted is called **alpha decay**. (An alpha particle is often represented in equations and diagrams by the Greek letter α.)

The nature of alpha decay was discovered by Ernest Rutherford, the discoverer of the nucleus, in the first decade of the twentieth century. His simple and clever experiment, sketched in Figure 12-2, began with a small amount of radioactive material known to emit alpha particles in a sealed tube. After a number of months, careful chemical analysis revealed the presence of a small amount of helium in the tube, helium that hadn't been present when the tube was sealed. From this observation, Rutherford concluded that alpha particles must be associated with the helium atom. Today we would say that Rutherford observed the emission of the helium nucleus in radioactive decay, followed by the acquisition of two electrons to form an atom of helium gas.

Rutherford received the Nobel prize in chemistry for his chemical studies and his work in sorting out radioactivity. He is one of the few people in the world who made his most important contributions to science—in this case the discovery of the nucleus—*after* he received the Nobel prize.

When the nucleus emits an alpha particle, it loses two protons and two neutrons. This means that the daughter nucleus will have two fewer protons than the original. If the original nucleus is uranium-238 with 92 protons, for example, the daughter nucleus will have only 90 protons, which means that it is a *completely different chemical element* called thorium. The total mass of the new atom will be 234,

• **Figure 12-2** The Rutherford experiment led to the identification of the alpha particle, which is the same as a helium nucleus.

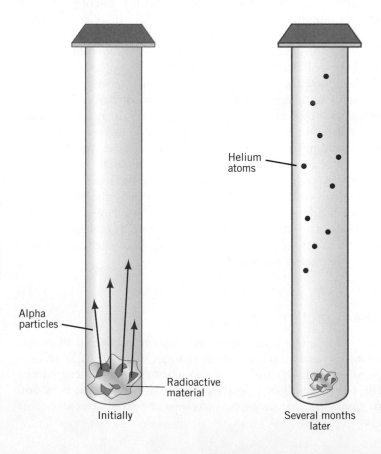

Helium atoms

Alpha particles

Radioactive material

Initially

Several months later

so alpha decay causes uranium-238 to transform to thorium-234. The thorium nucleus with 90 protons can accommodate only 90 electrons in its neutral state. This means that, soon after the decay, two of the original complement of electrons will wander away, leaving the daughter nucleus with its allotment of 90. The process of alpha decay reduces the mass and changes the chemical identity of the decaying nucleus.

Radioactivity is nature's "philosopher's stone." According to medieval alchemists, the philosopher's stone was supposed to turn lead into gold. The alchemists never found their stone because almost all of their work involved what we today would call chemical reactions; that is, they were trying to change one element into another by manipulating electrons. Given what we now know about the structure of atoms, we realize that they were approaching the problem from the wrong end. If you really want to change one chemical element into another, you have to manipulate the nucleus, precisely what happens in the process of radioactivity.

When the alpha particle leaves the parent nucleus, it typically travels at very high speed (often at an appreciable fraction of the speed of light) so it carries a lot of kinetic energy. This energy, like all nuclear energy, comes from the conversion of mass: the mass of the daughter nucleus and the alpha particle, added together, is somewhat less than the mass of the parent uranium nucleus. If the alpha particle is emitted by an atom that is part of a solid body, then it will undergo a series of collisions as it moves from the parent nucleus into the wider world. In each collision it will share some of its kinetic energy with other atoms. The net effect of the decay is that the kinetic energy of the alpha particle is eventually converted into heat, and the material warms up. About half of the Earth's interior heat comes from exactly this kind of energy transfer. As we shall see in Chapter 17, this heat is ultimately responsible for many of the Earth's major surface features.

2. Beta Decay

The second kind of radioactive decay, called **beta decay**, involves the emission of an electron. (Beta decay and the electron it produces are often denoted by the Greek letter β.) The simplest kind of beta decay that can be observed is for a single neutron. If you put a collection of neutrons on the table in front of you, they would start to disintegrate, with about half of them disappearing in the first 10 minutes or so. The most obvious products of this decay are a proton and an electron. Both particles carry an electrical charge and are therefore very easy to detect. This production of one positive and one negative particle from a neutral one does not change the total electrical charge of the entire system.

In the 1930s, when beta decay of the neutron was first seen in a laboratory, the experimental equipment available at the time easily detected and measured the energies of the electron and proton. Scientists looking carefully at beta decay were troubled to find that the process appeared to violate the law of conservation of energy, as well as some other important conservation laws in physics. When they added up the mass and kinetic energies of the electron and proton after the decay, the total amounted to less than the mass tied up in the energy of the original neutron. If only the electron and proton were given off, the conservation law of energy, as well as other important laws of nature, would be violated.

Rather than face this possibility, physicists at the time followed the lead of Wolfgang Pauli (see Chapter 8) and postulated that another particle had to be emitted in the decay, a particle that they could not detect at the time, but that carried away the missing energy and other properties. It wasn't until 1956 that physicists were able to detect this missing particle—the *neutrino*, or "little neutral one"—in the laboratory. This particle has no electrical charge, travels close to the speed of light, and, if modern theories are correct, carries a very tiny mass. Today, at giant particle accelerators (see Chapter 13), neutrinos are routinely produced and used as probes in other experiments.

When beta decay takes place inside a nucleus, one of the neutrons in the nucleus is converted into a proton, an electron, and a neutrino. The lightweight electron and the neutrino speed out of the nucleus, while the proton remains. The electron that comes off in beta decay is not one of the electrons that was originally circling the nucleus in a Bohr orbit. The electrons emitted from the nucleus come out so fast that they are long gone from the atom before any of the electrons in orbit have time to react. The new atom has a net positive charge, however, and eventually may acquire a stray electron from the environment.

The net effect of beta decay is that the daughter nucleus has approximately the same mass as the parent (it has the same total number of protons and neutrons), but has one more proton and one less neutron. It is therefore a different element than it was before. Carbon-14, for example, undergoes beta decay to become an atom of nitrogen-14. If you were to place a small pile of carbon-14 powder—it would look like black soot—in a sealed jar and come back in 20,000 years, most of the powder would have disappeared and the jar would be filled with colorless, odorless nitrogen gas. Beta decay, therefore, is a transformation in which the chemical identity of the atom is changed, but its mass is virtually the same before and after. (Remember: the electron and neutrino that are emitted are extremely lightweight and make almost no difference in the atom's total mass.)

What force in nature could cause an uncharged particle such as the neutron to fly apart? The force is certainly not gravitational attraction between masses. It is not the electromagnetic force that causes oppositely charged particles to fly away from each other. And beta decay seems to be quite different from the strong force that holds protons together in the nucleus. In fact, beta decay is an example of the operation of the fourth fundamental force in nature, the weak force.

3. Gamma Radiation

The third kind of radioactivity, called **gamma radiation**, is different in character from alpha and beta decay. (Gamma decay and gamma radiation are often denoted by the Greek letter γ.) A "gamma ray" is simply a generic term for a very energetic photon—electromagnetic radiation. In Chapter 6 we saw that all electromagnetic radiation comes from the acceleration of charged particles, and that is what happens in gamma radioactivity.

When an electron in an atom shifts from a higher energy level to a lower one, we know that a photon will be emitted, typically in the range of visible or ultraviolet light. In just the same way, the particles in a nucleus can shift between different energy levels. These shifts, or nuclear quantum leaps, involve energy differences thousands or millions of times greater than those of orbiting electrons. When particles in a nucleus undergo shifts from higher to lower energy levels, some of the emitted gamma radiation is in the range of X-rays, while others are even more energetic.

A nucleus emits gamma rays any time its protons and neutrons reshuffle. Neither the protons nor the neutrons change their identity, so the daughter atom has the same mass, the same isotope number, and the same chemical identity as the parent. Nevertheless, highly energetic radiation is produced by this process.

Moving Down the Chart of the Isotopes

The three kinds of radioactivity, summarized in Table 12-1, affect the nuclei of isotopes. Gamma radiation changes the energy of the nucleus without altering the number of protons and neutrons—the isotope doesn't change into a different

Table 12-1 Types of Radioactive Decay

Type of Decay	Particle Emitted	Net Change
alpha	alpha particle	new element with two less protons, two less neutrons
beta	electron	new element with one more proton, one less neutron
gamma	photon	same element, less energy

element. Alpha and beta radiation result in a new element by changing the numbers of protons and neutrons. Think about how alpha and beta radiation might be represented on the chart of the isotopes (Figure 12-1). Alpha decay removes two protons and two neutrons, so we shift diagonally down and to the left two squares on the chart. Alpha decay thus provides a way to move from heavier to lighter elements.

Beta decay, on the other hand, results in one less neutron and one more proton. On the chart of the isotopes we move diagonally up to the left by one square. Beta decay provides a way to reduce the ratio of neutrons to protons, which is generally greater for heavier elements. Combinations of beta and alpha decays, therefore, provide a means to move from heavier radioactive isotopes to lighter stable isotopes.

Radiation and Health

Why is nuclear radiation so dangerous? Alpha, beta, and gamma radiation all carry a great deal of energy—enough energy to damage the molecules that are essential to the workings of the cells that make up your body (Figure 12-3). The

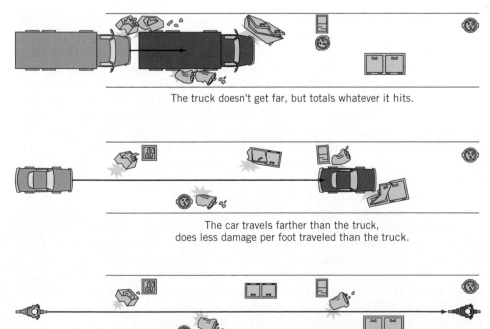

The truck doesn't get far, but totals whatever it hits.

The car travels farther than the truck, does less damage per foot traveled than the truck.

The motor bike makes it through the alley, doing less damage per foot traveled.

• **Figure 12-3** The damage to atoms and molecules from different kinds of radiation can be compared to the damage to objects in an alleyway caused by different types of vehicles. The truck resembles an alpha particle, the car resembles a beta particle, and the motorcycle resembles a gamma ray. Although you might conclude that the gamma ray does the least amount of damage, its high energy and ability to penetrate deeply makes it especially dangerous in large quantities.

most common type of damage is *ionization,* the stripping away of one or more of an atom's electrons. An ionized atom cannot bond in its normal way, and any structures that depend on that atom—a cell wall or a piece of genetic material, for example—will be damaged. Prolonged exposure to ionizing radiation can so disrupt an organism's cells that it will die.

It takes a great deal of radiation to cause sickness or death. Only in unusual circumstances, such as the aftermath of nuclear weapons used on the Japanese cities of Hiroshima and Nagasaki at the end of World War II, or the nuclear reactor accident at Chernobyl in Ukraine in 1986, do people die shortly after exposure. There are, however, possible long-term effects of exposure to lower levels of radiation. While such exposure will not cause death, it may affect a body's ability to replace old cells and can increase the risk of cancer. Radiation may also damage the genetic material that carries the coded information required to reproduce. Birth defects may not appear until decades after exposure to radiation.

No one can escape high-energy radiation entirely. Radioactive decay of uranium and other elements in rocks and soils, as well as cosmic radiation from space, bombard us all the time. Radioactive elements even occur in our bones and tissues. Certain kinds of radiation—medical X-rays, for example, and radioactive isotopic tracers for diagnosis—have saved countless lives. Human beings have always lived in a radioactive environment. Nevertheless, it is wise to minimize exposure to unnecessary sources.

THE SCIENCE OF LIFE •

Robert Hazen's Broken Wrist

I once had an experience that gave me a whole new perspective on radioactivity. A decade ago while playing beach volleyball I dove for a ball and bent back my wrist. It hurt a lot, but it was early in the season, so I taped up the wrist and kept on playing. After a couple of weeks it didn't hurt too much, so I forgot about the injury.

Years later, when the wrist started hurting again, I saw a doctor, who said, "Your wrist has been broken for a long time. When did it happen?" Because the break was so old, my doctor had to find out whether the broken bone surfaces were still able to mend. They sent me to a specialized hospital facility where I was given a shot of a fluid containing a radioactive phosphorus compound—a compound that concentrates on active growth surfaces of bone. After a few minutes this material circulated through my body, with some of the phosphorus compound concentrating on unset regions of my wrist bones. Radioactive molecules constantly emitted particles that moved through my skin to the outside; as I lay on a table, my broken wrist glowed on the overhead monitor. The process produced a clear picture of the fracture, so my doctor was able to reset the bones. My wrist has healed, and I'm back to playing volleyball.

Today numerous different radioactive materials are useful in medicine and industry because all radioactive isotopes are also chemical elements. The chemistry of atoms is governed by their electrons, while the radioactive properties of a material are totally unrelated to the chemical properties. This means that a radioactive isotope of a particular chemical will undergo the same chemical reactions as a stable isotope of that same element. If a radioactive isotope of iodine or phosphorus is injected into your bloodstream, for example, it will collect at the same places in your body as stable iodine or phosphorus.

Medical scientists can use this fact to study the functions of the human body and to make diagnoses of diseases and abnormalities (Figure 12-4). Iodine, for example, concentrates in the thyroid gland. Instruments outside the body can study the thyroid gland's operation by following the path of iodine isotopes that are injected into the bloodstream. Radioactive or nuclear tracers are also used extensively in the earth sciences, in industry, and in other scientific and technological applications to follow the exact chemical progressions of different elements. Small amounts of radioactive material will produce measurable signals as they move through a system, allowing scientists and engineers to trace their pathways. •

Half-Life

A single nucleus of an unstable isotope left to itself will eventually decay in a spontaneous event. That is, the original nucleus will persist up until a specific time, then radioactive decay will occur, and from that point on you will see only the fragments of the decay.

Watching a single nucleus undergo decay is like watching one kernel in a batch of popcorn. Each kernel will pop at a specific time, but all the kernels don't pop at the same time. Even though you can't predict when any one kernel will pop, you can predict the time during which the popping will go on. A collection of radioactive nuclei behaves in an analogous way. Some nuclei decay almost as soon as you start watching; others persist for much longer times. The percentage of nuclei that decay in each second after you start watching remains more or less the same.

Physicists use the term **half-life** to describe the average time it takes for half of a batch of radioactive isotopes to undergo decay. If you have 100 nuclei at the beginning of your observation and it takes 20 minutes for 50 of them to undergo radioactive decay, for example, then the half-life of that nucleus is 20 minutes. If you were to watch that sample for another 20 minutes, however, not all the nuclei would have decayed. You would find that you had about 25 nuclei at the end, then at the end of another 20 minutes you would most likely have 12 or 13, and so on (Figure 12-5).

• **Figure 12-5** The graph shows the number of radioactive nuclei left in a sample as the number of half-lives increases.

Saying that a nucleus has a half-life of an hour does *not* mean that all the nuclei will sit there for an hour, at which point they will all decay. The nuclei, like the popcorn kernels in our example, decay at different times. The half-life is simply an indication of how long on average it will be before an individual nucleus decays.

Radioactive nuclei display a wide range of half-lives. Some nuclei, such as uranium-222, are so unstable that they persist only a tiny fraction of a second. Others, such as uranium-238, have half-lives that range into the billions of years, comparable to the age of the Earth. Between these two extremes you can find a radioactive isotope that has almost any half-life you wish.

We do not yet understand enough about the nucleus to be able to predict half-lives. On the other hand, the half-life is a fairly easy number to measure and therefore can be determined experimentally for any nucleus. The fine print on most charts of the isotopes (expanded versions of Figure 12-1) usually includes the half-life for each radioactive isotope.

Radiometric Dating

The phenomenon of radioactive decay has provided scientists who study the Earth and human history with one of their most important methods of determining the age of materials. This remarkable technique, which depends on our knowledge of the half-life of radioactive materials, is called **radiometric dating**.

The best-known radiometric dating scheme involves the isotope carbon-14. Every living organism takes in carbon during its lifetime. At this moment, your body is taking the carbon in your food and converting it to tissue, and the same is true of all other animals. Plants are taking in carbon dioxide from the air and doing the same thing. Most of this carbon, about 99%, is in the form of carbon-12, while perhaps 1% is carbon-13. But a certain small percentage, no more than one carbon atom in every trillion, is in the form of carbon-14, a radioactive isotope of carbon with a half-life of about 5700 years.

As long as an organism is alive, the carbon-14 in its tissues is constantly renewed in the same small proportion that is found in the general environment. All of the isotopes of carbon behave the same way chemically, so the proportions of carbon isotopes in the living tissue will be the same everywhere, for all living things. When an organism dies, however, it stops taking in carbon of any form. From the time of death, therefore, the carbon-14 in the tissues is no longer replenished. Like a ticking clock, carbon-14 disappears atom by atom to form an ever-smaller percentage of the total carbon. We determine the approximate age of a bone, piece of wood, cloth, or other object by carefully measuring the fraction of

The Shroud of Turin, with its ghostly image of a man, was dated by carbon-14 techniques to centuries after the death of Christ.

carbon-14 that remains, and comparing it to the amount of carbon-14 that we know must have been in that material when it was alive. If the material happens to be a piece of wood taken out of an Egyptian tomb, for example, we have a pretty good estimate of how old the artifact is and, probably, when the tomb was built.

Carbon-14 dating often appears in the news when a reputedly ancient artifact is shown to be from more recent times. In a highly publicized experiment, the Shroud of Turin, a fascinating cloth artifact reputed to be involved in the burial of Jesus, was shown by carbon-14 techniques to date from the twelfth century A.D.

 Stop and Think! In Chapter 2 we described the monument known as Stonehenge and gave an age for it. This age came from the carbon dating technique we've just described. Because the monument is made of stone (which has no carbon), how do you suppose this dating was done?

Carbon-14 dating has been instrumental in mapping human history over the last several thousand years. When an object is more than about 50,000 years old, however, the amount of carbon-14 left in it is so small that this dating scheme cannot be used. To date rocks and minerals that are millions of years old, scientists must rely on similar techniques that use radioactive isotopes of much greater half-life. Among the most widely used radiometric clocks in geology are those based on the decay of potassium-40 (half-life of 1.25 billion years), uranium-238 (half-life of 4.5 billion years), and rubidium-87 (half-life of 49 billion years). In these cases, we measure the total number of atoms of a given element, together with the relative percentage of a given isotope, to determine how many radioactive nuclei were present at the beginning. Most of the ages that we will discuss in the chapters on the earth sciences and evolution are ultimately derived from these radiometric dating techniques.

The oldest human fossils are too ancient to be dated by carbon-14 methods. An alternative technique, called potassium-argon dating, is employed for dating the rocks in which these skulls, which are up to 3.7 million years old, were found.

SCIENCE BY THE NUMBERS •

Dating a Frozen Mammoth

Russian paleontologists occasionally discover beautifully preserved mammoths frozen in Siberian ice. Carbon isotope analyses from these mammoths often show that only about $\frac{1}{4}$ of the original carbon-14 is still present in the mammoth tissues and hair. If the half-life of carbon-14 is 5700 years, how old is the mammoth?

To solve this problem it's necessary to determine how many half-lives have passed, with the predictable decay rate of carbon-14 serving as a clock. In this case, only $\frac{1}{4}$ of the original carbon-14 isotopes remain ($\frac{1}{4} = \frac{1}{2} \times \frac{1}{2}$), so the carbon-14 isotopes have passed through two half-lives. After 5700 years about half of the original carbon-14 isotopes will remain. Similarly, after another 5700 years only one-half of those remaining carbon-14 isotopes (or $\frac{1}{4}$ of the original amount) will remain. The age of the mammoth remains is thus two half-lives, or about 11,400 years. •

Decay Chains

When a parent nucleus decays, the daughter nucleus will not necessarily be stable. In fact, in the great majority of cases, the daughter nucleus is as unstable as the parent. The original parent will decay into the daughter, the daughter will decay into a second daughter, on and on, perhaps for dozens of different radioactive events. Even if you start with a pure collection of atoms of the same isotope of the same chemical element, nuclear decay will guarantee that eventually you'll have many different chemical species in the sample. A series of decays of this sort is called a *decay chain*. The sequence of decays continues until a stable isotope appears. Given enough time, all of the atoms of the original element will eventually decay into that stable isotope.

To get a sense of a decay chain, consider the example we used at the beginning of this chapter—uranium-238, with a half-life of approximately 4.5 billion years. Uranium-238 decays by alpha emission into thorium-234, another radioactive isotope. In the process uranium-238 loses 2 protons and 2 neutrons. Thorium-234 undergoes beta decay (half-life of 24.1 days) into protactinium-234 (half-life of about seven hours), which in turn undergoes beta decay to uranium-234. Each of these beta decays results in the conversion of a neutron into a proton and an electron. After three radioactive decays we are back to uranium, albeit a lighter isotope with a 247,000-year half-life.

The rest of the uranium decay chain is shown in Figure 12-6. It follows a long path through eight different elements before it winds up as stable lead-206. Given enough time, all of the uranium-238 now in the Earth will eventually be converted into lead. Since the Earth is only about 4.5 billion years old, however, there's only been time for about half of the original uranium to decay, so at the

• **Figure 12-6** The uranium-238 decay chain. The nuclei in the chain decay by both alpha and beta emission until they reach lead-208, a stable isotope. Some isotopes may undergo either alpha or beta decay, as indicated by splits in the chain. Nevertheless, all paths eventually arrive at lead-208 after 14 decay events.

moment (and for the foreseeable future) we can expect to have all the members of the uranium decay chain in existence on the Earth.

Indoor Radon

The uranium-238 decay chain is not an abstract concept, of interest only to theoretical physicists. In fact, the health concern over indoor radon pollution is a direct consequence of the uranium decay chain. Uranium is a fairly common element—about two grams out of every ton of rocks at the Earth's surface are uranium. The first steps in the uranium-238 decay chain produce thorium, radium, and other elements that remain sealed in ordinary rocks and soils. The principal health concern arises from the production of radon-222, about halfway along the path to stable lead. Radon is a colorless, odorless, inert gas that does not chemically bond to its host rock.

As radon is formed, it seeps out of its mineral host and moves into the atmosphere, where it undergoes alpha decay (half-life of about four days) into polonium-218 and a dangerous sequence of short-lived, highly radioactive isotopes. Historically, radon atoms were quickly dispersed by winds and weather, and they posed no serious threat to human health. In our modern age of well-insulated, tightly sealed buildings, however, radon gas can seep in and build up, occasionally to hundreds of times normal levels, in poorly ventilated basements. Exposure to such high radon levels is dangerous because each radon atom will undergo at least five more radioactive decay events in just a few days.

The solution to the radon problem is relatively simple. First, any basement or other sealed-off room should be tested for radon. Simple test kits are available at your local hardware store. If high levels of radon are detected, then the area's ventilation should be improved.

Energy from the Nucleus

Most scientists who worked on understanding the nucleus and its decays were involved in basic research (see Chapter 1). They were interested in acquiring knowledge for its own sake. But, as frequently happens, knowledge pursued for its own sake is quickly turned to practical use. This certainly happened with the science of the nucleus.

The atomic nucleus holds vast amounts of energy. One of the defining achievements of the twentieth century was the understanding of and ability to harness that energy. Two very different nuclear processes can be exploited in our search for energy: processes called nuclear fission and nuclear fusion.

Nuclear Fission

Fission means splitting, and nuclear fission means the splitting of a nucleus. In most cases, energy is required to tear apart a nucleus. Some heavy isotopes, however, have nuclei that can be split apart into products that have less mass than the original. From such nuclei, energy can be obtained from the mass difference.

The most common nucleus from which energy is obtained by fission is uranium-235, an isotope of uranium that constitutes about 7 of every 1000 uranium atoms in the world. If a neutron hits uranium-235, the nucleus splits into two roughly equal-sized large pieces and a number of smaller fragments.

Among these fragments will be two or three more neutrons. If these neutrons go on to hit other uranium-235 nuclei, the process will be repeated and a *chain reaction* will begin, with each split nucleus producing the neutrons that will cause more splittings. By this basic process, large amounts of energy can be obtained from uranium.

The device that allows us to extract energy from nuclear fission is called a **nuclear reactor** (Figure 12-7). The uranium in a reactor contains mostly uranium-238, but it has been processed so it contains much more uranium-235 than it would if it were found in nature. This uranium is stacked in long fuel rods, about the thickness of a lead pencil, surrounded by a metallic protector. Typical reactors will incorporate many thousands of fuel rods. Between the fuel rods is a fluid called a moderator, usually water, whose function is to slow down neutrons that leave the rods.

The nuclear reactor works like this: A neutron strikes a uranium-235 nucleus in one fuel rod, causing that nucleus to split apart. These fragments include several fast-moving neutrons. Fast neutrons are very inefficient at producing fission, but as the neutrons move through the moderator they are slowed down. In this way, they can initiate other fission events in other uranium atoms. A chain reaction in a reactor proceeds as neutrons cascade from one fuel rod to another. In the process, the energy released by the conversion of matter goes into heating the fuel rods and the water. The hot water is pumped to another location in the nuclear plant, where it is used to produce steam.

The steam is used to run a generator to produce electricity as described in Chapter 5 (see Figure 5-10). In fact, the only significant difference between a nuclear reactor and a coal-fired generating plant is the way in which steam is made. In the former, the energy to produce steam comes from the conversion of mass in uranium nuclei; in the latter, it comes from the burning of coal.

Nuclear reactors must keep a tremendous amount of nuclear potential energy under control while confining dangerously radioactive material. Modern reactors are thus designed with numerous safety features. The water that is in contact with the uranium, for example, is sealed in a self-contained system and does not touch

• **Figure 12-7** A nuclear reactor, shown here schematically, produces heat that converts water to steam. The steam powers a turbine, just as in a conventional coal-burning plant.

The nuclear power plant at Three Mile Island, near Harrisburg, Pennsylvania, had to shut down after suffering a partial meltdown. Safety measures insured that no radioactive material was released into the environment.

the rest of the reactor. Another built-in safety feature is that nuclear reactors cannot function without the presence of the moderator. If there should be an accident in which the water was evaporated from the reactor vessel, the chain reaction would shut off. Thus a reactor cannot explode and is *not* analogous to the explosion of an atomic bomb.

The most serious accident that can occur at a nuclear reactor involves processes in which the flow of water to the fuel rods is interrupted. When this happens, the enormous heat stored in the central part of the reactor can cause the fuel rods to melt. Such an event is called a *meltdown*. In 1979, a nuclear reactor at Three Mile Island in Pennsylvania suffered a partial meltdown, but released no radioactive material to the environment. In 1986, a less carefully designed reactor at Chernobyl, Ukraine, underwent a meltdown accompanied by large releases of radioactivity.

Fusion

Fusion refers to a process in which two nuclei come together to form four hydrogen nuclei. Under special circumstances it is possible to push two nuclei together and make them fuse. When elements with low atomic numbers fuse, the mass of the final nucleus is less than the mass of its constituent parts. In these cases, it is possible to extract energy from the fusion reaction by conversion of that "missing" mass.

The most common fusion reaction combines four hydrogen nuclei to form a helium nucleus (Figure 12-8). (Remember that an ordinary hydrogen nucleus is a single proton, with no neutron. Thus we use the term "hydrogen nucleus" and "proton" interchangeably.) This nuclear reaction powers the Sun and other stars and thus is ultimately responsible for all life on Earth.

You cannot just put hydrogen in a container and expect it to form helium, however. Two positively charged protons must collide with tremendous force in

• **Figure 12-8** A fusion reaction releases energy as nuclei combine. Hydrogen nuclei enter into a multistep process whose end product is a helium nucleus. The red balls are protons, the blue ones are neutrons.

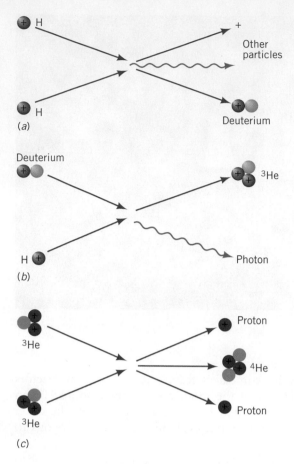

order to overcome their electrostatic repulsion and allow the strong force to kick in (remember, the strong force operates only over extremely short distances). In the Sun, high pressures and temperatures in the star's interior trigger the fusion reaction. The sunlight falling outside your window is generated by the conversion of 600 million tons of hydrogen into helium each second. The helium nucleus has a mass about half a percent less than the original hydrogen nuclei. The "missing" mass is converted to the energy that eventually radiates out into space.

Since the 1950s there have been many attempts to harness nuclear fusion reactions to produce energy for human use. The problem has always been that it is very difficult to get protons to collide with enough energy to overcome the electrical repulsion between them and initiate the nuclear reaction.

One promising but technically difficult method is to confine protons in a very strong magnetic field while heating them with high-powered radio waves. Alternatively, powerful lasers can be used to heat pellets of liquid hydrogen. This rapid heating produces shock waves in the liquid, and these shock waves raise the temperature and pressure to the point where fusion is initiated.

A number of rather expensive programs are now underway in the United States, Europe, and Japan, where researchers are investigating ways to produce commercially feasible nuclear fusion reactors, perhaps sometime in the twenty-first century. The development is slow and costly, but if researchers are successful, the energy crisis will be over forever, because there is enough hydrogen in the oceans to power fusion reactions virtually forever.

The Princeton Tokomak is a ring-shaped magnetic chamber. Hydrogen plasma is confined in this ring during attempts to achieve nuclear fusion reactions.

The National Ignition Facility attempts to initiate a fusion reaction in hydrogen-rich pellets that are simultaneously irradiated by dozens of high-powered lasers.

TECHNOLOGY •

Nuclear Weapons

Whenever humans have discovered a new source of energy, that source has quickly been turned into weapons. Nuclear energy, the most concentrated energy source known, is no exception. The earliest atomic bombs, developed in the

Science News | Muon Manna
(SCIENCE NEWS, VOL. 163, MARCH 22, 2003, P. 179)

The Earth is constantly being bombarded by high-speed particles created in nuclear reactions in stars. High in the atmosphere these particles hit nuclei in the atmosphere, breaking them up and creating sprays of particles, one of which is known as muon (pronounced MEW-on).

Recently, scientists have experimented with using the flood of muons at the Earth's surface to detect radioactive material and even nuclear weapons being smuggled into the United States. The idea is simple: detectors are placed above and below a truck being inspected at a border crossing and the number of muons entering and leaving is detected. If there is a heavy metal like plutonium or enriched uranium in the truck, the muons will be scattered through a larger angle than would be the case for scattering from lighter materials. In tests at Los Alamos, a piece of tungsten the size of a hamburger bun was easily detected. So, although much work remains to be done, this new technique may mark a significant advance in border security.

United States as part of World War II's Manhattan Project, relied on fission reactions in concentrated uranium-235 or plutonium-239. The problem faced by the designers of the atomic bomb was that there have to be a certain number of uranium-235 atoms to sustain a chain reaction to the point where large amounts of energy can be released. This quantity of uranium-235, called the *critical mass,* is about 60 kilograms—a chunk of uranium about the size of a grapefruit.

At the instant of an atom bomb explosion, a critical mass of the radioactive isotope is compressed into a small volume by a conventional chemical explosive. A chain reaction of fission reactions releases a flood of neutrons, which splits much of the nuclear material and releases a destructive wave of heat, light, and other forms of radiation. The first atomic bombs carried the explosive power of many thousands of tons of chemical explosive.

Shortly after World War II, the United States and the Soviet Union developed the hydrogen bomb, which relies on nuclear fusion. In a hydrogen bomb, a compact hydrogen-rich compound is surrounded by atom bomb triggers. When the atomic fission bombs are set off, they trigger much more intense fusion reactions in the hydrogen. Unlike atom bombs, which are limited by the critical mass of nuclear explosive, hydrogen bombs have no intrinsic limit to their size. The largest nuclear warheads, which could fit in a closet, carry payloads equivalent to many millions of tons (megatons) of conventional explosive. •

SCIENCE IN THE MAKING •

Superheavy Elements

Uranium, with 92 protons, is the heaviest element commonly found in nature, but ever since the mid-twentieth century scientists have been able to build heavier ones in the laboratory. If you look at the periodic table of the elements in Chapter 8, all of the elements past uranium are seen only in specialized experiments. The technique used is to bombard a heavy nucleus like lead with other nuclei and hope that, occasionally, enough protons and neutrons will stick together to form the nucleus of a still heavier atom. Although these heavier atoms will be unstable and decay quickly, they can last long enough to be identified by their spectra.

A group at the Lawrence-Berkeley Laboratory in California recently ran an experiment in which a lead target was bombarded with krypton ions. In the debris of the collisions, they saw evidence for elements 116 and 118. Even though the atoms lived only 1.2 milliseconds and 200 microseconds, respectively, they were the heaviest and most complex nuclei ever seen. •

Thinking More About | The Nucleus

Nuclear Waste

When power is generated in a nuclear reactor, many more nuclear changes take place than those associated with the chain reaction itself. Fast-moving debris from the fission of uranium-235 strike other nuclei in the system—both the ordinary uranium-238 that makes up most of the fuel rods, and the nuclei in the concrete and metal that make up the reactor. In these collisions, the original nuclei may undergo fission or absorb neutrons to become isotopes of other elements. Many of these newly produced isotopes are radioactive. The result is that even when all of the uranium-235 has been used to generate energy, a lot of radioactive material remains in the reactor. This sort of material is called *high-level nuclear waste*. (The production of nuclear weapons is another source of this kind of waste.) The half-lives of some of the materials in the waste can run to hundreds of thousands of years. How can we dispose of this waste in a way that keeps it away from living things?

The management of nuclear waste begins with storage. Power companies usually store spent fuel rods at a reactor site for tens of years to allow the short-lived isotopes to decay. At the end of this period, long-lived isotopes that are left behind must be isolated from the environment. Scientists have developed techniques for incorporating these nuclei into stable solids, either minerals or glass. The idea is that the electrons in radioactive isotopes form the same kind of bonds as stable isotopes, so that with a judicious choice of materials, radioactive nuclei will be locked into a solid mass for long periods of time.

Plans now call for nuclear waste disposal by the incorporation of radioactive atoms into stable glass that is surrounded by successive layers of steel and concrete. These stable containers are to be buried deep under the surface of the Earth in stable rock formations. Ultimately, if a long sequence of public hearings, construction permits, and other hurdles are passed, the U.S. Department of Energy hopes to confine much of the nation's nuclear waste at the Yucca Mountain repository in a remote desert region of Nevada. The hope is that long-lived wastes can be sequestered from the environment until after they are no longer dangerous to human beings.

The Yucca Mountain project continues to be a controversial subject. Supporters of the site argue that a single, remote long-term site is vastly preferable to the present 131 temporary repositories now located in 39 different states. Such scattered sites are difficult to monitor and protect from terrorist threats. Opponents of Yucca Mountain counter that hauling thousands of tons of nuclear waste on interstate highways poses a far greater danger to the public than the present sites. Some geologists, furthermore, fear that Yucca Mountain may be subject to occasional earthquakes and that its location, less than 100 miles from Las Vegas, is not sufficiently remote.

What should we do with our increasing quantities of nuclear waste? What responsibility do we have to future generations to ensure that the waste we bury stays where we put it? Should the existence of nuclear waste restrain us in our development of nuclear energy? Should we, as some scientists argue, keep nuclear waste materials at the surface and use them for applications such as medical tracers and fuel for reactors?

SUMMARY

The nucleus is a tiny collection of massive particles, including positively charged *protons* and electrically neutral *neutrons*. The nucleus plays a role independent of the orbiting electrons that control chemical reactions, and the energies associated with nuclear reactions are much greater. The number of protons—the *atomic number*—determines the nuclear charge, and therefore the type of element; each element in the periodic table has a different number of protons. The number of neutrons plus protons—the *mass number*—determines the mass of the *isotope*. Nuclear particles are held together by the *strong force*, which operates only over extremely short distances.

While most of the atoms in objects around us have stable, unchanging nuclei, many isotopes are unstable—they spontaneously change through *radioactive decay*. In *alpha decay*, a nucleus loses two protons and two neutrons. In *beta decay*, a neutron spontaneously transforms into a proton, an electron, and a neutrino. A third kind of radioactivity, involving the emission of energetic electromagnetic radiation, is called *gamma radiation*. The rate of radioactive decay is measured by the *half-life*, which is the time it takes for half of a collection of isotopes to decay. Radioactive half-lives provide the key for *radiometric dating* techniques based on carbon-14 and other isotopes. Unstable isotopes are also used as radioactive tracers in medicine and other areas of science. Indoor radon pollution and nuclear waste are two problems that arise from the existence of radioactive decay.

We can produce nuclear energy in two ways. *Fission* reactions, as controlled in *nuclear reactors*, produce energy when heavy radioactive nuclei split apart into fragments that together weigh less than the original isotopes. *Fusion* reactions, on the other hand, combine light elements to make heavier ones, as in the conversion of hydrogen into a smaller mass of helium in the Sun. In each case, the lost nuclear mass is converted into energy.

KEY TERMS ABOUT THE NUCLEUS

proton	mass number	beta decay	fission
neutron	strong force	gamma radiation	nuclear reactor
atomic number	radioactivity, or radioactive decay	half-life	fusion
isotope	alpha decay	radiometric dating	

REVIEW QUESTIONS

1. Compare the size of a nucleus to the size of an atom.

2. Which are heavier, electrons or protons?

3. What fact about atomic nuclei suggests the existence of the neutron?

4. What is the difference between mass number and atomic number? Is one always greater than the other?

5. What is an isotope?

6. How do you know that the strong force exists?

7. How is the strong force different from gravity and electromagnetism?

8. What happens to atomic nuclei during radioactive decay?

9. Explain the term "half-life."

10. Explain how radioactivity can be used to date (a) a piece of wood, and (b) a rock.

11. Describe the major achievement of Marie Curie.

12. What is alpha decay? How does it change the nucleus?

13. Why does beta decay not change the total electrical charge of an atom?

14. What led physicists to hypothesize the existence of the neutrino?

15. How does gamma radiation differ from alpha and beta radiation?

16. How can we obtain energy from nuclear fission?

17. What is a chain reaction?

18. How does a nuclear reactor work?

19. How do fusion reactions produce energy?

20. What is a critical mass?

21. How are radioactive tracers useful in medicine? Give an example.

22. What is nuclear waste? Why is it a serious problem for society?

DISCUSSION QUESTIONS

1. What was the hypothesis behind Rutherford's experiment on alpha decay? What did he prove?

2. What are the potential benefits and risks in using nuclear tracers in medical diagnosis?

3. "Critical mass" is a term that is widely used outside of nuclear science. What is its everyday meaning, and how does that relate to its scientific meaning?

4. Almost all of the atoms with which we come into daily contact have stable nuclei. Given that most known isotopes are unstable, how could this state of affairs have arisen?

5. How is the principle of conservation of energy seen in (a) fission reactions, and (b) fusion reactions?

6. Discuss the pros and cons of nuclear power.

7. Can nuclear radiation escape from nuclear power plants? If so, how?

8. Suppose you are a scientist from the future who had discovered the ruins of the Empire State Building. How would you go about estimating the date when it was built?

PROBLEMS

1. Use the periodic table to identify the element, atomic number, mass number, and electrical charge of the following combinations:

a. 6 protons, 7 neutrons, 10 electrons

b. 6 protons, 8 neutrons, 10 electrons

c. 9 protons, 8 neutrons, 10 electrons

d. 9 protons, 8 neutrons, 9 electrons

2. Use the periodic table to determine how many protons and neutrons are in each of the following atoms:

a. C-13

b. Ni-56

c. Ag-108

d. Rn-222

3. The average atomic weight of cobalt atoms (atomic number 27) is actually slightly greater than the average atomic weight of nickel atoms (atomic number 28). How could this situation arise?

4. Imagine that a collection of 1,000,000 atoms of uranium-238 was sealed in a box at the formation of the Earth 4.5 billion years ago. Use the uranium-238 decay chain (Figure 12-4) to predict some of the things you would find if you opened the box today.

5. Isotope X has a half-life of 100 days. A sample is known to have contained about 1,500,000 atoms of isotope X when it was put together, but is now observed to have only about 100,000 atoms of isotope X. Estimate how long ago the sample was assembled. Explain the relevance of this problem to the technique of radiometric dating.

INVESTIGATIONS

1. Read a historical account of the Manhattan Project. What was the principal technical problem in obtaining the nuclear fuel? Why did chemistry play a major role? What techniques are now used to obtain nuclear fuel?

2. What is the current status of U.S. progress toward developing a depository for nuclear waste? How do your representatives in Congress vote on matters relating to this issue?

3. What sorts of isotopes are used for diagnostics in your local hospital? Where are supplies of those radioisotopes purchased? What are the half-lives of the isotopes, and how often are supplies replaced? What is the hospital's policy regarding the disposal of radioactive waste?

4. How much of the electricity in your area comes from nuclear reactors? What fuel do they use? Where are the used fuel rods taken when they are replaced? If the facility offers public tours, visit the reactor and observe the kinds of safety procedures that are used.

5. Obtain a radon test kit from your local hardware store and use it in the basement of two different buildings. How do the values compare? Is either at a dangerous level? If the values differ, what might be the reason?

6. Only about 90 elements occur naturally on Earth, but scientists are able to produce more elements in the laboratory. Investigate the discovery and characteristics of one of these human-made elements.

7. Read an account of the so-called cold fusion episode. At what point in this history were conventional scientific procedures bypassed? Ultimately, do you think that the scientific method worked or failed?

8. Soon the U.S. government will take over responsibility for the nuclear wastes of the 50 states. What options do we have for waste storage? Do you think all the waste should be stored in one place? Should we try to separate and use the radioactive isotopes? What are the factors—social, political, and economic—that will help determine what happens to this nuclear waste?

WWW RESOURCES

See *The Sciences* homepage at: **http://www.wiley.com/college/trefil** for valuable web links.

1. **http://www.accessexcellence.org/AE/AEC/CC/radioactivity.html**
The Discovery of Radioactivity: The Dawn of the Nuclear Age, an interesting story.

2. **http://www.lbl.gov/abc**
The ABC's of Nuclear Science, from Lawrence Berkeley National Laboratory, where you'll find a brief introduction to nuclear science.

3. **http://www2.slac.stanford.edu/vvc/default.html**
SLAC Virtual Visitor Center, where you can learn about accelerators, synchrotrons, and particle detectors.

4. **http://www.ocrwm.doe.gov**
Issues surrounding the disposal of radioactive wastes in Yucca Mountain.

13

The Ultimate Structure of Matter

How can antimatter be used to probe the human brain?

GREAT IDEA

*All matter is made of quarks and leptons,
which are the fundamental building blocks of the universe.*

PHYSICS

Matter is composed of six kinds of quarks
and leptons, whose actions are governed by
a single unified force.

CHEMISTRY

Elementary particles can be
detected by measuring the changes
they cause in stable atoms.

GEOLOGY

The structure of the Earth is stable
because of the balance
between chemical and gravitational forces.

HEALTH & SAFETY

Particle accelerators are now used in
the treatment of some types of cancer.

ASTRONOMY

The Sun and other stars produce cosmic
rays, which gave scientists their first view
of elementary particles.

TECHNOLOGY

The largest particle accelerators
use electromagnets with
superconducting wire.

BIOLOGY

Positrons, a form of
antimatter, play an important role in
the study of the living brain.

Red = applications of the great idea
discussed in this chapter.

Orange = other applications, some of
which are explored in other chapters.

As you lie on the beach you let a handful of sand sift through your fingers. Look at a single tiny grain, and think about its microscopic structure. Imagine that you could magnify that grain a thousandfold, a millionfold, even more. What would you see?

At a thousand magnification the rounded grain would appear rough and irregular, but no hint of its atomic structure could be seen. At a million magnification individual atoms, each about a ten-billionth of a meter across, would begin to be visible. And at a trillion magnification the atomic nuclei would appear as tiny points, surrounded by almost nothing.

But is that it? Or is there even more to the submicroscopic structure of the atom? What are the ultimate building blocks of matter?

Of What Is the Universe Made?

The Library

The next time you head over to the library, wander through the stacks and think about what constitutes the fundamental building blocks of the library. Your first reaction might be to say that books are fundamental building blocks—row after row, shelf after shelf, of bound volumes. But a library is not just a collection of books; the volumes are arranged with an order to them. You could describe the set of rules that dictates how books are arranged in libraries—the Dewey decimal system, or the Library of Congress classification scheme, for example. Thus a complete description of a library at this most superficial level includes two things: books as the fundamental building blocks, and rules about how the books are organized.

Inside a book, the various volumes are not as different from each other as they might seem at first. They are all made of an even more fundamental unit—the word. You could argue that the word is the fundamental building block of the library; and, as was the case for cataloged books, we require a set of rules, called grammar, that tells us how to put words together to make books. Words and grammar, then, take you down to a more basic level in your probe of a library's reality.

You probably wouldn't be content very long with the notion of the word as the fundamental building block, because all of the thousands of words are different combinations of a small number of more fundamental things—letters. Only 26 letters (at least in the English alphabet) provide the building blocks for all the thousands of words on all the pages in all the books of the library. Furthermore, we need a set of rules (spelling) that tells us how to put letters together into words. The discovery of letters and spelling would constitute perhaps the ultimate description of a library and its organization.

In a library, letters form words and words form books. Letters can thus be thought of as the fundamental unit of the library.

So the library can be described in this way: We use spelling to tell us how to put letters together into words. Then grammar tells us how to put words together into books. Finally, we use organizing rules to tell us how to put books together into a library.

And this, as we shall see, is how scientists attempt to describe the entire physical universe.

Reductionism

How many different kinds of material can you see when you look up from this book? You may see a wall made of cinder block, a window made of glass, a ceiling made of fiberglass panels. Outside the window you may see grass, trees, blue sky, and clouds. We encounter thousands of different kinds of materials every day. They all look different—what possible common ground could there be between a cinder block and a blade of grass? They all look different, but are they really?

For at least two millennia, people who have thought about the physical universe have asked this question. Is the universe just what we see, or is there some underlying structure, some basic stuff, from which it's all made? You could even say that herein lies one of the most fundamental scientific questions.

The quest for the "ultimate building blocks" of the universe is referred to by philosophers as *reductionism*. Reductionism is an attempt to reduce the seeming complexity of nature by first looking for underlying simplicity, and then trying to understand how that simplicity gives rise to the observed complexity. This pursuit is a continuation of an old intellectual belief that the appearances of the world do not tell its true nature, but that its true nature can be discovered by the application of thought and, in the case of science, experiment and observation.

The Greek philosopher Thales (625?–546 B.C.) suggested that all materials are made of water. This supposition was based on the observation that, in everyday experience, water appears as a solid (ice), a liquid, and a gas (water vapor). Thus, alone among the common substances, water seemed to exhibit all the states of matter (see Chapter 10). To Thales, this observation suggested that water was in some sense fundamental. We no longer accept the idea that water is the fundamental constituent of matter, but we do believe that we can find other fundamental constituents.

The Building Blocks of Matter

To many people, the library analogy presents a profoundly satisfying way of describing complex systems. Some would even argue that everything you could possibly want to know about the library is contained in letters and their organizing principles. In just the same way, scientists want to describe the complex universe by identifying the most fundamental building blocks and deduce the rules by which they are put together.

At first, you might say the most fundamental building block of the universe is the atom. All the myriad solids, liquids, and gases are made of just 100 or so different kinds of chemical elements. The complexity of materials that appears to the senses results from the many combinations of these relatively few kinds of atoms. The rules of chemistry tell us how atoms bind together to make all of the materials we see.

Early in this century, scientists learned that atoms are not really fundamental, but are made up of smaller, more fundamental bits—nuclei and electrons. These particles arrange themselves according to their own set of rules, with massive neutrons and protons in the positively charged nucleus, and negatively charged electrons in shells around the nucleus. A picture of the universe with only three fundamental building blocks—protons, neutrons, and electrons—is very simple and appealing. Protons and neutrons together form nuclei, and electrons surround the nucleus to form atoms. Electrons combine and interact with each other to form all the materials we know about.

But, just as words and grammar gave us a false level of simplicity in the analogy of the library, this simple picture of the universe didn't stand up to more detailed experiments and observations. As we have hinted, the nucleus contains much more than just protons and neutrons, although this fact did not become clear to physicists until the post–World War II era. If we are going to follow the reductionist line in dealing with the universe, we have to start thinking about what makes up the nucleus. By common usage, the particles that make up the nucleus, together with particles such as the electron, were called *elementary particles,* to reflect the belief that they comprised the basic building blocks of the universe (Figure 13-1). The study of these particles and their properties is the domain of a field known as **high-energy physics**, or **elementary-particle physics**.

10^{-9} m	10^{-10} m	$10^{-15} - 10^{-14}$ m	10^{-15} m	Less than 10^{-18} m
Molecule	Atom	Nucleus	Neutron (or proton)	Quark

• **Figure 13-1** The modern picture of the fundamental building blocks of the universe. Molecules are made from atoms, which contain nuclei, which are made from elementary particles, which in turn are made from quarks.

Discovering Elementary Particles

Nowhere in nature is the equivalence of mass and energy more obvious than in the interactions of elementary particles. Imagine that you have a source of protons traveling at very high velocities, approaching the speed of light. This source might be astronomical in nature, or it might be a machine that accelerates particles. Once the proton has been accelerated, it has a very high kinetic energy. If this high-energy proton collides with a nucleus, the nucleus can be split apart. In this process, some kinetic energy of the original proton can be converted into mass according to the equation $E = mc^2$. When this happens, new kinds of particles that are neither protons nor neutrons can be created.

Cosmic Rays

During the 1930s and 1940s, physicists used a natural source of high-energy particles, so-called **cosmic rays**, to study the structure of matter. Cosmic rays are particles (mostly protons) that rain down continuously on the atmosphere of the Earth after being emitted by stars in our galaxy and in other galaxies.

Space is full of cosmic rays. When they hit the atmosphere, they collide with molecules of oxygen or nitrogen and produce sprays of very fast-moving secondary particles. These secondary particles, in turn, can make further collisions and produce even more particles, building up a cascade in the atmosphere. It is not uncommon for a single incoming particle to produce billions of secondary particles by the time the cascade reaches the surface of the Earth. Indeed, on average, several of these rays pass through your body every minute of your life.

Physicists in the 1930s and 1940s set up their apparatus on high mountaintops and observed what happened when fast-moving primary cosmic rays or slightly slower-moving secondary particles collided with nuclei. A typical apparatus incorporated a gas-filled chamber several centimeters across (Figure 13-2). Midway in the chamber was located a thin sheet of target material—lead, for example. Cosmic rays occasionally collided with one of the nuclei in the piece of lead, producing a spray of secondary particles. By studying particles in that spray, physicists hoped to understand what was going on inside the nucleus.

By the early 1940s, when the international effort in physics research shut down temporarily because of World War II, physicists working with these cosmic ray experiments had discovered particles in addition to the proton, neutron, and electron. And when the research effort started up again after the war, these discoveries multiplied as more and more particles were found in the debris of nuclear collisions, both by cosmic ray physicists and by those working at the new particle accelerators we will discuss shortly.

The net result of these discoveries was that the nucleus could no longer be considered as a simple bag of protons and neutrons. Instead, we had to think of the nucleus as a very dynamic place. All kinds of newly discovered elementary particles in addition to protons and neutrons were found there. These exotic particles are created in the interactions inside the nucleus, and they give up their energy (and, indeed, their very existence) in subsequent interactions to make other kinds of particles. This constant dance of the elementary particles inside the nucleus has been well documented since these early explorations.

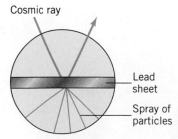

• **Figure 13-2** In a typical cosmic ray experiment, cosmic rays hit a lead nucleus, producing a spray of particles.

TECHNOLOGY •

Detecting Elementary Particles

If elementary particles are smaller even than an individual nucleus, how do we know they're there? Experimental physicists have raised detection of elementary particles to a fine art over the years. Nevertheless, the basic technique used in any detection process is the same: the particle in question interacts with matter in some way, and we measure the changes in matter that are the effects of that interaction.

If an elementary particle has an electrical charge, it may tear electrons loose as it goes by an atom. Thus a charged elementary particle moving through material such as a photographic emulsion will leave a string of ions in its wake, much as a speedboat going across a lake leaves a trail of troubled water.

A more modern detection method is to allow the particles to pass though a grid of thin conducting wires (usually made of gold). As a particle passes a wire, it exerts a force on the electrons in the metal, creating a small pulse of current. By measuring the time that this pulse arrives at the end of the wire, and by putting together such information from many wires, a computer can reconstruct the particle's path with high precision.

Uncharged particles such as neutrons are much more difficult to detect because they do not leave a string of ions in their path. Typically, the passage of an uncharged particle cannot be detected directly; instead, we wait until it collides with something. If that collision produces charged particles, then we can detect them by the techniques just outlined and can work backward and deduce the property of the uncharged particle. •

Particle Accelerators: The Essential Tool

For a time, physicists had to sit around and wait for nature to supply high-energy particles (in the form of cosmic rays) so that they could study the fundamental structure of matter. The arrival of cosmic rays could not be controlled, and it could be very time consuming waiting for one to hit. Physicists quickly realized that they had to build machines that could produce streams of "artificial cosmic rays"—**particle accelerators** that scientists could turn on and off at will, and that would take the place of the sporadic cosmic rays in experiments. At the beginning of the 1930s at the University of California at Berkeley, Ernest O. Lawrence began producing a new kind of accelerator called a *cyclotron*, an invention for which he won the 1939 Nobel prize in physics.

The cyclotron works by applying an electrical force to groups of charged particles that are forced to move in circles by large magnets, usually electrons or protons, producing a large acceleration according to Newton's second law. (Force = mass × acceleration: see Chapter 2.) The force is entered over and over again, and the particles are accelerated almost to the speed of light. Once they have acquired this much kinetic energy, they are allowed to collide with other particles. Those collisions provide the interactions that scientists wish to study.

Lawrence's first cyclotron was no more than a dozen centimeters across and produced energies that were pretty puny by today's standards. A modern particle accelerator is a huge, high-tech structure capable of producing energies as high as all but the most energetic cosmic rays. Called a **synchrotron**, its main working part is a large ring of magnets that keep the accelerated particles moving in a circular track.

One aspect of Maxwell's equations that we didn't explore in detail in Chapter 5 is that magnetic fields exert a force on moving charged particles. That force tends to

Ernest O. Lawrence posed in the 1930s with his invention, the cyclotron, which was the first particle accelerator.

The four-story-high Fermi-lab CDF particle detector. Particle detectors have gone from being small, desktop pieces of apparatus to huge high-technology instruments like the one shown.

make charged particles move in a circular track. As a particle in a synchrotron moves around the circle, the large electromagnets are adjusted to keep its track within a small chamber (typically several centimeters on a side) in which a near-perfect vacuum has been produced. This chamber, in turn, is bent into the large circle that marks the particle's orbit. Each time the particles come around to a certain point, an electric field boosts their energy. As the velocity increases, the field strength in the magnets is also increased to compensate, so that the particles continue around the circular track. Eventually, the particles reach the desired speed and they are brought out into an experimental area where they undergo collisions.

As the energy required to stay at the frontier of particle physics increases, so too does the size of accelerators. The highest-energy accelerator in the world today is at the Fermi National Accelerator Laboratory (Fermilab) outside of Chicago, Illinois. There, protons move around a ring almost 2 kilometers (about a mile) in diameter and achieve energies of a trillion volts. By 2005, scientists expect to complete the construction of the Large Hadron Collider in Geneva,

(a)

(b)

(*a*) Fermilab in Illinois and (*b*) Stanford Linear Accelerator Center (SLAC) in California are two of the world's most powerful accelerators.

Switzerland. Located in an underground tunnel about 8 km (5 miles) across, it will accelerate protons to over 7 trillion volts.

The **linear accelerator** provides an alternative strategy for making high-velocity particles. This device relies on a long, straight vacuum tube into which electrons are injected. The electronics are arranged so that an electromagnetic wave travels down the tube, and electrons ride this wave more or less the way a surfer rides a wave on the ocean. The largest linear accelerator in the world, at the Stanford Linear Accelerator Center in California, is about 3 kilometers (almost 2 miles) long.

THE SCIENCE OF LIFE •

Accelerators in Medicine

The ability to build machines that accelerate charged particles has had an important effect in many areas of medicine, most notably in the treatment of cancer. Often the goal of this treatment is to destroy malignant cells in tumors, and subjecting those cells to high-energy X-rays or gamma rays is a particularly effective way of doing this for some cancers.

To produce a beam of gamma rays for cancer therapy, a small accelerator produces an intense beam of high-speed electrons. These electrons are then directed into a block of heavy metal such as copper, where they are stopped abruptly. As we learned in Chapter 5, electrically charged objects that are accelerated (or, in this case, decelerated) emit electromagnetic waves. In the case of electrons accelerated to an appreciable fraction of the speed of light and suddenly stopped, those waves will be in the form of gamma rays. The direction of the electron beam is arranged so that the gamma rays pass through the tumor, killing cells as they pass through.

A form of cancer therapy still under development involves using beams of accelerated protons, which are allowed to hit a metal target and produce another kind of elementary particle called a pi-meson. When beams of pi-mesons enter tissue, the distance they travel depends on their energy. Thus the accelerator can be set so that the particle beam stops in the tumor itself, delivering large amounts of energy to a relatively small region. •

The Elementary Particle Zoo

At the beginning of the 1960s, the first generation of modern particle accelerators began to produce copious results, and the list of "elementary particles" known to reside inside the nucleus began to grow rapidly. The list now numbers in the hundreds. A few important groups of particles are summarized in the following sections and in Table 13-1.

Table 13-1 Summary of Elementary Particles

Type	Definition	Examples
leptons	do not take part in holding together the nucleus	electron, neutrino
hadrons	participate in holding nucleus together	proton, neutron, roughly 200 others
antiparticles	particles with same mass, but opposite charge and other properties	positron

Leptons

Leptons are elementary particles that do not participate in the strong force that holds the nucleus together, and they are not part of the nuclear maelstrom. We have encountered two leptons so far—the *electron*, which is normally found in orbit around the nucleus rather than in the nucleus itself, and the *neutrino*, a light neutral particle that hardly interacts with matter at all. Since the 1940s, physicists have discovered four additional kinds of leptons, for a total of six. If you keep in mind that the electron and the neutrino are typical leptons, you will have a pretty good idea of what they're like. The six leptons seem to be arranged in pairs—in each pair there is a particle like the electron, which has a mass, and a specific kind of neutrino.

Hadrons

All of the different kinds of particles that exist inside the nucleus are referred to collectively as **hadrons**, or "strongly interacting ones." The array of these particles is truly spectacular. Hadrons include particles that are stable like the proton, particles that undergo radioactive decay in a matter of minutes like the neutron (which undergoes beta decay), and still other particles that undergo radioactive decay in 10^{-24} seconds. The latter kind of particles do not live long enough even to travel across a single nucleus! Some hadrons carry an electrical charge, while others are neutral. But all of these particles are subject to the strong force, and all participate in holding the nucleus together; thus they help in making the physical universe possible.

Antimatter

For every particle that we see in the universe, it is possible to produce an antiparticle. Every particle of **antimatter** has the same mass as its matter twin, but the particles have opposite charge and opposite magnetic characteristics. The antiparticle of the electron, for example, is a positively charged particle known as the *positron*. It has the same mass as the electron, but a positive electrical charge. Antinuclei, composed of antiprotons and antineutrons and orbited by positrons, can form antiatoms.

When a particle collides with its antiparticle, both masses are converted completely to energy in a process called *annihilation*, the most efficient and violent process that we know in the universe. The original particles disappear, and this means that energy appears as a spray of rapidly moving particles and electromagnetic radiation. This fact has long been adopted by science fiction writers in their descriptions of futuristic weapons and power sources. (The starship *Enterprise* on *Star Trek*, for example, has matter and antimatter pods as its power source.)

Although antimatter is fairly rare in the universe, it is routinely produced in particle accelerators. High-energy protons or electrons strike nuclear targets, and the energy of the particles is converted to equal numbers of other particles and antiparticles. Thus the existence of antimatter is verified daily in laboratories.

SCIENCE IN THE MAKING •

The Discovery of Antimatter

In 1932, Carl Anderson, a young physicist at the California Institute of Technology, was performing a rather straightforward cosmic ray experiment of the type described in the text. Cosmic rays entered a type of detector called a "cloud chamber." In Anderson's cloud chamber, a cosmic ray particle would move

(b)

(a)

• **Figure 13-3** Carl Anderson identified the positron (the antiparticle of the electron) from the distinctively curved path left in a bubble chamber. In Anderson's original photograph (a) the positron path curves upward and to the left. In a more recent photograph (b) an electron (e⁻) and a positron (e⁺) curve opposite directions in a magnetic field.

through a moisture-laden gas, leaving behind a string of ions. By pulling out a piston at the bottom of the chamber, the gas pressure was lowered, and the liquid (usually alcohol) that had been in gaseous form condensed out into droplets. The ions acted as nuclei for the condensation of these droplets, so that the path of the particle was marked by a string of droplets in the chamber.

The key innovation in Anderson's experiment was the positioning of the cloud chamber between the poles of powerful magnets. These magnets caused electrically charged cosmic rays to move in curved tracks, with the amount of curving dependent on the particle's mass, speed, and charge. Furthermore, the tracks of positively and negatively charged particles curved in opposite directions under the influence of the magnetic field.

Soon after he switched on his apparatus, Anderson saw tracks of particles whose mass seemed to be identical to that of the electron, but whose tracks curved in the opposite direction from those of electrons being detected (Figure 13-3). This feature, he concluded, had to be the result of a "positive electron," a phrase he contracted to positron. Although no one realized it at the time, Anderson was the first human being to see antimatter. •

 Stop and Think! How might Anderson have interpreted his results if he had seen tracks of particles curving the same direction as electrons, but curving a different amount? (*Hint:* Remember Newton's second law of motion.)

THE ONGOING PROCESS OF SCIENCE •

How Does the Brain Work?

The study of elementary particles often seems quite abstract, but situations do arise where elementary particles play a very important role in understanding the real world. The new technology of positron emission tomography (PET), for example, is helping scientists probe the mysterious workings of the brain.

In this medical technique, molecules such as glucose (see Chapter 21) that have been made using an unstable isotope of an element like oxygen (an isotope produced in nuclear reactors) are injected into a patient's bloodstream. Organs in the body, including the brain, take up these molecules. They will go to the parts of the brain that need it; the parts that require extra energy at the time (see Figure 13-4). Alternatively, they may be molecules shaped in such a way that they attach to specified spots on the cells in the brain (see Chapter 22).

• **Figure 13-4** Positron emission tomography, commonly called the PET scan, reveals activity in the human brain. (*Left*): A patient undergoing a PET scan. (*Right*): A scan of a normal brain is seen at the top of the figure. The bright spots are places where large amounts of glucose (a simple sugar used by most cells for energy) are being used by the brain. The bottom half of the figure shows a scan of a person suffering from Alzheimer's disease.

The isotopes are chosen for this technique because they emit a positron, the antiparticle of an electron, when they decay. These positrons quickly annihilate with nearby electrons, emitting energetic gamma rays in the process. These gamma rays are relatively easy to detect from outside the body. A PET scan works like this: After the material is injected into the bloodstream, the patient is asked to do something—talk, read, do mathematical problems, or just relax. Each of these activities uses a different region of the brain. Scientists watching the emission of positrons can see those regions of the brain "light up" as they are used. In this way, scientists use antimatter to study the normal working of the human brain without disturbing the patient, as well as to detect and study abnormalities that can perhaps be treated. •

Quarks

When chemists understood that the chemical elements could be arranged in the periodic table, it wasn't long before they realized what caused this regularity. Different chemical elements were not "elementary," as Dalton had suggested, but were structures made up of things more elementary still. The same thing is true of the hundreds of elementary hadrons, or nuclear particles. They are not themselves elementary, but are made up of units more elementary still—units that are given the name **quark** (pronounced "quork"). First suggested in the late 1960s, quarks have come to be accepted by physicists as *the* fundamental building blocks of hadrons. Even though they never have been (and probably cannot be) seen in the laboratory, the concept of quarks has brought order and predictability to the complex zoo of elementary particles. (It is important to remember that only hadrons, not leptons, are made from quarks).

Quarks are different from other elementary particles in a number of ways. Unlike any other known particle, they have fractional electrical charge, equal to $\pm \frac{1}{3}$ or $\pm \frac{2}{3}$ the charge on the electron or proton. In this model of matter, quarks in pairs or triplets make up all the hadrons, but once they are locked into these particles, no amount of experimental machination will ever pry them loose. Quarks existed as free particles only briefly in the very first stages of the universe (see Chapter 15).

In spite of these strange properties, the quark picture of matter is a very appealing one. Why? Because instead of dealing with numerous hadrons, only six kinds of quarks (and six antiquarks) occur in the universe. The quarks, like many things in elementary-particle physics, have been given fanciful names: *up, down, strange, charm, top,* and *bottom* (see Table 13-2). We have seen elementary particles that contain all of these six. (The discovery of the top quark was announced in May 1994.)

From these six simple particles, all of the hadrons that we know about—all those hundreds of particles that whiz around inside the nucleus—can be made. The proton, for example, is the combination of two up quarks and one down quark, while the neutron is the combination of two down quarks and one up quark. In this scheme, the charge on the proton, equal to the sum of the charges on its three quarks, is

$$\tfrac{2}{3} + \tfrac{2}{3} + \left(-\tfrac{1}{3}\right) = +1$$

while the charge on the neutron is

$$\tfrac{2}{3} + \left(-\tfrac{1}{3}\right) + \left(-\tfrac{1}{3}\right) = 0$$

In the more exotic particles, pairs of quarks circle each other in orbit, like some impossible star system.

Quarks and Leptons

The quark model gives us a picture of the universe that restores the kind of simplicity that was brought by both Dalton's atoms and Rutherford's nucleus. All of the elementary particles in the nucleus are made from various combinations of six kinds of quarks. These elementary particles are then put together to make the nuclei of atoms. The six different leptons—primarily the electrons—are stationed outside the nucleus to make the complete atoms, and different atoms interact with each other to produce what we see in the universe. In this scheme, the quarks and leptons are the letters of the universe; they are the basic stuff from which everything else is made. The fact that there are six leptons and six quarks has not escaped the notice of physicists. This phenomenon is built into almost all theories of elementary particles. The question of *why* nature should be arranged this way remains unanswered.

Table 13-2 **Quark Properties**

Name of Quark	Symbol	Electrical Charge*
down	d	$-\tfrac{1}{3}$
up	u	$+\tfrac{2}{3}$
charm	s	$-\tfrac{1}{3}$
strange	c	$+\tfrac{2}{3}$
bottom	b	$-\tfrac{1}{3}$
top	t	$+\tfrac{2}{3}$

* Quarks with the same charge differ from each other in mass and other properties.

Quark Confinement

It would be nice to be able to study individual quarks in the laboratory, and physicists have conducted extensive searches for them. Yet there has been no generally accepted experimental isolation of a quark, and many particle theorists suspect that quarks can never be pried loose from the particles in which they exist. In these theories, once a quark is taken up into a particle, it is "confined" in that particle forever.

Here's an analogy that may help you think about quark confinement. Suppose you cut a rubber band and then try to isolate just one end of it. (Think of the rubber band as being a particle and the very end of it as being the quark.) You could grab hold of the rubber band and pull it, perhaps even break it. You would then have two shorter rubber bands, but you would never have the end of a rubber band by itself. No matter how many times you broke the rubber band apart, you would get the same result. There just is no such thing as an "end" not attached to something else.

Elementary particles seem to be the same. You can hit them as hard as you like in an attempt to shake the quarks loose, but every time you start to pull out a quark, you've also supplied enough energy to the system to make more quarks and antiquarks, and those new particles will immediately be taken up into ordinary particles. If you hit one particle hard enough, you will wind up with lots of other elementary particles, the things that correspond to the short pieces of the rubber band in our analogy.

The Four Fundamental Forces

In our excursion into the library, finding the letters of the alphabet wasn't enough to explain what we saw. We had to know the rules of spelling and grammar by which letters are converted into words and then books. In the same way, if we are going to understand the fundamental nature of the universe, we have to understand not only the quarks and leptons, but also the forces that arrange them and make them behave the way they do.

One useful analogy is to think of the quarks and leptons as the bricks of the universe. The universe appears to be built of these two different kinds of bricks that are arranged in different ways to make everything we see. But you cannot build a house using bricks alone. There has to be something like mortar to hold the bricks together. The "mortar" of the universe—the things that hold the elementary particles together and organize the physical universe into the structures we know—are the forces. At the moment, we know of only four fundamental forces in nature. Two of these, *gravity* (Chapter 2) and *electromagnetism* (Chapter 5), were known to nineteenth-century physicists and are part of our everyday experience. They are forces with infinite range—that is, objects such as stars and planets can exert these forces on each other even though they are very far apart.

The other two forces are less familiar to us, because they operate in the realm of the nucleus and the elementary particle. They have a range comparable to the size of the nucleus (or smaller) and hence play no role in our everyday experience. The *strong force* holds the nucleus together, while the *weak force* is responsible for processes such as beta decay (see Chapter 12) that tear nuclei and elementary particles apart.

Each of the four fundamental forces is different from the others in strength and range (see Table 13-3). The important point about the four forces is that whenever anything happens in the universe, whenever an object changes its motion, it happens because one or more of these forces is acting.

Table 13-3 The Four Forces

Force	Relative Strength*	Range	Gauge Particle
gravity	10^{-39}	infinite	graviton
electromagnetic	$\frac{1}{137}$	infinite	photon
strong force	1	10^{-13} cm	gluon
weak force	10^{-5}	10^{-15} cm	W and Z

* Relative to the strong force.

• **Figure 13-5** The exchange of a ball between two skaters provides an analogy for the exchange of a gauge particle. Skater *A*, who throws the ball, recoils, and skater *B* recoils when the ball reaches her. Thus both skaters change direction, and, by Newton's first law, we say that a force acts between them.

Force as an Exchange

We know that forces cause matter to accelerate—nothing happens without a force. We have talked about the gravitational force, the electromagnetic force, the strong force, and the weak force. Each has its own distinctive effects on nature. We have not, however, asked how these forces work.

The modern understanding of forces may be thought of schematically as illustrated in Figure 13-5. Every force between two particles corresponds to the exchange of a third kind of particle, called a *gauge particle* for historical reasons. That is, a first particle (an electron, for example) interacts with a second particle (say another electron) by the exchange of a gauge particle. The gauge particles produce the fundamental forces, such as electricity, that hold everything together.

In Chapter 2 we used the analogy of someone standing on skates throwing baseballs to explain Newton's third law of motion. Suppose a person on skates throws a baseball, and another person standing on skates catches the baseball some distance away. The person who threw the baseball would recoil, as we discussed. The person who subsequently caught the baseball would also recoil. We could describe the situation this way: Two people stand still before anything happens. After some time, the two people are moving away from each other. From Newton's first law, we conclude that a repulsive force had acted between those two people. Yet it's very clear in this analogy that that repulsive force is intimately connected with (a physicist would say "mediated by") the exchange of the baseball.

In just the same way, we believe that every fundamental force is mediated by the exchange of some kind of gauge particle (Figure 13-6). For example, the electrical force is mediated by the exchange of *photons*. That is, for example, the magnet holding notes onto your refrigerator is exchanging huge numbers of photons with atoms inside the refrigerator metal to generate the magnetic force.

In the same way, the gravitational force is mediated by particles called *gravitons*. Right now you are exchanging large numbers of gravitons with the Earth, an exchange that prevents you from floating up into space. The four fundamental forces and the gauge particles that are exchanged to generate each of them are listed in Table 13-3.

The two familiar forces of gravity and electromagnetism act over long distances because they are mediated by massless, uncharged particles (of which the familiar photon is one). The weak interaction, on the other hand, has a short range because it is mediated by the exchange of very massive particles—the *W* and *Z particles*—that have masses about 80 times that of the proton. Like the photon, the W and Z are particles that can be seen in the laboratory—they were first discovered in 1983, and are now routinely produced at accelerators around the world.

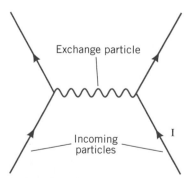

• **Figure 13-6** Exchange diagrams, introduced by physicist Richard Feynman, provide a model for particle interactions and the fundamental forces. Two incoming particles (such as two electrons) exchange a gauge particle (a photon) and thus are deflected by the force.

Richard Feynman
(1918–1988).

The situation with the strong force is a bit more complicated. The force that holds quarks together is mediated by particles called *gluons* (they "glue" the hadrons together). These particles are supposed to be massless, like the photon; but, like the quarks, they are confined to the interior of particles.

Unified Field Theories

Although a universe with six kinds of quarks, six kinds of leptons, and four kinds of forces may seem to be a relatively simple one, physicists have discovered an even greater underlying simplicity. The four fundamental forces turn out not to be as different from each other as their properties might at first suggest. The current thinking is that all four of these "fundamental" forces may simply be different aspects of a single underlying force.

Scientists suggest that the four forces appear to be different because we are observing them at a time when the universe has been around for a long time and is at a relatively low temperature. The situation is somewhat analogous to freezing water. When water freezes it can adopt many apparently different forms—powdered white snow, solid ice blocks, delicate hoarfrost on tree branches, or a slippery layer on the sidewalk. You might interpret these forms of frozen H_2O as very different things, and in some respects they are distinct. But heat them up and they are all simply water.

Similarly, the four forces look different at the relatively low temperatures of our present existence, but heat matter up to trillions of degrees and the different forces are not really different at all. Theories in which fundamental forces are seen as different aspects of one force are called **unified field theories**.

The first unified field theory in history was Isaac Newton's synthesis of earthly gravity and the circular motions observed in the heavens. To medieval scientists, earthly and heavenly motions seemed as different as the strong and electromagnetic forces do to us. Nevertheless, they were unified in Newton's theory of universal gravitation. In the same way, scientists today are working to unify the four fundamental forces.

The general idea of these theories is that if the temperature can be raised high enough—that is, if enough energy can be pumped into an elementary particle—the underlying unity of the forces will become clear. At a few laboratories around the world, it is possible to take protons and antiprotons (or electrons and positrons), accelerate them to extremely high energies, and let them collide. (As we have noted, proton–antiproton collisions involve the process of annihilation between particle and antiparticle.) When these collisions occur, for a brief moment the temperature in the volume of space about the size of a proton is raised to temperatures that have not been seen in the universe since it was less than a second old. In the resulting maelstrom, particles are produced that can be accounted for only if the electromagnetic and weak forces become unified.

In 1983, experiments at the European Center for Nuclear Research and the Stanford Linear Accelerator Center demonstrated that this kind of unification does occur. When protons and antiprotons (at the former laboratory) or electrons and positrons (at the latter) were accelerated and allowed to collide head-on, W and Z particles were seen in the debris of the collisions. Not only were the reactions seen, but the properties of the resulting particles and their rates of production were exactly those predicted by the first unified field theories.

The expectations of today's physicists regarding the unification of forces can be illustrated in a simple flow diagram (Figure 13-7). Scientists have already seen

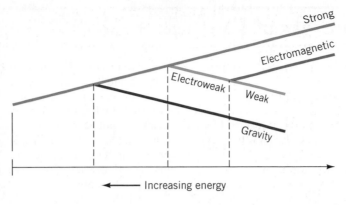

• **Figure 13-7** The four forces become unified at extremely high temperatures, equivalent to those at the beginning of the universe. At 10^{-43} second after the moment of creation, the universe had already cooled sufficiently for gravity to have separated from the other three forces. The strong force separated at 10^{-33} second, while the weak and electromagnetic forces separated at 10^{-10} second.

the unification of the electromagnetic and weak force in their laboratories. The resulting force, which physicists call the *electroweak force,* will be studied in great detail by the next generation of particle accelerators. At much higher energies, energies that will probably never be attained in Earth-based laboratories, we expect the strong force to unify with the electroweak. The theories that make this prediction constitute the *standard model*—the best model we have today of the elementary particles. Physicists have accumulated a fair amount of experimental evidence supporting the standard model.

Finally, at still higher energies, we hope to see the force of gravity unify with the strong electroweak force. No theory yet describes this unification successfully, and attempts to develop a successful model are very much a frontier issue. Scientists have, only half in jest, started to refer to theories that combine all four forces as TOEs—*theories of everything.*

The unification of the four forces has no obvious effect on our everyday world, because it requires such exotic high-energy conditions to see it happen. Nevertheless, the unification of forces played a crucial role in the formation of the universe. Much of our understanding of what the universe is and how it came to be in its present state (Chapter 15) revolves around the various kinds of unification of the forces of nature.

Science News | Rare Events—Exotic Processes Probe the Heart of Matter
(SCIENCE NEWS, VOL. 163, APRIL 12, 2003, P. 227)

Scientists cannot study quarks directly, but they can learn a great deal about them by studying the way that ordinary particles (which are made from quarks) interact with each other. They have known for decades that a particular kind of interaction, involving what are known in the jargon of physics as "charge conjugation violation," would yield particularly interesting information about the nature of the up and down quarks, but because these reactions are rare, have never been able to follow-up on this insight.

Recently two groups working at Canada's TRIUMF particle accelerator in Vancouver have reported the first sighting of these rare reactions. Directing an intense beam of neutrons at a container of liquid hydrogen, they observed the spray of elementary particles that were produced when the neutrons collided with protons in the hydrogen. They found that in approximately 17 of every 10,000 events, pions came off at angles that indicated that the rare reaction was actually taking place. According to our theories, the details of how these pions move depend on the difference between the masses of the up and down quarks. Thus, by observing ordinary collisions between ordinary particles, scientists may be able to determine the details of the structure of the underlying quarks.

Thinking More About | Particle Physics

Searching for the Ultimate Theory

The search for a theory of everything (TOE) is the culmination of millennia of human thought and effort, and represents a clear example of basic research. Unlike basic research in the past, however, this search is very expensive.

The problem is not that we don't have theories that are candidates for the TOE—far from it. One group of candidates are the so-called "string theories." These complex mathematical models of the subatomic world depict quarks as the result of vibrations of tiny multidimensional strings (think of vibrating guitar strings). In these theories, the different quarks are seen as different kinds of vibrations of these strings, which exist in spaces of 10 and 11 dimensions. There is no end to the ingenuity of theorists trying to solve this ultimate puzzle.

The problem is that to test these theories experimentally, we need to build huge particle accelerators—machines more complex than anything ever built by human beings. In 1993, for example, Congress pulled the plug on an ambitious project called the Superconducting Supercollider, a $10 billion project under construction south of Dallas. Today, the machine that will lead the world in particle physics is being built in Switzerland by the European Center for Nuclear Research (CERN). When it comes on-line in 2005, it will be able to test some (but not all) of the current candidates for the TOE.

How much money do you think ought to be spent on pursuing something like the TOE, given that we have so many pressing problems in the world? How much do you think your generation should invest in knowledge that probably won't have any practical benefits for decades?

SUMMARY

High-energy physics, or *elementary-particle physics,* deals with bits of matter that we cannot see, and forces and energies that we can barely imagine. Nevertheless, the study of the subatomic world holds the key to understanding the structure and organization of the universe.

All matter is made up of atoms, which are made up of even smaller particles—electrons and the nucleus—but these are not the most fundamental building blocks of the universe. Physicists originally examined collisions between energetic *cosmic rays* and nuclei to study elementary particles. They now employ *particle accelerators,* including *synchrotrons* and *linear accelerators,* to collide charged particles at near-light speeds. These scientists have discovered hundreds of subatomic particles.

One class of particles, the *leptons* (including the electron and neutrino), are not subject to the strong force and thus do not participate in holding the nucleus together. Nuclear particles called *hadrons* (including the proton and neutron), according to present theories, are made from *quarks*—odd particles that have fractional electrical charge and cannot exist alone in nature. Together, leptons and quarks are the most fundamental building blocks of matter that we know. Each of these particles has an *antimatter* particle, such as the positron, the positively charged antiparticle of the electron.

The four known forces—gravity, electromagnetism, the strong force, and the weak force—cause particle interactions that lead to all of the organized structures we see in the universe. Particle interactions are mediated by the exchange of gauge particles, with a different gauge particle for each of the different forces. Two masses, for example, will exchange gravitons (the gauge particle of gravity) as they attract each other, and two charged particles will exchange photons, much the same way that two skaters will be "repelled" by each other if a mass is thrown (exchanged) from one to the other.

While the four known forces appear to us to be quite different from each other, we believe that early in the universe, when temperatures were extremely high, the four forces were unified into a single force. At the forefront of modern physics research is the search for a *unified field theory* that describes this single force.

KEY TERMS ABOUT PARTICLE PHYSICS

high-energy physics, or elementary-particle physics	particle accelerator	linear accelerator	antimatter
cosmic rays	synchrotron	leptons	quarks
		hadrons	unified field theory

REVIEW QUESTIONS

1. How is the search for elementary particles an example of reductionism? Why is reductionism appealing?

2. What are building blocks of a library? Why is there more than one correct answer?

3. What is a synchrotron? (Is there a synchrotron at a laboratory near you?)

4. How do scientists detect the presence of subatomic particles?

5. Why are leptons, such as electrons and neutrinos, said to be weakly interacting particles?

6. Why are there so many different kinds of hadrons, but only a few kinds of leptons? Are hadrons or leptons more elementary?

7. What is antimatter, and how do we know it exists?

8. How do quarks differ from other elementary particles? Is there any way to prove that quarks exist?

9. Describe how quarks and leptons are put together to make all the matter we see.

10. Explain what it means for quarks to be confined.

11. List the four fundamental forces from strongest to weakest.

12. What particle is exchanged to generate each of the four fundamental forces?

13. What is a unified field theory? Give an example.

14. What is a PET scan? How does it employ elementary particles?

15. Why is big science needed in the study of elementary particles?

DISCUSSION QUESTIONS

1. Identify what might be considered the "fundamental units" and rules of organization of (a) a grocery store, and (b) a parking garage. How many levels of organization can you identify? (Remember, not all questions have only one correct answer.)

2. Which particle–antiparticle interaction releases more energy: an electron–positron annihilation, or a proton–antiproton annihilation? How does the law of conservation of energy come into play?

3. What are the similarities in the modern argument over the reality of quarks and the nineteenth-century argument over the reality of atoms? What are the differences?

4. Why is it appealing for physicists to think that there are only six kinds of quarks, as opposed to more than a hundred hadrons?

5. What observations led Carl Anderson to conclude that he had discovered a particle with the same mass as the electron, but with a positive electrical charge?

6. What does it mean to say that all four fundamental forces were unified?

7. How might you detect the presence of a charged elementary particle?

8. How will we know when we have identified the truly fundamental building blocks?

PROBLEMS

1. What is the electrical charge of an antiproton? An antineutron? Why?

2. A hadron called the lambda particle is made from two down quarks and one strange quark. What is the charge of the lambda particle?

3. A particle called the pi-meson is made from an up quark and an antidown quark. What is the charge of this particle?

INVESTIGATIONS

1. How did your congressional representative and senators vote on SSC funding in Congress? Why did they vote that way? Why do you agree or disagree with their vote?

2. Locate the nearest PET-scan facility and arrange a visit. Where do the physicians obtain the special form of glucose used in the procedure? What kind of edu-

cational training would you need to operate such a facility?

3. Watch an episode of *Star Trek* and discuss the use of matter and antimatter in the propulsion system of the *Enterprise*. Can you find any other uses of antimatter in science fiction stories?

4. What does it mean that the fundamental building blocks of the universe are things we can never isolate and study? Does that mean they aren't real? You might want to think about the question of the reality of atoms (see Chapter 8) for a historical precedent to this situation.

WWW Resources

See *The Sciences* homepage at: **http://www.wiley.com/college/trefil** for valuable web links.

1. **http://www.sciencenet.org.uk/database/Physics/Lists/Quarks**
   Quarks—learn about leptons, gluons, neutrinos, and more.

2. **http://www.cern.ch/Public/ACCELERATORS/Welcome.html**
   http://public.web.cern.ch/public/about/how/microscope/microscape.html
   Accelerators from CERN—as good as CERN's other sites.

3. **http://www.fnal.gov/pub/about/tour/index.html**
   Guided Tour of Fermilab Exhibit on high-energy physics.

4. **http://www-ed.fnal.gov/painless/htmls**
   High Energy Physics Made Painless, from Fermilab, written in plain English.

14

The Stars

How much longer can the Sun sustain life on Earth?

GREAT IDEA

The Sun and other stars use nuclear fusion reactions to convert mass into energy. Eventually, when a star's nuclear fuel is depleted, the star must burn out.

CHEMISTRY

All chemical elements heavier than hydrogen are being produced in the nuclear reactions of stars.

PHYSICS

The Sun's heat energy flows outward from its core into space first by conduction, then primarily by convection, and finally by radiation.

GEOLOGY

The Sun's radiant energy drives the Earth's weather patterns. (Ch. 18)

ENVIRONMENT

Since the Sun first entered its main sequence, the total amount of energy generated has stayed roughly constant, providing a stable energy supply for life on Earth.

HEALTH & SAFETY

Exposure to ultraviolet radiation emitted by the Sun increases the risk of skin cancer. (Ch. 24)

ASTRONOMY

A star's life cycle can be measured in stages that correspond to the amount of energy being generated.

TECHNOLOGY

A variety of satellite observatories detect a wide range of electromagnetic radiation from stars.

BIOLOGY

The Sun provides virtually all of the energy for life on Earth. (Ch. 22)

Red = applications of the great idea discussed in this chapter.

Orange = other applications, some of which are explored in other chapters.

The glaring Sun blazes down with midday brilliance. You make sure to use sunblock before stretching out on the beach towel. It's hot, but that's the way it's supposed to be at the beach. And the cooling ocean is just a few steps away.

What is the Sun—this distant glowing object that gives our planet light and warmth? Is the Sun unique? Has it always graced Earth's sky? Will it ever stop shining?

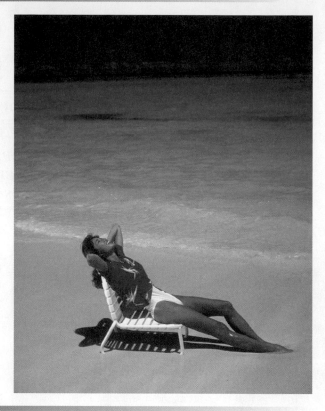

The Nature of Stars

Astronomy, the study of objects in the heavens, is perhaps the oldest science. When you examine the night sky, the most striking feature is the thousands of visible stars. Each **star** is an immense fusion reactor in space—a large ball of gas, consisting mostly of hydrogen and helium, which are the two most abundant elements in the universe. Every star is held together by gravity and every star radiates energy that is generated via nuclear fusion. The Sun, the nearest star to Earth, is just one of countless trillions of stars in our universe.

You have already learned enough about the way the universe works to understand some of the implications of your nighttime view of the stars. The fact that you can see the stars, for example, means that they are emitting electromagnetic radiation in the form of photons (see Chapter 6). Every star you see sends this radiant energy into space—energy that provides the essential data for all astronomers. Your eye intercepts a tiny fraction of that energy and converts it into the image you see, but similar amounts of energy radiate out in every direction from the star.

The laws of nature, including the laws of thermodynamics that describe the behavior of energy, apply everywhere in the universe. If a star sends radiant energy out into space, then the star must have a source of that energy. Furthermore, because every star is a finite object, it must have a finite store of energy. This simple observation leads to perhaps one of the most profound insights about the universe.

> **All stars have a beginning and an ending.**

In other words, the magnificent display that we see in the nighttime sky is a temporary phenomenon. It has lasted from the time that stars first formed until the present, a span of about 13 billion years. However, the view we see in the heavens will not last forever. Each star will eventually run out of energy. Before we look at the life cycle of stars, it's worth examining the kinds of data that astronomers use to understand the history and dynamic processes of stars.

Measuring the Stars with Telescopes and Satellites

Our only source of data on distant stars is electromagnetic radiation—energy in the form of photons streaming through space at 3×10^8 meters per second. The art and science of astronomy lies in the collection, analysis, and interpretation of these data. Most astronomers spend their lives measuring four aspects of photons from space:

1. Their wavelength, which is measured by spectroscopy
2. Their intensity, which is measured by a device like a light meter
3. Their direction, which is measured by recording two angles—one up from the horizon, and the other around from north
4. The variations of these wavelengths, intensities, and positions with time

These data, in turn, enable astronomers to understand many aspects of stars, including their distribution in space, their physical characteristics such as mass and composition, and their histories and future behavior. For example, astronomers find that many stars possess spectra that are virtually identical to that of the Sun. The fact that the intensity of light from these stars is many orders of magnitude weaker than the Sun indicates that they are vary far away.

Telescopes

To collect and analyze radio waves, microwaves, light, and other radiation, astronomers have devised a variety of **telescopes**, which are devices that focus and concentrate radiation from distant objects.

The first telescopes could examine only visible light, and when most people use the word telescope today, they mean an instrument for gathering and concentrating this form of radiation. The classic reflecting telescope (see Figure 14-1*a*) has a large mirror that reflects and focuses light to produce an image of the object being studied. (See Chapter 6 for a review of the reflection and refraction of light.)

Many modern light-gathering telescopes are built differently. Instead of having a solid block of glass for a mirror, they have an array of small, independently controlled, lightweight mirrors that, taken together, produce an image. The Keck telescope on Mauna Kea in Hawaii, the biggest of these new-age instruments with a collection of more than a dozen mirrors, together forming a reflective surface about 10 meters (30 feet) in diameter, was put into operation in 1992. Other factors being equal, the larger the telescope, the more useful it will be, because it will be able to collect more photons and thus detect fainter objects.

In the 1930s, astronomers built radio receivers that did for radio waves what the reflecting telescope did for light waves (see Figure 14-1*b*). For the first time, they could look at another kind of electromagnetic radiation. Today, large radio telescope facilities can be found all around the world.

Thousands of stars are visible in the night sky.

• **Figure 14-1** Schematic diagrams of telescopes. In an optical telescope (*a*), light strikes a curved mirror and is focused on a light-sensitive detector such as the eye or a piece of film. In a radio telescope (*b*), radio waves from space strike a curved metal dish that focuses the waves onto an antenna. Signals are amplified and processed by computer.

Orbiting Observatories

Except for visible light and radio waves, the atmosphere of the Earth is largely opaque to the electromagnetic spectrum. Most infrared and all ultraviolet radiation, long-wavelength microwaves, X-rays, and gamma rays entering the top of the atmosphere are absorbed long before they can reach instruments at the surface. The use of satellite observatories during the last half of the twentieth century has ushered in a golden age of astronomy. In this period, we have been able to put instruments into orbit far above the atmosphere and, for the first time, record and analyze the entire flood of electromagnetic radiation coming to us from the cosmos. *NASA* (the *National Aeronautic and Space Administration*) is in the process of creating a fleet of observatories high above atmosphere that will allow astronomers to probe every part of the electromagnetic spectrum. A description of some components of this "Great Observatories" program follows.

The Keck Telescopes in Hawaii are the world's largest.

The Very Large Array in Socorro, New Mexico, features a Y-shaped arrangement of linked radio telescopes. The effect of many small telescopes is equivalent to one very large telescope.

- *Hubble Space Telescope (HST)*. Launched in 1990, HST is a reflecting telescope with a 2.4-meter mirror designed to give unparalleled resolution in the visible and ultraviolet wavelengths. Despite a troubled beginning, the HST has proven to be one of the greatest scientific instruments in history. The HST was designed so that astronauts in the Space Shuttle could visit it periodically and install updated equipment, most recently in 2002. Thus, although the telescope has been in orbit for over a decade, it continues to be the premier astronomical instrument in the world. Some HST accomplishments are photographs of the comet Shoemaker-Levy hitting Jupiter in 1994, detection of the most distant supernovae and most distant quasars (1997), and accurate determination of the Hubble constant (2001).

- *Space Infrared Telescope Facility (SIRTF)*. Scheduled for launch in mid-2003, this orbiting observatory surveys the infrared radiation coming to the Earth from objects in space. Because everything radiates in the infrared, the telescope has to be cooled in a bath of liquid helium to keep it from "seeing" itself. This telescope sees the cool objects in the universe—clouds of dust around new stars, for example.

- *Chandra X-Ray Observatory*. Launched in 1999, the Chandra produces high-resolution X-ray images of objects in the sky. Its orbit carries it high above the belts of charged particles that surround the Earth, giving it a clear view of the X-ray sky. It is named for the Indian-American astrophysicist

The Hubble Space Telescope.

Subramanian Chandrasekar, the first scientist to understand the final stages in the lives of stars like the Sun.

The Anatomy of Stars

Astronomical observations reveal that stars are much more than uniform balls of gas. They have a complex and dynamic interior structure that is constantly changing and evolving. The Sun is the only star that is near the Earth, and thus it's the only star for which we have the kind of detailed knowledge that allows us to talk about how the various parts function. In this sense, the Sun is not only the giver of life on our planet, but also the giver of knowledge. Without such a star close by to study, we would probably not know much about the billions of stars that are farther away.

The Structure of the Sun

Based on comparisons with literally millions of other more distant stars, the Sun appears to be a rather ordinary star. While we can't peer into the Sun's center, theorists have learned to apply the principles of nuclear reactions to model processes deep inside stars. At its center is the stellar core, comprising about 10% of the Sun's total volume. This core is the Sun's furnace, where nuclear reactions rage, and energy generated in the core streams out from the center. Deep within the Sun, this energy transfer takes place largely through collisions of high-energy particles—gamma rays and X-rays, for example—that are generated by the core's nuclear reactions. About four-fifths of the way out, however, the energy-transfer mechanism changes, and the hydrogen-rich material in the Sun begins to undergo large-scale convection. This outer region, comprising the turbulent upper 200,000 kilometers (about 125,000 miles) of the Sun, is called the *convection zone*. Thus energy is brought from the core to the surface in a stepwise process, first by collisions, then by convection.

The only part of the Sun that we actually see is a thin outer layer. We can observe perhaps 150 kilometers (about 100 miles) into the Sun; any deeper and

The surface of the sun, showing hot material following magnetic field lines.

• **Figure 14-2** The Sun's chromosphere and corona become visible during a total eclipse. This halo of incandescent plasma is normally blotted out by light from the Sun's main disk.

the stellar material becomes too dense to be transparent. The outer part of the Sun, the part that actually emits most of the light we see, is called the *photosphere*. The Sun does not have a sharp outer boundary, but gradually becomes thinner and thinner farther away from the surface. These gaseous layers are not usually visible from the Earth. During a total eclipse of the Sun, however, when the Moon passes in front of the Sun, the Sun's spectacular halo, called the *chromosphere* and the *corona*, may become visible for a few minutes (Figure 14-2).

The Sun constantly emits a stream of particles—mainly ions (electrically charged atoms) of hydrogen and helium—into space around it. This stream of particles, called the **solar wind**, blows by Earth and the other planets all the time. Because the particles are charged, they affect the magnetic fields of the planets, compressing the fields on the "upstream" side and dragging them out on the "downstream" side (Figure 14-3). The interaction of the solar wind with the outer reaches of the Earth's atmosphere also gives rise to the aurora borealis, or northern lights.

The flow of energy from the Sun is a complex affair. Beginning with the conversion of mass in fusion reactions, the energy slowly percolates outward, first in collisions and later in great convection cells under the solar surface. It takes a few tens of

Solar wind

Magnetic field lines

N

S

Solar wind

• **Figure 14-3** The magnetic field of the Earth is swept out into a long tail by the solar wind.

Northern lights result from interactions of the solar wind with the Earth's magnetic field.

thousands of years for the energy to work its way to the photosphere, but only eight minutes for photons to cover the distance between the Sun and the Earth.

Once the sunlight reaches our planet, a tiny fraction of it is converted by the process of photosynthesis in plants into chemical energy stored in large molecules (see Chapter 22). This is the primary source of energy for most living things on the planet. Another fraction of the energy in sunlight heats the air at the equator and, as we shall see in Chapter 18, drives the Earth's weather patterns.

THE SCIENCE OF LIFE •

Why Is the Visible Spectrum Visible?

In Chapter 5 we saw that, of all the possible waves in the electromagnetic spectrum, the human eye can detect only the small interval of wavelengths between red and violet. One reason why the human eye is made this way was discussed in Chapter 5—the Earth's atmosphere is transparent to these wavelengths, so it is possible for the waves to travel long distances through the air. But there is another aspect to the development of the human eye that has to do not with the Earth, but with the Sun. Because of the fusion reactions at its core, the temperature of the outer part of the Sun is quite high, about 5500°C (for reference, gold melts at about 1065°C). Every object above absolute zero radiates electromagnetic waves, and both the total amount of energy and the wavelengths of the radiation depend on the body's temperature.

In Figure 14-4, we show the amount of energy that the Sun radiates at each wavelength, with the visible spectrum represented by the vertical lines. We see that the Sun's peak output of energy is in the middle of the visible spectrum. Thus the wavelengths between red and violet are visible for two reasons—the air is transparent to them, and the Sun, our main source of light, emits the greatest proportion of its energy in that form.

Science fiction writers often use this fact when they portray imaginary beings from other planets. Those from planets around cooler stars than the Sun may be given large eyes so they can absorb more of the scarcer photons. For the reasons we have cited, however, humans don't require such large optical collectors. •

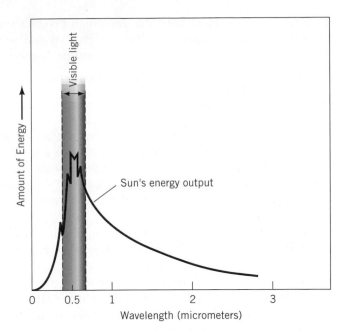

The Sun's Energy Source: Fusion

Once people came to understand conservation of energy—that energy has to come from somewhere, and that the total amount of energy in a closed system is constant—two key questions about the stars arose naturally: What is their energy source? How can they continue to burn, emitting huge amounts of energy into space, yet remain seemingly unchanged for such long periods of time?

In the nineteenth century, several scholars attempted to explain the Sun's energy source. One astronomer, for example, calculated how long the Sun could burn if it were composed entirely of the best fuel available at that time—anthracite coal. (The answer turns out to be about 10,000 years.) The Sun's energy source also figured in the famous debate at the end of the nineteenth century regarding the age of the Earth (see Chapter 3).

Today, we understand that the Sun is indeed "burning" a fuel, but that fuel is hydrogen, which is consumed through nuclear fusion reactions (see Chapter 12). Stars are made primarily of hydrogen gas, because that is the most common material in the universe. As a star forms, gravity pulls the hydrogen into a dense ball that heats up. Electrons are torn from the hydrogen and other atoms, creating a plasma made up primarily of protons (the nucleus of the hydrogen atom) and electrons.

Normally, protons would repel each other (see Chapter 5). As matter accumulates in the new star, however, the protons move faster as the temperature increases. Eventually, they acquire enough energy to overcome the electrical repulsion between them. They start to fuse.

The fusion process in the Sun's core does not take place all at once, with four particles suddenly coming together to make a helium-4 nucleus. Instead, it takes place in three steps.

$$\text{Step 1: } P + P \rightarrow D + e^+ + \text{neutrino}$$

Two protons come together to form a deuterium nucleus (an isotope of hydrogen made up of one proton and one neutron), a positron (e^+, the antiparticle of the electron as described in Chapter 13), and a neutrino.

$$\text{Step 2: } D + P \rightarrow {}^3\text{He} + \text{photon}$$

Another proton collides with the deuterium produced in the first step to form ³He, the isotope of helium that has two protons and one neutron in its nucleus. A photon in the form of an energetic gamma ray is also produced.

Step 3: ³He + ³He → ⁴He + 2 protons + photon

Two ³He nuclei collide to form ⁴He, two protons, and a photon (another gamma ray).

The net effect of this three-step process, called *hydrogen burning*, is that four protons are converted into a ⁴He nucleus with a few extra particles thrown in. As we saw in Chapter 12, the sum of the masses of all the particles produced in this reaction amounts to *less* than the mass of the original four protons. The lost mass has been converted into energy—the nuclear energy that powers the Sun and eventually radiates out into space.

How long could the Sun burn hydrogen at its present rate? If you simply add up all the hydrogen in the Sun and ask how long it could last, the answer turns out to be something like 75 billion years. Actually, no star ever consumes all of its hydrogen in this way. The hydrogen burning is generally confined to a small region in the center of the star called the core. The best current estimate of the total lifetime of our Sun is about 11 billion years—that is, our star is almost halfway through its hydrogen-burning phase.

 Stop and Think! Why do you suppose fusion proceeds in a stepwise manner, rather than having four protons come together all at once?

THE ONGOING PROCESS OF SCIENCE •

The Solar Neutrino Problem

Our explanation of the Sun's energy source is a theory—a very plausible one—that is subject to experimental verification. In fact, a great deal of observational evidence supports the notion that hydrogen-burning reactions account for the Sun's energy. One crucial piece of evidence, however, seemed to indicate that we might not have known as much about the interior of the Sun as we'd like to think. Beginning in the early 1970s, a large experiment located a mile underground in a gold mine in Lead, South Dakota, has been returning results that were puzzling, to say the least.

The idea behind this experiment is that, as we have just seen, nuclear fusion reactions in the Sun's core produce neutrinos. Most of these neutrinos escape from the Sun without being absorbed or changed, and arrive at the Earth unchanged. Most of them will pass through the Earth as well, but occasionally one will interact with an atom in the apparatus of this experiment, so that it can be detected. Thus the experiment provides us with a "telescope" that can "see" right down to the center of the Sun. If we believe we know what reactions are going on there, we should be able to predict how many neutrinos should be seen.

When these measurements are taken, scientists see only about one-third to one-half of the number of neutrinos they had expected to see. Other experiments of this type, being run in Europe, the former Soviet Union, and Japan, bore out this result. Explaining the missing one-half to two-thirds of the expected neutrinos was known as the "solar neutrino problem."

One possible explanation of the solar neutrino problem was tied to the nature of elementary particles such as neutrinos, and the fact that there are three different kinds of neutrinos. According to this idea, the predicted number of ordinary neutrinos (or electron neutrinos) is produced in the Sun, but while they're in transit to the Earth, some of them are converted into the two other kinds of neutrinos (the ones associated with the mu and tau particles). Such transitions between neutrino types are possible in some versions of modern unified

Scientists inspect the Super Kamiokande neutrino detector in Japan.

field theories. In this way, by the time the neutrino stream reaches the Earth, only a fraction of the original particles would be ordinary neutrinos capable of interacting with ordinary atoms in an experimental apparatus.

In 2001, results from a new observatory located in an old nickel mine in Sudbury, Ontario, Canada, gave a spectacular confirmation of this idea, and solved the solar neutrino problem once and for all. This detector contains 8000 tons of pure water, and, at its core, another 1000 tons of what is called "heavy water"—water in which one hydrogen atom contains an extra neutron in its nucleus. That extra neutron can undergo interactions only with electron neutrinos, while all three kinds of neutrinos can scatter from ordinary water. Thus, by comparing reaction rates in the two parts of the detector, scientists were able to show that roughly two-thirds of the neutrinos that leave the Sun have been converted, by the time they reach the Earth, into something other than electron neutrinos. •

TECHNOLOGY •

Dyson Spheres, an Ultimate Technology

Sometimes it's fun to speculate about how an extremely advanced technological civilization would use the energy from a star. One approach to the question is to note that most of the energy generated by stars is radiated into space and, from the point of view of planet dwellers, wasted. Physicist Freeman Dyson has suggested that one way to avoid this energy loss would be to dismantle a large planet and convert its material into a sphere surrounding a star—a hypothetical structure now called a Dyson sphere. A Dyson sphere would not only intercept and utilize all of a star's energy, it also could support a tremendous population. Such an immense structure would have an internal surface area comparable to more than 500 million Earth-like planets, and it would be uniformly heated in eternal daylight.

A star enclosed in a Dyson sphere would radiate its energy in the visible and higher energies, as usual, but all that energy would be absorbed by the sphere, which would then be warmed and radiate the energy into space as infrared radiation. •

The Variety of Stars

Knowing how one star, our own Sun, works should help us understand the variety of other stars we see. When you look at the stars in the night sky, one of the first things you notice is that they don't all look the same. For example, some stars appear reddish, while others are almost blue. Your everyday experience with flames provides a simple explanation: different stars must be at different temperatures. Very hot flames, such as a gas burner, emit a greater percentage of high-energy blue photons; cooler fires feature lower-energy orange and red photons.

Stars also differ in their brightness; some appear as brilliant points of light, while others are barely visible. Differences in brightness arise from two factors—distance and energy output. Brightness varies in part because the stars are different distances from the Earth. An unusually bright star located far away will appear dim to us, while an average star located nearby might appear very bright. The brightness of a star is also related to the amount of energy it is producing. Astronomers often refer to the total energy emitted by a star as its *luminosity*. These differences in a star's appearance are taken into account by distinguishing between a star's *apparent brightness*, which is the brightness it appears to have when viewed from the Earth, and its *absolute brightness*, which is the brightness it would have if viewed from a standard distance.

Much of the differences in the stars' appearances arise from the many varieties of stars themselves. Some stars shine a thousand times brighter than the Sun, while others are a thousand times dimmer. Some stars contain 40 times more mass than the Sun, while others have much less. As we shall see, we can bring order to this tremendous diversity of stars by recognizing that the behavior of every star depends primarily on just two factors: its total mass, and its age.

The Astronomical Distance Scale

When we look at the sky, we see a two-dimensional display—all stars look equally distant. Before characterizing the different varieties of stars, we need to add the third dimension, to determine their distances. Only then can we relate apparent brightness (what we see from Earth) to absolute brightness (the luminosity or energy output of the star). Astronomers customarily measure these great distances in **light-years**, which is the distance light travels in one year, or about 10 trillion kilometers (about 6.2 trillion miles).

In practice, no single method can be used to find the distance to every star. Just as you might use a ruler, a tape measure, and a surveyor's tape to measure successively larger distances, astronomers measure distances to stars with a series of "yardsticks," each appropriate to a particular distance scale.

For short distances (up to a few hundred light-years), several different methods involving simple geometry can be used. For nearby stars, the angle of sight to the star measured at opposite ends of the Earth's orbit (Figure 14-5) can be used

• **Figure 14-5** The triangulation of stellar distances. By measuring the angle of sight to a given star from two points of known separation, we can determine the star's distance from us.

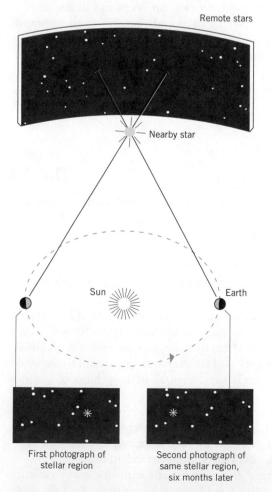

Remote stars

Nearby star

Sun

Earth

First photograph of stellar region

Second photograph of same stellar region, six months later

to work out the distance. For centuries, navigators on the Earth's surface have used a similar method, called *triangulation,* to determine the position of ships.

For greater distances, a standard type of star called a *Cepheid variable* is used. These stars, the first of which was discovered in the constellation of Cepheus, show a regular behavior of steady brightening and dimming over a period of weeks or months. Henrietta Leavitt (1868–1921) of Harvard College Observatory showed that the absolute magnitude of these stars is related to the time it takes for them to go through the dimming-brightening-dimming sequence. Thus we can watch a Cepheid variable for a while and deduce how much energy it is pouring into space. This measurement, together with knowledge of how much energy we actually receive, tells us how far away it is.

The method of Cepheid variables can be used to measure distances of many millions of light-years. As we shall see in Chapter 15, it was a crucial ingredient in the birth of modern cosmology.

The Cepheid variable scale is an example of what astronomers call a "standard candle." The idea is that if you know how much energy an object is giving off, and compare that with how much energy you are actually receiving, you can figure out how far away from you the object is. The development of other kinds of standard candles is a major thrust of modern research.

Annie Jump Cannon (*left*) and Henrietta Swan Leavitt (*right*) contributed important studies of the spectroscopy of stars at the Harvard College Observatory.

The Hertzsprung-Russell Diagram

Early in this century, two astronomers, Ejnar Hertzsprung of Denmark and Henry N. Russell of the United States, independently discovered a way to find order among the diversity of stars. The product of their work, called the *Hertzsprung-Russell (H-R) diagram,* is a simple graphical technique widely used in astronomy. It works like this: On a graph's vertical axis, astronomers plot the amount of energy given off by a star, as measured by estimating the star's distance and brightness. On the graph's horizontal axis, they plot the star's surface temperature, as determined by its color, or spectrum (see Chapter 6). Each star has its own characteristic combination of energy and temperature, and so it appears as a single point on the Hertzsprung-Russell diagram. The Sun, for example, is one of the points highlighted in Figure 14-6.

When stars are plotted this way, the majority (the ones like the Sun) fall on a band that stretches from the upper left to the lower right in the diagram. That is, most stars conform to a trend from very hot stars emitting lots of energy, down to relatively cool stars emitting less energy. Objects in this grouping are called **main-sequence stars**. All of these stars are in the hydrogen-burning phase of their lives, and their energy is produced in the fusion reactions that we described earlier in this chapter.

Two additional clumpings of stars appear in the H-R diagram. One clumping, in the upper-right corner, corresponds to stars that emit a lot of energy but whose surfaces are very cool. These stars must be very large—many times the size of our Sun—so that the low temperature (and thus the low-energy emission of each square foot of surface area) is compensated by the large surface area. Stars of this type are called **red giants**, and they often do appear somewhat reddish in the sky.

Another grouping of stars appears in the lower-left corner of the H-R diagram. These stars, called **white dwarfs**, have very low emission of energy but very high surface temperatures. Consequently, white dwarf stars must be very small—typically about the size of Earth. Both red giants and white dwarfs play crucial roles in the life cycles of stars, as we shall see shortly.

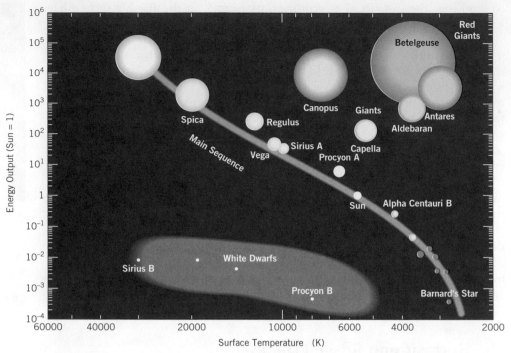

• **Figure 14-6** A Hertzsprung-Russell diagram plots a star's temperature versus its energy output. Stars in the hydrogen-burning stage, including the Sun, lie along the main sequence, while red giants and white dwarfs represent subsequent stages of stellar life.

The Life Cycles of Stars

Every star passes through a cycle that includes formation from dust and gas, a period of nuclear fusion, and an end to nuclear reactions. As we shall see, the duration and violence of that cycle depends almost entirely on the initial mass of the star.

The Birth of Stars

The Eagle Nebula, a birthplace of stars.

All stars are born in the depths of space, in clouds of gases and other debris. The modern theory of star and planet formation was first put forward by the French mathematician and physicist Pierre Simon Laplace (1749–1827). His was a simple idea that takes into account many of the distinctive characteristics of our solar system, which contains both the Sun and planets (see Chapter 16). According to the model, called the *nebular hypothesis*, long ago (about 4.5 billion years ago based on radiometric dating) a large cloud of dust and gas collected in the region now occupied by the solar system. Such dust and gas clouds, called **nebulae**, are common throughout our galaxy, the Milky Way. They typically contain more than 99% hydrogen and helium, with lesser amounts of all the other naturally occurring elements.

Under the influence of gravity, a nebula slowly, inexorably, collapses on itself. This collapse causes the cloud to spin faster and faster. The rapid spin means that some of the material in the outer parts of the nebula begins to spin out into a flat disk. This common consequence of fast rotation is familiar to anyone who has watched a pizza maker create a flat disk of dough by spinning a mass overhead. You can imagine a nebula at this stage of its formation as a large pancake with a big

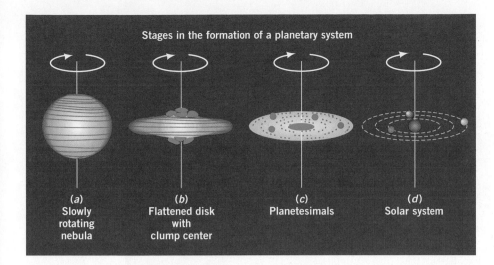

Stages in the formation of a planetary system

(a)
Slowly
rotating
nebula

(b)
Flattened disk
with
clump center

(c)
Planetesimals

(d)
Solar system

• **Figure 14-7** As the nebula that formed the Solar System collapsed, it began to rotate and flatten into a disk. The stages in solar system formation include (*a*) a slowly rotating nebula, (*b*) a flattened disk with massive center, (*c*) planets in the process of birth represented as mass concentrations in the nebula, and (*d*) the solar system.

lump in the middle. The big lump represents material that eventually will become a star, and the material in the thin flattened disk eventually will become the planets and the rest of the solar system (Figure 14-7). As a new star begins to form, and as more and more mass pours into it from the surrounding region of the nebula, the pressure and temperature at the center of the proto-star begins to climb.

Once this central mass achieves a critical size, the pressure and temperature deep inside will become high enough to initiate nuclear fusion reactions. At that moment, a star is born.

The Main Sequence and the Death of Stars

Every star begins as an immense ball of hydrogen and helium, formed by the gravitational collapse of a nebula. The ultimate fate of any given star, however, depends on the total mass of hydrogen and helium. The Hertzsprung-Russell diagram provides the key to understanding the very different fates of stars.

Stars Much Less Massive Than the Sun

All stars begin their lives in the hydrogen burning stage—the stage represented by main-sequence stars on the Hertzsprung-Russell diagram. If a star is much less massive than the Sun—perhaps only 10% of the Sun's mass—it will be just barely large enough to begin hydrogen burning in a slow and fitful way. Such a small star, called a *brown dwarf,* shines faintly compared to the Sun, with surface temperatures of only a few thousand degrees. Nuclear fusion proceeds relatively slowly, so such a star will continue to glow steadily for a hundred billion years without any significant change in size, temperature, or energy output.

Stars About the Mass of the Sun

The Sun and other stars of similar mass enjoy a more central position on the Herzsprung-Russell main sequence (Figure 14-8, position 1). The greater mass of the Sun, relative to brown dwarf stars, means that core temperatures and pressures are much higher and hydrogen burning proceeds at a much faster rate. The Sun, consequently, has a higher surface temperature and it completes its hydrogen-burning phase much more quickly—in a matter of a few billion years.

One way to look at the life of a star like the Sun is to think of it as a continual battle against the force of gravity. From the moment when the Sun's original gas

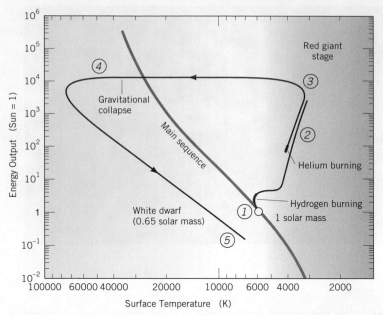

• **Figure 14-8** The life cycle of the Sun on a Hertzsprung-Russell diagram. The Sun started hydrogen burning in its core more than 4.5 billion years ago on the main sequence (at point 1), and it will remain near that point on the diagram for several billion years more. As the hydrogen in the core is consumed, however, a short period of helium burning (point 2) will move the Sun's position on the diagram rapidly upward toward the red giant stage (point 3). Once the helium is consumed, the nuclear fusion reactions will cease and gravitational collapse will cause the Sun to heat up (point 4). Eventually the Sun will cool to a white dwarf (point 5).

cloud started to contract, the force of gravity acted on every particle, forcing it inward and trying to make the entire structure collapse on itself. When the nuclear fires ignited in the core of the Sun 4.5 billion years ago, gravity was held at bay. The increase in temperature in the center raised the pressure in the star's interior and balanced the inward pull of gravity. But, in the long view of things, this balance can be only a temporary state of affairs. The Sun can stave off the inward tug of gravity only as long as it has hydrogen to burn. When hydrogen fuel in the core is depleted, the amount of energy generated in the core will decrease, and gravity will begin to take over. The Sun will begin to contract and heat up.

This dramatic situation will have two effects. First, the temperature in the region immediately surrounding the core will begin to rise. Any remaining hydrogen in that region, which had not burned because it had been at too low a temperature, will begin to burn. Thus a hydrogen-burning shell will begin to form around the extinguished core. The second effect is that the temperature in the core will rise until helium, the "ash" of hydrogen burning, will begin to undergo nuclear fusion reactions. The net reaction will be

$$^4He + {}^4He + {}^4He \rightarrow {}^{12}C$$

a process called *helium burning,* in which the helium in the core burns to make carbon. The Sun will then resemble an onion, with a helium burning core surrounded by a layer where hydrogen is being burned. At this stage the Sun will begin to move off of the main sequence (Figure 14-8, position 2).

This notion, that the ashes of one nuclear fire serve as fuel for the next, is central to an understanding of what goes on in stars. In stars like the Sun, the temperature never gets high enough to ignite the carbon, so helium burning is the final energy-producing stage. In more massive stars, this process of successive burning cycles can go on for quite a while, as we shall see.

The Sun will burn at more or less its present size and temperature for billions of years more. Since it first entered the main sequence 4.5 billion years ago, for example, the amount of energy generated by the Sun has increased by only about 30%. This long-term stability has important implications for the development of life on this planet. But, in its final stages, our star will undergo dramatic changes. When the core burns out, the hydrogen-burning shells surrounding the central region are pulled in. This temporary collapse increases the amount of energy generated by fusion, and the increased energy causes the surface of the Sun to balloon out. At its maximum expansion, the dying Sun extends out past the orbit of Venus. Because the solar wind also increases during this period, however, the Sun's mass drops and the planets move outward. In the end, only Mercury is actually swallowed. During this phase of its life, the Sun will emit almost 10,000 times more energy than it does today, but it will do so through a much larger surface. Consequently, that surface will appear to be very cool—red hot to our eyes. In fact, our Sun will become a red giant, and the helium in the Sun's core will burn to produce an inner core primarily of carbon (Figure 14-8, position 3).

As carbon accumulates in the core, a slow collapse will ensue until some other force intervenes. In the case of the Sun, that force will come from the Pauli principle—the principle (see Chapter 8) that tells us that no two electrons can occupy the same state. As the core starts to collapse, its electrons are compressed into a smaller and smaller volume. For a time the Sun continues to emit prodigious amounts of energy through a shrinking surface that reaches temperatures in excess of 70,000 degrees (Figure 14-8, position 4). Ultimately, the electrons reach the point (what we called the "full parking lot") where they can no longer be pushed together. At this point, the Pauli principle takes over and the collapse stops for the simple reason that the electrons can't be pushed together any closer than they already are. A permanent outward force is exerted on every element in the star—an outward force that cancels the inward force of gravity.

When the Sun reaches this stage, it will be rather small—probably about the size of the Earth (though still hundreds of thousands of times more massive than Earth)—and it will no longer be generating energy through nuclear reactions. It will be very hot and will take a long time to cool off. During this phase, the temperature of each part of the Sun's surface will be very high, but, because the Sun will be so small, the total amount of radiation coming from it will not be very large. It will be, in other words, a white dwarf (Figure 14-8, position 5). Most of the carbon that is the end product of helium burning will remain locked in the white dwarf and will not be returned to the cosmos.

Stars up to five or six times the mass of the Sun will follow approximately the same path on the H-R diagram (Figure 14-8). Such stars will have different lifetimes; one of the paradoxes of astronomy is that larger stars—those with the most hydrogen fuel—have the shortest lifetimes. This paradox arises because the largest stars have to burn hydrogen at a prodigious rate in order to overcome the intense force of gravity. Thus a star four times as massive as the Sun will complete its cycle in a relatively short time—less than a billion years—compared to the Sun's 11-billion-year span. But all of these stars will have essentially the same life history: main sequence → red giant → white dwarf.

Very Large Stars
Stars more than 10 times as massive as the Sun end their lives quite differently, in explosions of unimaginable power. For these stars, the pressure exerted by gravity is high enough so that the helium in the core not only burns to carbon, but the

• **Figure 14-9** The interior of a large star displays concentric shells of fusion reactions, yielding progressively heavier elements toward the core.

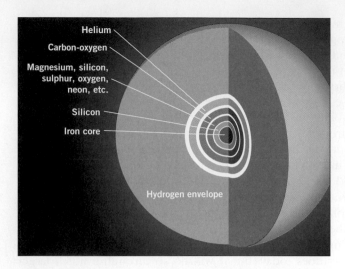

Helium

Carbon-oxygen

Magnesium, silicon, sulphur, oxygen, neon, etc.

Silicon

Iron core

Hydrogen envelope

carbon can also undergo fusion reactions to produce oxygen, magnesium, silicon, and other larger nuclei. For such a star, the successive collapses and burnings will produce a layered, onion-like structure such as that shown in Figure 14-9.

In fact, in the largest stars this chain of nuclear burning goes on until iron, the element with 26 protons, is produced. As we noted in Chapter 12, iron is the most tightly bound nucleus. The addition of energy is required to break the iron nucleus apart (nuclear fission) and to add more protons and neutrons to it (nuclear fusion). Thus it is impossible to extract energy from iron by any kind of nuclear reaction.

The cores of large stars will eventually fill up with iron "ash," and, no matter how high the pressure and temperature get, iron simply will not burn to produce a countervailing force to gravity. In fact, the iron core builds up until the force of gravity becomes so great that even the pressure of the electrons pushing for elbow room cannot prevent collapse. At the incredible pressures and temperatures at the center of the star, the electrons actually combine with protons inside the iron nuclei, forming neutrons, a process that is the exact opposite of radioactive beta decay (see Chapter 12). Within a second or so all of the protons in the iron nuclei are turned into neutrons, and all of the electrons disappear. At this point, the core of the star begins a catastrophic collapse. The collapse will go on until another force appears on the scene to counteract gravity. In this case, the force is provided by the degeneracy pressure of the neutrons, which, like electrons, are subject to the Pauli exclusion principle.

The core collapses so fast that it falls inward beyond the point where the degeneracy pressure of the neutrons can balance gravity. Like an acrobat jumping on a trampoline, the star's falling matter first bounces inward, and then rebounds as the neutrons exert a counter pressure. Meanwhile, the outer gaseous envelope of the star has suddenly lost its support and begins a free-fall toward the interior of the star. When the collapsing envelope of dense gas meets the rebounding core of neutrons, intense shock waves are set up in the star, and the entire outer part of the star literally explodes. From a distance the star suddenly appears to brighten in the sky, usually in a matter of a day or so. We call this dramatic event a supernova.

During the explosion, intense shock waves tear back and forth across the exploding star, raising the temperature enough to form all of the chemical elements in the periodic table. In a complex set of collisions, some of the nuclei up to iron that have been created by the successive fusion reactions soak up neutrons and undergo beta decay (see Chapter 12) to form nuclei up to uranium and beyond. All elements beyond iron are created in the short-lived maelstrom of the supernova explosion.

Supernovas probably happen about every 30 years in our own Milky Way galaxy. We don't see most of these events because of intervening dust, but we do see them in neighboring galaxies. On February 23, 1987, for example, a supernova was seen in the Large Magellanic Cloud, a small galaxy-like structure near the Milky Way galaxy. Although the supernova was 170,000 light-years from the Earth, it caused a great stir in science because it was the first supernova to be observed with modern observatories, including satellites. It was seen by large neutrino detectors and many ordinary telescopes on the Earth, and by X-ray and gamma-ray observatories above the atmosphere. Because it was the first supernova observed in 1987, it was given the name "1987A." Perhaps the biggest surprise to come out of the experience was that there were so few surprises. The intricate theories of nuclear reactions that take place in those incredibly complex few hours when a star explodes were largely confirmed.

The striking NASA Hubble Space Telescope picture shows three rings of glowing gas encircling the site of supernova 1987A, a star that exploded in February 1987.

Neutron Stars and Pulsars

For a while after a star explodes, the supernova is surrounded by a cloud of ejected material. This expanding cloud dissipates into interstellar space, leaving behind the core of neutrons that was created in the collapse. A star that is being held up by degeneracy pressure of neutrons, called a **neutron star**, is in essence a giant nucleus—incredibly dense and very small. A typical neutron star might be 10 miles across, small enough to fit within the city limits of even a moderate metropolis. Several significant changes occur when a large star shrinks down into something the size of a city. For one thing, the rate of rotation of the star goes up substantially. Just as an ice skater increases her spin when she pulls in her arms, a star rotates faster and faster as it contracts. In fact, some neutron stars in our galaxy rotate 1000 times a second. Compare this to the sedate motion of the Sun, which rotates once every 26 days.

Neutron stars do not give off much light, and they would probably have gone undetected if some of them didn't exhibit unusual behavior in the radio part of the spectrum. The reason for this behavior can be understood if you follow the collapse that leads to the neutron star. As the star collapses, the strength of its magnetic field increases. If a normal star has a dipole field (see Chapter 5), for example, then during the collapse the field lines are dragged in with the material of the star so the field becomes much more concentrated and intense. Some neutron stars in our galaxy possess fields as much as a trillion times that of the magnetic field at the surface of the Earth.

These two effects—a strong magnetic field and rapid rotation—may combine to produce a special kind of neutron star, which astronomers call a **pulsar**. Fast-moving particles speed out along the intense magnetic field lines of the rotating neutron star, and these accelerating particles give off electromagnetic radiation, as shown in Figure 14-10. Most of this radiation is in the radio range, so the neutron star's signal is seen primarily with radio telescopes.

One way of thinking about a pulsar is to imagine it as being somewhat like a searchlight in the sky. Radio waves are continuously emitted along an axis that goes between the north and south magnetic poles of the neutron star, and this line describes a circle in space as the neutron star rotates. If you are standing in the line you will see a burst of radio waves every time the north or south pole of

Jocelyn Bell Burnell detected the first pulsars in 1967.

• **Figure 14-10** A schematic diagram of a pulsar reveals its two key attributes—rapid rotation and an intense magnetic field. This combination of traits produces a pulsing, lighthouse-like pattern of energetic radiation.

the pulsar is pointing toward you, and nothing when it's not. You will, in other words, see a series of pulses of radio waves. The signature of a pulsar in the sky is a series of regularly spaced pulses, typically some tens to thousands per second. The pulsar represents one possible end state of a supernova. All pulsars are neutron stars, although all neutron stars are probably not seen as pulsars by earthbound astronomers.

We know of several pulsars that are the remnants of previous supernovas. One of the first pulsars discovered lies at the core of the Crab Nebula, a supernova seen from Earth in A.D. 1054. Likewise, Supernova 1987A is also expected to reveal a pulsar when all the dust clears.

Our current theories of stellar evolution say that stars more than 10 times as massive as the Sun will go through the supernova process we've just described, and eject large amounts of heavy elements into space.

Black Holes

Occasionally, a large star may die in a way that does not lead to the formation of a pulsar. If a star is large enough—perhaps 50 or more times as massive as the Sun—there may be processes, as yet only imperfectly understood, by which even the degeneracy pressure of neutrons is overcome and the star collapses. The result is the ultimate triumph of gravity, a **black hole**. A black hole is an object so dense, a mass so concentrated, that nothing, not even light, can escape from its surface.

We do not know how often black holes are formed. Indeed, it comes as a surprise to most people to learn that no widely accepted astronomical black holes have been detected in our galaxy. Black holes are difficult to detect because you can't see them. Several promising candidates have been spotted, but none you could point to and say, "Yes, this is beyond doubt an example of a black hole."

The search for black holes concentrates on double star systems in which one star has evolved into a black hole. The idea is that even though we can't see the black hole itself, we can see its effect on its partner. The most striking thing to look for is material falling into the black hole. The enormous gravitational energy released in the process is partially converted into X-rays and gamma rays, which can be detected by orbiting observatories.

Science News | Fiber Helper
(SCIENCE NEWS, VOL. 163, JAN. 25, 2003, P. 53)

One of the great technological challenges facing our information systems is the question of how to speed up the rate at which computers can exchange information through optical fibers. Today, our maximum rate of transmission is about 10 billion bits per second, but engineers want to increase this to 40 billion bits per second over the next several years. One fundamental stumbling block comes from the fact that in optical fibers light waves whose electrical fields point in different directions move at slightly different speeds. This means that a pulse of light, which might carry one bit of information, will spread out as it travels from one place to another, and this limits the number of pulses that can be fed into the fiber each second.

Now scientists at Lucent Technologies in New Jersey have developed a device that not only overcomes this problem, but does so in a way that is unexpectedly cheap and easy to install. The device consists of two small gold electrodes that sandwich a thin layer of liquid crystal. When this device is installed at the junction of two optical fibers, a small voltage current applied to the electrodes causes the direction of the electric field of the light waves to change in a way that makes it easy to re-compress light pulses in the signal. With this device, the scientists say, transmission rates of 40 billion bits per second will soon be achievable, a fact which will make the information revolution even more revolutionary.

Thinking More About | Stars

Generation of the Chemical Elements

Think about the remarkable range of elements you can buy at your local shopping center. The hardware store stocks aluminum siding, copper wire, and iron nails. The drugstore sells iodine for cuts, zinc and calcium compounds as dietary supplements, and perhaps bottles of oxygen for patients with breathing difficulties. The jeweler displays rings and necklaces of silver, gold, and platinum set with diamonds, a form of carbon. And your local electronics dealer offers an amazing assortment of audio and video equipment made possible by integrated circuits of silicon, perhaps doped with small amounts of aluminum or phosphorus.

It may come as a surprise to you that almost everything you see about you was made in a supernova. Your body, for example, is made primarily from elements that formed in some distant exploding star more than 4.5 billion years ago. We say this because, as we shall see in Chapter 15, the universe began its life with only light elements—hydrogen, helium, and small amounts of lithium. These elements formed the first stars and were processed in the first stellar nuclear fires. In stars like the Sun, elements heavier than helium may be made, but they remain in that star and never return to the cosmos.

In large stars, however, all the elements up to uranium (the element with 92 protons) and beyond are made and spewed back into the interstellar medium in the titanic explosions we call supernovas. These heavy elements enrich the surrounding galaxy, and when new stars are formed these elements are incorporated into them. The Sun, which formed fairly late in the history of our own galaxy, thus incorporated many heavy elements that had been made in previous supernovas.

You can think of the history of our galaxy as successive and cumulative enrichments by nuclear processing in large, short-lived stars. These stars, with lifetimes as short as tens of millions of years, take the original hydrogen in the galaxy and convert it into heavier elements. Thus we expect that older, smaller stars that have been shining since the early history of the universe will have fewer heavy elements than relatively young stars like the Sun, a prediction that is borne out by astronomical observations.

Think about what this means as you look around you. All the objects in your life—this book, your clothes, even your skin and bones—are made of atoms that formed in the hearts of giant stars long ago.

SUMMARY

Astronomy is the study of objects in the heavens. Astronomers have discovered much about the nature and origins of *stars.* We study stars with *telescopes,* instruments that gather and focus electromagnetic radiation. Earth-based telescopes detect visible and radio waves, while orbiting observatories detect all other regions of the electromagnetic spectrum. The most powerful telescopes can detect stars that are hundreds of millions of *light-years* away.

Extreme temperatures and pressures deep inside a star cause its hydrogen core to undergo nuclear fusion reactions, burning to create helium and heat energy. Ignition of these nuclear fires creates an outward flow of particles, called the *solar wind*. The fusion reaction proceeds in three steps, in which (1) two protons come together to form deuterium, (2) a proton and a deuterium nucleus come together to form helium-3, and (3) two helium-3 nuclei fuse to make helium-4. This energy creates the pressure that balances the force of gravity that pulls the star inward.

Stars such as our own Sun form from giant clouds of interstellar dust called *nebulae*—clouds that gradually collapse under the force of gravity. This collapse subjects the star's atoms, primarily hydrogen, to tremendous temperatures and pressures. The life of a star is a continuous struggle against this gravitational force.

Stars that are burning hydrogen to produce energy are said to be *main-sequence stars*. Larger stars burn hotter and emit more energy, while smaller stars are cooler and radiate less energy. Main-sequence stars are found in a simple band-like pattern on a Hertzsprung-Russell diagram, which graphs a star's energy output versus its temperature.

When a star like the Sun consumes most of its core hydrogen, a helium-rich central region remains. The star once again begins to collapse under gravity, and internal temperatures rise again. Hydrogen burning begins in shells outside the core, while the core's helium may also combine in nuclear fusion reactions to form carbon. These new nuclear processes may cause a star like the Sun to expand briefly and become a *red giant*, a star whose relatively cool outer layers glow red. Eventually, however, nuclear fuel must be exhausted. Gravity will dominate and the carbon-rich star will collapse to a very small, very hot *white dwarf*.

Stars much larger than the Sun may evolve beyond hydrogen and helium burning. If temperatures and pressures are high enough, carbon can undergo additional nuclear reactions to form elements as heavy as iron, the ultimate nuclear ash. Once iron is formed, however, there can be no more energy produced by these reactions and burning will cease. The sudden extinguishing of a star causes a catastrophic gravitational collapse and rebound—a *supernova*—in which the star literally explodes and spews all the chemical elements into the heavens. A dense, spinning *neutron star* or *pulsar* may be the only remnant of the original star. The largest stars may collapse into a *black hole*, an object so massive that not even light can escape its gravitational pull.

KEY TERMS ABOUT STARS

astronomy	solar wind	red giant	supernova	pulsar
star	light-year	white dwarf	neutron star	black hole
telescope	main-sequence star	nebulae		

REVIEW QUESTIONS

1. What is a star?

2. What is the nature of the energy emitted by stars?

3. What conditions are present in stars that cause hydrogen to form helium? What is this process called?

4. What are the major layers of the Sun?

5. What two properties of stars do scientists plot on a Hertzsprung-Russell diagram? Why do they choose these properties?

6. In what ways is the Sun a typical star?

7. What are the effects of the solar wind on Earth?

8. What are four aspects of photons that astronomers measure?

9. Describe two kinds of telescopes. How are they similar?

10. What causes stars to vary in brightness? In color?

11. What are the advantages of placing a telescope in orbit?

12. What is a "standard candle" in astronomy?

13. Describe two ways to determine the distance to another star.

14. How are stars formed?

15. Why must the Sun eventually burn out? What changes will the Sun undergo before it burns out?

16. Why don't larger stars burn longer than smaller stars?

17. Why won't the Sun become a supernova or a black hole?

18. How are supernovas and neutron stars related to each other?

19. How are neutron stars and pulsars related to each other?

20. If iron is the ultimate nuclear ash, where do elements heavier than iron come from?

21. Why is it difficult to detect a black hole from Earth?

DISCUSSION QUESTIONS

1. Why do we see stars only at night? Do they shine during the day?

2. How might you determine the age of a star from an Earth-based telescope? What measurements might you make?

3. What was happening on Earth when the energy in the sunlight falling outside your window today was first produced in fusion reactions at the Sun's core? Were the Pyramids built yet? Did people live in cities? Was Neanderthal still around?

4. Given the connection between the Sun and the human eye, speculate about the kinds of stars that might be found in solar systems from which different fictional extraterrestrials are supposed to have come.

Would the Klingon and Vulcan stars in *Star Trek* have been much different from our own? Why or why not?

5. How can we talk about the evolution of stars over billions of years when human beings have been observing stars for only a few thousand years?

6. How does the principle of conservation of energy apply to a supernova?

7. Most stars we see are on the main sequence. Stars spend most of their lives consuming their initial stock of hydrogen. Is there a connection between these two statements? If so, what is it?

8. In view of the neutrino problem, why haven't physicists rejected the theory that stars obtain energy by hydrogen burning?

PROBLEMS

1. How far away is Alpha Centauri, the nearest star? How long would it take to get there at a speed of 2000 miles per hour (the speed of a fast jet plane?)

2. How much more light-gathering ability does the Keck telescope with its 10-meter diameter mirror array have than the 2.5-meter Hubble Space Telescope? [*Hint:* Light-gathering ability is proportional to the area of the mirror.]

INVESTIGATIONS

1. Locate some stars in the sky and find out their apparent magnitude. (You might want to start with some familiar stars such as those in the Big Dipper.)

2. The Crab Nebula formed from a supernova event that was sighted on Earth almost 1000 years ago. It must have been visible as a brilliant object for several days. What cultures left a record of this astronomical event? How did they explain what they saw?

3. Astronomers often debate the relative merits of Earth-based versus orbiting telescopes. What are some of the arguments on both sides of this issue?

4. You can set up an analog to the astronomical distance scale by using two "yardsticks"—a ruler and a tape measure, for example—to measure distances. Measure the dimensions of your classroom this way. How would you make sure that distances on each yardstick were the same? Does this exercise suggest a way for astronomers to check the consistency of their distance scale?

5. The nineteenth-century American poet Walt Whitman (1819–1892) wrote the following poem about astronomy:

When I Heard the Learn'd Astronomer

When I heard the learn'd astronomer,
When the proofs, the figures,
were ranged in columns before me,
When I was shown the charts and diagrams,
to add, divide, and measure them,
When I sitting heard the astronomer where he
lectured with much applause in the lecture-room,
How soon unaccountable I became tired and sick,
Till rising and gliding out I wander'd off by
    myself,
In the mystical moist night air, and from time
    to time,
Look'd up in perfect silence at the stars.

Although Whitman was unimpressed by the facts and figures of the "learn'd astronomer," astron-omers of the past century have changed the way we think about our place in the universe. In this respect, how does science complement poetry? How do poetry and astronomy differ as ways of understanding why we are here? How would you answer the poet today?

WWW Resources

See *The Sciences* homepage at: **http://www.wiley.com/college/trefil** for valuable web links.

1. **http://itss.raytheon.com/cafe/cafe.html**
   The Astronomy Cafe, a site with something for everyone. (Beware, if your computer automatically places an acute accent over the "e" in cafe, and you don't change it to an accentless "e," you won't reach this site.)

2. **http://www.dibonsmith.com/stars.htm**
   Constellations Web Page

3. **www.sunspotcycle.com**
   Sunspots, aurora, and magnetic disturbances—interesting subjects off the beaten track.

15

Cosmology

Will the universe ever end?

GREAT IDEA

The universe began billions of years ago in the big bang, and it has been expanding ever since.

PHYSICS

At the moment of creation, the four fundamental forces were unified as a single force. They have subsequently "frozen" into the forces we see today.

CHEMISTRY

The relative cosmic abundances of the elements hydrogen, helium, and lithium were established when the universe was approximately 500,000 years old.

ASTRONOMY

The cosmic microwave background, the universal expansion, and the abundance of light elements provides strong evidence for the big bang theory.

TECHNOLOGY

The Hubble Space Telescope and other orbiting observatories have provided key data for understanding the origin of the universe.

Red = applications of the great idea discussed in this chapter.

Orange = other applications, some of which are explored in other chapters.

While you were lying down, soaking up the Sun's rays, a couple of your friends started a charcoal fire on a small grill. If you observe closely, you may notice that the color of the coals in the fire changes, depending on how hot the fire is. They are ordinarily red, but in a roaring blaze they can glow blue-white. Then, as the fire starts to go out, the coals glow a dull orange and eventually stop glowing altogether.

But even when the coals aren't glowing, they are giving off energy in the form of infrared radiation, which you can feel if you put your hand out to the fire. Even the next day, you might still be able to feel the radiation given off by the cooling embers.

Believe it or not, a phenomenon like this campfire experience led twentieth-century scientists to a completely new understanding of the structure and history of the universe in which we live.

Galaxies

On any given night, as we look into the sky with modest-sized telescopes, we can see that the hazy band of the **Milky Way** is composed of countless millions of stars. Those stars appear as tiny pin-pricks of light. But there are lots of other less distinct objects that appear as fuzzy masses, too distant to resolve. And those cloud-like objects, called *nebulae*, were the subject of intense debate in the early twentieth century.

The Nebula Debate

Some astronomers thought nebulae were nearby dust clouds that are illuminated by other stars. In that case, they would be fairly close by and have no resolvable structures, even in the most powerful telescope. Other astronomers suggested that nebulae were much more distant clusters of stars. They're composed of lots of individual stars, but are much too far away for those stars to be resolved.

This controversy came into sharp focus on April 26, 1920, when rival American astronomers Harlow Shapley and Heber D. Curtis engaged in a public debate at the National Academy of Sciences. The younger Shapely had come into prominence by discovering that the Milky Way is much larger than previously thought—more than 100,000 light years across. Given that immense size, he couldn't imagine that much more distant objects existed. It's ironic that Shapley, who dramatically increased the size of the known universe, just couldn't accept how much larger the universe really is.

Curtis, on the other hand, argued that nebulae are much more distant collections of stars like our own. He saw the distinctive shapes of nebulae with spiral arms and central bulges, and concluded that a cloud wasn't likely to adopt that shape.

The more senior Curtis is said to have been the more eloquent of the two, and some attendees found him to have been more persuasive. But in science, debaters don't settle controversies. The scientific method demands that independently verifiable measurements and observations are the ultimate arbiter of any scientific question. The fact of the matter is that no one could make such observations with the tools available before 1920.

Edwin Hubble and the Discovery of Galaxies

As so often happens in science, improved instruments were the key to discovery. In this case a larger telescope, quite literally, resolved the issue. In 1900, the world's largest telescopes were reflectors with mirrors in the range of 50 or 60 inches in diameter—not large enough to reveal nebular structure. So it was that the Carnegie Institution of Washington decided to build a mammoth new telescope with an unprecedented 100-inch diameter mirror on Mount Wilson, near Los Angeles, California. At the time, Mount Wilson was a lonely outpost on the outskirts of a small city. Today it has been engulfed by the Los Angeles metropolitan area, but in those days it afforded astronomers a chance to look at the sky through clear, unpolluted air.

In 1919, the young American astronomer Edwin Hubble (1889–1953), fresh from distinguished service in World War I, went to work at Mount Wilson and used this magnificent instrument to tackle the mystery of the nebula. Because his new telescope allowed him to see individual Cepheid variable stars in some nebulae, which no one had been able to do before, Hubble was able to measure the distance to them. (Recall from Chapter 14 that Cepheid variable stars can be used as standard candles.) It turned out that the Cepheid variable stars were extremely faint, so the distance to the nearest one, located in the Andromeda nebula, was some 2 million light-years, far outside the bounds of the Milky Way. Thus, with a single observation, Hubble established one of the most important facts about the universe we live in: it is made up of billions of galaxies, of which the Milky Way is but one.

We now know that each of these countless **galaxies** is an immense collection of millions to hundreds of billions of stars, together with gas, dust, and other materials, that is held together by the forces of mutual gravitational attraction. In making these discoveries, he set the tone for a century of progress in the new branch of science called **cosmology**, which is devoted to the study of the structure and history of the entire universe.

Kinds of Galaxies

The Milky Way is a rather typical galaxy. As shown in Figure 15-1, it is a flattened disk about 100,000 light-years across. A central bulge known as the nucleus holds most of our galaxy's hundreds of billions of stars. Bright regions in the disk, known as spiral arms, mark areas where new stars are being formed. About 75% of the brighter galaxies in the sky are of this spiral type (Figures 15-1 and 15-2).

Edwin Hubble (1889–1953) at the 100-inch telescope of California's Mount Wilson Observatory.

 Stop and Think! What is the connection between the flat, spiral shape of our galaxy and the appearance of the Milky Way in the night sky?

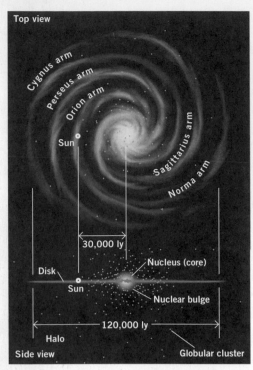

Top view

Cygnus arm

Perseus arm

Orion arm

Sun

Sagittarius arm

Norma arm

30,000 ly

Disk

Nucleus (core)

Sun

Nuclear bulge

120,000 ly

Halo

Side view

Globular cluster

• **Figure 15-1** A map of the Milky Way galaxy, showing the nucleus and spiral arms.

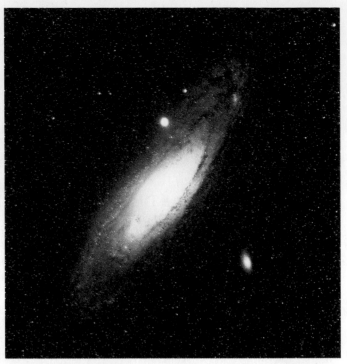

• **Figure 15-2** A typical spiral galaxy, with a bright core and spiral arms where new stars are forming.

A typical elliptical galaxy. This one is known as M84 and is located in the constellation Virgo.

Other galaxies, known as ellipticals, resemble nothing so much as cosmic footballs. The brightest elliptical galaxies tend to have more stars than spiral galaxies do and comprise about 20% of bright galaxies. In addition to the relatively large and bright elliptical and spiral galaxies, the universe is littered with small collections of stars known as irregular and dwarf galaxies. Even though these galaxies are faint and therefore difficult to detect, many of them have been identified. Astronomers thus think that these are probably the most common galaxies in the universe.

The total number of galaxies in the universe has been estimated by taking long exposure photographs of small regions in the sky with no stars—regions that would appear as black voids in smaller telescopes. The results of these so-called "deep-field images" are astonishing (Figure 15-3). The more we look, the more galaxies we see—perhaps 100 billion galaxies, each with countless stars.

Larger elliptical and spiral galaxies and smaller irregular and dwarf galaxies can be thought of as quiet, homey galaxies, where the process of star formation and death goes on in a stately, orderly way. But a small number of galaxies—perhaps 10,000 among the billions known—are quite different and are referred to collectively as active galaxies. The most spectacular of these unusual objects are the *quasars* (for quasi-stellar radio sources). Quasars are wild, explosive, violent objects, where as-yet-unknown processes pour vast amounts of energy into space each second from an active center no larger than our solar system. Astronomers suggest that the only way to generate this kind of energy is for the center of a quasar to be occupied by an enormous black hole (with masses, in some cases, millions of times greater than that of the Sun), and for the energy to be generated by huge amounts of mass falling into this center. Because they are so bright, quasars are the most distant objects we can see in the universe.

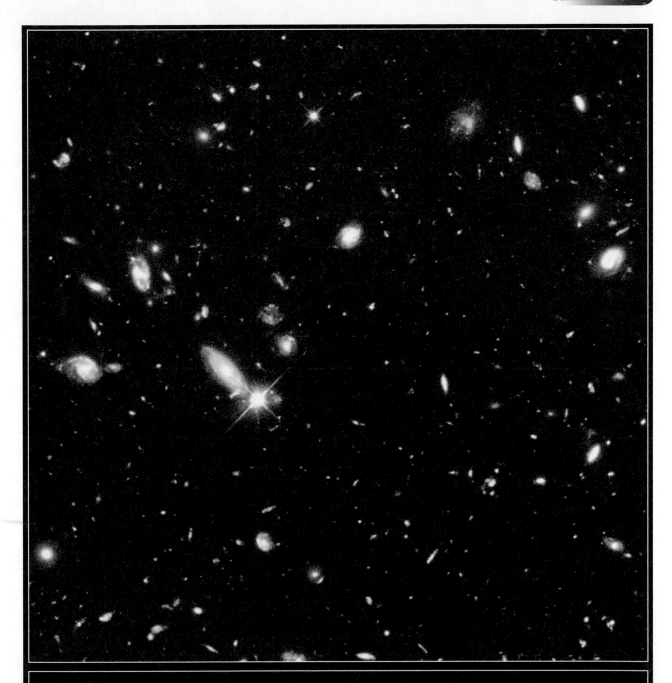

Hubble Deep Field
Hubble Space Telescope · WFPC2

PRC96-01a · ST ScI OPO · January 15, 1995 · R. Williams (ST ScI), NASA

• **Figure 15-3** This deep-field image of galaxies depicts a tiny patch apparently "empty" sky. Several hours of exposure by the powerful Hubble Space Telescope reveals more than 100 galaxies—evidence that the universe holds tens of billions of galaxies, each with hundreds of billions of stars.

The Redshift and Hubble's Law

Hubble's recognition of galaxies other than our own Milky Way wasn't the end of his discoveries. When he looked at the light from nearby galaxies, he noticed that the distinctive colors emitted by different elements seemed to be shifted toward the red (long-wavelength) end of the spectrum, compared to light emitted by atoms on Earth. Hubble interpreted this **redshift** as an example of the Doppler effect (see Chapter 6), the same phenomenon that causes the sound of a car whizzing past to change its pitch. Hubble's observation meant that distant galaxies are moving away from the Earth. Furthermore, Hubble noticed that the more distant a galaxy, the faster it moves away from us (Figures 15-4 and 15-5).

• **Figure 15-4** Photographs of galaxies as seen through a telescope (on the left), with spectra of those galaxies (on the right). The distance to each galaxy in megaparsecs is also given. Double dark lines in the spectra, characteristic of the calcium atom, are shifted farther to the right (toward the red) the farther away the galaxy is. Thus more-distant galaxies are traveling away from us at higher velocities. This phenomenon was used by Edwin Hubble to derive his law.

CLUSTER GALAXY IN   Distance in million ly (Mpe)   RADIAL VELOCITIES IN KM/S

Virgo — 63 (19) — 1210

Ursa Major — 990 (300) — 15000

Corona Borealis — 1440 (430) — 21600

Bootes — 2740 (770) — 39300

Hydra — 3960 (1200) — 61200

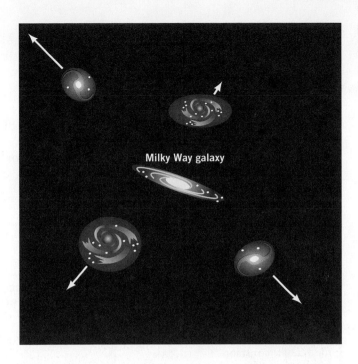

On the basis of measurements of a few dozen nearby galaxies, Hubble suggested that a simple relationship exists between the distance of an object from the Earth, and that object's speed away from the Earth. Comparing two galaxies—one twice as far away from the Earth as the other—the farther galaxy moves away from us twice as fast. This statement, which has been amply confirmed by measurements in the subsequent half-century, is now called **Hubble's law**. Hubble's law says:

▶ **In words:** The farther away a galaxy is, the faster it recedes.
▶ **In equation form:**

galaxy's velocity = (Hubble's constant) × (galaxy's distance)

▶ **In symbols:**

$$v = H \times d$$

Hubble's law tells us that we can determine the distance to galaxies by measuring the redshift of the light we receive, whether or not we can make out individual stars in them. Astronomers continue to debate the exact value of Hubble's constant of proportionality, but most experts agree that it is between 50 and 100 kilometers per second per megaparsec (a megaparsec, or Mpc, is a distance of a million parsecs or 3.3 million light-years). In this view of the cosmos, the redshift becomes the final "ruler" in the astronomical distance scale (see Chapter 14).

One way of interpreting Hubble's constant is to notice that if a galaxy were to travel from the location of the Milky Way to its present position with a velocity v, then the time it would take to make the trip would be distance divided by speed:

$$t = \frac{d}{v}$$

Substituting for v from Hubble's law,

$$t = \frac{d}{(H \times d)}$$
$$= \frac{1}{H}$$

Thus the Hubble constant provides a rough estimate of the time that the expansion has been going on and, hence, of the age of the universe. A Hubble constant of 50 km/s/Mpc corresponds to an age of the universe of about 16 billion years, while a constant of 100 km/s/Mpc corresponds to an age of about 8 billion years.

EXAMPLE 15-1

The Distance to a Receding Galaxy

Astronomers discover a new galaxy and determine from its redshift that it is moving away from us at approximately 100,000 km/s (about one-third the speed of light). Approximately how far away is this galaxy? Assume an intermediate value of 75 km/s/Mpc for the Hubble constant.

Reasoning: According to Hubble's law, a galaxy's distance equals its velocity divided by the Hubble constant.

Solution:

$$\text{distance (in Mpc)} = \frac{\text{velocity (in km/s)}}{\text{Hubble's constant (in km/s/Mpc)}}$$
$$= \frac{(100{,}000 \text{ km/s})}{(75 \text{ km/s/Mpc})}$$
$$= \frac{100{,}000}{75} \text{ Mpc}$$
$$= 1333 \text{ Mpc}$$

Remember, a megaparsec equals about 3.3 million light-years, so this galaxy is more than 4 billion light-years away. The light that we observe from such a distant galaxy began its trip about the time that our solar system was born.

SCIENCE BY THE NUMBERS •

Analyzing Hubble's Data

In his original sample, Hubble observed 46 galaxies, but was able to determine distances to only 24. Some of his data are given in Table 15-1.

How does one go about analyzing data like these? One common way is to make a graph. In this case, the vertical axis is the velocity of recession of the

Table 15-1 Some of Hubble's Data

Distance to Galaxy (in megaparsecs)	Velocity (in km/s)
1.0	620
1.4	500
1.7	960
2.0	850
2.0	1090

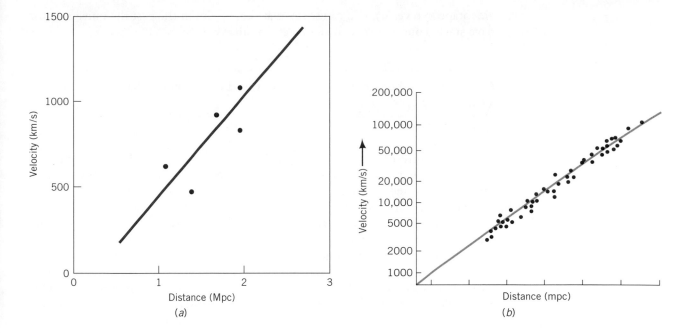

• **Figure 15-6** (*a*) Hubble's original distance versus velocity relationship. (*b*) Modern graphs of distance versus velocity record data from hundreds or thousands of galaxies.

galaxy, and the horizontal axis is the distance to the galaxy. In Figure 15-6a we show the data as originally plotted by Hubble, while Figure 15-6b presents a more recent compilation of many galaxies.

Looking at the original data (Figure 15-6a), the general trend of Hubble's law is obvious—the farther you go to the right (i.e., the farther away the galaxies are), the higher the points (i.e., the faster the galaxies are moving away). You also notice, however, that the points do not fall on a straight line, but are scattered. Confronted with this sort of situation, you can do one of two things. You can assume that the scattering is due to experimental error, and that more accurate experiments will verify that the points fall on a straight line; or you can assume that the scatter is a real phenomenon and try to explain it. Hubble took the first alternative, so the only problem left was to find the line about which experimental error was scattering his data.

The way this is usually done is to find the line for which the sum of the distances between the line and each data point is smaller than for any other line. In effect, you find the line that comes closest to all the data points. The slope of this line, which measures how fast the velocity increases for a given change in distance, is the best estimate of Hubble's constant. •

The Big Bang

Hubble's law reveals an extraordinary aspect of our universe: it is expanding. Nearby galaxies are moving away from us, and far-away galaxies are moving away even faster. The whole thing is blowing up like a balloon. This startling fact leads us, in turn, to perhaps the most amazing discovery of all. If you look at our universe expanding today and imagine moving backward in time (think of running a videotape in reverse), you can see that at some point in the past the universe must have started out as a very small object. In other words:

> The universe began at a specific point in the past, and it has been expanding ever since.

This picture of the universe—that it began from a small, dense collection of matter and has been expanding ever since—is called the **big bang theory**. This theory constitutes our best idea of what the early universe was like.

Think how different the big bang theory of the universe is from the theories of the Greeks or the medieval scholars, or even the great scientists of the nineteenth century whose work we have studied. To them, the Earth went in stately orbit around the Sun, and the Sun moved among the stars, but the collection of stars you can see at night with your naked eye or with a telescope was all that there was. Suddenly, with Hubble's work, the universe grew immeasurably. Our own collection of stars, our own galaxy, is just one of perhaps 100 billion known galaxies in a universe in which galaxies are flying away from each other at incredible speeds. It is a vision of a universe that began at some time in the distant past and will, presumably, end at some time in the future.

The Large-Scale Structure of the Universe

The Milky Way is part of a group of galaxies known as the Local Group, made up of ourselves, the Andromeda galaxy, and perhaps a dozen small "suburban" galaxies. The Andromeda galaxy is visible with the naked eye from the Earth—you can see it from a dark spot on a clear summer night as a fuzzy patch of light in the northeast. The Local Group, in turn, is part of the Local Supercluster, a collection of galaxies about 100 million light-years across.

We now know that literally billions of galaxies populate the universe, each a collection of billions of stars. Like the Milky Way, most galaxies seem to be clumped together into *groups* and *clusters,* many of which, in turn, are grouped into larger collections called *superclusters* of thousands of galaxies.

In the 1980s, astronomers began to make "redshift surveys" of the sky, in which they observe distant galaxies and measure their redshifts so we know how far the galaxies are. In this way, it is possible to construct a full, three-dimensional picture of the distribution of matter in the cosmos. With the results from these observations, led primarily by the team of Margaret Geller and John Huchra at the Harvard-Smithsonian Astrophysical Observatory, astronomers have put together a picture of the universe that is very different from what you might expect. Instead of finding galaxies scattered more or less at random through space, they find that galaxies are collected into large structures that run for billions of light-years across the sky. In fact, you can get an excellent picture of the structure of the universe by imagining the distribution of galaxies as something like a big pile of soapsuds. The result will give you a structure in which large empty spaces are surrounded by soap film. In exactly the same way, matter in the universe seems to be concentrated in superclusters on the surfaces of large empty areas called voids (Figure 15-7). Attempting to understand the reason for this very complex structure in the universe remains one of the major tasks of modern cosmology.

One theory that accounts for universal expansion is the *big bang*—the idea that the universe began at a specific moment in time and has been expanding ever since. Evidence from the *cosmic microwave background radiation* and the relative abundances of light elements, in addition to expansion, support the big bang theory.

At the moment of creation, all forces and matter were unified in one unimaginably hot and dense volume. As the universe expanded, however, a series of six "freezings" led to the universe we see today. Freezings at 10^{-43} second, 10^{-35} second, and 10^{-10} second caused a single unified force to split into the four forces we observe today: the gravitational, strong, electromagnetic, and weak forces. At that early stage of the universe, when all matter and energy were contained in a volume no larger than a grapefruit, matter was in its most elementary form of quarks and leptons.

At 10^{-5} second, the quarks bonded together to form heavy nuclear particles such as protons and neutrons. Subsequent freezings saw these particles first fuse to nuclei at three minutes, and ultimately join with electrons to form atoms at 500,000 years. Stars, which formed from those atoms, then could begin the processes that provided all the other chemical elements.

The search for *dark matter*—mass that we cannot see with our telescopes—is a research frontier that may help us determine whether the universe will continue expanding forever.

KEY TERMS ABOUT COSMOLOGY

Milky Way	cosmology	Hubble's law	cosmic microwave background radiation
galaxy	redshift	big bang theory	dark matter

REVIEW QUESTIONS

1. What is cosmology? How does cosmology differ from astronomy?

2. What is a galaxy? How does a galaxy differ from a star?

3. How are galaxies distributed in the universe?

4. How did Edwin Hubble discover that there are galaxies in the universe other than the Milky Way?

5. Name the different types of galaxies and their distinguishing characteristics.

6. Describe Hubble's law. How did Hubble discover it?

7. What kinds of evidence support the big bang theory?

8. How is the redshift related to the Doppler effect? What does the redshift say about the universe?

9. Make a table with ages of the universe in the left column (10^{-43} seconds, 10^{-35} seconds, 10^{-10} seconds, 10^{-5} seconds, 3 minutes, 500,000 years) and the major events in the history of the universe in the right column.

10. What is the significance of the discovery by Penzias and Wilson of cosmic microwave background radiation?

11. What are "ripples at the beginning of time," and why are they important?

12. What is dark matter and what evidence exists for it?

DISCUSSION QUESTIONS

1. Why does the Earth seem to be at the center of the Hubble expansion?

2. If the universe is closed, describe the results that some future Hubble would get when he looked through a telescope during the period of contraction. Would he still see other galaxies? Would he still see a redshift?

3. Why was the steady-state theory of the universe abandoned? How does this episode fit into the discussion of the scientific method in Chapter 1?

4. What measurements or observations contribute to the question of whether the universe is closed or open?

5. Louis Pasteur once said that "chance favors only the mind that is prepared." Apply this saying to the discoveries of Edwin Hubble, and of Penzias and Wilson.

6. Some advances in our knowledge have been made possible through better equipment, such as Hubble's discoveries using the 100-inch Hooker telescope at Mount Wilson. What other major discoveries in cosmology have relied on improvements in existing apparatus?

PROBLEMS

1. Assuming a Hubble constant of 75 km/s/Mpc, what is the approximate velocity of a galaxy 10 Mpc away? 250 Mpc away? 5000 Mpc away?

2. If a galaxy is 700 Mpc away, how fast is it receding from us?

3. An observer on one of the raisins in our bread-dough analogy measures distances and velocities of neighboring raisins. The data look like the following:

Distance (cm)	Velocity (cm/hr)
0.5	1.02
0.9	2.00
1.4	2.90
2.1	4.05
3.0	5.90
3.4	7.10

Plot these data on a graph and use the plot to estimate a "Hubble constant" for the raisins.

4. From the data in Problem 3, estimate the time that has elapsed since the dough started rising. Estimate the largest and smallest values of this number consistent with the data.

5. Some theories say that in the inflationary period, the scale of the universe increased by a factor of 10^{50}. Suppose your height were to increase by a factor of 10^{50}. How tall would you be? Express your answer in light-years and compare it to the size of the observable universe.

6. Suppose a proton (diameter about 10^{-13} cm) were to inflate by a factor of 10^{50}. How big would it be? Convert the answer to light-years and compare it to the size of the observable universe.

7. How fast is a galaxy 5 billion light-years from Earth moving away from us? What fraction of the speed of light is this?

INVESTIGATIONS

1. The Milky Way is a band of stars that, seen from Earth in the summer months, stretches all the way across the sky. Given what you know about galaxies, why do you suppose that our own galaxy appears this way to us? Who was the first natural philosopher to figure this out?

2. Will the constellation of Andromeda be above the horizon tonight? If so, go out and try to spot the Andromeda galaxy.

3. Look up the "Great Attractor." How does the existence of such an object fit in with the concept of the Hubble expansion? How would you modify the raisin-bread dough analogy to put in the Great Attractor?

4. Investigate the cosmologies of other societies. How do they think the universe began? Do they predict how it will end?

5. What agencies or organizations fund cosmological research? What was the role of the Carnegie Institution of Washington in Edwin Hubble's research?

WWW RESOURCES

See *The Sciences* homepage at: **http://www.wiley.com/college/trefil** for valuable web links.

1. **http://hou.lbl.gov/ISE/new/index.html**
Tour of the Universe—visit comets, planets, moons, stars, galaxies, and nebulae.

2. **http://seds.lpl.arizona.edu/**
Students for the Exploration and Development of Space Home Page—a professional site with vast resources.

3. **http://www.thetech.org/exhibits/online/hubble/**
Eye on the Universe: The Hubble Space Telescope—everything you ever wanted to know about the Hubble, but never thought to ask.

16

The Earth and Other Planets

Is Earth the only planet with life?

GREAT IDEA

The Earth, one of nine planets that orbit the Sun, formed 4.5 billion years ago from a great cloud of dust.

PHYSICS
The force of gravity caused the solar nebula to collapse on itself, forming our solar system.

CHEMISTRY
The Earth's early atmosphere was rich in the elements carbon, hydrogen, oxygen, and nitrogen.

ENVIRONMENT
Large meteors or comets, left over from the initial period of planetary formation, still occasionally hit the Earth, and may cause mass extinctions. (Ch. 25)

GEOLOGY
Differentiation caused the Earth's interior to become layered into the core, mantle, and crust.

HEALTH & SAFETY
The low force of gravity in space may cause gradual bone deterioration and thus limit the duration of long space voyages.

ASTRONOMY
The Earth and the other planets in our solar system orbit in the same direction around the Sun, and are more or less in the same plane.

TECHNOLOGY
Scientific instruments on board the Voyager 1 and 2 satellites have provided detailed images and information about the outer planets in our solar system.

BIOLOGY
The ancestors of living things could not have come into existence until after the great bombardment.

Red = applications of the great idea discussed in this chapter.

Orange = other applications, some of which are explored in other chapters.

It's shortly after noon; the Sun is blazing overhead. As you scan the horizon you see a perfect half Moon rising in the East. The rough, cratered surface stands out even in daylight. But you recall that just a few days ago you saw the Moon as a thin crescent in the evening sky. And a couple of weeks before that, the night's full Moon was so bright you could almost read by it. The Moon, like other objects in our solar system, is constantly changing in the sky.

As you stare at our nearest neighbor in space it's amazing to think that a few decades ago humans actually walked on that hostile world and brought precious pieces of its surface back to Earth. What did scientists learn from those alien rocks? What do they tell us about the ancient origin and dynamic state of our home, the solar system?

The Sun and Its Planets

Walk outside and look at the sky tonight just after sunset. Chances are you will find two or three particularly bright objects that stand out among the stars, even in the haze and illumination of a city. They don't seem to twinkle like stars, but shine steadily. If you looked at them through binoculars, they would appear to be small disks.

If you look at the same bright objects on successive nights, you'll notice that over a period of weeks or months, they seem to wander among the stars, never appearing in exactly the same place two nights in a row. The Greeks called them "wanderers," or planets, and assigned them the names of the gods (although today we use the Roman names). In the evening and morning, for example, you are likely to see Venus, named for the goddess of love, and swift-moving Mercury, the messenger of the gods; and the night sky is often dominated by Jupiter, the king of the gods.

Today we know that those disks of light in the sky are objects similar in many ways to our own planet, Earth. They show us that we are part of a system that includes not only the Earth, but the Sun and the other planets as well. Our probes have visited all of them and landed on two—Mars and Venus. Visionaries talk of the day when science fiction will become reality and human beings will work and live on these, our nearest neighbors in the cosmos. In every sense of the word, the planets are the next frontier.

The Solar System

The Copernican revolution radically altered human perceptions of our place in the universe (see Chapter 2). Rather than occupying what was assumed by many to be the center of creation, the Earth became just one of a number of planets

• **Figure 16-1** The solar system.

orbiting the Sun. The **solar system**, which includes the Sun, the planets and their moons, and all other objects gravitationally bound to the Sun, displays several distinctive characteristics. Describing these features and explaining in detail how they came to be remains one of the main challenges faced by planetary scientists today.

How can we deduce the origin and present state of the solar system? Until recently, all our observations of the Sun and planets had been made from the surface of the Earth. We see points of light moving in the sky, but how can that information be translated into a vivid picture of a dynamic system?

Humans have studied the solar system for thousands of years, making observations and proposing models. Ancient scholars recorded the changing positions of the brightest planets, such as Venus and Jupiter. Application of the telescope by Galileo and many subsequent astronomers (see Chapter 2) led to the discovery of numerous new, faint objects, including several moons and other small bodies. More recently, orbiting space probes and flyby missions have returned closeup photographic images of several planets, while spacecraft have landed on Venus and Mars. Our present understanding of the solar system, therefore, represents the cumulative effect of centuries of observation.

As astronomers gathered data on the solar system, they noticed several striking regularities regarding the orbits of planets and the distribution of mass, patterns that provide the key to understanding the evolution of our home (Figure 16-1).

Planetary Orbits

Think about what Newton's laws tell us regarding satellites orbiting a central body. A satellite can go in any direction: east to west or west to east, around the equator or over the poles. There are no constraints regarding the orientation of the orbit, and planets could orbit any which way around the Sun. Yet in our solar system we see three very curious features:

1. All planets, and most of their moons, orbit in the same direction around the Sun, and this direction is the same as that of the rotation of the Sun.

2. All orbits of planets and their larger moons are in more or less the same plane. The solar system resembles a bunch of marbles rolling around on a single flat dish.

3. Almost all planets and moons rotate on their axes in the same direction as the planets orbit the Sun.

(STOP) Stop and Think! If you had only the preceding information, what scenarios for the origin of the solar system would you construct?

The Distribution of Mass

You could imagine a solar system in which mass is evenly distributed, with all planets more or less the same size and same chemical composition. But our solar system is not that way at all (Figure 16-2). Instead:

- Virtually all of the material of the solar system is contained within the Sun, with only a small fraction in the planets and other objects in orbit.

- There are two distinct kinds of planets. Near the Sun, in the "inner" solar system, are planets like the Earth—relatively small, rocky, high-density worlds. These are called the **terrestrial planets**, and include **Mercury**, **Venus**, **Earth**, **Mars**, and (although it isn't really a planet) **Earth's Moon**. Farther out from the Sun, in the "outer" solar system, are huge worlds made primarily of hydrogen and helium. We call them "gas giants," or **Jovian planets**, and they are **Jupiter**, **Saturn**, **Uranus**, and **Neptune**. **Pluto**, the outermost planet, is something of an anomaly, being small and rocky. The planets of the solar system and some of their characteristics are listed in Table 16-1.

- Interspersed with the planets are a large number of other kinds of objects. All the planets except the innermost, Mercury and Venus, are orbited by one or

• **Figure 16-2** Most of the mass in the solar system is in the Sun, and most of the rest is in the Jovian planets. (Distances in this figure are not to scale.)

Table 16-1 **The Planets and Their Characteristics**

	Mercury	Venus	Earth	Mars	Jupiter	Saturn	Uranus	Neptune	Pluto
Diameter (km)	4,880	12,104	12,756	6,787	142,800	120,000	51,800	49,500	6,000
Mass (Earth = 1)	0.005	0.815	1.0	0.108	317.8	95.2	14.4	17.2	0.003
Density (gm/cm3) (water = 1)	5.44	5.20	5.52	3.93	1.30	0.69	1.28	1.64	2.06
Number of moons	0	0	1	2	16	18	15	8	1
Length of day (Earth hours)	1416	5832	24	24.6	9.8	10.2	17.2	16.1	154
Period of one revolution around Sun (Earth years)	0.24	0.62	1.00	1.88	11.86	29.50	84.00	164.90	247.70
Average distance from Sun (millions of km)	58	108	150	228	778	1427	2870	4497	5900

more **moons**. While some moons are little more than boulders a few kilometers across, others are much larger, and Saturn's largest moon Titan is about the same size as Mercury. Saturn also has dramatic rings composed of millions of tiny moons. Small, rocky **asteroids** that circle the Sun like miniature planets are found primarily in orbits between Mars and Jupiter, in what is called the **asteroid belt**, although some have orbits that cross the Earth's. Far beyond Pluto, we find a swarm of icy **comets** with compositions something like a "dirty snowball." Occasionally, one is jostled loose from its orbit and becomes part of the realm of the planets, creating a spectacular display in the sky.

These regularities in the distribution of the solar system's mass give us important hints as to how the system was formed—new theories that will lead to even more observations of the heavens.

The Nebular Hypothesis

In Chapter 14 we examined the modern theory of star formation—the *nebular hypothesis,* which was first put forward by the French mathematician and physicist Pierre Simon Laplace (1749–1827). His model of star formation also helps to explain many of the distinctive characteristics of the solar system—the rotation of the Sun, the orbits of the planets, and the distribution of mass into one large central object and lots of much smaller orbiting bodies. According to the nebular hypothesis, long ago (about 4.5 billion years ago based on radiometric dating) a large cloud of dust and gas collected in the region now occupied by the solar system. Such dust and gas clouds, called **nebulae**, are common throughout our galaxy, the Milky Way. They typically contain more than 99% hydrogen and helium, with lesser amounts of all the other naturally occurring elements.

Under the influence of gravity, the nebula slowly, inexorably, started to collapse on itself. As was the case for the formation of stars from a nebula, the collapse caused the cloud to spin faster and faster. The rapid spin had several consequences. For one thing, it meant that some of the material in the outer parts of the cloud began to spin out into a flat disk. This common consequence of fast rotation is familiar to anyone who has watched a pizza maker create a flat disk of dough by spinning a mass overhead. If you imagine the solar system at this stage of its formation as a large pancake with a big lump in the middle, you won't be far wrong. The big lump represents the material that will eventually become the Sun and the material in the thin, flattened disk will eventually become the planets and the rest of the solar system (Figure 16-3).

The flattening of the nebula into a disk explains another feature of the solar system. The planets had to form in this rotating disk of material, and hence their eventual orbits had to lie close to the disk's plane. The fact that all planetary orbits lie near the same plane, then, is a simple consequence of the solar system's rapid rotation as the nebular cloud began to contract.

In any clump of matter like the spinning disk, by chance, matter is more densely collected in some regions than elsewhere. These regions exert a stronger gravitational force than their neighbors, so that nearby matter tends to gravitate to them. Once the nearby matter has come in, the concentration of matter at that point is even greater, and it will pull even more material into it. As material accumulates, solid grains start to stick together.

This ultimate consequence of gravitational force leads to the rapid breakup of the disk into small objects called *planetesimals,* which range in size from boulders to masses several kilometers across. Once this has happened, the process of gravitational attraction goes on at a grander scale. Planetesimals collide with each other; larger objects capture smaller ones and continue growing.

About the time that this process was going on in the early solar system, the material at the center—more than 99% of the nebula's original mass—began to turn into a star. Light energy began to radiate out from the Sun, and temperature differences began to develop in the disk. Those parts nearest the Sun warmed up, while those farther out warmed only a little. As a result, the inner and outer solar systems developed differently. In the warm inner system, compounds such as water, methane, and carbon dioxide were in gaseous form, while farther out they were frozen into solids.

Thus, everyday physical processes having to do with phases of matter and the response to temperature—processes as familiar as boiling water and making ice—

• **Figure 16-3** As the nebula that formed the solar system collapsed, it began to rotate and flatten into a disk. The stages in solar system formation include (*a*) a slowly rotating nebula, (*b*) a flattened disk with massive center, (*c*) planets in the process of birth represented as mass concentrations in the nebula, and (*d*) the solar system.

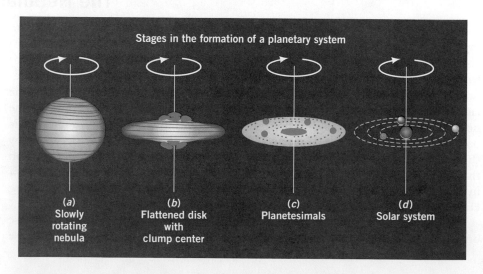

Stages in the formation of a planetary system

(a) Slowly rotating nebula

(b) Flattened disk with clump center

(c) Planetesimals

(d) Solar system

The inner planets, like Mars, are small and rocky.

explain one of the crucial facts about the solar system. The terrestrial planets, including Mercury, Venus, Earth, and Mars, were formed from those materials that could remain solid at high temperatures. Consequently, they are small, rocky worlds.

Farther out in the solar system we find the Jovian planets, including Jupiter, Saturn, Uranus, and Neptune. The compositions of those planets are essentially the same as the material concentrated in the original nebula; that is, they contain large amounts of hydrogen and helium. These planets formed from material that condensed and accumulated because of lower temperatures so far from the Sun. Consequently, these outer Jovian planets have a markedly different chemical composition from the inner terrestrial planets of the solar system.

In passing, we should note that the Jovian planets probably had their own complement of high-density materials. Scientists suspect that beneath the thousands of kilometers of helium, hydrogen, and other condensed gases on these planets is concealed a core like a small terrestrial planet, whose composition is much like that of the Earth and its neighbors. But this rocky matter represents only a small fraction of these planets' total mass.

Some astronomers argue that the largest planets, Jupiter and Saturn, formed by a process more like that of a small star than through the accretion of planetesimals. The details of the structure and formation of the Jovian planets remains a rich ground for debate in the sciences.

Just as any construction site has a pile of leftover materials lying around when the building is finished, so too does the solar system have its "scrap pile." These

Gas giants, like Jupiter, are large and are composed mainly of hydrogen and helium. Note the Great Red Spot—a storm that has raged on Jupiter for centuries.

leftovers take the form of the rocky asteroids and icy comets that still orbit the Sun. They represent the matter that never got taken up into planets.

THE SCIENCE OF LIFE •

Gravity and Bones

The planets of our solar system vary greatly in mass, from tiny Pluto with only 1/500th the mass of Earth, to Jupiter, which is 317 times more massive than our own planet. Consequently, the force of gravity at the surface of each planet is different; you would weigh a small fraction of what you do now on the surface of Pluto, but many times your present weight on Jupiter. (The connection between mass and weight is reviewed in Chapter 2.)

In humans, bones in the skeleton support our weight. Bone is not a static material, like concrete, but changes in response to its environment. It constantly rebuilds itself, replacing the calcium-rich minerals that form the solid structure. In fact, you can think of what goes on in bones as being analogous to the remodeling of a house. First, the old material is removed (a process called resorption), then new material is added. If a bone is subject to unusual stress (or lack of it), it will change gradually in response, adding or subtracting mass.

On the surface of the Moon, for example, you would weigh one-sixth of your Earth weight. Your bones would start to remodel themselves in response to the lower force of gravity, unless you kept them under stress by an extended program of vigorous exercise. Astronauts spending a few weeks or months in the weightless environment of space have experienced significant bone loss that, fortunately, is eventually made up after they return to Earth. Scientists are less certain, however, of the extremely long-term effects of low gravity on bone loss. What might happen during the long months of a space flight to Mars, for example? Studies on astronauts now may well determine whether such ambitious interplanetary flights take place in the foreseeable future. •

 Stop and Think! What advantages to a living thing do you suppose arise from the features of bones we've just discussed? Why do you suppose bones aren't built like bridges, which are designed to carry the heaviest load possible?

Bones respond to the absence of gravitational stress.

The Formation of the Terrestrial Planets

The collapse of the solar nebula into the Sun and planets began the solar system's evolution. Following the formation of planets each object evolved in its own distinctive way. For the terrestrial planets, this history had to do with the churning, colliding, roiling cloud of planetesimals. Once they were formed, the formation of planets followed quickly. As planetesimals moved in their orbits, they collected smaller planetesimals through the process of gravitational attraction. Then these larger planetesimals collided and coalesced into the beginnings of a planet. As the process of accumulation went on, the growing planet gradually swept up all the debris that lay near its orbit.

If you had been standing on the surface of a newly forming planet like the Earth during this stage, you would have seen a spectacular display. A constant rain of debris left over from the initial period of planetary formation fell to the surface, steadily adding mass to the planet. During this period, called the **great bombardment**, the large amounts of kinetic energy carried by the shower of stones were converted into heat, which was added to the newly forming planet. By some accounts, much of the planetary surface would have glowed bright red from this accumulating heat and each large impact would have been accompanied by a spectacular splash of molten rock. Although in the case of the Earth the addition of material has slowed considerably since the beginning, it has not stopped. Every time you see a **meteor** (often called a shooting star), for example, you are seeing an object roughly the size of a grain of sand being added to our planet. Scientists estimate that the mass of the Earth grows by about 20 metric tons (20,000 kg, or 2×10^7 g) per day by accretion of material falling from space.

When the nebular hypothesis was first proposed in the eighteenth century, there seemed little chance that any direct observational evidence could be found to support it. In 1992 astronomers using the Hubble Space Telescope (see Chapter 14) detected thick masses of dust encircling newborn stars in a region of space called the Orion nebula. Subsequent observations have confirmed the existence of numerous disks around young stars. It appears that in these cases we are seeing distant solar systems in the process of being born—observations that give us a measure of confidence in our model of how planets come into existence.

An artist's impression of the surface of the Earth during the great bombardment.

These Hubble Space Telescope pictures show a disk around a young star.

HD 141569 Circumstellar Disk
Hubble Space Telescope • ACS HRC Coronagraph

NASA, M. Clampin (STScI), H. Ford (JHU), G. Illingworth (UCO/Lick Observatory),
J. Krist (STScI), D. Ardila (JHU), D. Golimowski (JHU), and the ACS Science Team • STScI-PRC03-02

SCIENCE BY THE NUMBERS •

The Growth of the Earth

The Earth's mass is approximately 6×10^{27} grams. If 2×10^7 grams are added per day, how long would it take to double the Earth's mass?

Reasoning and Solution: First, we have to calculate how many grams are added to the Earth each year by multiplying the daily added mass by the number of days in a year. The Earth's total mass, divided by the mass added each year, gives us the time it would take to double the present mass.

First we determine the yearly mass added to the Earth.

$$\text{mass added per year} = (365 \text{ days/year}) \times (2 \times 10^7 \text{ g/day})$$
$$= 730 \times 10^7 \text{ g/year}$$
$$= 7.3 \times 10^9 \text{ g/year}$$

Then, divide the Earth's total mass by the mass added every year.

$$\text{number of years} = \frac{(6 \times 10^{27} \text{ g})}{(7.3 \times 10^9 \text{ g/year})}$$
$$= 0.82 \times 10^{18} \text{ years}$$
$$= 8.2 \times 10^{17} \text{ years}$$

This number is the time (in years) that would be required to double the mass of the Earth at its present rate of growth. This immense time, nearly a billion-billion years, is vastly greater than the lifetime of our planet, which is a paltry 4.5 billion years. From this calculation we see that the total amount of mass now being added to the Earth is trivial. •

Differentiation

Each time another planetesimal hit a newly forming planet, all of its kinetic and potential energy was converted into heat. That heat diffused through the planet. In the case of the Earth, the surface glowed red hot and the deep interior reached temperatures of thousands of degrees. Eventually, the Earth either melted completely or else was heated to high enough temperatures so that it was very soft all the way through. Heavy, dense materials (like iron and nickel) sank under the force of gravity toward the center of the planet, while lighter, less-dense materials floated to the top. The result of this process, called **differentiation**, is that the present-day terrestrial planets have a distinctively layered structure (the Earth's structure is shown in Figure 16-4).

In a sense, what happened to these planets long ago isn't too different from what happens to a mixture of oil and water that is shaken up and then allowed to stand. Eventually, the lighter oil will float to the top and the heavier water will sink to the bottom under the influence of gravity. The Earth also separated into layers of different density when it underwent differentiation.

The Interior of the Earth

At the center of the Earth, with a radius of about 3400 kilometers (2000 miles), is the **core**, made primarily of iron and nickel metal. Temperatures at the center of the Earth are believed to exceed 5000°C, but pressures are so high—about 3.5 billion grams per square centimeter (almost 50 million pounds per square inch)—that the iron-nickel inner core is solid. A little farther out the pressures are somewhat lower, so that the outer region of the iron-nickel core is actually a liquid.

The metal core is overlain by a thick layer, the **mantle**, which is rich in the elements oxygen, silicon, magnesium, and iron. Metallic bonding predominates in

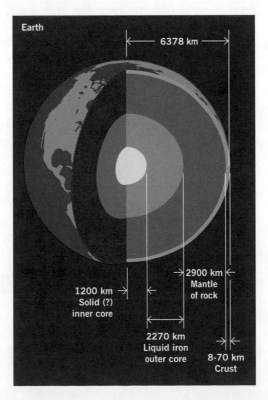

Earth

6378 km

1200 km
Solid (?)
inner core

2270 km
Liquid iron
outer core

2900 km
Mantle
of rock

8-70 km
Crust

• **Figure 16-4** The layered Earth. The principal layers, which differ in chemical composition and physical properties, are the core, the mantle, the crust, and the atmosphere (not shown). When looked at in detail, each of these layers is itself composed of smaller layers.

the core, but the mantle features minerals with primarily ionic bonds between negatively charged oxygen ions and positively charged silicon, magnesium, and other ions. Mantle rocks are similar in composition to some familiar surface rocks, but the atoms in these high-pressure materials are packed together in much denser forms.

At the very outer layer of the Earth is the **crust**, which is made up of the lightest materials. The crust's thickness ranges from less than 10 kilometers (about 6 miles) in parts of the oceans, to as much as 70 kilometers (about 45 miles) beneath parts of the continents. The crust is the only layer of the solid Earth with which human beings have had contact, and it remains the source of almost all the rocks and minerals that we use in our lives.

You might wonder how scientists could describe parts of the Earth that no human being has ever seen. In the next chapter we introduce seismology, a branch of science that has provided (among other things) our present picture of the Earth's interior.

TECHNOLOGY •

Producing World-Record High Pressures

The force of gravity, pulling inward on all of the Earth's layers, results in immense internal pressures, exceeding 3 million times the atmospheric pressure at the Earth's center. What changes affect rocks and minerals at these extreme conditions? High-pressure researchers, who have learned to sustain laboratory pressures greater than those at the center of the Earth, are providing surprising answers.

Of all the materials from the Earth's deep interior, none holds more fascination than diamond, the high-pressure form of carbon. This magnificent gemstone is also the hardest known substance and the most efficient abrasive for machining the tough metal parts of modern industry. Until the mid-1950s, diamonds were available only from a few natural sources, but in 1954 scientists at General Electric discovered how to manufacture diamonds by duplicating the extreme temperatures and pressures that exist hundreds of kilometers beneath the Earth's surface. The researchers squeezed carbon between the jaws of a massive metal vise and heated their sample with a powerful electrical current. Early experiments yielded only a fraction of a carat of diamond, but large factories now produce dozens of tons of diamonds annually, an output exceeding the total amount of diamonds mined since Biblical times.

The Earth taught us how diamonds are made, and now scientists use diamonds to learn how the Earth was made. The highest sustained laboratory pressures available today are obtained by clamping together two tiny pointed anvils of diamond. Samples squeezed between the diamond-anvil faces are subjected to pressures of several million kilograms per square centimeter, greater than at the center of the Earth. At such extreme conditions, rocks and minerals compress to new, dense forms occupying less than half their original volumes. Dramatic changes in chemical bonding are also observed, with many ionically and covalently bonded compounds transforming to metals at high pressure. •

Researchers attain high pressures, equivalent to those deep inside the Earth and other planets, using the diamond anvil cell. Looking through such diamond cells you can observe pressurized samples such as this high-pressure ice crystal that was formed at room temperature by squeezing water.

EXAMPLE 16-1

The Density of the Moon

Scientists can measure the mass of the Moon by observing satellites in orbit or by measuring tides on Earth. This mass is approximately 7.4×10^{22} kg. They can also measure the radius of the Moon by observing its apparent size in the sky. Its radius is approximately 1.7×10^6 km. What is the average density of the Earth's nearest neighbor?

Reasoning: The density of an object is defined to be its mass divided by its volume. The first step, then, is to find the volume of the Moon. Once we have this, the density will be given by:

$$\text{density} = \text{mass of Moon}/\text{volume of Moon}$$

The volume of a sphere of radius R is given by:

$$\text{volume of sphere} = 4/3 \times \text{pi} \times \text{radius}^3$$

Solution: The volume of the Moon is then

$$\begin{aligned} \text{vol} &= 4/3 \times 3.14 \times (1.7 \times 10^6)^3 \\ &= 2 \times 10^{19} \text{ m}^3 \end{aligned}$$

So that the density is

$$\begin{aligned} \text{density} &= \frac{7.4 \times 10^{22} \text{ kg}}{2 \times 10^{19} \text{ m}^3} \\ &= 3700 \text{ kg/m}^3 \end{aligned}$$

For reference, the density of water is 1000 kg/m^3 and the average density of the Earth is about 5500 kg/m^3. Thus, the overall density of the Moon is considerably less than that of the Earth. In fact, it is about the same as the comparatively light material in the Earth's mantle, a fact that plays an important role in our theories of the Moon's formation.

The Formation of the Moon

The origin of the Moon, the only large body in orbit around the Earth, poses one of the oldest puzzles in planetary science. The Moon is one of the largest bodies in the solar system—larger than the planets Mercury and Pluto, and almost as large as Mars. The Moon's density and chemical composition, subjects of intense study by the astronauts of the *Apollo* lunar missions, are quite different from the Earth as a whole, though they are remarkably similar to those of the Earth's mantle. The problem of the Moon's origin can be stated simply: How could such a large body have arisen in the same region of space as the Earth, when its composition is so different?

The current theory is called the "big splash" (Figure 16-5). In this theory, the Earth underwent differentiation as described earlier, but while it was still in a formative state an object about the size of Mars struck it. This collision blew a huge quantity of mantle rocks out into orbit around the Earth. The Moon then formed from this material, which explains the Moon's unusual composition, density, and large size.

(a) Time: 403s

(b) Time: 1204s

(c) Time: 2003s

• Figure 16-5
The "big splash" theory of the Moon's formation points to a gigantic impact of a Mars-sized body with Earth (*a*). A large quantity of material from Earth's mantle was blasted into orbit (*b*) and eventually coalesced into the Moon (*c*).

The 1200-meter-wide Meteor Crater in Arizona formed from a collision about 20,000 years ago. The meteorite was approximately the size of a small car.

As for the Earth, the theories predict that as a result of the collision, large-scale melting occurred. When the planet cooled off, no trace of the mammoth impact was left.

Formation of the Other Terrestrial Planets

The natural processes that occurred during the Earth's formation affected the other planets as well. Mercury, Mars, and the Moon, for example, display surface cratering that suggests that large chunks of rock bombarded all of these planets late in their formation. The Earth undoubtedly looked like this over 4 billion years ago, but all evidence of those early craters has been weathered away. On Mercury and the Moon, which have no atmosphere, no weathering has affected the craters and so they are still there.

The early bombardment may also have affected other characteristics of the terrestrial planets. The direction of rotation of Venus, for example, is opposite that of the Earth. (Planets revolve around the Sun, but rotate about their axes.) The Earth's axis of rotation, furthermore, is tilted at 23 degrees to the plane of its orbit, while Uranus has its axis of rotation close to the plane of its orbit, a full 90 degrees from an upright orientation. Current thinking is that these differences resulted from the more or less random collisions with large objects, perhaps hundreds of kilometers in diameter, which marked the end of the main phase of planetary formation. You might expect that the details of these late-stage collisions were different for each planet. Thus the nebular hypothesis not only explains how it is that the planets all have their orbits in the same plane and move in the same direction around the Sun, but also allows us to explain why the rotations of individual planets can be so different.

THE SCIENCE OF LIFE •

When Could Life Begin?

This scenario for Earth's formation also has important implications for the origins of life on our planet. During the period of the great bombardment, the Earth was constantly being hit by huge objects—chunks of rock the size of a state or even a country. At the very least, the tremendous energy released by such collisions would be enough to vaporize any oceans that had formed. Each collision would, quite literally, sterilize the planet. Even if life had come into existence during this period, it would have been wiped out by the impacts. Thus the ancestors of modern living things could not have gotten their start until the end of the bombardment, which occurred between 4.2 and 3.8 billion years ago. This fact will become very important when we discuss the origins of life in Chapter 25. •

The Evolution of Planetary Atmospheres

The Earth didn't always have the kind of atmosphere it has today. In fact, scientists now suggest that originally it had no atmosphere at all, and that once an atmosphere formed, its chemical composition gradually evolved to that of the present. The question of how the Earth's atmosphere arose and changed is extremely important, because this history is inseparable from understanding the origin and evolution of life on our planet.

The early Earth may have collected some gases by gravitational attraction. During the early formation of the Sun, large amounts of material and radiation were thrown off. This flood of materials would have blown off any atmosphere the Earth had accumulated. Thus, for all intents and purposes, the early Earth atmosphere was an airless ball of hot (or even molten) rock.

During the period of cooling that followed the great bombardment and melting, large amounts of water vapor, carbon dioxide, and other gases would have been released from deep within the solid Earth. Countless volcanoes and fissures, all belching steam and other materials, would have blown their gases into the newly forming atmosphere. In other words, the gases that formed the ancestor of today's atmosphere were probably originally locked into the rocks near the Earth's surface when the original atmosphere was swept away. Subsequently, a process called *outgassing* released a completely new atmosphere.

Outgassing, which was violent and rapid early in the Earth's history, has not ended today. We tend to think of volcanic eruptions as involving the flow of red-hot lava, but if you remember pictures of eruptions, you probably recall large clouds of smoke and steam that accompany the glowing lava flows. Even today, more than 4.5 billion years after the planet's formation, volcanoes release large amounts of gases from the interior of the Earth.

One estimate is that the principal result of outgassing in the early Earth was the production of an atmosphere composed primarily of methane (CH_4), ammonia (NH_3), carbon dioxide (CO_2), hydrogen (H_2), and water (H_2O), though scientists are engaged in a spirited debate on the subject of the exact atmospheric composition. Presumably, the same sort of process was occurring on the other terrestrial planets. For a time, the atmosphere was probably too hot for water to condense from a gas to a liquid, but eventually the atmospheric temperature dropped and torrential rains began to fill the ocean basins.

Once a planet has acquired an atmosphere by outgassing, there are several ways that its atmosphere can evolve and change. The simplest is *gravitational escape*. The molecules in an atmosphere heated by the Sun may move sufficiently fast so that appreciable fractions of them can actually escape the gravitational pull of their planet. The Moon, Mercury, and Mars are examples of bodies that had denser atmospheres early in their history, but lost much of these gases through gravitational escape long ago. Most of the light elements such as hydrogen and helium were presumably lost in the same way from the Earth, but the heavier gases such as carbon dioxide and water vapor remained because they were too heavy to escape the Earth's gravitational force.

The surface of Mars might have been covered by an ocean at one time.

A second cause of atmospheric change that operates only on Earth is the effect of living things. To the best of our knowledge, no life exists anywhere else in the solar system (although some scientists argue that there may have been life at one time on Mars). By the time the Earth was 1 billion years old, photosynthetic organisms had evolved to use the Sun's energy to power the chemical reactions essential for life. In photosynthesis, carbon dioxide and water are taken into the structures of living things, and oxygen is given off as a waste product. As life flourished on the planet, the amount of free oxygen increased as well, until today it comprises about 20% of the atmosphere.

We tend to think of oxygen as a benign and beautiful substance, but from a chemical point of view it's really rather nasty stuff. As we saw in Chapter 8, oxygen reacts violently with many materials (think of fire burning or the explosion of hydrogen or gasoline). In fact, the production of oxygen by living things on the early Earth can be thought of as the first global pollution event. Thus, life forms both affect and are affected by the atmosphere of the planet on which they reside. In fact, many scientists now suggest that you can tell whether a planet has life on it simply by looking at its atmosphere.

Exploring Mars

The exploration of Mars will occupy a great deal of the attention of the space community in the coming decades. In the 1990s the Pathfinder mission and the Mars Global Surveyor collected unmistakable evidence that there was once liquid water on the Martian surface—perhaps even a large ocean. In 2001 and 2002, the Mars Odyssey mission provided new striking evidence that a substantial quantity of water remains locked in the Martian crust. In fact, the current thinking is that early in its history, before it lost its atmosphere to gravitational escape, Mars would have looked much like the Earth. And, so the reasoning goes, since life seems to have developed quickly on Earth, it may well have done the same on Mars. Even if the cooling and loss of atmosphere wiped out that early life, we should be able to find evidence for it in the form of fossils.

Current plans call for several Mars orbiter and lander missions during the next decade, with a "sample return" mission to be launched toward Mars sometime after 2010. NASA planners are working closely with the Centers for Disease Control to ensure that these samples neither contaminate nor are contaminated by the Earth. A high-security containment structure will be constructed to house the Mars samples when they return.

The Outer Solar System

Space probes sent out from Earth in the 1970s and 1980s have visited most of the outer planets and provided a new view of the outer solar system. The distances to the giant outer planets are immense. The closest gas giant, Jupiter, orbits at five times the Earth–Sun distance, over 800 million kilometers away. Saturn is twice that far, while Uranus and Neptune are several billion kilometers away. This far out in the system, the Sun looks like a small marble in the sky, and its warming effects are feeble indeed. Csompounds that are normally gases on Earth, such as carbon dioxide, nitrogen, and methane, are found in liquid or even solid form under the intense pressures that exist in the interiors of the Jovian planets.

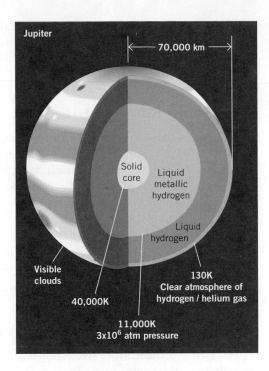

• **Figure 16-6** A theoretical view of the interior of Jupiter, one of the Jovian planets. Most of the planet's volume is highly compressed hydrogen and helium.

Jupiter

70,000 km

Solid core

Liquid metallic hydrogen

Liquid hydrogen

Visible clouds

130K
Clear atmosphere of hydrogen / helium gas

40,000K

11,000K
3×10^6 atm pressure

The structure of the outer giant planets is layered, like that of the terrestrial planets, but they do not have a well-defined solid surface like the Earth and Moon. Moving down from space into the body of Jupiter or Saturn would be a strange experience. You would move through progressively denser and denser layers of clouds and then pass imperceptibly into a layer where the gases change into liquids because of the high pressure. In fact, landing on Jupiter would be more like landing on a giant ice cream sundae than landing on the planet Earth or the Moon. In Figure 16-6, we show a typical structure for one of the Jovian planets.

During the mid-1990s, astronomers got two unique opportunities to study the atmosphere of Jupiter. One of these was fortuitous. From July 16 to 22, 1994, a string of objects known collectively as Comet Shoemaker-Levy collided with Jupiter. For days, most of the telescopes on Earth were trained on Jupiter as one impact after another roiled its upper layer of swirling gases. The collisions were more powerful than thousands of hydrogen bombs. The effect of these collisions was to bring gases that normally lie hundreds of miles deep up to the top of the atmosphere where scientists could see them. Shoemaker-Levy gave astronomers a chance to test their ideas about what was beneath the visible part of the Jovian atmosphere, as well as theories about how the atmosphere would cause the ripples created by the impacts to damp out. The net effect of the impacts, other than providing a spectacular show, was to allow astronomers to fine-tune their notions about the composition of the Jovian atmosphere.

Then, in December 1995, the spacecraft *Galileo* arrived in orbit around Jupiter to begin a study of the planet. *Galileo* was launched on October 18, 1989. Its orbit took it around the Sun and the Earth for an extra boost from gravity. When it arrived at Jupiter, the satellite launched a small probe into the Jovian atmosphere. Its descent slowed by a parachute system, the probe sank into the atmosphere, sending back information about the material through which it was passing. After 57 minutes of operation, the probe (as expected) was destroyed, but during its brief lifetime it gave scientists a library of new information about the

This infrared image of Jupiter shows the many impact sites, or splashes, due to fragments of Comet Shoemaker-Levy 9 in July 1994.

atmosphere of the largest planet. Since that time, *Galileo* has been in orbit around Jupiter, sending back a treasure trove of information about that planet and its moons.

Moons and Rings of the Outer Planets

Astronomers have found dozens of moons circling Jupiter, Saturn, Uranus, and Neptune. These bodies range from small rocks to planet-sized objects. Each of these moons is its own world, with its own history and formed by its own unique collection of physical processes. Each can be thought of as a small laboratory that sheds some light on the formation of terrestrial planets, but three are of special interest.

Io

The moon Io, which circles close to Jupiter, is the only moon in the solar system known to have active volcanoes. Scientists think that Jupiter's powerful gravitational forces flex and twist the moon to produce the energy to drive those volcanoes.

Europa

Jupiter's second moon has become one of the most studied objects in the solar system, because the *Galileo* spacecraft results hold out the possibility that conditions there may be appropriate for the development of life. The *Voyager* spacecraft photographs of Europa showed a smooth surface made of water ice. The relative absence of craters means that the surface must have formed recently, which would be puzzling in a moon in the frigid outer depths of the solar system.

 Stop and Think! Why should the absence of craters indicate a young surface on Europa?

When *Galileo* arrived at Jupiter, it sent back closeup photographs of the surface that looked more like the Arctic ice pack than a perpetually frozen world. Giant blocks of ice seemed to be jumbled together, welded together at their boundaries by what looked like ridges of freshly frozen material. Scientists began to speculate that under Europa's icy surface, heated by the same kind of gravita-

Saturn with its rings and moons.

tional twisting that powers Io's volcanoes, there might actually be liquid water— an entire ocean, in fact. Later measurements showed that Europa has a magnetic field that could arise from a salty ocean in its interior, and produced pictures of craters that look as if they had been filled in by a slushy fluid after impact. Right now, the consensus is that Europa might have the only nonterrestrial ocean in the solar system.

Since life on Earth developed in the oceans, the possibility exists that life (in microbial form, at least) might have arisen on Europa. NASA is busy planning a major exploration effort for this moon, with the possibility of sending robot probes to melt their way through the ice to explore this new and totally unexpected environment.

Titan

Saturn's moon Titan, one of the largest moons in the solar system (it is about the same size as the planet Mercury), may well be something of a laboratory for the early Earth. It may have frigid lakes of methane (CH_4) and ethane (C_2H_6) on its surface, and, from the beginning of the solar system, simple chemical reactions in its atmosphere have probably produced a layer of organic materials there. Thus, Titan may have something to tell us about how organic materials accumulate, and about how cellular life developed on our own planet.

Rings

In addition to these numerous moons, each of the four Jovian planets has a system of rings that are formed from countless small particles of ice and rock. Saturn features the most spectacular of these ring systems—an array of dozens of fine bands, separated by larger objects called shepherd satellites.

Pluto

The outermost planet, Pluto, remains something of a mystery. It can be studied through telescopes, but has yet to be visited by a space probe. Pluto is a small planet, only about 0.3% of the mass of the Earth, and is circled by a moon called Charon that is only slightly smaller than the planet. Its orbit is highly elliptical and, for a period of its orbital "year" (about 250 Earth years), is inside the orbit of Neptune. Because it is a small planet of rock and ice, unlike the neighboring gas giants, some scientists argue that Pluto actually formed as a captured comet or asteroid, rather than a planet in the usual sense of the word. Indeed, the origin of Pluto is very much an open question in planetary astronomy.

The surface of Pluto as seen by the Hubble Space Telescope.

SCIENCE IN THE MAKING •

The Discovery of Pluto

Five of the planets—Mercury, Venus, Mars, Jupiter, and Saturn—are visible to the naked eye and have been known from ancient times. The other three, most-distant planets—Uranus, Neptune, and Pluto—were discovered after the invention of the telescope. The most recent discovery of a planet occurred on February 18, 1930, by 23-year-old Clyde Tombaugh, who had been brought up on a Kansas farm. Employed as a technician at Lowell Observatory in Flagstaff, Arizona, Tombaugh uncovered convincing evidence for the existence of a new planet.

As a teenager, Tombaugh had built a small telescope, using parts from an old cream separator to make its stand. He drew sketches of the surface of Mars and sent them to Lowell Observatory, which was then engaged in observations of the red planet. The sketches, made with a small amateur's instrument, corresponded so well to what astronomers at Lowell were seeing through their state-of-the-art telescope that Tombaugh received a job offer by return mail.

At Lowell, he began a systematic search for what was then called Planet X. The founder of the observatory, American astronomer Percival Lowell, had predicted the existence of such a planet based on some rather questionable data on variations in the orbit of Neptune. Tombaugh's task was straightforward, if tiring. He would take photographs of each section of the sky, then a second photograph of the same section a few days later. The two photographs were then put into a machine that would show first one photograph, then the other, in an eyepiece. As the photographs were "blinked," any object that had moved between the time of the two photographs would appear to jump back and forth, while stars would remain stationary.

The main problem is that the plane of the solar system is littered with asteroids, each of which could show up as a moving light on such photos. The key point wasn't that Tombaugh found something out there that moved—there were plenty of such objects. The point was to find a point of light that moved by as much as Kepler's laws tell us that a planet out beyond Neptune would move in a few days. That is exactly what Tombaugh found on that day in February, some 10 months into his search.

After becoming one of only three human beings to have discovered a new planet, Tombaugh went back to college. Much to his surprise, he was not allowed to take introductory astronomy. "They cheated me out of four hours!" he says.

And his old telescope? When one of the authors asked him before his death a few years ago whether he was going to donate it to the Smithsonian Institution, the 83-year-old astronomer replied, "They want it, but they can't have it. I'm not through using it yet!" •

The discovery photos for Pluto reveal the shift of one point of light between January 23, 1930 (left), and January 29, 1930 (right). The white arrows point to Pluto.

SCIENCE IN THE MAKING •

The *Voyager* Satellites

On August 20, 1977, a rocket blasted off from Cape Canaveral in Florida, to set a small space probe on its course. Sixteen days later, another rocket did the same. These two probes, called *Voyager 1* and *2,* respectively, spent the next 15 years moving past the planets of the outer solar system, providing scientists with their first closeup look at the Jovian planets and their moons.

Each spacecraft had 10 scientific instruments on board, each designed to measure a different aspect of the deep-space environment. The ones that had the greatest public impact were the cameras that took pictures of moons, rings, and planets, but measurements were also made of magnetic fields, cosmic ray abundances, and infrared and ultraviolet radiation. Taken together, the *Voyager* probes produced a good deal of the detailed information about the outer solar system contained in this chapter.

One interesting feature of spaceflights like this is that by the time a spacecraft has been in flight for a while, all of its instrumentation has become obsolete. Between its encounters with Jupiter and Neptune, for example, the computers on *Voyager 2* were reprogrammed to make significant changes in the way they analyzed and transmitted data. As a result, the rate of transmission during the Neptune flyby in 1989 was not significantly different from that of the Jupiter encounter in 1979, despite the greater distance and lower light levels at Neptune.

Among their discoveries, the *Voyagers* found ring systems around all the Jovian planets, recorded a volcanic eruption on Io, tripled the number of known moons around Uranus, and clocked record winds on the surface of Neptune. Today, both *Voyagers,* together with a couple of earlier space probes called *Pioneers,* have moved out of the solar system and into interstellar space. *Voyager 2* is expected to keep returning data until its plutonium power supply runs down, sometime around 2020. By that time, it may have reached the place where the Sun's magnetic field blends into the magnetic field of our galaxy, thereby becoming the first human-made object to have broken free from all the dominant influences of the Sun. •

Asteroids, Comets, and Meteors

As the solar system formed, not all the material in the planetary disk was taken up into the bodies of the planets and moons. Even after hundreds of millions of years of accumulation and bombardment, a lot of debris was still floating around out there and remains even today. This debris comes in two main forms, asteroids and comets, which in a sense mimic the compositional differences of the inner and outer planets.

Asteroids

Asteroids are small rocky bodies in orbit around the Sun, like miniature versions of the inner terrestrial planets. Most asteroids are found in a broad, circular asteroid belt between Mars and Jupiter—material thought to be a collection of planetesimals that never managed to collect into a stable planet. The most likely explanation is that the nearby planet Jupiter had a disrupting gravitational effect. In addition, many asteroids possess orbits that cross the Earth's orbit, and they produce occasional large impacts on our planet.

Comets

Comets can best be thought of as "dirty snowballs." Unlike asteroids, they consist of chunks, sometimes many miles in diameter, of material such as water ice and methane ice in which a certain amount of solid, rocky material or dirt is embedded. Also, unlike asteroids, most of the comets in the solar system circle the Sun outside the orbit of Pluto. Two main reservoirs of comets are found in the solar system. One of these is a large spherical array called the *Oort cloud* (named after Dutch astronomer Jan Oort, 1900–1992, who first postulated its existence), located far from the solar system. The other is a disk of comets closer in to the solar system called the *Kuiper belt* (after the Dutch astronomer Gerard Kuiper, who first suggested its existence).

Occasionally, when the orbit of a comet is disturbed, the comet will be deflected so that it falls toward the Sun. When this happens, the increasing temperature of the inner solar system begins to boil off materials, and we see a large "tail," blown away from the Sun by the solar wind, that reflects light to us.

Sometimes a comet will be captured and fall into a regular orbit around the Sun. The most famous of these periodic comets is Halley's Comet (see Chapter 2), which returns to the vicinity of the Earth about every 76 years. Halley's return in 1910 was quite spectacular, because the comet passed near the Earth when it was at its highest temperature and therefore had its largest and most spectacular tail. The return in 1986 was much less spectacular because the comet was on the far side of the Sun when it was at its brightest. The next predicted return in 2061, unfortunately, will probably be just as unspectacular.

Astronomers have actually detected many objects in the inner Kuiper belt with the Hubble Space Telescope. These objects are several hundred miles across. Current thinking is that over the course of time, collisions in the Kuiper belt have gradually removed most of the original comets from it, leaving these objects as the last occupants. In fact, some astronomers have suggested that Pluto, far from being a true planet, is simply a survivor of the process by which the Kuiper belt was emptied early in the life of the solar system.

 Stop and Think! How do you suppose astronomers knew that the Oort cloud and Kuiper belt existed before objects in the latter could actually be seen?

A comet develops a tail as it approaches the Sun.

Table 16-2 Major Meteor Showers

Name	Date for Maximum	Extreme Limits	Hourly Rate of Meteors
Quadrantid	January 3	January 1–4	30
Aquarid	May 4	May 2–6	5
Perseid	August 12	July 29–August 17	40
Orionid	October 22	October 18–26	13
Taurid	November 1	September 15–December 15	5
Leonid	November 17	November 14–20	6
Geminid	December 14	December 7–15	55

THE SCIENCE OF LIFE •

Comets and Life on Earth

In addition to providing us with one of the first historical tests of the law of universal gravitation, comets may have had an important effect on the evolution of life on Earth. Many scientists suspect that the impacts of comets or asteroids may have drastically altered the Earth's climate and produced mass extinctions, or killings, at various times in the Earth's history (see Chapter 25). Most Earth scientists, for example, now believe that the dinosaurs and other life forms that thrived 65 million years ago were driven to extinction following the impact of a large comet or asteroid that hit the Earth at a site near Mexico's Yucatan Peninsula.

Meteoroids, Meteors, and Meteorites

Meteoroids are small pieces of ancient space debris in orbit around the Sun. Occasionally one of these bits, perhaps the size of a sand grain, will fall into the Earth's atmosphere where it becomes briefly visible as a meteor. Most meteors burn up completely to microscopic particles of ash that slowly, imperceptibly, rain down on Earth. The meteors' bright streaks of light record the path of this burning. Occasionally, if the object is big enough so that only the outer surface burns, a piece of rock may actually reach the Earth's surface. Any such rock that has fallen to Earth from space is called a **meteorite**.

Meteor showers are spectacular, regularly occurring events in the night sky. During a shower, every minute or so you can see brilliant streaks in the sky, each one caused by the collision of the Earth with swarms of small debris that travel around the orbits of comets. Some of these swarms may be comets that were broken up by the gravitational pull of one of the planets. Table 16-2 lists some of the most spectacular meteor showers.

Meteorites are extremely important in the study of the solar system because they represent the material from which the system was originally made. They are analyzed intensely by scientists, both to get a notion of how and when the Earth was made, and to learn what kinds of materials human beings will find when they leave the Earth to explore the rest of the solar system. •

SCIENCE IN THE MAKING •

Discovering New Planetary Systems

In 1994, Alexander Wolszczan at Penn State University announced the discovery of the first planetary system outside of our own. Since that time more than 100 *extrasolar planets* have been discovered, and more are announced every month.

• **Figure 16-7** Periodic changes in the red shift or blue shift of light may reveal the presence of a planet. This graph illustrates such a red/blue shift versus time or a nearby star. These data indicate a planet that orbits the star every 4.4 days.

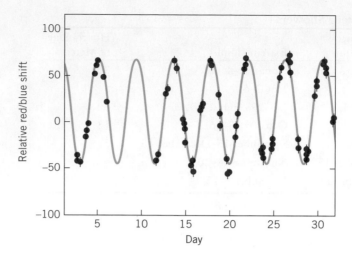

All of these planets are much too faint and distant to be seen directly in today's telescopses, but two clever observational approaches have led to most of these discoveries. Most of these distant planets are identified using the Doppler effect (see Chapter 6). As a planet orbits a star, its gravitational pull causes the star to wobble slightly. By monitoring a star over many nights—sometimes for more than a decade—this regular wobble is revealed by alternating periods of redshift and blueshift of starlight (Figure 16-7).

Alternatively, if an extrasolar planet orbits in a plane viewed edge on, then from time to time the planet will pass in front of the larger star. This transit of the planet slightly reduces the light reaching us—a reduction that can be measured with a sensitive light meter.

Keep watching the news for more reports of new extrasolar planets. •

Artist's conception of the transit of a planet in front of a star in a distant solar system.

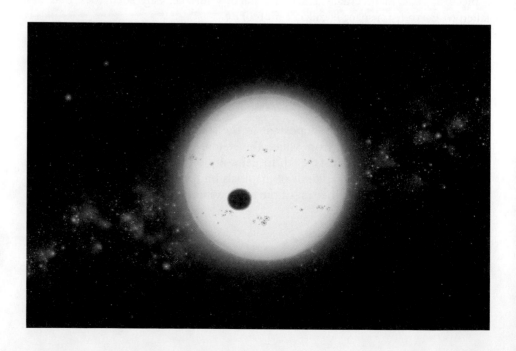

Since the first discovery of planets orbiting distant stars, astronomers have been able to document no fewer than 100 solar systems, and the number keeps growing. The most important feature of these systems is that most of these systems do not seem to be like our own, but contain giant planets, bigger than Jupiter, in close orbits around their stars. Recently, scientists at the Harvard-Smithsonian Center for Astrophysics in Cambridge, Massachusetts, have discovered a star that breaks all the records. Circling close to a star 5000 light years away, this planet orbits closer to its star than any planet discovered up to this point. So high is its temperature, that scientists calculate that liquid iron may rain down in its gaseous surface!

The planet was discovered by a new technique, as well. Instead of watching the tiny changes in the star's position caused by the gravitational pull of its planets, scientists monitor thousands of stars and look for a telltale drop in brightness as the planet passes in front of it. If the orbits of the planets are such that they will pass between the star and the Earth, this is a very efficient way of doing a planet search. A group of ground-based telescopes called the Optical Gravitational Lensing Experiment (OGLE), whose main function is to search for dark matter, turns up planets as a side benefit. In 2006, NASA will launch the Kepler satellite, which will use the transit method to search for Earth-type planets around other stars.

THE ONGOING PROCESS OF SCIENCE •

How Are Extrasolar Planets Formed?

When scientists had only our solar system to observe, it was fairly easy to devise a theory that explained all of the observed facts. However, with the rapidly growing inventory of extrasolar planets, scientists can test their theories against data obtained from other solar systems. Not surprisingly, these new data are raising problems with the nebular hypothesis outlined in the text.

In the nebular hypothesis, you would expect large planets to be located far from a star, in the region where materials could stay solid. Surprisingly, a number of the new planets don't seem to follow this pattern. Many large planets orbit close to their respective stars. These planets have been dubbed "hot Jupiters" by astronomers, because they are Jupiter-sized objects in their star's warm zone.

The best theories we have to date suggest that these planets were formed far from their stars, in the "cold Jupiter" region, and then, slowed down by clouds of dust that for some reason weren't present in the early solar system, they spiraled into their present orbits. One piece of evidence for this picture: photographs of distant stars that seem to be in the process of formation often show thick dust clouds around the plane of rotation. •

 Stop and Think! Given the way new planets are detected, can you think of a reason why "hot Jupiters" would be the easiest ones to discover?

Thinking More About | Planets

Human Space Exploration

Since before astronaut Neil Armstrong became the first human to walk on the surface of the Moon in 1969, the scientific community has debated the question of how the exploration of the solar system should be carried out. The question is this: Should future missions to the planets carry people, or should they carry only machines?

Those who advocate exploration by machines point to the enormous technical difficulties involved in providing a safe habitat for human beings in the harsh environment of space. Why, they ask, should we make the enormous, expensive effort to put a human being on the surface of Mars, for example, when just as much can be learned by sending instrument packages and robots controlled from the Earth?

On the other side of the issue, scientists advocating space exploration by astronauts argue that no machine has the flexibility and ingenuity of a human being. They note that no matter how well designed a machine might be, when it is millions of miles from Earth things can go wrong, and only a trained astronaut can salvage the mission. They point out that even a mammoth project like the Hubble Space Telescope needed astronauts to replace flawed optical systems. Besides, they argue, if one goal of the space program is to establish human colonies on other bodies in the solar system, you can't do that with machines.

What do we hope to learn from our studies of the solar system? Is colonization of the rest of the solar system the real long-term goal of the space program? How much extra effort (and taxpayers' dollars) is it worth expending to put people instead of machines on the surface of Mars?

SUMMARY

The Earth formed along with the Sun and other planets in our *solar system* from a *nebula*—a large gas and dust cloud rich in hydrogen and helium—approximately 4.5 billion years ago. As that cloud began to contract as a result of gravitational forces, it also began to rotate and flatten out into the disk that now defines the planetary orbits. More than 99% of the original nebula's mass concentrated at the center, which became the Sun.

Gradually, the matter in the flat disk began to form clumps under the influence of its own local gravitational forces. The largest of these masses swept up more and more debris as they orbited the early Sun, and they began to define a string of planets. *Terrestrial planets,* those nearest the Sun, were subjected to high temperatures and strong solar winds, so that most gases such as hydrogen, helium, and water vapors were swept out into space. Thus the inner four planets, including *Mercury, Venus, Earth,* and *Mars,* are dense, rocky places with a relatively low content of gaseous elements.

The Earth's formation was probably typical of these planets. After the principal mass of the Earth had been collected together, additional rocks and boulders showered down in the *great bombardment,* adding matter and heat energy to the planet. Dense iron and nickel separated from lighter materials by the process of *differentiation* and sank to the center to form a metallic *core.* Most of the Earth's mass concentrated in the thick *mantle,* while the lightest elements formed a thin *crust.* The *Moon,* Earth's only large satellite, may have formed when a planet-sized body hit the Earth early in its history.

The solar system's outer *Jovian planets,* including *Jupiter, Saturn, Uranus,* and *Neptune,* are quite different from the inner planets. Lying beyond the strong effects of solar heat and wind, they accumulated large amounts of gases such as hydrogen, helium, ammonia, and water. These outer planets are thus giant balls of ice, with thick atmospheres and great frigid oceans of nitrogen, methane, and other compounds that are gases on Earth. Beyond the Jovian planets lies *Pluto,* a rocky body that is the smallest planet. All of the planets except Mercury and Venus, the two closest to the Sun, have *moons* in orbit.

Interspersed with the planets and their moons are many other kinds of objects. Small, rocky *asteroids,* most of which are concentrated in an *asteroid belt* between Mars and Jupiter, circle the Sun like miniature planets. Far outside the solar system, swarms of "dirty snowballs" called *comets* are concentrated in the Oort cloud. If a comet's distant orbit is disturbed, it may fall toward the Sun and create a spectacular display in the night sky. When a piece of interplanetary debris hits the Earth's atmosphere, it creates a *meteor,* sometimes called a shooting star, which burns up with a fiery trail. Occasionally, a meteor fragment will hit the Earth and become a *meteorite.*

KEY TERMS ABOUT THE SOLAR SYSTEM

solar system	nebula	core	comet
terrestrial planets (Mercury, Venus, Earth, Earth's Moon, Mars)	Pluto	mantle	meteor
	moons	crust	meteorite
Jovian planets (Jupiter, Saturn, Uranus, Neptune)	great bombardment	asteroid	
	differentiation	asteroid belt	

REVIEW QUESTIONS

1. Identify three distinctive characteristics of the orbits of planets and moons in the solar system.

2. Identify two distinctive characteristics of the distribution of mass in the solar system.

3. Briefly describe two classes of planets found in the solar system.

4. State the nebular hypothesis. How does it explain the orbits of the planets?

5. What are planetesimals and what role do they play in the formation of planets?

6. What is differentiation? How has this process affected the Earth?

7. Describe the layered structure of the Earth's interior.

8. How does the high pressure in the core affect chemical bonds?

9. What is the Earth's mantle? Of what elements is it made?

10. Describe the "big splash" theory of the Moon's origin.

11. Explain the importance of outgassing to the history of the Earth. Is it still going on today?

12. Explain the role of gravity in the evolution of a planet's atmosphere.

13. What is an asteroid? Where are most asteroids found?

14. What is the difference between a meteor and a meteorite?

15. What are comets made of? Where are most comets found?

16. How could asteroids and comets affect life on Earth?

17. Which planets have moons?

18. If Titan is almost as large as the planet Mercury, why is it considered a moon and not a planet?

DISCUSSION QUESTIONS

1. What distinctive characteristics of the Earth make it suitable for life? How has life altered the chemistry of the Earth's atmosphere?

2. Why are meteorites important to our study of the solar system?

3. Review the history of studies of the solar system. What new technologies have enhanced our ability to make observations on objects in the solar system?

4. What factors might influence the development of life on other planets?

5. What sources of data might help us determine more about how the Earth's Moon formed?

6. How does Clyde Tombaugh's work fit into the scientific method?

7. Do you think that we should continue to explore space? Why or why not?

8. Why do you suppose scientists worry about material from Earth contaminating the Mars sample?

9. Could material from Earth contaminate Mars? What effect might such contamination have on future missions to the planet?

PROBLEMS

1. Given the diameters of the planets in Table 16-1, what are the relative volumes of Earth, Mercury, and Jupiter? From the same table, what are the relative masses?

2. From the values of mass in Problem 1, calculate the densities (mass divided by volume) for Earth, Mercury, and Jupiter. Why do you think they are different?

3. How many asteroids 10 kilometers in diameter would be required to make a planet about the size of Mars? Neglect the effects of compression in the planet's interior.

4. If the average thickness of the Earth's crust is 10 kilometers, what fraction of the solid Earth's total volume is in the crust? What fraction is in the mantle?

INVESTIGATIONS

1. Investigate the history of unmanned planetary probes. What are the names, dates, and target planets of these probes? What countries sponsored them? What kinds of data did they return?

2. What planetary missions are now planned or underway? When will they begin to return data? What kinds of data are going to be gathered?

3. Read a history of the *Apollo* missions to the Moon. What theories about the Moon's origins prevailed before these missions? What new data changed theories about the origin of the Moon?

4. Investigate the discovery of the planet Uranus by William Herschel. What other astronomical contributions did members of the Herschel family make?

5. How would you respond to an argument that went as follows: No one was present when the Earth was formed, so how can scientists talk about the details of the formation process?

6. Listen to *The Planets*, a suite for orchestra by the British composer Gustav Holst. In what ways do the musical descriptions of each planet reflect the physi-

cal characteristics of that planet? What other sources of inspiration, besides scientific data, did Holst use in creating these pieces? Which planets did he omit and why?

7. There are many more meteor showers than the ones listed in Table 16-2. Find out which ones may be coming in the next month or two and plan a meteor-watching party.

8. Scientists are attempting to document the paths of asteroids with Earth-crossing orbits. Investigate this research and comment on the probability that a large asteroid might hit the Earth. Should we increase funding for asteroid monitoring?

WWW Resources

See *The Sciences* homepage at: **http://www.wiley.com/college/trefil** for valuable web links.

1. **http://www.seds.org/nineplanets/nineplanets/**
The Nine Planets: A Multimedia Tour of the Solar System—don't miss it.

2. **http://www.thetech.org/exhibits/online/satellite/**
The Satellite Site—besides learning about satellites, you can construct your own.

3. **http://space.jpl.nasa.gov**
Solar System Simulator, from NASA—view anything in the solar system from any perspective within it.

17

Plate Tectonics

Can we predict destructive earthquakes?

GREAT IDEA

The entire Earth is still changing, due to the slow convection of soft, hot rocks deep within the planet.

PHYSICS
Heat energy moves from the Earth's core to the surface primarily by the process of mantle convection.

CHEMISTRY
Chemical processes contribute to the gradual weathering of rocks. (Ch. 18)

ENVIRONMENT
Scientists have speculated that giant volcanic eruptions 250 million years ago caused mass extinctions of life on Earth. (Ch. 25)

GEOLOGY
New crustal rocks are created at divergent plate boundaries.

HEALTH & SAFETY
New buildings in earthquake-prone regions are designed to withstand violent wave-like motions of the ground.

ASTRONOMY
Radio astronomers have used distant quasars to measure the slow process of seafloor spreading.

TECHNOLOGY
Sensitive instruments developed to detect submarines during World War II were later used to measure the magnetism of rocks on the seafloor.

BIOLOGY
The shifting of continents has affected the distribution of land animals on Earth.

Red = applications of the great idea discussed in this chapter.

Orange = other applications, some of which are explored in other chapters.

Early afternoon at the beach: A cooling breeze has picked up off the water. The steady flow of air is wonderfully refreshing, though occasional gusts of wind kick up sand and grit. Some of that sand blows onto your beach towel and into your hair.

The wind is constantly moving soil at the Earth's surface, shifting and changing what is there. Shifting sand may seem a trivial phenomenon, but such gradual tiny daily changes add up to extraordinary transformations of the land over countless millions of years. Similar gradual movements of matter deep within our planet accomplish even more remarkable changes. The seemingly permanent continents and oceans of the Earth are also in constant motion. The continent of North America is about a meter farther from Europe than it was when you were born, the result of forces deep within the Earth.

The Earth's surface is always changing. No feature of the Earth—no desert or broad plain, no mountain or ocean—is permanent. Every feature is constantly evolving into something different.

The Dynamic Earth

Think about the last time that you passed a new construction site after a rain shower. You could probably see little valleys freshly carved by water running over the bare earth, and shallow pools where fine-grained material collected in layers—features that are small-scale examples of the erosion of soil by rain. If the earthmovers had dug a deep pit you might have noticed different layers of earth and rock freshly exposed—layers that represent sediments deposited by water long ago.

These sorts of small-scale changes in the Earth's surface are mirrored by much more dramatic large-scale changes. When Mount St. Helens, a volcano in Washington State, erupted in 1980, the entire side of a mountain was blown away and many square kilometers of forest were flattened. Large earthquakes in our lifetime will change the course of rivers and destroy villages and towns.

But how do we know that the Earth's surface is changing at larger scales? We rarely observe significant changes in the landscape, but you can make a simple estimate that will convince you that the Earth must be a very dynamic planet. Mountains appear to be as permanent as anything could be, yet, as we see in the following section, it is easy to convince yourself that mountains must wear away in times much shorter than the 4.5-billion-year age of the Earth. We will also see that continents are not as permanent as they appear to be.

SCIENCE BY THE NUMBERS •
How Long Could a Mountain Last?

While there is no such thing as a "typical" mountain, for the purposes of this rough estimate let's think of a mountain as a rectangular mass about 2 kilometers high, 4 kilometers long, and 4 kilometers wide (that's about 1.2 miles by 2.5 miles by 2.5 miles). The volume of this midsized mountain is

$$\text{volume} = \text{length} \times \text{height} \times \text{width}$$
$$= 2 \text{ km} \times 4 \text{ km} \times 4 \text{ km}$$
$$= 32 \text{ km}^3$$

Expressed in cubic meters, that is

$$2000 \text{ m} \times 4000 \text{ m} \times 4000 \text{ m} = 3.2 \times 10^{10} \text{ m}^3$$

Think about a stream running down a mountainside. You know that such a stream carries a certain amount of sand, silt, and dirt with it. You can see this because the stream has a sandy bottom, and you can watch it depositing sand in little eddies and still water along its side. You might also see gravel and boulders in the stream, evidence that, from time to time, heavy rains cause much more violent movement of material down the mountainside. That material had to be worn off of materials higher up on the mountain, so the existence of the stream means that the mountain is constantly being eroded away.

You can estimate how long a mountain might survive against erosion by a stream. Suppose, for example, that four principal streams run off the sides of the mountain, and that each stream carries an average of one-tenth of a cubic meter of earth per day off the mountain. (The actual amount would vary from day to day depending on the kind of rock, the amount of water flowing downhill, and other factors.) One-tenth of a cubic meter per day is not very much material. It's like a pile of sand, dirt, and gravel about 50 centimeters (a foot and a half) on a side, a pile that could fit under an ordinary kitchen chair. If you think about the amount of material you might collect if you put your hand down into a stream for a while, you'll see that the number is reasonable. Over a period of a year, the four streams might thus remove

$$4 \text{ streams} \times 0.1 \text{ meter}^3/\text{stream-day} \times 365 \text{ days/year} = 146 \text{ meter}^3/\text{year}$$

Every year, therefore, close to 150 cubic meters of material—about six dumptrucks full—could be removed from a mountain by normal erosional processes of streams.

Pike's Peak near Colorado Springs, Colorado, may be approximated as $2 \times 4 \times 4$ km rectangular block of rock.

(a)   (b)

Steep slopes and angular peaks characterize young mountains such as the 65-million-year-old Rocky Mountains in Alberta, Canada (*a*) photographed from Mt. Rae. The 400-million-year-old Great Smoky Mountains in North Carolina (*b*) display the rounded character of older mountains.

If the mountain streams remove about 150 cubic meters each year, then the lifetime of the mountain can't be much longer than the volume of the mountain divided by the volume lost each year:

$$\frac{3.2 \times 10^{10} \text{ m}^3}{(150 \text{ m}^3/\text{year})} = 0.0213 \times 10^{10} \text{ years}$$

$$= 213{,}000{,}000 \text{ years}$$

This estimate, while very rough and not directly applicable to any specific mountain, tells us that under normal circumstances, mountains can't last more than a few hundred million years. All mountains must disappear and be eroded away to low, rounded hills in times much shorter than the 4.5-billion-year age of the Earth. •

The Case of the Disappearing Mountains

We must conclude that if the erosion of mountains takes a few hundred million years, then any mountain that existed when the Earth first formed 4.5 billion years ago would have been worn away long ago, and the Earth's surface by now should be smooth and featureless. The only way that mountains could still exist on the surface of the Earth is for mountains to be continuously formed.

Everyday observations of erosion and some very simple arithmetic thus lead us to a startling conclusion: tremendous forces must be acting on the Earth, creating new mountain chains as the old ones are worn down. The surface of the Earth cannot be static. Although mountains seem to human beings to symbolize eternal solidity, they are transitory. Geologists who map the distribution and ages of rocks have shown that the Appalachian Mountains were formed a few hundred million years ago, and the Rocky Mountains only about 60 million years ago.

Newton's laws of motion (Chapter 2) tell us that nothing happens unless a force acts. What forces in the Earth could create entire mountain ranges? Until recently, this question remained one of the greatest puzzles in geology.

Volcanoes and Earthquakes—Evidence of Forces in the Earth

Most geological processes such as mountain building and erosion are slow by human standards and take thousands or millions of years to produce noticeable change. But volcanoes and earthquakes may transform a landscape in an instant, thus revealing the tremendous energy stored in our dynamic planet.

Volcanic eruptions provide the most spectacular process by which new mountains are formed. In a typical **volcano**, subsurface molten rock called *magma*, concentrated in the Earth's upper mantle or lower crust, breaks through to the surface, as shown in Figure 17-1. This breakthrough may be sudden, giving rise to the kind of dramatic events seen when Mount St. Helens exploded in 1980, or it may be relatively slow, with a stately surface flow of molten rock, known as *lava*. In both cases, however, magma eventually breaches the surface and hardens into new rock.

An **earthquake** occurs when rock suddenly breaks along a more-or-less flat surface, called a *fault*. Have you ever stretched a thick, strong elastic band, only to have it snap back painfully against your hand? You gradually added elastic potential energy to the band, and that energy was suddenly released—converted to violent kinetic energy. The same thing happens in an earthquake when stressed rock suddenly snaps.

When a brittle rock breaks, tremendous amounts of potential energy are released. The two sides of a fault can't fly apart like an elastic material can, so the energy is transmitted in the form of a sound wave or seismic wave (see Chapter 6). These waves, traveling at speeds of several kilometers per second, cause the ground

Mount St. Helens in Washington erupted in a violent explosion on May 18, 1980.

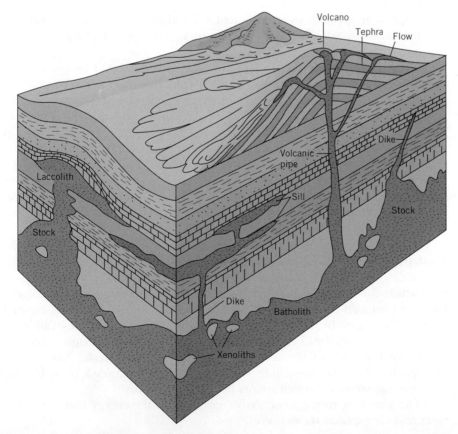

• **Figure 17-1** A cross section of a volcano reveals a magma chamber, which stores molten rock, and a system of pipes, cracks, and vents that lead to the surface. The terms in the orange area refer to the kinds of rock formations resulting from cooled magma. Xenoliths are the original rocks encased in this cooled magma.

In January 1995, a magnitude-7.2 earthquake caused extensive damage and loss of life in the city of Kobe, Japan.

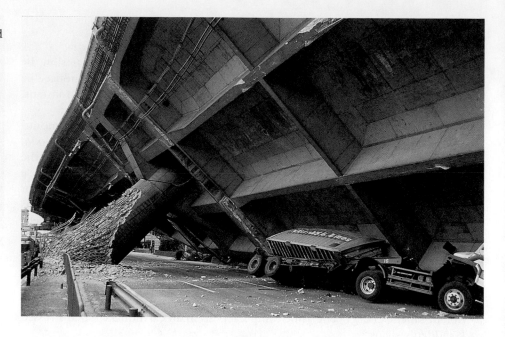

to rise and fall like the surface of the ocean. Normally "solid" ground sways and pitches in a motion that can cause severe damage to buildings and other structures. If an earthquake occurs under or near a large body of water, these violent motions of the ground can transfer energy into great waves that can devastate low-lying coastal areas. Such waves are often referred to as "tidal waves," though they are not caused by tides. A more correct term is *tsunamis,* a Japanese word for harbor or bay waves.

Great earthquakes, such as the one that killed 20,000 people in India in September 1993, are fortunately relatively rare. But smaller earthquakes, barely noticeable to the average person, occur every day by the thousands. Earthquakes were traditionally rated on the *Richter scale,* named after Charles Richter, the U.S. geologist who devised it. Technically, the Richter scale refers to the amount of ground motion that would be measured by an instrument a fixed distance from the center of the earthquake. The scale is such that each increase of 1 unit corresponds to 10 times more ground motion. Thus an earthquake that measures 7 will have 100 times more ground motion than one that measures 5, and so on. Today, a similar magnitude scale, based on energy release, is used.

Earthquakes that measure around 5 on the magnitude scale will be felt by most people, but will do little damage in areas with well-constructed buildings. An earthquake between 6 and 7 will do considerable damage to buildings, and a magnitude-8 earthquake will level large areas. The earthquake that occurred in the San Francisco Bay area in October 1989 measured 7.1, and was dubbed the "Pretty Big One" by Californians who are waiting for what they call the "Big One." The January 1993 earthquake that caused so much damage to the freeway system of Los Angeles measured 6.7 on the magnitude scale. No earthquakes greater than 9 on the magnitude scale have ever been recorded, probably because no rocks can store that much energy before they let go.

The puzzle remains, however: Where does all the energy that powers volcanoes and earthquakes come from?

The Movement of the Continents

Geologists have faced other mysteries as well. Think about a large map of the world. In your mind, move North and South America eastward toward Eurasia and Africa. Have you ever noticed how the two seem to fit together (Figure 17-2)?

English statesman and natural philosopher Francis Bacon (1561–1626) pointed out this fact in 1620. It wasn't until the beginning of the twentieth century, however, that anyone took the parallel coastlines seriously enough to ask about the origin of this pattern. In 1912, a German meteorologist named Alfred Wegener (1880–1930) proposed that Earth's continents are in motion. The reason that the Americas fit so well into the coastline of Europe and Africa, he suggested, is that they were once joined and have since been torn apart.

Wegener's theory, called *continental drift,* was dismissed by most earth scientists. He amassed some geological evidence to back it up, such as the matching locations of distinctive rock formations on opposite sides of the Atlantic Ocean. But most of this evidence was fragmentary and unconvincing to other scientists; indeed, some of Wegener's arguments later turned out to be wrong. Furthermore, he failed to provide a reasonable mechanism by which continents could move. For most of the twentieth century, continental drift was regarded as a far-fetched exercise in theory, and few geologists paid much attention to it. Beginning about 1960, however, geologists and oceanographers obtained new evidence to support one aspect of Wegener's notion—the idea that the continents are not fixed.

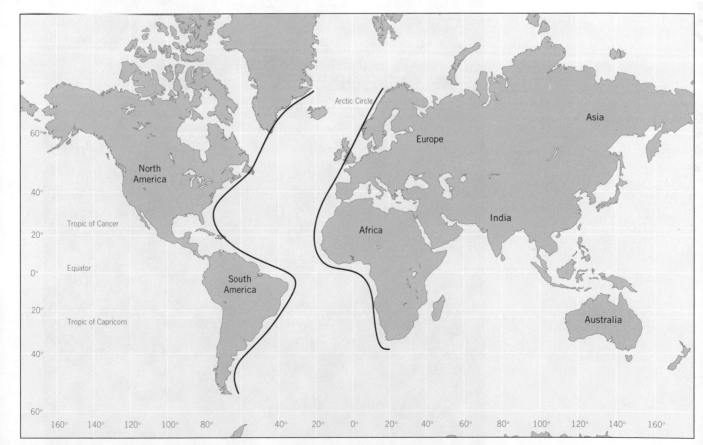

• **Figure 17-2** A map of the world's continents reveals the similar shapes of coastlines on the two sides of the Atlantic Ocean.

The discovery that continents do indeed move required the merging of very different kinds of newly acquired geological evidence—topographic profiles of the oceans' floors, maps of rock magnetism, and data on rock ages.

1. Ocean Floors

When the contours of ocean floors were mapped in the years following World War II, oceanographers discovered remarkable, unsuspected features. Most scientists thought that the deep ocean bottoms were simply flat plains, passively collecting the sediments that gradually eroded off the ancient continents. Instead they found steep-walled canyons and lofty mountains, indicating that the seafloor is as dynamic and changing as the continents themselves (Figure 17-3). The

• **Figure 17-3** A topographic map of ocean floors reveals dramatic mountain chains, deep flat planes, canyons, and trenches. These features suggest that ocean basins are active geological regions.

longest mountain range on Earth, for example, is not on a continent, but in the middle of the Atlantic Ocean. Called the *Mid-Atlantic Ridge,* this feature extends from Iceland in the North Atlantic to the South Sandwich Islands in the South Atlantic. These ridges are sites of continuous geological activity, including numerous earthquakes, volcanoes, and lava flows. Similar ridges, also called rises, were found on the floors of all the Earth's oceans. In fact, oceanographers have now mapped more than 85,000 km of ocean ridges.

2. Magnetic Reversals

To understand the nature of magnetic data, the second kind of evidence that pointed to continental motion, you have to recall that the Earth has a magnetic field with north and south magnetic poles. For reasons that are not fully understood, this field changes direction sporadically over time—something like an electromagnet in which the direction of current in the coils changes occasionally (see Chapter 5). Well over 300 reversals of the Earth's magnetic field have been recorded in ancient rocks spanning about 200 million years. During recent episodes of reversed fields, the north magnetic pole of the Earth was located somewhere in what is now Antarctica, and the south magnetic pole somewhere in the Canada-Greenland region.

When lava flows out of a fissure in the Earth, it contains small crystals of natural iron oxides, including the naturally magnetic mineral magnetite. These bits of iron ore act as tiny magnets, and because the rock is still in a fluid state, their magnetic dipoles are free to turn around and align themselves in a north–south direction parallel to the Earth's magnetic field. Think of them as small compass needles embedded in the fluid rock. Once the rock hardens, however, the bits of magnetite are frozen in place—they can no longer move. Thus the volcanic rock carries within it a memory of where the magnetic north pole was when the rock solidified. If we examine the tiny compass needles, we can tell whether the magnetic field of the Earth was oriented as it is today, or whether it was reversed. The field devoted to the study of this sort of effect is called *paleomagnetism,* and it came into maturity in the early 1960s.

In the mid-1950s, an oceanic exploration ship named *Pioneer* began taking magnetic measurements near the ocean floor off the coast of Washington State. At first the data made little sense, but as more and more profiles were obtained, a puzzling pattern of stripes on the ocean floor began to emerge. It seemed that there were parallel strips of rock in which the magnetic direction in neighboring strips alternated. (We show some of the original data in Figure 17-4.) Through the mid-1960s, Earth scientists collected more and more data of this type, and it soon became clear that the Mid-Atlantic Ridge, the East Pacific Rise, and many other places on ocean floors show the same pattern of alternating magnetic stripes.

How could these magnetic stripes be explained? In an environment in which the orientations of north and south magnetic poles were switching back and forth over time, the only way to get the observed striping is shown in Figure 17-5. The seafloor must be getting wider, a process called *seafloor spreading,* as new molten rock comes from deep within the Earth and erupts through fissures on the ocean bottom. Over time, this new rock will be pushed aside as the continents move apart and as more magma comes up to take its place. The "compass needles" in this newer rock will point to the location of the magnetic north pole when they reach the surface. Each new batch of magma will solidify and lock in the current magnetic orientation, despite any further reversals. Each time the Earth's magnetic field reverses, the dipole direction of the planet's magnetic field changes and gets locked into the newly formed rock. Thus, over long periods of time, we would expect to see alternating bands of magnetic orientation—exactly the kind of zebra-striped pattern of alternating north and south compass orientations shown in Figure 17-4.

• **Figure 17-4** Measurements in the late 1950s and early 1960s revealed magnetic stripes running nearly parallel to the Vancouver province and Washington State coastlines.

• **Figure 17-5** Magnetic stripes that parallel ocean ridges must form as new magma wells up from the fissure and pushes out to the sides. In this cross-sectional view, older rocks lie farther from the ridge. (The "lithosphere" includes the uppermost mantle and all of the crust.)

3. Rock Ages

The conclusions from magnetic data were reinforced by studies of the age of volcanic rocks in the oceanic crust. Volcanic rocks contain radioactive isotopes that can be used for dating (see Chapter 12). Rocks near the Mid-Atlantic Ridge and other similar features were found to be quite young, a few million years old or less. Rocks collected successively farther away from the ridge proved to be successively older.

 Stop and Think! Given what you know about the scientific method, why do you suppose scientists accept the movement of continents as a fact today, but didn't accept it in Wegener's time?

New Support for the Theory

The new data on the topography of ocean floors, as well as the magnetic properties and ages of its rocks, suggested to many scientists that the width of the Atlantic Ocean must be increasing yearly as the seafloor spreads. Eurasia and North America, it appears, are moving apart. Could the hypothesis that this distance is increasing be tested by an experimental measurement?

Up until the late 1980s no one was able to measure the motion of continents directly. The breakthrough came from an unexpected source—radio astronomy. Astronomers in North America and Europe trained radio telescopes on distant quasars (see Chapter 15). By measuring the times of arrival of the crests of the same radio wave, astronomers were able to get very accurate measurements of the distance between their telescopes. By repeating these sorts of experiments over a period of a few years, they were able to measure exactly the separation of the continents. Their work shows that North America is separating from Europe at the rate of about 5 centimeters (about 2 inches) a year.

SCIENCE BY THE NUMBERS •

The Age of the Atlantic Ocean

If continents are constantly moving at speeds up to several centimeters per year, what would a map of Earth's surface have looked like millions of years ago? We can make an educated guess by using present rates of movement and "reversing the tape," so to speak. We know, for example, that the floor of the Atlantic Ocean is spreading at about 5 cm per year. Assuming that the rate of spreading has remained more or less constant, how old is the Atlantic Ocean?

To calculate the answer, we need to apply the familiar equation for travel time:

$$\text{time of travel} = \text{distance/speed}$$

(You use the same relationship every time you estimate the driving time for a vacation.) The speed in this equation is the spreading rate, 5 cm per year, and the present width of the Atlantic is approximately 7000 km, or 7×10^8 cm. The Atlantic Ocean began to open, therefore, at

$$\text{time} = \frac{7 \times 10^8 \text{ cm}}{(5 \text{ cm/yr})}$$
$$= 1.4 \times 10^8 \text{ years}$$
$$= 140 \text{ million years}$$

By this calculation, 140 million years ago Europe and the Americas must have been joined together because there was no Atlantic Ocean! In fact, by retracing

• **Figure 17-6** Once the motion of continents was determined, scientists could predict how the Earth's surface might have looked in the past. More than 200 million years ago, the present-day continents were joined together as the ancient continent Pangaea.

240 million years ago

120 million years ago

Present

the wandering paths of continents, earth scientists have discovered that 200 million years ago what we now call the continents of North America, South America, Eurasia, and Africa were locked together in one giant continent called *Pangaea* (Figure 17-6). A globe of that ancient Earth would be all but unrecognizable, with a huge landmass on one side and a giant ocean on the other.

By the same token, 100 million years from now the Earth's continents will have moved thousands of kilometers and appear completely different from today's arrangement. •

Plate Tectonics: A Unifying View of the Earth

The compelling model of the dynamic Earth that has emerged from studies of paleomagnetism, rock dating, and much other data is called **plate tectonics**. "Tectonics" is related to the word "architect" and carries the connotation of building or putting things together. Plate tectonics develops a picture of the world that explains many of the Earth's large-scale surface features and related phenomena.

The central idea of the plate tectonics theory is that the surface of the Earth is broken up into about a dozen large pieces (as well as a number of smaller ones) called **tectonic plates** (Figure 17-7). Each plate is a rigid, moving sheet of rock up to 100 km (60 miles) thick, composed of the crust and part of the upper

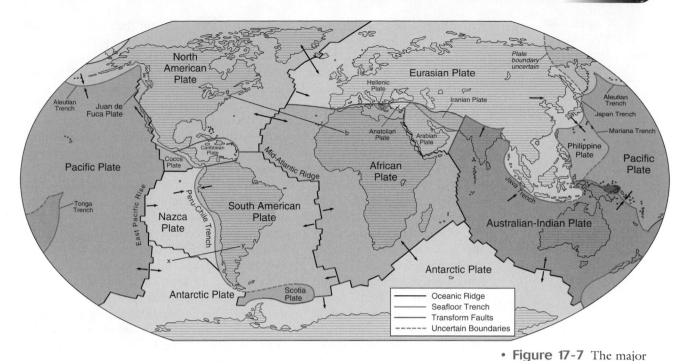

• **Figure 17-7** The major plates of the Earth with their directions of motion shown by arrows.

mantle. Oceanic plates have an average 8- to 10-km thickness of dense rock known as *basalt* on top of the mantle rock. Continental plates have an average 35-km thickness of lower-density rock, such as *granite*, capping the basalt.

The tectonic plate boundaries are not the same as those of the continents and oceans. Some plates have continents on all or part of their surface, while some are covered only by oceanic crust. Most of the North American continent, for example, rests on the 8000-km-wide North American Plate, which extends from the middle of the Atlantic Ocean to the Pacific Plate on the West Coast.

About one quarter of the Earth's surface is covered by continent; the rest is ocean. On time scales of millions of years, the plates shift about on the planet's surface, carrying the continents with them like passengers on a raft. Thus it is not the motion of the continents themselves that is fundamental to understanding the dynamics of the Earth, but the constant motion of the underlying plates. Continental motion (what Wegener called continental drift) is just one manifestation of that plate motion.

The Convecting Mantle

Nothing happens without a force. What force could possibly be large enough to move not only the continents, but also the plates of which they are a part? Many geophysicists accept the theory that continents move as a result of the force generated by **mantle convection** deep within the Earth—motions driven by our planet's internal heat energy.

Two sources of energy contribute to Earth's interior heat. Some of this heat energy is left over from the gravitational potential energy released during the great bombardment and differentiation of the mantle and core as the Earth formed (see Chapter 16). The decay of uranium and other radioactive elements (see Chapter 12), which is fairly common throughout the Earth's core and mantle, provides a second important source of heat energy. These elements decay over time and produce energetic, fast-moving decay products, particles that collide with atoms and molecules in surrounding rocks and give up their energy as heat. Deep in the Earth, all this heat energy softens rocks to the point that they can flow slowly like hot taffy.

In Chapter 4 we saw that heat energy, once generated, must move spontaneously toward cooler regions. The heat generated in the interior of the Earth, for example, must eventually be radiated into space. If the Earth were somewhat smaller, or if only small amounts of heat were generated, the energy could be carried to the surface entirely by conduction—the movement of heat by atomic collisions. This process operates in the Moon and Mars, for example. In the case of the Earth, however, there is too much internal heat to be carried by conduction alone. Rocks in the mantle have been heated to the point where they are able to flow, and deep within the mantle of the Earth immense convection cells are set up. According to this model, the rocks of the mantle behave like water in a boiling pot.

There are, of course, very important differences between the Earth's mantle and a boiling pot—in particular, the time scales. Solid rock cannot flow significantly on time scales comparable to human lifetimes. But give soft, hot rocks a few hundred million years and they can move large distances. Earth scientists now estimate that the Earth's convection cells go through a full cycle—with hot rocks rising from the lower mantle, cooling near the surface, and falling back to be replaced by other, warmer rocks—on a time scale of about 200 million years. In effect, the Earth behaves something like a giant spherical stove, with burners on the inside and circulating rocks bringing the heat to the surface.

At the very top, these partially molten, circulating mantle rocks encounter the comparatively thin plates that cover the surface in a relatively cool, brittle layer. Along the oceanic ridges the brittle plates fracture and basaltic lava erupts, initiating seafloor spreading and plate motion. The plates move along with the convection cells underneath them, more or less as a film of oil on boiling water would move along on top of the water. The plates shift around, bash into each other, join each other, and are split apart in a constant dance. And on top of these plates, floating along like a thin scum, with no control whatsoever over their destiny, are the continents—the places that we call the "solid Earth."

THE ONGOING PROCESS OF SCIENCE •

A Competing Model

Recently, a number of geophysicists have challenged their colleagues with a new twist on models of plate tectonics. In the "old" model, seafloor spreading is driven primarily from the inside by mantle convection; hot upwelling mantle rocks push apart thin, brittle plates at the surface. In the new model, the process is driven primarily from the outside, with gravity pulling cold, dense plate material at the surface down into the mantle. According to this model, seafloor spreading results from two plates being pulled apart, which leaves a gaping trench that must be filled with magma from below. Both models are now being put to the test by geophysicists around the world. •

 Stop and Think! How might you test the two competing models described above? Could both be correct?

The theory of plate tectonics caused a revolution in the earth sciences. For the first time, evidence from many different earth science disciplines had been brought together to form a single, coherent picture of our planet. This theory includes the oceans, the landmasses, the planet's deep interior, and the interconnections between all these systems. There was a time when geologists of different specialties—women and men who studied the ocean currents or ancient fossils, ore deposits or the planet's deep interior—had little to say to each other. That situation is no longer true. All of these different disciplines now share a common way of looking at the Earth, and thus are able to give each other ideas and gain breadth and depth from interactions with each other. It may be that your college or university no longer has a department of geology but instead has a department called earth sciences or environmental sciences. These changes in name are more than just bureaucratic shufflings. They represent a very real change in the way scientists view and study the Earth.

SCIENCE IN THE MAKING •

Reactions to Plate Tectonics

At first, geologists confronted by the observations of magnetic stripes on the ocean floors, rock ages, and other seemingly odd data tried to find an explanation that did not require new seafloor to be created. All geologists had been taught a "fixed Earth" model in their college courses, and that was the standard picture of our planet they used in their work. Most of these scientists were not prepared to accept this radical new idea, that the continents might actually move, without a fight.

Some experts questioned the statistical significance of the magnetic data, and they wondered whether the distinctive striped patterns weren't the result of some as-yet-unknown effect (such as small electrical currents running around the ocean floor). Others simply tried to ignore the whole thing. But as geologists and oceanographers collected more data—as new measurements of magnetic patterns and more precise rock ages were obtained—the evidence for seafloor spreading simply became overwhelming.

In a very short time, less than a decade from the time the first puzzling data from the *Pioneer* expedition came in, geologists had for the most part accepted a theory that radically changed many of the central principles of their discipline. This dramatic change in perspective brings us back to a point we made in Chapter 1. Good scientists will eventually accept the implications of their observations, whether those implications violate preconceived concepts or not. A scientist can't look at data without some preconceived notions. Few scientists, for example, took the original continental drift arguments of Wegener seriously because, in part, no obvious mechanism could cause entire continents to move.

We should note in passing that, although Wegener's theory contained one feature of modern theories, namely moving continents, continental drift was not plate tectonics. It predicted, for example, that the average elevation of continents would increase with time—a prediction not confirmed by careful measurements. But as more and more data supported the more-convincing plate tectonics model, the majority of earth scientists readily changed their notions as the data demanded it.

The fact that the fixed Earth—one of the most revered and widely accepted geological theories—could be abandoned in the space of a few years when confronted by powerful contrary evidence indicates that the scientific method works. It also shows that many of the arguments one hears from the proponents of pseudosciences such as UFOs, astrology, creation science, and the like—arguments to the effect that the scientific community routinely closes its mind to new ideas and will not accept them—are simply wrong. Scientific theories, unlike the untestable claims of pseudoscience, are subject to repeated scrutiny and can be falsified. When confronted with overwhelming evidence, scientists are, indeed, prepared to accept new ideas and abandon the old "conventional wisdom." •

A satellite photograph of a portion of Africa's Great Rift Valley. The narrow body of water defines a divergent plate boundary where new plate material is being created and plates are moving out to either side.

Plate Boundaries

The boundaries between the Earth's tectonic plates are active sites that determine much of the geological character of the surface. Three main types of boundaries separate the Earth's tectonic plates: divergent, convergent, and transform.

1. Divergent Plate Boundaries

We saw one aspect of plate motion when we talked about seafloor spreading at the Mid-Atlantic Ridge, where new plate material is formed. We can now understand how such a spreading feature arises. In Figure 17-8, we show what happens when plates happen to lie above a zone where magma comes to the surface. Not only does the volcanic action form a chain of mountains, but the motion of the magma also pushes the two adjoining plates farther and farther away from each other. The newly erupted molten material cools to rock and becomes new plate material. As the brittle tectonic plates crack and separate, shallow earthquakes of relatively low energy occur. This mechanism drives the seafloor spreading that gave us our first indication of the nature of continental motion. Such a spreading zone of crustal formation is called a **divergent plate boundary**.

When a divergent plate boundary occurs on the ocean floor, the seafloor spreads, basalt lava erupts from the newly created fissures, the two plates are pushed apart, and any continents that might be located on other portions of those plates are pushed apart as well. Eurasia and North America, for example, are separating right now at the rate of about 5 cm per year; consequently, the Atlantic Ocean is getting wider. Note that old spreading centers, such as the Mid-Atlantic Ridge, are always located in the middle of an ocean.

New spreading centers, on the other hand, may begin anywhere, even in the middle of a continent. If a continent happens to be sitting above what will eventually become a divergent plate boundary, then the continent itself will be literally torn apart. The Great East African Rift Valley, which extends south from Ethiopia, along the east coastal interior of central Africa to the coast of Mozambique, and north into Israel and Syria, is a modern-day example of this motion. Millions of years in the future, an ocean may separate the western part of Africa from the eastern part. In fact, at the point where the Great Rift Valley crosses the African coast, this sea is already beginning to form. Look at the Dead Sea, Red Sea, and Gulf of Aqaba and you will see this rift in progress.

2. Convergent Plate Boundaries

The Earth is not getting any larger. If new material pushes tectonic plates apart at places such as the oceanic ridges, then old plate material must be pushed together

• **Figure 17-8** A divergent plate boundary defines a line along which new plate material is formed from volcanic rock.

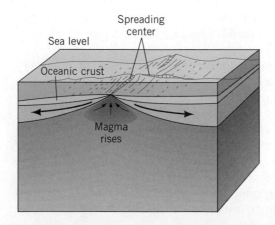

and taken into the Earth somewhere else. A place where two plates are coming together is called a **convergent plate boundary**.

At most convergent plate boundaries, one plate sinks beneath another to form a **subduction zone**. The plate that is subducted, or "taken beneath," in this way sinks down to rejoin the mantle material from which it came.

Earth scientists observe three broadly different kinds of surface features associated with convergent plate boundaries, all shown in Figure 17-9. First, if no continents are on the leading edge of either of the two converging plates, the result will be a *deep ocean trench*. As one plate penetrates into the Earth, it can bend and buckle the adjacent plate to produce a deep furrow in the ocean floor. Melting of the subducting slab at depths of 100 or 200 km can generate magma. The hot magma slowly rises toward the surface and, if the magma penetrates the overlying ocean crust, continuing eruptions of lava will build a chain of volcanic

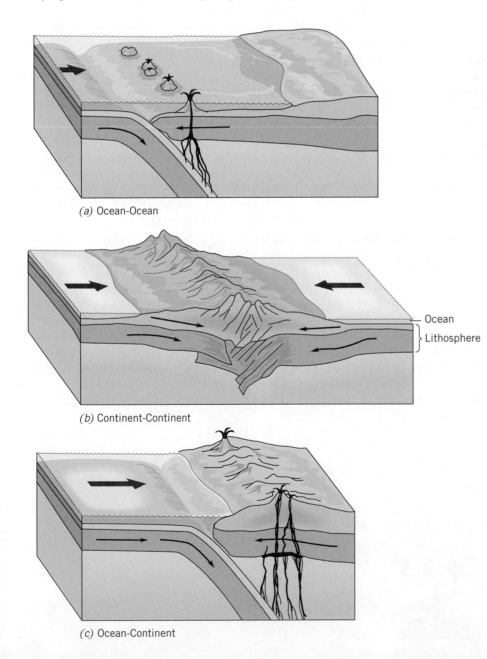

(a) Ocean-Ocean

(b) Continent-Continent

Ocean
Lithosphere

(c) Ocean-Continent

• **Figure 17-9** Convergent plate boundaries may display a variety of surface features, depending on the distribution of continental material. (*a*) When neither tectonic plate carries continental material at the convergent boundary, then a subduction zone is formed. A deep ocean trench and chain of island volcanoes are often created in this case. (*b*) When both tectonic plates carry continental material at the boundary, the continental materials buckle and fold to form nonvolcanic mountains. (*c*) When only one tectonic plate carries continental material at the boundary, the oceanic plate will subduct beneath the continent. A deep trench may form offshore and a coastal mountain range will form on land.

The San Andreas Fault in California marks the transform boundary between the North American Plate and the Pacific Plate.

islands adjacent to the trench. The Marianas Trench, the deepest point in the world's oceans (11 km or about 7 mi deep, 2 km deeper than Mt. Everest is high) near the volcanic coastline of the Philippines, is an example of just such a subduction zone and volcanic terrain.

If continents ride on top of both converging plates, they will collide. Continental material will be compressed together like crumpled cloth and pushed up to form a high, jagged mountain chain. The Himalayas, for example, which began to form about 30 million years ago, are still growing taller at about 1 cm per year as the once-separate Indian subcontinent collides with Asia. Similarly, the Ural Mountains mark the point at which Europe and Asia were welded together, and the Alps mark the point at which the Italian peninsula was joined to Europe. All of these geological processes involve the production of midcontinent mountain chains.

Finally, if a continent rests at the leading edge of only one of the two colliding plates, the denser oceanic plate will subduct beneath the continent. Just as in the case where two oceanic plates converge, a deep trench may form a short distance offshore, while the continental material may be crumpled into a coastal mountain range. In addition, the subducting tectonic slab may partially melt and thus provide magma that rises to form a chain of volcanic mountains parallel to the coast. The Andes Mountains of South America and the Cascade Mountains of the northwestern United States are spectacular examples of this phenomenon.

Roughly speaking, oceanic plate material on the Earth renews itself about every 200 million years. The process of seafloor spreading and subduction is constantly replacing the ocean crust, while the lower-density continental plate material experiences no subduction. This process explains why, whereas some rocks on ancient continents formed billions of years ago and are still preserved there, no rocks on the ocean floor are older than about 200 million years.

3. Transform Plate Boundaries

The third kind of boundary between plates occurs when one plate scrapes past the other, with no new plate material being produced. This kind of plate contact is called a **transform plate boundary** and is shown in Figure 17-10. The most famous transform boundary (and the only active plate boundary in the continental United States) is the San Andreas Fault in California. At the San Andreas Fault, the Pacific Plate is moving northwestward with respect to the North American Plate at the rate of several centimeters a year.

The process by which two plates slide past each other is not smooth. Over time, the motion of plates compresses and strains rocks at the boundary. Friction normally prevents the stressed rocks from moving, but periodically the rocks sim-

• **Figure 17-10a** A transform plate boundary, showing the relative motions of the adjacent plates.

ply break, moving as much as several meters in one sudden burst. When they do so, an earthquake occurs. No mountain building or volcanism is associated with transform boundaries.

THE SCIENCE OF LIFE •

Upright Posture

Have you ever wondered why human beings are among the very few animals on the Earth that walk upright? Most scientists today suspect that it was the adaptation of upright walking, which freed our hands, that led eventually to the use of tools and development of increased brain size in humans. Richard Leakey, a well-known anthropologist, has suggested that our upright posture might have resulted indirectly from movements of the Earth's tectonic plates.

His argument goes like this: 30 million years ago, most of eastern Africa was covered by a lush jungle. No fewer than 20 different species of apes, including our ancestral species, flourished in that environment and were especially well adapted to living in trees. When a divergent boundary started to pull the continent apart along the East African Rift Valley, the environment started to change. The forest began to disappear, to be replaced first by open plains dotted with stands of trees, and finally, 3 million years ago, by the savannah that exists there today. Most of the apes became extinct long before our 3-million-year-old ancestors, but Leakey argues that walking upright and being able to get from one forest "island" to another would have been a distinct advantage in that sort of environment. The result, according to Leakey, is that today there are only three kinds of descendants from those apes in Africa—gorillas, chimpanzees, and human beings. •

The Geological History of North America

The epic movements of tectonic plates provided geologists with a new way of thinking about the history of the Earth's surface. Earth scientists now use our understanding of plate tectonics to tell us something about the formation of our own continent. The oldest parts of the North American continent are in northeastern Canada and Greenland. Here we find large geological formations of rocks several billion years old that form the core of the continent (see Appendix C for the geological time scale). Over long periods of time, land was added to this continent by tectonic activity. Most of the western part of the United States, for example, is made up of small chunks of land called *terranes*—masses of rock several hundred kilometers across. Originally, these terranes were large islands in the Pacific Ocean, but they were carried toward the North American continent by plate activity and added to the mainland as tectonic plates converged. The hills near Wichita, Kansas, for example, are old mountains that once marked the addition of a large South American terrane onto what then comprised North America. (The idea that Wichita might have once had oceanfront property is one of the strange discoveries that comes out of plate tectonics.)

The Appalachian Mountains, which may at one time have rivaled the Himalayas in majesty, were formed over a period from about 450 to 300 million years ago when the continents that are now Eurasia and Africa rammed into the continent that is now North America. A series of long folds and fractures, structures that formed the present-day Appalachian Mountains, appeared in the surface rocks. This process explains, for example, why roads in the mountainous regions of the eastern part of the United States tend to run from southwest to

Kaibab-Toroweap Limestone

Permian period
290 mya–248 mya

Coconino Sandstone

Hermit Shale

Pennsylvanian period
323 mya–290 mya — Supai Sandstone

Mississippian period
354 mya–323 mya — Redwall Limestone

Ordovician period
490 mya–443 mya — Muav Limestone

Brighter Angel Shale

Cambrian period
543 mya–490 mya

Tapeats Sandstone

• **Figure 17-10b** The dramatic rock exposures of the Grand Canyon reveal hundreds of millions of years of Earth history. Rock formations are successively older as you approach the canyon floor.

northeast. They follow the mountain valleys that were created by erosion of these folded rocks. Thick wedges of sediments eroded off the mountains, forming the Coastal Plains of eastern North America and contributing to the sediments of the Great Plains.

The dramatic geological features of the western United States record a great variety of mountain-forming events. The Rocky Mountains rose approximately 60 million years ago from a broad warping and subsequent folding and fracturing of continental material. The Colorado Plateau, comprising parts of the states of Colorado, Arizona, and New Mexico, experienced a more gentle uplift, as rivers incised features such as the Grand Canyon. The Sierra Nevada range formed more recently when molten rock pushed up a huge block of sediments. These processes of uplift and erosion continue to this day in many places around the world.

Another Look at Volcanoes and Earthquakes

Plate tectonics provides us with a dynamic picture of the Earth. Plates are continually moving over the hot, partially molten rocks in the mantle. They crash together, rip apart, and scrape by each other. In the process, tall mountain chains are uplifted and worn down, and wide ocean basins are opened and closed as continents come together and split apart. Nothing on Earth is permanent, because heat continuously flows from the hot interior to the cooler surface, and mantle convection provides the primary mechanism for that heat transfer. The scale of these ongoing processes is vast, nearly outside our ability to comprehend, but we are occasionally reminded of the power of geological processes.

For thousands of years humans have realized that the Earth's most violent events—volcanoes and earthquakes—do not occur randomly. Earthquakes are common in California and Alaska, but extremely rare in Kansas or Florida. Volcanoes are commonplace in Hawaii and the Pacific Northwest, but never appear in New York or Texas. Why should this be? Plate tectonics provides an answer.

Plates and Volcanism

The global distribution of volcanoes may be understood in terms of the principles of plate tectonics. Volcanoes are common in three geological situations: along divergent plate boundaries, near convergent plate boundaries, or above places called "hot spots."

1. Divergent Plate Boundaries

The formation of new crust along volcanic spreading ridges of divergent plate boundaries is the principal way that new crustal rocks are formed. New basaltic plate material forms at the rate of a few centimeters per year along about 85,000 km of oceanic ridges around the world.

2. Convergent Plate Boundaries

Volcanoes are also common near subduction zones, except where two continental tectonic plates collide. As water-rich crustal material plunges into the mantle it becomes hotter and may partially melt. This magma, which is highly mobile fluid rock, rises to the surface to form chains of volcanoes, typically about 200 km inland from the line of subduction. The "Ring of Fire," a dramatic string of volcanoes that borders much of the Pacific Ocean, is a direct consequence of plate subduction (Figure 17-11).

The volcanoes that form the Cascade Mountain chain along the northwestern coast of the United States (including Mount Rainier and Mount St. Helens) are striking examples of the processes associated with subduction of an oceanic plate beneath a continent. Frequent dramatic eruptions of similar volcanoes in Central America, Japan, and the Philippines point to other places where subduction and volcanism occur in tandem.

3. Hot Spots

Finally, **hot spots** are a dramatic type of volcanism indirectly associated with plate tectonics. Earth scientists recognize dozens of hot spots around the world,

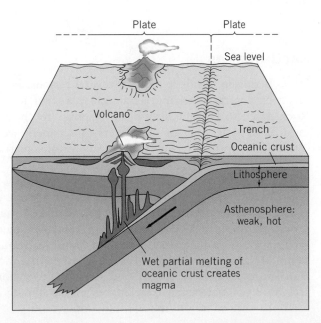

• **Figure 17-11** Volcanoes form above a subduction zone when heated plate material partially melts. The hot magma rises through the overlying crust to form a chain of volcanic islands.

• **Figure 17-12** The Hawaiian Islands stretch along a northwest–southeast line that reveals the north-westerly motion of the Pacific Plate over a fixed hot spot. As the Pacific Plate moves, new volcanic islands are created to the southeast, while older islands erode away. The island of Kauai, currently the oldest, is between 3 and 5.5 million years old, while Hawaii, the youngest island, is less than 0.8 million years old.

including Hawaii, Yellowstone Park, Iceland, and others where large isolated chimney-like columns of rising hot rock, also known as mantle plumes, rise to the surface more or less like bubbles coming to the surface in water being heated on a stove. These plumes may originate in the lower mantle or even at the core–mantle boundary. On a geological time scale, sources of hot spots are rela-tively stationary, so if a tectonic plate slowly moves over the fixed hot spot, the result will be a chain of volcanoes like the Hawaiian Islands that are built through a series of basaltic lava eruptions (Figure 17-12). These islands were created one at a time as the Pacific Plate moved above the localized hot spot. The present-day volcano Kilauea on the "big island" of Hawaii, the site of most of the island chain's active volcanism, is directly over a hot spot. The volcanic islands to the northwest are progressively older, as well as smaller owing to erosion, revealing that the motion of the Pacific Plate is also toward the northwest. In fact, a series of eroded submarine peaks that were islands millions of years ago stretches hun-dreds of kilometers farther to the northwest. In several million years, the most northwesterly of the present Hawaiian islands will have been eroded beneath the waves, but new volcanic activity has already begun on the ocean floor southeast of Kilauea, promising a new island that has already been given the name "Loihi" by islanders.

Earthquakes

Stress builds up in brittle rock for several reasons. Heated rock expands and cool-ing rock contracts—changes that cause a solid formation to warp and distort. Rock may also become stressed in response to changes in pressure, as overlying mountains wear away or new layers of sediment weigh down. And, of course, stress builds up to extreme levels as two tectonic plates attempt to move past each other at a transform plate boundary.

Earthquakes may be felt near any plate boundary. Minor shallow earthquakes occur near divergent plate boundaries as two oceanic plates move apart. Stronger earthquakes, including "deep-focus" earthquakes originating more than 100 km down, occur near subduction zones. Many of the most destructive shocks in Japan are of this type. In the United States, earthquakes at the transform plate boundary along the San Andreas Fault receive the most attention because of the fault's unusual activity, length, and proximity to major population centers. There are, however, occasional earthquakes in the middle of plates—in Missouri, for example—whose origins are not fully understood.

Seismology: Exploring the Earth's Interior with Earthquakes

Scientists who study earthquakes have discovered that these violent events provide the best means for exploring the deep interior of our planet. Geologists can't get their hands on much more than the outer 10 km or so of rock layers. Everything we know about the interior of the Earth deeper than a few kilometers has to be obtained by indirect means. The science of **seismology**, the study and measurement of sound vibrations within Earth, is dedicated to deducing our planet's inner structure.

The basic idea of seismology is simple. When an earthquake or explosion occurs, waves of vibrational energy (see Chapter 5) move out through the rocks. Some of these waves travel through the center of the Earth, some move along the surface, and still others bounce off layers deep within the planet.

So-called seismic waves come in two principal types. *Compressional* or *longitudinal waves* are like sound—the molecules in the rock move back and forth in the same direction as the wave. *Shear waves*, on the other hand, are *transverse waves*, like water waves in which the molecules move up and down perpendicular to the direction of wave motion. These kinds of waves travel through rock at different velocities depending, among other things, on the rock type, its temperature, and the pressure. After a major earthquake scientists at laboratories around the world record the intensity and time of arrival of the various kinds of waves, both those that pass along the surface and those that pass through the interior of the Earth (Figure 17-13). By comparing the arrival behavior of waves from the

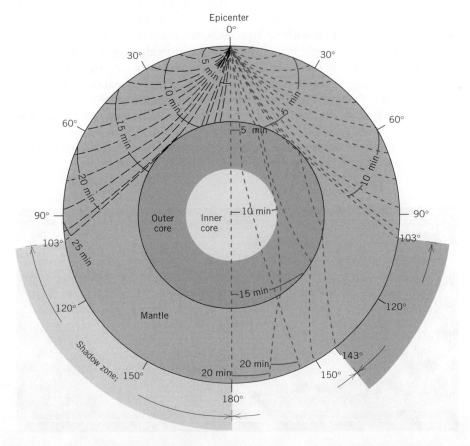

• **Figure 17-13** Seismic waves passing through the Earth can take a variety of paths. The speeds of *P* or compressional waves (shown in red) and *S* or shear waves (in black) will be different depending on the type of rock, its temperature, and the pressure. *S* waves, furthermore, cannot travel through the liquid outer core.

same earthquake at many different sites on the Earth, a computer can construct a picture of the material through which those waves passed.

THE ONGOING PROCESS OF SCIENCE •

Seismic Tomography

The picture of the Earth we give in Chapter 16, in which we talk about the solid and liquid core, the layered mantle, and the thin brittle crust, comes from studies of seismic waves. Now, as more and more seismic data are collected, and ever-faster computers permit new ways to process those data, a new branch of Earth science called *seismic tomography* is enabling geophysicists to obtain astonishing three-dimensional pictures of the Earth's interior (Figure 17-14). We are now able to document the basic movements of cold subducting slabs, hot upwelling mantle plumes, and the convection cells that characterize plate tectonics. •

TECHNOLOGY •

The Design of Earthquake-Resistant Buildings

Most of the people who die in earthquakes die because of falling buildings, not because of the violent shaking. Over the past few decades, structural engineers have learned a great deal about how to design buildings so that they do not collapse during an earthquake. The basic problem they face is how to construct a building that will maintain its integrity when the ground on which it sits moves. There are two general solutions to this problem—make it flexible, or make it rigid.

The first strategy, widely used in designing tall buildings, is best typified by a tree bending in the wind. A building with a specially reinforced steel skeleton can be designed so that it will bend and vibrate as the ground shakes, but come back to its original orientation without damage when the quake stops.

The second approach is widely used in individual houses and apartment buildings. The idea is to construct the building so that it tosses about on the moving surface like a ship on the ocean. The main preoccupation of the engineers is to guarantee that the building's corners are maintained at 90 degrees, no matter how much it moves around, by reinforcement of corners and rigid connections to the foundation and roof. Sometimes this rigidity can be obtained simply by covering all the walls of the building with plywood sheets before the outer siding is installed. •

• **Figure 17-14** A seismic tomograph provides a picture of the Earth's deep interior, based on millions of individual measurements of seismic wave velocities. This image reveals hot rocks (red) around the Pacific Ocean rim, and cooler rocks (blue) under the continents.

Science News | Mapping with Grace
(SCIENCE NEWS, JAN. 4, 2003, P. 6)

The gravitational pull of the Earth would be the same everywhere on the surface if the Earth were a perfect sphere and if the density of the planet were perfectly uniform. In point of fact, however, neither of these conditions is actually met. The Earth bulges slightly at the equator (so that you weigh less there than at the poles), and the density of the planet varies from one point to the next, with the pull of gravity being stronger over a point of high density than it is over one of low density. Scientists map out the gravitational field of the Earth by measuring the way that irregularities affect the orbits of satellites in orbit.

In March 2002, a pair of spacecrafts called the Gravity Recovery and Climate Experiment (GRACE) was launched to carry out this task to unprecedented accuracy. By measuring how the distance between the satellites changes (for example, when one is pulled forward in its orbit by a massive object like a mountain), the Earth's field can be mapped. Preliminary results indicate that this map will be 1000 times more accurate than the ones we have had to date. Some scientists have suggested that maps of this accuracy could be used to monitor changes like the growth or shrinkage of the Antarctic ice sheet.

Thinking More About | Plate Tectonics

Earthquake Prediction

One of the most important roles scientists can play in modern society is to provide warnings of natural disasters such as earthquakes, volcanic eruptions, and large storms. In the fall of 1999, for example, early warnings allowed thousands of Florida residents to escape the path of Hurricane Andrew. The storm caused billions of dollars of property damage, but surprisingly little loss of life. Similarly, volcanic eruptions, which are usually preceded by numerous small earthquakes, also can be forecast with some certainty. The successful prediction of Mount Pinatubo's 1991 eruption in the Philippines gave thousands of people living on the flanks of the long-dormant volcano time to flee.

But earthquake prediction is another story. Earthquakes occur because of the predictable and measurable gradual buildup of stresses in the Earth's crust. But the sudden failure of rock is not so predictable. You are familiar with this situation if you've ever gradually bent a pencil to the breaking point. It's easy to predict that a bent pencil will eventually break, but it's very hard to say exactly at what point the failure will occur. Much of the scientific effort related to earthquake prediction centers on the careful documentation of stress buildup in earthquake-prone areas. But these measurements alone tell us little about the exact time when failure will occur.

In their efforts to predict earthquakes, many scientists search for "precursor events"—measurable phenomena that precede a quake. There is much anecdotal evidence that such events may indeed occur. Folklore has it that some domesticated animals become highly agitated before a strong earthquake, or that changes are seen in the flow of well water or hot springs. Recognition of such changes enabled Chinese scientists to save many lives prior to a major 1975 earthquake. Similarly, scientists have noticed changes in the regularity of geysers and have recorded swarms of minor quakes just prior to some big earthquakes. Nevertheless, no reliable methods for predicting earthquakes have yet been devised. At best, we can reliably predict the probability that a large earthquake might occur in a given area during a period of a few decades.

Ironically, if we do develop a way to predict the timing of earthquakes precisely, a whole new series of problems could arise. Suppose you could predict with 80% certainty that there will be a major earthquake in the Los Angeles Basin sometime in the next 30 days. Would you then announce it? What would happen in the Los Angeles Basin if you made such an announcement? What would happen if you made the announcement and the earthquake never occurred? What would happen if you didn't make the announcement and the earthquake did occur? These are not easy subjects to deal with.

SUMMARY

The surface of the Earth constantly changes. Mountains are created and worn away, while entire continents slowly shift, opening up oceans and closing them again. *Plate tectonics,* a relatively new theory that explains how a few thin, rigid *tectonic plates* of crustal and upper mantle material are moved across the Earth's surface by *mantle convection,* provides a global context for these changes. According to this theory, plates move over a partially molten, underlying section of the Earth's mantle, like rafts on the ocean, in response to convection of hot mantle rocks.

Three different kinds of observations—the geological features of ocean floors, parallel stripes of magnetic rocks situated symmetrically about volcanic ridges on the ocean floor, and the ages of these rocks—provided direct evidence that new crust is being created at *divergent plate boundaries.* Meanwhile, old crust returns to the mantle in *subduction zones,* where plates converge. *Convergent plate boundaries* in the ocean create deep trenches and associated volcanic islands. When an oceanic plate subducts beneath a plate carrying a continent, an offshore trench and chain of continental volcanoes parallel to shore result. The collision of two plates that carry continents at their margins produces mountain ranges of crumpled continental rocks. *Transform plate boundaries* occur where two plates scrape past each other.

Most *volcanoes* form near plate boundaries, either along the volcanic ridges of diverging plates, or above subducting plates. Other volcanoes such as the Hawaiian Islands form above *hot spots* originating in the Earth's mantle. *Earthquakes* occur when stressed rock ruptures. Earthquakes may be felt at all plate boundaries. The only plate boundary in the United States, California's San Andreas Fault, is a transform boundary in which one block of crust moves horizontally past the opposing block. The science of *seismology,* which documents the passage of earthquake-generated waves through the Earth, is providing new insights into the dynamic processes that drive plate tectonics.

KEY TERMS ABOUT PLATE TECTONICS

volcano

earthquake

plate tectonics

tectonic plates

mantle convection

divergent plate boundary

convergent plate boundary

subduction zone

transform plate boundary

hot spots

seismology

REVIEW QUESTIONS

1. What evidence suggests that mountain ranges are not permanent features on the Earth's surface?

2. What evidence suggests that Europe, Africa, and North and South America were once joined?

3. What evidence pointed to the process of seafloor spreading, or diverging plates?

4. Describe the three kinds of plate boundaries.

5. Describe the three different kinds of surface features that might occur at a convergent boundary.

6. Explain how mountains might form as a result of plate motions.

7. Identify a mountain range in North America that formed as a result of plate motions.

8. Why does a ring of volcanoes and earthquakes surround much of the Pacific Ocean?

9. What North American mountain range may have been the tallest in the world approximately 300 million years ago?

10. How do we know that tectonic plates move?

11. What is the Richter scale? Where might you read about it?

12. How do the ages of rocks on the ocean floor help support the theory of seafloor spreading?

DISCUSSION QUESTIONS

1. Identify two kinds of volcanic mountain chains that bear a close relationship to plate boundaries.

2. What plate do you live on? How many adjacent plates are there? What kinds of boundaries do you find to the north, south, east, and west?

3. Why are all three types of plate boundaries essential if plate tectonics is to work?

4. The continent of Antarctica has rocks with plant and animal fossils that suggest the Antarctic climate was once temperate. Explain at least two different ways in which these warm-climate fossils might have ended up in what is now a polar region. How might you test your hypotheses?

5. Volcanic islands, including the Azores, Canaries, and Iceland, lay scattered across the Atlantic Ocean. If you were to date the rocks on these and other Atlantic islands, what pattern do you predict you would find?

6. Geologists estimate that as much as 80% of the Earth's surface is covered by volcanic rocks. Is this estimate reasonable? What role might plate tectonics have played in producing these rocks?

7. Geology has been called an integrated science, because it calls on several scientific disciplines to help explain features and processes of the Earth. Explain how geologists have used other sciences to answer the following questions:

a. How old is a piece of rock?

b. How is heat transferred from the Earth's deep interior to the surface?

c. How does the Earth's magnetic field change over time?

d. What is the structure of the Earth's interior?

e. What is the topography of the seafloor?

8. Could the Earth's continents form into a single, Pangaea-like mass again? Why or why not? If they could, can you estimate how long it would take for them to do so?

9. At some convergent plate boundaries, deep ocean trenches lie a short distance from tall mountains. Why are these two contrasting features related to each other?

10. Popular media sometimes describe the California coast as poised to "slide into the ocean." Based on your understanding of plate tectonics, is this a plausible occurrence? Why or why not?

11. Public administrators are concerned that an earthquake early warning system might create more panic and threat to lives than it alleviates. For example, upon receiving a warning, a father might jump in the car to find his daughter, threatening his own life and the future well being of his child. What do you think about this issue?

PROBLEMS

1. If the African Rift Valley opens up at the rate of 5 cm per year, how long will it be before a body of water 1000 km wide divides the African continent?

2. Estimate the probable lifetime of your favorite mountain. [*Hint*: First get its dimensions from a map, then estimate its volume.]

INVESTIGATIONS

1. Examine original sources related to Wegener's continental drift theory. Why was this theory rejected by the majority of earth scientists in the 1920s? Compare and contrast the major features of the continental drift theory with plate tectonics theory.

2. How did ancient civilizations explain the occurrence of earthquakes and volcanoes?

3. Does plate tectonics operate on any other planet or moon in our solar system? Why or why not?

4. In your library, examine newspaper reports of major volcanoes and earthquakes during the past 20 years (each student could take one year). Plot these events on a world map. Do you see any obvious geographic patterns? How do the locations of these events relate to the plate boundaries shown in Figure 17-7?

5. Recent satellite images reveal Jupiter's moon Io to be the most volcanically active object in the solar system. What is the nature of these volcanoes? What provides their energy?

6. A few years ago someone predicted an earthquake on the New Madrid Fault in Missouri, the site of a destructive shock in 1812. He was widely believed and schoolchildren were trained in what to do in case of an earthquake. The earthquake did not take place and still has not occurred. What evidence did the amateur scientist use to make his case? How would you analyze that evidence?

7. Scientists have recently discovered astonishing deep-ocean communities of life forms associated with plate boundaries. Investigate the nature and distribution of these deep ecosystems. Why are they found close to these boundaries and not elsewhere?

WWW RESOURCES

See *The Sciences* homepage at: **http://www.wiley.com/college/trefil** for valuable web links.

1. **http://vquake.calstatela.edu**
   Electronic Desktop Project—click on "*Virtual Earthquake*" and determine the epicenter and Richter magnitude of an earthquake.

2. **http://www.thetech.org/exhibits/online/topics/30a.html**
   Earthquakes—learn about seismograms, waves, faults, plate tectonics, and more.

3. **http://volcanoes.usgs.gov/warn.html**
   Volcanoes!—good links to volcano observatories and seismic laboratories.

4. **http://pasadena.wr.usgs.gov/latest/shakingmaps.html**
   TriNetSHAKEMAP Home Page, where you can view the shakemaps mentioned in the Science News summary in this chapter.

18

Cycles of the Earth

Will we ever run out of fresh water?

GREAT IDEA

All matter above and beneath the Earth's surface moves in cycles.

PHYSICS

The movement of heat by convection drives ocean currents.

CHEMISTRY

The Earth has a finite number of atoms, which are constantly moving and recycling in repositories of rocks, water, and air.

ENVIRONMENT

Humans are removing water from aquifers faster than they can be replenished, depleting the supply of available fresh water.

GEOLOGY

The rock cycle creates, alters, and destroys the solid materials of the Earth.

HEALTH & SAFETY

Elements move through the human body in cycles; your body depends on a regular intake of elements to help replace dying cells.

ASTRONOMY

Variations in the Earth's rotation are partly responsible for the cycle of ice ages on the Earth.

TECHNOLOGY

Doppler radar measures the motions of air currents and thus can detect the approach of violent weather.

BIOLOGY

Coral reefs are limestone deposits built by the gradual action of microscopic plants and animals; each generation grows on the remains of the previous one.

Red = applications of the great idea discussed in this chapter.

Orange = other applications, some of which are explored in other chapters.

The beautiful day continues, bright and clear. As the Sun gradually arcs overhead into the western sky, the afternoon shadows begin to lengthen and the cool wind picks up off the water. By 2 P.M. there's a steady seaward breeze blowing close to 20 miles per hour.

Day after summer day it's the same story at the shore: refreshing off-shore breezes pick up during the day, while warm on-shore breezes blow in the evening. This familiar atmospheric behavior is just one of Earth's countless cycles.

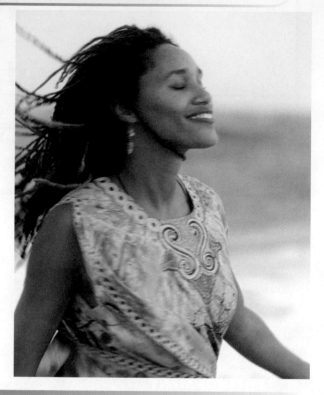

Cycles Small and Large

Every place we go, every day of our lives, we experience Earth's cycles. A day may start out clear and sunny, with mild temperatures and gentle breezes. But, suddenly, the wind picks up as a line of dark clouds presses in from the west. With the wind comes the first threatening rumble of thunder, flashes of distant lightning, and spurts of rain. A heavy downpour and powerful gusts of wind follow, as thunder booms and lightning illuminates the gray sky around us. Trees sway, windows rattle, and limbs come crashing down at the height of the storm.

Within an hour skies are sunny again, though the temperature is noticeably cooler. The air has a fresh, clean smell, and the sky seems more deeply blue than before. In the span of a few hours we have experienced one of Earth's many cycles—the atmospheric cycle called weather.

Day and night, summer and winter, life and death—these and many other cyclical changes characterize our dynamic planet. As the author of the *Book of Ecclesiastes* wrote 3000 years ago:

> *One generation passeth away, and another generation cometh: but the earth abideth forever;*
>
> *The sun also ariseth, and the sun goeth down, and hasteth to the place where he arose;*
>
> *The wind goeth toward the south, and turneth about unto the north; it whirleth about continually, and the wind returneth again according to his circuits;*

All the rivers run into the sea; yet the sea is not full; unto the place from whence the rivers come, thither they return again . . .

The thing that hath been, it is that which shall be; and that which is done is that which shall be done: and there is no new thing under the sun.

Recycling

Think about the last time that you drank a can of soda. What did you do with the aluminum can when you were through? You may have taken the time to place the can in a recycling bin. Alternatively, you may have tossed it into a trash container, or even by the side of the road. What difference does it make? Where do the aluminum atoms end up?

The atoms that make up the Earth, with the exception of a few radioactive isotopes (Chapter 12), will last virtually forever. A single aluminum atom, for example, will appear in many different guises during its lifetime. It may form part of a swirling lava flow in which it is tightly bonded to oxygen atoms. It may then be incorporated with those oxygen atoms into a solid rock. As the rock weathers away, the atom may be concentrated in soil with other aluminum atoms, where it is mined. Giant smelters separate the aluminum atom—a process that consumes prodigious amounts of energy—to produce the aluminum metal that made your soda can. Once discarded, the atom may be recycled into new cans, or it may go back to the soil where it once again bonds to oxygen.

 Stop and Think! One of the main points in Chapter 3 is that energy flows through the Earth. Does this apply to matter also? Explain.

The Earth has a vast, though finite, number of aluminum atoms that take part in the aluminum cycle. The advantage to recycling aluminum is that we save all the energy that went into finding concentrated aluminum sources and breaking aluminum-to-oxygen bonds. But no matter what you do with your can, the aluminum atoms still are part of the Earth.

The Nature of Earth's Cycles

The history of an aluminum atom is just one example of the many paths within the three great cycles of materials in the Earth's oceans, atmosphere, and rocks. Two central ideas frame our understanding of the movement of matter in our changing planet:

Earth materials move in cycles.

and

A change in one cycle affects the others.

The story of the aluminum atom suggests a useful two-step strategy for analyzing any of the many cycles by which each type of Earth material moves. The first step is to make an inventory of all the different **reservoirs** in which that substance is found. Earth's water, for example, is found in oceans, rivers, ice caps, and several other reservoirs. The second step is to identify the varied ways that the material is transferred from one reservoir to another. In the case of water, for example, movement may occur by precipitation, evaporation, or gravity.

Each of Earth's cycles illustrates a central theme: our planet's atoms are constantly moving and recycling. Water moves from rivers to oceans to glaciers and to clouds as it takes part in the Earth's dynamic hydrologic cycle. Above the Earth's surface, the gases of the atmosphere flow in the great cycles of weather, the seasons, and global climate. And the solid surface of the Earth slowly alters, erodes away, and forms again in the stately rock cycle.

Many of the Earth's cycles are driven by the tendency of heat to spread out—to flow from hot to cold in what we described as the second law of thermodynamics (see Chapter 4). The Earth has two primary sources of heat energy: the Sun, and its own geothermal processes, each of which drives its own thermal cycle. More heat energy from the Sun falls at the equator than at the poles, and heat transfer by convection moves gases in the atmosphere and water in the oceans in the great cycles that control weather and climate. Similarly, heat energy in the Earth's core and mantle drives the convection cycles that move the tectonic plates.

Thus Earth's cycles reflect the most basic properties of matter and energy. These cycles may be studied at many levels, from an atomic scale for an individual element such as aluminum, to the global cycles involved in plate tectonics. We find it especially useful to consider the Earth in terms of the three most familiar cycles around us: the cycles of water, air, and rock.

● The Hydrologic Cycle

Water plays a vital role in the unique chemistry of Earth's outer layers. Water saturates the air, falls to the ground as precipitation, moves through a complex system of rivers and streams, and is stored for long periods in underground reservoirs, oceans, and ice. Water shapes the surface of our planet, and it provided the medium in which life began. The combination of processes by which water moves from repository to repository above, below, and on the Earth's surface is called the **hydrologic cycle**.

Reservoirs of Water

The total amount of water on the Earth's surface has stayed roughly the same from very early times. Water first reached the surface during the outgassing of the young, volcano-covered Earth (see Chapter 16). When the planet's surface temperature finally fell below 100°C, this water condensed into liquid form and began to fill the ocean basins. Relatively minor processes still add and remove water from the Earth. High in the atmosphere, ultraviolet rays from the Sun break up water molecules, freeing hydrogen atoms, which because of their low mass may escape into space. At the same time, at converging and diverging plate boundaries and other sites of volcanism, small amounts of new water are emitted from the Earth's deep interior. These losses and gains are in rough equilibrium, and in any case both are rather small—by one estimate, no more than one or two Olympic-sized swimming pools of water per year. Thus, for all intents and purposes, we can treat the Earth as if it has had a fixed amount of water at its surface for billions of years. The water that we have now is all there is.

The Earth boasts several major water repositories, as summarized in Table 18-1. In addition to oceans, lakes, and rivers, significant amounts of water are locked into Earth's polar ice caps and glaciers, bodies of ice that form in

Table 18-1 **Reservoirs of Water**

Reservoir	Percent of Earth's Supply
Oceans	96.0
Lakes, rivers, and streams	0.009
Ice caps and glaciers	3.0
Groundwater	1.0
Clouds	0.001
Living things	0.0001

regions where snowfall exceeds melting. **Ice caps** are layers of ice that form at the north and south polar regions of the Earth. **Glaciers** are large bodies of ice that slowly flow down a slope or valley under the influence of gravity. Approximately 96% of glaciers (by volume) occur in Antarctica and Greenland, while the rest are widely scattered in mountainous areas. All of these places where water occurs tap into the same central supply. During its lifetime, a given molecule of water will cycle through many different reservoirs, over and over again.

A vast part of the hydrologic cycle remains unseen. Some of the water that falls on the continents does not immediately return to the ocean; rather it seeps into the Earth to become **groundwater**. There, it goes into large *aquifers*— reservoirs that are, in effect, underground storage tanks of water. By some estimates, more than 98% of the world's fresh water is stored as groundwater. Water typically percolates into the ground and fills the tiny spaces between grains of sandstone and other porous rock layers. Impermeable materials, such as clay, which keeps the water from seeping away, often bound these layers of water-saturated rock.

Movements of Water Between Reservoirs

Earth's water is in constant motion both within and between reservoirs—a process that may gradually change the distribution of water on Earth's surface. The hydrologic cycle with which most of us are familiar involves the short-term back-and-forth transfer of water molecules between the oceans and the land. Water evaporates off the surface of the ocean, forms into clouds, falls as rain on the land, and then returns to the oceans via rivers and streams. Most terrestrial life depends on this simple cycle (Figure 18-1).

Much of the movement of Earth's water occurs within the oceans, which are far from static. Each ocean basin has great **currents**, which are like rivers of moving water within the larger ocean (see Figure 18-2). These currents play a vital role in redistributing heat across the surface of the planet, and thus in determining climate. Some surface currents carry warm water from the equator, where a large amount of heat energy from the Sun is absorbed, toward the cooler poles. At the same time, other surface currents carry cold water from the poles back to the equator to be heated and cycled again. These great gyres as they are called have a profound effect on the weather of the land they flow past. In the North Atlantic, for example, the Gulf Stream current starts in the Caribbean and flows past the eastern coast of the United States. It comes near England, making the British Isles much warmer than you might expect them to be based on their latitude, which is farther north than Maine. A much colder current, on the other hand, flows along the western coast of Europe back to the tropics to complete the cycle.

• **Figure 18-1** A diagram of the hydrologic cycle showing the transfer of water molecules between oceans and land. The numbers in parentheses show the volume of water that cycles through the continental United States in millions of cubic meters each day.

• **Figure 18-2** Ocean currents play a major role in redistributing the Earth's heat.

In addition to this rather rapid circulation of water at the surface, we find deeper three-dimensional circulation of water in the ocean. When the effects of surface currents and wind along a coast act in such a way as to push surface water away from the land, colder water from the depths comes up to create an area of upwelling. The waters along the coast of California display this phenomenon, which helps explain why the ocean there is so cold. On a larger scale, water from the Arctic and Antarctic, which is both cold and salty because so much fresh water is removed to form ice, sinks to the bottom of the sea and rolls sluggishly toward the equator. This dense, cold water forms the slow, deep flow that characterizes much of the bottom currents in the world's ocean basins.

Humans also participate in the water cycle by tapping into deep aquifers when they drill wells to supply water for cities and agriculture. One problem with using aquifers as a water supply is that it may take many thousands of years to fill them, but only a few years to drain them. For example, when farmers in the central United States take water from the High Plains aquifer, one of the great underground reservoirs, they are in effect mining the water. Underground water is not a renewable resource except over very long time scales.

THE SCIENCE OF LIFE •

Sobering Facts About Water

Although Earth's supply of water is vast, about 96% is salty and most of the remaining fresh water is locked into ice caps and glaciers. Thus less than 1% of Earth's water is readily available for human use.

Modern society places tremendous demands on this limited resource. Agriculture, industry, and personal needs result in an average daily water consumption of about 2000 gallons per person in North America. As supplies of groundwater are reduced, and pollution contaminates other reservoirs, shortages of fresh water may become a serious concern in the future. •

Chemical Cycles in the Oceans

Just as the water in the oceans is in constant physical motion, so too are the chemicals that make it salty. Scholars once thought that the oceans were passive receptacles for materials washed into them from the land. The old argument went that rivers flowing into the ocean carried dissolved minerals and salts with them, and when water evaporated, these minerals were left behind, leaving the oceans saltier and saltier with time. In this view, the extremely salty Dead Sea in Israel was always cited as a place where salts had accumulated over the longest period of time.

In fact, we now know that the saltiness of the oceans has not changed appreciably over several hundred million years, and they probably have been salty since soon after they formed. Instead of thinking of the oceans as passive receptacles, it is more accurate to think of them as large test tubes in which a constant round of chemical reactions goes on that affects and is affected by the input of minerals from the world's rivers.

The saltiness of the oceans comes primarily from the presence of sodium and chloride ions, but many other dissolved minerals occur in seawater as well. Each element follows different reactions, and each will remain in solution for different periods of time. Calcium, for example, may be dissolved out of limestone by water and carried into the ocean. Once there, an average calcium ion can be expected to float around for about 8 million years, but eventually it will be taken up into the skeleton of some sea creature and sink to the bottom when that creature dies.

Table 18-2 **Some Typical Residence Times for Elements in the Ocean**

Element	Concentration (parts per million)	Residence Times (millions of years)
Sodium	10,800	260
Calcium	413	8
Chlorine	19,400	infinite
Gold	0.00005	0.042
Potassium	387	11
Copper	0.003	0.05

There it may once more be formed into limestone, lifted up by tectonic forces, and eventually carried back to the sea through erosion or dissolution.

The average length of time that an atom will stay in ocean water before it is removed by some chemical reaction is called the *residence time* (see Table 18-2). Sodium (one of the atoms that gives seawater its distinctive taste) enters the ocean after dissolving out of various kinds of rocks. A sodium ion will stay in suspension on average for about 260 million years before it is incorporated again into various kinds of clay and mud on the ocean bottom. Once so incorporated, it can go through the same cycle of uplift and erosion as limestone. Chloride ions, on the other hand, tend to stay in the ocean almost forever, though these atoms may leave the ocean for short periods of time.

Only when a body of salt water is evaporated, forming dry salt deposits like those surrounding the Great Salt Lake in Utah, is chlorine removed from its water environment for any appreciable length of time. But even these deposits, slowly buried and compressed, could eventually (in perhaps a few hundred million years) rise to the surface as salt domes, where they would weather away, returning the salt once again to the sea.

Thus chemical cycles in the ocean can be simply pictured. The Earth's rivers continuously transport various elements into the sea. Each of these elements resides for a certain amount of time in the ocean and then is removed by chemical reactions. The supply of every kind of atom is being constantly renewed, and the oceans may never be any less salty than they are today.

THE SCIENCE OF LIFE •

Element Residence Times

Your body, like the oceans, constantly recycles atoms. Some of your body's cells, such as the lining of the intestines, are replaced every few days. You need fresh supplies of carbon, oxygen, and nitrogen every day to help replace these cells. Red blood cells last much longer—120 days on average—but you need a regular intake of iron to produce these important cells. Failure to digest enough iron can lead to anemia, a condition characterized by fatigue due to insufficient red blood cells.

Atoms in your bones and tendons last much longer—a decade or more, on average—but even those atoms are constantly being replaced. Gradual loss of calcium in bone, for example, is of special concern in older people who may not consume enough replacement calcium. Osteoporosis, a disease in which bones become weak and brittle, may result from this calcium deficiency. A similar mysterious loss of bone calcium affects astronauts who spend more than a few days in the weightless environment of space.

Some harmful elements, including lead, mercury, and other so-called heavy metals, do not easily recycle once taken into the body, because we have no effective biological process to remove them. Their average residence times, in other words, are much longer than a human lifetime. Concentrations of these atoms can thus build up over time and can result in sickness or even death. You may hear about local efforts to test drinking water for high concentrations of lead that are sometimes found in old plumbing systems. •

SCIENCE BY THE NUMBERS •

The Ocean's Gold

We've just said that every element can be found in seawater. How much gold is there in a cubic kilometer of seawater?

According to Table 18-2, gold is present in the ocean at a concentration of 0.00005 parts per million (ppm). A concentration of 1 ppm corresponds to 1 milligram (mg) of a solid dissolved in a liter (l) of water. A liter is a volume measurement equal to a thousandth of a cubic meter (10^{-3} m^3). The total amount of gold in a cubic meter of seawater, therefore, is 0.00005 milligrams per liter times 1000 liters per meter cubed:

$$(0.00005 \text{ mg/l}) \times (1000 \text{ l/m}^3) = 0.05 \text{ mg/m}^3$$

A gram contains 1000 milligrams, so

$$(0.05 \text{ mg/m}^3) \times (1 \text{ g/1000 mg}) = 0.00005 \text{ g/m}^3$$

A cubic kilometer contains $(1000 \text{ m}) \times (1000 \text{ m}) \times (1000 \text{ m}) = 10^9$ m^3, so the total amount of gold in a cubic kilometer of seawater is

$$(10^9 \text{ m}^3) \times (0.00005 \text{ g/m}^3) = 5 \times 10^4 \text{ gm}$$

Every cubic kilometer of ocean water holds about 50,000 grams (about 100 pounds) of gold. At $300 an ounce, that much gold is worth about half a million dollars.

The total amount of gold dissolved in the world's oceans is vast, but no economical way to extract these riches is known. The equipment and energy required to process that much water would cost far more than the value of any gold recovered. •

Ice Ages

From time to time, much of the Earth's water supply becomes locked into glaciers that advance across land from the poles—a period called an **ice age**. We are now in the middle of an ice age, a period of several million years during which glaciers have repeatedly advanced and retreated. Within the present ice age we are living in an *interglacial period*, which is occurring between two major advances of glaciers. About 20,000 years ago, massive glaciers spread down from eastern and central Canada, covering a good deal of northern North America, and then receded to Greenland about 10,000 years ago, as illustrated in Figure 18-3. Glaciers have come and gone many times, and periods of cyclic glaciation like the one in which we now live have occurred relatively often during the past 2 million years of Earth history.

The total amount of Earth's water is fixed, so as ice caps and glaciers grow, the amount of water available to fill the ocean basins decreases and the sea level drops. During the most recent advance of glaciers some 20,000 years ago, for example, as much as 5% of Earth's water was locked into ice. Sea level dropped to

• **Figure 18-3** The extent of the most recent North American glaciation, approximately 20,000 years ago, looking down on the North Pole. Arrows indicate the direction of the glaciers' advances.

the point that the East Coast of what is now the United States was about 250 km farther east than it is today. A land bridge joining western North America and eastern Asia made it possible to walk from Alaska to Siberia. This land bridge provided a route that was taken by the ancestors of many Native Americans when they moved into the Americas from Siberia.

Milankovitch Cycles

The main causes of periodic glaciation were first explained by Milutin Milankovitch, a Serbian civil engineer, in the early part of the twentieth century. His theory was simple: The relation between the Earth and the Sun is affected by a number of variations in the Earth's rotation and orbit. These variations cause slight changes in the amount of solar radiation absorbed by the Earth, as shown in Figure 18-4.

The easiest of the orbital effects to understand is the precession of the Earth's axis of rotation. If you have ever watched a child's top spinning, you know that sometimes as the top spins rapidly around its axis, the axis itself describes a lazy circle in space. This circular motion is called a *precession*. In the same way that a top may precess every second or two, the Earth's axis, which is tilted at an angle of 23 degrees, precesses once every 23,000 years. While precession occurs, the axis of the Earth's elliptical orbit also moves around the Sun due to the gravitational effects of the other planets. The net effect of these two motions is that when the Earth is farthest from the Sun, during the summer, the axis of the Earth tilts the Northern Hemisphere toward the Sun for half of a 23,000-year cycle.

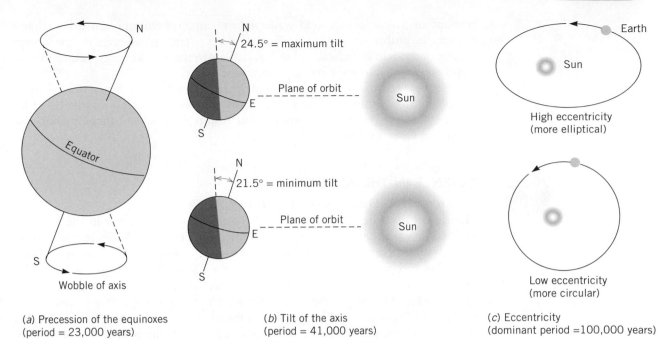

(a) Precession of the equinoxes
(period = 23,000 years)

(b) Tilt of the axis
(period = 41,000 years)

(c) Eccentricity
(dominant period =100,000 years)

• **Figure 18-4** The precession of the Earth's axis (*a*). Small changes in the tilt of the axis (*b*), and changes in the shape of the orbit induced by the other planets (*c*), contribute to recurring ice ages.

The axis gradually shifts so that the Southern Hemisphere is tilted toward the Sun for the other half of the cycle. Today Earth's axis is oriented such that the Northern Hemisphere is tilted away from the Sun during the winter months (the period in which the Earth is actually closest to the Sun). About 11,500 years from now, however, the situation will be reversed, and the Northern Hemisphere will be tilted toward the Sun during the same period.

 Stop and Think! Why are winter months in the Northern Hemisphere colder than summer months, even though the Earth is closer to the Sun during the winter?

Other orbital effects involve a slow change in the angle of the axis of rotation (it rocks back and forth by about a degree every 41,000 years), as well as a small change in the shape of the Earth's orbit caused by other planets (about a 100,000-year cycle). Milankovitch proposed that the global climate varies in cycles (now called *Milankovitch cycles*) when all three of these effects reinforce each other. If we find ourselves in a period of decreasing solar energy absorption and increased precipitation, more snow will fall in the winter and it will stay on the ground longer in the summer. Snow and ice reflect sunlight, so this extra snow and ice further cool the Earth and more snow falls and stays on the ground even longer. Thus a decline in absorption of sunlight may trigger a sequence of events that can lead eventually to glacial advance. By the same token, a period of increased absorption of sunlight will result in warmer periods during which glaciers will tend to retreat.

Several other factors play a role in controlling the extent and distribution of glaciers. Large glaciers can form only on land masses, which gradually shift because of tectonic motion. The locations of mountain chains also play a significant role by altering wind and precipitation patterns. Recent evidence also suggests that the amount of volcanic dust and gases in the atmosphere can cause short-term changes in global temperatures. Finally, some scientists suspect that the energy output of the Sun is cyclical and that variations in the Sun's energy output impose a cyclical variation in the Earth's temperature.

For the record, most scientists think that we are heading into a new phase of glacial advance within the next 10,000 years. This cooling trend may be offset for a time, however, by global warming that results from an enhanced greenhouse effect (see Chapter 19).

SCIENCE IN THE MAKING •

Milankovitch Decides on His Life's Work

Milutin Milankovitch didn't seem to be headed toward a career in the sciences. Trained in Vienna as a civil engineer, he designed reinforced-concrete structures in central Europe prior to becoming a professor of mathematics in his native Belgrade just before World War I. Swept up in the nationalistic movements that were then (as now) prominent in the Balkans, he became friendly with some poets who specialized in writing patriotic verse. One evening, drinking coffee to celebrate a new book of verse, Milankovitch and his friends came to the attention of a banker at a neighboring table. The banker was so taken with the poems that he bought 10 copies on the spot.

With new money in their pockets, the friends celebrated with wine. After the first bottle, Milankovitch says in his journal, "I looked back on my earlier achievements and found them narrow and limited." By the third bottle, he had decided to "grasp the entire universe and spread light to its farthest corners."

He then methodically set apart a few hours each day to study and interpret climate records. Even during World War I, when he served as an engineer on the Serbian general staff and became a prisoner of war, he kept at it. A member of the Hungarian Academy of Sciences arranged for him to have a desk at the Academy after he gave his word of honor that he would not try to escape, and a good deal of the work described in the text was done under those conditions. The final work, published in 1920, was quickly recognized and accepted by the scientific community. •

The Atmospheric Cycle

The Earth's atmosphere and oceans play the most important role in redistributing heat across the surface of the planet. The atmosphere also has chemical cycles involving oxygen and carbon, but those cycles are intimately bound up with the presence of living things on the Earth, and we will wait to discuss them until we look at the Earth's ecosystems (Chapter 19). The circulation of gases near the Earth's surface—both the short-term variations of weather, and the longer patterns of climate—is called the **atmospheric cycle**.

Air Masses: Reservoirs of the Atmosphere

At first glance it might seem odd to speak of an atmospheric cycle. After all, the atmosphere appears to be one continuous mass of air rather than several different reservoirs. However, at any one time the atmosphere can be divided into many separate "air masses," each of which has more or less uniform properties. Each air mass can be thought of as a separate reservoir of air, and adjacent air masses differ in physical properties. Adjacent air masses may occupy different regions close to the ground, such as a low-pressure system in the Midwest and an adjacent high-pressure system off the New England coast. On the other hand, adjacent air masses may represent different atmospheric layers high above the surface.

In order to understand the properties of air masses, we need to define two closely related terms—the weather, and the climate. **Weather** is the state of the atmosphere at a given time and place. At any given place, the weather is influenced by many factors and may be highly variable from day to day, not to mention from season to season. **Climate**, on the other hand, is a long-term average of weather for a given region. A regional climate may be hot or cold, wet or dry, though the weather on any given day might be quite different. Climate may remain unchanged for centuries, or it may shift quite dramatically, often for reasons that are as yet uncertain.

Weather

Five variables define the state of the atmosphere: temperature, air pressure, humidity, cloudiness, and prevailing winds. Your local weather report typically covers all of these variables.

1. The *temperature* reported in daily weather predictions refers to temperature at ground level. Temperature varies strongly with altitude above the ground. In fact, the major layers of the atmosphere—regions such as the stratosphere and troposphere—are defined by these temperature variations.

2. The second variable that defines the state of the atmosphere is *pressure,* which decreases significantly with altitude, because air is compressed by its own weight. At a height of 5.5 km, air pressure is only half of its value at sea level.

A satellite photo of a low-pressure system that is centered over Ireland and moving toward the European continent. Notice the counterclockwise rotation of the air.

• **Figure 18-5** The jet stream is a fast-moving, high-altitude air current above North America. (*a*) The jet stream often follows a relatively straight path, with minor undulations. (*b*) Strongly developed undulations may pull a mass of cold arctic air to the south.

(*a*) Jet stream with small undulations

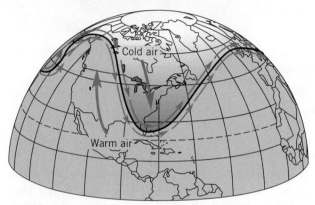

(*b*) Strongly developed undulations pull a trough of cold air south

Pressure also varies laterally, because air masses tend to move and rotate with respect to each other. Air piles up in some places to form a high-pressure system, while it stretches out in other places to form a low-pressure system. Air in low-pressure systems tends to rise, which causes cooling and increased clouds; conversely, high-pressure systems tend to feature warmer, dry air. Significant air pressure differences, which can arise at boundaries between layers high in the atmosphere, cause high-speed air currents called the **jet stream** (Figure 18-5). The jet stream moves west-to-east across the United States; it causes flights from New York to Los Angeles to average almost an hour longer than flights from Los Angeles to New York.

3. The third atmospheric variable is *humidity,* which is a measure of the atmosphere's highly variable water content. The bulk composition of the atmosphere is remarkably uniform; nitrogen and oxygen make up 99% of dry atmosphere. The atmosphere also always contains some water vapor, though the amount is highly variable, depending on the temperature and relative humidity. Air on a cold, dry winter day might hold less than 0.1% water by volume, whereas air on a hot, humid summer day may contain several percent water by volume.

4. *Cloudiness,* the fourth weather variable, is closely tied to humidity. Clouds are a concentration of tiny water droplets or ice crystals. These substances scatter light, so clouds appear white. Clouds form when air becomes saturated with water—a process that often occurs when a mass of air rises and cools. Clouds often dramatically outline the contact between two adjacent air masses. A band of clouds may mark a front, where two air masses at different temperatures

collide near ground level. Dramatic anvil-shaped thunderhead clouds often form when a warmer air mass collides with a cooler air mass. The warmer air mass is less dense, and so it rides up over the cooler air. This increase in elevation cools the warm, wet air, causing clouds and rain. Large gradients in temperature and pressure generate strong winds and violent lightning. Similarly, clouds and rain often form on the windward side of mountain ranges as an air mass is forced to rise up the mountain flanks. The leeward side is usually much drier. Some mountainous areas of Hawaii receive more than 100 inches of rain per year on the eastern side, while experiencing near-arid conditions a few kilometers away on the western slopes.

5. The fifth atmospheric variable is the direction and strength of *winds*. Winds are a consequence of atmospheric convection—a process that helps to redistribute heat. Ocean breezes on a tranquil summer day illustrate how winds can occur. During a sunny day, the land heats up more than water, so warmer air rises from the land and cooler air flows in from the water, producing a refreshing sea breeze. In the evening, as the land cools, the pattern reverses; warmer air over the water rises and the breeze comes from the land.

The General Circulation of the Atmosphere

The atmosphere circulates in vast rivers of air that cover the globe from the equator to the poles. These prevailing winds arise in much the same way as local winds, though on a much larger scale. As in local winds, this circulation is powered by the energy of the Sun. Air in the tropics is heated and rises. If the Earth did not rotate, we would expect to have a situation like the one shown in Figure 18-6. Warm air would rise at the equator, cool off, and sink at the poles. This pattern of flow is the familiar convection cell we saw in Chapter 4. Such a pattern arises whenever a fluid is heated nonuniformly in a gravitational field.

If the Earth did not rotate, prevailing winds in the Northern Hemisphere would flow from north to south. In fact, they do nothing of the kind. The weather patterns in much of the Northern Hemisphere, including North America, move, in general, from west to east—we live in a region of what meteorologists call *prevailing westerlies*. This behavior of the Earth's atmosphere results

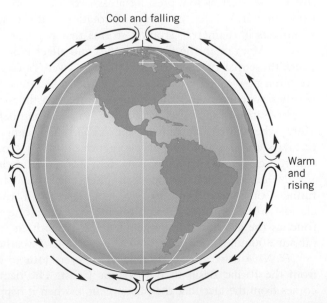

Cool and falling

Warm and rising

• **Figure 18-6** If the Earth did not rotate, the circulation of the atmosphere would take place in convection cells that create high-altitude winds from equator to pole, and low-altitude winds from pole to equator.

• **Figure 18-7** Atmospheric convection on the rotating Earth, showing the principal air circulation cells. Compare this diagram with the opening photograph in Chapter 16.

from the fact that the Earth rotates. The rotation breaks the north–south atmospheric convection cell that would exist in the absence of rotation into three cells in each hemisphere as shown in Figure 18-7. In addition, the rotation "stretches out" the shape of the air circulation pattern in each cell. In the cell nearest the equator, the winds at the surface tend to blow from east to west—the so-called *trade winds* that drove sailing ships from Europe to North America. In temperate zones, the effect is to cause the winds to blow from west to east, creating regions in which weather patterns also usually move from west to east. Finally, in the Arctic and Antarctic, the winds blow once again from east to west.

Similar patterns of atmospheric motion can be seen on all the planets in the solar system that have atmospheres. In some cases, like the planet Jupiter, the rapid rotation of the planet and the atmospheric dynamics cause more than 3 convection cells. Jupiter, in fact, has no fewer than 11.

Common Storms and Weather Patterns

Many kinds of severe weather conditions affect our world. *Tropical storms* are severe storms that start as low-pressure areas over warm ocean water. They draw energy from the warm water, growing and rotating in great *cyclonic* patterns hundreds of kilometers in diameter. Tropical storms that begin in the Atlantic Ocean off the coast of Africa or in the Caribbean Sea and affect North America are called *hurricanes;* those that begin in the North Pacific were once called *typhoons,* though they are often now called hurricanes by weather forecasters. Until recently these violent weather systems frequently hit unprotected coastlines with little warning. Today, weather satellites spot and track tropical storms long before they approach land. In 1992, when Hurricane Andrew approached the Miami area, residents received several days warning and were able to get out of the way of the storm. This event was widely regarded as a triumph of modern storm prediction.

Tornadoes, much smaller-scale phenomena than hurricanes, are rotating air funnels some tens to hundreds of meters across. Tornadoes descend from storm clouds to the ground, causing intense damage along the path where the funnel touches the ground. The largest tornadoes, with air speeds in excess of 500 km (about 300 miles) per hour, are the most violent weather phenomenon known.

El Niño, a weather cycle that recurs every four to seven years, affects weather from the Pacific Basin to the Atlantic Coast. The name means Christ Child and comes from the fact that the phenomenon, when it happens, usually begins around

Christmas time. El Niño can cause severe storms and flooding all along the western coast of the Americas, and drought from Australia to India. El Niño is an example of a coupling between two of the Earth's cycles—in this case, the atmospheric and water cycles. It requires both winds and ocean currents to work. Here's what happens: Normally, the winds off the coast of Peru blow westward. They move the warm ocean water westward, like water sloshing in a bathtub, to the western Pacific. As the surface water moves west, the colder, nutrient-rich water from the deep ocean wells up and supports marine life and fish-eating birds. Because the eastern Pacific is cooler, the atmosphere cools and descends there, forming a zone of high pressure and dry weather off the coast of South America. Meanwhile, the western Pacific is warmer, so air warms and rises above it in a rainy, low-pressure zone.

Every four to seven years, however, this pattern changes, signifying the beginning of an El Niño event. Warm surface water sloshes to the east, the water temperature in the eastern Pacific increases by a few degrees and the normal atmospheric patterns switch places. Westerly winds replace the normally easterly flowing trade winds. This wind reversal reinforces the movement of warm water eastward to the coast of South America, where air warms and rises, creating rainy conditions. The marine life and birds are no longer supported by the nutrients of the cold, deep water. The western Pacific becomes relatively cool and dry. Eventually, the water sloshes back and the whole cycle repeats. Historical records tell us that this cycle has been repeating in the Pacific basin since the 1600s, and may have been going on since the last ice age.

Climate

Climate, as opposed to weather, seldom changes much on the scale of human lifetimes. In spite of many uncertainties about climate change, several factors that strongly influence regional climate are now well documented. Large bodies of water and ocean currents, such as the Gulf Stream, can greatly change a region's climate by transferring heat. Oceans and large lakes can also add moisture to an air mass. Northwest New York State, for example, receives heavy rains and snows as Canadian air masses pass over the Great Lakes. Mountain ranges disrupt the movement of air masses, and can efficiently remove moisture from an air mass. We have seen how tall mountains on Hawaii affect rainfall; nearby locations on opposite sides of a volcanic mountain can have radically different rainfalls.

These effects of oceans and mountains on climate reveal that movements of tectonic plates play a major long-term role in Earth's climate. As plates move, bodies of water open and close and mountain ranges are formed. In addition, the presence of continents near one or both poles strongly influences the severity of ice ages, because thick accumulations of ice require a solid base. Thus, Earth's atmospheric cycle is strongly influenced by other global cycles.

THE ONGOING PROCESS OF SCIENCE •

How Steady Is Earth's Climate?

Through most of recorded history, Earth's climate has been pretty much as we know it today, but recorded history covers only 4000 years—a blink of an eye in geological time. Until recently, scientists assumed that climate change always happened slowly in response to factors such as the tectonic movement of the continents. However, since the early 1990s thinking on this subject has started to change. It turns out that Earth's climate can change more drastically, and more quickly, than anyone had realized.

Key evidence came from deep-sea cores drilled in the floor of the North Atlantic Ocean. During times corresponding to the last ice age, scientists found layers of rocks in these cores, spaced between 7000 and 11,000 years apart, that are identical to rocks found in northern Canada. The first clue as to what these layers might mean came from geophysicist Douglas MacAyael at the University of Chicago. His explanation was based on the behavior of the ice sheets that covered North America and the rock underneath them. Over most of northeastern Canada, the underlying rock is hard and strong. In Hudson Bay, however, the rock is softer. MacAyael's calculations showed that when the ice over Hudson Bay piled up several miles deep, the soft underlying rock would fracture and, when mixed with melted water, turn into a layer about the consistency of toothpaste. When this happened, the ice sheet would slide out to sea and huge armadas of glaciers would sail out into the North Atlantic. In this scheme, the mysterious Canadian rocks were simply material incorporated into the icebergs that dropped to the ocean floor whenever the iceberg melted.

However, from the point of view of climate stability the important thing about these events is that they are accompanied by huge swings in temperature—the data seem to indicate that the average temperatures changed by 5°C (9°F) in a matter of 10 years or so. For reference, this change would be roughly like moving the climate of Florida to Boston. The most likely explanation is that the fresh water added to the North Atlantic by melting ice temporarily shut down the ocean currents that distribute heat around the globe, and that these currents stayed "off" until the water had been mixed and become salty again.

Since the discovery of the first of these sudden climate swings during the last ice age, scientists have found evidence for many more. Today, scientists are trying to understand how sudden changes in climate can be caused not only by glaciers, but also by changes in the brightness of the Sun and a host of other effects. It appears that our comfortable view of a stable Earth won't survive long as we unravel the history of the climate. •

Understanding Climate

While the daily weather is often dominated by the position of the jet stream and the creation of high- and low-pressure zones, the long-term climate depends on more lasting features of the Earth's surface. These factors include the distribution of heat due to the stabilizing temperature of oceans, and the presence of mountains, which force air masses up over them. The climate is also extremely sensitive to the amount of sunlight that falls on the atmosphere and the amount of heat that is radiated back to space.

At the moment, our best attempts at predicting long-term climate depend on complex computer models of the atmosphere called *global circulation models (GCMs)*. In a typical GCM, a computer splits the world's surface into squares several hundred kilometers on a side, and slices the atmosphere into about 10 vertical compartments. In each of these boxes the laws of motion and thermodynamics are used to calculate the amount of heat that flows in and out, how much water vapor comes out of the air, and so on. The computer balances the inflow and outflow from all of the boxes in the atmosphere and projects forward in time to try to predict long-term climate trends. Our current models are still rather crude (they have a great deal of difficulty accounting for the effects of clouds or the ocean, for example), but they represent the best attempts to date to understand what affects the Earth's climate. These models also play a critical role in discussing various types of ecological changes such as global warming (see Chapter 19).

A computerized radar weather map shows areas of cloud cover and precipitation.

TECHNOLOGY •

Doppler Radar

Radar has been a vital tool for weather forecasters for decades, and you may see radar maps of local weather conditions on TV every night. The way radar works is simple. Microwaves are sent out from a central antenna. When they encounter objects such as raindrops, snowflakes, or ice in the air, the waves are reflected back. Each kind of material produces a distinct pattern of reflected waves because its density is different from that of the surrounding air. These reflection patterns are used to assemble a map of local storm activity.

Ordinary radar, however, cannot detect winds, even winds of high velocity. The reason is that the densities of moving air and stationary air are usually not very different, and the two produce the same reflection pattern. But in many situations it's important to detect air currents. Near airports, for example, sudden downdrafts create violent air turbulence called *wind shear*, an extremely dangerous condition that we need to be able to detect.

Doppler radar is designed to detect motions of the air. It works like this: Reflected waves are analyzed not only for their intensity, as in ordinary radar, but for their frequency as well. From the difference between the emitted and reflected frequencies, a simple analysis of the Doppler effect yields the velocity of the object from which the wave was reflected. In this way, high winds and atmospheric turbulence can be detected at a safe distance. As you might expect, Doppler radar requires powerful computers and is much more expensive than ordinary radar, but the increased safety is well worth the expense. •

The Rock Cycle

When the Earth formed there were no rocks. About 4.5 billion years ago, the great bombardment, the process that built the Earth from the solar nebula, released prodigious amounts of energy as swarms of meteorites crashed into the growing planet, converting gravitational potential energy into heat. That heat produced a molten ball orbiting the Sun. There was no land, no oceans, and no atmosphere. Only when the bombardment subsided and the Earth began to cool did rocks appear. First, as the temperature dropped below the melting point of surface rocks, the outer crust of the Earth gradually solidified like the first layer of ice on a pond in winter. Then, when surface temperatures dropped below the boiling point of water, the first rains must have fallen. Together, these two events began the **rock cycle,** a cycle of internal and external Earth processes by which rock is created, destroyed, and altered.

Rock *formations,* which are bodies of rocks that form as a continuous unit, may be thought of as the "reservoirs" of the rock cycle. The atoms that make up the solid Earth spend most of their lives cycling among igneous, sedimentary, and metamorphic rocks—three principal types of rocks that differ in the processes by which they are formed.

Igneous Rocks

Igneous rocks, which solidify from a hot liquid and thus were the first to appear on the Earth, come in two principal types. **Volcanic** or **extrusive rocks** solidify on the Earth's surface in what are by far the most spectacular of all rock-forming events, volcanic eruptions. Red-hot fountains and flows of lava ooze down the slopes of the growing volcanic cone. The most common variety of volcanic rock is *basalt,* a dark, even-textured rock rich in oxides of silicon, magnesium, iron, calcium, and aluminum. Basalt makes up most of the rock in Hawaii, as well as most of the new material formed at midocean ridges. Other volcanoes feature rocks richer in silicon; if these magmas mix with a significant amount of water or other volatile (easily boiled) substance, the volcanic rock can become the frothy rock called *pumice.*

Igneous rocks that harden underground are called **intrusive rocks.** Dark-colored basalt often exploits underground cracks near volcanoes to form layers or

(a)   (b)

Igneous rocks. (*a*) Devil's Tower in Wyoming represents the neck of a would-be volcano that may have never quite reached the surface. The surrounding sediments have subsequently eroded away. (*b*) Granite from a quarry in Barre, Vermont, solidified from magma deep underground.

sheets of igneous rock. The Palisades on the Hudson River near New York City formed in this way. Lighter in color and density, *granite* is perhaps the most common intrusive rock in the Earth's crust. Hard, durable granite, with its attractive pink or gray colors and speckled array of light and dark minerals, makes an ideal ornamental building stone. New England is particularly famous for its many fine granite quarries.

Igneous rocks are still being formed on Earth—for example, when new plate material is formed at diverging boundaries (see Chapter 17) or in active volcanoes. In other places, such as the Yellowstone Park region, hot springs and geysers reveal hidden sources of underground heat and may indicate places where intrusive igneous rocks are forming today.

Sedimentary Rocks

When the first rains began to fall on the first igneous rocks, the process of *weathering* began. Small grains washed off the recently hardened volcanic rocks, flowed down through streams and rivers into the seas, and were deposited on the seafloors when the fast-moving waters of the rivers met the slower currents of the oceans. Weathering also occurred as water dissolved rocks, and by the mechanical action of water freezing in cracks. Over time, layers of sediment accumulated, especially at the mouths of rivers near the shores of the Earth's new oceans. As more and more sediment collected, these layers became thicker and thicker. In many places on the Earth right now—the Mississippi River Delta that extends into the Gulf of Mexico, for example—layers of sediment may reach several kilometers in thickness.

As the first sediments were buried deeper, temperature and pressure on them increased. In addition, water flowed through the layers of sediments, dissolving and redepositing glue-like chemicals—something like the crusty deposits that can build up on an ordinary faucet when water drips continuously. The net result of all of these processes—pressure, heat, and the effects of mineral-laden water—was to weld the bits of sediment together into new layered rocks. This kind of rock, appropriately called **sedimentary rock**, is made up of grains of material worn off previous rocks. Other common sedimentary rocks, including salt deposits, may form from layers of chemical precipitates.

While uniform sedimentary rocks can form at the base of a single mountain or cliff, the collection of grains often comes together from many different places. The grains in a single fragment of sedimentary rock being formed in the Mississippi delta, for example, may have come from a cliff in Minnesota, a valley in Pennsylvania, and a mountain in Texas. Similarly, sediments deposited near the mouth of the Colorado River carry bits of history from much of the North American West. Deltas inevitably contain particles from all rocks in their rivers' drainage area.

As you travel across the United States you will encounter many common varieties of sedimentary rock. They are easy to spot in road cuts and outcrops because of their characteristic layered appearance, like the pages of a book or a many-layered cake. *Sandstone* forms mostly from sand-sized grains of quartz (silicon dioxide or SiO_2), the commonest mineral at the beach, and from other hard mineral and rock fragments. Sandstone often formed from ancient beaches, deserts, or stream beds—places where concentrations of sand are found today. Sandstone usually feels rough to your touch, and you can just barely see the individual grains that have been cemented together.

Shale and *mudstone* form from sediments that are much finer grained than sand. These rocks commonly accumulate beneath the calm waters of lakes or in

A spectacular example of sedimentary rocks in Utah. The different colored bands correspond to layers of different kinds of materials that were deposited on the floor of a long-vanished ocean. The surrounding sediments have been eroded away to provide material for new sedimentary rocks downstream.

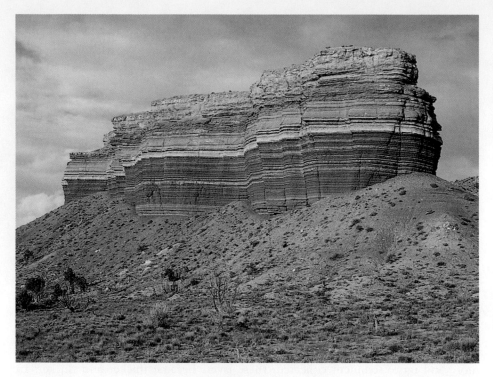

the deep ocean basins—places often teeming with life. There organisms, both large and small, die and are buried in muddy ooze, where they may eventually form into *fossils* that provide us with much information about the evolution of life on Earth (see Chapter 23).

Limestone, another distinctive type of sedimentary rock, forms from the calcium carbonate ($CaCO_3$) skeletons of sea animals, or by chemical precipitation directly from ocean water. Some limestone grows from a gradual rain of microscopic debris or broken shells, while others represent a coral reef that spread across the floor of a shallow sea. Like shale and mudstone, limestone commonly bears fossils.

Given what we know about plate tectonics, and about the constant movement of materials around the surface of the Earth, it should come as no surprise that just because sedimentary rocks originally formed at the bottom of the ocean, they have not necessarily stayed there since their formation. Indeed, it is not at all unusual to see sedimentary rocks in mountain passes thousands of meters above the ocean, or in the middle of continents thousands of kilometers from the nearest open water. Spectacular limestone formations form cliffs above Chattanooga, Tennessee, mountains near El Paso, Texas, and the heart of the Canadian Rockies, all far removed from the ocean.

One of the best places to get an appreciation of sedimentary rocks is at the beach. If you pick up a handful of sand, you will notice that each grain is different. Some are dark colored, some are light. Some have sharp, angular edges, some are smooth and worn down. Each of these grains of sand once was part of a rock in a drainage system of the rivers that feed into the ocean. As the rock weathered away, each grain was chipped off and carried to the sea by wind and water. Eventually, the grains of sand you hold in your hand will be formed into solid rock and subjected to the forces of plate tectonics. That sandstone may some day be uplifted to an altitude far above sea level, where the grain may be weathered again and start the whole cycle all over. Each grain of sand in your hand, then, may have made the trip from rock to beach to sandstone many times in its life.

The story of the grain of sand provides a good model for the way materials move about the surface of the Earth. The atoms of rocks, just like those of the air, water, or your body, are always shifting around, but it is always the same matter—the same atoms—recycling.

THE SCIENCE OF LIFE •

Coral Reefs

Coral reefs are the abodes of countless billions of creatures that build their homes, bit by bit, from calcium carbonate. Reefs thrive in shallow, clear, ocean water with temperatures above 18°C (about 64°F). *The Pelican Island* by British poet James Montgomery (1771–1854) captures the extraordinary phenomenon of entire oceanic islands rising from this biological process:

> *I saw the living pile ascend,*
> *The mausoleum of its architects,*
> *Still dying upwards as their labours closed;*
> *Slime the material, but the slime was turn'd*
> *To adamant, by their petrific touch;*
> *Frail were their frames, ephemeral their lives,*
> *Their masonry imperishable. . . .*
> *Atom by atom, thus their burthen grew,*
> *Even like an infant in the womb, till Time*
> *Deliver'd ocean of that monstrous birth,*
> *—A coral island, stretching east and west.*

Massive limestone reefs like the one in Montgomery's poem once thrived in ancient shallow seas of New York, Illinois, Montana, Texas, and many other places where limestone mountains now stand. •

Coral reefs form around this island in the Pacific.

Metamorphic Rocks

It may happen that sedimentary rocks are buried deep within the Earth and thus subjected to intense pressure and heat. There they will be turned into yet another kind of rock, transformed by the Earth's extreme conditions into **metamorphic rock**. If a shale or mudstone formation is buried like this it may eventually turn into a brittle, hard *slate*, the kind of rock from which school blackboards used to be made. Even higher temperatures and pressure can transform slate into spectacularly banded rocks, called *schists* and *gneisses,* which often boast fine crystals of garnets and other high-pressure minerals. Roadcuts and outcrops of these metamorphic rocks can look like an intensely folded cloth or a giant cross-section of swirled marble cake. Sandstone, when exposed to high temperature and pressure, also metamorphoses, recrystallizing to a durable rock in which the original sand grains fuse into a solid mass known as *quartzite*.

The Story of Marble

Of all the metamorphic rocks, none tells a more astonishing tale than *marble,* a rock of extraordinary beauty. If you ever travel the roads of Vermont, chances are you will pass an outcrop or roadcut of distinctive greenish-white cast, a rock with intricate bands and swirls. These marbles take a high polish and have been prized for centuries by sculptors and architects. But no works of humans can match the epic process that formed the stone.

Most marbles began as limestone, rocks that originate primarily from the skeletal remains of sea life. Over the ages, limestone in the area we now call Vermont was buried deeper and deeper, crushed under the weight of many

The Green Mountains in New Hampshire are made of metamorphic rocks—rocks that have been altered by intense pressure and temperature deep within the Earth, and then uplifted and eroded into mountains.

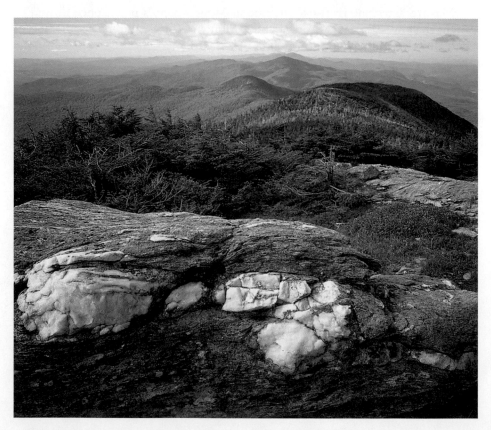

kilometers' thickness of sand, shale, and more limestone in an ancient sea. But no ocean or sea can last forever in our dynamic planet. An ancient collision of the Eurasian and North American plates compressed and deformed this ocean basin, crumpling the layered rock into tight folds and subjecting the sedimentary pile to intense temperatures and pressures. The buckled and contorted formations were uplifted to high elevations when the Appalachian Mountains formed. During the intense pressures and high temperatures associated with the converging tectonic plates, the limestone was metamorphosed to the marble that we use today. Many millions of years of erosion and uplift have exposed these ancient rocks, which are gradually weathering away to begin the cycle again. And humans, in a futile quest for immortality, quarry the marble for their monuments and tombstones and other transient reminders of Earth's incessant change.

Igneous, sedimentary, and metamorphic rocks all participate in the rock cycle. Igneous rocks, once formed, can be weathered to form sedimentary rocks, or they can undergo metamorphism. Layers of sedimentary rocks also can be transformed into metamorphic rocks. All three kinds of rocks can be subducted into the Earth, partially melted, and reformed as new igneous rocks. Thus the rock cycle never ceases.

The Lincoln Memorial is one of many famous monuments carved from marble, a metamorphosed limestone.

SCIENCE IN THE MAKING •

Hutton and the Discovery of "Deep Time"

Near the town of Jedburgh in Scotland is a curious cliff that reveals vertical layers of rock overlain by horizontal layers. How could such a sequence have occurred? In the last decades of the eighteenth century, Scottish scientist James Hutton (1726–1797), a man who is often called "the father of modern geology," studied this remarkable cliff and realized that he was seeing the result of an incredibly long period of geological turmoil.

Knowing what you now know about sedimentary rocks, you will realize when you look at this cliff that you are seeing the end product of a long chain of events (Figure 18-8). First, a series of sedimentary rocks was laid down in the usual horizontal fashion, one flat layer on top of another. Then some tectonic activity disrupted those layers, breaking and folding them until they were tilted nearly

James Hutton recognized the immense spans of time required to form this spectacular outcrop at Siccar Point, Berwickshire, Scotland.

• **Figure 18-8** This series of diagrams shows several stages in the history of the Jedburgh outcrop. (*a*) Layers of sediment were gradually deposited in water. (*b*) Those sediments, deeply buried, were compressed and tilted during tectonic activity. (*c*) Uplift brought the tilted sediments to the surface, where they were partly eroded. (*d*) The rocks subsided, and a new cycle of sedimentation began.

(*a*) Gradual sedimentation

(*b*) Burial and deformation

(*c*) Uplift and erosion

(*d*) Gradual sedimentation

vertically. Then, after still more tectonic activity, the rocks found themselves at the bottom of an ocean and another layer of sedimentary rocks formed on top of them. Finally, an episode of uplift and erosion has brought the rocks to our view.

Hutton realized that geological forces must have been operating for very long times indeed. Each step of the formation process—gradual sedimentation, burial, folding, uplift, more sedimentation, and so on—would require countless generations, based on observations of ongoing geological processes. In the words of nature writer John McPhee, Hutton had discovered "deep time." In order for a formation like the one at Jedburgh to exist, the Earth had to exist not for thousands of years or even hundreds of thousands of years, but for many millions of years.

Today, we know that the age of the Earth is calculated in billions of years, and the existence of structures like this is not surprising. At the time of its interpretation by James Hutton, however, the rocks at Jedburgh provided a totally new insight into the inconceivable antiquity of our planet.

In the words of Hutton himself, the testimony of the rocks offered "no vestige of a beginning, no prospect of an end." •

Science News | Slippin' Slide
(SCIENCE NEWS, VOL. 163, MARCH 8, 2003, P. 149)

Ice on the Antarctic continent plays a major role in the hydrological cycle on our planet. In the western part of the continent, the glaciers flow toward the sea, forming large floating structures known as ice shelves. In 1995, one of these shelves, known as the Larsen A ice shelf, broke off and drifted out to sea. Since that time, scientists in Buenos Aires have been monitoring the rate of flow of glaciers on land, and have found some rather puzzling results.

Antarctic glaciers do not move all together, but in what are called ice streams—rivers of ice flowing through their more stationary counterparts. Using satellite photos, the scientists have discovered that glaciers near the sea have sped up since 1995. One, for example, has been clocked at 2 meters per day, over four times its speed before 1995 and twice its speed in 1999. Similar results have been seen for other streams near the ocean. Farther inland, however, ice on higher elevations has either not increased its speed at all or done so only modestly. Consequently, they are seeing the formation of ice terraces—20- to 40-meter-tall structures—as the differential movement stretches the ice out.

If the speedup continues and brings more new ice into the ocean, it could contribute to a rise in the world's sea levels (ice already floating does not make such a contribution when it melts, since it has already displaced an amount of water equal to its mass).

The Interdependence of Earth's Cycles

We have described the hydrologic, atmospheric, and rock cycles as if they were completely independent of each other, as if they operated alone in splendid isolation. In fact, each cycle affects and is affected by the others.

The amount of rainfall in a given location affects the rate of erosion and thus the amount of sediment being deposited in deltas—and therefore the amount of sedimentary rock being formed. In this way the atmospheric and water cycles affect the rock cycle. In the same way, the breakdown of rock is essential to the formation of soils in which plants grow. The presence of plants, in turn, affects the absorption of sunlight at the Earth's surface and thus the energy balance that controls the movement of the winds and ocean currents. And, over hundreds of millions of years, the global cycle of plate tectonics, which controls the distribution of the Earth's mountains and oceans, influences all other cycles. Thus, although Earth's cycles operate on very different time scales, they constantly influence each other.

Thinking More About | Cycles

Beach Erosion

Something about the shore appeals to people. Beach-front property is considered to be highly desirable, and over the past half-century America's prosperity has resulted in large-scale development of the Atlantic and Gulf coastlines. As a result, Americans are becoming very aware of the effects of natural cycles on property values.

Beaches, like all other systems in nature, are not static but change in response to environmental forces. The action of waves transports sand grains from one place and deposits them somewhere else. Large waves tend to move sand away from a beach and deposit it in offshore bars, while smaller waves tend to move the sand back toward the beach. Thus a seasonal movement of sand occurs on many beaches—offshore in the winter (when storms send in large waves), and onshore during the summer. In addition, waves normally strike a beach at a slight angle, a phenomenon that moves sand along the beachfront. Large storms may completely destroy beaches and dunes, which are rebuilt farther inland over time. Thus every beach is a dynamic, shifting system. Left to itself, a beach will move around in response to the forces of wave and storm.

If the beach were left to itself this cycle of change would cause no problems. If, however, waterfront properties worth many millions of dollars have been developed on or near the beach, such movements have enormous economic consequences for homeowners. Should governments use public funds to try to protect such homes? Should the government provide low-cost insurance to indemnify the owners for loss? Should insurance be issued to allow people to rebuild beach-front homes after a storm?

SUMMARY

Matter that forms the outer layers of the Earth follows many cycles, driven by the energy of the Sun and the Earth's inner heat energy. Each cycle can be analyzed in terms of *reservoirs* that hold matter, and by the movement of matter between reservoirs.

The *hydrologic cycle* traces the path of water as it evaporates from the oceans, falls back to Earth as rain, and forms lakes, rivers, *ice caps, glaciers,* and *groundwater* reservoirs. During unusually cold climatic periods, more water falls as snow, creating a white reflective blanket that further reduces the amount of absorbed solar radiation. This situation, if prolonged, can lead to an *ice age,* during which ocean levels drop significantly and great sheets of ice cover the land at high and middle latitudes. Temperatures in these latitudes may be moderated, however, by ocean *currents* that are important in redistributing temperatures at the Earth's surface.

The *atmospheric cycle* of the *weather* redistributes solar energy from the warmer equatorial regions to higher latitudes through the development of global convection cells of air. The prevailing westerly flow of weather across North America marks one of these large cells, while the *jet stream* delineates the boundary between this flow and the contrary cell to our north. *Climate,* in contrast to weather, varies much more slowly in response to ocean circulation, the Sun's energy output, the positions of continents and mountain ranges, and other relatively fixed conditions.

The solid materials of the Earth's crust are subject to the *rock cycle.* The first solids to form on the cooling planet were *igneous rocks,* which are formed from hot, molten material. *Volcanic* or *extrusive* igneous rocks solidify on the surface, while *intrusive* igneous rocks cool underground. The first igneous rocks were subjected to weathering by wind and rain, which eventually produced layers of sediment and the first *sedimentary rocks.* Sandstone, shale, limestone, and other sedimentary rocks were deposited in ocean basins, layer upon layer, in sequences often many kilometers thick. Igneous and sedimentary rocks were subsequently buried and transformed by the Earth's internal temperature and pressure to form *metamorphic rocks.* Each of the three major rock types—igneous, sedimentary, and metamorphic—can be converted into the others by the ongoing processes of the rock cycle.

KEY TERMS ABOUT EARTH CYCLES

reservoirs	groundwater	weather	igneous rock	sedimentary rock
hydrologic cycle	current	climate	volcanic or	metamorphic rock
ice caps	ice age	jet stream	extrusive rock	
glaciers	atmospheric cycle	rock cycle	intrusive rock	

REVIEW QUESTIONS

1. What happens to matter during a cyclical process?

2. What form of energy drives the hydrologic cycle, the movement of tectonic plates, and weather patterns?

3. What are two steps in the analysis of a cycle of Earth material?

4. What are the principal repositories of water on Earth?

5. Identify three ways that water moves between repositories.

6. How does water move within the oceans? How does it move within glaciers?

7. By what processes does the amount of water on Earth change from year to year? What is the magnitude of this change from year to year?

8. What are the differences between ice caps and glaciers?

9. What factors might cause glaciers to advance from polar areas to more temperate zones?

10. How do ocean currents affect local climate?

11. Why do we call groundwater in most areas a "nonrenewable resource?"

12. What is the difference between weather and climate? Describe the weather and climate of your area.

13. In what ways are air masses like reservoirs of the atmosphere?

14. What are the five variables that describe the weather?

15. Why does air pressure vary from place to place?

16. What is the prevailing direction of the jet stream? How does it influence your weather?

17. How does the atmosphere distribute heat across the Earth's surface?

18. If land heats up more quickly than water, what does this tell you about their relative heat capacities?

19. Why were igneous rocks the Earth's first rocks?

20. What are three main kinds of rocks? How do they form?

21. If you were driving past a large roadcut through rock, what features might you observe to tell you its origin?

DISCUSSION QUESTIONS

1. In the case of the cycle of an aluminum atom, what are some of the reservoirs of aluminum?

2. Describe three places where you might find volcanic rocks forming today. Describe three places where you could watch sedimentary rocks forming today. Where would you have to go to watch metamorphic rocks form?

3. The thickness of polar ice caps depends critically on the location of continents; much thicker ice can accumulate on land than in water. Where is the only polar continent now?

4. What kind of rock underlies your campus? Are any rock outcrops nearby? Was your area ever under a large body of water?

5. How do oceans redistribute Earth's heat? How does the atmosphere accomplish this? Do rocks redistribute heat? Which global cycle is most efficient in transferring heat? Why?

6. You can often distinguish surface ocean currents because their color is different from the surrounding ocean. Why do you think this is so?

7. On the Jovian planets, the amount of heat coming from the interior of the planet is about equal to the amount that falls as sunlight. Should this affect the way the atmosphere circulates on these planets? Why or why not?

PROBLEMS

1. How much calcium is in a cubic kilometer of seawater? [*Hint*: Refer to Table 18-2.]

2. If copper is worth 20 cents per kilogram, what is the value of the copper in a cubic kilometer of seawater?

3. An impressive limestone deposit in north-central Montana is 2000 meters thick. If limestone grows at an average rate of 1 millimeter per year, how long did it take to form this limestone deposit?

4. Record the temperature, atmospheric pressure, and cloudiness at both noon and midnight in your area for a period of at least 15 days. (You can find these data on the Internet.)

a. Graph the temperature versus pressure. Is there a systematic trend? Why?

b. Is there a relationship between atmospheric pressure and cloudiness? Why?

c. Is there a correlation between cloudiness and the difference between temperatures at noon and midnight? Why?

INVESTIGATIONS

1. Look at some weather maps in your local newspaper over a period of several weeks and see if observing weather patterns to the west of your location is a good predictor of your weather. Why should this be so?

2. Where does water come from at your college? Is the water processed or treated in any way? How long might that source of water last? What alternatives exist if that supply is depleted?

3. The three kinds of rocks—igneous, sedimentary, and metamorphic—are described in this chapter as being quite distinct, yet some earth scientists have engaged in an intense debate about the origins of certain rocks, such as granites, that formed at high

temperature deep within the Earth. Some scientists claim that these rocks are igneous, while others say they are metamorphic. How could such a debate arise, and how could it be resolved? [*Hint*: Think about making taffy.]

4. Investigate the biological cycle of calcium in your body. Where in your body is calcium used? How often is it replaced? How much calcium do you need to con-sume each day? What are the best food sources of this element?

5. What are the "doldrums" and how do they form? What role have they played in poetry and literature?

6. Many movies have been made about weather dis-asters—hurricanes, tornadoes, blizzards, and so on. Watch such a movie and comment on the accuracy of the science portrayed.

WWW Resources

See *The Sciences* homepage at: **http://www.wiley.com/college/trefil** for valuable web links.

1. http://college.hmco.com/geology/resources/geologylink/index.html
Geologylink—don't miss the "Virtual Fieldtrip"—great site!

2. http://www.yellowstone.net/geysers
Yellowstone Net Geyser Information—this site will make you want to see it for yourself.

3. http://www.glacier.rice.edu
Glacier, a site about Antarctica, where you can learn about ice, oceans, and meteorology.

4. http://www.noaa.gov/
NOAA Home Page, a vast and diverse wealth of information from the National Oceanic and Atmospheric Administration.

19

Ecology, Ecosystems, and the Environment

Are human activities affecting the global environment?

GREAT IDEA

Ecosystems are interdependent communities of living things that recycle matter while energy flows through.

PHYSICS

Smokestacks equipped with electrostatic precipitators rely on electromagnetic forces to collect ash and soot particles.

CHEMISTRY

Burning fossil fuels releases nitrogen and sulfur compounds, which react with water in the air to form acid rain.

ENVIRONMENT

A gradual buildup of atmospheric carbon dioxide may lead to global warming caused by the greenhouse effect.

GEOLOGY

Acid rain has increased the rate of weathering of rocks, most notably limestone and other sedimentary rocks used in buildings and statues.

HEALTH & SAFETY

The release of CFCs into the atmosphere has caused a decrease in the concentration of protective ozone, and may contribute to an increase in skin cancer.

ASTRONOMY

The intense output of ultraviolet radiation from the Sun is largely absorbed by the Earth's ozone layer.

TECHNOLOGY

New methods of recycling, such as the use of surfactants, play a significant role in reducing solid waste in the United States.

BIOLOGY

Energy in ecosystems flows from the Sun through plants to herbivores, then carnivores.

Red = applications of the great idea discussed in this chapter.

Orange = other applications, some of which are explored in other chapters.

Y̲ou and a friend decide to take a walk down the beach, away from the crowd. Along a deserted stretch you watch as dozens of small shorebirds scurry back and forth, poking their long pointed bills into the wet sand. They seem to be searching for food. A closer look reveals tiny air holes in the sand—the telltale signs of tiny crustaceans. Father down the beach, the sand is littered with small shiny shells; a golfball-sized crab scurries by, and smelly strands of seaweed wash up onto the shore.

But those life forms are only the most obvious members of the oceanside community. If you could take a small sample of beach sand and examine it under a microscope, you would observe countless bacteria and other tiny organisms that thrive in the tidal environment. The beach turns out to be a richly varied community of organisms.

In much the same way, a full understanding of our living planet will come if you view it not as a series of isolated individuals, but as one vast interconnected community.

Ecology and Ecosystems

Think about the wonderful communities of living things that you've seen in your travels—deep woods and flowering meadows, shallow ponds and ocean beaches, dry deserts and stagnant swamps. Perhaps you've been lucky enough to hike in high-mountain tundra or go snorkeling at a coral reef. Each of these places boasts a collection of interdependent living organisms in a distinctive physical environment.

 Stop and Think! What characteristics do all the living communities that we have just listed have in common?

The word **ecology**, derived from the Greek word for household or housekeeping, is the branch of science that focuses on natural living systems in the broadest sense. An **ecosystem** includes all the different kinds of living things that live in a given area, together with their physical surroundings. In every ecosystem, some organisms, such as plants, act as producers; they obtain atoms and energy from their physical surroundings and convert them into the essential carbon-based molecules of life. These biomolecules then sustain other organisms, such as animals, which act as *consumers* in ecosystems. In addition, still other lifeforms, including bacteria and fungi, act as *decomposers* that renew the raw materials of life. Together, these diverse organisms form an interdependent *community*.

An ecosystem can be as small as a single community of organisms on and near a bush in a tropical forest. It can be an aquarium in your living room, or a lake, including all the fish, insects, plants, and microrganisms in it. Or an ecosystem can be a mountain meadow, a salt marsh, a continent, even an entire planet. No matter what size ecosystem we talk about, however, the emphasis of ecology is to look at the system—its matter and its energy—as a whole, rather than as a group of independent parts.

Every living organism, from single cells to complex animals and plants, relies on its ecosystem to sustain life. Indeed, the continuance of life on Earth is not a property of isolated individual organisms or even of species, but rather of ecosystems. One key to understanding living organisms, therefore, is to examine the ecosystems in which they survive.

Much can be learned from looking at living things as part of integrated natural systems, but this realization is relatively recent. Throughout the nineteenth century, for example, biologists were concerned with cataloging living things, and paid little attention to how they were affected by (and, in turn, affected) their environment. Only within the last few decades have many of the insights discussed in this chapter come to be recognized as different aspects of the study of ecology.

Characteristics of Ecosystems

Ecosystems are richly varied. They occur on virtually every body of water and parcel of land on Earth, from the deepest ocean trench to the highest mountain range. Yet, in spite of this diversity, all ecosystems share a few basic characteristics. As you read about these characteristics, think about how they apply to an ecosystem near your home.

1. Every Ecosystem Consists of Both Living and Nonliving Parts

Nonliving or *abiotic* parts form the chemical and physical **environment** of the ecosystem—the water, soil, atmosphere, and so forth. Local climate, including average temperature, rainfall, winds, and Sun exposure, are important physical properties of land ecosystems, whereas water temperature, pressure, salinity, and acidity help to characterize ecosystems in oceans, lakes, and other bodies of water.

Living organisms form the *biotic* part of an ecosystem; they form an *ecological community,* which may be defined as all the individuals in an area that interact with each other to maintain life. In a forest ecosystem, for example, an ecological

Complex coral reef ecosystems are extremely sensitive to changes in local conditions, such as salinity and water temperature. Large areas of coral near the coasts of North and South America are endangered by human activity.

community will include trees, shrubs, insects, birds, snakes, and squirrels, as well as fungi, bacteria, and a host of other microscopic organisms in the soil.

2. Energy Flows Through Ecosystems

The most important interactions of organisms in an ecological community are by way of a *food chain* or *food web,* which indicates who feeds on whom. Each species in a food web obtains energy and chemicals from other organisms; in turn, each species provides energy and chemicals for other organisms. Insects eat plants, birds eat insects, bacteria and fungi in the soil decompose birds and other organisms when they die, and plants obtain vital nutrients from the soil. Food webs for ecological communities may be extremely complex.

The flow of energy between *trophic levels* (see Chapter 3) is an important unifying characteristic of all ecosystems. The first trophic level of photosynthetic plants, which use only the Sun's energy, provides energy for herbivores in the second trophic level. Herbivores, in turn, pass some of their energy to carnivores of the third trophic level, and so on. Decomposers, including bacteria and fungi, obtain energy from all other trophic levels. In each energy transfer from one trophic level to another, most of the available energy cannot be recovered in a useful form; it eventually radiates into space as waste heat (see Chapter 4). In fact, only about 10% of the energy available at one trophic level finds its way to the next. Thus as energy flows through an ecosystem it must be replaced continuously.

3. Matter Is Recycled by Ecosystems

Atoms continuously cycle from one part of the Earth to another. Perhaps the easiest way to understand the cycling of atoms through the Earth's biosphere is to follow the *carbon cycle.* This cycle can be illustrated by looking at the possible path of a single atom of carbon that leaves your lungs the next time you breathe out a molecule of carbon dioxide. This carbon atom enters the atmosphere, where many different things can happen to it (Figure 19-1). It can, for example, be taken up by a plant during photosynthesis and then be incorporated into the tissues of a tree or a blade of grass. The plant can then be eaten so that the carbon atom becomes part of the tissue of a herbivore. Alternatively, the carbon can simply return to the atmosphere if the plant dies and rots without being eaten.

If the carbon atom is taken into the tissue of a herbivore, then it may show up on your dinner plate one day and be taken into your body as part of some food you eat. It might even be incorporated into your own body to stay there until you die, or to move through the chemical cycles described in Chapter 22. In either case, the carbon atom, in time, will enter the atmosphere again.

Another possible track for a carbon atom is shown in Figure 19-1. It can enter the ocean by being added to a mollusk shell or the skeleton of a microscopic organism. Upon the death of the organism, these hard parts sink to the ocean bottom, where, in the form of calcium carbonate, they are turned into limestone. In this case, the carbon atom can remain locked up for hundreds of millions of years until the limestone is weathered and the carbon is released into the atmosphere.

A single atom of carbon, in other words, may have gone through many different chemical reactions during the 4.5-billion-year life of the planet, and will continue to do so as long as the Earth has living things on it. The one thing it will not do, however, is leave the planet. A similar story can be told for an atom of nitrogen or phosphorus or any other chemical element in the Earth.

 Stop and Think! Some toxic chemicals, such as the heavy metal mercury and the pesticide DDT, may gradually concentrate to harmful levels in living things, because cells have no mechanisms to remove them. These

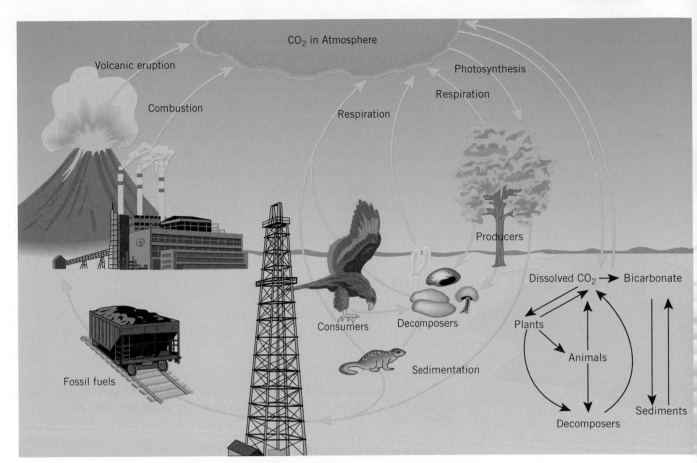

• **Figure 19-1** The carbon cycle. Carbon atoms cycle through both living (biotic) and nonliving (abiotic) parts of the Earth's ecosystem. They are found in carbon dioxide in the air, then taken into plants to become part of their structure. If a plant is eaten, the carbon may be returned to the air through respiration or become part of an animal's tissue. When the animal dies, the carbon dioxide returns to the air. Carbon atoms may also be locked into sedimentary rocks such as shale and limestone.

dangerous substances are observed to be most concentrated in species at the top of the food chain—a phenomenon known as *bioconcentration* or *biological magnification*. Based on the characteristics of ecosystems, why should this phenomenon occur?

4. Every Organism Occupies an Ecological Niche

The **ecological niche**, a central concept in ecology, refers to a particular mode of survival—a particular way of obtaining matter and energy—within an ecosystem. In a forest ecosystem there may be a niche that can be filled by one or more kinds of warm-blooded, insect-eating, nocturnal animals—bats, for example. Mushrooms growing in shaded wooded areas may fill another niche. Each plant or animal in an ecosystem fills an ecological niche, and different organisms compete for dominance in their preferred ecological niche.

5. Stable Ecosystems Achieve a Balance Among Their Populations

This balance, called *homeostasis*, reflects the fact that matter and energy are limited resources that must be shared among all individuals of an ecosystem. An ecosystem in homeostasis will exhibit some variations in population sizes, as food supplies and other factors vary from season to season and year to year. But the overall distribution of species is usually relatively constant. A one-acre sunny meadow, for example, will boast a large but limited amount of grasses, flowering plants, and other vegetation. Year in and year out, those plants support a limited population of insects, which in turn will feed perhaps a few dozen birds.

6. Ecosystems Are Not Permanent, but Change Over Time

While ecosystems may appear to be stable, in fact we know that they change over time. On the longest time scales, the effects of plate tectonics will change the climate in a given area, converting a desert into a fertile plain, for example. On shorter time scales, the advance and retreat of glaciers can have a similar effect, as can changes in patterns of precipitation. Even on very short time scales, the introduction of a new species, by humans or by nature, can profoundly change the pattern of life in a given area. As the science of ecology progresses, understanding and predicting these sorts of changes is becoming a major research goal.

The Law of Unintended Consequences

The complex interweaving of living things in their environment leads to a central insight in the science of ecology, an idea called the **law of unintended consequences.**

> **It is virtually impossible to change one aspect of a complex system without affecting other parts of the system, often in as-yet unpredictable ways.**

Whenever we change something in an ecosystem other changes will follow, and we have to consider what that might be. Examples of this "law" appear in the news almost daily: building levees on the Mississippi River has caused unintended intensification of flooding; extracting petroleum and water from underground reservoirs has caused unintended land subsidence; building jetties into the ocean has resulted in unintended erosion of beaches. Each of these systems is interdependent, so the whole responds to every stimulus.

As often happens when scientists and engineers encounter complex systems for the first time, a good deal of observation and trial and error has to take place before an understanding of the system begins to emerge. Unfortunately, during that period of study serious mistakes can be made (see the discussion of Lake Victoria below). Eventually, however, people learn how to proceed, and begin to undertake large-scale projects with some confidence. At the moment, for example, the largest reconstruction project ever attempted is being undertaken in the Everglades of South Florida. The Everglades Restoration Plan is designed to restore the Everglades by changing the flow of water in the entire southern part of the state. As the plan proceeds, you can be sure that everyone—engineers and environmentalists alike, will have the law of unintended consequences firmly in mind.

The Lake Victoria Disaster

Millions of people who live on the shores of Lake Victoria, the largest freshwater lake in Africa, know firsthand about the law of unintended consequences. What was once a rich fishing ground and source of most of their protein has been radically altered by the introduction of a single new species—the Nile perch.

About 30 years ago, sport fishermen, seeking a greater challenge for the growing tourist market, introduced this large, aggressive predator into the lake. The perch thrived and rapidly ate up populations of smaller fish that not only provided an essential part of the local diet but also controlled populations of algae and parasite-bearing snails. Unchecked, live algae spread over the lake's surface, while dead algae sank, decayed, and consumed oxygen in deeper water where fish used to live. Snails have also multiplied and become a serious health hazard because they carry parasites that can affect humans.

Native fishermen now rely on Nile perch, which weigh up to several hundred pounds each, rather than smaller fish, but this change carries its own ecological consequences. Unlike the small fish that were sun dried, Nile perch must be roasted over fires. Lake Victoria's shoreline, each year stripped of more trees for this purpose, is suffering extensive soil erosion and further unanticipated changes to the lake's ecosystem. A single new species has thus drastically altered a vast ecosystem.

 Stop and Think! The ecologist Garrett Hardin has stated as a principle of ecology that "We can never do merely one thing." What do you think he meant by this?

SCIENCE IN THE MAKING •

Island Biogeography

Because ecosystems are so complex, it is sometimes difficult to draw unambiguous conclusions from field studies. In 1963, however, American ecologists Robert MacArthur and Edward O. Wilson looked at the populations on islands, small ecosystems separated from the rest of the terrestrial world by water. From their study, they were able to frame a hypothesis: Whenever a new species migrates to an island that already has a thriving and stable ecosystem, it will flourish only if another species becomes extinct. According to this so-called equilibrium hypothesis, only a fixed number of species exist in any ecosystem, and if a new species invades, one of the old species will be driven to extinction.

The hypothesis was supported a few years later by Wilson and Daniel Simberloff in a classic ecological experiment. They first surveyed all the insects and crustaceans on a series of small mangrove islands off the coast of southern Florida. They then removed all living animals on the islands by draping large plastic sheets over them and fumigating. Over a period of years, they watched the islands undergo the process of repopulation as new animals migrated from the mainland or from other islands. As expected, the total number of species on each island at the end was about the same as it had been at the beginning. Perhaps less expected, however, was the fact that the kinds of animals on the repopulated islands were often quite different from those that had been there before. New species that happened to be carried to an island on the tides were able to establish themselves in particular ecological niches, which were then unavailable to competitors that arrived later.

In 1995, nature began a similar experiment on its own. A violent hurricane propelled a large raft of fallen trees along with 15 green iguanas—spiny lizards up to four feet in length—from the Caribbean island of Guadeloupe to the island of Anguilla, 200 miles away. A new colony of green iguanas has begun to breed on Anguilla, and it soon will be competing for resources with the native species of brown iguanas. Ecologists are keeping close tabs on this dramatic example of changing island ecology. •

New species migrate to islands like this, reestablishing ecosystems.

Threats to the Global Ecosystem and Environment

The resources of our global ecosystem are vast but limited, and we often don't know enough about them to predict accurately how they will respond to change. These two inescapable facts, coupled with the growing pressure of human populations for energy and material goods, have led to a number of large-scale environmental problems. We are going to look at four of those problems—the disposal of solid waste, the degradation of the ozone layer, acid rain, and the greenhouse effect. All of these problems are serious, but their solutions entail different levels of national and international commitment. Taken together, they provide a sense of how ecosystems respond to human activities, as well as the difficulties that will have to be solved in order for our industrial society to keep functioning.

The Problem of Urban Landfills

The fact that nothing is ever really thrown away has become very much a concern in urban America (Figure 19-2). The problem is that garbage (so-called solid waste) is generated at an enormous rate in American cities today. New York City alone adds 17,000 tons of solid waste to its landfill on Staten Island every day. Environmental engineers estimate that, at current rates, every individual American will generate solid waste equivalent in volume to the Statue of Liberty in only about five years.

To make matters worse, the nature of modern landfills is such that the normal process of breakdown and decay in the carbon and nitrogen cycles is slowed enormously. In a landfill, solid waste is dumped on the ground and compacted, then covered with a layer of dirt, then another layer of compacted waste, then another layer of dirt, and so on. Material in such a landfill is cut off from air and water, and the bacteria that normally operate to decompose the waste cannot thrive. Archaeologists digging into landfills have discovered, for example, that newspapers from the 1950s are still readable after having been buried for a half century! This situation means that, unlike an ordinary garden compost pile, in which materials are

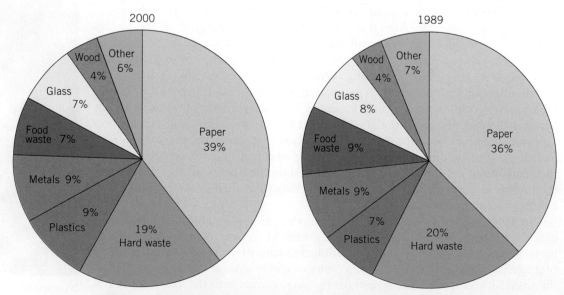

• **Figure 19-2** The percentage of different kinds of trash in urban landfills in 1989 (right) and percentages for 2000 (left). Not much progress, is there?

quickly broken down by the action of bacteria, the landfill is really more like a burial site than a location for recycling.

Two approaches respond to the problem of solid waste. One strategy is recycling; every aluminum can that is recycled is one that won't be taking up space in a landfill. The other approach is the creation in rural areas of large depositories that are designed to accept waste shipped from distant locations. Cities pay more to ship and dump trash in facilities like this, but the costs are relatively modest compared to building new landfills close to home.

SCIENCE BY THE NUMBERS •

Trash

How much solid waste is produced in the United States every year? Engineers estimate that the average American each year is responsible for about 40 tons (80,000 pounds) of trash, including everything from disposable containers, newspapers, and mail-order catalogs to old automobiles and appliances, as well as the industrial wastes necessary to manufacture the things we buy. What is the total volume of this waste? Compacted trash typically weighs about 80 pounds per cubic foot—somewhat denser than water, but less dense than rock (of course, it takes up much more volume before it's compacted). Forty tons, therefore, is equivalent to a volume of

$$\frac{80,000 \text{ pounds}}{80 \text{ pounds per cubic foot}} = 1000 \text{ cubic feet}$$

That's enough compacted trash to fill two large dump trucks for every man, woman, and child in the United States every year. Thus 250 million Americans produce a total annual volume of trash of

$$250,000,000 \text{ people} \times 1000 \text{ cubic feet/person} = 2.5 \times 10^{11} \text{ cubic feet}$$

That's almost two cubic miles of trash every year, enough to build a solid 500-foot-wide wall across the Grand Canyon at its widest and deepest point. •

TECHNOLOGY •

The Science in Recycling

Because land that can be used for dumps near big cities is growing ever more scarce, and because the environmental cost of using materials once and then throwing them away is growing steadily, governments have recently begun to pay more attention to recycling. Every recycled plastic milk jug or sheet of paper means less material in landfills, as well as less petroleum taken from the ground or less energy used to convert wood pulp to paper.

But recycling is not as easy as it sounds. A great deal of science and engineering has to be done before even the simplest materials can be reused. In addition, the processes that have to take place to recover one kind of material are, in general, different from those needed to recover another. The recycling of different kinds of plastics (see Chapter 10), for example, requires different kinds of chemical reactions, and processes that work for plastic soft-drink bottles will not necessarily work for ketchup containers. As a result, each kind of material that is to be recycled poses its own unique problems to an engineer.

Take white paper, for example. The average office worker generates about 250 pounds of high-grade paper waste per year, and many offices around the country have paper recycling programs. The first step in this process is simple: the paper is ground up into a pulp and added to water to make a slurry. Ink particles from typewriters and pens rise to the surface of the slurry and can be skimmed off, leaving a material that can be added to fresh pulp to make new paper. As we pointed out in Chapter 5, however, copying machines and laser printers work by melting bits of carbon mixed with resins onto the paper. That sort of ink makes heavier particles when the paper is ground up, and those particles sink to the bottom along with the paper fibers. Until quite recently, such paper could be recycled only into products such as cardboard or tissue paper, for which color quality is not important.

The new technology for dealing with this problem involves the addition of substances called surfactants to the pulp. The molecules in these substances bind to the heavier ink particles on one end, and to bubbles of gas on the other. Once the molecules are attached to the ink, various gases are bubbled through the slurry. The surfactants and their load of ink rise to the surface with the bubbles and are skimmed off, leaving clean paper fibers for reuse.

A national recycling effort will involve hundreds of different processes such as this, each geared to a specific material, but each doing its part to make a coherent whole. •

The Ozone Problem

In Chapter 14 we pointed out that, although the Sun gives off most of its radiation in visible light, a certain amount of that radiation comes in the form of ultraviolet light from the higher-energy part of the spectrum. Ultraviolet radiation can be very damaging to living organisms; indeed, it is routinely used to sterilize equipment in hospitals. If the surface of the Earth were not shielded in some way from the Sun's ultraviolet rays, life on land would be very different, if not impossible.

Ozone, a molecule made up of three oxygen atoms instead of the usual two, absorbs ultraviolet radiation. If enough ozone molecules exist in the atmosphere, they will absorb most of the ultraviolet radiation from the Sun and keep it from reaching the ground. In fact, a protective shield of ozone formed high in the Earth's atmosphere several hundred million years ago, and it was only after this shield formed that life moved onto land.

The Ozone Layer

Scientists detect ozone in the atmosphere by using several techniques. One is simply to fly specialized aircraft into the region where ozone is common and collect samples. For the past decade or so, this kind of sampling has been done routinely by organizations such as the National Oceanic and Atmospheric Administration (usually called "Noah" after its acronym NOAA) and its counterparts in other countries. Another way to detect ozone is to measure characteristic spectral lines given off by the ozone molecule (see Chapter 6). These measurements can be made from satellites, from aircraft, or by ground-based observers. In general, all these techniques are now used to give us a picture of the health of the ozone layer.

Measurements reveal that ozone is a trace gas that constitutes less than one molecule in a million in the Earth's atmosphere. Although ozone is found at every altitude (you are breathing a small amount even as you read this), most of the ozone is found some 30 kilometers (about 20 miles) up (Figure 19-3). In this region, concentrations of ozone are significantly higher than they are in other parts of the atmosphere, although even here the amounts are very small. This region of enhanced ozone concentration is called the **ozone layer**. Most of the absorption of ultraviolet radiation goes on in this layer, but it should not be thought of as anything analogous to a cloud bank in the sky.

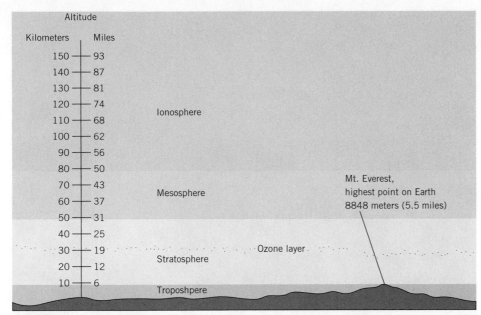

• **Figure 19-3** The ozone layer. Although ozone is found everywhere in the atmosphere, even at ground level, it is concentrated in a layer some 20 miles above the Earth's surface. The labels on the left are the standard terms scientists use to describe different levels of the atmosphere.

The Ozone Hole

In 1985, British scientists working in Antarctica noticed that during the Antarctic spring (roughly the months of September through November) the amount of ozone in the ozone layer dropped significantly. Later studies from satellites and ground-based experiments confirmed these results. During this period of the year, the concentration of ozone above Antarctica falls by different amounts in different years. The region over the Antarctic where this phenomenon occurred was dubbed the **ozone hole** (see Figure 19-4). The ozone hole is not a place where the atmosphere has disappeared, but is a volume of the atmosphere in which the concentration of the trace gas ozone has declined significantly. Scientists became concerned about the appearance of the ozone hole, because the ozone layer worldwide is so vital to the existence of life on our planet.

In the 1950s, scientists introduced a new class of chemicals—*chlorofluorocarbons (CFCs)*—that were a boon to industry. Chlorofluorocarbons are very stable and nontoxic gases; they last a long time and do not break down readily when they are released into the atmosphere. Inexpensive CFCs were ideal for increasingly popular aerosol spray products, and they were valued replacements for rather nasty chemicals such as ammonia that had been used in refrigerators and air-conditioners. Thus CFCs played a key role in the great air-conditioning boom that made the southern part of the United States comfortably habitable during the summer.

In the mid-1970s, before the ozone hole was discovered, a group of researchers realized that CFCs might cause destruction of ozone in the atmosphere. Once the annual appearance of the ozone hole was firmly established in the 1980s, concerns over the role of CFCs increased. In a classic example of the law of unintended consequences, seemingly benign CFCs turned out to present a very real danger to the Earth's ozone layer. Over periods of time that range into the decades, molecules of CFCs work their way into the upper regions of the atmosphere, where they can be broken apart by high-energy ultraviolet radiation

• **Figure 19-4** The dark area marks a region of lower ozone concentration over Antarctica.

Sep 6 2000

from the Sun. The chlorine atoms that are freed in this way act as a catalyst in a reaction that can be written as follows:

▶ **In words:** (ozone plus chlorine plus sunlight) become (ordinary oxygen plus chlorine)

▶ **In symbols:**

$$2O_3 + Cl + \text{sunlight} \rightarrow 3O_2 + Cl$$

While this reaction proceeds very slowly, each chlorine atom liberated from a CFC can, over time, destroy millions of ozone molecules before it is safely locked into another chemical species in the atmosphere.

Over most of the Earth, the effect of the chlorine atoms is not striking because new ozone molecules are being created all the time. In the Antarctic, however, a number of unusual circumstances come together to create the ozone hole. For one thing, during the months immediately preceding the hole, no sunlight falls in the Antarctic region of the Earth. This period of darkness leads to the appearance of high clouds made entirely of ice crystals, the so-called polar stratospheric clouds. Crystals of ice in these clouds provide sites on which molecules that contain chlorine atoms undergo a series of chemical reactions. These chemical reactions proceed up to the final step before ozone molecules are actually broken down. As soon as high energy in the form of ultraviolet sunlight returns in the Antarctic spring, the destruction of ozone proceeds very quickly because large quantities of ozone-destroying chlorine atoms are released all at once. The ozone is destroyed in a matter of days or weeks, and the ozone hole results.

You might think that the disappearance of the ozone shielding in the Antarctic spring would not be a major environmental problem. After all, life is sparse on the Antarctic continent. The real danger of the ozone hole, however, is that it points to chemical reactions that could have long-term effects on the entire ozone layer. Not only has the ozone hole grown larger over the past decade, but also recent measurements suggest that the ozone layer has been depleted by a few percent worldwide.

Dealing with the Threat to the Ozone Layer

In 1986, an international congress meeting in Montreal produced a treaty by which all the industrial nations of the world agreed first to limit, then to eliminate, their production of CFCs. This decision triggered a lot of activity in major chemical companies, where people are looking to find replacement substances. In 1992, the reduction of CFCs was proceeding so quickly that the target date for elimination of most CFCs was set at 1996. Government mandates prohibited use of Freon in automobile air-conditioning systems by 1994, and called for its complete elimination by 1996. Current calculations suggest that these restrictions are having the desired effect, and that the ozone layer will return to normal sometime early in the twenty-first century.

The ozone hole is an example of a serious environmental concern, but one that has a relatively straightforward solution. Scientists have established the cause of the problem. The effects of the ozone hole, while serious, are not totally devastating to life on Earth, and the cost of solving the problem is relatively low. The problem of ozone depletion appears to be well on its way to being solved.

Acid Rain and Urban Air Pollution

Burning—the chemical reaction of oxidation—inevitably introduces chemical compounds into the atmosphere. For example, carbon dioxide and water vapor, the common products of hydrocarbon combustion (see Chapter 11), are always released. But burning produces three other significant sources of pollution: nitrogen oxides, sulfur compounds, and hydrocarbons.

1. *Nitrogen oxides.* Whenever the temperature of the air is raised above about 500°C, nitrogen in the air combines with oxygen to form what are called NO_x compounds (pronounced "nox"): nitrogen monoxide (NO), nitrogen dioxide (NO_2), and others. The "x" subscript indicates that these compounds contain different numbers of oxygen atoms.
2. *Sulfur compounds.* Petroleum- and coal-based fossil fuels usually contain small amounts of sulfur, either as a contaminant or as an integral part of their structure. The result is that chemical combinations of sulfur and oxygen, particularly sulfur dioxide (SO_2), are released into the atmosphere as well.
3. *Hydrocarbons.* The long-chain molecules that make up hydrocarbons are seldom burned perfectly in any real-world situation. As a result, a third class of pollutants, bits and pieces of unreacted hydrocarbon molecular chains, enters the atmosphere.

The Effects of Air Pollution and Acid Rain

The emission of NO_x compounds, sulfur dioxide, and hydrocarbons gives rise to a number of serious environmental problems. One of these, which has immediate consequences for urban residents, is **air pollution**. Sunlight hitting nitrogen compounds and hydrocarbons in the air triggers a set of chemical reactions that, in the end, produce ozone. And, whereas ozone in the stratosphere is essential to life on Earth, ozone at ground level is a caustic, stinging gas that can cause extensive damage to the human respiratory system. This "bad ozone" is a major product of modern urban air pollution associated with photochemical *smog*—the brownish stuff that you often see over major cities during the summer.

Urban air pollution is a serious problem, but it can sometimes seem to be an immediate and transitory one. If the air quality in a city declines then people can be alerted about it immediately as part of the weather forecast. Just like the weather, the intensity of air pollution varies on a daily basis and it can change swiftly with the arrival of a thunderstorm or stiff winds.

A comparison of Los Angeles during a clear day (top) and on a smoggy day (bottom).

• **Figure 19-5** The formation of acid rain and its effect on ecosystems. Pollutants from urban and industrial areas can travel great distances, affecting lakes and forests hundreds of miles away.

However, long-term problems are associated with the presence of nitrogen and sulfur compounds in the air; these problems may not have an immediate effect on the place where the emissions occur. When these compounds are in the air, they interact with water, sunlight, and other atmospheric chemicals to form tiny droplets of nitric and sulfuric acid. (The latter is the type of acid normally used in automobile batteries.) When it rains, these droplets of acid wash out and they become, in effect, a rain of dilute acid rather than water. This phenomenon is known as **acid rain** (Figure 19-5). (In fact, rain is normally slightly acid because carbon dioxide dissolves in raindrops to make a weak solution of carbonic acid. The term acid rain refers to the considerable extra acidity produced by human activities.)

You can see one effect of this sort of acid rain in cities. Many of the great historical monuments in European cities, for example, are made from limestone, which is particularly susceptible to the effect of acid. Over the years, the acid rain simply dissolves the fabric of the building (Figure 19-6).

In the mid-twentieth century, the local effects of acid rain and other kinds of pollution in the United States were dealt with by the construction of tall smoke-

• **Figure 19-6** The effects of acid rain. Over a period of 60 years, this sandstone statue on a castle in Germany has been completely destroyed.

stacks, particularly in the industrial parts of the Midwest. The effect was to put the pollutants high enough in the atmosphere to be taken away by the prevailing winds. But, in keeping with our dictum, "you can't throw anything away," that approach didn't really solve the problem. It merely displaced it. The nitrogen and sulfur compounds emitted in Midwest smokestacks fell as acid rain on the forests of New England.

Acid rain may not be the only cause of damage to forests and lakes. Other agents, such as local climate changes, may be responsible in some cases. As in other ecosystems, scientists cannot be sure of every cause and effect. Nevertheless, in a society that is more and more concerned with preserving nature, the added stress on forests and lakes due to acid rain receives a great deal of attention.

Dealing with Acid Rain

The response of governments to urban air pollution has centered on reducing the levels of emissions associated with the burning of fossil fuels. In California, for example, strict new regulations on average automobile emissions are encouraging the production of hybrid gasoline/electric cars (see Chapter 5). Because of the size of the California automobile market, it is expected that this requirement will lead to the rapid development and reduced cost of hybrid cars nationwide. In addition, in many states large facilities such as power plants, which emit huge amounts of pollutants, are required to install complex engineering devices known as scrubbers, whose job it is to remove the sulfur compounds from the smoke-stack before they become part of the atmosphere.

Acid rain and air pollution are examples of moderate environmental problems. We understand in a general way what the problems are, what at least some of the consequences of pollution are, and what has to be done to prevent the pollution. The costs of dealing with these problems, however, are considerably higher than the costs of reversing the depletion of the ozone layer. Political and economic questions become very important. How much are we willing to pay for clean air? This is not an easy question, nor is it a question answerable by science alone.

The Greenhouse Effect

The temperature at the Earth's surface is determined primarily by the extent to which gases in the atmosphere absorb outgoing infrared radiation (see Chapter 6). The atmosphere is largely transparent to the Sun's incoming visible and ultraviolet

(a)

(b)

Smokestacks equipped with an electrostatic precipitator create an electric field that attracts ash and soot and collects them before they can pollute the atmosphere (*a*). When the precipitator is turned off (*b*), thick clouds rise from the stacks.

• **Figure 19-7** The greenhouse effect. Just as the Sun's energy passes through the glass of a greenhouse and becomes trapped inside as heat, the atmosphere acts as a greenhouse to warm up the Earth.

Solar radiation passes through the greenhouse glass and is converted to heat, which is trapped within the greenhouse.

Solar radiation passes through the atmosphere and is converted to heat, which is trapped within the planetary atmosphere.

Solar radiation

Atmospheric shell of CO_2 and other greenhouse gases

Panes of greenhouse glass

radiation that warms the surface, but it is somewhat opaque to the infrared (heat) energy that radiates out into space (Figure 19-7). If it were not for the trapping of heat by the atmosphere, the average temperature of the Earth (i.e., the average day–night, winter–summer temperature) would be about −20°C. Thus, like a greenhouse, the atmosphere raises the temperature of the Earth from about −20°C to its present temperature. This temperature increase is the so-called **greenhouse effect**.

In today's news, "greenhouse effect" usually refers to possible increases in global temperatures—both a change in average global temperature, and a change in the temperature contrast between equator and poles. Three points of general agreement frame debates about global warming.

1. All scientists agree that carbon dioxide absorbs infrared radiation and acts as a greenhouse gas. Our neighboring planet, Venus, which has a thick carbon dioxide atmosphere and surface temperature exceeding 400°C (see Chapter 16), demonstrates this effect most dramatically. In fact, many atmospheric gases contribute to Earth's less severe greenhouse effect and CO_2 accounts for only about 10% of the total infrared absorption. Water vapor, especially in clouds, is the dominant greenhouse gas, while the trace gases methane and CFCs, which make up less than a few millionths of the atmosphere, are molecule-for-molecule the most efficient infrared absorbers.

2. All scientists agree that the burning of fossil fuels by human beings has increased the amount of carbon dioxide in Earth's atmosphere. This dramatic trend is illustrated in Figure 19-8, which is a graph of the amount of carbon dioxide in the Earth's atmosphere as measured at a high mountaintop observatory in Hawaii during the past several decades. The small wiggles in the graph correspond to annual cycles by which carbon dioxide is taken into leaves in the spring, and then returned to the atmosphere in the fall. In a sense, the wiggles in this graph show the Earth breathing.

3. And scientists agree that the average global temperature has increased significantly during the past several decades, with the 1990s being the warmest on record: 15 of the 20 warmest years in recorded history have occurred since

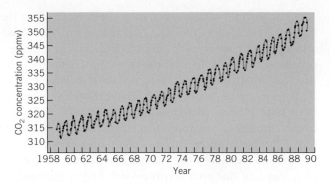

• **Figure 19-8** Measurements of atmospheric CO_2 concentrations reveal an annual cycle, as well as a gradual increase.

1980. The year 1998 was the warmest on record by a whopping $\frac{1}{4}$ degree, and that year was a full degree warmer than the 30-year average. Most individual months also set historic records, and the subsequent years have also been significantly warmer than the long-term average. So there can be little doubt that the Earth became warmer in the last quarter of the twentieth century.

Debates About Global Warming

Global warming debates focus on whether increased CO_2 is entirely responsible for the observed increase in global temperature. The reasons for these uncertainties stem from the fact that our only way of predicting the behavior of Earth's atmosphere is through global circulation models (see Chapter 17). These models, which break the atmosphere into unrealistic uniform chunks several hundred kilometers on a side, are at best imperfect ways of predicting changes in climate. For example, such a coarse-grained look at the atmosphere cannot possibly hope to deal with effects of clouds that typically are only a few miles on a side. Clouds reflect more incident sunlight into space and thus play a critical role in climate. If the effect of increased carbon dioxide is to increase atmospheric temperature slightly, one consequence might be increased evaporation of water from the ocean and, hence, increased formation of clouds on some parts of the globe. Thus, some scientists argue, the clouds produce an automatic feedback that counteracts some of the effects of carbon dioxide.

During a period known as the "Little Ice Age" the Earth's temperature was lower than it is now, and canals like this one in Holland froze over all winter.

The world's oceans are another important effect that is difficult to incorporate in global circulation models. A constant interplay takes place between water and atmosphere at an ocean's surface, and carbon dioxide moves into and out of the oceans all the time. In fact, the amount of carbon dioxide locked in the oceans and their sediments is much greater than that stored in the atmosphere. Even small changes in the way that oceans interact with atmospheric carbon dioxide can thus have huge effects on the world's climate. In addition, as we saw in Chapter 17, ocean currents are instrumental in spreading heat around the surface of the Earth. Small changes in those currents could have enormous effects on the Earth's climate.

It's also conceivable that at least some of the recent observed temperature rise might be due to a relatively short-term increase in solar energy output. Such solar variations have occurred in the recent past, for example, during a short period of global cooling—the "mini ice age" from about 1645 to 1715. During that interval the Sun is estimated to have been about 1% cooler, so it's essential to get better and longer-term measurements of the Sun's energy output.

It has become standard practice in the greenhouse debate to make all calculations and predictions about the Earth's temperature for the case in which atmospheric carbon dioxide doubles. A group called the Intergovernmental Panel on Climate Change (IPCC) relies on the participation of thousands of scientists around the world and issues reports every five years. Their most recent report suggests that the Earth's temperature will increase between 2°C and 6°C over the next century, with a "best guess" of about 4°C.

The range of possible consequences of greenhouse warming in North America is also the subject of debate. As a general rule, for every 0.5°C of greenhouse warming, a global line of a given temperature will move about 100 miles northward. Thus, for 2°C warming, temperatures in Washington, D.C., will become comparable to those in Atlanta, and temperatures in Minneapolis will be comparable to those in St. Louis. The effects on the Earth's biosphere and ecosystems might be large or small depending on the magnitude and rate of warming. The total warming in the Northern Hemisphere after the last ice age, for example, was about 5°C, and took place over a period of several thousand years. We know from studies of pollen deposited in the bottom of lakes that this warming, though large, was sufficiently gradual that plant populations were able to adapt and migrate north with the retreat of the glaciers. More recently, studies of the northern Atlantic Ocean have indicated that there have been periods in which the temperature in that region has changed by 5°C over a much shorter period, perhaps as little as a few decades. No known ecological disasters appear to be associated with these events. The predictions of consequences of greenhouse warming, should it occur, thus are also surrounded with a great deal of uncertainty.

Whatever the consequences, a growing international consensus holds that global warming is real and should be a matter of concern. One of the first strong international statements was produced in 1995 following a gathering of 1000 experts from around the world. They endorsed the conclusion that warming is occurring in a report produced by the United Nations Intergovernmental Panel on Climate Change. These studies led to a proposed international agreement on the reduction of carbon dioxide emissions called the Kyoto accord. You may have read about the U.S. refusal to sign that accord—a complex political issue that's confused by controversial ways of calculating each country's net contribution of greenhouse gases to the environment.

From the point of view of government policy, the central question remains: What will be the social and economic consequences? Unfortunately, it is extraordinarily difficult to answer this question with the scientific knowledge we now have. Global warming could cause dramatic changes in coastal flooding, agricultural production, distribution of infectious diseases, and other factors that influence the well being of societies. But how much will it cost in social and economic terms to wean ourselves from fossil fuels? Any effort to reduce drastically the consumption of fossil fuels will cost consumers money, and they might require significant changes in lifestyles, as well. Just think about all the ways we use carbon-based fuels. They're the basic energy source for automobiles, jet planes, ships, and most of our electric power plants. Thus, finding ways out of this dilemma is not easy.

THE ONGOING PROCESS OF SCIENCE •

Dealing with the Greenhouse Effect

The greenhouse effect may be both the most difficult and the most potentially alarming of the many environmental problems that face the global ecosystem. On the one hand, it is the most difficult to model because the effect of adding carbon dioxide to the atmosphere is uncertain, and the cost of doing something about it is very high. The idea that you can take the world economy, which runs almost entirely on fossil fuels, and change it over to other sources of energy in a very short period of time is unrealistic. In the past, it has taken many decades to make similar changes in a society's energy use and consumption. Figure 19-9, for example, shows the transitions from wood to coal and from coal to oil and gas in the U.S. economy. As you can see, it takes 30 to 50 years for a new fuel to work its way into the economy. If the more disastrous predictions of greenhouse warming are true, in about 50 years the warming will already have occurred, and it will be too late to do anything about it.

In addition, the best scientific estimates now indicate that if warming occurs, it will not cause severe environmental changes for several decades, far beyond the planning horizon of corporations, governments, and other major institutions in any society. The question comes down to something like this: Are you willing to change your driving habits now because a possibility exists that global warming will adversely affect the lifestyles of your grandchildren? Human beings find it difficult to suffer real hardship in the present to prevent an uncertain event from happening in the future. •

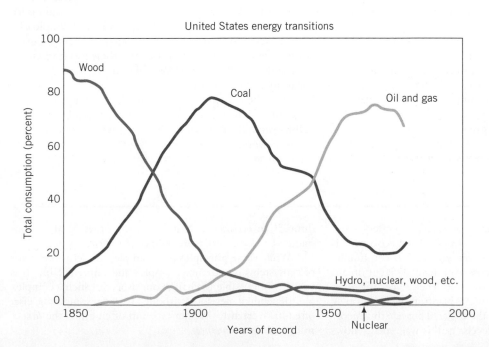

• **Figure 19-9** U.S. energy transitions. In the past, it has taken 30 to 50 years to make the transition from one type of fuel to another. We could expect a transition to solar energy (as an example) to take about this long.

Science News | Hawaii's Hated Frogs
(SCIENCE NEWS, JAN. 4, 2003, p. 11.)

In normal ecosystems, the population of each species is limited by something, be it food supply, space, or the presence of predators. When a species is introduced into a new environment, however, these limits may not exist. In this case, the species may begin to multiply exponentially and cause problems. Problems with these so-called exotic species are common in today's world, where the movement of people and goods between countries is common.

In the mid-1980s, shipments of potted plants from the Caribbean to Hawaii inadvertently carried a couple of species of small frogs to an environment in which there were no amphibians and no natural predators. As you might expect, the populations of these frogs began to grow, and it was not long before problems began to appear in their new home.

The most obvious problem to humans in Hawaii was noise. During the mating season, one of the frog species (called coquies) emit loud calls. In areas with high frog populations, noise levels of between 70 and 90 decibels have been measured—the equivalent of what people might experience during takeoffs and landings near an airport. In addition, the frogs consume large amounts of insects and spiders, which means that native species which feed on these animals will have problems.

Fortunately, it appears that the frog invasion of Hawaii has been detected early enough for effective measures to be taken. It turns out that common substances, such as caffeine, citric acid (an ingredient of orange juice), and ordinary garden lime can act as "frogicides" without affecting native species. With judicious spraying, Hawaiians may soon return to the quiet nights they used to enjoy.

Thinking More About | Global Warming

How Certain Do You Have to Be?

As we have seen, the problem of global warming is a complex one. Uncertainties remain about what the effects of the continued use of fossil fuels will be, and whatever those effects are, they are unlikely to be made manifest for decades. Nevertheless, decisions will be made over the next decade that will, at least potentially, have enormous consequences for future generations. In this situation, even doing nothing—pursuing business as usual—is a decision.

On the one hand, if the lower-level predictions of the GCM turn out to be correct—if the Earth warms only a degree or so—the consequences will be relatively mild, and it would probably make sense not to take drastic measures to curtail greenhouse gases. On the other hand, if the higher-end predictions turn out to be true, the consequences could be severe and far reaching, and include effects like increased droughts in many areas of the world and the flooding of low-lying coastal areas.

The problem, of course, is that we have to act now, and incur real costs, to prevent something that will happen far in the future. How much sacrifice should people be willing to make today to reduce risks in the future? What sorts of sacrifices are you willing to make? Would you give up driving your car a couple of days a week? Would you buy a lower-performing but more efficient vehicle, or lower the thermostat in your house during the winter? Would you pay more for heating and electricity?

On the other hand, are you willing to ignore the risks of global climate change and rising sea levels? Unfortunately, this is a problem for which there are no easy answers.

SUMMARY

Ecology is the branch of science that studies interdependent groups of living things, called *ecosystems*. Each ecosystem is characterized by its physical *environment* and its community of living organisms. In every ecosystem many different organisms, each competing for matter and energy, occupy their own *ecological niches*. Photosynthetic plants in the first trophic level use energy from the Sun; these plants provide the energy for animals in higher trophic levels. In this way, energy flows through an ecosystem. Matter, on the other hand, is constantly recycled as atoms are used over and over again.

While these principles seem simple, the actual behavior of ecosystems is extremely complex and unpredictable. It is virtually impossible to change one aspect of such a complex interdependent network without affecting something else, often inadvertently—a phenomenon often called the *law of unintended consequences*.

Human actions are causing changes in the Earth's global environment—changes that may affect ecosystems. The use of chlorofluorocarbons (CFCs) during the past several decades, for example, is having a pronounced effect on *ozone,* a molecule of three oxygen atoms found as a trace gas in the *ozone layer* of the upper atmosphere. Ozone provides important protection on Earth from the Sun's harmful ultraviolet radiation, but chlorine atoms from CFCs hasten the breakdown of ozone molecules, thus creating a growing *ozone hole.*

Burning coal and other fossil fuels releases sulfur and nitrogen compounds into the atmosphere—chemicals that contribute to *air pollution* and *acid rain.* Dealing with acid rain will require cleaning up emissions from automobiles and power-generating plants.

Carbon dioxide, a necessary product of all combustion of carbon-based fuels, adds to the atmosphere's store of infrared-absorbing gases, and thus contributes to the *greenhouse effect.* At present, scientists are not able to predict the consequences of these global changes with much certainty.

KEY TERMS ABOUT ECOSYSTEMS

ecology
ecosystem
environment

ecological niche
law of unintended
    consequences

ozone
ozone layer
ozone hole

air pollution
acid rain
greenhouse effect

REVIEW QUESTIONS

1. Give an example of an ecosystem near your home.
2. What is an ecological niche? Give an example.
3. Describe six characteristics shared by all ecosystems.
4. What is a trophic level? In which trophic level are you?
5. What is bioconcentration? Which trophic levels are most affected?
6. State the law of unintended consequences. Give an example of the law in operation.
7. How does carbon cycle through the Earth's ecosystem? What other elements undergo a similar kind of cycle?
8. How does energy move in ecosystems?
9. Why doesn't trash decompose in a modern landfill?

10. What is the ozone layer? Where is it located? Why is it important to life on Earth?
11. What is the ozone hole? How have governments responded to the discovery of the ozone hole?
12. Why is ozone in the stratosphere considered beneficial whereas ozone at ground level is not?
13. What is acid rain? What steps would have to be taken to solve the acid rain problem?
14. Why is the greenhouse effect a current area of scientific concern when the Earth has had carbon dioxide, methane, and water vapor for several billion years?
15. Why are predictions of global warming so uncertain?
16. What steps would have to be taken to reduce the severity of the greenhouse effect?

DISCUSSION QUESTIONS

1. Would you expect the number of species present on an island to depend on the size of the island? Why or why not?
2. Cite five examples of environmental changes that have been made in your area. Can you identify any unintended consequences of these changes?
3. What environmental changes might result from a global warming of 2°C? What countries might be most affected?
4. Do you think Wilson and Simberloff's experiment was ethical? Why or why not? Was there any other way to get this information?
5. One of the problems of understanding the workings of ecosystems is that it is not possible to hold everything constant and change only one variable.

Why is this true? What effects might this have on the interpretation of observations or experiments?
6. How did you affect your environment today? How did it affect you?
7. What would the political, social, and economic consequences be in your community if serious steps were taken to reduce acid rain or air pollution?
8. Suppose that the United States decided today to undergo a conversion from fossil fuels to solar energy. How long do you think it would take to make a complete transition? What are some of the changes that would have to be made? Who would benefit, and who would be hurt by such a change?
9. Of what ecosystem is the squirrel on your lawn or the bird flying across your campus a part?

Are there any threats to the well-being of that ecosystem?

10. Where do electric cars obtain their energy? Is it true that they do not generate pollution because they have batteries?

11. Suppose that scientists concluded that an appreciable fraction of any measured global warming was due to warming of the Sun. What would the policy implications of such a finding be?

PROBLEM

If a global warming of 4°C takes place, what kind of weather might your town experience? [*Hint*: Find a town to the south of you that has that sort of weather now.]

INVESTIGATIONS

1. Do commercial jet airliners fly through the ozone layer? What effects might this have?

2. How are solid wastes such as plastics handled in your community? Does that method represent a long-term or short-term solution to the problem? What other options are available to your community?

3. Write a short story chronicling the passage of a nitrogen or phosphorus atom through 10 different stages.

4. What is an environmental impact statement? Are there any projects in your area that have required environmental impact statements? Where should they be required?

5. Identify an environmental law or court ruling that has been enacted in the last year. What impact will this law have? Who benefits from the decision? Will anyone lose his or her job as a result?

6. What happens to your garbage? Is there a recycling program in your town? What materials can be recycled?

7. Read about the "pea-soup fogs" that used to plague London. What caused them? How many people could be killed in one?

WWW RESOURCES

See *The Sciences* homepage at: **http://www.wiley.com/college/trefil** for valuable web links.

1. **http://www.cbl.umces.edu/~bonda/ATLSS.html**
Across Trophic Levels System Simulation, focuses on South Florida ecosystems—this is a challenging site.

2. **http://www.epa.gov/students/**
EPA Student Site.

3. **http://www.nwf.org**
National Wildlife Federation Home Page.

4. **http://www.mp1-pwrc.usgs.gov/birds.html**
USGS Biological Survey, where you can track the migration of wild geese.

20

Strategies of Life

What is life?

GREAT IDEA

Living things use many different strategies to deal with the problems of acquiring and using matter and energy.

PHYSICS

Stems and trunks support plants and allow them to grow upward against the force of gravity.

CHEMISTRY

All life depends on chemical reactions that take place in cells. (Ch. 22)

ENVIRONMENT

Evidence from fossils suggests that the average lifetime of a species on earth is a few million years.

GEOLOGY

Lichens often grow on rocks to absorb the minerals they need, and thus play an important role in the breakdown of rock into soil.

HEALTH & SAFETY

The common mold *Penicillium* was found to secrete a substance that kills bacteria, making it the first effective antibiotic.

ASTRONOMY

The Sun provides energy for life on Earth. (Ch.3)

TECHNOLOGY

Microscopes play an important role in the discovery of new life forms.

BIOLOGY

Living things are classified according to their shared physical characteristics.

Red = applications of the great idea discussed in this chapter.

Orange = other applications, some of which are explored in other chapters.

Look at how many different living things you can find at the beach. You've already seen birds, seaweed, crustaceans, a variety of shells, and a crab near the water's edge. Higher up the beach you notice an abundance of dune grasses and small weeds, along with countless flies, ants, and other insects. A rocky tidal pool holds starfish, sea urchins, and myriad tiny swimming creatures. Schools of fish roil the surface of the water close to shore, while a few jellyfish (fortunately not the stinging kind) also inhabit the shallow water. You even remember seeing a majestic whale spouting far offshore during an earlier trip to this very beach.

There's not a place on the surface of the Earth where you won't find living things. The frigid Arctic seas teem with life, while the frozen wastes of Antarctica yield up hardy lichens and single-celled organisms. Living things may be found in the deepest, darkest parts of the ocean and in the most dry and forbidding deserts. In fact, you could argue that what makes the Earth different from every other place we know in the solar system (and perhaps even every other place in the galaxy) is the existence of varied and abundant life.

The Organization of Living Things

Biology is the branch of science devoted to the study of living things, by far the most complex systems that scientists study. Every single cell is astonishingly complex—vastly more intricate than the most advanced machines—and each human being contains tens of trillions of cells. Yet, despite this complexity, living things operate according to the same laws of nature as everything else we've studied. The laws of motion, energy conservation, the laws of electricity and magnetism, and the chemical bonding of atoms, for example, all operate in and govern the behavior of all living things. We have underscored this point by using examples from biology to illustrate all of the preceding chapters.

Ways of Thinking About Living Things

An ant provides a useful way to begin thinking about the study of living things. We can study the ant in many ways. We can, for example, examine it as an individual organism, in which case we ask questions such as "How big is it?" "How much food does it consume?" "Where does it get its energy?" We could take a more microscopic view and consider the individual ant as a collection of specialized organs. In this case we might ask about how the ant moves oxygen from the air to its cells, or how its hard outer covering protects it and supports its weight. Penetrating still deeper, we could look at the ant as a collection of cells, and ask how a single one of those cells operates. Questions such as "How does this cell carry out its chemical functions?" and "What are the pieces from which this cell is made?" would then be appropriate. Finally, we could look inside the cell and think about its ultimate constituents—the atoms and molecules that combine and react chemically to make the cell what it is. Here we would ask, "What are the molecules that operate in a cell?" and "How do they interact as chemicals?"

An ant can be studied at many scales, from individual microscopic molecules and cells, to the structure of individual organs and appendages, to the behavior of a solitary ant, to the complex interactions of an ant colony.

We could also choose to look at the big picture. Instead of probing ever-smaller parts of the ant, we could choose to view the ant as part of larger and larger structures. The single ant, for example, is part of the social organization of an ant colony, which in turn forms part of an ecosystem of living and nonliving things—a sand dune or a field or a patch of forest. This small community, in turn, represents part of the great global system that encompasses all living things on the planet.

Learning about a single living thing such as an ant thus can take place on many levels. Different branches of biology deal with these levels, which we will discuss in the following chapters. The important point to remember, however, is that all of these ways of viewing the ant are important. Each approach complements, and is complemented by, the others.

In spite of this range of approaches, a profound change has occurred in the life sciences during the last half of the twentieth century. Traditional biology concerned itself largely with discovering, understanding, and cataloging organisms and their interactions. Beginning in the nineteenth century, however, chemists began increasingly to study the molecules found in living systems. This work culminated in the 1950s, when scientists discovered the singular role played by the molecule deoxyribonucleic acid (DNA) in determining what traits living organisms inherit from their parents (see Chapter 23). This discovery opened up an entire new world in the life sciences. As a result, during the past few decades the study of living things has undergone a fundamental realignment. Today the great majority of biologists are studying living systems at the level of molecules, rather than at the level of the organism. Why this should be so will become clear in the following chapters.

What Is Life?

We all have a sense of what it means to be alive. We recognize some living things by their use of energy to grow and repair themselves, their response to external stimuli, and their ability to reproduce. But the more we learn about the world around us, the harder it becomes to provide a precise definition of life. Some objects, such as the mule, are clearly alive but are unable to reproduce. Certain seeds may lie dormant for centuries without any sign of life, but then suddenly awaken. Furthermore, as technology advances, machines take on more and more of the qualities we usually associate with life. As a result of these sorts of problems, most scientists prefer not to try to define what life is in the abstract, but rather to describe the collective properties of living systems at some level, as we will do.

Other medical, legal, and ethical questions relating to the definition of life concern when life begins and when it ends. How should our society define human life? Is it possible that we could develop machines that are in some way alive? These are ethical questions that must take scientific knowledge into account, but their ultimate answers lie outside the realm of scientific inquiry.

The Characteristics of Life

The diversity of living things is truly staggering. You have only to think of whales, palm trees, mold, and mosquitoes to recognize this fact. Yet biologists have found that beneath this diversity many characteristics link all life together. In fact, the general principles that govern all living things will occupy us for most of the rest of this book. We list them here, however, to make the point that, despite their seeming diversity, living things are really not that different from each other.

1. *All living things maintain a high degree of order and complexity.* Objects can be ranked according to their *complexity,* which is related to the number of different parts that are organized to make the whole. In this sense, a jet airplane is more complex than a wristwatch, which is more complex than a pencil. Even the simplest living thing is vastly more complex than any object ever constructed by humans.

2. *All living things are part of larger systems of matter and energy.* Living things and their surroundings form complex ecosystems (see Chapter 19). Matter continuously recycles in a given system, while energy flows through it. All organisms need energy to continue living. Plants use photosynthesis, by which the Sun's radiant energy is used to produce energy-rich molecules from water and carbon dioxide. Animals and fungi, on the other hand, obtain energy-rich molecules from plants and other animals.

3. *All life depends on chemical reactions that take place in cells.* As we shall see in Chapters 21 and 22, most living things share a basic set of molecular building blocks and chemical reactions. By the same token, specific chemical reactions are what make one living thing different from another—what makes you

The chameleon gets its energy like all animals—by eating other living things.

different from a kumquat. Cells, the chemical factories of life, are the highly organized building blocks of life. Many organisms such as bacteria and blue-green algae are single-celled, whereas larger organisms such as human beings may incorporate trillions of interdependent cells.

4. *All life requires liquid water.* Liquid water possesses several unusual properties, including its ability as a solvent (see Chapter 10) and its high heat capacity (see Chapter 4), which make it an essential medium in the cells of all living things.

5. *Organisms grow and develop.* All organisms change in form and function at different stages in their lifetimes. In this chapter we will survey some of the varied ways that organisms accomplish these changes.

6. *Living things regulate their use of energy and respond to their environments.* During periods of extreme cold or dryness, for example, many plants will lie dormant and animals will become sluggish. During warmer or wetter periods, on the other hand, plants may flower and animals may enter their reproductive cycle. You experience this kind of change all the time. When your body temperature increases significantly, you sweat, and heat is removed from the body as the sweat evaporates from your skin. When you get cold, you shiver and the extra heat generated by your muscles warms you up.

7. *All living things share the same genetic code, which is passed from parent to offspring by reproduction.* The chemical reactions in a cell are governed by a code written in the language of the molecule DNA (see Chapter 23). Just as all books in English are written with the same alphabet, so too the heredity information that passes traits from parents to offspring uses a single genetic language. Sometimes the process of reproduction can be as simple as the splitting of a single cell into two offspring, and other times as complex as human sexual reproduction. In all cases, though, life consists of a chain of parents and offspring moving through time.

All organisms, from single-celled microbes to these complex hummingbirds, grow and develop.

8. *All living things are descended from a common ancestor.* In Chapter 25 we will review the long chain of evidence that led Charles Darwin and others to recognize the evolution of life. We will see that the many similarities among living things arise from their common ancestry.

SCIENCE IN THE MAKING •

Measuring Plant Growth

We can see the similarity between biology and the other sciences by looking at how the scientific method was used to answer an old question. All animals derive their nourishment from the food they eat, but where do plants get theirs? Throughout most of recorded history, people thought that plant nourishment must come from the soil—that plants "eat" soil in the same way that animals eat meat or fruit.

In 1648, Joannes Baptista Van Helmont (1579–1644), a Flemish physician and the discoverer of carbon dioxide, reported an experiment that changed this view. He planted a willow tree weighing five pounds in a pot containing 200 pounds of soil and watered it for five years as it grew. At the end of that time, he weighed the tree and found that its weight had increased to 169 pounds while the amount of soil in the pot had decreased by at most a few ounces. He concluded that all the material used to construct the fabric of the willow tree came from the water.

Subsequent experiments showed that he was wrong; much of the tissue in plants comes from carbon dioxide in the air. The point of the Van Helmont story, however, is that in science a good quantitative experiment, even one with an incorrect conclusion, can clear the way for progress. In this case, Van Helmont's proof that plants did not take their fabric from the soil led eventually to our present understanding of the role of plants in removing carbon dioxide from the atmosphere and producing oxygen. •

Classifying Living Things

In Chapter 1 we saw that science begins with observation. People must start their exploration of a new area by looking to see what's there. Astronomers watched the skies for thousands of years and named many celestial objects before Newton could explain the motion of the solar system. Alchemists mixed chemicals and observed countless chemical reactions long before modern ideas of the atom or chemical bonding were developed. Similarly, humans spent thousands of years observing and naming living things before they could begin to recognize order in the variety of organisms they encountered. **Taxonomy**, the field devoted to cataloging living things, describing them, and giving them names, plays a central role in science, because our search for patterns in the universe depends on recognizing similarities and differences.

Classification provides us with more than just a way of describing our world. It helps us fit new objects and phenomena into an existing framework. Classification enables a biologist who finds a new organism to group it with similar organisms and thereby to make a number of intelligent conjectures about that organism—about its diet, for example, or mating habits. The same holds true of classification schemes for nonliving objects. Astronomers who classify stars, for example, know by systematic comparisons that a Sun-like star will have a lifetime of about 10 billion years, will become a white dwarf (Chapter 15), and so on.

Cataloging Life

Biologists, confronted by the amazing variety of living things, realized that they had to find some systematic way of cataloging life's diversity. Indeed, the earliest attempts to classify life must extend back to the origins of language, itself. In ancient times, the Greek philosopher Aristotle (384–322 B.C.) tackled this problem in his extensive biological writings. He noted, for example, that whales and dolphins, though fish-like, are actually mammals.

The most successful systematic attempt to devise a systematic scheme was begun by Swedish naturalist Carolus Linnaeus (1707–1778). His work was based on observation. When you look at living things it becomes obvious that some characteristics are shared, while others are not. A human being, for example, is more like a squirrel than like a blade of grass; a sparrow is more like a fish than like algae in a pond. The purpose of the **Linnaean classification** was to group all living things according to their shared characteristics so that each organism is as close as possible to those other organisms that it resembles and as far as possible from those it does not (Figure 20-1).

The basic unit of the classification scheme is the **species**, which we define today as an interbreeding population of individual organisms that produces fertile offspring. Linnaeus, who worked at a time when European scientific institutions were being flooded with new types of plants from around the world, realized that simply describing species would not be enough. Instead, he introduced a system in which all species can be placed into a *hierarchy*—a sequence of categories that places all species into a larger framework based on similarities and differences among organisms.

Linnaeus's original goal was to organize the entire structure of nature, and to this end he published classification schemes for three "kingdoms" of plants, animals, and minerals. As you might expect in the first attempt to achieve such an ambitious goal, there were some errors in his work. (For example, he mistakenly

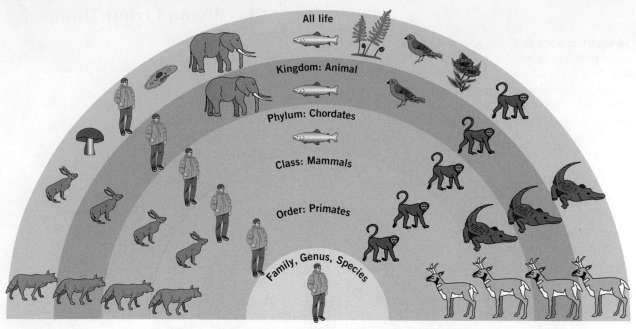

All life

Kingdom: Animal

Phylum: Chordates

Class: Mammals

Order: Primates

Family, Genus, Species

• **Figure 20-1** The Linnaean classification scheme recognizes the relationship of each living thing to every other. We can arrange species into groups that are more and more closely related. Although human beings are not treated differently from other organisms in this classification system, we are naturally more familiar with our own species than with any other.

classified the rhinoceros as a rodent.) But Linnaeus's work showed that it is possible to define relationships among different species.

The task of classifying living things is something like the problem of pinpointing one particular building in the entire world—a problem you face every time you mail a letter. You might start by specifying the continent on which the building stands, then the country, then the state or province, the town, the street, and finally the street number. Each step in this list of designations represents a separation, a splitting off. Houses on different continents are more distant than those on the same continent, houses in different towns more distant than those in the same town, and so on. Eventually, you get to an exact designation—a street address in a given town—that specifies the building uniquely.

The modern biological classification scheme uses the same kind of hierarchical scheme, with narrower and narrower divisions. However, instead of political and geographical distinctions such as city or country, the Linnaean scheme uses divisions based on the biological similarities of different species—similarities that point to common evolutionary pathways (see Chapter 25).

The main categories that biologists use, going from broadest to narrowest, are *kingdom, phylum, class, order, family, genus,* and *species.* (A useful mnemonic to help you remember this sequence is the sentence "King Phillip Came Over For Good Spaghetti.") As the number of known species has grown to more than a million, additional divisions such as suborder (a subdivision of an order) and superfamily (a few closely related families) have been added to the Linnaean scheme. You can think of this classification as being represented by a series of ever-smaller circles, with the specifications of kingdom, phylum, class, order, family, genus, and species serving to guide you to ever-smaller groupings. At the end, you come to a single kind of organism sitting in a circle all its own. Each step in

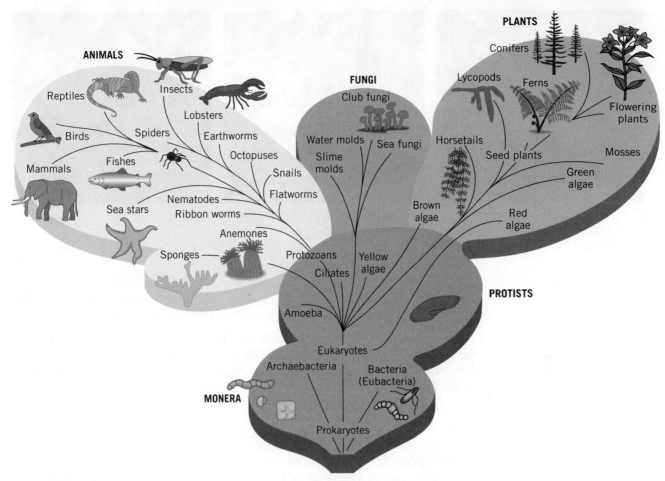

• **Figure 20-2** The five kingdoms of the biological classification system are illustrated by this diagram, which also suggests the progression from simple monera to more-complex life forms.

this narrowing process involves a judgment about which organisms are like each other and which organisms are not.

This narrowing leads ultimately to the familiar two-part scientific names of organisms. When you go to a zoo or read a biology textbook, you will probably notice that the scientific names of plants and animals are given in terms of two Latin words—*Homo sapiens* or *Tyrannosaurus rex,* for example—that indicate the genus and species. (By convention, the two words are italicized and the genus is capitalized.) This *binomial nomenclature* is an important legacy of Linnaeus's work.

The **kingdom** is the broadest classification, corresponding to the coarsest division of living things. Until the 1960s, most biologists recognized only two kingdoms—plants and animals. For the past several decades most biologists have classified living things into five kingdoms (Figure 20-2), though, as we shall see, this view is also changing as new data come to light. In the five-kingdom scheme, two of the kingdoms consist primarily of single-celled organisms.

1. **Monera.** Single-celled organisms without an internal structure called the *cell nucleus* (see Chapter 22). Monera are the most primitive living things.

(a)   (b)   (c)

Monera—single-celled organisms without a nucleus—come in a variety of shapes. These microscope photographs show bacteria in the shape of (*a*) spheres, (*b*) rods, and (*c*) spirals.

2. **Protista.** Mainly single-celled organisms with a cell nucleus, but also a few multicellular organisms that have a particularly simple structure.

The remaining three kingdoms in the prevailing current classification scheme include *multicellular* organisms, in which several different kinds of interdependent cells combine in a single species. Members of these kingdoms are distinguished primarily by the way that they obtain energy.

3. **Fungi.** Multicellular organisms that get their energy and nutrients by absorbing materials from their environment.

4. **Plants.** Multicellular organisms that get their energy directly from the Sun through photosynthesis. (This process will be described in detail in Chapter 22. For now, all you need to remember is that in *photosynthesis,* a plant takes carbon dioxide from the air and combines it with water and sunlight to form the energy-rich molecules known as sugars, plus some oxygen.)

5. **Animals.** Multicellular organisms that get their energy and nutrients by eating other organisms.

Some protista (single-celled organisms with a nucleus) develop beautiful microscopic shells. This shell of foraminifera houses amoeba-like cells.

THE ONGOING PROCESS OF SCIENCE •

A Different Division of Kingdoms

Biologists, employing the techniques of molecular genetics (see Chapter 24), have recently discovered a large group of extremely simple one-celled organisms that have dramatically altered our view of life's diversity. These microbes, collectively known as *Archaea,* often thrive in extreme environments, including acidic springs, arctic ice, deep-ocean hydrothermal vents, and in solid rock kilometers below the surface. Genetic studies reveal that these cells have remarkably distinctive and varied chemical processes that set them apart from all other cellular life. The profound differences reflected in the unique genetic makeup of *Archaea* have led many biologists to adopt a dramatically new division of life into just three kingdoms.

According to this new view, *Archaea* and *Bacteria* are distinct kingdoms of single-celled life without nuclei. Even though these organisms can look quite similar to each other, they differ in many of their internal chemical mechanisms. The third kingdom in this new scheme is *Eucaryea,* which encompasses *all* life based on cells with nuclei, including plants, animals, fungi, and a host of single-celled species. This new three-kingdom classification scheme reflects the fact that fungi, plants, and animals are chemically and genetically extremely similar, at least compared to *Archaea* and *Bacteria*. •

 Stop and Think! Does it matter how many kingdoms biologists recognize? How might the proposed change to three kingdoms, two of which are microbes, affect our view of life on Earth?

SCIENCE BY THE NUMBERS •

How Many Species Are There?

Biologists are now engaged in a lively debate on one of the most fundamental questions you can ask about the world: How many species inhabit our planet? Estimates range from 3 million to 30 million species.

For large animals, such as the birds and mammals that command human attention, the situation is not too bad. All experts agree, for example, that the Earth is populated by about 9000 species of birds and 4000 of mammals, and only a few new ones are discovered each decade. For other kinds of organisms, however, we are still in a state of relative ignorance. For one thing, there is no central database where information on new species is summarized, and so we can't even make a firm statement about the total number of species that have been discovered, much less about ones that haven't been. At the moment, the number of known species—species that have been examined and recorded by scientists somewhere—is estimated to be between 1.5 million and 1.8 million. The distribution of these species is shown in Figure 20-3.

Scientists have a number of methods for using current data to make estimates about the total number of species on Earth. If we make a graph of the total number of known species as a function of time, for example, we should get a curve like the one in Figure 20-4. As time goes by and more species become known, the curve should flatten. If we assume that the discovery curve for insects, for example, will follow this same pattern, then by making a guess as to where we are on the curve, we can estimate what the final level will be. Using this notion, estimates of the total number of insect species of from 5 million to 7 million are obtained.

Another estimation technique is to do an exhaustive survey of organisms in a small geographic area, determine the ratio of known to unknown species in that

• **Figure 20-3** A pie graph of species distribution among different kinds of living things reveals that insects account for more than half of all known species.

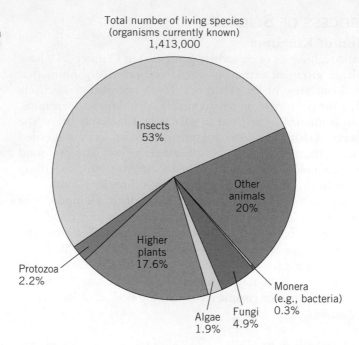

Total number of living species
(organisms currently known)
1,413,000

Insects
53%

Other animals
20%

Higher plants
17.6%

Protozoa
2.2%

Algae
1.9%

Fungi
4.9%

Monera
(e.g., bacteria)
0.3%

area, and assume that this ratio applies worldwide. A study in the Indonesian rain forest, for example, focused on a particular type of insect of which 1065 species were known. A new exhaustive survey came up with 625 additional species, for a total of 1690 species. Thus the ratio of previously unknown to previously known species is:

$$\frac{\text{previously known species}}{\text{previously unknown species}} = \frac{1065}{625} = 1.7$$

If we assume that this number applies to all insects worldwide (and that's a very big if) and accept that there are about 900,000 known species of insects, the total number of insect species in the world would then be about

$$\text{total species} = 1.7 \times \text{known species}$$
$$= 1.7 \times 900,000 \text{ species}$$
$$= 1,530,000 \text{ species}$$

• **Figure 20-4** The total number of species of a given kind of living thing can be estimated by a graph that plots the number of known species versus year. As fewer and fewer species remain to be discovered, the plot should eventually flatten out to indicate the approximate number of species.

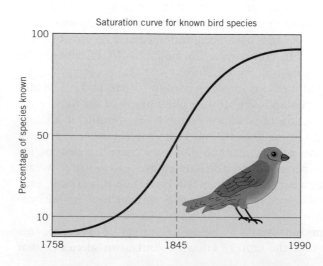

Saturation curve for known bird species

Percentage of species known

100

50

10

1758   1845   1990

Other studies of this type, making longer strings of assumptions about how to apply local numbers to the global system, have produced estimates for the number of insect species as high as 30 million. We will have to know a lot more about the kinds of species that actually exist before we can be comfortable with these sorts of estimates. •

Classifying Human Beings

Human beings are one member of the kingdom of animals. With that decided, we can go on to work out the rest of our address in the classification scheme. Among animals, there is one phylum called *chordates,* whose members have a thickened set of nerves down their back. Most chordates (and most of the organisms that come to mind when we hear the word "animal") have the nerve encased in bone. These animals form the subphylum **vertebrates**—animals with backbones. Because human beings have backbones, we belong to this subphylum, as do amphibians, fish, reptiles, and birds.

Among vertebrates, one class is made up of individuals that maintain the same body temperature regardless of the temperature of the environment, that have hair, and whose females nurse their young. Humans belong to this class, which is called **mammals**, as do wolves, rabbits, whales, and antelopes.

Among mammals, we belong to the order **primates**, which have grasping fingers and toes, eyes at the front of the head, a large brain, and fingernails instead of claws. Monkeys and apes are also members of this order. Human beings are members of the *hominid* family (primates who walk erect) and the genus *Homo* (hominids who satisfy still more detailed anatomical criteria having to do with factors such as face shape, tooth shape and size, and brain size).

At this point in the process of zeroing in on our own species we encounter an anomaly. Most animals have several close cousins, which are members of the same genus but different species, but this situation is not true of humans. The grizzly bear (*Ursus horribilis*) and the polar bear (*Ursus maritimus*), for example, are two species within the genus *Ursus* (bear). In the genus *Homo,* though, there is only one species: *Homo sapiens* (us). In the past, there were other members of the family hominid and the genus *Homo* on Earth (we discuss some of them in Chapter 25) but at present we have no near relatives. All of those who might have been our near relatives are now extinct, perhaps by our own doing.

In any case, all humans can interbreed, so we are all part of a single species, *Homo sapiens*, and we all inhabit the same smallest circle in the classification scheme.

Implications of Linnaean Classification

As we have presented it here, and as Linnaeus originally conceived it in the eighteenth century, biological classification concerns itself solely with segregating living things according to their degree of physical similarity to each other. No attempt is made to explain why living things can be grouped in this way.

Today, however, most scientists would argue that there are compelling reasons why a classification scheme like the one we have outlined should exist. For one thing, scientists no longer have to be content with describing organisms purely in terms of their physical structure. In Chapter 23, for example, we will see that the information carried in the DNA molecules found in all organisms

Primates, such as this bonnet macaque from India, are characterized by grasping fingers and toes, eyes at the front of the head, a large brain, and fingernails instead of claws.

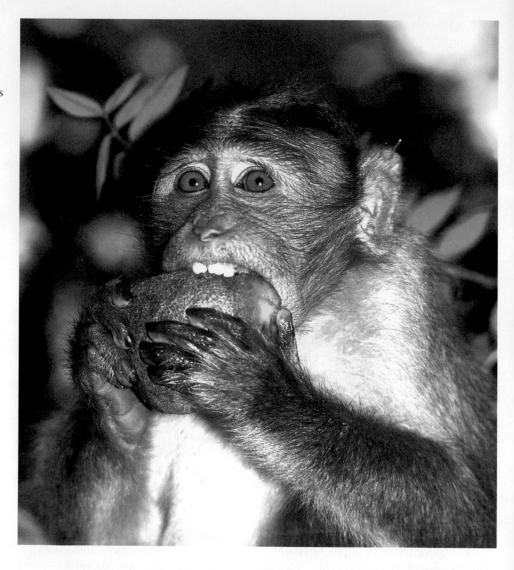

provides an alternative way of describing the organisms. One way of talking about how closely two organisms are related to each other, therefore, is to discuss how closely their DNA molecules resemble each other. The closeness of the relationship between two living things—the property that tells us where to draw the circles in Figure 20-1—can thus be determined in a quantitative way by comparing DNA and other specific molecules.

More important, the fact that living things can be grouped in successive layers strongly suggests that Linnaeus and his followers had discovered a kind of family tree. If, as we shall argue in Chapter 25, all living things descended from the same primordial ancestor, then the Linnaean groupings follow naturally. The amount of similarity or difference between two organisms depends on the amount of time and rate of change because the two shared a common ancestor. In addition, each classification group results from real events in the past when species split off from each other.

 Stop and Think! How does the classification of living things reflect the scientific method?

Survival: A New Look at the Life Around You

A single-celled organism is one of the most remarkably complex structures known to science. Even the smallest cell features hundreds of interacting chemical processes that must be exquisitely balanced and regulated. Nevertheless, the survival strategies of single-celled organisms are relatively simple.

The first order of business for a cell is to absorb from its environment all the material it needs to maintain itself. In some simple cells, called *heterotrophs,* the cell must consume a variety of biomolecules including amino acids, lipids, and carbohydrates to survive. Other more chemically complex cells, called *autotrophs,* are able to manufacture these essential building blocks from simple molecules like H_2O, CO_2, and NH_3. Inside the cell, these materials are used in the chemical reactions needed to keep the cell alive and for it to reproduce. Waste products generated by these reactions leave the cell the same way that materials came in: they pass through the cell boundary and out into the surrounding environment. For most of Earth's history, the operation of single cells was all there was to life.

With the advent of multicellular life, however, strategies became more complicated. Molecules that provided the cell's chemical energy could no longer simply move into individual cells from the environment (most cells in a multicellular organism, after all, are shielded from the environment by other cells). Instead, those molecules must be carried from distant parts of the organism to the cells where they are to be used. Similarly, waste products must be carried away from individual cells to the environment.

Some very primitive multicellular organisms (sponges, for example) are merely collections of cells that could just as well survive on their own. In higher organisms, however, specialized cells group together into organs and organ systems to take care of jobs such as moving energy-rich materials to cells and removing wastes. In humans, for example, the organ we call the heart and those we call blood vessels form an organ system known as the circulatory system, whose task it is to circulate the blood.

One way to think about living things, then, is to identify tasks that all organisms must perform and then ask what processes have evolved that allow a particular organism to perform those tasks. Every multicellular organism, for example, must obtain and distribute molecules that supply energy and build the fabric of the organism, and every organism must reproduce itself.

Let's look at the marvelous diversity of living things with an eye toward seeing what strategies they have evolved to deal with these two basic tasks of life.

Strategies of Fungi

Fungi, a group that includes such diverse organisms as molds, mushrooms, and yeast, were once classified as plants, but they are so different from true plants that they are now given their own kingdom. Some types of fungi (yeast, for example) are single-celled, but most of the ones with which we are familiar, such as mushrooms, are multicellular. Fungi grow by sending out filaments, which are slender, thread-like stalks sometimes no more than one or two cells across, and absorbing food directly through these stalks. In this way, the fungi play an important role in nature by breaking down dead organic material. For example, fungi often grow like shelves out of the sides of fallen trees in a forest.

The structure of fungi is fairly simple, consisting of little more than a mass of filaments. Because of this structure, complex systems to move materials around aren't necessary. No cell is far from the material on which the fungus lives; hence that material can be absorbed directly.

Fungi have developed a variety of reproductive strategies. First, they can reproduce by having their filaments break off and grow. More often, they produce spores, which are usually asexual reproductive organs through which a fungus can produce offspring without interacting with any other fungus. Spores can travel long distances through air and water, but once growth starts, fungi are as immobile as plants. Spores can also be produced by "mating," which is accomplished by the fusion of two cells in the filaments from different plants. Spores are often held in small containers that grow on top of stalks; in effect, they get a "running start" by being above the ground when the container breaks. The fuzzy appearance of mold on the old food in your refrigerator often comes from the spore containers on top of the stalks.

One of the most remarkable lifestyles displayed by fungi is observed in organisms called *lichens,* which are often seen as crusty coatings on rocks, and which play an important role in the breakdown of rock into soil. Each lichen is actually a combination of two interdependent species, a fungus and a single-celled organism that can use the Sun's energy in photosynthesis. Lichens typically absorb most of the minerals they need from the air and rainfall, and hence can grow in inhospitable places such as mountaintops and deserts (Figure 20-5).

Fungi

Algea

Fungi

Rootlike
connection
to substrate

• **Figure 20-5** Lichens, which grow on solid rock, sustain life through a complex cooperative effort by fungi and algae.

SCIENCE IN THE MAKING •
The Discovery of Penicillin

When you get an infection, or even just a bad cut, your doctor will very likely prescribe an *antibiotic,* a medicine capable of destroying foreign bacteria that otherwise would flourish in your body. It's hard for us, living in an age where antibiotics are common, to realize that a half-century ago bacterial diseases such as pneumonia and minor cuts that became infected were major killers.

The discovery in 1928 of penicillin, the best known of the modern antibiotics, was the result of a botched experiment in the London laboratory of bacteriologist Alexander Fleming (later Sir Alexander). He was growing cultures of *Staphylococcus* (a common infectious bacterium) in dishes when he noticed that one of his experimental dishes had been contaminated by a common mold called *Penicillium,* and that the bacteria didn't grow in that dish.

Other scientists had probably seen the same thing but had just thrown the contaminated plates away and continued with their experiments. Fleming, however, realized that the mold must have been secreting a substance that killed bacteria. When he finally isolated that substance, he named it *penicillin,* after the mold.

For a period after Fleming's discovery, penicillin could not be made in large quantities or in pure enough form to have much medical effect. In 1938, however, Howard Florey and Ernst Chain at Oxford University succeeded in producing relatively pure forms of the substance. Under the pressure of World War II, a major development program had the drug in mass production by 1943. It saved countless lives on the battlefields of that war and is now one of an array of substances used to maintain human health around the world. Fleming, Florey, and Chain shared the Nobel prize for medicine in 1945.

The action of penicillin is a good illustration of how molecules function in living systems. The outside cell covering or cell membrane of the bacteria responsible for many infectious diseases is built from molecules that have short tails. Each bacterium cell also contains specialized molecules that link the tails together to create the *cell membrane.* Penicillin locks onto these specialized molecules and prevents them from attaching to the tails of the covering molecules, thus preventing the cell membrane from growing. Human cells don't use the same specialized molecules to build cell membranes, so the drug does not have this effect on us (although it can trigger allergic reactions in some people). •

Strategies of Plants

Plants and algae, through the process of photosynthesis (see Chapter 22), take energy from the Sun and lock it up in the form of chemical energy in their tissues and cells. At the same time, they remove carbon dioxide and water from the air and produce oxygen as a waste product, including the oxygen you are breathing right now.

Biologists have not been able to agree about how to assign plants to various phyla, classes, orders, and so forth, or even on how to draw the boundaries of the plant kingdom. Algae, for example, are single-celled organisms (or simple multicellular ones) that carry out between 50% and 90% of the Earth's photosynthesis. *Blue-green algae,* or *cyanobacteria,* are single-celled organisms and are normally classified as monera; but other kinds of algae, including primitive multicellular organisms such as seaweeds and kelp (including green, red, and brown algae), are called plants in some schemes and protista in others.

For our purposes, we will define plants to be multicellular organisms that perform photosynthesis. Plants are found primarily on land, and the main divisions between them have to do with the way they reproduce and how they acquire and circulate water.

The Simplest Plants

The most primitive terrestrial plants are in the phylum of bryophytes, whose most familiar members are mosses and liverworts. These plants do not have roots, as more advanced plants do, but absorb water directly through their aboveground structures. For this reason, mosses are found in moist environments. They are anchored to the ground by filaments, as are fungi. Unlike fungi, however, bryophytes use the Sun's energy to produce their own food by photosynthesis.

Like all other plants, mosses and liverworts reproduce both sexually (involving sperm and egg) and asexually (involving spores). A generation produced sexually from the union of sperm and egg produces its offspring by means of spores. Then that asexually produced generation reproduces sexually, the two pathways alternating down through the generations.

As we shall see in Chapter 25, life on Earth began in the oceans and migrated to land only about 400 million years ago. This history is evident in today's bryophytes, in that they are not equipped to get moisture directly out of the soil, and that they cannot reproduce in a dry environment.

Vascular Plants

By far the greatest number of plants that play a role in our everyday life are in the phylum of **vascular plants** (Figure 20-6). These plants have an internal "plumbing" system consisting of roots, stems, and leaves capable of carrying fluids from one part of the plant to another. They also have ways of controlling water loss and protecting the sperm and egg so that they can survive outside of water. The development of internal plumbing not only adapted plants to life in the dry terrestrial environment, but it also began the process of providing internal structures to overcome the downward pull of gravity—both abilities crucial for land plants.

The most primitive vascular plants, a group whose most familiar members are in the class called *ferns*, still reproduce by producing sperm that must swim through water to fertilize eggs and generate spores. You can see the small yellow spore containers on the underside of the leaves of ferns. In this way they differ from the more advanced vascular plants, which, as we shall see, reproduce by means of seeds.

Although seedless vascular plants such as ferns play a relatively minor role on the Earth today, they were the main form of plant life 300 million years ago. Huge forests of ferns and related trees blanketed the land, where they used photosynthesis to store the Sun's energy in plant tissues. When these plants died, they were buried and, over millions of years, turned into coal. Thus you could say that the Industrial Revolution, which dramatically altered the structure of Western society in the nineteenth century, depended on seedless vascular plants, as does much of modern technological civilization.

The most common classes of vascular plants today are the **gymnosperms** (plants that produce seeds without flowers; e.g., fir trees) and the **angiosperms** (plants that produce seeds and flowers). The distinguishing feature of these plants, which have dominated the plant kingdom for the last 250 million years, is that they reproduce by means of seeds. All seeds contain a fertilized egg and some nutrient, both wrapped in a protective coating. Like spores, seeds are capable of lying dormant for long periods and hence can wait through times of cold

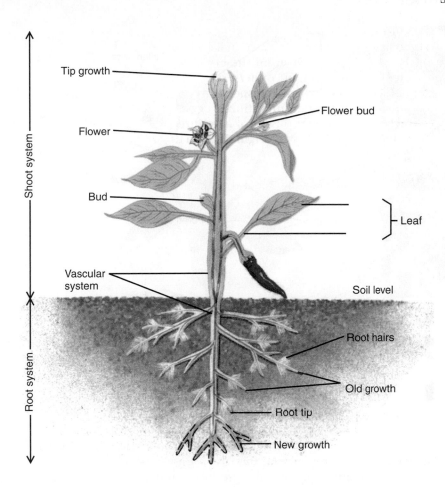

Tip growth

Flower bud

Flower

Bud

Leaf

Shoot system

Vascular
system

Soil level

Root system

Root hairs

Old growth

Root tip

New growth

• **Figure 20-6** The basic design of all vascular plants includes a root system below ground and a system of stems and leaves above ground.

or drought before they sprout. One way that seed-producing plants have become fully adapted to life on land is that the sperm part of these plants, familiar to us as pollen grains, typically moves through the air or is carried by insects. Thus, though seed plants may need water to grow, they do not need to be near standing water in order to reproduce.

The name gymnosperm means "naked seed" and refers to the fact that the seeds grow unprotected from the elements. The most familiar gymnosperms are evergreen trees, or conifers, such as the pine. On these trees, some cones produce pollen, which is dispersed by the wind. When pollen grains land on cones that contain unfertilized eggs, fertilization takes place. The seed, which as mentioned consists of a fertilized egg plus some stored nutrients, develops on the cone that originally held the egg, and, when conditions are right, is released and carried by the wind to a new location. Typically, hundreds or even thousands of seeds have to be released to get one new seedling.

Angiosperms, which have been around for at least 100 million years and have dominated the Earth's plant life for the last 65 million years, comprise the great bulk of known species of modern plants. These plants reproduce through the complex structure of their flowers. In a flower, the pollen grains containing the sperm grow on stalks known as stamens (Figure 20-7). Wind or insects carry the grains either to another part of the same flower or to other flowers. Once in its new location, each pollen grain grows a tube and enters the ovary, where the eggs are found. After fertilization, a seed forms within the ovary, and the ovary itself develops into fruit. When you cut into an apple or a peach, you can see the

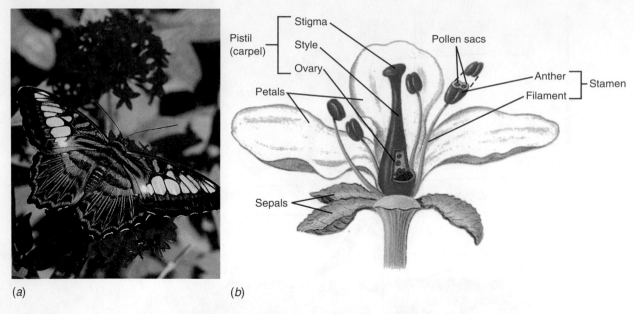

(a)   *(b)*

• **Figure 20-7** Flowers produce sperm and eggs for sexual reproduction. (*a*) Pollinators such as bees and butterflies transport pollen from one flower to the next. (*b*) The structures of a flower are represented schematically.

seeds and ovary quite clearly. When the fruit is ripe, it detaches itself from the plant. Many adaptations allow seeds to be carried long distances, from winged seeds (like those of some trees) to small seeds on berries that are eaten and passed through the digestive tracts of animals.

Although angiosperms can reproduce through fertilization, they also reproduce by sending out runners or shoots. Grass on a lawn, for example, reproduces this way if it is prevented from producing seeds by constant mowing. In the first case, reproduction is sexual (because a sperm and an egg come together); in the second case, it is asexual.

Strategies of Animals

Animals are multicellular organisms that must get their nourishment by capturing and consuming molecules produced by other life forms. The variety of organisms in this kingdom is truly staggering, ranging from sponges to tiny worms to eagles to students. Although the mass of all the plants on Earth far exceeds that of all the animals, the animal kingdom, with over 1.3 million known species, takes the prize for diversity. Depending on how lines are drawn, the kingdom can include more than 30 phyla. This diversity is summarized in Figure 20-8.

It's not easy to make generalizations about animals because of the great variety in this kingdom. However, the essential tasks of reproducing and acquiring energy and nutrients can help us get an overview. As you read the following, remember that respiration in animals is the reverse of photosynthesis in plants. In photosynthesis, a plant takes in carbon dioxide and gives off oxygen as a waste product. Animals, on the other hand, use lungs or gills to breathe in the oxygen that is used in the body's chemical reactions, and then they exhale carbon dioxide as a waste product.

- **Figure 20-8** The family tree of animals, showing some of the major phyla.

Invertebrates

When we think about animals, we usually visualize large organisms that fall under the subphylum of vertebrates, such as birds, fish, or elephants. Most animal species, however, are **invertebrates**—organisms without backbones that make up the 30 or so other animal phyla. The simplest invertebrates, such as sponges, exhibit characteristics somewhere between those of an aggregate of individual cells and those of true multicellular organisms. If a sponge is passed through a sieve, the individual cells not only survive, but also eventually reorganize themselves into a sponge. Corals, too, are colonies of countless separate minute organisms; break up the collection and each individual can function on its own.

Most of the phyla of the animal kingdom consist of worms, mollusks, and various microscopic organisms. Some of these animals have become incredibly specialized; one phylum of worms, for example, contains more than 70 species found as parasites in the noses, sinuses, and lungs of vertebrates. Sea cucumbers, jellyfish, earthworms, mollusks, snails, and tapeworms are all examples of the diverse invertebrate forms to be found in the animal kingdom.

Arthropods are by far the most successful phylum in the animal kingdom, in terms of both number of species and total mass. Arthropods include familiar forms such as spiders, insects (including beetles, ants, butterflies, and many other

(a)

(b)

Most known animal species are arthropods, with segmented bodies and jointed limbs. They include (*a*) spiders, with eight legs and often several pairs of eyes; and (*b*) insects, with six legs and three segments.

kinds of "bugs"), and crustacea (e.g., crabs, shrimp, and lobsters), all of which are animals with segmented bodies and jointed limbs. The more than 900,000 recognized species of insects account for at least 70% of all known animal species. There are more species of beetles than of any other type of animal, and more individual ants than individuals of any other type. These facts prompted a famous comment by evolutionary theorist J.B.S. Haldane (1892–1964) who, when asked what his studies of biology had taught him about God, replied, "He has an inordinate fondness for beetles."

One of the problems that all land-dwelling organisms have to deal with is finding a way to support their structures against the pull of gravity. Arthropods solve this problem with a hard external covering known as an exoskeleton. This strategy is different from that of the vertebrates, whose weight is supported by an internal skeleton and whose outer coatings are usually soft. You can see this same difference in strategy illustrated architecturally in the contrast between old buildings held up by massive stone walls, and modern skyscrapers, whose weight is held up by a steel skeleton and whose outer skin may be nothing more substantial than thin sheets of glass.

🛑 **Stop and Think!** Can you think of any other strategies that living things could use to maintain their structures?

The hard exoskeleton provides an evolutionary advantage to arthropods: it is a "coat of armor" that protects the animal from predators. Because the exoskeleton cannot grow, arthropods usually shed their exoskeletons periodically, a process known as molting. A typical insect (Figure 20-9) has a body divided into three segments. Three pairs of legs originate from the central segment, or thorax, while a pair of antennae for sensing the environment adorns the head. Many insects also have one or two pairs of wings. Insects have a heart, but no lungs; they bring oxygen into their bodies through a set of tubes.

Vertebrates

Familiar vertebrate animals such as rabbits, birds, frogs, or fish have spinal cords encased in a backbone. The easiest way to understand the connection between the several branches of the vertebrate family tree is to think of each new branching up to reptiles as another step in the transition from water-dwelling animals to those fully adapted to life on land. As we shall see in Chapter 25, this line of thought follows the actual evolution of modern vertebrates, whose ancestors developed in the ocean and later made the move to a terrestrial environment.

The earliest fish, which became common about 400 million years ago, had no jaws; they fed by moving water through their mouths and filtering materials out. Lampreys (which look like eels without jaws) are modern descendants of these primitive fish. Over the following 100 million years, jaws evolved, and the advantage of speed over heavy protection led to a loss of bone. Modern fish such as sharks and stingrays, for example, have no bone at all, but skeletons made from cartilage, which is a structural material less rigid than bone. Modern fish absorb oxygen from water that flows through their gills.

Bony fish are a class of vertebrates that includes salmon, perch, trout, and most other organisms we think of when we hear the word "fish." Their skeletons are, as the name implies, made from bone. Oddly enough, the ancestors of these fish developed in fresh water and had both lungs and gills. In modern fish, these

• **Figure 20-9** The generic insect.

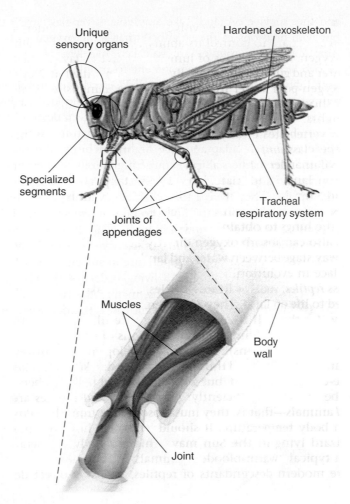

Unique sensory organs

Hardened exoskeleton

Specialized segments

Joints of appendages

Tracheal respiratory system

Muscles

Body wall

Joint

lungs have evolved into the swim bladder, an internal sac the fish can inflate to control its ability to float, while the gills function to supply oxygen. A few species of lungfish survive today. These fish live in stagnant water and gulp air occasionally to supplement what they can extract from the oxygen-poor water in which they live. Lungfish can also live out of water for short periods, allowing them to move from one pool to another during droughts.

The first vertebrates clearly adapted to live at least part of their lives on land were the class *amphibians,* whose modern descendants include frogs, toads, and salamanders. Most amphibians spend part of their life cycle in water, part on land. Frogs hatch in water as tadpoles, complete with gills and fins, and then develop into land-living adults with lungs and legs. They have a three-chambered heart and a circulatory system in which blood is pumped to the lungs to obtain oxygen, then returned and sent out into the body. Frogs also can absorb oxygen directly through their skin. Amphibians mark a halfway stage between water and land, in terms of both their anatomy and their place in evolution.

The class *reptiles,* including lizards, turtles, and snakes, were the first animals fully adapted to life on land. They are covered with hard scales, cutting down the loss of water through the skin. Eggs are fertilized within the body of the female, instead of relying on chance unions of egg and sperm in water, as with fish and amphibians. The young develop in eggs surrounded by a shell that can retain water and thus survive on land. Like amphibians, reptiles have a three-chambered heart, but with divisions in the chambers that allow oxygen to be used more efficiently. Amphibians and reptiles are so-called *cold-blooded* animals—that is, they must absorb heat from their environment to maintain body temperature. It should be noted, however, that a "cold-blooded" lizard lying in the sun may achieve a body temperature much higher than typical "warm-blooded" animals.

Birds are now widely thought to be modern descendants of reptiles, probably direct descendants of dinosaurs. Their anatomy differs from that of reptiles because of their adaptation to flight. In birds, the scales of the reptiles have evolved into feathers. Birds require high levels of energy to sustain flight, so their respiratory and circulatory systems are more complex than in reptiles and amphibians. They have a four-chambered heart, as do humans. One side of the heart pumps blood to the lungs to take in oxygen, and the other side pumps this oxygen-rich blood around the body. This feature allows the bird to use the energy in its food with maximal efficiency, so that it is *warm-blooded*, maintaining a relatively constant body temperature in any environment.

Taxonomists recognize 18 living orders of the class *mammals* in the world today (Figure 20-10). Like birds, mammals maintain a constant body temperature by burning food. In almost all cases, the development of the fertilized egg

• **Figure 20-10** The mammalian family tree.

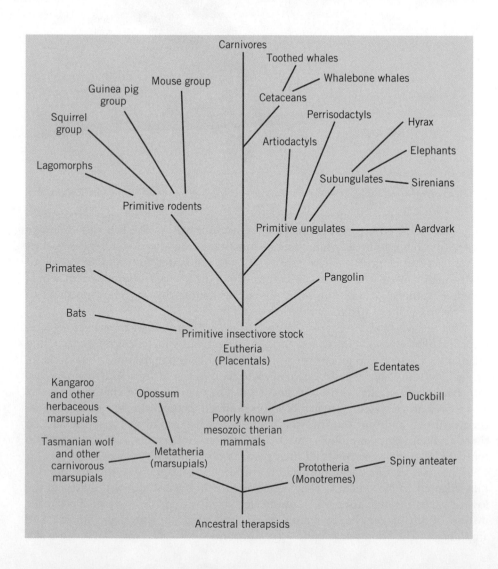

Science News | Camelid Comeback
(SCIENCE NEWS, JAN. 11, 2003, P. 26)

One of the issues that concerns scientists who catalogue and study the Earth's life forms is the problem of extinction. On the surface, this seems to be a simple issue—once a species has gone extinct, it will no longer be seen on the planet, and it seems to be a simple matter to decide when this has happened. In the real world, however, particularly when dealing with closely related organisms, the situation is not nearly so clear cut.

Animals in the camel family originated in North America about 30 million years ago, and 11 million years ago the population split. One group migrated to Asia across the Bering Straits and gave rise to the modern Bactrian (two-humped) camel and the more common dromedary (one hump). The other group migrated to South America and gave rise to modern llamas and alpacas (which are domesticated), and vicunas and guanacos (which are wild). The vicuna is highly prized for its wool, which is used to produce high-quality clothing. Indeed, the ancient Inca emperors forbad anyone but royalty to wear vicuna garments. By 1960, the population of wild vicuna had shrunk to about 10,000, and trade in their wool was suspended.

Today, the population has rebounded as a result of government conservation policies, and some limited trade is permitted, but a new problem has arisen. In most South American countries, vicuna are no longer allowed to run wild, but are fenced in large enclosures. In addition, there is some genetic evidence that over the past centuries, wild vicuna have interbred to some extent with their domesticated cousins. The question: does the existence of a population of fenced, interbred animals allow us to say that the vicuna is no longer in danger of extinction? It's not an easy question to answer.

---

takes place entirely inside the body of the mother, so that the young are born live. Once born, the young are nourished by milk from special glands in the female. Other adaptations to the terrestrial environment include hair to aid in temperature regulation, specialized teeth for breaking up food, legs located under the body, and, perhaps most important, an enlarged brain.

Thinking More About | Life's Strategies

Eating Through the Phyla

Human beings consume an amazing variety of foods. One way to make the diversity of life more real to you is to think about the variety of kingdoms and phyla your meals come from. Consider, for example, a slice of mushroom pizza. The crust derives from wheat, a vascular plant. The mushrooms, of course, are fungi. The cheese comes from milk produced by a cow, a vertebrate animal, and the milk is converted into cheese through the action of a single-celled member of the kingdom monera. The remains of these organisms are still in the cheese when you eat it, so with one bite of pizza you are consuming representatives of four kingdoms. If you could imagine adding a dash of seaweed or kelp, which are protista (at least in some classification schemes), you could get all five kingdoms in one bite.

Biologist Harold Morowitz, in his book *Entropy and the Magic Flute* (Oxford University Press, 1993), points out that traditional Japanese cuisine incorporates more phyla than any other. It includes such delicacies as seaweeds and sea cucumbers (animals in the same phylum as starfish), as well as the usual crustaceans (arthropods), shellfish, and various bony fish. But even a Western meal such as seafood

A slice of mushroom pizza incorporates foods from many phyla.

pasta accompanied by a salad with oil and vinegar dressing contains a wide variety of phyla. It has vascular plants (lettuce, tomato, and olive oil), a phylum of monera (which ferments the vinegar), clams and squid (phylum mollusca), and bony fish (vertebrates), not to mention flour (from angiosperms) and perhaps eggs (from vertebrates) in the pasta.

How many phyla combine to make your favorite meal?

SUMMARY

Biology, the study of living systems, began with efforts to describe the great variety of organisms on Earth. *Taxonomy,* the grouping of living things by their distinctive characteristics, has been aided by the *Linnaean classification* scheme, which groups organisms according to similarities in structure. Scientists now recognize five *kingdoms: monera* and *protista,* the two kingdoms of one-celled organisms; *fungi,* which eat dead organic matter; *plants,* which make their own food by photosynthesis; and *animals,* which eat other organisms. A given *species* is placed in groups making up a series of increasingly specialized labels. The categories are, from most general to most specific, phylum, class, order, family, genus, and species.

The species, defined to be an interbreeding population of individuals that produces fertile offspring, is the basic unit of classification. *Homo sapiens* (the human species) is in the phylum chordata, the subphylum *vertebrates,* the class *mammals,* the order *primates,* the family hominids, and genus and species *Homo sapiens.* The fact that living things can be grouped in this way can be interpreted as evidence that they all descended from a common ancestor.

Every multicellular organism must develop ways to obtain and distribute molecules for energy and structure, and to reproduce itself. Different life forms have evolved different ways to deal with these problems. Fungi absorb materials through slender filaments and reproduce through the production of spores. *Vascular plants,* the most abundant plants, use thin tubes to distribute water to their leaves. The two largest groups of vascular plants are *gymnosperms,* which have exposed seeds, and *angiosperms,* which have flowers. The most abundant animals are *invertebrates,* which are dominated by *arthropods* such as insects and spiders.

KEY TERMS ABOUT LIFE

biology	species	vertebrates	*Homo sapiens*	angiosperms
taxonomy	kingdoms (monera, protista,	mammals	vascular plants	invertebrates
Linnaean classification	fungi, plants, animals)	primates	gymnosperms	arthropods

REVIEW QUESTIONS

1. How can you tell if an object is alive?

2. What is complexity?

3. Identify eight characteristics of all living things.

4. List the levels in the modern system of biological classification. At each level, identify the name of the group that includes humans.

5. What are some distinctive characteristics of the five kingdoms of living things?

6. Why do some biologists think there are more than five kingdoms?

7. Why do some biologists think there are fewer than five kingdoms?

8. How do the energy-gathering strategies of fungi, plants, and animals differ?

9. Name two tasks that all living things carry out.

10. What are bryophytes? Give some examples.

11. What characteristics distinguish vascular plants from others? Give examples of different kinds of vascular plants.

12. What are the differences between gymnosperms and angiosperms?

13. Why are angiosperms the most successful group of plants?

14. What are the four main structures of flowering plants? What is the function of each structure?

15. What are arthropods? How do they support their weight?

16. List the major groups of vertebrates and their distinguishing characteristics. Give an example of an animal from each group.

17. How are reptiles better adapted for life on land than amphibians?

18. What classes of animals are warm-blooded? What are the advantages of being warm-blooded?

DISCUSSION QUESTIONS

1. In what ways is the Linnaean classification scheme like a postal address? In what ways is it different?

2. How does the fact that living things can be classified in ever more specialized groups support the idea that they all descended from a common ancestor?

3. What is the range of estimates of the number of species on Earth? Why is the number so uncertain?

4. Given the definition of a species, how many different species of dogs are in the United States? How many species of humans are in the United States?

5. What are some of the reasons that two scientists might disagree on the Linnaean classification of a new kind of worm? Is the Linnaean system an "exact" science, with only one possible correct answer?

6. Why are biologists more confident of the total number of bird species than of insect species? Do you think we know a greater percentage of butterfly species or of worm species? Why?

7. What environmental conditions might favor the development of ferns instead of cherry trees?

8. Speculate on why vascular plants are more widely distributed than bryophytes.

9. Why might there be so many species of insects compared to species of birds or mammals?

10. What characteristics might distinguish two species of trees?

11. In what ways might changes in the nature of land plants have affected the evolution of land animals?

12. Where are the Earth's main coal deposits? What does this tell you about the location of forests hundreds of millions of years ago?

INVESTIGATIONS

1. Think about courses at your university other than those in biology. In what ways does classification play a role in chemistry? In psychology? In English? Is there any field of study that does not use classification in one way or another?

2. Examine recent issues of scientific journals and find an article that describes a new species of animal or plant. How was this new species classified?

3. In the eighteenth and nineteenth centuries, many well-educated amateur naturalists made significant contributions to the study of plants, animals, and fossils. Statesman Thomas Jefferson, artist John James Audubon, and explorers Lewis and Clark are among the famous Americans who described unusual plants and animals. Read a biography of an amateur naturalist and discuss how his or her work contributed to the science of biology.

4. Investigate the research of Carl Woese of the University of Illinois. How did his discoveries alter thinking about the classification of living things?

5. Take a walk around your campus and see how many of the four major plant groupings—bryophytes, seedless vascular plants, gymnosperms, and flowering plants—you can identify. On most campuses you should be able to find all four, and even in the middle of a city you should be able to find two or three.

6. Go to your favorite supermarket and try to count how many different phyla of plants and animals are for sale. What is the average number of phyla per aisle? Does this number vary much from one store to another?

7. Many medicines were derived originally from plants. List some of them. Are any of the plants that produced those medicines now endangered?

8. Many single-celled organisms appear as tiny round objects about a millionth of a meter in diameter. Investigate the procedures a biologist might use to classify such an organism.

WWW RESOURCES

See *The Sciences* homepage at: **http://www.wiley.com/trefil** for valuable web links.

1. *Classification of Living Things*. A stylish introduction to Linnaean classification, by Prof. Dennis O'Neil of Palomar College, San Marcos, California.) **http://anthro.palomar.edu/animal/**

2. *The Tree of Life*. A wonderful exploration of life's diversity and connections, developed at the Dept. of Agriculture of the Univ. of Arizona.) **http://tolweb.org/tree/phylogeny.html**

3. *Introduction to the Fungi*. Cool page with information on the many varieties and extraordinary uses of fungi.) **http://www.ucmp.berkeley.edu/fungi/fungi.html**

4. *The Arthropod Cabinet*. A virtual museum of neat arthropod specimens.) **http://www.priweb.org/collections/arth/arthropod_cabinet.html**

5. *Vertebrate Evolution*. The American Museum of Natural History's site for vertebrate paleontology.) **http://www.amnh.org/Exhibitions/Expeditions/treasure_fossil/Fossils/**

21

Molecules of Life

What constitutes a healthy diet?

GREAT IDEA

*A cell's major parts are constructed
from a few simple molecular building blocks.*

PHYSICS

Sugar molecules transfer energy in the cells of living things.

CHEMISTRY

The shape of organic molecules determines their chemical function in the cell.

GEOLOGY

Rocks, like cells, are modular; they are formed from many mineral grains.

HEALTH & SAFETY

Your body needs a constant supply of minerals and organic molecules such as proteins to sustain itself and continue growing.

ASTRONOMY

The action of the Sun's ultraviolet radiation on the skin can produce minute quantities of vitamin D in the body.

TECHNOLOGY

Synthetic molecules like Olestra are used as additives in food without affecting the body's digestive system.

BIOLOGY

Most of the structures of living things are made of proteins, carbohydrates and lipids.

Red = applications of the great idea discussed in this chapter.

Orange = other applications, some of which are explored in other chapters.

A granola bar makes a tasty, energy-rich, mid-afternoon snack. You lie back on your beach towel, take a bite and start to think about food. Why do we get hungry? What chemicals make up food? Why do some foods taste better than others?

Take a close look at the colorful granola bar wrapper and find the "Nutrition Facts" printed on the back. At the top of the list is "Calories"—a measure of food energy. Our bodies require energy to do work, just like every other physical system. That's why we get hungry.

The nutrition facts also include information on specific kinds of molecules, notably fat, carbohydrates and protein. These molecules are fundamental building blocks of every living thing and so are an essential part of our diets. We need a steady supply of these molecules because we are, quite literally, what we eat. Food tastes good because our tastebuds are fine-tuned to these critical molecules.

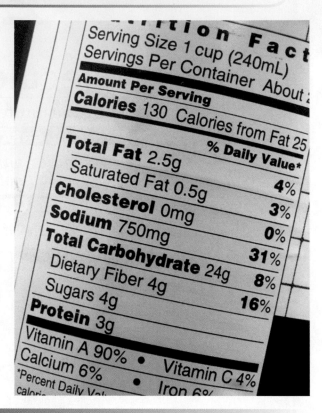

Organic Molecules

Next time you're outside, look closely at a tree. The trunk and limbs divide over and over again, a branching that is mirrored by the hidden root system. The tree has countless almost identical leaves on every limb, as well as myriad seeds in their season. Repeating the same basic patterns over and over again results in the complex structure of the tree.

Structures in your city or town reveal the same kind of patterns. Buildings feature stacks of identical bricks, row after row of identical windows, and numerous identical shingles, slates, or other roofing materials. The sidewalk is made of slab after slab of concrete, while street lamps, signs, fence posts, and telephone poles also repeat over and over again.

Indeed, almost any complex structure found in nature or designed by humans is modular, composed of a few simple pieces that combine to form larger objects. Molecules of water form the ocean, mineral grains form rocks, and countless identical hydrogen atoms form stars. The chemicals of life are no different. A few basic molecules combine to create the wonderful complexity of life around us.

Four Basic Characteristics

Wood. Leather. Hair. Cotton. Skin. All of these materials originated in living systems on our planet. And like all other materials found in living things, they share some basic chemical characteristics.

1. Most Molecules in Living Systems Are Based on the Chemistry of Carbon

In Chapter 10, we saw that carbon atoms possess the ability to form long chains, branches, and rings. In fact, chemists usually refer to molecules containing carbon as **organic molecules**, whether or not they are part of a living system. The branch of science devoted to the study of such carbon-based molecules and their reactions is called *organic chemistry*.

2. Life's Molecules Form from Very Few Different Elements

In terms of the percentages of atoms, just four elements—hydrogen, oxygen, carbon, and nitrogen—comprise 97.5% of our bodies' weight. Calcium in bones accounts for 2%, while phosphorus, sulfur, and all the other elements make up the remaining 0.5% (see Table 21-1). These elements combine to form the molecules that control chemical reactions in all living things.

3. The Molecules of Life Are Modular, Composed of Simple Building Blocks

Large and complicated molecules could be put together in two contrasting ways. One way would be to build each one from scratch, so that no piece of one molecule would be part of another. Another very different way would be to make the molecules modular, that is, to build them from a succession of simpler, widely available parts so that each large molecule differs from another only in the arrangement of those parts. Nature, for the most part, displays modularity in the molecules of living systems.

Modern buildings illustrate the versatility of modular construction. All kinds of buildings, from a humble cottage to a soaring skyscraper, can be built from a few basic parts—bricks, beams, windows, doors, stairs, and so on. The skyscraper and the cottage differ from each other both in the amount of material in them and in the arrangement of those materials, but they contain many of the same basic modules. This kind of modular construction is extremely efficient. It takes a great deal of work, time, and money to custom-design every door, window, and other component of your home. You might end up with a better-designed structure, but at a very high price. By building your home with widely available parts, you save money and still end up with a very satisfactory dwelling.

Similarly, though life's molecules come in an extraordinary variety of shapes and functions, they are made from collections of just a few smaller molecules. This modularity does not mean that the final products are simple, just as there's nothing particularly simple about a skyscraper. It merely means that if we wish to understand how large molecules behave, we first have to talk about the simple pieces from which they are built.

Table 21-1 **Atoms in the Human Body**

Element	Percent
Hydrogen	61.2
Oxygen	23.5
Carbon	11.7
Nitrogen	1.1
Calcium (mostly in bones)	2.0
Phosphorus	0.2
Sulfur	0.1
All others	0.2

Side Group

Amino group   Carboxyl group

• **Figure 21-1** An amino acid, showing the amino (NH₂) and carboxylic acid (COOH) groups and the side group. The side group varies from one type of amino acid to another, and gives that particular amino acid the chemical properties that distinguish it from any other.

4. Shape Helps to Determine the Behavior of Organic Molecules—In Other Words, Molecular Geometry Controls the Chemistry of Life

The connection between geometry and the behavior of organic molecules can be understood if you remember one important thing about chemical bonds. All chemical bonds result from the shifting of electrons among specific pairs or groups of atoms. This bonding property is particularly true of atoms that tend to form ionic, covalent, and hydrogen bonds (see Chapter 10).

A very large and complex molecule may have millions of atoms arranged in a complicated shape. If this large molecule is to take part in chemical reactions—if it is to bind to another molecule, for example—then that binding must take place through the actions of the valence electrons of atoms near the outsides of the two molecules. Specific atoms in each molecule must be able to get near enough to each other so that their electrons can form the bond. Consequently, the geometrical shape of a molecule plays a crucial role, because it determines whether atoms that can form bonds in each molecule will be able to get close enough together for the bonds actually to form.

In principle, an infinite number of molecules could be constructed according to these four rules. In fact, when we examine natural systems we find that only four general classes of molecules govern most of life's main chemical functions. We'll discuss three of these classes—proteins, carbohydrates, and lipids—in this chapter (the fourth important group of molecules, nucleic acids, are introduced in Chapter 23 on the genetic code). Throughout this discussion, you should keep in mind that all of these molecules conform to the four rules: they are carbon-based, they form from just a few elements, they are modular in structure, and their behavior depends on shape.

Chemical Shorthand

If we kept showing all of the atoms and bonds, as we do for an amino acid in Figure 21-1, diagrams of molecules would get very cluttered as the molecules become more complex. Consequently, chemists have adopted several standard shorthand ways of representing organic molecules. Many molecules can be represented by the following rules:

1. *No hydrogen atoms or bonds to hydrogen atoms are shown in the diagram.*
2. *Carbon atoms are not shown explicitly.*

As an example of how this notation works, look at the following diagram. Both of these drawings show molecules of benzene (a volatile liquid sometimes used as a

All atoms and bonds are shown.   Only carbon–carbon bonds are shown. Carbon atoms, hydrogen atoms, and carbon–hydrogen bonds are implied.

motor fuel). On the left, all the atoms are shown, and you can see that each carbon atom forms four bonds to its neighboring atoms. On the right, the carbon atoms are not shown, but we know they are located at the points where the bonds come together. Similarly, the hydrogen atoms are not shown, but we see that each carbon atom has only three bonds shown. We infer the existence of the hydrogen atom by the "missing" bond.

SCIENCE IN THE MAKING •

The Synthesis of Urea

In the early 1800s, scientists were not convinced that molecules in living systems are formed according to the same chemical rules that govern those in nonliving systems. Such molecules, after all, had not been produced in the laboratory. In 1828, a German chemist by the name of Friedrich Wöhler (1800–1882) performed a series of experiments that were crucial in establishing the ordinariness of organic molecules.

Like many scientists at that time, Wöhler had a breadth of experience that is unusual today. Before he began his career as a chemistry teacher, for example, he became a medical doctor and qualified in the specialty of gynecology. He was also interested in the practical aspects of chemistry, and he collected minerals from the time he was a child. He described his crucial experiments this way: "I found that whenever one tried to combine cyanic acid (a common laboratory chemical) and ammonia, a white crystalline solid appeared that behaved like neither cyanic acid nor ammonia."

After extensive testing, Wöhler found that the white crystals were identical to urea, a substance routinely found in the kidneys and (as the name suggests) urine, where it helps remove nitrogen wastes from the body. In other words, the appearance of that "white crystalline solid" showed that it is possible to take ordinary chemicals off the shelf and produce a substance found in living systems. He had demonstrated that the same chemical processes typical of abiotic materials might form organic molecules.

With humor uncharacteristic of most academicians, Wöhler announced his findings in a letter as follows: "I can no longer, as it were, hold back my chemical urine: and I have to let out that I can make urea without needing a kidney, whether of man or dog." •

Proteins: The Workhorses of Life

The molecules we call proteins play many key roles in living systems. Some proteins form building materials from which large structures are formed. Your hair, your fingernails, the tendons that hold your muscles in place, and much of the connective tissue that holds your body together, for example, are made primarily of protein molecules. Proteins also serve to regulate the movement of materials across cell walls, and thus control what goes into and out of each cell in your body. Proteins play many specialized roles in our bodies—for example, as hormones that regulate bodily functions and as antibodies that protect against infection and disease. In addition, proteins serve as enzymes (see the following section), molecules that control the rate of complex chemical reactions in living things.

Because of these and many other functions, proteins are vital components of your diet, as you have probably heard. You must regularly take in proteins to supply your body with building materials to effect repairs and growth.

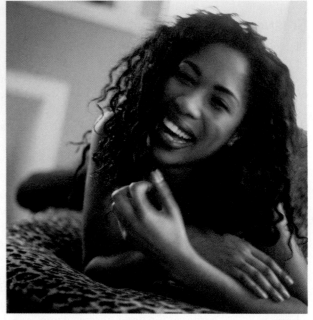

A spider's silk, fingernails, and hair are everyday examples of structural proteins.

Amino Acids: The Building Blocks of Proteins

Proteins are modular just like all complex biological molecules. They are made up of strings of basic building blocks called **amino acids**. A typical amino acid molecule is sketched in Figure 21-1. All biological amino acids incorporate a characteristic backbone of atoms. One end terminates in a *carboxylic acid group* (COOH), a combination of carbon, oxygen, and hydrogen. On the other end is an *amino group* (NH_2), a nitrogen bonded to two hydrogen atoms. (These two groups give this category of molecules their name.) Between these two ends a carbon atom completes the backbone.

Branching off the central carbon atom is another atom or cluster of atoms, the "side group" that makes each kind of amino acids unique and interesting. Hundreds of different amino acids can be made in the laboratory, each with its different characteristic side group. A few common amino acids are sketched in Figure 21-2 to give you a sense of the kind of diversity that is possible within this basic structure.

Two amino acids can bond together in a very simple way. A hydrogen atom (H) from the amino end will connect to the hydroxyl (OH) group of the carboxylic acid end of another amino acid to form a molecule of water (H_2O). This water molecule moves off (you can think of this process as "squeezing out" the water), leaving the two amino acids bonded together in what is called a *peptide bond*. This process is identical to the *condensation polymerization* reaction that is often used to manufacture plastics and other polymers (see Chapter 10). Indeed, chemists often refer to a bonded chain of amino acids as a *polypeptide*.

Once two amino acids have joined together with a peptide bond, more amino acids can be hooked onto either end by the same process to form a long

• **Figure 21-2** Several amino acids. Each has a distinctive side group (blue type) that branches off the central carbon atom.

string of amino acids. A **protein** is a large molecule formed by linking amino acids together in this way. There are many different amino acids to choose from, and different proteins correspond to a different ordering (as well as a different total number) of the amino acids in the string.

One of the great surprises that came out of the study of biochemistry in the early part of the twentieth century was that although chemists can synthesize hundreds of different amino acids, only a small number of amino acids actually appear in the proteins of living systems on Earth. Only 20 different amino acids are produced in cells, although some of these are modified once the amino acid string is put together. The mystery of why only 20 amino acids are found in living things has a possible explanation in terms of the theory of evolution, which we explore in Chapter 25. Note, however, that even with only 20 basic building blocks, an almost infinite variety of different strings or proteins can be formed (see the following "Science by the Numbers" section).

The Structure of Proteins

Proteins are extremely complex molecules, sometimes consisting of many thousands of amino acids and millions of atoms. One of the great triumphs of modern science has been to determine the exact atomic structures of many of these large molecules. To accomplish this feat, biochemists first have to isolate quantities of pure protein, form delicate single crystals in which the large molecules line up in a regular array, and examine the crystals by X-ray techniques that reveal the distribution of atoms in space.

A protein's structure is usually described in four stages, each representing an increasing order of complexity (Figure 21-3).

1. Primary Structure
The exact sequence of amino acids that go into a given protein is called its *primary structure*. Every distinct protein has a different primary structure—that is, it has a different sequence of amino acids along its string.

2. Secondary Structure
Depending on the arrangements of amino acids in the primary structure, hydrogen bonds can form that give the final protein a specific shape. Some proteins, for example, take the form of a long helix or long spring. Others fold back on themselves repeatedly to form rough spheres. Shapes taken by the string of amino acids that makes up the primary structure of a protein are called its *secondary structure*.

When you cook an egg, you can see the effect of secondary structure. The proteins in egg white are wrapped up into tiny spheres scattered throughout the

• **Figure 21-3** The structure of a protein can be described in four steps. Primary structure (*a*) is the sequence of amino acids. Secondary structure (*b*) is the way the sequence kinks or bends. Tertiary structure (*c*) is the shape of the completely folded protein. Quaternary structure (*d*) is the clustering of several proteins to form the active structure, in this case, hemoglobin, which carries oxygen in your bloodstream.

fluid. This is why normal egg white is transparent. When you cook the egg white, you break the hydrogen bonds that keep the protein wrapped up and allow the molecules to unfold. The tough mat they form when they interlock gives the cooked egg white its characteristic texture and appearance.

3. Tertiary Structure

As parts of the amino acid chain fold back on itself, atoms in the side groups can come into contact with each other. As a result, additional cross-linking chemical bonds form between side groups in amino acids in different parts of the chain. One common link occurs between sulfur atoms in different side groups. The distinctive shape of human insulin, for example, arises because of bonds that form between sulfur atoms in the amino acid cystine.

As a result of these links, a protein will twist around, kink up, and fold itself into a complex shape, much as a string will fold itself into a complex shape if it's dropped on a table. This complex folding is the *tertiary structure* of the protein.

4. Quaternary Structure

Finally, two or more long chains, each with its own secondary and tertiary structure, may come together to form a single larger unit. This joining of separate protein chains determines the *quaternary structure* of the protein.

Predicting the exact shape that will be assumed by a given sequence of amino acids remains one of the great goals of modern biochemistry, a goal that we are still far from reaching. But whether or not we can predict the ultimate shape of a protein, the fact remains that each different sequence of amino acids will produce a large molecule with a different three-dimensional shape. This fact will become important when we consider the role of proteins in the cell's chemistry.

SCIENCE BY THE NUMBERS •

How Many Proteins Can You Make?

At first, it may seem that with only 20 different amino acids available to build proteins in living systems, the number of different kinds of proteins you could make would be rather limited. Let's do some calculations to see why this isn't the case.

Suppose we start by asking a simple question: How many different proteins, each 10 amino acids long, can we make from amino acids found in living systems? (Once you've seen the answer to this question, you'll be able to figure out for yourself how to calculate the answer for a protein with any number of amino acids.)

One way of thinking about this question is to imagine that each protein consists of 10 amino acids on a string, and each amino acid can be selected from one of 20 different boxes. We could choose the first amino acid of the string from any one of 20 boxes. For each of these 20 choices for the amino acid in the first position, there are 20 choices we could make for the amino acid in the second position. Thus we could choose amino acids to fill the first two vacancies on the string in $20 \times 20 = 400$ different ways.

Following this logic, the number of ways to arrange 10 amino acids in a string is

$$20 \times 20 \times 20 \times 20 \times 20 \times 20 \times 20 \times 20 \times 20 \times 20 = 1.028 \times 10^{13}$$

Thus we could make about 10 trillion different proteins that contain 10 amino acids. This number is huge—100 million times larger than the number of proteins used in the human body. And, of course, this is just the number of different proteins you could make containing exactly 10 amino acids. Typical proteins in living systems contain many more amino acids, usually hundreds to thousands of them. The bottom line of this calculation is that, although only 20 different amino acids appear in living systems, this number still allows for a tremendous diversity of proteins. •

Proteins as Enzymes

One of the key roles that proteins play in living systems is to act as enzymes in chemical reactions in cells. An **enzyme** is a molecule with a specific shape and structure that facilitates bonding between two other molecules, but which is not permanently altered or taken up in that overall reaction. Because of the presence of the enzyme, the chemical reaction takes place at a much faster rate than it otherwise would.

Enzymes play a role in chemical reactions similar to a broker or an agent in a business deal. The broker brings together a buyer and seller, but does no buying or selling. The buyer and seller eventually might find each other without the help of the broker, but the deal goes through much quicker if the broker is there. In the same way, a molecule that plays the role of an enzyme possesses a shape and structure that may bring together two other molecules and facilitate their forming a bond, or it may tear a molecule apart without itself being included in the chemical reaction. Because of the enzyme, the reaction takes place relatively quickly.

Enzymes illustrate the primary importance of geometrical shape in determining how chemical reactions take place among large molecules. You can easily visualize the workings of an enzyme (see Figure 21-4). Each large molecule has places on it, atoms or small groups of atoms, where chemical bonding can take place. Think of these locations as sticky spots somewhere on a large, convoluted molecular shape. In order for two or more molecules to interact, their respective sticky spots have to come into contact. More precisely, the atoms whose electrons will eventually form the bonds must be brought close enough together for the electrons to interact. This proximity is unlikely to happen at random.

Imagine each molecule as a large pile of string that is dumped in the corner of a room, and think of the spots that could form chemical bonds as patches of glue located at random places along the string. If you took two such pieces of string and tossed them together in the corner, the chances are very slight that any of the sticky spots would come near each other. If, on the other hand, you picked up the strings and arranged it so that the sticky spots were next to each other, you could make sure that they formed a bond. In this "chemical reaction," you are playing the role of the enzyme. You cause bonds to form that probably wouldn't form without you, but you do not become a part of the bond.

Enzymes perform an analogous function in organic reactions. Typically, an enzyme is a large molecule that has particular spots on its surface into which reacting molecules will just fit. The enzyme attracts first one of the molecules and then the other. In some enzymes, two specific molecules attach themselves in only one way, so it is guaranteed that their "sticky spots" will be near each other. The chemical bonds that hold them together will form. Once the bonds have formed, the overall shape of the resulting composite molecule suddenly becomes different from that of either of the two molecules that went into it. Consequently, the new large molecule no longer fits into the appropriate grooves and valleys of the enzyme, and it spontaneously breaks free and wanders off by itself. This separation leaves the enzyme free to mediate the same reaction again, each time with two new pieces. Another kind of enzyme, like those in your stomach, performs

• **Figure 21-4** An enzyme in action joins two molecules (designated A and B) and produces a product (C). The product is released and the enzyme is free to repeat the process.

Molecules

Enzyme

Enzyme-molecule complex

A

B

Active site

Enzyme is recycled

Molecule modification

Product C

(a)

(b)

A computer-generated image of an enzyme in action. A glucose molecule approaches the enzyme hexokinase (*a*). When the two molecules combine, the shape and function of the enzyme change (*b*).

the opposite function, breaking apart large molecules into smaller units over and over again.

If you think about the way an enzyme works, you will realize why molecular shape is so important. The ridges and grooves on the surface of an enzyme serve as resting places for the molecules that interact on the enzyme's surface. Tens of thousands of different protein molecules, each of which adopts a different shape and therefore provides a resting place for different interacting molecules, are ideally suited to function in this way. For precisely this reason, proteins participate in most of the chemical reactions in living organisms.

Enzymes mediate the reactions of complex molecules in living systems. Thus the molecules that act as enzymes in living systems play a crucial role in determining the properties of those systems.

 Stop and Think! The relationship between an enzyme and the molecules that it reacts with is sometimes compared to a "lock and key" mechanism. What do you think is meant by this statement and in what ways does it apply to enzymes?

THE SCIENCE OF LIFE •

Proteins and Diet

Because proteins play such an important role in living systems, the cells in your body need a constant supply of all 20 amino acids. In adults, 12 of the 20 amino acids are synthesized in the body. The rest, the so-called *essential amino acids*, have to be taken into the body in the proteins and other foods that we eat. Because amino acids, unlike fat, cannot be stored by the body, the essential amino acids have to be present in every meal in roughly the proportion in which they occur in the body's own proteins.

Foods vary widely in their total protein content, from about 1% in bananas and carrots to almost 30% in peanuts and some cheese. Foods that supply amino acids in roughly the same proportion as those in human proteins are called *high-quality proteins*, while those that supply too little of one or more amino acid are called *low-quality proteins*. In general, meat and dairy products supply high-quality proteins, while plant products supply low-quality proteins.

In Figure 21-5, we make this point by comparing the amount of each of the eight essential amino acids found in eggs (the food whose amino acids most closely match human protein proportions) and cornmeal. You should note, however, that it is not necessary for each food we eat, in and of itself, to supply all

• **Figure 21-5** Proportion of essential amino acids in egg and cornmeal. The amino acid proportions for egg are close to those in the human body, whereas the cornmeal contains too little of the amino acids lysine, methionine, and tryptophan.

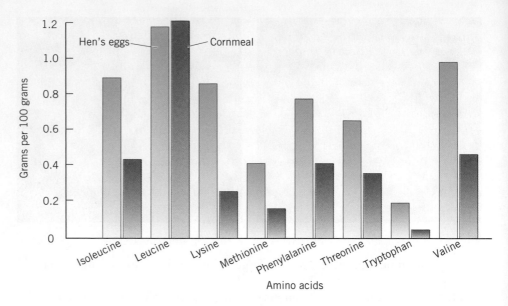

essential amino acids. It is possible to plan meals so that amino acids from one food make up for deficiencies of that amino acid in the other. Many traditional meals have this property. Milk, for example, provides the lysine that breakfast cereal lacks. The American staple, the peanut butter and jelly sandwich, provides the same kind of matching proteins. In fact, many traditional foods from around the world do pretty well in supplying complementary sources of amino acids. Some examples: corn tortillas and beans (Mexico), rice and tofu (Japan), and rice and ground nuts (West Africa). Because of the fact that plants provide low-quality protein, however, individuals on vegetarian diets must plan their food intake carefully to compensate for possible protein deficiencies.

By the way, have you ever wondered why we cook meats and other foods? High temperatures quickly depolymerize proteins (see Chapter 10), thus transforming long polymer chains into individual amino acid molecules. This chemical reaction breaks down tough protein fibers so foods are more tender and easily digested. At the same time, any potentially harmful bacteria are killed when their proteins are destroyed. •

How Drugs Work

Many of the drugs we take produce their effect because of the shape of their molecules. Some drugs, for example, alter our body chemistry by blocking the action of enzymes. You can understand how such a drug might work by looking at Figure 21-4. The efficiency of the enzyme depends on the fact that the shape of its surface matches the shape of the molecules involved in the reaction. A drug molecule that attached itself to one of those crucial sites on the enzyme would block that site, preventing one of the molecules involved in the original reaction from occupying it. As a result, the enzyme would not be able to facilitate the reaction as it normally does, and the chemical balance of the cell would be changed. When you take an aspirin, for example, you are blocking the action of an enzyme that facilitates the production of molecules called prostaglandins. These molecules, among other things, affect the transmission of nerve signals.

Other drugs work in similar ways on other cellular processes. We shall see in Chapter 22, for example, that part of the process of moving materials in and out of a cell across the cell membrane involves the fit between the molecules being moved and specialized proteins, called receptors, in the membrane. A drug that attaches to the receptor or to the material that is being brought in or out of the cell will block this match and alter the traffic in and out of the cell. Similarly, in Chapter 5, we noted that nerve impulses are transmitted from one nerve cell to the next by special molecules called neurotransmitters. These molecules are shaped so that they fit into specific sites on the "downstream" nerve cell. Many drugs, including alcohol and Valium, gain their effect because they have the right shape to bind to the synapses and alter their operation.

As our understanding of the geometry of organic molecules has increased, scientists are increasingly able to produce molecules with the right shape from scratch. Products made in this way have been nicknamed "designer drugs" (you'll learn more about them in Chapter 24). One such drug, called captopril, has been in use since 1975. This drug blocks the action of an enzyme that produces molecules that contribute to hypertension, and so is used to control that condition. Designer drugs for treating psoriasis, glaucoma, AIDS, and some forms of cancer and arthritis are in advanced stages of testing and may be on the market soon.

Carbohydrates

• **Figure 21-6** The structure of glucose.

Carbohydrates, the second important class of modular molecules found in all living things, are made up of carbon, hydrogen, and oxygen. They play a central role in the way that living things acquire and use energy, and they form many of the solid structures of living things. You use carbohydrates every day in many of the foods you eat, the fuels you burn, the clothes you wear, and even the paper of this book.

The simplest carbohydrates are **sugars**, molecules that usually contain five, six, or seven carbon atoms arranged in a ring-like structure. *Glucose*, an important sugar in the energy cycle of living things, is sketched in Figure 21-6. Glucose figures prominently in the energy metabolism of every living cell; it supplies the energy that we use to move and grow.

The general chemical formula for sugar is $C_nH_{2n}O_n$ or $C_n(H_2O)_n$. Glucose, for example, has the formula $C_6H_{12}O_6$. As often happens with organic molecules, other forms of the molecule have the same chemical composition, but have the components arranged differently. In Figure 21-7, for example, we show the sugar fructose. As the name implies, this sugar is commonly found in fruit. It has the same number of carbon, hydrogen, and oxygen atoms as glucose, but the atoms are arranged slightly differently, and this different arrangement gives fructose a different chemical behavior.

Chemists call individual sugar molecules *monosaccharides*, meaning "one sugar." (The same root word is used when an overly sentimental story is described as "saccharine.") The carbohydrates that we eat, however, are usually formed from two or more sugar molecules. Ordinary table sugar, for example, is made from two sugars, glucose and fructose, linked together by covalent bonds.

When many sugars are strung together in a chain, the resulting molecule is called a *polysaccharide* ("many sugars"). The two most familiar polysaccharides are starch and cellulose. Both of these kinds of molecules are made from long chains of glucose molecules. They differ from each other only in the details of the way the glucose molecules bind to each other (Figure 21-8.)

Starches, a common component of the human diet, are a large family of molecules in which the glucose constituents link together at certain points along the ring. Starches are found in many plants, such as potatoes and corn. Animals also

The fibers that hold these plants up are made from glucose.

Fructose

• **Figure 21-7** The structure of fructose. It has the same number and kinds of atoms as glucose, but is a different arrangement.

form a glucose polymer, called *glycogen* or *animal starch*, which is stored in the liver and in muscle tissues. Humans break down starch molecules with an enzyme in the digestive system, thus releasing individual glucose molecules, which provide the fundamental energy fuel used by cells.

Cellulose, a long, stringy polymer that provides the main structural element in plants, from stems and leaves to the trunks of trees, also forms from glucose molecules. Because the glucose molecules are linked in a different way, however, human beings cannot digest cellulose. We do not manufacture an enzyme that can separate individual glucose molecules from the cellulose polymer. Consequently, humans don't go out and graze on the lawn at lunchtime, though people on diets often eat celery and other "roughage" or "fiber." On the other hand, cellulose can be digested and broken down by many bacteria. Cows, for example, have bacteria in their stomachs that perform this function for them, as do wood-eating termites.

STOP **Stop and Think!** Why do long-distance runners often load up on carbohydrates before a race?

The wood fibers in the paper on this page are made from glucose molecules bonded into cellulose, basically the same chemical as in the stalk of a celery stick. The same glucose molecules, bonded in a different way, form the flour in the spaghetti you ate the last time you had a pasta dinner. An amazing diversity can be built into organic molecules through modular construction.

• **Figure 21-8** An individual glucose molecule (*a*) has six carbon atoms as numbered. These molecules can be linked into polymers such as cellulose (*b*) and starch (*c*), which differ in the way that glucose molecules are linked together.

(*a*)

Glucose

(*b*)

Cellulose

(*c*)

Starch

Lipids encompass a grab bag of vital organic molecules that go into making up every living thing. **Lipids** include a variety of molecules that will not dissolve in water, including fats in food, waxes in candles, greases for lubrication, and a wide variety of oils. If you think of drops of oil or bits of fat floating around on top of a pot of soup, you have a pretty good picture of what large clumps of lipid molecules are like.

At the molecular level, lipids play two important roles in living things. First, they form cell membranes that separate living material from its environment, as well as separate one part of a cell from other parts. They are also used to store energy. In fact, in the human body excess weight is usually carried in the form of fat, which is a different kind of lipid from those in cell membranes. Lipids are extremely efficient storehouses for energy. A typical gram of fat, for example, contains twice as many calories as a gram of either protein or carbohydrate.

Like proteins and carbohydrates, numerous lipid molecules can come together to form large modular structures in every cell. An important class of these molecules, called *phospholipids*, are long and thin with a carbon backbone, as shown in Figure 21-9. In phospholipids, a phosphate group (one phosphorus and four oxygen atoms) is incorporated into one end of the molecule. The oxygen atoms in this group tend to be negatively charged, so that this end of the molecule is attracted to water (we say it is hydrophilic). The other end of the molecule, however, is repelled by water (we say it is hydrophobic). These particular types of lipids play an extremely important role in living systems because, as we shall see, they are the materials from which cell membranes are made.

Saturated and Unsaturated Fats

Every carbon atom in a lipid chain forms exactly four bonds to neighboring atoms (see Chapter 10). In a straight chain, each carbon atom bonds to two adjacent carbon atoms along the chain and two hydrogen atoms on the sides. Carbon atoms of this type are *saturated*—fully bonded to four other atoms.

In some lipids, adjacent carbon atoms will have only three neighbors, including two carbon and one hydrogen atoms. An angled "double bond" will thus

• **Figure 21-9** A phospholipid molecule, showing the negatively charged phosphate group at one end, and ordinary hydrocarbon chains at the other. The end with the phosphate group is attracted to water, and the hydrocarbon end is repelled by it. Different collections of molecules in the group labeled "R" correspond to different kinds of phospholipids.

form between the two carbon atoms (see Figure 21-10). A chain with one double bond is *monounsaturated*, while two or more double bonds yield a *polyunsaturated* lipid.

Saturated fats in the diet provide the raw materials from which the body can synthesize *cholesterol*, an essential component of all cell membranes. Unfortunately, high levels of cholesterol in the blood can also lead to fatty deposits that clog arteries. For these reasons, many food producers emphasize their use of cholesterol-free foods, rich in polyunsaturated fats. Advertising often suggests that unsaturated foods are "good for you."

Be warned, however. Many of these polyunsaturated products require a further processing step, called *hydrogenation*, to give them a pleasing texture and consistency. Popular chocolate candies, for example, must be made from fats and oils that soften near body temperature. Hydrogenation—the addition of hydrogen atoms back into the carbon chains—eliminates carbon–carbon double bonds. Each added hydrogen atom pulls one of the carbon bonds apart and thus partially saturates the lipid chains. Many popular cooking oils that begin with highly unsaturated lipids are "partially hydrogenated for freshness and consistency" at the manufacturing plant, a process that undoes the good of the unsaturated bonds.

• **Figure 21-10** Lipid molecules with saturated, unsaturated, and polyunsaturated forms, showing the resulting kinks.

TECHNOLOGY •

Nonfattening Fats

For most of human history, energy-rich fat was a rare delicacy, something enjoyed only occasionally by most people. Consequently, we acquired a taste for fat that remains with us today in our more affluent situation. A taste for fat combined with widespread availability has led to a serious problem with excess weight in the United States.

Until recently, there was little that people could do to keep their weight down except reduce their food intake and exercise. Now, however, new abilities in molecular technology have added a third option—we can eat foods that taste like fat, but which cannot be digested, and hence supply the body with no energy.

The first "no-fat fat" was approved for use in 1995 under the trade name Olestra. One ordinary fat found in foods consists of three long-chain molecules connected to a small alcohol molecule. The whole thing looks something like a capital Y, with the alcohol molecule at the center. In the intestines, specialized molecules from the digestive system attach to the alcohol and break off the "legs," which are then broken down further by other molecules. Olestra is shaped very similarly, except that it has eight chains attached to the alcohol instead of three. Because of the extra chains, the molecules from the digestive system can't get at the alcohol and the Olestra passes undigested through the human body. It tastes like fat, but adds no calories. Manufacturing specialized molecules like this to use in the human diet will be a growth industry in the future. •

Cell Membranes

The most important single function of lipids in our bodies is the formation of *cell membranes*, the structure that separates the inside of every cell from its environment. Phospholipids, with their hydrophobic and hydrophilic ends, perform this function because when placed in water, these molecules typically adopt a double-layered

Potato chips made with "no-fat fat."

• Figure 21-11 The structure of a lipid bilayer. The hydrophobic ends of the molecules face each other, while the hydrophilic ends are in the surrounding water.

structure like the one shown in Figure 21-11. The hydrophobic ends of the molecule line up facing each other, while the hydrophilic ends face to the outside. In this way, water is kept away from the hydrophobic ends and nearer the hydrophilic ends. A double-layered structure of molecules like this functions very well as a membrane of a cell. It is flexible and can change its shape, but it also provides a tough barrier. Special mechanisms have to be in place in order for anything to elbow its way through the bimolecular layer.

The structure of the lipid bilayers that make cell membranes is remarkably similar to liquid crystals (see Chapter 10). The lipid molecules are highly ordered in their orientation and spacing, but they are somewhat disordered in their exact positions side-to-side. This loose structure provides an important measure of flexibility to cell membranes.

Minerals and Vitamins

Though most of our body is made and operates with proteins, carbohydrates, lipids, and nucleic acids (see Chapter 23), other chemicals are also vital to life. These essential chemicals include the familiar minerals and vitamins that must form part of our diet.

Minerals

Minerals, in a nutritional context, include all chemical elements in our food other than carbon, hydrogen, nitrogen, and oxygen. The most abundant mineral in our bodies is calcium, which is concentrated in bones and teeth and comprises almost 2% of our total weight. Even though bones appear to be solid, permanent structures, your calcium is constantly being replenished. Gradual loss of calcium, particularly in older women, is a major cause of bone disease and injury.

Citrus fruits are an important source of vitamin C in our diets.

Cellular fluids require small amounts of the elements potassium, chlorine, sodium, and magnesium to maintain proper body acidity and control electrical charges in nerve processes. A grab bag of minor or trace elements, from iodine in the thyroid gland to iron in the blood, are also involved in the body's chemistry.

Every few years the National Research Council publishes a list of Recommended Dietary Allowances (RDA, sometimes referred to as Recommended Daily Allowances) for minerals (see Table 21-2). These values are gradually being replaced by new Dietary Reference Intakes (DRI), which differ from earlier values.

Table 21-2 Selected Recommended Dietary Allowances (RDAs and DRIs) for Minerals[a]

Gender	Age	Weight kg	lb	Height cm	ft'in"	CA (mg)	P (mg)	FE (mg)	Mg (mg)	Zn (mg)	I (μg)[b]	Se (μg)[b]
Both	0–0.5	6	13	60	2'	210	100	6	30	5	40	10
	0.5–1	9	20	71	2'4"	270	275	10	75	5	50	15
	1–3	13	29	90	2'11"	500	460	10	80	10	70	20
Men	15–18	66	145	176	5'9"	1300	1250	12	410	15	150	50
	19–24	72	160	177	5'10"	1000	700	10	420	15	150	70
	25–50	79	174	176	5'10"	1000	700	10	420	15	150	70
	51+	77	170	173	5'8"	1200	700	10	420	15	150	70
Women	15–18	55	120	163	5'4"	1300	1250	15	360	12	150	50
	19–24	58	128	164	5'5"	1000	700	15	310	12	150	55
	25–50	63	138	163	5'4"	1000	700	15	320	12	150	55
	51+	65	143	160	5'3"	1200	700	10	320	12	150	55
—Pregnant						1000	700	30	320	15	175	65
—Lactating												
(First 6 months)						1000	700	15	320	19	200	75
(Second 6 months)						1000	700	15	320	16	200	75

[a] Condensed version of Recommendations by the Food and Nutrition Board of the National Research Council. For up-to-date information visit their web site: http://www4.nationalacademies.org/IOM/IOMHome.nsf/Pages/Food+and+Nutrition+Board.
[b] 1μg (one microgram) = 10^{-6} g = 10^{-3} mg.

Calcium DRIs, for example, are significantly greater for most men and women than the earlier recommendations, while phosphorus DRIs are significantly less.

Vitamins

Biologists have discovered a host of complex organic molecules that, in small quantities, play an essential role in good health. These chemicals, though unrelated to each other in any chemical or physiological sense, are known collectively as **vitamins**. They are generally designated by a letter, such as vitamin A. For historical reasons, a number of different vitamins were grouped together under vitamin B and have been given a series of numbers such as B_1 (thiamine) and B_2 (riboflavin).

With one exception, vitamins are not made in the body and must be taken in with our food. The exception, vitamin D, can be produced in the body through the action of ultraviolet radiation on the skin. However, in most parts of the world exposure to sunlight is normally too low to produce enough vitamin D. Thus, as a practical matter, all vitamins must be taken in as part of the diet.

The vitamins in the B category, along with vitamin C, are *water-soluble vitamins*. As the name implies, these vitamins dissolve in water and hence are not retained by the body. The supply of water-soluble vitamins must be renewed daily. Vitamins A, D, E, and K, however, are *fat-soluble vitamins*. They can be stored in the body (in the liver, for example). In some cases, taking in too much of a fat-soluble vitamin can have unwanted or even harmful consequences. Too

Table 21-3 Selected Recommended Dietary Allowances (RDAs and DRIs) for Vitamins[a]

Gender	Age	Weight kg	Weight lb	Height cm	Height ft'in"	A (RE[b])	D (µg[c])	E (mg α-TE[d])	Folacin (µg[c])	Niacin (mg NE[e])	Riboflavin (mg)	Thiamine (mg)	B_6 (mg)	B_{12} (µg[c])	C (mg)
						Fat-Soluble Vitamins			**Water-Soluble Vitamins**						
Both	0–0.5	6	13	60	2'	375	5	3	25	5	0.4	0.3	0.3	0.3	30
	0.5–1	9	20	71	2'4"	375	5	4	35	6	0.5	0.4	0.6	0.5	35
	1–3	13	29	90	2'11"	400	5	6	50	9	0.8	0.7	1.0	0.7	40
Men	15–18	66	145	176	5'9"	1000	5	10	200	20	1.8	1.5	2.0	2.0	60[f]
	19–24	72	160	177	5'10"	1000	5	10	200	19	1.7	1.5	2.0	2.0	60
	25–50	79	174	176	5'10"	1000	5	10	200	19	1.7	1.5	2.0	2.0	60
	51+	77	170	173	5'8"	1000	10	10	200	15	1.4	1.2	2.0	2.0	60
Women	15–18	55	120	163	5'4"	800	5	8	180	15	1.3	1.1	1.5	2.0	60
	19–24	58	128	164	5'5"	800	5	8	180	15	1.3	1.1	1.6	2.0	60
	25–50	63	138	163	5'4"	800	5	8	180	15	1.3	1.1	1.6	2.0	60
	51+	65	143	160	5'3"	800	10	8	180	13	1.2	1.0	1.6	2.0	60
—Pregnant						800	5	10	400	17	1.6	1.5	2.2	2.2	70
—Lactating (First 6 months)						1300	5	12	280	20	1.8	1.6	2.1	2.6	95
(Second 6 months)						1300	5	11	260	20	1.7	1.6	2.1	2.6	90

[a] Published in 1989; vitamin D values revised in 1997. For up-to-date information visit their web site: http://www4.nationalacademies.org/IOM/IOMHome.nsf/Pages/Food+and+Nutrition+Board.

[b] RE represents the number of retinol equivalents.

[c] 1µg (one microgram) = 10^{-6} g = 10^{-3} mg.

[d] α-TE represents the number of α-tocopherol equivalents.

[e] NE represents the number of niacin equivalents.

[f] These represent recommended RDAs for nonsmokers. The RDAs of vitamin C for smokers are 67% greater than those for nonsmokers.

Science News | Unnatural Biochemistry
(SCIENCE NEWS, JAN 25, 2003, P. 53)

Almost all living things use the same 20 amino acids to assemble their proteins, using those proteins to run their cellular chemistry. There has always been a question about whether or not other amino acids could be incorporated into proteins in living things, or whether there was some reason that these 20, and only these 20, appear in cells. Now scientists at Scripps Research Institute in La Jolla, California, have succeeded in engineering a bacterium that both uses and synthesizes a 21st amino acid in its proteins. Using the common *E. coli* bacterium, the scientists modified the cell's DNA so that it would integrate the 21st amino acid into its proteins (the 21st acid is actually produced by another bacterium as part of its chemical defense, but doesn't function in enzymes).

There are technical possibilities that come from this work. You can imagine, for example, using genetically modified bacteria to produce the sorts of polymers now made in chemical plants. Scientists are also testing the new bacteria to see whether they function well in stressful situations. If they don't, it might help to explain why amino acids other than the standard 20 were weeded out during the course of evolution.

much vitamin D, for example, can lead to calcium deposits forming in the heart and kidneys, and too much vitamin A can be seriously toxic. (Too much beta-carotene, a precursor of vitamin A, can even turn your skin orange, but only temporarily.)

Vitamins serve a wide variety of functions in the body. Many of them assist enzymes in mediating the body's chemical reactions. In fact, most vitamins were discovered through the study of diseases that are caused by a chemical deficiency. The disease scurvy, for example, causes degeneration of tissues when the body fails to obtain enough vitamin C, a chemical abundant in citrus fruits. Scurvy was particularly common among sailors on long ocean voyages until the connection between diet and disease was made. Subsequently, sailors on British naval vessels were fed a regular diet of limes (hence the nickname "limeys"). Similarly, the bone disease rickets results from a deficiency of vitamin D. The modern diet with vitamin-enriched foods and vitamin supplements can virtually eliminate these deficiency diseases. As with minerals, the National Research Council publishes DRIs for vitamins. The DRIs for some vitamins are shown in Table 21-3.

Thinking More About | The Molecules of Life

Dietary Fads

The realization that the functioning of the body depends on the foods we eat is an old one, and is bolstered by the understanding that the cell's basic structures are built from molecules brought in through the digestive system. This understanding, coupled with the current preoccupation with health and fitness in the United States, leads occasionally to fads in which one food or another is touted as a new cure-all. It's hard to get enough information to analyze a fad while it's in full swing, but studies of fads after the fact can teach us a lot about them. The rise and fall of oat bran is a particularly enlightening case.

In the mid-1980s, people began to understand that high levels of cholesterol in the blood were correlated to the incidence of heart disease. Studies available at the time indicated that the inclusion of fiber in the diet, particularly oat bran, helped lower blood cholesterol levels. Oat bran became a fad food, and for a time it was virtually impossible for stores to keep it in stock.

Then, in 1990, newspaper headlines blared that a study in the prestigious *New England Journal of Medicine* (vol. 322: 147 [1990]) showed that oat bran did not, in fact, lower cholesterol levels. The oat bran industry, running at $54 million a year, collapsed. Processing plants closed and people lost their jobs.

Was this a reasonable response to the *New England Journal* paper? Let's look at the study that was reported and try to find out. The study took 20 people, all healthy hospital employees of ages 23 to 49 with low cholesterol levels, and tested them on diets with high-fiber oat bran and low-fiber foods for six-week periods. The result? The mean cholesterol levels of the subjects was 172 ± 28 milligrams per deciliter on the low-fiber diet, and 172 ± 25 on oat bran. (Physicians usually start to worry when your cholesterol level gets to the neighborhood of 220.) This inconclusive result, based on 20 healthy people, provided the basis for the headlines.

Does this study tell you anything about what would happen if someone with high cholesterol went on an oat bran diet? How representative of the entire population are 20 healthy hospital employees in Boston? Given the spread of cholesterol levels in the group, could the actual levels have gone down (or up) without the researchers being able to detect it?

Summary

Organic molecules share the following characteristics: (1) they are based on carbon, (2) they usually form from only a few elements, (3) they are generally modular structures (that is, no matter how large or complex they are, they are formed from a few simple building blocks), and (4) their chemical function is largely determined by their geometrical shape. Three important types of biological molecules are proteins, carbohydrates, and lipids.

Proteins form from chains of *amino acids* to make many of the body's physical structures, such as hair and muscle. Proteins in cells also function as *enzymes*, which are molecules that increase reaction rates between other molecules, but are, themselves, unaffected by the reaction. Proteins thus mediate many of life's chemical reactions.

Carbohydrates are modular molecules built from *sugars*, which are relatively simple molecules built from carbon, oxygen, and hydrogen. Carbohydrates provide an essential source of energy for all animals, and they provide much of the solid structure in the cellulose of plants.

Lipids, including fats and oils, are molecules that will not dissolve in water. If the carbon atoms form single bonds, the lipid is said to be saturated, whereas molecules on which adjacent carbon atoms form double bonds are said to be unsaturated. All cell membranes are constructed from bilayers of lipids, which are terminated by one end that attracts water and the other end that repels water.

In addition to the major nutrients proteins, carbohydrates, and lipids, humans also require small amounts of other chemicals—*minerals* and *vitamins*—that perform specialized chemical functions in the body. The National Research Council publishes Dietary Reference Intakes for both minerals and vitamins.

Key Terms About Life's Molecules

organic molecules   protein   carbohydrates   lipids   vitamins
amino acids   enzymes   sugars   minerals

Review Questions

1. What is the difference between an organic and inorganic molecule? Give an example of each.

2. What is an enzyme? How does it work?

3. What is a protein? Why are proteins sometimes referred to as "polypeptides"?

4. What are some of the biological functions of proteins?

5. What is an amino acid? What groups of atoms are common to all amino acids?

6. How is a protein constructed from amino acids?

7. How are drugs able to affect chemical reactions in living things?

8. What are the basic building blocks of carbohydrates?

9. What is the difference between saturated and unsaturated fats? Give examples of each.

10. What is the difference between cellulose and starch at the molecular level? Give examples of each substance.

11. What is the relationship between cellulose and fiber?

12. What roles do lipids play in the human body?

13. How does the structure of cell membranes enable them to carry out their functions?

14. Why are minerals an important part of a balanced diet? Give some examples of minerals and describe their functions.

15. What are vitamins? Which are water soluble? Which are fat soluble?

16. What is a DRI? How does it differ from an RDA?

DISCUSSION QUESTIONS

1. There are several different forms of vegetarianism. Some people simply avoid red meat, but will eat fish and chicken. Others avoid all meat, but will consume milk and eggs. Still others avoid all animal products. What precautions would people in each group have to take to assure that they had the proper supply of amino acids?

2. Given what you know about the structure of protein molecules, why might a single mistake in the sequence of amino acids make a significant difference in the shape of a protein?

3. Look at a typical menu at your campus food service. Does it provide a balanced source of nutrition? If not, how would you change it to do so?

4. Regulations require that drugs meet certain advertising standards. If a drug is claimed to stop hair loss or promote weight gain, for example, there has to be evidence that the drug actually works. Should vitamin and mineral supplements have to meet the same standard? Why or why not?

5. Almost any table salt you buy in a store has iodine added to it. Why do you suppose this is done?

6. In the novel *Jurassic Park* by Michael Crichton, the scientists who create modern-day dinosaurs had, as a last-ditch safety measure, what they called the "lysine defense." The idea was that the metabolism of the dinosaurs had been manipulated so that they could not manufacture the amino acid lysine. How would this defense work? Can you think of some way the dinosaurs might get around it?

7. Should people be cautious before eating manufactured foods like Olestra? Why or why not?

INVESTIGATIONS

1. Read the nutritional information on a box of standard cereal and on one that claims to be "natural." Which actually supplies more of the RDA of minerals and vitamins?

2. Make a detailed record of one week's intake of food, vitamins, and other supplements. Consult nutrition charts and determine the percentage by weight of protein, carbohydrate, fats, and other substances that you consumed. What percentage of the fat you consumed was saturated? What changes in your diet could reduce the total percentage of fat consumed, and lower the ratio of saturated to unsaturated fat?

3. Read about a vitamin-deficiency disease. How was it discovered and how was it cured?

4. Investigate dietary sources of vitamin C, and review how the body uses this vitamin. Is there a difference between the vitamin C in freshly squeezed orange juice and in a vitamin C tablet? Some years ago the Nobel prize–winning chemist Linus Pauling advocated vitamin C as a defense against cancer. How did he justify these claims? What was the response of the medical community?

5. Visit a health food store in your community. How do the claims made on labels square with what you know about the chemical basis of nutrition?

6. How would you design an experiment to study the effectiveness of oat bran in reducing cholesterol?

7. Investigate the relationship between health and cholesterol levels. Is it possible for your cholesterol level to be too low?

WWW RESOURCES

See *The Sciences* homepage at: **http://www.wiley.com/college/trefil** for valuable web links.

1. *Protein Crystallography on the Web.* The University of London web site gives a sense of the research behind protein structures. **http://px-1.cryst.bbk.ac.uk**

2. *Complex Carbohydrates.* Neat structure views from the University of Oxford. **http://www.chem.ox.ac.uk/mom/carbohydrates**

3. *Model of a Lipid Bilayer Membrane.* A revealing movie of the lipid bilayer structure. **http://www.life.uiuc.edu/crofts/bioph354/membrane_phase.html**

4. *Food and Nutrition Board.* The National Research Council's guide to diet and health. **http://www.nap.edu/books/0309041392/html/index.html**

5. A good government nutrition site is **www.nutrition.gov**. You can get anywhere in the government nutrition arena from there, including the research sites: the FDA food safety site, **www.foodsafety.gov** and **www.nationalacademies.org**.

22

The Living Cell

What is the smallest living thing?

GREAT IDEA

Life is based on chemistry, and chemistry takes place in cells.

PHYSICS
Nerve cells transmit electrical impulses over a distance. (Ch. 5)

CHEMISTRY
Molecules such as ATP transfer energy in cells to power the chemical reactions necessary for life.

ENVIRONMENT
The amount of carbon dioxide in the atmosphere rises and falls in an annual cycle, as plants take in carbon dioxide in the spring and release it in the fall. (Ch. 19)

GEOLOGY
When living things go through the rock cycle, a fossil is created, providing a record of life at a given point in time. (Ch. 25)

HEALTH & SAFETY
Some viruses mimic the shape of food molecules to gain entrance into cells.

ASTRONOMY
Plants convert radiant energy from the Sun into carbohydrates.

TECHNOLOGY
Electron and optical microscopes play a critical role in the study of cells.

BIOLOGY
Cells, the basic building blocks of life, come in a variety of shapes and carry out many different functions.

Red = applications of the great idea discussed in this chapter.

Orange = other applications, some of which are explored in other chapters.

It's late afternoon at the beach when you notice that the tops of your feet are bright red. You've got sunburn. Hours earlier you used sunblock but you missed those areas. Now they hurt!

Past experience tells you what will happen. For the next couple of days the tops of your feet will be tender and painful, especially when you get into a hot shower. Then the outer layers of skin will peel off. But within a week or so new skin will grow and your feet will be back to normal.

The human body is amazing. When injured, parts of the body like sunburned skin may die, but the skin is quickly regenerated. How is that possible? The answer lies in the behavior of cells—the fundamental building blocks of life.

The Nature and Variety of Cells

For centuries, scientists have tried to answer questions about nature's fundamental building blocks. In this context, dealing with living things is particularly complex. Although all living things are made out of atoms and molecules, as we saw in the previous chapter, living things are more than just collections of atoms. An entity must do many things such as reproduce and take in matter and energy for us to say that it is alive. These functions cannot be performed by a random collection of atoms; rather, they result from the collective behavior of large numbers of atoms organized into some kind of system. For our purposes, the **cell** can be considered to be the smallest identifiable unit capable of carrying on the basic tasks that we associate with living things.

An enormous number of different kinds of cells can be found in nature. Cells come in a wide range of sizes and shapes, and perform all sorts of functions. While typical animal cells are about one-hundredth of a millimeter (a thousandth of an inch) in diameter, they can range in size from bacteria only a few hundred-thousandths of a centimeter across (much too small to see in most light microscopes, and smaller than some large molecules), to the yolk portion of an ostrich egg that is much larger than most species of animals. Most cells are too small to be seen with the unaided eye, but are easily studied with a microscope (see below).

Cells also come in a wide variety of shapes. Plant cells are often rectangular or polygonal, while egg cells are usually spherical. Bacteria may be rod-shaped or spiral in form, muscle cells are extremely elongated, nerve cells sport a complex array of branching fibers, and a sperm cell has a tail-like flagellum that helps it swim. The recognition of common characteristics in this extraordinary collection represents one of the great advances in biology.

These differences in shape reflect the differences in the functions that the cells perform. Elongated muscle cells exert forces when they contract. Branching nerve cells (see Chapter 5) transmit impulses to many other cells. To fulfill their functions, cells constantly require raw materials and energy to live and reproduce. Living things use two very different strategies to satisfy these needs. Some cells (such as bacteria and protozoa) operate as separate entities, ensuring their survival by reproducing in vast numbers. Multicellular organisms such as plants and animals, on the other hand, employ cells collectively. In these more complex life forms, different groups of cells serve very different functions, with each group depending on others in a complex web of interdependence.

 Stop and Think! The fact that cells require energy implies that they do work. What kind of work do cells do?

SCIENCE IN THE MAKING •
The Discovery of Cells

An essential and distinctive feature of all cells is a membrane that isolates and protects the interior from the outer environment. In 1663, Robert Hooke (1635–1703), a brilliant and contentious contemporary of Isaac Newton, used one of the first microscopes to observe honeycomb structures in a thin slice of cork. It was Hooke who first called the tiny, box-like units "cells."

Within the next few years, Dutch merchant and self-taught scientist Anton van Leeuwenhoek (1632–1723) employed superb microscopes of his own design and construction to discover a rich variety of cells, including those in blood, saliva, semen, and the intestines. On October 9, 1676, van Leeuwenhoek sent a letter to the president of the Royal Society in London. He wrote, "In the year 1675 I discovered living creatures in Rain water, which had stood for a few days in a new earthen pot . . . ," and he went on to describe a series of "animacules" that were visible through his microscope. •

The Cell Theory

In spite of van Leeuwenhoek's colorful descriptions, it was not until the nineteenth century that scientists finally accepted the idea that animals and plants are essentially aggregates of cells. In 1838, the German botanist Matthais Schleiden proposed that all plants are made of cells. In the following year his countryman, zoologist Theodor Schwann, extended this idea to animals and proposed what is now known as the *cell theory*. Three tenets of the Schwann's cell theory are:

1. All living things are composed of cells.
2. The cell is the fundamental unit of life.
3. All cells arise from previous cells.

Thus, biologists recognized that only cells can produce other cells, and that these tiny objects represent the indivisible units of life—a discovery as fundamental as the discovery of atoms in chemistry and quanta in physics. The cell theory initiated the field of cell biology, which remains one of the central efforts in biology.

How Does a Cell Work?

As the fundamental unit of life, the cell must perform all of the varied tasks that we associate with living things (see Chapter 20). The cell must obtain atoms and energy from its environment, grow, respond to changes in environmental conditions, and

The cell is like an oil refinery.

reproduce. As we shall see, each of those tasks is accomplished by remarkable cellular mechanisms. But before examining those complex processes it's useful to imagine the cell in a different way—as a factory that produces and distributes chemicals.

Have you ever driven by an oil refinery or other kind of chemical plant? It's a place of bewildering complexity, laced with a maze of pipes and towers, bustling with diverse activity as energy and materials constantly flow in and out.

As complex and diverse as chemical plants might seem, they all share a few basic features. Every chemical plant must have walls, a control room, and facilities to provide and distribute energy. There must be loading docks to bring in supplies and remove trash, conveyer belts or pipes to move materials from one place to another, and storage rooms to keep a stock of critical items at the ready. And at the heart of every plant must be pieces of machinery that control chemical reactions and manufacture the desired chemical products.

A chemical plant is, in fact, a lot like a living cell.

Observing Cells: The Microscope

Advances in understanding how cells work have relied in large part on the development of microscopes. Early microscopes were rather primitive affairs; consequently, scientists were unable to see many details of cell structure. Indeed, until the middle part of the twentieth century, science textbooks often spoke of something called "protoplasm." This substance was supposed to be a kind of uniform, molasses-like fluid that filled cells. Today, with much better microscopes we know that cells are very complex indeed. Advanced cells are full of specialized structures, as complicated in their own way as larger life forms such as human beings. In fact, we shall see that the molecules of life introduced in Chapter 21 play a crucial role in the complex workings of the cell, with each performing a separate vital function. Today, we refer to the fluid that takes up the spaces between all this complexity as *cytoplasm*.

Early microscopes and their modern high-tech descendants all operate on the same basic principle shown in Figure 22-1*a*. Ordinary visible light passes through a sample between two transparent layers of glass or plastic. The light transmits

Ocular lens

Objective lens
Specimen

Condenser lens

Light source

(a)

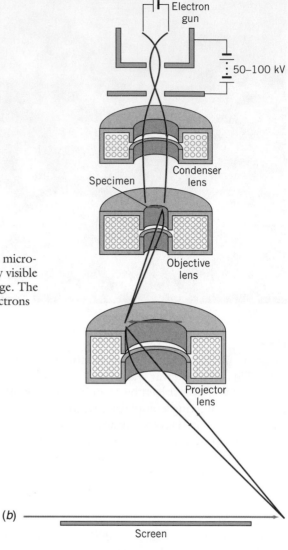

Electron
gun

50–100 kV

Specimen

Condenser
lens

Objective
lens

Projector
lens

(b)

Screen

• **Figure 22-1** Light microscope (*a*) and electron microscope (*b*). In the light microscope, waves of ordinary visible light travel through a series of lenses to form an image. The electron microscope uses the wave-like nature of electrons (see Chapter 8) to accomplish the same purpose.

through a series of lenses so that a magnified image is presented in the eyepiece. This kind of apparatus is called an *optical microscope* and today these instruments can magnify more than 1000 times and resolve details less than a ten-thousandth of a centimeter across—enough to make an ordinary cell look as big as a quarter. In many modern optical microscopes, a miniature video camera in the eyepiece allows the image to be displayed on a television screen.

Special dyes that are taken up by only one part of a specimen are often used to increase contrast in the image, and hence to make internal structures clearer. For example, we shall see that parts of cells called *chromosomes* play an important role in reproduction. These features were first seen as colored structures in cells that had been stained, a fact that is reflected in their name.

The ability of a microscope to differentiate objects that are close to each other is called its resolving power. The resolving power of all microscopes is limited by the wavelength of the light used: objects about the size of one wavelength appear blurred. Light microscopes, for example, typically employ light waves with wavelengths on the order of a ten-thousandth of a centimeter; thus objects about that size or smaller will appear as undifferentiated blurs in even the most perfectly designed instrument. This limitation means that many of the smaller structures in the cell cannot be seen with this sort of microscope.

In the 1930s, German scientist Ernst Ruska, working at a university in Berlin, introduced the *electron microscope,* a major new advance in microscopes that uses electrons instead of light to illuminate objects. In Chapter 9, we discussed the notion that quantum objects such as the electron can be thought of as tiny particles, but also as energetic waves. The electron's wavelength depends on its energy—the greater the energy, the shorter the wavelength—and typical electron wavelengths in modern instruments are comparable to the size of a single atom. In a situation such as that shown in Figure 22-1*b*, where an electron beam is shot at a target, we are in effect examining the target with very short wavelengths, and thus achieving resolving powers up to 100,000 times that of optical microscopes. Modern electron microscopes are often used to resolve atomic-scale features.

The electron microscope works this way: An electric current heats a tungsten filament in a strong electric field—typically about 100,000 volts—to produce an electron beam. Electrons leave the negatively charged tungsten wire and accelerate toward the positive end of a tube. This beam of electron "waves" is focused by specially designed ring-shaped electromagnets, the analogs of glass lenses in a conventional microscope. The focused beam strikes the sample, and the electrons then hit a detector that converts the beam into an image, as shown in Figure 22-2.

Modern electron microscopes are very expensive; it's not unusual for one to cost more than $500,000. Nevertheless, electron microscopes are an invaluable tool in all areas of science and industry that require examination of objects at extremely high magnification—particularly in the study of cells.

A scientist operates an electron microscope.

• **Figure 22-2** Electron microscope photograph of a fruit fly with a wing mutation.

Cell Membranes

Every cell must be isolated from its environment—that is, there must be an "inside" that is distinct from an "outside." In addition, complex cells also require different parts of the cell to be separated from each other by inner partitions.

Both of these requirements are satisfied by **cell membranes**. The simplest cells will have only one external membrane (Figure 22-3). More complex cells have many internal membranes in addition to the outer envelope. The basic molecular structure of cell membranes is the lipid bilayer, of the type we discussed in Chapter 21.

• **Figure 22-3** All cells possess a lipid bilayer membrane, which is studded with protein receptors. The membrane separates the inside of the cell from the outside.

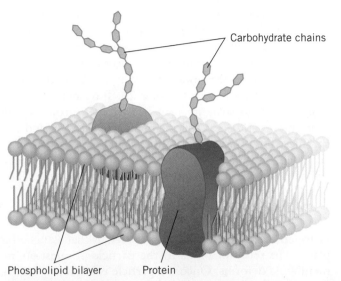

Carbohydrate chains

Phospholipid bilayer   Protein

The chain-like lipid molecules are arranged in a double layer with the hydrophobic ends of the molecules pressed against each other and the hydrophilic ends on the outside. Because cells almost invariably exist in a watery fluid, this arrangement is the lowest possible energy state in which the molecules can arrange themselves. Water is squeezed out from the space between the layers, thereby ensuring that the hydrophobic parts of the membrane are not in contact with it. In the same way, the hydrophilic parts find themselves in a watery environment.

One way to visualize the cell membrane is to think of a technique that is often used in moderate climates to protect swimming pools from freezing in the winter. Instead of draining water from the pool, an expensive and time-consuming operation, owners simply throw a large number of Styrofoam balls into the pool. These balls float next to each other. They cover the water, constantly touching, but also constantly jostling and moving around. They lift up and down when waves move across the water, but the covering retains its integrity. In the same way, cell membranes are made up of molecules stacked or arranged next to each other. These molecules can change shape and move around according to the dictates of their environment, but they retain their integrity and do not rupture. Thus they perform the function of separating a cell from its environment.

Transporting Material Across a Cell Membrane

If a cell membrane were totally impermeable, life would not be possible. In order to be alive, a cell must take in raw materials from its surroundings and pass wastes and other chemicals into the environment, just like the loading docks and pipelines that run to and from a chemical plant.

Materials are transported across cell membranes in many ways. The simplest is the movement of small individual molecules across the cell membrane. You may see this process at work in your local supermarket, where produce managers often spray fresh vegetables with water. They do not do this for decoration—they put water on the carrots, lettuce, and other vegetables so that it will move through the membranes into the cells, making up for water that has evaporated out. In this way, vegetables maintain a fresher appearance for longer periods of time.

Cell membranes also incorporate various kinds of channels and molecular-sized openings, which allow specific materials to go back and forth. When nerve signals move through the human body, as we saw in Chapter 5, sodium and potassium ions move back and forth across nerve cell membranes to create the signal. The various kinds of channels that exist in different kinds of cells allow different kinds of atoms and molecules to pass through.

One important means of bringing material through a cell membrane, however, depends on the notion that "molecular geometry controls the chemistry of life," as we discussed in Chapter 21. Interspersed here and there in a cell membrane are large structures made of folded proteins, called **receptors**. Receptor molecules each have a specific geometrical shape, and each receptor will bind to a specific type of molecule in the environment. When that molecule is present, it is attracted to the receptor's binding site. Thus receptors can be thought of as the cell's "door guard" looking over prospective molecular entrants and picking out only those nutrients whose shape is exactly right.

When a receptor "recognizes" a particular molecule, the molecule and receptor are attracted to each other, for example, through hydrogen bonds, and they fit together. A sequence of events such as that sketched in Figure 22-4 thus takes place. The receptor binds to the particle in question and holds it while the cell membrane deforms. Once the particle is inside, as shown, the membrane may nip

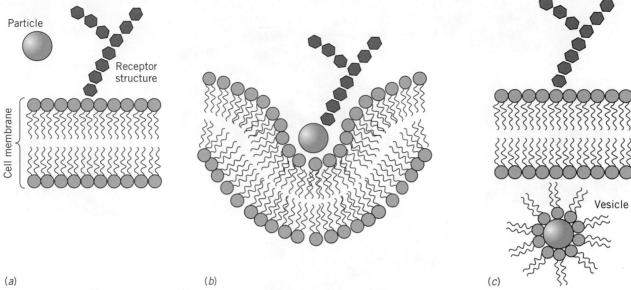

(a)   (b)   (c)

• **Figure 22-4** The action of receptors in a cell. (*a*) A food particle (in green) approaches a receptor. (*b*) The receptor bonds to the particle and draws it close to the cell membrane. (*c*) The particle is taken inside the cell and surrounded by lipids to form a vesicle.

off, enclosing the particle in its own special wrapping, and the cell membrane reforms behind it. The tiny container, called a *vesicle,* then becomes the vehicle by which the particle moves around inside the cell. A similar process that works in reverse is used when molecules from inside the cell are moved out. Once in a while a receptor can be fooled. As we'll see in Chapter 23, some tiny disease-causing objects called viruses gain entrance into cells by mimicking the shape of food molecules and thus triggering the receptor mechanism.

The outer covering of plant cells contains an additional structure in addition to the kind of flexible membranes we have described. Plant cells may also be connected to each other by a **cell wall**, which is a solid framework made of cellulose molecules and other strong polymers. Cell walls, which often account for about a third of a living plant's mass, give tree trunks and leaves the strength to grow upright against the force of gravity. In fact, it was cell walls (as opposed to cells per se) that Robert Hooke saw when he looked at his piece of cork in 1663 (see Figure 22-5).

 Stop and Think! From a thermodynamic point of view, are cells open or closed systems? Explain.

The Nucleus

In most cells, the most prominent and important interior structure is the **nucleus**. The nucleus forms a relatively large enclosed structure that contains the cell's genetic material—its DNA (see Chapter 23). This DNA contains the instructions for the day-to-day chemical operation of the cell, as well as the mechanism by which the cell reproduces itself. If we think of the cell as being analogous to a large chemical factory, then the nucleus can be thought of as the front office. There, the blueprints are stored and instructions for the operation of the entire system go out.

(a)

(b)

• **Figure 22-5** A typical plant cell. (*a*) A generalized drawing with electron micrographs of some key organelles (see Table 22-1). (*b*) Photograph of a cell of maize rust. The dark boundary is the cell wall, made from cellulose. The nucleus takes up almost half the area of the central part of the cell.

Not all cells have nuclei. In some cells, the DNA is present in a tight coil, but is not separated from the rest of the material in the interior. Presumably, these sorts of primitive cells, called *prokaryotes* ("before the nucleus"), evolved first. The kingdom monera (see Chapter 20), including bacteria and their relatives, includes all cells that do not have a nucleus.

The more advanced single-celled organisms, the *eukaryotes* ("true nucleus"), as well as all multicellular organisms (including human beings), are made from cells that do contain nuclei. The kingdom protista includes single-celled eukaryotic organisms. Virtually all of the organisms with which we are familiar are made up of eukaryotic cells (Figure 22-5).

One interesting feature of the nucleus—a feature that may contain a good deal of information about the evolution of higher life forms—can be found in its confining membranes. The nucleus has not one, but two membranes, as shown in Figure 22-6. The standard explanation of the double membrane in the nucleus is that it is a vestige of an earlier stage of development. The idea is that at some point in the past, a large cell engulfed a small one, much as modern cell membranes use receptors to engulf molecules. Over time, a symbiotic relationship developed between those first two cells. Each cell was able to do better in a partnership than it could do alone. The double-membrane nucleus is interpreted as having an inner membrane,

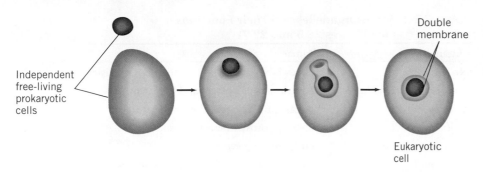

• **Figure 22-6** The nucleus has a double membrane, perhaps because it evolved from an earlier stage in which a large cell engulfed a small one, as shown.

descended from the original membrane of the swallowed cell, and an outer membrane, descended from the vesicle that formed when the first cell was enveloped.

Other structures in the cell also have a double membrane (see the following section), suggesting that, while cells are indeed the basic unit of life, individual cells in complex organisms may be more like colonies of smaller cells than a single cell.

The Energy Organelles: Chloroplasts and Mitochondria

Eukaryotic cells have many inner structures similar to the nucleus. Each of these structures carries out a special chemical function in the cell. Any specialized structure in the cell, including the nucleus, is called an **organelle**. Important organelles are shown in Figures 22-5 and 22-7, and a listing of some of their primary functions is given in Table 22-1.

• **Figure 22-7** A typical animal cell showing the nucleus, mitochondria, and various other organelles (see Table 22-1).

Table 22-1 **Some Organelles and Their Functions**
(See Figures 22-5 and 22-7)

Organelle	Primary Function
Nucleus	Stores DNA and controls the cell's chemistry
Endoplasmic reticulum	Contributes to protein and lipid synthesis
Mitochondria	Release energy from food by metabolism
Chloroplasts	Site of photosynthesis (in plants only)
Ribosomes	Site of protein synthesis
Nucleoli	Manufacture the subunits of ribosomes
Golgi apparatus	Processes proteins previously synthesized at the ribosomes
Lysosomes	Contain digestive enzymes for breakdown of wastes
Vesicles	Small containers for chemical raw materials
Cytoskeleton	Provides cell structure and internal transport of vesicles
Vacuoles	Waste and water storage
Amyloplasts	Storage of starch (in plants only)
Plasmodesmata	Water conduits between plant cells

Every chemical factory requires energy, and living cells gather energy in two very different ways. Plants rely on the Sun for their energy, while animals ultimately depend on the chemical energy stored in plants.

Chloroplasts are the main energy transformation organelles in plant cells. As the name suggests, they are the places where molecules of *chlorophyll* are found. Chlorophyll absorbs the energy from sunlight and uses that energy to transform atmospheric carbon dioxide and water into energy-rich sugar molecules such as glucose. Chloroplasts have a double cell membrane, which suggests that they once may have been independent cells.

Mitochondria, sausage-shaped organelles, are places where molecules derived from glucose react with oxygen to produce the cell's energy. Mitochondria are, in effect, the furnaces where fuels are oxidized. A typical eukaryotic cell will have anywhere from a few hundred to a few thousand mitochondria.

Like the nucleus, chloroplasts and mitochondria have double cell membranes and even their own complement of DNA. Most scientists have concluded, therefore, that chloroplasts and mitochondria were originally independent cells in the early history of life on Earth.

Cytoskeleton

The *cytoskeleton* gives the cell its shape, keeps things anchored in place, and, in some cases, allows the cell to move. The cytoskeleton is a series of protein filaments that extend throughout the cell, more or less like a complex of spider webs. Inside the cell, the cytoskeleton serves as the transport system along which the vesicles that carry material from one place to another move. In some cases, cells can move by shortening and lengthening filaments inside the cell, or by causing structures related to the cytoskeleton that extend outside the cell to move like little oars.

Metabolism: Energy and Life

The cell's process of deriving energy from its surroundings is called **metabolism**. Cells need a means to transfer that energy from one place to another, to power the varied pieces of chemical machinery necessary for life.

The Cell's Energy Currency

Several molecules are used to store and distribute energy in all living cells. One way to think about this suite of molecules is to think about the money in your wallet. You may have some cash, but you also probably have credit cards, and perhaps even a check or two. Each of these items provides a way of moving money around, and each is appropriate for different situations. You pay cash for small purchases, make larger purchases with a credit card, and pay some of your bills by check. In the same way, a cell has different molecules that store different amounts of energy, each of which is appropriate to a particular use.

The most common of these energy carriers is *adenosine triphosphate (ATP)*— a molecule that provides energy for countless chemical processes in all living cells. A sketch of this molecule is given in Figure 22-8. The structure of ATP is a good illustration of the argument given in Chapter 21 that important molecules in nature tend to be built from the same simple building blocks. ATP contains three phosphate groups (collections of phosphorus and oxygen atoms) at the end of the molecule (these three phosphates are what give ATP the "tri" part of its name). The other parts of the molecule consist of the sugar ribose, which is also a building block of the RNA structure (see Chapter 23), and the base adenine (part of both DNA and RNA).

A considerable amount of energy is required to put phosphate groups onto the ends of the tail of an ATP molecule. In the language of Chapter 10, putting the last phosphate group on the ATP tail is an endothermic process. If the phosphate group is subsequently removed in another chemical reaction, that energy is available to drive other chemical reactions. Thus the ATP molecule can carry energy in the form of phosphorus–oxygen bonds from one part of the cell to another.

In one place in a cell—in the mitochondria, for example—chemical reactions produce energy. This energy is used to produce a molecule of ATP. The molecule then moves out of the place where it is made to a place where energy is needed. At this point, the ATP acts something like a tiny battery: the ATP molecule attaches to part of the cell's chemical machinery, a phosphate group is removed,

• **Figure 22-8** Sketch of ATP, the energy "money" of cells. Note that it is built from a sugar (ribose), a base (adenine), and three phosphate groups.

and the stored chemical potential energy becomes available to drive the desired chemical reactions. The triphosphate (three phosphates) then becomes a diphosphate (two phosphates), ADP:

$$ATP \rightarrow ADP + PO_4 + energy$$

ATP is the molecule that serves as the cell's "cash" in the cell's energy system. A typical cell will have several million ATP molecules doing their job at any given time. Other, more-complex molecules (represented by the letters FADH and NADH) correspond to the "credit cards" in the cell's energy system. They store up energy and can be cashed in on short notice when extra energy is required. One way of thinking about the role of ATP is to say that when a chemical reaction adds the last phosphate group to ATP, the molecule picks up the equivalent of a pocketful of money. That money can be spent later for almost any purpose.

Photosynthesis

Photosynthesis, the mechanism by which plants convert the energy of sunlight into energy stored in carbohydrates, provides the chemical energy for almost all species (Figure 22-9). In plants, this complex process operates as follows: A large molecule, usually chlorophyll, absorbs sunlight. After a series of chemical reactions, this energy is ultimately stored in a set of molecules that includes ATP. Once the energy has been captured in this way, it is used in another complex series of reactions to produce carbohydrates. The most important carbohydrate molecule is glucose, an energy-rich sugar that also provides the module from which all cellulose and starch polymers are made (see Chapter 21). The end result is the conversion of the energy in the electromagnetic radiation from the Sun into chemical energy stored in the bonds holding the carbohydrate molecules together.

The shorthand way of thinking about photosynthesis is to say:

▶ **In words:** Energy plus carbon dioxide plus water react to produce carbohydrate plus oxygen.

▶ **In equation form:**

$$energy + CO_2 + H_2O \rightarrow carbohydrate + O_2$$

The rate at which plants produce oxygen and carbohydrates is usually limited by the amount of carbon dioxide in the air.

The most familiar molecule involved in photosynthesis, chlorophyll, occurs in various forms that can absorb red and blue light. The energy that falls as sunlight on a leaf is white light, roughly equal mixtures of all colors of the visible spectrum (see Chapter 6). The leaf absorbs red and blue components of light from the Sun, while green light is reflected—a situation that explains why leaves appear green. In addition to chlorophyll, a number of secondary molecules are involved in photosynthesis. These molecules tend to absorb blue light, so they appear to be red and orange. A normal leaf contains much more chlorophyll than secondary molecules, so the color of the secondary molecules is masked. In the fall, however, when the leaf dies and chlorophyll is no longer produced, its underlying color can be seen. We say that the leaves "change color" although, in fact, the brilliant fall colors were there all the time.

• **Figure 22-9** The process of photosynthesis. Chloroplasts in the leaf absorb energy from the Sun. That energy is then used to convert carbon dioxide from the atmosphere and water into carbohydrates, such as glucose.

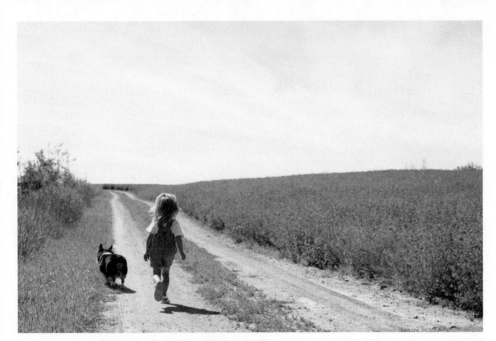

Plants are green because of the presence of chlorophyll.

Glycolysis: The First Step in Energy Generation in the Cell

The primary source of energy for living things comes from the oxidation of carbohydrates such as glucose. These sorts of reactions, called **respiration**, are taking place in all of your cells at this very moment. Your lungs breathe in oxygen produced by plants, while blood in your circulatory system transports that oxygen to every cell in your body. At the same time carbon dioxide, which is the end product of the breakdown of carbohydrates that you ingest in your food, is removed by the circulatory system to the lungs and breathed out as waste.

Respiration retrieves the energy stored in glucose in a complex series of cellular chemical reactions. Chemical bonds of the glucose molecule store chemical potential energy. The more glucose bonds that are broken, that is, the smaller the pieces of the final molecules, the more energy the cell will have transferred.

The first step in the extraction of energy from glucose is called **glycolysis** (the "lysis," or splitting, of glucose). This rather complex process takes place in nine separate steps, each of which is governed by a specific enzyme. At the end of the process, a single molecule of glucose, which contains six linked carbon atoms, is split into two smaller molecules called pyruvic acids, each containing three carbon atoms. In addition, the reaction makes two molecules of ATP and two molecules of other energy carriers. In most cells, the energy stored in these other carriers is converted into two or three more molecules of ATP before they leave the mitochondria. Thus each glucose molecule can ultimately yield six to eight molecules of ATP through the process of glycolysis.

After glucose has been split by glycolysis, energy can be generated in two separate and distinct ways: respiration and fermentation. Respiration requires the presence of oxygen, and is therefore said to be *aerobic*. The primary function of your lungs and circulatory system is to maintain this aerobic respiration. Fermentation, on the other hand, can occur in the absence of oxygen, and is said to be *anaerobic*.

Fermentation: A Way to Keep Glycolysis Going

Pyruvic acid molecules still hold a great deal of chemical potential energy. In the absence of oxygen, however, that energy cannot be liberated to run cellular metabolism. In this situation, a process called **fermentation** can be used to provide energy to keep glycolysis going. As long as there is a supply of glucose, the cell can go on generating energy, albeit somewhat inefficiently. In some cases, as in single-celled yeast, the end product of fermentation is ethanol—ordinary beverage alcohol. This sort of fermentation provides the basis for the production of wine and other alcoholic drinks.

When cells have to use glucose in the absence of oxygen, only a fraction of the available energy is used, and a great deal of energy is left stored in other molecules. Yeast is a good example. You know that alcohol, which is produced by yeast during the process of fermentation, contains a great deal of energy—it can,

Microscopic organisms undergo fermentation—a process that is critical to the production of cheese, bread, and wine.

after all, be burned as a fuel. The chemical energy in alcohol is left behind by the yeast cells that made it—energy that the cells could not use because they were not able to metabolize it.

A somewhat different kind of fermentation takes place in cells of animals. The energy in pyruvic acid is normally tapped by the process of respiration (see the following section). In the absence of oxygen, however, our muscles can use fermentation to keep glycolysis going (often taking glucose from materials stored in the muscles themselves). The end product of this sort of fermentation is lactic acid, a three-carbon molecule that then accumulates in the muscle. When we undergo strenuous exercise, if our bodies are not prepared to deliver all the oxygen that is needed, the cells will eventually fall back on this simpler process. The stiffness and aches that you feel in your muscles after unusually strenuous exercise is caused by the buildup of lactic acid that must be removed once you are through exercising. One benefit of that lactic acid buildup is that it signals the body to increase the size of muscle cells—a process familiar to body builders. Hence the expression, "No pain, no gain."

The fact that some of our cells can operate both with and without oxygen—the fact that they have this reserve process to fall back on—is taken by some scientists to indicate that cells evolved fermentation reactions first and only later developed the ability to burn oxygen. You can think of the body's use of fermentation as analogous to writing a term paper with a pencil when a power outage makes a computer unavailable. It's not the most efficient way to work, but it gets the job done. In a sense, then, the stiffness that you feel in your muscles is a reminder of the origin of our species in simple cells.

The Final Stages of Respiration

In human cells, the energy-rich products of glycolysis react in the mitochondria, and all the available energy that was stored in the glucose is retrieved. The end effect of these chemical reactions is that oxygen and the pyruvic acids take part in a complex series of reactions to produce carbon dioxide, water, and a large amount of energy stored in ATP molecules.

In cells where oxygen is available, pyruvic acids (three-carbon molecules) are first broken down into two-carbon groups, and then enter a complex series of chemical reactions called the *Krebs cycle*. In the course of this cycle, the original glucose is broken down and its carbon is converted into carbon dioxide, some energy is released to ATP molecules, and the rest of the energy is stored in some of the other energy-carrying molecules. In the final stage of respiration, the energy in these other carriers is used to produce even more ATP molecules.

The exact number of ATP molecules produced from a single glucose molecule depends on details of the structure of the mitochondrial membranes, and varies slightly from one cell to another. As a general rule, however, the metabolism of a single glucose molecule ultimately produces 36 to 38 molecules of ATP, which can then be used by the cell to run all the rest of its chemical machinery. Compare this production to the 6 to 8 ATP molecules produced by glycolysis alone.

Thus aerobic reactions yield significantly more energy per molecule of glucose than anaerobic ones yield. It can be argued that the large amounts of energy needed to maintain a multicellular organism would not have been available to organisms that had not developed respiration. The outcome of this line of thought is that before a significant amount of oxygen became available in the

The process of respiration expels water vapor, which appears as condensation on a cold day.

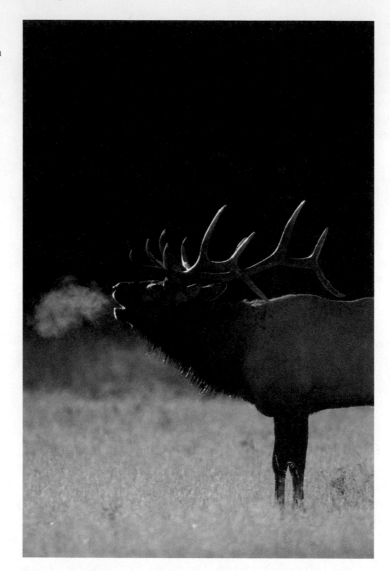

atmosphere, complex life forms could not have developed. We will discuss the development of complex organisms in Chapter 25.

STOP **Stop and Think!** Where did you get the energy that keeps you alive today?

Cell Division

A key principle of the cell theory is that all cells arise from previous cells, but how does this process occur? Individual cells do not last forever. As you read this, cells are dying and being replaced throughout your body. In order for this sort of replacement to occur, cells must be able to reproduce. Microscopic observations of living cells have revealed that cells divide and reproduce by two separate processes, called mitosis and meiosis.

Mitosis

In the great majority of cell divisions in living organisms, a single cell splits, so that two cells appear where once there was only one. It is by means of this process of cell division, called **mitosis**, that organisms grow and maintain themselves. When you get a cut or sunburn, this process quickly replaces damaged cells. Mitosis involves the reproduction of individual cells, but is not involved in sexual reproduction in higher plants and animals.

In Chapter 23, we will discover that DNA governs the chemical workings of any cell. DNA in eukaryotes is contained within the cell nucleus in structures called *chromosomes*. When chromosomes were first discovered in the nineteenth century, there was an intense debate about their function. Today, we understand that each chromosome is a long strand of the DNA double helix, with the strand wrapped around a series of protein cores like tape around a spool.

Chromosomes come in pairs, but there is no connection between the number of chromosomes and the complexity of an organism. Humans have 46 chromosomes (23 pairs), but the number of pairs varies from one species to another. Mosquitoes, for example, have 6 while dogs have 78. In other words, there does not appear to be any particular connection between an organism's complexity and the number of its chromosomes.

The process of mitosis is shown schematically in Figure 22-10. Assume for simplicity that we begin with a cell that has just two pairs of chromosomes, one shown larger than the other in Figure 22-10a. Each individual chromosome of the pair, furthermore, differs slightly from the other because (as we shall see in the discussion of meiosis, below) one comes from the male parent and the other from the female parent. Individual chromosomes in a pair are thus illustrated in red and green. These differences in size and color will help you follow the path of each chromosome through cell division.

The first step in mitosis is the copying of the chromosomes (a process we will describe in more detail in the next chapter). As shown in Figure 22-10b,

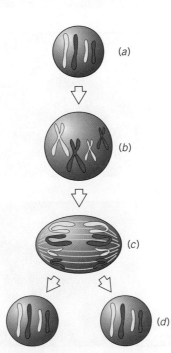

• **Figure 22-10** Mitosis, shown schematically for a cell with two pairs of chromosomes, one larger and one smaller (*a*). In each pair, red and green individual chromosomes are from different parents. (*b*) Chromosomes duplicate, resulting in two identical sets of two pairs. (*c*) Matched pairs of chromosomes are pulled along spindles to opposite ends of the cell. (*d*) A new membrane forms and separates the parent cell into two identical daughter cells.

a cell that is about to divide has twice the normal number of chromosomes, neatly paired off like socks that have been sorted after going through the laundry.

After duplication of the chromosomes, the nuclear membrane dissolves and a series of fibers called *spindle fibers* develop (Figure 22-10*c*). The matched chromosome pairs are pulled apart and migrate to opposite ends of the cell. After this separation, the nuclear membranes reform and the cell splits down the middle (Figure 22-10*d*). The result is two cells, each of which carries a set of chromosomes that are identical to the original. Powerful microscopes can capture photographs of these stages of mitosis in progress (Figure 22-11).

• **Figure 22-11** Mitosis, shown in actual photographs of a dividing cell. (*a*) Chromosomes are duplicated and thicken. (*b*) They align along the center of the cell. (*c*) They are sorted into two groups. (*d*) The matched pairs migrate to opposite poles of the cell. Finally, the cell divides, and each daughter has a full complement of chromosomes.

(a)

(b)

(c)

(d)

A human cell dividing. Genetic material shows as dark pink in this false-color photomicrograph.

Some cells in your body divide often; the cells in the lining of the small intestine, for example, are replaced every few days. Other cells, such as those of the nervous system, don't divide at all after maturity.

Meiosis

A remarkable, specialized kind of cell division called **meiosis** takes place in a few cells in organisms that reproduce sexually. In this process a single cell with a full complement of chromosomes splits to form four daughter cells, or *gametes,* each of which has half the number of chromosomes found in most normal cells. The central function of meiosis is to generate the sperm and eggs (or ova) that will later combine in sexual reproduction to produce a new member of the species. Recall that in mitosis, two daughter cells are genetically identical to the original cell, but in meiosis each gamete has its own unique new combination of genetic material.

Key steps of meiosis are illustrated in Figure 22-12. As in Figure 22-10, we begin with a cell that has two pairs of chromosomes, one shown larger than the other and with distinctively colored individual chromosomes (Figure 22-12*a*). The first step of meiosis is the same as for mitosis—the chromosomes are copied so the cell has twice the usual amount of DNA—two larger identical green chromosomes, two smaller identical red chromosomes, and so on—in "X"-shaped pairs (compare Figures 22-10*b* and 22-12*b*). But from this point, meiosis differs from mitosis in several important and striking ways.

By an extraordinary mechanism, two X-shaped pairs of chromosomes (one all-red and one all-green) cross over each other and can exchange short lengths of genetic material, thus generating chromosomes with a new mix of genetic material from both parents (Figure 22-13; this effect is illustrated as mixed red and green in Figure 22-12*c*). Note that at this point the cell has eight chromosomes, some of which differ from any of the four original red or green chromosomes.

The remaining steps of meiosis consist of a sequence of changes that sort out these eight chromosomes into smaller groups. First, the four X-shaped pairs of chromosomes segregate along spindle fibers so that each of two daughter cells has two X-shaped pairs of chromosomes—one longer and one shorter (Figure 22-12*d–f*). Then the X-shaped pairs of chromosomes in each daughter cell are pulled apart along more spindle fibers and these cells split again, producing a to-

• **Figure 22-12** Meiosis, shown schematically (see text). As in mitosis, the chromosomes are duplicated and paired. The pairs separate and the cell divides for the first time. The chromosome pairs then separate and each daughter divides again, producing a total of four cells, each with half the normal complement of DNA.

• **Figure 22-13** Crossing over between pairs of chromosomes results in the shuffling of genetic material to yield chromosomes with a new genetic makeup.

Homologous chromosome pair in tetrad formation

tal of four gametes (Figure 22-12*g–j*). Each of these four sex cells has two individual chromosomes, or half the normal complement. These chromosomes eventually are incorporated into sperm or egg.

At first glance this elaborate process of meiosis may seem to be an extravagant and unnecessary way to divide cells. However, as we shall see in Chapter 25, the ability of sexually reproducing organisms constantly to vary their genetic makeup can provide a tremendous advantage in the struggle to survive.

Science News | Teasing Out Tongue's Taste Receptors
(SCIENCE NEWS, JAN. 4, 2003, P. 8)

As you read these words, you are breathing. The muscles of your diaphragm expand and contract, air moves in and out of your lungs, and all of this happens without any conscious thought on your part. Awake or asleep, conscious or unconscious, the mechanisms of breathing just keep going on.

Since ancient times, scientists have wondered how the body regulates its breathing. The Greek physician Galen, for example, noted that gladiators could still breathe if injured below the neck, but that head injuries often caused breathing to stop. He concluded that breathing was governed by the brain, a conclusion that has become part of medical lore. Later, modern scientists were able to pinpoint a small group of neurons in the brain stem that produce periodic bursts of electrical activity. These neurons seem to be the ones that regulate the process of breathing. Subsequent work indicated that a specific chemical, called 'substance P', was taken in by these neurons, and seemed to be essential for the maintenance of the breathing cycle. When rats were injected with a toxin that destroyed the substance P receptors in the neurons in their brain stems, they began to breathe irregularly and, in many cases, died. Autopsy studies of infants who died of natural causes seem to indicate that human brains have substance P receptors in roughly the same location as those in the brains of rats.

Some scientists have suggested that SIDS (Sudden Infant Death Syndrome), a disease that kills newborn children, may be related to problems with substance P chemistry. If this turns out to be true, then this basic research into one of the body's functions may show us how to save lives in the future.

Thinking More About | Cells

Biochemical Evidence for Evolution

The most striking thing about the energy metabolism of cells is that every single living thing on Earth, from the lowest bit of pond scum to the cells in our own bodies, uses part or all of the same chemical reaction cycles to obtain energy. In other words, they share a common biochemical background.

Most cells get energy from glucose by the process of glycolysis. Cells in advanced organisms—those in your own body, for example—can get more energy by adding more oxidation steps to the process of glycolysis. Some cells cannot do this, and therefore obtain less energy from each glucose molecule. This difference turns out to be a universal feature of living things; that is, when you examine life's chemical reactions, you find that more-specialized cells tend to use more chemical processes, but those specialized reactions are built up from chemical reactions present in more primitive cells.

You can think of the situation in cells as something like the way a complex chemical factory might develop. Long ago the factory may have made just one kind of chemical, perhaps white powdered lime for your lawn. As the factory grew and expanded, many new chemicals were produced—fertilizers and insecticides, for example. But the lime-making operation was still intact, ready to be used any time. We could, in fact, deduce the history of the factory by taking it apart and seeing how various chemical operations have been added on.

Scientists suspect that cells, the chemical factories of life, behave the same way. Biochemical evidence demonstrates that older, simpler chemical reactions lie at the heart of the more-complex operations of today's cells. Some biologists argue that this fact implies that all life descended from a common ancestor. How could you make such an argument based on what you know of respiration and fermentation? What do you think the more-primitive ancestors must have been like? Do you think the ancestors must have been in an environment that was rich in oxygen? Why or why not?

SUMMARY

Cells, complex chemical systems with the ability to duplicate themselves, are the fundamental units of life. All cells are bounded by a *cell membrane* consisting of a lipid bilayer. Most plants also have a *cell wall* made of cellulose and other strong polymers. Nutrients move into and wastes pass out of the cell through the cell membrane at protein *receptors,* which bind to specific molecules because of their distinctive shapes.

Cells possess a complex internal structure with many different kinds of chemical machinery. All but the most primitive cells have a *nucleus,* a structure surrounded by a double cell membrane that contains DNA. Other discrete structures, or *organelles,* in the cell perform various specialized functions.

Every cell must have a chemical mechanism for obtaining and distributing energy—the process of *metabolism.* Plants absorb light from the Sun and convert this radiant energy into chemical energy in *chloroplasts* by the process of *photosynthesis.* Animals must eat food with chemical potential energy, primarily carbohydrates such as glucose originally derived from plants. The first step in getting energy from glucose is *glycolysis,* a series of chemical reactions that takes place in *mitochondria,* by which the glucose molecule is split into pyruvic acids. In the process of *fermentation,* pyruvic acids are broken down into molecules such as ethanol and lactic acid and the energy is used to keep fermentation going. In the process of respiration, pyruvic acid molecules are broken down to carbon dioxide and water, liberating much more energy in the process.

Most cells divide by the process of *mitosis,* in which chromosomes are first duplicated, then separated. The cell then divides, producing two daughters, each of which has the same complement of DNA as the original cell. In *meiosis,* which produces sperm and ova for sexual reproduction, chromosome duplication is followed by two divisions that result in a set of four cells, each of which has half the normal complement of DNA.

KEY TERMS ABOUT THE CELL

cell	cell wall	chloroplasts	photosynthesis	fermentation
cell membrane	nucleus	mitochondria	respiration	mitosis
receptor	organelle	metabolism	glycolysis	meiosis

REVIEW QUESTIONS

1. What is a cell?
2. How big are the largest and smallest cells?
3. Give an example of how the shape of a particular type of cell is well suited to its function.
4. State three tenets of the cell theory.
5. What is the difference between a light microscope and an electron microscope? What are the smallest things that can be seen with each?
6. Describe the structure of a cell membrane.
7. How do materials move across cell membranes?
8. What is the function of receptors in the cell membrane? What is their chemical composition? How are receptors similar to enzymes?
9. How do cell walls differ from cell membranes?
10. What is the difference between a prokaryote and a eukaryote? Give examples of each.
11. What are the differences between chloroplasts and mitochondria? How are they similar?
12. What does the double membrane of the nucleus tell us about the evolution of eukaryotes?
13. What is ATP? What role does it play in the energy balance of a cell?
14. In what ways are chloroplasts and mitochondria similar? How do they differ?
15. Why do leaves appear green? What happens when they change color?
16. What are the products of photosynthesis? What molecules are involved in making photosynthesis happen in plants?
17. What is fermentation? How does it provide energy for living cells?
18. What is respiration? How does it provide energy for living cells?
19. Compare the energy released by the conversion of glucose in respiration versus fermentation.
20. In what ways are mitosis and meiosis similar? How do they differ?

DISCUSSION QUESTIONS

1. Could wine ferment if it were left exposed to the air? [*Hint*: Think about the word "anaerobic."]
2. What does it mean to say that almost all life on Earth depends on photosynthesis?
3. What sources of energy other than the Sun might some organisms use?
4. In what ways do the cells of plants and animals differ? In what ways are they the same?
5. List all the ways you can think of in which cells are analogous to chemical factories.
6. The text says that all life on Earth's surface depends on photosynthesis. Trace the foods you had for dinner last night back to specific plants.
7. List four ways in which the working of a cell illustrates the importance of geometry in molecular interactions.
8. Why is it that if you cut your hand it will heal, but if someone's spinal cord is severed in an accident that person is permanently paralyzed? What kind of research might change this situation? [*Hint*: Can nerve cells undergo mitosis?]

INVESTIGATIONS

1. Examine a drop of your own blood in a light microscope. What kinds of cells do you see?
2. Locate an electron microscope on your campus or at a nearby laboratory. Arrange a visit to watch the microscope in action. All analytical equipment has three major components: hardware to produce and control a source of energy (in this case the electron beam), hardware to mount and manipulate the specimen, and hardware to detect the interaction of the sample with the energy. Sketch the microscope and control panels and indicate which parts are associated with which of these three components.
3. Many everyday products, including vinegar, Swiss cheese, and bread dough, rely on the process of fermentation. Investigate some of these varied products and the microorganisms that enable their manufacture.
4. We often hear of "aerobic" exercises. Is there any connection between these exercises and aerobic processes in cells?
5. Look at water from a local pond or lake under a microscope. If you were van Leeuwenhoek, seeing this for the first time, how would you describe it?
6. Investigate the relative division rates of the body's different kinds of cells. Which cell types divide most

rapidly? Which divide most slowly? Why are there such different rates?

7. Investigate what diseases are associated with cells that divide too rapidly or too slowly.

WWW Resources

See *The Sciences* homepage at: **http://www.wiley.com/college/trefil** for valuable web links.

1. **http://commtechlab.msu.edu/sites/dlc-me/zoo**
The Microbe Zoo—an enjoyable site where you can visit Dirtland, Safari Hut, and more.

2. **http://www.thetech.org/exhibits/online/genome/**
DNA: The Instruction Manual for Life, an extensive general overview of DNA.

23

Classical and Modern Genetics

Why do offspring resemble their parents?

GREAT IDEA

*All living things use the same genetic code
to guide the chemical reactions in every cell.*

PHYSICS
Nuclear radiation can damage DNA,
causing mutations.

CHEMISTRY
Molecules of DNA and RNA carry the genetic
code and produce proteins in the cell.

ENVIRONMENT
Oxidizing chemicals in the environment
may cause an increase in the rate of
genetic mutations.

GEOLOGY
Mineral-like combinations of iron and sulfur
atoms play a role in the transfer of energy
to cells.

HEALTH & SAFETY
The principles of genetics have been used
to trace cases of hereditary or genetic
diseases. (Ch. 24)

ASTRONOMY
A recently discovered meteorite containing
organic molecules and tiny structures
reminiscent of bacteria suggests that primitive
life may have once existed on Mars. (Ch. 25)

TECHNOLOGY
New methods of altering the genetic code are
used to develop new varieties of plants and
animals. (Ch. 24)

BIOLOGY
Genetic information is passed from parents to
offspring when reproductive cells divide.

Red = applications of the great idea
discussed in this chapter.

Orange = other applications, some of
which are explored in other chapters.

It's just about time to head back home after a great day in the sun. You'll have company during the drive, because a friend has asked you to give her brother a ride back to campus. You've never met him before, but there's no mistaking the family relationship: the same wavy brown hair, the same wide-set eyes, the same distinctive shape to the nose.

One of life's most familiar characteristics is the similarity of offspring to their parents. Countless generations of animal breeders have relied on this fact, as have farmers who developed more productive strains of crops. And we see the same hereditary links in the faces of our families and friends.

From penguins to potatoes to people, like begets like.

Classical Genetics

Genetics, the study of ways in which biological information is passed from one generation to the next, was pioneered by an Austrian monk named Gregor Mendel (1822–1884). Perhaps more than any other prominent scientist, Mendel closely matches the popular image of the lonely genius conducting exacting research in isolation. Working at the monastery in Brno, in what is now the Czech Republic, Mendel began to ask the kinds of questions we have been posing: Why do offspring resemble parents? And why do offspring differ from parents?

Mendel attempted to answer these questions, as any good scientist should, that is, by observing nature, doing experiments, and seeing what there was to see. In a series of studies with pea plants in his monastery garden, he delineated the basic laws that govern the inheritance of physical characteristics.

The technique that Mendel used is simple to describe, although it was difficult and tedious to carry out. He cross-pollinated different varieties of peas. For example, he would fertilize the flowers of **purebred** tall pea plants—plants that always produced tall offspring—with the pollen from short ones, and then observe the characteristics of the "children" and "grandchildren," as shown in Figure 23-1. The offspring of two different strains, such as tall and short pea plants, are called **hybrids**.

When Mendel made these observations, he found that there were remarkable regularities in the characteristics of the offspring. All offspring from the first generation of a tall–short cross were tall. If these offspring were bred with each other, however, the results were quite different. On average, three-fourths of second-generation offspring were tall, while one-fourth reverted to being short. Thus, in hybridization, shortness disappears for one generation, only to reappear

1 Parent
Tall and dwarf
varieties are
cross-fertilized.

Tall   x   Dwarf

2 All the hybrid
progeny are tall.

Tall

3 First Generation
The hybrid
progeny are
self-fertilized.

Tall   x   Tall

4 Second Generation
Tall and dwarf
plants appear
among the
offspring of
the hybrids
approximately
in a ratio of
3 tall : 1 dwarf.

787 Tall   277 Dwarf

in the next. Mendel observed the same kind of behavior in half-a-dozen other pea plant traits: seed pod shape, flower color, and so on.

Mendel invented the "unit of inheritance," what we now call the **gene**, to explain his findings. He had no idea what a gene might be, or even whether it had a real physical existence. Today, as we shall see shortly, the gene can be identified as part of a long molecule of DNA. For Mendel, however, the existence of DNA was unknown, and he deduced the presence of genes purely from mathematical analysis of how traits of his plants were inherited.

Stop and Think! In what ways were Mendel's experiments with peas similar to Galileo's experiments with falling bodies?

In the simplest version of Mendelian or **classical genetics**, we assume that every offspring receives two genes for every characteristic—one from the father and one from the mother. In the experiment with pea plants, for example, every offspring in every generation received a gene for height (either tall or short) from its mother (the plant that provided an egg) and another gene for height from its father (the plant that provided the pollen). Mendel concluded that pairs of genes determined every characteristic he observed, and that the offspring may receive a different gene from the father than from the mother. So, if two genes are present, which characteristic is actually seen in the offspring? In the language of modern geneticists, we phrase the question by asking, Which gene is "expressed"?

Returning to our example of the pea plants, we recall that Mendel produced plants with both a gene for tallness and a gene for shortness in the first generation. The fact that all of these first-generation plants were tall means that, in all cases, the gene for tallness was expressed. Mendel stated this fact by saying that the gene for tallness is **dominant**. By this he meant that if an offspring receives a "tall gene" from one parent and a "short gene" from the other, that offspring will be tall. In this situation, the short gene is said to be **recessive**. The gene is present in the offspring, but it does not determine the offspring's physical characteristics; it is not expressed. That gene, however, can be passed along to subsequent generations. You should note that, in spite of the name, "dominant" is not the same as "good" or "strong" in the world of genes. Many fatal genetic diseases are passed from generation to generation by dominant genes.

Mendel's experiment can be understood in very simple terms. In the first generation, every hybrid receives a tall gene and a short gene. Because the tall gene is dominant, all of the first generation of hybrid plants will be tall. In the next generation, there are four possible gene combinations, as shown in Table 23-1. Each plant in the second generation can receive either a tall or a short gene from each of its parents. On average, the distribution of genes will be random so that we can argue as follows: In roughly one-fourth of the cases, the offspring will receive a tall gene from its mother and a tall gene from its father. In another one-fourth of the cases, the offspring will receive a short gene from its mother and a short gene from its father. In the remaining half of these cases, the offspring will receive a tall gene from its father and a short gene from its mother, or vice versa.

Consequently, in the second generation approximately three out of every four offspring will have at least one gene for tallness, and only one in four will have two genes for shortness. Given the fact that tallness is a dominant characteristic, this distribution means that three of four offspring in the second generation will be tall, while only one will be short. This situation is precisely what Mendel observed.

Table 23-1 **Tall (T) versus Short (t) Hybrids**

		Father's Genes	
		Tall	Short
Mother's genes:	Tall	TT	Tt
	Short	tT	tt

EXAMPLE 23-1

Breeding Peas

You are given two purebred pea plants. One plant has smooth pea pods and purple flowers (dominant traits). The other plant has wrinkled pea pods and white flowers (recessive traits). These characteristics are expressed independently of each other. What distribution of characteristics would you expect in the first generation of plants bred from these two parent plants? What distribution of traits would you see in the second generation?

Reasoning: Every plant in the first generation of offspring receives dominant genes for a smooth pea pod (S) and purple flower (P) from one parent, and recessive genes for a wrinkled pod (s) and white flower (p) from the other. Every plant in the first generation, therefore, has exactly the same gene combination, abbreviated SsPp. All of these plants will appear with smooth pods and purple flowers because S and P are dominant.

The second generation, however, will display a mixture of traits. The easiest way to predict the distribution of these traits is to set up a matrix, similar to the one shown in Table 23-1. In this case, however, we must deal with four different genes in each parent (SsPp), so the matrix must be 4×4, as shown in Table 23-2.

This table shows that there are 16 different possible combinations of the four genes. On average, 9 out of every 16 plants will appear with smooth pods and purple flowers—both dominant genes will be expressed. In addition, 3 of 16 on average will display wrinkled pods but purple flowers, and 3 of 16 will have white flowers but smooth pods. Finally, only 1 in 16 of the second generation will display both recessive traits: white flowers and wrinkled pea pods.

Mendel's observation of this characteristic 9:3:3:1 distribution of second-generation traits for two different genes was instrumental in his development of the genetic theory.

Table 23-2 **SsPp Matrix with Resulting 9:3:3:1 Distribution**

	SP	Sp	sP	sp
SP	SSPP	SSPp	SsPP	SsPp
Sp	SSpP	SSpp	SsPp	Sspp
sP	sSPP	sSPp	ssPP	sspP
sp	sSpP	sSpp	sspP	sspp

1 SSPP   2 SSPp   2 SsPP

4 SsPp   1 SSpp   2 Sspp

1 ssPP   2 ssPp   1 sspp

Smooth + Purple = 9

Smooth + white = 3

wrinkled + Purple = 3

wrinkled + white = 1

The Rules of Classical Genetics

Mendel's research can be summarized by three rules that frame classical genetics.

- *Rule 1.* Physical characteristics or traits are passed from parents to offspring by some unknown mechanism (we call it a gene).
- *Rule 2.* Each offspring has two genes for each trait, one gene from each parent.

- *Rule 3.* Some genes are dominant and some are recessive. When present together, the trait of a dominant gene will be expressed in preference to the trait of a recessive gene.

The rules of classical genetics were deduced during the early twentieth century. Careful records were kept on many kinds of organisms, from humans to cattle to agricultural plants, and large lists of dominant and recessive genes were compiled. In human beings, for example, dark hair and eye color are dominant over light, the ability to roll your tongue is dominant over inability, and hairy toe knuckles are dominant over hairless.

Qualitative versus Quantitative Genetics

In one sense, the qualitative aspects of Mendelian genetics have been understood for many centuries. Early human societies knew, for example, that if you saved the largest potatoes and planted them in the spring, the resulting crop would be better than if you just planted potatoes at random. They also knew that if you had a bull that gained weight rapidly and produced lots of meat, you should breed that bull to as many cows as possible so some of the offspring would share the characteristics of the father.

But Mendel's careful statistical analysis of pea plant traits carried genetics beyond the qualitative level. By discovering the distinctive 3:1 and 9:3:3:1 ratios of traits in second-generation plants, Mendel was able to propose a predictive model of genetics—a model that recognized the equal importance of both parents, and the distinction between dominant and recessive traits. When Mendel's rather obscure publications were "discovered" at about the turn of the century, they provided a model that allowed breeders to approach their work in a far more controlled and directed manner.

The traits of prize bulls and racehorses, for example, are carefully documented, as are the pedigrees of their offspring. The success of plant and animal breeders in controlling the flow of genes from one generation to the next is attested to by the appearance of cattle such as Black Angus (which are little more than a rectangular block of beef on very short legs) and the many varieties of vegetables and fruits that stock supermarket shelves.

Of equal importance, the laws of Mendelian genetics can now be used to trace cases of hereditary or genetic disease, such as the many cases of families with cystic fibrosis, a disease that affects approximately one in every 2000 Caucasian children in North America. Individuals with cystic fibrosis suffer from thick mucus deposits that obstruct the lungs, as well as other abnormalities of the body's chemistry. When both parents carry the recessive gene for cystic fibrosis, their children have about a one-in-four chance of acquiring the disease.

Although we have chosen examples in which one physical characteristic is correlated to one gene, most cases of inheritance are not this simple. Human height and skin color, for example, are affected by the action of several genes, and nutrition as well as genetics can influence height. Thus, while the principles of classical genetics have widespread validity, the way that they work out in practice may be quite complex.

Many varieties of tomatoes have been bred selectively to achieve desired qualities, such as color, size, or taste.

DNA and the Birth of Molecular Genetics

The key to understanding Mendel's genetic principles is **molecular genetics**, which is the study of the mechanism that passes genetic information from parents to offspring at the molecular level. In Chapter 22 we saw that cellular functions, the basic mechanisms of all life, depend on chemical interactions between molecules. Chromosomes, the distinctive elongated structures that appear to divide just prior to cell division, became an obvious focus for genetic study. Could these structures carry information and pass it from one generation to the next? Studies of cell division by meiosis pointed strongly in that direction. Recall that meiosis produces gametes—sex cells with half the usual number of chromosomes. Gametes from two parents are subsequently joined during sexual reproduction to yield a full complement of chromosomes.

By the mid-twentieth century, biochemists analyzed chromosomes and showed that they are made primarily of DNA, deoxyribonucleic acid. The discovery of the nature and function of nucleic acids has fundamentally transformed the study of biological systems in the past three decades. **Nucleic acids**, so called because they were originally found in the nucleus of cells, include **DNA** and **RNA**, the molecules that carry and interpret the genetic code. These chemicals govern both the inheritance of physical traits by offspring and the basic chemical operation of the cell. These extraordinary molecules conform to the twin principles of modularity and geometry that are followed by all other organic materials (see Chapter 21).

Nucleotides: The Building Blocks of Nucleic Acids

Proteins (chains of amino acids) and carbohydrates (clusters of sugar molecules) can form large structures from a single kind of building block. Nucleic acids, on the other hand, are assembled from subunits that are themselves made from three different kinds of smaller molecules. The assemblage of three molecules is called a *nucleotide,* and nucleic acids are made by putting nucleotides together in a long chain.

The first of the smaller molecules that go into an individual nucleotide is a sugar. The sugar in DNA is *deoxyribose* (thus giving DNA its complicated name, *deoxyribonucleic acid*), while in RNA (*ribonucleic acid*) the sugar is *ribose*. Ribose is a standard sugar containing five carbon atoms. Deoxyribose, as the name implies, is missing one oxygen atom (Figure 23-2).

The second small molecule of the nucleotide is the phosphate ion, which includes one phosphorus atom surrounded by four atoms of oxygen.

Finally, each nucleotide incorporates one of four different kinds of molecules in DNA that are called *bases*. The four different base molecules are often abbreviated by a single letter—A for adenine, G for guanine, C for cytosine, and T for thymine.

Ribose   Deoxyribose

• **Figure 23-2** Ribose and deoxyribose are 5-carbon sugars that differ in the number of oxygen atoms.

• **Figure 23-3** A nucleotide, formed by a sugar, base, and phosphate group.

Each nucleotide combines the three basic building blocks: a sugar, a phosphate, and a base (Figure 23-3). These three molecules bond together, with the sugar molecule in the middle. Think of a nucleotide as something like a prefabricated wall in a house. Both DNA and RNA are made by linking nucleotides together in a specific way.

DNA Structure

We can start putting DNA together by assembling a long strand of nucleotides. In this strand, the alternating phosphate and sugar molecules form a long chain, and the base molecules hang off the side. The whole thing looks like a half-ladder that has been sawn vertically through the rungs.

DNA consists of two such strands of nucleotides joined together to form a complete "ladder." The bases sticking out to the side provide the natural points for joining the two single strands. As you can see from Figure 23-4, however, the distinctive shapes of the four bases ensure that only certain pairs of bases can form hydrogen bonds. Adenine, for example, can form bonds with thymine, but not with any of the other bases or with itself. Similarly, cytosine can form a bond with guanine, but not with itself, thymine, or adenine.

As a consequence, there are only four possible rungs that can exist in a DNA ladder. They are:

AT
TA
CG
GC

With the bonding of these base pairs, the complete DNA molecule is formed into a ladder-like double strand. Because of the details of the shape of the bases, each rung is twisted slightly with respect to the one before it. The net result is that this ladder comes to resemble a spiral staircase—a helical shape that gives DNA its common nickname, the **double helix**.

RNA Structure

RNA is built in a manner similar to DNA with three important differences. First, RNA is only half the ladder; that is, it consists of only one string of nucleotides put together. Second, the sugar in the RNA nucleotide is ribose instead of deoxyribose. And third, the base thymine is replaced by a different base, uracil, abbreviated U. The shape of uracil is such that, like thymine, it will bond to the

• **Figure 23-4** The structure of DNA. AT and CG base pair linkages are shown above the DNA strand. The dotted lines are hydrogen bonds.

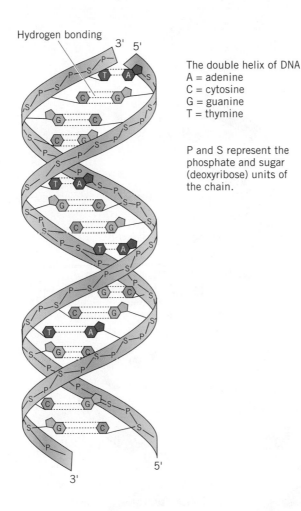

The double helix of DNA
A = adenine
C = cytosine
G = guanine
T = thymine

P and S represent the phosphate and sugar (deoxyribose) units of the chain.

base adenine. As we shall see, the ability of uracil to bond to adenine plays an important role in regulating chemical reactions in the cell. Several different kinds of RNA operate in the cell at any given time. All of them, however, have the same basic structure.

The Replication of DNA

In Chapter 22, we described the processes by which cells divide. Prior to both mitosis and meiosis, DNA in the chromosomes is copied. Thus DNA replication is one of the first steps in the passing of genetic information from one generation to the next.

DNA replication is possible because the geometry of the base pairs allows only certain kinds of bindings; that is, adenine (A) binds only to thymine (T), and cytosine (C) binds only to guanine (G). No other pairings are allowed. When a cell is about to divide, special enzymes move along the DNA double helix, breaking the hydrogen bonds that link the bases—in effect, breaking the "rungs of the ladder," as shown in Figure 23-5. As a result, the two split arms of the DNA ladder have exposed bases.

Consider, just for the sake of argument, an adenine (A) base that is no longer locked into its partner on the other side of the double helix. In the fluid around

• **Figure 23-5** DNA replication. A DNA double helix may be split, thus exposing bases on both strands. Two new identical double helices may then be formed from the original.

the DNA are many nucleotides, some of which contain an unattached thymine (T). With the aid of another enzyme, this thymine will bind to the exposed adenine in the original DNA strand.

In the same way, an exposed cytosine (C) will bind to a nucleotide containing guanine (G) from the fluid in the nucleus. No other type of nucleotide can bind to that particular site.

The net result of these preferential bindings along a single strand of exposed DNA is that the missing strand is reconstructed, base by base. The same thing happens in mirror image to the other half of the exposed DNA strand. Thus, once the DNA is unraveled, each strand replicates its missing partner. The end product is two double-stranded DNA molecules, each of which is identical to the original molecule.

When a cell divides by means of mitosis, the genetic information contained in the DNA of one cell is passed on to its daughters. Thus each daughter cell will have chromosomes identical to those of the parent. In meiosis, on the other hand, each daughter cell has only one chromosome from each pair of chromosomes in the original. When a sperm and an egg come together during fertilization, the resulting cell once again has a full set of chromosomes, but now one chromosome in each pair comes from the father, the other from the mother.

The simple chemistry of the base pairs provides a mechanism for reproducing DNA. This feature of DNA molecular structure accounts for one of the striking facts about life—offspring do share many traits of their parents. Ultimately, chemical binding of base pairs results in the inheritance of parental traits.

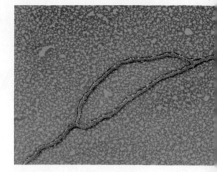

Electron microscope image of the DNA in a dividing human cancer cell.

The Genetic Code

DNA carries all our genetic information; this molecule is, in effect, the book of life. But how is the book read? How are the almost endless strings of DNA nucleotides translated into flesh and blood? That is the role of RNA.

Transcription of DNA

In addition to replicating itself so that cell division can take place, DNA also supplies the information that runs the chemistry within each individual cell. This process depends on the fact that all cells are governed by protein enzymes that run chemical reactions (see Chapter 21). Thus the question of how cell chemistry is regulated boils down to how the information in DNA can be used to produce proteins. If we understand this step, then we will understand how DNA governs the chemical functioning of every cell in our body.

DNA is a very large molecule. In eukaryotic cells it is found outside the nucleus only in mitochondria and chloroplasts. Thus the first question we have to ask is how information in the DNA gets out into the cell at large. The answer to this question involves a process called *transcription*, which uses the other nucleic acid, RNA.

When it is time to fabricate a new protein to act as an enzyme in a cell, other enzymes "unzip" a section of DNA as shown in Figure 23-6. Nucleotides of RNA that are always floating in the nuclear material are then hooked, with the aid of enzymes, onto the appropriate bases by a process exactly analogous to that which occurs in the replication of DNA. Each of the exposed bases on the "unzipped" strand of DNA binds to its appropriate nucleotide—A to U, C to G, and so forth. (Remember that in RNA, the base uracil, U, substitutes for the thymine in DNA.) In this way, a short strand of RNA is created that carries information from the

mRNA 5'
U A G U A A U C G U U U C G A U U C G G A U

One strand of DNA being transcribed

3'

5'

C G A T T C G G A T T A G C G C T A G C T T A G C T T A G T C G A

Locally unwound segment of double helix

• **Figure 23-6** Transcription of DNA occurs when a segment of DNA is split and a single-stranded messenger RNA segment forms. The mRNA carries the same information that was on the original DNA segment.

original exposed strand of DNA. Think of the RNA as being the "negative" of the true picture, which is the DNA.

Because it is relatively short and not connected to anything else, the RNA strand can move out through tiny pores in the wall of the nucleus and into the cell at large. Thus the function of this kind of RNA is to carry the information that was contained in the central DNA molecule out into the region of the cell where chemical reactions are going on. Because it carries a message, this kind of RNA (one of three important types in every cell) is called **messenger RNA**, or **mRNA** for short.

The Synthesis of Proteins

The exact sequence of base pairs on messenger RNA carries a coded message that contains chemical instructions. Once the mRNA arrives at the place in the cell where proteins are to be synthesized, it encounters a second type of RNA—a molecule called **transfer RNA**, or **tRNA** for short. The job of tRNA is to read that coded message. Transfer RNA, whose shape is shown in Figures 23-7 and 23-8, has a shape at one end that attracts 1 of the 20 amino acids found in living things (see Chapter 21). At the other end is a small loop of molecule with three exposed bases on it. One of four different bases can be found in each of the places on the top loop, so there are 64 ($4 \times 4 \times 4$) different kinds of tRNA molecules. Of these, 61 tRNA molecules attach to a specific amino acid at its other end, while the remaining 3 act as "stop" signs, which end the construction of a protein.

The sequence of bases along the mRNA is, as we have seen, a transcription of the information contained in the sequence of bases along the original DNA. Messenger RNA in effect carries a coded message, spelled out in four letters: A, U, C, and G. Each group of three exposed bases on the mRNA chain is like a word—a sequence of three letters that will bind to one, and only one, of the sets of bases on 1 of the 64 tRNA molecules. If a segment along the mRNA reads A-A-U, for example, then the tRNA molecule that has U-U-A as its unpaired bases will bond to that particular spot. Thus, after time, the mRNA and tRNA will form a sequence as shown in Figure 23-8.

The set of three bases on the mRNA, called a *codon*, determines which of the possible tRNA molecules will attach at that point. Each codon on the mRNA determines a single amino acid, and the string of codons determines the sequence of amino acids—what we have called the primary structure of the protein that is being assembled. This connection between the codons and the amino acid they select is called the **genetic code**, as detailed in Table 23-3. All living things share this code.

• **Figure 23-7** Computer-generated model of tRNA. The triplet of bases is shown in red, the spot that binds to the amino acid (in this case, serine) is shown in yellow.

As the tRNA molecules attach themselves along the mRNA, a string of amino acids in a specific order—a protein—is assembled as shown in Figure 23-9. Once its amino acid has been incorporated into the protein, a tRNA molecule moves away to be replenished with another amino acid and used again.

The protein synthesis actually takes place on ribosomes, which are large, irregularly shaped organelles made of proteins and yet another kind of RNA, called *ribosomal RNA,* or *rRNA.* As shown in Figure 23-9, the process of synthesis is somewhat more complex than the simple discussion we have given here. Ribosomes align the messenger RNA and transfer RNA during protein assembly.

Table 23-3 **The Genetic Code**

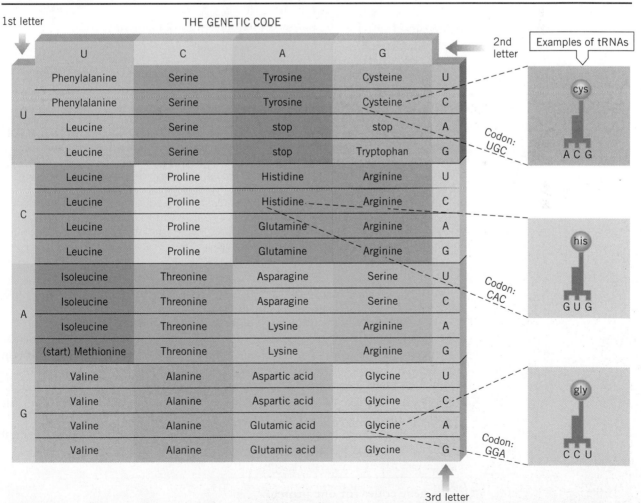

THE GENETIC CODE

1st letter	U	C	A	G		Examples of tRNAs
U	Phenylalanine	Serine	Tyrosine	Cysteine	U	
	Phenylalanine	Serine	Tyrosine	Cysteine	C	cys / A C G
	Leucine	Serine	stop	stop	A	
	Leucine	Serine	stop	Tryptophan	G	Codon: UGC
C	Leucine	Proline	Histidine	Arginine	U	
	Leucine	Proline	Histidine	Arginine	C	
	Leucine	Proline	Glutamine	Arginine	A	his / G U G
	Leucine	Proline	Glutamine	Arginine	G	
A	Isoleucine	Threonine	Asparagine	Serine	U	Codon: CAC
	Isoleucine	Threonine	Asparagine	Serine	C	
	Isoleucine	Threonine	Lysine	Arginine	A	
	(start) Methionine	Threonine	Lysine	Arginine	G	
G	Valine	Alanine	Aspartic acid	Glycine	U	gly / C C U
	Valine	Alanine	Aspartic acid	Glycine	C	
	Valine	Alanine	Glutamic acid	Glycine	A	
	Valine	Alanine	Glutamic acid	Glycine	G	Codon: GGA

2nd letter

3rd letter

• **Figure 23-9** The formation of a protein requires three kinds of RNA. (*a*) A strand of messenger RNA fits into a groove in a ribosome (an organelle formed from proteins and ribosomal RNA). (*b*) The ribosome attracts the appropriate transfer RNA, which carries with it an amino acid (shown in blue). (*c*) A second tRNA attaches to the ribosome and the two adjacent amino acids are linked. (*d–f*) The ribosome begins to shift along the mRNA, attracting new tRNA molecules and adding amino acids to the chain. Once the amino acids and tRNA are disconnected, the tRNA floats off to find another amino acid. (*g–h*) The completed protein is assembled and released by the ribosome, and all the components are available to start the process over again.

Thus three different kinds of RNA—transfer, messenger, and ribosomal—are involved in the synthesis of a single protein.

As a net effect of this rather complex molecular manufacturing process, the information encoded in the DNA molecule has been expressed as a particular sequence of amino acids that determines the identity of the appropriate protein enzyme. Thus a specific stretch of DNA located on one chromosome produces the enzyme that runs a particular chemical reaction in the cell. This stretch of DNA is what we have called a gene. That chemical might control skin color, hair texture, or any of the other traits that we recognize.

One of the central rules of modern biology, often referred to as the "central dogma of molecular biology," is:

One gene codes for one protein.

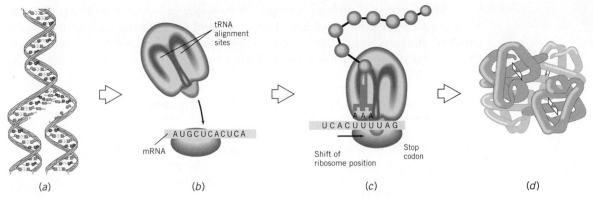

(a)   **(b)**   **(c)**   **(d)**

• **Figure 23-10** A schematic diagram of protein production from DNA. (*a*) One stretch of DNA codes for one mRNA molecule. (*b*) One messenger RNA molecule attaches to a ribosome. (*c*) Transfer RNA molecules match an amino acid to each codon on the messenger RNA. (*d*) Amino acids link together to make one protein, which will drive one chemical reaction in the cell.

That is, one stretch of DNA will code for one mRNA molecule, which will code for the sequence of amino acids in one protein, which will drive one chemical reaction in the cell (Figure 23-10). While a number of more complex processes produce a few specialized proteins, this rule holds for the vast majority of protein molecules. More than a century ago, Mendel postulated the existence of a gene, without knowing what it was. Now molecular biologists can tell you exactly where many specific genes lie along a stretch of DNA, as well as the sequence of base pairs along them.

Genes in prokaryotes are usually found on one continuous stretch of DNA, but in eukaryotes like human beings the geometry of genes is often more complicated. A gene on human DNA does consist of a stretch of DNA, but the coding sections of the DNA of a single gene are often separated from each other by stretches of noncoding DNA. The parts of the DNA that code for the protein are called *introns,* while the noncoding sections that are interspersed between them are called *exons*. The cellular machinery that transcribes the gene is able to cut out the exons and assemble the protein only from introns. In the assembly process, however, the introns can be put together in different ways, so that a single gene can code for more than one protein. In humans, for example, a single stretch of DNA may contribute to three or more different proteins.

All living systems employ the genetic mechanism we have just described. The transfer of genetic information by DNA and the production of proteins by RNA is a process shared by every cell on Earth. Each species, and each individual within a species, has a slightly different message written on its DNA. The identity of every cell, as well as the organism of which the cell is a part, is determined by the chemical reactions that take place there. The enzymes determine the chemical reactions, and the enzymes are coded for in the DNA. Thus DNA is truly the molecule that contains the code of life.

What is perhaps most remarkable about this process is that all living things use essentially the same code to translate between the messages carried in the genes of DNA, the messages carried in RNA, and the string of amino acids in proteins. This relationship explains why biologists speak of "the genetic code" when they refer specifically to the relationship between a triplet of base pairs on the mRNA, and the corresponding amino acid in the protein. The basic "word" of the molecular world, then, is the triplet of bases along DNA—the codon. Each codon eventually codes to one amino acid in a string of proteins.

The fact that all living organisms, from single-celled yeast to human beings, use precisely the same biochemical apparatus and precisely the same technique for making proteins and running their chemistry is one of the great unifying ideas in the science of biology. Indeed, one of the great principles of science is:

> **All living things on Earth use the same genetic code.**

This finding in no way limits the tremendous variety and diversity one can find in living things. Just as many different books can be written using the 26 letters of the English alphabet, so too can many different life forms be constructed using the four "letters" in the genetic code.

Mutations and DNA Repair

If DNA were copied faithfully from one generation to the next, no living thing could be much different from its ancestors. But mistakes do happen, and many agents in nature can damage the DNA molecule. Numerous chemicals (particularly those that cause oxidation reactions in cells), nuclear radiation, X-rays, and ultraviolet light (which also produces oxidizing chemicals) are all examples of such agents.

If the DNA of a parent's egg or sperm is altered, then the alteration will be faithfully copied by the process we have just described. The offspring will inherit the change, just as they inherit all other genetic information from the parents. Such a change in the DNA of the parent is called a **mutation**. As we shall see in Chapter 25, mutations have played a very important role in the development of life on Earth.

Recently, scientists have begun to realize that DNA is damaged at a far higher rate than had previously been thought. Careful chemical analyses indicate that damage to DNA in humans goes on at the rate of about 10,000 "hits" per cell per day. Fortunately, the body has developed repair mechanisms that take care of almost all of this damage as soon as it happens. The study of DNA repair, and the hope that it may help us deal with diseases such as cancer, represents a major frontier in science today and will be discussed more fully in Chapter 24.

Why Are Genes Expressed?

Every cell in your body except the reproductive cells contains an identical set of chromosomes—the exact same set of DNA molecules—yet your cells are not all alike. In fact, chemical reactions that are critical to one set of cells—those that produce insulin in your pancreas, for example—play no role whatsoever elsewhere. The genetic coding for making insulin is contained in every cell in your body, but turned on only in a few. How do the cells in the pancreas "know" that they are supposed to activate the particular gene for insulin, while the cells in the brain know they are not supposed to?

The mystery of DNA's operation runs even deeper than this. It now appears that only about 5% of all DNA in human beings is actually taken up by the genes. The other 95% used to be called "junk DNA" because nobody understood why it was there. Scientists are increasingly coming to believe, however, that at least some of the rest of the DNA contains instructions for turning genes on and off. The study of gene control is a frontier field and we understand very little about how it works. We do know, however, that genes are activated at certain times in the growth of plants or animals and the triggers for this activation appear to be enzymes or other chemical agents.

Many scientists also believe that the failure of these instructions leads to diseases such as cancer. If a cell is dividing and the mechanism that tells it when it's time to stop is faulty, the cell may continue to multiply and produce a tumor. Damage to the control mechanisms in a cell thus may be much more serious than damage to the genes themselves.

Viruses

If you have ever had influenza ("the flu") or a common cold you've experienced the consequences of viruses. Viruses aren't alive in the sense that bacteria and other single-celled organisms are. Unlike the life forms we discussed in Chapter 20, viruses do not metabolize and are not capable of reproduction on their own. Rather, they rely on the genetic mechanisms of cells to reproduce.

A **virus** consists of a short length of RNA or DNA wrapped in a protein coating (Figure 23-11). The protein is shaped so that it fits cell receptors and is taken into a cell. Once inside the cell, a variety of events may occur, depending on the exact nature of the virus. The viral DNA may replicate itself, producing its own mRNA, or viral RNA may serve directly as messenger RNA. Thus the virus takes over the cell's machinery, using the cell's enzymes and tRNA to produce more viruses like itself, eventually killing the cell.

Alternatively, as in the HIV (human immunodeficiency virus) that causes AIDS, the virus contains an RNA sequence that can be transcribed back into DNA, along with some enzymes that insert the DNA into the cell's own DNA. Once that stretch of DNA is inserted, it acts just like any other gene and co-opts the cell into making more viruses. No matter what the mechanisms, however, the result is the same: the cell eventually dies.

The surface of the HIV contains protein structures that fit perfectly into one of the molecules in the outer membrane of one type of human T cell, which is a critical part of the human immune system. T cells are thus "fooled" into pulling the virus inside. The virus then attacks and ultimately destroys cells that are essential to the operation of the human immune system.

Note that a "computer virus" operates in the same way. This kind of virus is a set of instructions taken into a computer that co-opts all the computer's machinery to its own ends.

Protein coat — — Nucleic acid

• **Figure 23-11** Viruses can have a wide variety of shapes and sizes. This diagram of a bacterial virus shows the protein coat containing DNA at the head. The tail fibers at the bottom attach the virus to the cell wall. DNA is then injected into the cell through the cylindrical core.

An electron microscope photograph of herpes viruses reveals the regular protein coating that surrounds a strand of DNA.

Viral Epidemics

There is an old joke about someone who goes to a doctor with a cold and is told to take a shower and stay outside in the cold with wet hair and without a coat.

"But if I do that, I'll get pneumonia," the patient protests.

"Of course," says the doctor, "but I can cure pneumonia."

The medical profession has enjoyed a great deal of success in dealing with diseases such as pneumonia that are caused by invading bacteria. Antibiotics often work by blocking particular enzymes in the bacteria. Because these enzymes don't operate in human cells, antibiotics can destroy the bacteria without harming the human whose body they are invading.

Viruses, on the other hand, co-opt most of the host cell's machinery and antibiotics do not affect them. This difference is why viral diseases such as the common cold cannot be treated as effectively with commonly available drugs as bacterial infections. The most effective countermeasure for viral diseases has been vaccination, which stimulates the human immune system to produce antibodies that neutralize the virus. These antibodies are molecules that have a precise shape that binds to the virus and prevents them from attaching to cells. Poliomyelitis, smallpox, and yellow fever have all been dealt with in this way.

Viruses not only hide inside cells, many of them also have the ability to change very rapidly, producing new forms as quickly as we find vaccines against them. The copying of DNA in cell division is subject to the cell's "proofreading" mechanisms so that daughter cells are the same as the parents. However, some viruses like HIV have no such proofreading and consequently they mutate at a rate up to a million times faster than normal eukaryotic cells. The influenza virus adopts a different strategy. If two influenza viruses invade the same host, they have the ability to swap sections of their nucleic acids, producing a new strain in the process. This rapid rate of mutation in influenza viruses is the main reason that Americans are urged to get new flu shots each year. The new vaccine attempts to counteract whatever virus has developed since last year's shot.

As the AIDS epidemic should remind us, viral diseases remain a very real threat to the human race. Several features of modern life make human beings particularly susceptible to viral attack. For one thing, we now tend to live together in cities, providing a large host population for new viruses. We also travel a great deal so that a virus that develops in one part of the world will quickly spread.

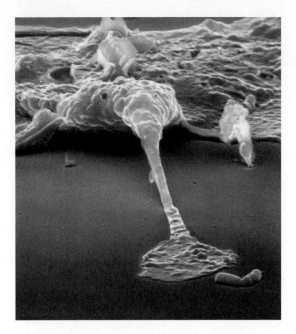

The human body produces immune system cells, called phagocytes, that destroy viruses, bacteria, and other foreign substances. This photo shows a phagocyte stalking a small bacterium.

Finally, humans are coming into more contact with isolated wilderness areas and therefore into contact with whatever viruses are already living on hosts in those areas. One example is the virus responsible for AIDS, which is believed to have arisen from a virus affecting monkeys in remote African forests. A hunter cutting his finger while skinning an infected monkey, for instance, could have introduced the virus to the human population.

 Stop and Think! How much attention do you think governments and scientists should pay to the dangers of new viral diseases? Do you think an international medical center should be established to monitor the appearance of new diseases? What good would such an early warning system do?

THE SCIENCE OF LIFE •

The Human Genome Project

The sum of all information contained in the DNA for any living thing—the sequence of all the bases in all the chromosomes—is known as that organism's **genome**. Determining a complete genome is a vast project that has become a major focus of modern molecular biology. The centerpiece of this global, multibillion-dollar effort is called the **Human Genome Project**. This massive undertaking has produced a complete tabulation of the human genome—all 23 pairs of chromosomes, all 3 billion base pairs—as well as an impressive and rapidly growing list of genomes of other organisms. The genomes of more than a dozen infectious microbes, plants, and a host of animals have been completed since the announcement of the yeast genome in 1997 and dozens more will appear in the coming years. For the first time, biologists can compare the genetic makeup of a diverse suite of organisms.

Researchers must accomplish two key tasks, mapping and sequencing, in the exploration of the human genome. They must first find the location of every gene on every chromosome, a process called **DNA mapping**. Creating a complete genetic map is no mean feat. Human DNA, for example, contains at least 30,000 (by some counts as many as 50,000) genes divided among the 23 pairs of chromosomes. Each chromosome is a long chain of DNA. Mapping all the genes, discovering where they lie along each chromosome, is time consuming, but it plays a vital

• **Figure 23-12** Two important goals of the Human Genome Project are DNA mapping and DNA sequencing. A genetic map shows the location and sequence of genes along a chromosome. It can be used to identify the genes for a specific trait. Scientists working on the Human Genome Project are creating physical maps that describe the chemical characteristics of the DNA molecule at any given point. The physical maps will then be used for DNA sequencing, which will determine the exact sequence of base pairs along a DNA molecule.

role in dealing with many kinds of hereditary diseases. Medical researchers investigating genetic diseases, for example, must find the exact chromosome and location of the defective gene in order to identify genetic markers for the disease and, perhaps, find a cure. In recent years, the locations of the defective genes for cystic fibrosis, sickle-cell anemia, and genetic forms of arthritis have been discovered on specific chromosomes, and many similar advances can be expected in the next few years.

The genetic map, like a good road atlas, tells us the general location of the most interesting places in our tour of the human genome. Genes are like villages and towns in our atlas, but these maps alone tell us little about the details of those places. We also need directories to each village and town if we are to really understand how the genome works. **DNA sequencing** is the process of determining, base pair by base pair, the exact order of bases along a DNA molecule. The net result of a sequencing operation is a string of letters (ATTGCGCATT . . . , and so on), a sequence that tells us how the DNA is put together in that particular stretch (Figure 23-12).

Many people are surprised to learn that a key goal of the Human Genome Project is the determination of the complete genomes of many other species, including the mouse, the fruit fly, yeast, and numerous microbes. These life forms, so crucial to ongoing genetic research, have many of the same genes, and thus reveal many of the same genetic mechanisms, that occur in humans. One result of this sort of knowledge is that a gene sequence can be used to deduce the sequence of amino acids in a protein and this information, in turn, may give some insight into the function of that protein in the organism.

Keep watching the news for announcements of the latest progress in this mammoth undertaking. •

SCIENCE BY THE NUMBERS •

The Human Book of Life

In Chapter 10 we saw that information can be quantified in units of the "bit"—a simple statement about "yes or no" or "on or off." We can use this notion to calculate the amount of information in the human genome.

Each site along the DNA molecule can be occupied by one of four bases. This information can be represented by two bits. We could, for example, set up a code as follows:

A = on on
T = on off
C = off on
G = off off

Using this code, we could go down the molecule specifying two bits of information at each nucleotide, and this would tell us the sequence. For example, the sequence AGT would be rendered:

on on; off off; on off

The human genome contains about 3 billion bases, so the total information content is:

3,000,000,000 bases × 2 bits/base = 6,000,000,000 bits

Let's compare this information content to that of a familiar object—this text-book. A textbook transmits information by letters, numbers, and other symbols, each of which can be represented by six bits (see Chapter 10). An average page of this book contains about 3000 characters, for an information content of

3000 characters/page × 6 bits/character = 18,000 bits/page

The number of pages required to carry the entire human genome equals the number of bits per genome, divided by the number of bits per page:

$$\frac{(6,000,000,000) \text{ bits/genome}}{(18,000 \text{ bits/page})} = 333,333 \text{ pages}$$

It would take almost 500 volumes the size of this book to record the entire blue-print for a human being. It's amazing to think that all of that information is con-tained in every one of your cells. •

TECHNOLOGY •

New Ways to Sequence

When the Human Genome Project was starting, scientists estimated that it would take decades and cost billions of dollars. Even well into the project, the official estimate was that it wouldn't be completed until 2005 and would cost 3 billion dollars (about one dollar per base pair).

This situation was changed drastically when molecular biologist J. Craig Ven-ter, who was then head of Celera Corporation, developed a new way of combin-ing computers with automatic DNA sequencing machines. As a result of his work, the Genome Project finished in 2000, five years ahead of schedule, with the cost of sequencing being only about 10 cents per base pair.

Venter's novel technique is called "shotgun," and here's how it works: Long stretches of DNA are broken up into many small pieces. These pieces are fed into an army of sequencing machines, each of which "reads" only a short segment—a few hundred base pairs of the original. By identifying overlapping segments from among the thousands of short DNA strands, powerful computers are able to reconstruct the entire DNA sequence.

It is important to realize that in this technique, the contributions of com-puters are just as important as those of the sequencers. This is why scientists

J. Craig Venter

Science News | Delivering the Goods
(SCIENCE NEWS, JAN. 18, 2003, P. 43)

In the next chapter we will discuss a medical technique known as gene therapy, whose goal is to replace damaged DNA in living cells. An important aspect of gene therapy, therefore, involves delivering healthy DNA to cells in the patient's body. The most common technique, which we'll discuss in the next chapter, is to use an inactivated virus as the so-called 'vector' to carry out this task. After all, viruses have evolved precisely to do the job of inserting their own DNA into host cells, so there's no reason that we shouldn't try to adapt that ability to our own needs. Unfortunately, there are some down sides to the use of viruses, such as severe immune reactions in some patients, so some groups of scientists are working on finding other sorts of vectors.

At the University of California at San Francisco, for example, scientists are using tiny vesicles made from lipid molecules as carriers of DNA. The size of large bacteria, these DNA loaded vesicles react to the pH of the fluid in which they find themselves. They are fine in ordinary blood, which has a pH of about 7.4, but when they enter a cell (pH 5 or 6) they dissolve, losing their cargo of DNA. The new genes move to the nucleus, where they can be expressed like any other gene.

Other scientists at the California Institute of Technology are building microscopic 'minivans' made from polymers—long chain molecules that can wrap around themselves to form microscopic tubes. In experiments with mice, these delivery systems seem to deliver DNA in a useful form, because the genes carried in this way are seen to be expressed in the mouse cells.

There are other entrants in the nonviral delivery system race. Teams at the Massachusetts Institute of Technology are screening thousands of polymers to find better candidates for this task. Other scientists are trying 'naked DNA'— DNA coated on the outside of tiny gold pellets or assisted by high-voltage electrical current.

Whether any of these techniques will replace viruses, and if so, which ones, remain questions that will be answered in the future.

often speak of the Genome Project as an example of the *bioinformatics* revolution.

Today, Celera's sequencing system continues to operate 24 hours a day, and each day they sequence a million base pairs and use $4,000 to $5,000 worth of electricity in the process. •

Thinking More About | Genetics

The Ethics of Genes

Advances in genetic research are dramatically altering our understanding of human health and behavior. Scientists now can detect many characteristics of an individual, including the presence of life-threatening diseases, before birth. Every year we learn more about genetic characteristics, and thus are better able to foresee aspects of a child's future. But with this knowledge comes an ethical challenge that will face every American in the coming decades. What should we do with genetic information?

Eventually we may be able to test every fetus for a variety of incurable genetic diseases. Should those tests be mandated? Should parents be informed of their future child's fate? Should the prospect of an incurable disease provide grounds for abortion? It has also been suggested (though not proven) that alcoholism and other behavioral disorders may be related, at least in part, to genetic factors. Suppose a person was found to carry a particular gene or combination of genes that were thought to predispose individuals toward alcoholism? To whom should that information be conveyed? To the individual? To his or her doctor? His or her employer? His or her insurance company?

Taking these issues a step further, it may soon be possible to alter an individual's DNA in utero, perhaps even in the first weeks of pregnancy. Many people would probably agree to genetic manipulation if it could cure their child of a fatal disease, but where does society draw the line? Would you allow such a procedure to improve genetically defective eyesight, or perhaps prevent crippling arthritis in later years? Would you be willing to enhance your child's IQ, or make her more athletic? What about changing his height or hair color? As with many other aspects of science and technology, we must come to grips with the question of whether it is ethical to do something simply because we are able to do it.

SUMMARY

Genetics, the study of the way in which biological information is carried from one generation to the next, is a field as old as the selective breeding of animals and the selection of seeds for crops. Gregor Mendel attempted to quantify aspects of this process by cross-pollinating *purebred* varieties of pea plants to produce *hybrids.* He discovered that all first-generation hybrids appeared the same, with the traits of just one parent plant, but the second generation displayed characteristics of both parents. Typically, three-fourths of the members of the second generation display one trait, one-fourth the other. Mendel explained his observations by developing laws of *classical genetics:* (1) traits are passed from parent to offspring by "units of inheritance" (we call them *genes*); (2) each parent contributes one gene for each trait; and (3) some genes are *dominant* and will be expressed, while others are *recessive* and will appear only if no dominant gene is present.

Modern *molecular genetics* seeks to understand the molecular basis for Mendel's observations. The key to understanding genetics lies in the unique structure of the *nucleic acids,* including *DNA,* with its *double helix,* ladder-like sequence of base pairs, and the closely related single-stranded *RNA.* The four different DNA bases, A, T, C, and G, which always come in the pairs AT or CG, act like letters of a coded message—the message of life. Because of its structure, DNA can replicate itself and store the information needed to make proteins.

Every cell has a set of chromosomes with the complete DNA blueprint in its nucleus. The process of copying DNA before cell division is called replication, and involves the splitting of the two sides of the DNA double helix, exposing the complementary base pairs. Each exposed base binds to its complement, and so two complete DNA strands form where before there was only one.

The coded DNA message is read by RNA, a process called transcription. *Messenger RNA,* a single-stranded molecule, copies the sequence for one gene and carries it out of the nucleus to the part of the cell where proteins are made. *Transfer RNA* matches sequences of three base pairs to corresponding amino acids; thus an RNA sequence translates into a string of amino acids—a protein. The correspondence between base-pair sequences and amino acids is called the *genetic code,* which is shared by every living organism.

While the DNA message is resilient to most damage, errors in the coded sequence can occur and cause *mutations. Viruses,* on the other hand, cause sickness by usurping a cell's chemical factories with foreign genetic instructions.

The complete description of an organism's genetic code is called its genome. Scientists determine a *genome* by first *mapping* the positions of every gene on every chromosome, and then *sequencing* the exact order of base pairs on every gene. The *Human Genome Project* has produced the 3-billion-base-pair sequence of the human genome, as well as genomes for many other organisms.

KEY TERMS ABOUT GENETICS

genetics	dominant	RNA	genetic code	Human Genome
purebred	recessive	double helix	mutation	Project
hybrid	molecular genetics	messenger RNA	virus	DNA mapping
gene	nucleic acids	(mRNA)	genome	DNA sequencing
classical genetics	DNA	transfer RNA (tRNA)		

REVIEW QUESTIONS

1. How did Mendel define the gene? How do we define it today?

2. Why was it important for Mendel to begin with purebred plants for each trait he was studying?

3. What is the difference between a dominant and a recessive gene?

4. What is a nucleotide?

5. Name the four bases that occur in DNA. What pairs can they form?

6. Describe the construction of the double helix structure of DNA.

7. How does RNA differ from DNA?

8. What are the main steps in the process of DNA replication?

9. How is the information of DNA copied onto mRNA?

10. What is the function of mRNA?

11. How does tRNA determine the primary structure of proteins?

12. What is a codon? What is the genetic code?

13. Why do genetic mutations occur? What agents cause them?

14. What is a virus? Why are they so difficult to control?

15. What is the difference between mapping and sequencing DNA?

DISCUSSION QUESTIONS

1. Could a recessive trait skip more than one generation? How could this happen?

2. If you were given two pea plants, one with waxy leaves and one with fuzzy leaves, how would you determine which leaf trait is dominant?

3. Why is DNA sequencing more time-consuming than DNA mapping?

4. What does the statement "one gene, one protein" mean? Why is this statement sometimes called the "central dogma of molecular biology"?

5. State some of the arguments for and against the use of genetic engineering.

6. Inbreeding, or the mating of closely related individuals, tends to perpetuate both good and harmful traits. Why should this be so?

7. If every cell in your body has exactly the same DNA, how can the cells perform such different functions?

8. Why do most biologists say that viruses are not alive?

9. Exposure to environmental chemicals or radiation may cause damage to children, even though those children have not even been conceived at the time of the exposure. Give a molecular explanation of how such harm could occur. What role should information on DNA repair play in such discussions?

PROBLEMS

1. The *Encyclopedia Britannica* has about 1500 words per page, 1000 pages per volume, and 30 volumes. How many sets of the *Encyclopedia Britannica* would it take to transmit the same amount of information as is contained in human DNA? [*Hint*: Remember, the average word has five characters and a single character has six bits of information.]

2. Suppose a particular breed of mice can be either white or gray, and have either clear or pink eyes. Suppose further that if purebred white mice are crossed with purebred gray mice, all the offspring are gray; and that if true-breeding clear-eyed mice and true-breeding pink-eyed mice are crossed, all the offspring have pink eyes. What will be the distribution of hair and eye color in the second generation if we start by crossing true-breeding gray pink-eyed mice with true-breeding white clear-eyed mice?

3. Scientists frequently use fruit flies, which breed every 10 days, to do genetics experiments. How long would it take to repeat one of Mendel's experiments on peas using fruit flies?

INVESTIGATIONS

1. Prepare a report on a genetic disease. What progress has been made in mapping the defective gene? Sequencing the gene? What kinds of medical treatments are now available?

2. Read *The Double Helix* by James Watson, codiscoverer with Francis Crick of the DNA structure. What data did they use to unravel the structure? What were the key steps in solving the double helix structure?

3. Some psychological disorders are now believed to be caused by defects in the body's chemistry. Read about one such disease, and summarize the argument between those who believe that psychological prob-

lems all have a molecular basis and those who believe that they are all due to the environment in which the individual has lived.

4. Make a family tree for your own family, recording characteristics such as eye and hair color, height, causes of death, and so on. Can you apply Mendel's rules to this tree?

5. A number of obscure viral diseases have arisen over the past few decades. Look up Korean hemorrhagic fever, dengue fever, Lassa fever, or the Ebola and Marburg viruses. What symptoms do these diseases or viruses produce? What danger do they pose to the larger human population?

WWW RESOURCES

 See *The Sciences* homepage at: **http://www.wiley.com/college/trefil** for valuable web links.

1. http://www.ornl.gov/TechResources/Human_Genome/publicat/publications.html
Human Genome Project Information, a primer.

2. http://www.accessexcellence.org/AB/GG

   Biotech Graphics Gallery contains illustrations and explanations covering cell processes, DNA replication, biotechnology, and more. Great site!

3. http://biologylab.awlonline.com/

   Electronic Desktop Project, click on "*Virtual Fly*" and mate Drosophila flies.

4. http://www.genome.gov/Education

   Educational resources for genetics education.

5. http://www.people.virginia.edu/~rjh9u/fugate.html

   Interesting description of a unique human trait, the so-called "Blue People of Kentucky."

24

The New Science of Life

Can we cure cancer?

GREAT IDEA

Our new understanding of genetic mechanisms is leading to enormous technological advances in medicine and other aspects of our lives.

PHYSICS

DNA fingerprinting relies on the fact that short segments of DNA move faster than long segments in an electric field.

CHEMISTRY

Chemical reactions in the cell are used to repair damaged DNA.

ENVIRONMENT

Both natural and commercially produced pesticides can cause damage to DNA; it makes no difference where the pesticide molecules came from.

HEALTH & SAFETY

Cancer and genetic diseases may soon be effectively treated with gene therapy.

ASTRONOMY

Ultraviolet light from the Sun may damage DNA.

TECHNOLOGY

Computers are being used to design drugs with a specific shape that will accomplish a particular function in the body.

BIOLOGY

Genetic engineering is based on the fact that all life uses the same genetic code.

Red = applications of the great idea discussed in this chapter.

Orange = other applications, some of which are explored in other chapters.

You head down the highway, listening to your favorite music station, when the program is interrupted for a news flash. New DNA evidence has led police to the arrest of a suspect in a highly publicized murder. A few skin cells under the victim's fingernails, analyzed at an FBI crime lab, cracked the case.

It seems as if DNA and genetic technologies are in the news every day. Paternity testing, cloning, tests for genetic diseases, DNA fingerprinting, stem cells, gene therapy, genetically modified foods—our world has been transformed by our understanding of the genetic code. What are these remarkable new technologies? How will they affect our lives and the lives of our children?

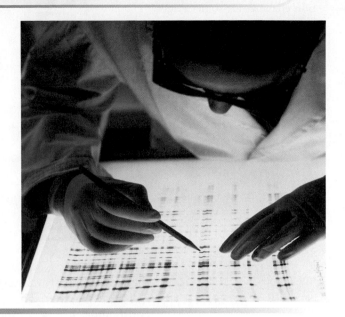

The Technology of Genes

Fundamental new insights into the workings of nature often trigger dramatic changes in the human condition. The discovery of the nature of electricity and magnetism, for example, led to the electrification of entire continents. The discovery of the basic laws of quantum mechanics eventually led to the modern information revolution. Now, our new understanding of the genetic mechanisms of all living things is leading to changes every bit as profound and pervasive. In fact, this revolution has already begun, although its consequences are not always immediately visible to the general public. At research centers and hospitals around the world the new molecular understanding of life is being put to work to cure disease and to better the human condition. In this chapter we present a few areas of current effort to give you a sense of what will soon become possible. Remember, though, that these advances are just the tip of the iceberg with respect to technologies of the new science of life.

Genetic Engineering

Every week, headlines referring to a remarkable technology known as genetic engineering appear in your newspaper. **Genetic engineering** is a procedure by which foreign genes are inserted into an organism, or existing genes are altered, to modify the function of living things. The basic technique of genetic engineering is very simple. Certain proteins, called *restriction enzymes*, have the ability to cut a DNA molecule (as shown in Figure 24-1) so that the DNA has several unattached bases at the cut end. Think of these exposed bases as something like pieces of Velcro at the ends of the DNA strands.

If another strand of DNA is cut in the same way, and if the exposed base pairs on that second strand are complementary to the base pairs on the original strand,

• **Figure 24-1** Restriction enzymes act something like a pair of scissors that break a DNA chain at specific sequences. Biologists can use this procedure to insert or remove segments of DNA.

then when the two strands are put together the bases will bind and the strands will stick together. This procedure allows researchers to take a stretch of DNA, cut it, and splice in another stretch of DNA that has the appropriate base pairs on its ends (Figure 24-2). The new DNA will contain an extra stretch of genetic information in it.

If the new stretch of DNA is a gene, then the same mechanism that drives the chemistry in every cell on Earth can start expressing that gene in its new environment. For example, more than 100 copies of the gene that makes human insulin have been spliced together into a loop of DNA called a *plasmid*. Biologists

• **Figure 24-2** The process of genetic engineering. Two strands of DNA are cut by restriction enzymes. Each cut is carefully made so that the exposed bases of each strand are complementary. The two strands are joined together to form one DNA molecule.

introduced that plasmid into the single-celled bacterium, *E. coli* (so-called because it is common in the human colon), and that genetically modified *E. coli* copies the plasmid along with its own DNA when it divides. A vat full of genetically engineered *E. coli* thus produces large quantities of human insulin that is almost indistinguishable from insulin produced in your own pancreas. In fact, most of the insulin used to treat diabetes is now made this way. This genetically based process is a great improvement over the old method, which involved tedious extraction of pig insulin from the pancreases of slaughtered animals— insulin that precipitated an adverse immune response in some patients.

The story of genetically engineered insulin is only a small part of the growing list of changes that are possible with genetic engineering. Genes that contain the natural insecticide Bt have been introduced into corn plants, making the plants resistant to the European corn borer, a major agricultural pest. In 2000, more than 40 million hectares (150,000 square miles) were planted in genetically modified corn worldwide, a strategy that is estimated to have prevented over a billion dollars' worth of crop damage. Plants engineered to be resistant to specific kinds of herbicides are widely used. These crops can be planted in unplowed fields, which can then be sprayed to eliminate weeds. This so-called "no-plow" agriculture is gaining wide acceptance as a way of preventing soil erosion.

Other applications of genetic engineering include strawberries that are highly resistant to frost, plants that are unaffected by specific diseases, colored varieties of cotton, and crops that manufacture natural insect repellents. Genetic engineering of animals has led to varieties that grow faster or have other agricultural advantages, and researchers have recently patented varieties of mice especially "designed" for medical research. There's even a patent for genetically engineered petroleum-eating bacteria to clean up oil slicks from tanker accidents.

Underlying all of this technology is the central fact that all life is based on the same genetic code—the translation of DNA sequences in a gene to amino acid sequences in a protein. The exact same geometrical shapes and chemical properties of the four base molecules occur in every living thing. That scientists can routinely switch genes from plants to animals and back again is simply another demonstration of the chemical unity of all life.

We have not even begun to imagine the changes that can take place through the use of this technology. The social issues involved in genetic engineering are profound. In 1974, scientists working in the field of genetic engineering voluntarily undertook a moratorium on further research until thought could be given to the question of how to keep potentially dangerous organisms from escaping into the environment. In most cases, such as the *E. coli* used in insulin production, the host bacteria are so specialized and so dependent on their laboratory culture that they could not survive in the wild. Nevertheless, the Andromeda strain scenario (named

(a)

(b)

Genetic engineering has produced a variety of modified organisms, including (*a*) pest-resistant crops and (*b*) genetically identical mice for medical research.

for Michael Crichton's popular novel, *The Andromeda Strain*), in which a genetically altered, destructive life form escapes into the environment, is something we must be concerned about. Is it possible that a genetically engineered disease, a common human bacterium with an inserted gene for a lethal toxin, for example, could be turned loose on the human race?

 Stop and Think! What harmful effects might result if a gene to prevent frost damage in strawberries were to get into other plants?

Recently there have been movements around the world to ban the introduction of genetically modified foods—what opponents call "Frankenfoods." This opposition is largely motivated by the fear that there may be unknown environmental and health consequences to the introduction of these kinds of foods. These sorts of concerns are justifiable and need to be addressed whenever a new strain of plant or animal is developed. Others point out, however, that the introduction of new strains of plants and animals has been occurring for centuries through carefully controlled selective breeding. What's new about genetic engineering is that, unlike the breeders of the past, modern biologists can usually control exactly what gene is being added to or deleted from the organism being developed.

TECHNOLOGY •

DNA Fingerprinting

The analysis of DNA in human tissue, a technique called **DNA fingerprinting**, is becoming increasingly important in the judicial system in the United States. Except for identical twins, no two human beings in the world have the same DNA. Thus analysis of blood, skin, or semen samples from the scene of a crime can be used to identify criminals in much the same way that fingerprints do.

Analysis of a DNA sample depends on the fact that all human DNA contains many regions called *variable number tandem repeat (VNTR)* sequences. In these regions, a particular nonsense phrase (for example, TAA or TAG, which do not code for an amino acid) is repeated over and over again—up to 256 times. The number of repeats in a given sequence varies from one individual to the next.

To begin the analysis, an enzyme splits apart DNA into segments containing VNTRs. The enzymes cut the DNA at places where there is a specific sequence of bases, so segments containing different VNTRs will be of different lengths. These numerous small DNA segments are placed in a gelatin-like material. When subjected to an electrical field, the segments move through the gel, with the shorter and less massive strands, in general, moving faster. (Remember Newton's second law of motion—acceleration equals force divided by mass, so smaller masses accelerate more under a given force.) The net result is that after a certain time, the different strands of DNA will have moved different distances. A strand containing a VNTR with 10 repeats, for example, will have moved farther than one containing 200.

Technicians then mark these segments with radioactive isotopes or fluorescent chemicals, and a piece of photographic film is laid over the gel. The radioactive or fluorescent emissions are recorded on standard photographic emulsion. The end result of this process is that the information in each person's DNA is reduced to something like a bar code (Figure 24-3). The "bar code" obtained from a tissue sample at the scene of a crime can be compared to that obtained from a suspect to make an identification.

The standard technique relies on cutting DNA at five different VNTR sites. Scientists and legal experts have engaged in considerable debate about whether this procedure provides enough evidence to rule out accidental identifications,

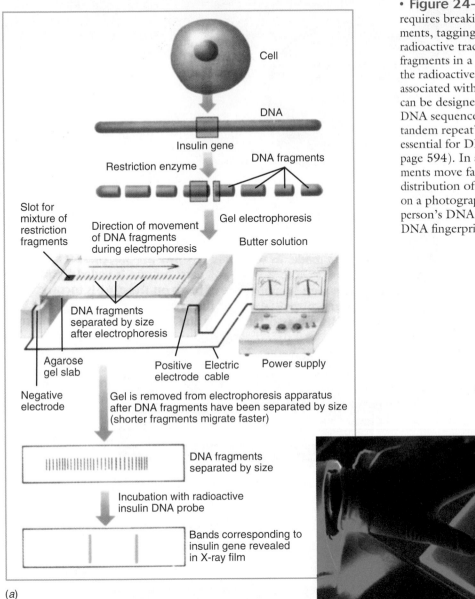

• **Figure 24-3** (*a*) DNA fingerprinting requires breaking DNA into short fragments, tagging those fragments with radioactive tracers, and then mixing the fragments in a gel. In the example shown, the radioactive tracer targets the gene that is associated with insulin. Radioactive tracers can be designed to attach to any desired DNA sequence, including "variable number tandem repeat" (VNTR) sequences that are essential for DNA fingerprinting (see text page 594). In an electric field, smaller fragments move farther along the gel, and the distribution of fragments can be recorded on a photographic film (*b*). Because each person's DNA sequence is unique, each DNA fingerprint is distinctive.

(a)

(b)

particularly among people who share some DNA, such as those in a given ethnic group. Some of the controversy was resolved in 1992, when the National Academy of Sciences issued a report suggesting guidelines for dealing with this problem. As a result, DNA fingerprinting is now routinely introduced in many courts. •

Copying DNA—The PCR Process

Development of a simple technique sometimes opens the door for all sorts of new applications. In biotechnology, the process called *polymerase chain reaction (PCR)* has played this role. In essence, PCR is a way of making copies of select strands of DNA so that, starting with a very small sample (a few cells, for example), investigators can produce as much of the desired DNA as they need.

• **Figure 24-4** The polymerase chain reaction (PCR) copies a sequence of DNA. (*a*) A strand of DNA is mixed in solution with DNA precursors (nucleotides), a primer that targets a specific piece of DNA, and an enzyme (polymerase) that helps to assemble DNA. The mix is heated to 95°C to separate DNA strands. (*b*) When cooled to about 60°C, primers attach to the DNA strands. (*c*) At 70°C nucleotides begin to attach to the DNA strands. (*d*) At the end you have two copies of the desired DNA.

The PCR technique is often used to amplify DNA prior to DNA fingerprinting, for example.

The process is illustrated in Figure 24-4. A sample that contains the DNA to be copied is mixed in solution with three ingredients: DNA nucleotides (the building blocks or precursors of DNA), a short stretch of DNA known as the "primer" (which is designed to identify the desired section of DNA to be copied), and an enzyme called DNA polymerase that helps to assemble DNA strands. First, the mixture is heated to about 90°C to separate the DNA into two strands (Figure 24-4*a*). Once the strands are separated, the solution is cooled to 60°C, at which temperature primers attach to the desired portion of the DNA (Figure 24-4*b*). In the third step the solution is heated to 70°C, which enables polymerase to attach nucleotides onto the DNA strands (Figure 24-4*c*). Eventually, we have two identical DNA strands in place of the original (Figure 24-4*d*). This process, repeated many times, can create as many copies of the original DNA strand as needed.

Cloning

One of the most striking scientific developments in the last decade was the appearance in 1997 of Dolly, the cloned sheep. **Cloning** is the process of engineering a new individual entirely from the genetic material in a cell from another individual. A clone is thus genetically identical to the cell donor. The birth of the first cloned mammal in history raised many questions both scientific and social, including the most troubling question of all—the possibility of cloning human beings.

What Is a Clone?

Before we get to those issues, we need to understand exactly how cloning works. We know that every cell in an organism like a sheep (or a human) contains the full DNA blueprint for producing an adult. We also know that during the development of the organism from a fertilized egg, most of the genes in most cells are shut down as cells differentiate. Cloning, as it exists today, is a technique that undoes that shutting-down process, and restores the DNA to its original full "blueprint" status.

Here's how it worked for Dolly. A team, led by British biologist Dr. Ian Wilmut, took an unfertilized egg from a Scottish Blackface ewe and removed the DNA from its nucleus. A cell from an adult sheep (a Finn Dorset ewe) was fused with this egg using a small electrical shock. The egg then began to divide, and the normal process of replication produced new copies of the Finn Dorset DNA in each cell. Finally, the embryo was implanted into the uterus of still another adult sheep and allowed to develop to maturity.

The key aspect to this procedure is that, although we do not know how to turn genes on and off in a cell, the unfertilized egg seems to be able to do it. The result is an offspring whose DNA is identical to that of the donor cell, and different from that of both the egg donor and the animal that carried the embryo. Since the birth of Dolly, many different mammals have been cloned, including mice, cows, and monkeys. Furthermore, there have been many generations of animals—clones of clones of clones—so that the process has become commonplace in the laboratory.

When Dolly first appeared, there was a great deal of concern that the cloning process would be applied to humans. Visions of armies of identical people, a basketball team made from clones of Michael Jordan, for example, abounded, along with darker visions of cloned humans being grown to supply organs for transplants. If you think about what a clone is, however, you will realize that

Dr. Ian Wilmut, the scientist who carried out the first successful cloning of a mammal and whose work led to Dolly.

A photograph showing a foreign gene being introduced into an animal cell.

these outcomes aren't what cloning is about. A cloned human would simply be a person whose DNA is identical to that of another, a phenomenon with which we are already familiar in twins. Just as we would not allow organs to be taken from one twin without his or her consent, we wouldn't allow the same procedure in clones. And as far as a basketball team cloned from Michael Jordan is concerned, his athletic skill is only partly derived from his genes. Unless his clone was willing to put in the unending hours of practice that made Jordan a star, that clone probably wouldn't be of much use to the team at all.

There are, however, many places where cloning (particularly in combination with genetic engineering) will be used. For example, it is possible to splice genes that code for specific human proteins (growth hormones, for example) in animals like cows and sheep. The protein could then appear in the milk, where it could be extracted easily. This procedure for making drugs, nicknamed "pharming," would depend on cloning to make sure that the gene appears in the offspring of the genetically engineered animal.

Two possible applications of cloning technology are being discussed for humans. The most controversial application would be to produce a new human being, a process known as *reproductive cloning*. Many scientists and government leaders oppose this use of the technique, and it is outlawed in many parts of the world. The other application, called *therapeutic cloning*, uses cloning as part of a medical procedure to improve human health and is being pursued in many countries.

Stem Cells

Every human being starts out as a single fertilized cell. That cell divides again and again until the organism is fully developed. As we saw in Chapter 23, as the development process advances and cells become more specialized, their ability to express some of their genes disappears until, in the fully developed organism, each cell expresses only a small fraction of the genes in its DNA.

For the first few cell divisions, however, each cell retains the ability to express all of its genes, and thus the ability to develop into any of the specialized cells that will eventually appear in the adult organism. These cells are said to be *totipotent*, and are referred to as *embryonic stem cells*. The term "stem" refers to the fact that the descendants of these cells can branch out and become any cells found in the adult organism. Normally, human cells lose this property after about two weeks of development.

During the mid-1990s, scientists began to develop the ability to keep stem cells in culture for long periods of time, and began to study the processes by which these cells "choose" what route they will take during the development process. If we could control this process, the medical consequences would be staggering. For example, nerve cells in adults do not divide, so that someone who suffers a spinal cord injury is condemned to permanent disability. If we could direct stem cells to grow into neurons (and scientists already have had some success in this effort), we could find ways to repair such injuries.

More promising (but farther away) is the possibility that stem cell research might lead to the ability to create tissue for transplant. At the moment, when a patient receives a transplanted heart or other organ, the host's immune system immediately attacks the new organ because it sees it as a foreign invader. However, if the transplanted tissue could be created from the patient's own cells this immune response would not happen and recovery from a transplant operation would be much easier.

Actor Christopher Reeve was paralyzed after a riding accident. Stem cell research holds the promise of regenerating damaged tissues, including severed nerve cells in people with spinal cord injuries.

In order to carry out this procedure, however, it would be necessary to use the patient's own DNA to create a cloned embryo, and then to destroy the embryo to obtain the stem cells. Consequently, this technique has become part of the difficult debate on abortion in the United States. One possible way around this difficulty is the suggestion by some scientists that some cells in the adult human body can be coaxed into acting as stem cells. Such cells, called *somatic stem cells*, show limited promise, but as of this writing the question of whether they can be made to perform in the same way as stem cells taken from embryos is unresolved.

Curing Disease

Many of the medical problems that human beings develop arise because of the malfunctioning of genes in their DNA. These medical conditions, collectively called **genetic diseases**, sometimes occur because a particular protein is not being made. As we saw in Chapter 23, proteins act as enzymes to drive chemical reactions in cells and each protein is coded from a single gene. If for some reason the sequence of bases on the gene is incorrect, then the correct protein will not be made, the chemical reaction will not move forward, and the disease associated with the lack of that protein would manifest itself.

Cystic fibrosis (see Chapter 23), for example, is an inherited defect that affects about 30,000 people in the United States. Although there are now treatments for this disease, and more than half the sufferers survive into their late twenties at least, until recently scientists had little idea of its ultimate cause. Then, in the early 1990s, scientists discovered that the most common form of cystic fibrosis was associated with a specific defect in a specific gene on chromosome 7. This gene codes for a protein that acts as a cell receptor regulating the flow of chloride ions across the cell membrane. In people suffering from this form of cystic fibrosis, however, three base pairs, corresponding to parts of the codons for the 507th and 508th amino acids in the protein's primary structure, are missing. That omission is enough to produce the disease.

Gene Therapy

Until quite recently, the only thing that physicians could do when faced with a genetic disease was to treat the symptoms. For example, in a disease such as diabetes, which is brought about by a failure of the body to produce the protein called insulin, treatment can run from modifying a patient's diet to injecting genetically engineered insulin on a daily basis. More recently, however, gene therapy, a new kind of treatment of these sorts of diseases, has become available.

Gene therapy is defined as a procedure for replacing a defective gene with a healthy one. Although still very much in the experimental stages, it holds enormous promise. Gene therapy can be done *in vitro* (that is, the gene can be injected into cells outside of the body, and the cells can then be introduced into the body) or *in vivo* (that is, the genes can be injected into cells in the body). As of this writing, only in vitro therapy has been accomplished in clinics, but there are many groups around the world trying to develop in vivo techniques.

The first successful gene therapy took place in the early 1990s at the National Institutes of Health (Figure 24-5). Ashanti de Silva was born with a disease known as severe combined immunodeficiency (SCID). Because of faulty coding in one gene in her DNA, she was unable to produce a protein called adenosine deaminase that is vital for the functioning of the immune system. Because her immune system didn't work, she had to be quarantined, and was able to leave home only to visit her doctor. She was always sick, and had a life that bore almost no resemblance to those of normal children.

Children who are born with this defect are extraordinarily sensitive to any kind of contact with disease. Before the late twentieth century, most SCID babies

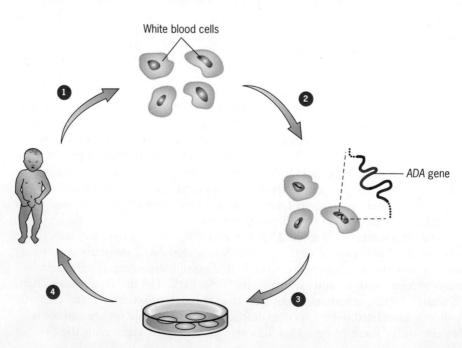

• **Figure 24-5** Gene therapy was first used successfully in the treatment of SCID. (1) White blood cells were removed from the patient. (2) Normal copies of the defective gene were inserted into the blood cells. (3) The cells were placed in a culture (a medium of nutrients) to verify that the DNA would replicate and proteins would form in the cell. (4) The genetically modified cells were returned to the patient's bloodstream. Because white blood cells have a relatively short lifespan, patients must undergo treatment regularly to maintain a constant supply of normal genes.

White blood cells

ADA gene

Ashanti de Silva was the first patient to be treated with gene therapy.

died within their first year. In the late twentieth century, a few of these children lived into their teens by being kept in complete isolation from the external environment—they were called "bubble babies."

In September 1990, Ashanti de Silva became the first person to undergo a new kind of medical treatment. Doctors removed white blood cells from her veins and, using the new technology of genetic engineering, inserted normal copies of the defective gene. Over a period of months, the corrected cells were returned to her bloodstream, where they could produce the missing protein. The results seemed miraculous. From a sick, reclusive child, she was transformed into a normal, active pre-teen.

As often happens when new medical techniques are introduced, these first treatments were not for diseases that are widespread, but rather for diseases for which there can be an unambiguous interpretation of the results. Although very few people have SCID, it is nonetheless a defect that can be traced to a particular gene, which therefore can be used to demonstrate that genes can be repaired in living human beings.

As of this writing, more than 200 programs for gene therapy protocols have been approved in the United States, and many are now underway. Unfortunately, the preliminary results of most gene therapy trials have not been very encouraging. Doctors have identified many gene defects that cause disease, and have even managed to insert corrected genes in some cells. Even so, in almost every case the new genes don't work—the modified cells cannot make the desired protein. The problem appears to be that the new genes are inserted into a chromosome more or less at random locations; the cell is, in effect, unable to find the gene and copy it with messenger RNA.

In addition, in 1999 the field of gene therapy suffered a major setback when a young man in one of the clinical trials died unexpectedly during the treatment. Investigation revealed that many of the standards normally in place in human clinical trials were not observed in his case—several months elapsed before the death was reported, for example. Even though this death was probably not related to the techniques of gene therapy, it emphasized that this procedure, despite its promise, will take a long time to develop.

The ultimate procedure in gene therapy would be to be able to introduce an agent into the body that would seek out the cells that have faulty genes, be taken into those cells, and then to insert healthy genes into the DNA of those cells at the correct location. While this may sound like science fiction, nature has many organisms that can insert genes in target cells: they are called viruses. The hepatitis virus, for example, can be taken into the human body, move to the liver, and be taken into the liver cells. Furthermore, as we saw in Chapter 23, many viruses are capable of inserting genes into existing DNA in a cell. Thus research efforts in gene therapy are beginning to concentrate on the construction of what are called "therapeutic viruses."

The idea of a therapeutic virus is that it will carry as its cargo a healthy human gene, rather than a normal viral gene. It will have an outer coating that is shaped so that it will be recognized by receptors on only certain cells in the body (just as the hepatitis virus is recognized only by cells in the liver). A therapeutic virus, when recognized, would be taken into the cell and its cargo of healthy genes inserted into an appropriate place in the cell's DNA.

Constructing a therapeutic virus is a tall order. As of the publication of this edition, research has progressed to the point where viruses can be constructed that can be recognized by specific cells in the human body. These viruses, if injected into the bloodstream, will be recognized only by certain cells. At the moment the main roadblock to gene therapy is the difficulty in having the viruses, once recognized, taken into the cell. It appears that more is involved than a single receptor, and working this mechanism out is a major task for molecular biologists.

If they succeed, however, it would be a major revolution in medicine, comparable in every way to the revolution associated with antibiotics. Before antibiotics, diseases such as pneumonia, tuberculosis, and various kinds of infections were often fatal and were greatly feared. Today, someone suffering from bacterial pneumonia simply has to go to the doctor's office and get a shot.

Cancer—A Different Kind of Genetic Disease

Cancer, a disease that strikes more than a million Americans every year, occurs when a group of cells in the body reproduces without restraint. The human body's trillions of cells have to maintain an exquisite balance. Regulatory processes orchestrate the death of old cells, while new cells arise to take their place. Cancer occurs when these processes fail—when genetic defects cause a cell to divide again and again in a runaway fashion to form a tumor.

Scanning electron micrographs showing the features of normal (*a*) and cancerous (*b*) rat kidney cells growing in culture. The normal cells adhere to the surface of the culture dish, forming monolayers of flat cells. The cancerous cells overgrow each other, forming clumps. Magnification: (*a*) 200X; (*b*) 280X.

(a)

(b)

Only recently have scientists begun to understand what's fundamentally different between a normal cell and a cancer cell. Normal cells have an internal clock and regulation mechanisms that keep track of the cell's life cycle. But the internal clock of a cancer cell is either turned off, or constantly reset, or just ignored.

Normal cells recognize several different kinds of damage. Have there been mistakes in DNA duplication during cell division? If so, then fix the mistake or kill the cell. Has the DNA been duplicated fully and only once? If not, fix the mistake or kill the cell. Are the chromosomes correctly segregated? Is the cell correctly oriented to partition the chromosomes? At each transition the cell stops to check whether everything is okay. Every step of mitosis—the cycle of DNA duplication and partitioning—has to be accomplished with the extraordinary fidelity that life demands. If not, kill the cell.

Cancer occurs when this fundamental guardianship fails. In cancer, the cell cycle continues unchecked, often despite profound damage to the DNA and to the chromosomes. And by ignoring chromosomal damage, additional harmful changes accumulate in the cell. The result is a terribly damaged cell that just keeps duplicating itself over and over again, making more copies of the defective cell.

Over the past several years, scientists have succeeded in identifying several specific genes whose protein products affect checkpoint pathways. No single genetic abnormality is sufficient for a normal cell to become a cancer cell. Rather, a handful of five or six such genetic abnormalities—perhaps 5 or 6 separate damaged genes in one single cell—are required. Many of these DNA changes are acquired or at least accelerated by exposure to mutagenic chemicals that damage DNA. Such chemicals are found in cigarette smoke, for example. Other carcinogenic chemicals include various organic solvents like benzene, atmospheric pollutants, and arsenic or other impurities in drinking water. Even a bad diet can accelerate the rate of gene damage.

The probability that any *single* cell will acquire the several gene abnormalities required to change the cell from normal to cancerous behavior is relatively low. However, there are tens of trillions of cells in your body and any one of them can accumulate errors along the path to cancer. So it's a matter of probabilities. This situation is considerably worse for some individuals who are born with genetic defects. In the United States, about a tenth of cancer patients diagnosed each year has inherited an abnormality in one of these genes. Because these individuals already carry what is called the first genetic hit on the road to cancer in *all* of their cells, the probability that any single cell will accumulate the additional 4 or 5 DNA cancer hits needed to make a tumor is much higher than normal. In fact, people with an inherited cancer gene can carry lifetime risks of developing cancer greater than 80 percent. The search for these cancer-related genes is one of the hottest areas of cancer research.

The growing recognition of a genetic basis for cancer points to new approaches for its cure. Today the treatment of cancer, while often successful, usually involves heroic measures such as surgery, radiation therapy, and the use of deadly chemicals to remove or kill these rogue cells. But some day that therapy will be tailored to the specific genetic fingerprint of each person's cancer. Missing proteins will be synthesized and supplied; damaged genes will be repaired or bypassed. As we discover and identify a growing list of inherited and acquired cancer susceptibility genes, we'll be able to determine the best preventative treatments for individuals at risk.

Try to imagine what it would be like to walk into a doctor's office, be diagnosed with cancer, and be given a virus-laden injection or a nose spray as your only treatment. Today this seems like a fairy tale, but if the work of molecular biologists in developing gene therapy is successful, having cancer in the future may be no worse than having an ear infection at the end of the twentieth century.

SCIENCE BY THE NUMBERS •

Double-Blind Clinical Trials

One of the great problems medical researchers face in testing new medical procedures like gene therapy is proving that the therapies actually work. It's often difficult for scientists to be certain that the treatment they prescribe is the cause of any improvement seen in the patient. To see why, imagine that you had a new medicine that you claimed cured the common cold. Suppose further that you tried the medicine on some people with colds and found that after a few days, all the people who tried the medicine got rid of their colds. Would this prove that your medicine was effective? Of course not. We know that the human immune system also battles the common cold, so if you had just left those people alone and gave them no treatment at all, they'd get better in a few days on their own. The medicine, as likely as not, was irrelevant.

To deal with these kinds of situations, researchers commonly use what is called the *double-blind clinical trial*. It works like this: A group of patients suffering from a particular disease is separated into two sections. Efforts are made to match the two sections in terms of age, sex, previous health history, and so on. One group is given the new treatment while the other group is given a placebo (that is, a sugar pill). For example, if the treatment being tested is a new drug, half the people will be given the new drug while the other half will be given a placebo. The patients are not told which treatment they are getting, nor do the physicians treating the patients know if a particular patient is getting the drug or a sugar pill. Thus neither the patients themselves nor the physicians who will be judging the efficacy of the treatment know which patients are receiving the drug and which are not. This is why it is called a "double-blind" trial.

In order for a drug to be judged effective, it has to pass a clinical trial of this type. Unfortunately, new "wonder cures" are often tested without such experimental rigor. For example, a man recently stood up in a conference and claimed that he had found a cure for a particular kind of cancer based on a new-age therapy involving meditation and natural foods. He was asked what evidence he had; his reply was that he had a patient who had a tumor, and when he started the patient on this treatment, the tumor began to shrink in size. He was asked, "How do you know that it was your treatment that caused the tumor to shrink?" His reply: "What else could it have been?"

In fact, tumors left to themselves often grow and shrink in irregular and unpredictable ways. This particular treatment, like any other, can be validated only by a double-blind trial, with two groups of people in the same medical condition, some of who are not receiving the treatment. Such rigor is rarely found in the sorts of activities that go by the name of alternative medicine. •

 Stop and Think! In a double-blind clinical trial half of the patients receive only a placebo, rather than a drug that might help their condition. Is this process ethical? Would you voluntarily participate in such a trial?

DNA Repair in the Cell

The transcription process we described in Chapter 23 shows how a specific sequence of bases along a DNA molecule is translated into the production of a specific protein in the cell. We also pointed out that if for some reason the DNA is damaged so that there is something wrong with the sequence of bases, the protein for which that gene codes will not be produced.

A common misconception about cellular DNA, one that is often encountered in popular writings on environmental problems, holds that the DNA in human cells is extremely fragile and is at the mercy of any kind of influence emanating from the environment. In fact, research that has been going on since the 1980s gives us a very different picture of DNA. It turns out that not all damage to DNA comes from outside the cell. In fact, most "hits" come from inside the cell itself. Cellular metabolism, for example, depends on respiration—a process with byproducts, some of which may be quite harmful. The best-known harmful byproducts of cellular respiration are a class of molecules called oxidants, such as the superoxide ion (O^{2-}). These ions are created copiously inside the cell and, if they make their way to the cell's nucleus, can cause damage to DNA. In addition, we ingest many kinds of molecules in our food, some processed, some natural, and these, too, can cause damage to the cells if they find their way to the cell's nucleus.

But the story doesn't end with the damage. Cells possess two different types of mechanisms for dealing with mistakes in DNA. Both of these mechanisms depend on sets of enzymes that wrap themselves around the DNA molecules and move up and down the spiral, looking for abnormalities. When abnormalities are found, these molecules call up one of two different kinds of repair mechanisms, depending on the kind of mistake that is found. Thus our picture of DNA in the cell's nucleus has to be a dynamic one, involving constant damage followed by constant repair.

One common kind of mistake in DNA, called a point defect, involves something like a simple misprint—the substitution of one base for another in the double helix. For example, the normal code for a particular spot on the DNA might require the base A, but for some reason we find the base T in that spot. In this case, the double helix will bulge slightly and the patrolling enzymes will detect the bulge. Other enzymes will come to that spot and snip out the offending bit of DNA, and allow the normal replication process to replace the blank spot with the correct base (Figure 24-6).

Other kinds of mistakes also occur. For example, two bases forming one side of the DNA double helix occasionally stick to one base on the other side. (This error may result when ultraviolet sunlight damages cells in the skin.) Alternatively, during the copying process, one strand of DNA can slide down, leaving a loop sticking out to the side. This kind of error is called a "mismatch." When these sorts of mistakes are encountered, a second kind of repair mechanism, called mismatch repair, is initiated, and the entire side of the DNA molecule that contains the offending section is removed. As before, the normal processes of DNA replication then reconstruct the missing stretch of DNA.

 Stop and Think! Given what you know about the effect of ultraviolet light on DNA, why should you wear sunscreen when you are outdoors?

What is perhaps most amazing about the way DNA operates in our cells is the sheer amount of damage that the molecules receive. Scientists measuring the chemical debris of the repair process estimate that every cell in your body sustains some 10,000 "hits" per day to its DNA, and succeeds in repairing almost all of them.

In fact, the process of DNA repair seems to be very similar to the process of repairing a house that has been damaged by a hurricane. In the case of the

• **Figure 24-6** DNA repair in the cell. Patrolling enzymes will identify defects in the DNA molecule, as indicated by a bulge in the double helix. Other enzymes will then remove the damaged section of DNA and allow the normal replication process to reconstruct the missing stretch.

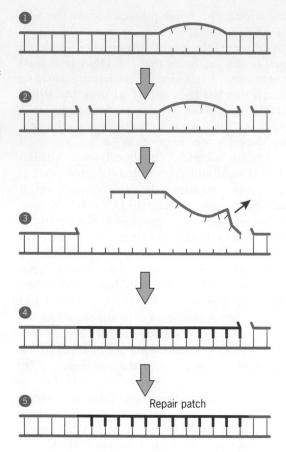

Repair patch

house, you would be sure that the roof and walls were repaired and the electricity restored before you started worrying about replacing the carpets. In the same way, in the DNA there seems to be a hierarchy in the repair mechanisms. Highest in the hierarchy is the repair of those genes that are actually expressed in the cell in which damage has occurred. The point is that this repair has to be finished before the cell divides. If it is not, then the process of replication discussed in Chapter 23 will ensure that every descendent of the particular cell will contain the defect. Thus, the life of every cell can be thought of as a race between the repair mechanisms that we just described and the normal process of mitosis.

One important message to learn from the DNA repair story is that molecules cause damage to DNA. If the shape of the molecule is right, it will produce a defect, regardless of where that molecule came from. *It makes no difference whether the molecule is a product of our society or of nature.*

To underscore this point think about pesticides, which are among the most commonly cited causes of DNA damage. Some pesticides are produced commercially, of course, but many occur naturally in plants as a defense mechanism. In fact, it is estimated that only about one-tenth of 1 percent of the pesticides that human beings take in each day are commercially produced, with the rest being a normal part of the plants we eat. Once inside the body, however, it makes no difference where the pesticide molecule came from. About half of both the synthetic and natural pesticides are capable of causing cancer in laboratory animals.

Pesticides are routinely sprayed on crops to cut down on insect pests, as in this field of snow peas in California.

Plants, like this common milkweed, have developed their own pesticides over the millennia.

AIDS

Society became aware of **acquired immune deficiency syndrome (AIDS)** in the 1980s. This disease is caused by a virus known as the *human immunodeficiency virus (HIV)*, and is transmitted by exchange of bodily fluids, most commonly in sexual contacts and the sharing of needles among drug abusers. The proteins in the virus's coat happen to fit the receptors in certain types of white blood cells (T cells) in the human immune system. Consequently, the virus is taken into these cells where it reproduces, destroying the immune system cell in the process. Thus AIDS is a viral infection that deprives the body of its principal defense system.

Of all the new diseases to come onto the scene since human beings began to acquire an understanding of the molecular basis of life, AIDS affects the greatest number of people—more than 40 million worldwide by recent United Nations estimates. Because of this widespread and growing number, the human response to AIDS is very different from the response to a disease like syphilis in previous centuries. The National Institutes of Health and other organizations have spent enormous amounts of money trying to understand the HIV replication cycle, in the hope that by documenting how the virus works on the molecular level, we can find ways to block its progress. The protease (PRO-tee-ace) inhibitors discussed in the next section are a direct outcome of this line of attack on the disease.

HIV is a complex virus (Figure 24-7) that comes with two coats of proteins. An outer coating fits onto the receptors of T cells, and an inner coating contains strands of RNA along with a few different types of enzymes. When the virus is taken into a cell, one class of enzymes in the virus initiates a process called reverse transcription. The net effect is to turn the virus's RNA into a corresponding stretch of DNA. This stretch of DNA contains nine genes. A second set of enzymes then inserts those genes into the cell's DNA. At this point, the cell starts turning out proteins and stretches of RNA needed to make new viruses. A third set of enzymes is then capable of forming these raw materials into new viruses, and moving them out through the cell membrane. The fact that we understand

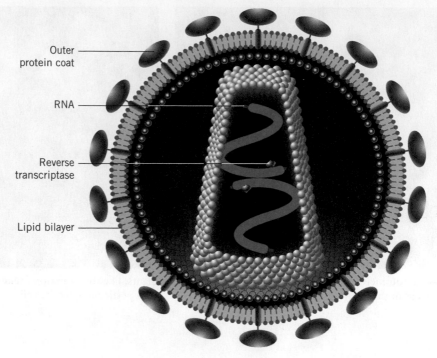

• **Figure 24-7** A diagram of the HIV virus. The reverse transcriptase is the enzyme in the virus that translates a strand of RNA into DNA .

Outer protein coat

RNA

Reverse transcriptase

Lipid bilayer

the life cycle of this virus and can explain it in this much detail is the result of an enormous amount of work done by scientists around the world to identify the virus and work out its properties.

What makes HIV so difficult to control is the fact that, like many viruses, its copying machinery is very sloppy. When DNA is replicated in the cell, constant proofreading and repair (as we have described) goes on to ensure that the correct type of DNA is being made. In the case of reverse transcription, however, no such proofreading mechanism is available. It is estimated, therefore, that the DNA made by this process differs from what is coded for in the viral RNA by about 1 base in 2000. In effect, every virus that comes out of the cell is slightly different from the one that went into it. This means that any treatment that depends on the fitting of a drug molecule onto the HIV will begin to lose its effectiveness as the virus continually mutates.

The most likely outcome for the battle against AIDS is that scientists will eventually manufacture several drugs that, when used in combination, are capable of blocking the life cycle of the virus at various points. This drug treatment may allow people who have the virus to live normal lives. In this case, we would say that the disease would be "managed," much like diabetes is managed, and it would no longer play the frightening role that it does today.

Computer-Assisted Drug Design

Every medicine is made of one or more molecules. When you take an aspirin or Tylenol, what you are doing is ingesting molecules that will play a particular role in your body. Some headache remedies, for example, alter your brain's chemistry to stop pain. Medicines work like any other molecules in living systems. Because of their shape and chemical characteristics, they are able to lock onto other specific molecules, thus altering your cellular chemistry.

Until very recently, the search for new medicines followed a standard course. Scientists in research laboratories (most commonly in pharmaceutical companies) would search in nature to find molecules that were useful against a specific condition. The search was hit or miss, and often scientists would develop drugs that they knew worked, but had no idea why they worked.

The new molecular understanding of living systems is changing all that. If we know the chemistry behind a certain condition, then we know the molecules that are involved and their shapes. It becomes possible to use that knowledge to design drugs "from scratch," rather than searching for them at random.

A simple analogy can be used to understand this new approach to pharmaceuticals. Think about a bottle. A bottle is designed to hold fluids, and does so by having a small open neck and a large holding area. You can stop the bottle from taking in fluids by placing a cork in the narrow opening. In this analogy, the cork plays the role of the medicine or drug, and the bottle the role of a molecule operating inside your cell. By finding a cork that fits a particular bottle, you can alter the functioning of that bottle. In the same way, by finding a "molecular cork" that fits a particular "molecular bottle" in the human body, you can alter the body's chemistry.

In terms of this analogy, the traditional search for drugs can be thought of as rummaging through a large pile of corks in hope of finding one that will fit a particular bottle. The rain forest, for example, with its enormous biological diversity, can be thought of as a very large pile of corks through which one can rummage to find the one cork that fits a particular bottle.

There is, however, another way of achieving the same objective. You can look at the bottle and measure its neck, then manufacture a cork that will fit it exactly. This new approach, which must rely heavily on the use of computers, is called *computer-assisted drug design (CADD)*. The idea of designing drugs to order is a fairly old one. In fact, the first such drug was put on the market in 1973. However, with the flood of new molecular knowledge, this field of technology is expanding rapidly.

The basic design strategy is very simple, and can be illustrated by talking about a molecule called a *protease inhibitor*, which was designed by several pharmaceutical companies to combat HIV. These drugs are the result of the long scientific study of the HIV virus.

At one stage in the life cycle of HIV, it inserts DNA produced from the virus's RNA into the DNA of the cell, at which point the cell starts manufacturing material for new viruses. Several proteins serve as enzymes for this insertion process, and some of these proteins have to be cut into pieces before they can play their role in making more viruses. A molecule known as a protease does this cutting. It is shaped something like a large convoluted donut. The proteins to be cut are pulled into the "hole" of the doughnut, where the actual cutting takes place. If they can't be pulled in they can't be cut, and if they can't be cut, the virus can't reproduce.

Starting with this understanding, scientists designed a molecule that would plug the hole, blocking access for the viral proteins. Protease inhibitors were one of the first sets of drugs designed with new computer visualization techniques. In 1996, these drugs got their first clinical trials and brought new hope that AIDS might not only be controlled, but perhaps even cured.

Whether or not the protease inhibitors succeed in this goal, they represent a technological milestone. More drugs like them will be designed in the future. In fact, it is not too much to expect that someday the main business of pharmaceutical companies will not be modifying molecules found in nature, but designing molecules to do specific jobs in the body, based on the knowledge of how those molecules work in the body.

A scientist examines a computer image of a molecule to evaluate its usefulness as a medicine. Quick procedures are common in computer aided drug design.

Science News | Losing Rhythm
(SCIENCE NEWS, JAN. 11, 2003, P. 21)

The term *atrial fibrillation* refers to a serious—sometimes fatal—heart condition in which the upper chambers of the heart (see Appendix A) beat irregularly and rapidly. The resulting disturbance in the flow of blood to the body can cause heart failure or blood clots, which are often implicated in strokes. Physicians know how to treat the condition if it is caught in time, but until recently little was known about its cause.

Now researchers in China have succeeded in locating a single gene that seems to be implicated in causing atrial fibrillation. Their study involved analyzing the DNA of four generations of a family in which the disease afflicted about a fourth of the individuals. They found that a single mistake on a single gene, located on chromosome 11, is responsible for the problem. This gene normally codes for a protein called KCNQ1, which is involved in forming the channels in nerve cells through which potassium and sodium ions move. The single defect in the gene changes one amino acid in the protein, and this, in turn, causes the ion channels in nerves around the heart to stay open longer than normal, affecting the heart's beating.

Although there are other causes of atrial fibrillation, such as infection or other heart disease, this finding will enable scientists to devise a test to screen for patients who might have a genetic predisposition to the disease.

 Stop and Think! Do you think computer-assisted drug design, when it becomes commonplace, will weaken arguments for preserving the rain forest based on potential new supplies of medicines?

Thinking More About | Drug Design

The Evolving Resistance to Antibiotics

About 100 different antibiotics are currently available commercially in the United States. These antibiotics block the life cycle of bacteria that invade the human body. The first of these antibiotics, penicillin (see Chapter 20), works by looking like a component of the bacterial cell wall. When incorporated into the bacterium, penicillin cannot be linked to the rest of the cell wall; hence the cell has a hole in that place. Eventually, the bacterium gets too "holey" and dies.

When penicillin was introduced during World War II, it was truly a "miracle drug." Until that time, anyone who was cut or wounded stood a great risk of bacterial infection. Once penicillin became available the situation changed. Not only wounded soldiers, but children with ear infections, old people with pneumonia, and many others began to benefit from the ability to introduce molecules into the body that would block the growth of bacteria.

While humanity may have won that particular battle against bacteria, the war is far from over. The reason is that in any bacterial population, there are bound to be a few bacteria that, for one reason or another, are not strongly affected by a particular antibiotic. For example, they may have a slightly differently shaped material that builds cell walls so that penicillin will not fit onto that particular shape. If so, then penicillin will not affect these bacteria. In fact, for that small group of resistant bacteria the introduction of the antibiotic is a real godsend. It doesn't affect them but it does wipe out much of their competition. They are thus free to multiply, and, over time, all of the bacteria will have whatever properties made those individuals resistant to the drug.

Traditionally, medical scientists have dealt with this phenomenon by developing a large number of antibiotics, each of which intervenes in the bacterial life cycle in a slightly different way. Consequently, if you happen to have a bacterium that is resistant to one antibiotic, it will probably succumb to the action of another. You may have had the experience of going to a doctor with an infection, being given an antibiotic, and then finding that it didn't work. In all likelihood, all your doctor had to do then was prescribe a different antibiotic and everything was fine.

The problem is that as time has passed more and more bacteria have become resistant to more and more antibiotics. In fact, as of this writing, there is one strain of bacteria, a common hospital *Staphylococcus*, that is resistant to every commercially available antibiotic except one, and in 1996 a bacterium with lowered resistance to that last antibiotic appeared in Japan.

The appearance of drug-resistant bacteria is not particularly surprising; in fact, it probably should have been anticipated. Nevertheless, in the late 1980s there was a general sense of complacency among scientists on the antibiotic question and a gap developed between the production of new antibiotics and the development of resistance among bacteria.

By the early 1990s, this gap was recognized and widely publicized in several national news magazines. More companies returned to the task of developing new kinds of antibiotics, and some of these new drugs are beginning to come on the market. For a time, at least, the problem may be "solved." What sort of policies do you think ought to be instituted to prevent another antibiotic gap opening up sometime in the twenty-first century?

SUMMARY

Our enhanced understanding of genetic mechanisms has led to new advances in *genetic engineering*, which involves the insertion of foreign genes into an organism, or the alteration of existing genes, to create modified life forms. A variety of genetically engineered plants for improved crops, animals for medical research, and single-celled organisms for drug production are now available. Our ability to manipulate genetic material has also been applied in *cloning*, by which genetically identical individuals can be produced, and *DNA fingerprinting*, which is used in many legal cases to establish the identity of individuals from their unique genetic makeup.

Much current research is being devoted to *genetic diseases*, which arise from one or more malfunctioning genes, and can cause sickness or death. Several thousand genetic diseases, some affecting tens of thousands of patients in the United States alone, are known. A promising future technology is *gene therapy*, which involves replacing a defective gene with a healthy one. More than 200 gene therapy trials are underway, though few of these have yet achieved positive results. Genetic research will continue to play a major role in medicine, especially in the study of *cancer*, which is the uncontrolled growth of cells in the body. Research will also focus on the processes by which cells repair the constant damage to DNA, the computer design of new drugs, the development of new antibiotics, and techniques to combat *acquired immune deficiency syndrome (AIDS)*, in which a virus (HIV) attacks cells of the body's immune system.

KEY TERMS ABOUT GENETICS

genetic engineering
DNA fingerprinting

cloning
genetic disease

gene therapy
cancer

acquired immune
deficiency syndrome (AIDS)

REVIEW QUESTIONS

1. What is genetic engineering?

2. What do restriction enzymes do? How are they used in genetic engineering?

3. Give an example of a genetically engineered product. Why is it appropriate to use the term "engineered" to describe it?

4. What is DNA fingerprinting and how does it work?

5. What is a genetic disease? Give an example.

6. What is gene therapy? Is it always successful?

7. How are viruses used in gene therapy?

8. What cell function appears to go awry in the case of cancer cells? How can this damage an individual?

9. What is a double-blind clinical trial? Why are such trials important in medical research?

10. How can computers be used to design drugs? What advantages would computer-designed drugs have over other drugs?

11. What is DNA repair, and where does it take place?

12. What is acquired immune deficiency syndrome? How is it transmitted?

13. Why do antibiotics, which kill bacteria, gradually lose their effectiveness? Why do we need new antibiotics?

DISCUSSION QUESTIONS

1. Suggest a possible product that might be genetically engineered. If available, would you use such a product?

2. In what ways is DNA fingerprinting like traditional fingerprinting? In what ways do they differ?

3. Why aren't all gene therapy trials successful?

4. What kinds of genetic damage can occur in cells to cause many cancers?

5. Why aren't stories of miracle cures by new drugs sufficient to bring these drugs quickly to market?

6. What difference would it make if the physicians knew which group in a clinical trial had treatment? What difference would it make if the patients knew?

7. What role does protease play in the reproduction of HIV? What does a protease inhibitor do? Do these new drugs cure AIDS?

8. Why do cells need a DNA repair mechanism? What kind of mistakes occur, what causes them, and how often do they occur?

9. Why is AIDS so difficult to cure? How does the AIDS virus attack the body?

10. How do mutations of HIV compare to the process by which bacteria acquire immunity to antibiotics, as was discussed in the text?

PROBLEMS

1. A pharmaceutical company claims that a new drug cuts in half the time an average patient suffers from a cold. Given a pool of 200 cold sufferers, describe a double-blind experiment that would test this claim.

2. A second company claims that two different drugs, working in combination, are even more effective than the single drug refered to in Problem 1. Given a pool of 200 cold sufferers, how would you test this claim in a double-blind clinical trial?

INVESTIGATIONS

1. Is DNA fingerprinting evidence used in your state or local courts? If so, investigate how such evidence has been used.

2. Find out if one of the more than 200 gene therapy trials is taking place near you (the National Institutes of Health in Bethesda, Maryland, maintains a list of such research projects). What disease is being treated, and what are the results so far?

3. Read Michael Crichton's novel *Jurassic Park*, which describes genetic engineering experiments. Is the scenario realistic? What precautions should the scientists have taken?

4. Look over the newspapers for the last few months and find an announcement that scientists have discovered the gene behind a particular disease or condition. How does that discovery fit in with the material in this chapter?

5. From time to time a new AIDS drug will receive publicity because of reportedly miraculous results. Should such a drug be made available immediately to AIDS sufferers? Why or why not?

6. Read the prize-winning novel *Arrowsmith* by Sinclair Lewis. How does the novel's hero, Martin Arrowsmith, test his new plague vaccine? Was this a double-blind procedure? What goes wrong with the experiment?

7. Identify a pharmaceutical company that uses computers to design drugs. Investigate one of their recent projects. Obtain promotional literature and clinical trial reports to learn how the drug is used and how it was designed.

WWW RESOURCES

See *The Sciences* homepage at: **http://www.wiley.com/college/trefil** for valuable web links.

1. http://biotech.icmb.utexas.edu/
Biotech, from Indiana University, a comprehensive site dedicated to enriching the public's understanding of biology and chemistry.

2. http://www.accessexcellence.org/AB/IE
Issues, examines issues connected to advances in biotechnology.

3. http://www.alife.org/index.php
Artificial Life, from the Santa Fe Institute.

25

Evolution

How did life arise?

GREAT IDEA

All life on Earth evolved from single-celled organisms by the process of natural selection.

PHYSICS

Radiation from the Sun or internal heat from the Earth may have provided the energy for synthesizing early life.

CHEMISTRY

Miller and Urey synthesized amino acids by subjecting a mixture of water and simple gases to electric sparks.

ENVIRONMENT

The impact of a giant asteroid with Earth may cause drastic changes in the global environment and trigger mass extinctions.

GEOLOGY

Fossils chronicle the history of life on Earth.

HEALTH & SAFETY

The appendix is a vestigial organ in humans; it can be removed without adverse effects.

ASTRONOMY

A meterorite that may have originated from Mars is thought by some scientists to carry fossils of minute bacteria-like organisms.

TECHNOLOGY

The first humans to use technology of fire lived about 500,000 years ago.

BIOLOGY

Life evolves by the competitive process of natural selection.

Red = applications of the great idea discussed in this chapter.

Orange = other applications, some of which are explored in other chapters.

A wonderful day is almost over. You close your eyes and relive some of the sensations; the sights, the sounds, the smells. But one aspect of the day stands out—how amazingly rich with life our planet is. The green fields and forests that lined the road, the birds and insects (and people) along the shore, the tidal pools crowded with strange, colorful creatures; everywhere you look life abounds.

How could such an incredible array of living things have developed on a once-lifeless planet? How could living things on our planet include such extraordinary variety, from seaweed to a whale? The answer to these questions requires us to think not only about what life is, but also how it got to be the way it is.

The Fact of Evolution

The Earth started out as a hot, lifeless ball of molten rock (see Chapter 16). The first rocks were formed when the planet cooled, but even then the Earth looked nothing like it does today. Water filled the ocean basins, but no fish swam in it and no algae floated on it. All of the countless millions of different life forms that would someday develop were absent in this early stage.

The transition from a lifeless planet to one that teems with living things came in two stages. The first stage involved the appearance of the first living cell from the lifeless chemical compounds—rock, water, and gases—that existed in the early Earth, and was governed by the laws of chemistry and physics that we have studied. The second stage was the multiplication, diversification, and evolution of that first living cell into the astonishing variety of life that we observe on Earth now. This ongoing process of change is called **evolution**.

Today, *virtually all scientists accept evolution as a historical fact*. Evolution—the concept that life has changed over vast spans of geological time—is an observational phenomenon that is as well established as the fact that the Earth goes around the Sun or that a ball falls when you drop it.

As we shall see later in this chapter, this acceptance of evolution as a fact does not mean that there aren't debates about different *theories* of evolution. For example, scientists debate how fast evolution proceeds and by what mechanisms. But differences in opinion about these details should not be confused with the unambiguous observational *fact* that life has evolved on Earth for billions of years. A tremendous body of scientific literature is devoted to this subject, and we will discuss here only three of the most important pieces of evidence for the process of evolution: the fossil record, the evidence of biochemical similarity, and the occurrence of vestigial organs.

The Fossil Record

The most dramatic and compelling evidence for life's changes over geological time comes from **fossils**, the tangible evidence of past life. When a plant or animal dies, the remains are usually lost. A tree will rot, the carcass of an animal will be torn apart by scavengers and dispersed, a crab shell will be broken up by the action of the surf. Occasionally, however, an organism is removed quickly from the environment, typically by being buried in sediments and sealed off. The hard parts of such an organism may remain underground for a long period of time.

As time goes by, two things may happen. First of all, the material around the organism may go through the rock cycle, as described in Chapter 17, and be turned into rock. Second, minerals in the water flowing through the surrounding area may gradually replace the calcium and other atoms in the buried hard parts, thus creating a fossil. We often think of fossils as the large dinosaur skeletons in a museum, but the term is also used to refer to other kinds of records of past life, such as a leaf imprint on mud that changes into rock, or an insect preserved in amber.

The term *fossil record* refers to all of the fossils that have been found, catalogued, and analyzed since human beings first began to study them in a systematic way in the early part of the nineteenth century. The fossil record reveals how different organisms came to be what they are. The fossil record of horses, for example, includes a series of precursor animals beginning with one about the size of a cat some 50 million years ago, and changing through many intermediate forms up to modern times. Throughout this sequence of fossil mammals is a gradual transition from a small, quick animal to a large, grazing one.

The fossil record also contains some examples of actual changes in species. In order to do this, the fossil record has to be very complete, with many thousands of years of continuous sediments. Such continuity is rare, but in some instances the transitions from one species to another can be documented.

Even so, the major problem with the fossil record is that it is very incomplete. It is estimated that only one species (*not* one individual) out of every 10,000 early life forms is represented in the fossil record. Thus, in interpreting the past, we must always be aware that we are dealing with a very small and select sample of what was actually there. This sample is strongly biased toward organisms that were more likely to have been buried soon after death. Thus, we have a much better record of mollusks and clams, which had hard shells and lived in sediments on the continental shelf, than we do of insects that flew around primeval forests. Nevertheless, the fossil record was the first (and for a long time, the only) evidence that backed up the notion that life is constantly changing and evolving.

A wide variety of fossils are found in rocks from every continent. (*a*) A fossil trilobite, an arthropod from 500 million years ago. (*b*) The fossil bird Archaeopteryx from 150 million years ago. (*c*) A fossil relative of the scorpion preserved in amber (hardened tree sap).

(a) (b) (c)

Stop and Think! From the preceding discussion, it is clear that animals with skeletons and shells will be fossilized more easily than those with soft bodies. What animals alive today are likely to be found as fossils a million years from now? Would future paleontologists get an accurate view of present-day life by examining those fossils?

Three key ideas quickly emerged from studies of fossils. First, the older the rocks, the more their animal and plant fossils differ from modern forms. Mammals in 5-million-year-old rocks are not terribly different from today's fauna, but few species that existed 50 million years ago would be recognizable today, and dinosaurs rather than mammals were dominant 150 million years ago. Similar patterns occur in shells, plants, fish, and all other forms. Often the earlier forms appear to combine characteristics of later organisms. Ancient insects preserved in amber, for example, show some forms that may be intermediate between ants and wasps. Early mammals, similarly, have general mammalian characteristics, but few of the specialized structures that have evolved in bats, whales, tigers, and rabbits.

Fossils also display general trends in overall complexity of form. All known fossils from before about 570 million years ago are either single-celled organisms or simple invertebrates such as jellyfish. Marine invertebrates with hard parts—mollusks, coral, and crustacea, for example—dominate the record for the next 200 million years or so. Simple land animals and plants appear next, followed by flowering plants and a much greater variety of large land animals. This long-term trend toward increasing complexity of organization is consistent with all theories of evolution.

Finally, the fossil record proves beyond a doubt that most species that have lived on Earth have died out and are now **extinct**. Scientists estimate that for every species on the planet today, as many as 999 species have become extinct at some time in the past. In fact, the average lifetime of a species in the fossil record seems to be a few million years. Species, like individuals, are born, live out their life, and die. This fact alone is ample evidence that some natural mechanism must exist to produce new species as the old disappear.

The Biochemical Evidence

We all carry within us evidence for the fact of evolution—a molecular record of our descent from the first primeval cell. The DNA of each living organism represents the sum of all the changes in the DNA that connect that organism back to the DNA in the first forms of life. If we can learn how to "read" the DNA in living organisms then we should be able to deduce some things about the way those organisms developed.

According to the standard picture of evolution, for example, human beings and the great apes had a common ancestor about 8 million years ago. Much farther back in time, about 250 million years ago, human beings and reptiles shared a common ancestor. DNA changes slowly under the influence of mutation and natural selection. The fact that we've had only 8 million years for human DNA and ape DNA to differentiate, compared to 250 million years during which human DNA differentiated from the reptiles, suggests that there ought to be more similarities between human and primate DNA than there are between DNA of humans and reptiles.

DNA strands from two different organisms cannot always be compared directly, but from Chapter 23 we know that the proteins in cells are related to DNA in much the same way as a negative is to a photograph. You can get the same kind of information by comparing sequences of amino acids along proteins as you can by comparing base pairs along the DNA molecule. In a protein called cytochrome C that every living cell uses in its energy metabolism, for example, the difference between humans and chimpanzees (our closest relative) is nonexistent. The cytochrome C molecules from the chimpanzee and human are exactly the same. As you move farther and farther away from human beings in the main classification scheme (see Chapter 20), the differences become greater. In a rattlesnake, for example, there is an 86% overlap in the molecules, whereas in common brewer's yeast only 58% of the molecules are the same. The fact that our DNA is very similar to those organisms with which we shared the most recent ancestors has been cited as one of the most important pieces of evidence for evolution. If, for example, each plant and animal were created separately and specially, there would be no reason at all to see this kind of progression.

Evidence from Anatomy: Vestigial Organs

Physical structures within our own bodies provide more compelling evidence for the fact of evolution. We have a number of internal features that serve no useful function whatsoever—**vestigial organs** that are reminders of our mammalian ancestors. Organs that are well adapted to their environment, surprisingly, *do not* provide unambiguous evidence for evolution. The perfection of the human eye, for example, was often claimed in the nineteenth century as proof of God's special creation of human beings. The evidence for evolution comes instead from considering organs that have no use or are even harmful to the organism in which they are found.

Consider the human appendix, a thin, closed tube connected to the upper part of the large intestine. This three-inch-long organ has no proven function in modern humans, and it actually poses a threat to every one of us. Before the invention of surgery, inflammations of the appendix were often fatal. The pressures of natural selection would never lead to the development of a harmful organ in a human being, yet the appendix sits there at the end of everyone's intestines. Unless the appendix has some as-yet-undiscovered function, it is hard to understand how this organ could come to be.

Vestigial organs such as the appendix can be explained by recognizing that they once had a function that they no longer have, and are in the process of disappearing.

The wings of a penguin are vestigial characteristics, because they can no longer be used to fly.

In a sense, modern human beings are a snapshot in a continuous process in which the appendix perhaps once served as an important part of the digestive system, but is no longer needed.

Numerous examples of vestigial characteristics have been identified, and they provide important evidence against the argument that every organ in every creature is part of a grand design. Penguins have vestigial wings now used to swim, some whales have tiny internal vestigial hind legs, and humans have vestigial tailbones and vestigial muscles to wag them. A striking example of vestigial organs is found in species of cave-dwelling worms that have no need of eyes, but have eye sockets *under their skin*.

Chemical Evolution

Chemical evolution, the first step in life's long history, is the process by which rocks, water, and gases combined to become the first living cell. The central question of chemical evolution is how one can start with the simple chemical compounds that were present in the early Earth and wind up with an organized, reproducing cell. This area of research is relatively new and immensely challenging; few clear answers have yet emerged. Perhaps the most important experiment relating to chemical evolution was performed in 1953 by Stanley Miller (b. 1930) and Harold Urey (1893–1981) at the University of Chicago. The novel apparatus of the **Miller-Urey experiment** is sketched in Figure 25-1.

Miller and Urey argued that the Earth's early atmosphere contained simple compounds composed principally of hydrogen, carbon, oxygen, and nitrogen—compounds including water vapor (H_2O), methane (CH_4), hydrogen (H_2), and ammonia (NH_3). Miller and Urey mixed these materials together in a large flask that was half-filled with water. Then, realizing that powerful lightning would have laced the turbulent atmosphere of the early Earth, they caused electrical sparks to

Figure 25-1 The Miller-Urey experiment. Several of the chemical compounds thought to have been present on the early Earth were mixed and subjected to electrical discharges. Within a few weeks, amino acids had formed.

jump between electrodes in the flask. After a couple of weeks, they noticed that the liquid in the flask became cloudy and started to turn a dark-brown color. Analysis revealed that this brownish liquid contained a large number of amino acids, one of the basic building blocks of life (see Chapter 21).

Thus, as early as the 1950s, experiments had shown scientists that natural processes in the oceans of the early Earth might generate the modules of at least one of life's important molecules, proteins. Since that time, it has been found that energy sources such as ultraviolet radiation (from the Sun) and heat (for example, from volcanoes) will also produce amino acids. In subsequent experiments at the University of Chicago and other laboratories scientists have used modified Miller-Urey devices to make other organic molecules, including lipids and bases, as well as complex substances such as long protein chains.

Some scientists suggest that this scenario has important implications for the early Earth. For perhaps several hundred million years, the hypothesis goes, the amino acids and other molecules created by the Miller-Urey process were concentrated in the ocean, producing a rich broth, sometimes called the *primordial soup*. Additional amino acids may have been added to this chemical mixture in the early oceans by other sources, such as meteorites and comets, which are known to carry carbon-based molecules. However the process happened, it seems clear that the enrichment of organic chemicals in the Earth's early oceans required nothing beyond normal chemistry. This small piece of the chemical evolution puzzle seems to be pretty well understood.

Our greatest gap in the evolutionary story comes next. Could the countless molecules floating in random patterns in the ocean have organized themselves into a functioning, reproducing cell? While mechanisms such as condensation polymerization (see Chapter 10) can join simple organic molecules together, sunlight tends to break these bonds apart.

We simply do not know how the first cell formed. However, a number of very interesting ideas may help close this significant gap in our knowledge. We know, for example, that molecules more than 10 meters or so deep in the primeval ocean would have been shielded from the Sun's ultraviolet radiation. In this environment polymers and other complex molecules might have grown and diversified. If the concentration of organic molecules was high enough then the sunlight breaking up these molecules would not have been able to overcome their formation rate, and the concentrations might have increased even more.

For example, some scientists have proposed that the first cell may have evolved in a tidal pool. If it turns out that something like a protected tidal pool is necessary for the development of life, then life may be a relatively rare thing in the universe. Our present understanding is that the formation of a terrestrial planet together with a large moon (and, thus, the generation of significant tides) is an unlikely event.

 Stop and Think! Many science fiction stories revolve around the ability of humans to synthesize life. Did Miller and Urey synthesize life? Do you think scientists will ever be able to synthesize living cells beginning with organic molecules?

A major weakness of chemical evolution theories is that they do not tell us about how organic molecules could become isolated from the environment and organized into the larger structures essential for life. How could a cell membrane form, for example? Early optimism that research on the primordial soup would lead quickly to an understanding of life's origins has faded and scientists now understand that major questions remain. On the other hand, this work has shown

A colony of living things three miles down at the midocean vent in the Atlantic.

clearly that the basic building blocks of life were available very early in the history of the Earth, perhaps within a few million years after the first oceans formed. This growing understanding has led to alternative hypotheses regarding life's origins.

Black Smokers

In 1979, biologists diving to the deep-ocean floor in the submersible *Alvin* discovered an unexpected diverse ecosystem surrounding vents of mineral-rich hot water, called *black smokers,* near midocean volcanoes (see Chapter 19). The remarkable bacteria that thrive in these extreme environments obtain their energy from the Earth's internal heat, rather than the Sun. These bacteria, among the most primitive life forms known, may be closer on the evolutionary tree to the first living cell than any organisms living at the Earth's surface. This discovery has led many scientists to wonder if deep, dark, hydrothermal zones on the ocean floor might have been the site of life's origin.

Some researchers now speculate that warm, gas-rich water circulating through cracks and fissures near midocean volcanic ridges provided an ideal protected environment for the origin of life. The surface of the early Earth was repeatedly bombarded by large meteorites, was constantly bathed in harmful ultraviolet radiation, and was continuously blasted by intense lightning. Deep-ocean environments were protected from these environmental insults.

Black smokers also provide an ideal chemical environment for organic synthesis, because water at high temperature and pressure has physical properties very different from those that are familiar to us. For one thing, water at these extreme conditions is much less polar and thus may facilitate the synthesis of amino acids, lipids, and other key biological molecules, while promoting their assembly into larger structures by polymerization reactions. One of the authors (RMH) is now engaged in experiments to understand how organic chemical reactions proceed—and how life may have originated—in hot, pressurized water.

RNA Enzymes

Today's cells run most of their chemistry by using protein enzymes, which, in turn, are coded for in DNA. On the other hand, in order to turn the DNA into a "working" protein, other enzymes are necessary. This cycle gets us into a kind of chicken-and-egg controversy. You need DNA to make the proteins, but you need the proteins to make the DNA. How could the first living cell have solved this dilemma?

Scientists have attempted to resolve this problem with a number of intriguing solutions, all of which share one assumption: that the very earliest life forms had a rather different (and much simpler) chemistry than the ones we see around us today. The problem facing scientists is something like trying to reconstruct the Wright Brothers' first airplane by examining a modern jetliner. Many of the original design features have been replaced by more efficient components. Similarly, the first cell's chemical mechanisms, being rather inefficient, may have been largely replaced when the DNA-RNA—protein system evolved later. Thus we do not see these chemical mechanisms in living systems today, but perhaps we can deduce their properties from studies of biochemistry.

One particularly interesting observation is that some kinds of RNA molecules have been found to act as enzymes for chemical reactions, in addition to their usual role as nucleic acids. This behavior suggests one way that the present system of cell chemistry could have evolved. RNA molecules catalyzed reactions that created proteins, and, over time, the proteins necessary for the development of the more complex (and presumably more efficient) DNA coding system were developed. Alternatively, other scientists have suggested that some kind of clay or other inorganic mineral may have provided sites for chemical reactions, as well as catalytic properties to help those reactions along.

Speculative ideas about black smokers and RNA enzymes are not necessarily exclusive. It may well be that the best place for chemistry involving RNA as an enzyme to occur is a deep-ocean fissure. What is certain is that life's chemical evolution will remain an exciting challenge for scientists.

The Window of Opportunity

Whatever the chemical processes were that led to the first organism capable of reproducing itself, we know that those processes had to take place rapidly. We know that the Earth, like all the other planets, went through the period of the great bombardment (see Chapter 16). During this period, large chunks of debris fell onto the planets from space, bringing enormous amounts of energy with them. An impact involving an asteroid several hundred miles across would heat the Earth enough to boil the oceans—the planet would literally be sterilized by such an impact. Any life that might have developed would be wiped out. There-fore, the process that led to the ancestors of all present life on Earth could not have begun until after the last big impact. The best estimate for this date is about 4 billion years ago.

On the other hand, recent discoveries have convinced some paleontologists that by at least 3.5 billion years ago life was not only present on Earth, but flour-ishing. In 1996, William Schopf of UCLA and his coworkers reported evidence for colonies of primitive bacteria in rocks that were laid down as sediment in a shallow bay in what is now Australia. When he takes thin slices of these old rocks and looks at them under a microscope (see Chapter 21), he sees the imprints that in size and shape resemble single-celled organisms (see Figure 25-2).

Although Schopf's original claims have been called into question, new evi-dence on distinctive carbon-based molecules extracted from Australian rocks of similar age support the idea that life was thriving at this ancient time. It would have taken quite a while for life to develop from the first cell to this microbial ecosystem, which means that the first cell must have appeared soon after the last big impact during the great bombardment.

The first cell had to develop during a well-defined window of opportunity. One side of the window is fixed by the time of the last big impact, the other by the appearance of fossils. Our present best estimates are that this window extended roughly from 4.0 to 3.5 billion years ago, and the origin of life may well have occurred early in that interval.

Figure 25-2 Some pale-ontologists argue that objects like this are clusters of bacteria that lived about 3.5 billion years ago—the earliest evidence of life on Earth. These bacteria may have been part of a complex ecosystem, so the earliest life must have appeared considerably before this time.

The First Cell

Think about the unique status of the very first cell on Earth. It need not have been particularly efficient in using the chemicals found in its environment—after all, it had no competition. There were no predators, and no other life forms to compete for the abundant stock of organic molecules that enriched the early ocean. Once the first cell formed, it may have multiplied rapidly.

Biologists have suggested that the special characteristics of the first cell may explain one of the great mysteries of modern biochemistry, the fact that living things today contain only 20 different kinds of amino acids (see Chapter 21). The notion is that, perhaps by chance or perhaps because this particular combination gave them a competitive edge, some early cells contained only these amino acids and it was the descendants of these cells that managed to dominate the Earth. In this way of thinking, the combination of these 20 amino acids is something of a "frozen accident," one of perhaps many chance events in the formation of life on Earth. Like so many other questions about the origin of life, this one will remain unanswered until we know more about the subject than we do now.

SCIENCE BY THE NUMBERS •

Cell Division

The first cell was a microscopic organism, but it may not have taken long for that first bit of life to spread great distances around the globe. To get a feel for this process, imagine how long it would take to fill up the Mediterranean Sea starting with a single microscopic cell that divides once a day, assuming all cells survive and continue to divide.

To get an answer, we must estimate the volume of an ordinary bacterium and compare it with the volume of the Mediterranean Sea. In Chapter 22 we learned that a typical bacterium is about a thousandth of a centimeter across, so its volume is approximately

$$(1/1000 \text{ cm})^3 = 10^{-9} \text{ cubic cm}$$

A recent world atlas gives the surface area of the Mediterranean Sea as about 2.5 million square kilometers, with an average depth of 1.4 kilometers, for a total volume of

$$2,500,000 \text{ km}^2 \times 1.4 \text{ km} = 3,500,000 \text{ km}^3 = 3.5 \times 10^6 \text{ km}^3$$

The question thus boils down to how many times you would have to double a 10^{-9} cm³ bacterium to fill 3.5×10^6 km³. To make things easier, we convert cubic kilometers to cubic centimeters:

$$1 \text{ km} = 10^5 \text{ cm}$$

so

$$1 \text{ km}^3 = 10^{15} \text{ cm}^3$$

The total volume of the Mediterranean in cubic centimeters is

$$3.5 \times 10^6 \text{ km}^3 \times 10^{15} \text{ cm}^3/\text{km}^3 = 3.5 \times 10^{21} \text{ cm}^3$$

How many bacteria would it take to fill this volume? We divide the immense volume of the Mediterranean Sea by the tiny volume of a single bacterium:

$$3.5 \times 10^{21} \text{ cm}^3/10^{-9} \text{ cm}^3 = 3.5 \times 10^{30} \text{ bacteria}$$

Starting with a single bacterium on the first day, there would be two on the second day, four on the third, eight on the fourth, and so on. After about three weeks there would be more than a million bacteria, taking up only about a thousandth of a cubic centimeter.

Day by day, however, the number would increase geometrically. After two months there would be more than 10^{18} bacteria; after three months 10^{27} individuals, occupying more than 10,000 cubic kilometers. And in just 10 days more—only 100 days after the first cell began to divide—the Mediterranean Sea would be completely filled with bacteria (Figure 25-3).

Naturally, no body of water could be "completely filled" with bacteria. In addition, early life probably did not spread this fast, nor was the process so regular

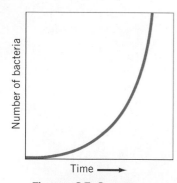

Figure 25-3 The number of bacteria grows rapidly, in what scientists call an exponential curve. In a matter of months, a single cell whose descendants divide once a day could easily populate a large ocean.

and predictable. But the implication is clear. While it may have taken hundreds of millions of years for the first cell to evolve, a large number of descendants of that first cell could have spread throughout the world's oceans relatively quickly. •

THE ONGOING PROCESS OF SCIENCE •

Did Life Also Originate on Mars?

The development of life on Earth would not have been possible without the presence of liquid water on the planet's surface. As we saw in Chapter 16, there was probably liquid water on the surface of Mars during its early history. In fact, some astronomers argue that the entire northern hemisphere of the planet was covered by an ocean and that the wet period of Martian history may have lasted for as much as a billion years. After this period the planet lost most of its atmosphere and hydrosphere to space and became the barren world it is today.

This scenario raises an interesting possibility. Since life on Earth seems to have developed rapidly once the great bombardment came to a halt, could the same thing have happened on Mars? Could life have evolved in those Martian oceans, only to perish when the oceans disappeared? If so, there should be fossil evidence to mark its existence.

In 1996 a team of scientists suggested that they had found such evidence in a meteorite that was blasted off the surface of Mars millions of years ago. The meteorite, labeled ALH84001 (because it was the first meteorite collected in 1984 from the Allen Hills region of Antarctica), contains tiny gas bubbles whose chemical composition matches that of the Martian atmosphere. The idea is that millions of years ago a large meteorite on our sister planet blew this rock fragment into space from which, after millions of years of wandering in the void, it fell to Earth. It is one of about 20 meteorites thought to come from Mars.

In a lively press conference and subsequent *Science* article in August 1996, scientists from the National Aeronautics and Space Administration (NASA) and

This 4.5-billion-year-old rock, labeled meteorite ALH84001, is believed to have once been a part of Mars and to contain fossil evidence that primitive life may have existed on Mars more than 3.6 billion years ago. The rock is a portion of a meteorite that was dislodged from Mars by a huge impact about 16 million years ago and that fell to Earth in Antarctica 13,000 years ago.

other laboratories presented several lines of evidence that might point to past life. They observed complex organic molecules laced through the meteorite, magnetic mineral grains typical of those deposited by Earth bacteria, isotopic compositions characteristic of living things, and tiny structures reminiscent of bacteria. Any one of these features, by itself, would be little cause for excitement. Carbon-rich molecules, for example, are well known in meteorites and comets, as are magnetic grains of iron minerals. But some NASA scientists argue that these observations, taken together, "are evidence for primitive life on early Mars."

Over time, other scientists produced evidence that called these initial claims into question and they are now generally discounted. The "fossils," for example, turned out to be layered mineral deposits viewed end on. Nevertheless, the excitement generated by the possibility that Martian life had already been discovered led NASA to initiate a program in *astrobiology*—the search for the origin and distribution of life in the universe. Thanks to the support of NASA's new Astrobiology Institute, hundreds of scientists are studying processes that may have led to life on Earth, Mars, and other worlds. •

 Stop and Think! Think about the possibility that life exists on planets orbiting the billions of stars in each of the billions of galaxies. Would such an abundance of life affect your view of life on Earth? Should we spend more tax dollars to search for extraterrestrial life?

Natural Selection and the Development of Complex Life

Once we get beyond the time when the first cell formed, our understanding of how life developed becomes much more detailed and precise. This understanding is due in large measure to the work of one man, Charles Darwin (1809–1882). His *Origin of Species,* published in 1859, is arguably one of the most influential books ever written. In it he sets forward a view of the development of living things that, since his time, has been expanded and developed to the point where it is fair to say that it is the single theory that unifies all of biology. A biochemist working on the transport of particular molecules across the cell membrane and a zoologist working on the ecology of a tropical lake will both share the central ideas of Darwin's theory, and hence will have a common vocabulary and a common way of attacking problems. Darwin's theory was influential and controversial because it identified a simple mechanism for evolving complex multicellular life forms from single-celled life. His entire theory is built around one central concept—natural selection.

Natural Selection

The easiest way to understand what Darwin meant by natural selection is to think first about the process that he called *artificial selection.* Farmers have known for millennia that the way to get bigger fruit, healthier plants, or animals with more meat on them is to carry out a conscious process of breeding. (Think back to Mendel's experiments discussed in Chapter 23.) If you want large potatoes, you should plant the eyes from only the largest potatoes in any given crop. Over long periods of time, this practice will give you a variety of potatoes that is significantly different from the one you started with. Because human choice, not nature, drives this process, it is given the name of artificial selection. It explains how you can get animals as different from each other as longhorn and Angus cattle, or Chihuahuas and Great Danes, from the same ancestral stock.

(a)

(b)

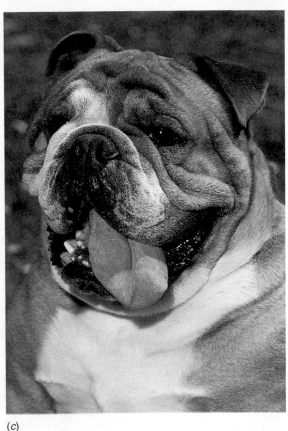

(c)

Contrasting breeds of dogs, including (*a*) Collie, (*b*) Chihuahua, and (*c*) Bulldog, illustrate the changes possible with artificial selection.

If human beings can introduce such wide-ranging changes in living things, Darwin reasoned, then nature should be able to do the same. The mechanism he proposed, which he called **natural selection**, depends on two basic facts for its operation:

1. *Every population contains genetic diversity.* The individual members of any population possess a range of characteristics. Some are able to run a little faster than others, some have a slightly different color than others, and so forth.

2. *Many more individuals are born than can possibly survive.* Therefore, those characteristics that make it more probable that a given member of the population will live long enough to reproduce will tend to be passed on to a greater percentage of the population's subsequent generations.

Think about a hypothetical example to see how natural selection works. Suppose an island supports a certain number of birds, and suppose that the environment of this island is such that having a color that blends in with the local vegetation makes it easier for those birds to avoid their predators. Just by chance, some members of the bird population will have colors that match the colors of local leaves and trees better than others. As we saw in Chapter 23, the cells' DNA would determine this property in those particular birds.

Better-camouflaged birds will be less likely to be eaten by predators, and, therefore, will be more likely to survive to adulthood and mate. You would expect, then, that the particular genes that give this advantage will be more likely to be passed to the next generation. In effect, natural forces influence the genes that are propagated in the next generation. In this case, the selection is based on the color of the feathers.

(a)

(b)

(c)

Figure 25-4 Light and dark versions of the peppered moth. The population shifted toward dark colors when coal burning became widespread in central England, then started to shift back when environmental controls were instituted.

If this process goes on for a long period of time, the entire population would eventually begin to share those advantageous genes for feather color. Natural selection works this way to modify a gene pool, just as populations of farm animals now share genes for rapid growth and meat production. Nature "selects" those characteristics that will be propagated in any given species. A structure, process, or behavior that helps an organism survive and pass on its genes is called an **adaptation**.

Natural selection, it should be remembered, is neither as controlled nor as rapid as artificial selection. It's always possible that birds that do not carry the selected gene will, in some generations, be more successful at mating than those who do. Over the long haul, however, the selective advantage granted by color will win. Thus Darwin envisioned natural selection as a process that operates over long time periods to produce gradual changes in populations, not a process that can explain short-term variations in a few individual traits. It's important to understand that natural selection relates to changes in populations over time. Each individual in that population retains the DNA it was born with, and does not change in response to environmental stresses.

About the time that Darwin's book came out a rather extraordinary example of the power of natural selection appeared in his native England. The Midlands area of England in the nineteenth century had become a vast industrial belt. Factories poured smoke into the air (this was before the time of environmental awareness) and covered much of the countryside with dark soot. The peppered moth, a small moth living in this region at the time, featured black-and-white wing patterns that blended in well with the light-colored lichen that had grown on trees in this area for centuries. At the time lighter individuals predominated, though an occasional dark one was seen. Light coloration gave the moth protection from predators in an environment that did not include soot, but the common lighter moths stood out clearly on trees darkened by industrial activity. Over a period of less than a century, the selective pressure on the moth population shifted in favor of darker individuals (Figure 25-4). By the turn of the century, most of the peppered moths to be found were almost black. Scientists point to this rapid shift in moth coloration as a modern example of natural selection in operation.

We should add that, since environmental controls have been adopted in England, soot emissions from Midlands factories have been cut significantly. As Darwin would have predicted, the peppered-moth population has started to lighten again, as the original mossy tree trunks become more common.

SCIENCE IN THE MAKING •

The Reception of Darwin's Theory

Charles Darwin formulated the basic outline of his theory of natural selection in 1838, but he waited more than 20 years to publish his findings. This delay was not simple procrastination. He realized that the central precepts of his theory would cause a furor. Eventually, learning that another British naturalist, Alfred Russell Wallace, had developed similar ideas, Darwin hastened to get his *Origin of Species* into print.

Written in accessible prose and published in a widely available edition, his theory evoked intense reactions. Some theologians denounced the book for its denial of a miraculous creation and relatively short Earth history, which they claimed were demanded by a literal reading of the Bible.

Equally disturbing to Darwin was the reaction of many readers who embraced the "theory of evolution" as scientific evidence for God's hand in the progress of nature and thus proof of man's moral and spiritual superiority. They seized Darwin's discovery as an example of God's wisdom and beneficence. Some intellectuals of the late nineteenth century even went so far as to cite Darwin in their defense of an economically and socially stratified society—the most "fit" individuals rose to the top of society, they claimed.

Ironically, Darwin never intended his theory to suggest the idea of inevitable "progress" in nature—only inevitable change. Indeed, Darwin never even used the word "evolution"—a word that connotes improvement—in his book, nor did he address the question of human origins in *Origin of Species*. Far from being guided by a divine hand, he saw natural processes as violent and amoral—a constant struggle for survival in which the ability to reproduce fertile offspring was the only measure of success. He observed successful natural strategies that his contemporaries would have viewed as repulsive in any moral sense—species whose females devour their mates, species whose offspring eat each other until just a few survive, and parasites and predators that kill without thought in the frantic quest for energy to survive. To Darwin, human ascendancy seemed an evolutionary accident rather than a divine plan,

The "progression" from chimpanzee to human is often used as an icon of Darwinian evolution. Darwin, however, did not see natural selection as leading inevitably from lower forms to humans.

and he saw no sign of God in the brutal process of natural selection. Nevertheless, in his own concluding words:

> *There is grandeur in this view of life, with its several powers, having been originally breathed by the Creator into a few forms or into one; and that, whilst this planet has gone cycling on according to the fixed law of gravity, from so simple a beginning endless forms most beautiful and most wonderful have been, and are being, evolved.* •

The Story of Life

As soon as the first cell split into two competing individuals, natural selection began to operate. In that early environment, where the first cells were surrounded by energy-rich molecules and very few neighbors, competition would not have been very intense. Before long, however, genetic mutations would have started to occur and some cells would have been different from others. Some of those differences involved the efficiency with which cells were able to utilize the molecules that they found in their environment. Certain cells, for example, might have been able to get energy more quickly from those molecules (and therefore reproduce faster) than others. Over time, the beneficial mutations would come to be shared throughout the entire population by the process of natural selection.

At this early stage, just as in today's life forms, the vast majority of mutations and the resultant differences were not beneficial. Random changes in DNA, after all, are not likely to produce organisms that can interact with their environment more efficiently than their fellows. Nonbeneficial mutations died out quickly, and only beneficial mutations remained. This process is a little like our view of movies from the 1930s and 1940s. A great many poor films were made in those days, but we don't see them anymore. What we remember and preserve are the most successful films, such as *Citizen Kane* and *Casablanca*. In the same way, only the "greatest hits" of all the mutations survived into the future.

Over time, you would expect the descendants of that first cell to spread around the Earth and occupy most of the oceans. Some scholars have suggested that this spread may have taken as little as a few years, given the lack of competition for the environmental resources. (The results we calculated in the "Science by the Numbers" section of this chapter suggest that such a scenario might be reasonable.) In this process of spreading, some cells would wind up in different environments than others. Some, for example, would be in tropical waters, while others would be in the Arctic. Some would be in deep oceans, while others would be next to the shore. Each of these environments would exert slightly different pressures on the cells. An adaptation that might be very advantageous in the tropics, for example, might not be advantageous near the poles, and vice versa. The driving force of natural selection, coupled with the fact that many different environments existed on our planet, would quickly have produced a number of very different living things. Thus we would expect the appearance of diversity— the process of speciation—to have begun quite early in the history of life.

Our knowledge of this early period of life is limited by the fact that we have very little in the way of hard physical evidence that pertains to it. As you might guess, it is difficult to find fossils of single-celled or microscopic organisms, though scientists have found them. As Figure 25-2 shows, we have found examples of suspected fossil bacteria. We have even unearthed a few cases of fossil bacteria caught in the act of dividing.

The best guess as to what went on until about a billion years ago is that the new living things spread around the world and differentiated, driven all the while by natural selection and changes in the Earth's climate. We suspect that in the early part of this evolutionary process, all cells were prokaryotic, and scientists often speak of this as the period dominated by cyanobacteria, single-celled life forms that produce oxygen as a byproduct of photosynthesis. To an outside observer, the Earth would have looked remarkably sterile. There was no life at all on land, but the margins of the oceans were covered with collections of green scum that was going about the business of taking in carbon dioxide and returning oxygen to the atmosphere.

About a billion years ago, symbiotic relationships were set up between cells that eventually led to the development of eukaryotes. At some point, smaller cells found that they did better living inside their larger neighbors than they could do on their own, and cells whose genetic materials were carried inside a nucleus were born. These cells, like their neighbors and ancestors the prokaryotes, remained as single-celled organisms.

Sometime during this period as well cells began to come together to form large colonies. At first, these objects were probably nothing more than clumps of single-celled organisms living next to each other. Later, however, they developed into larger bodies. Indeed, by about 600 million years ago the seas were probably full of large multicellular animals and plants. You can think of some of them as resembling modern jellyfish. The stage was set for one of the most important developments in the history of life, the hard shell.

About 545 million years ago a crucial development took place in living systems. By a process that we don't fully understand, but which may have involved a new enzyme that converted calcium in the ocean water into shell material, some animals began to grow hard shells. This new chemical trick was so advantageous that the seafloor was soon teeming with many different kinds of hard-shelled animals. As always happens when a new evolutionary path develops, there was a great deal of competition and experimentation among living things as they evolved outer shells, body designs, and metabolisms suited for each environment.

From the scientist's point of view, one of the most important aspects of this development was that, for the first time, living things left large numbers of fossils. In fact, for most of the nineteenth and twentieth centuries, before discovery of the fossils that indicated the presence of primitive forms of life, it looked to scientists as if life suddenly exploded at the beginning of this period. This sudden change in life on Earth, therefore, is often referred to as the *Cambrian explosion*. (Geologists refer to the time during which skeletons developed as the Cambrian

Table 25-1 **Major Steps**
           in the Evolution of Life

Time (millions of years)	Event
~3500	First cell
1000	Eukaryotes
700	Multicellularity
450	Vertebrates and land plants
400	Amphibians
350	Reptiles
140	Appearance of flowering plants
100	Placental mammals
65	Primates
3	Hominids

period, after Cambria, the old Roman name for Wales, where rocks from this period were first studied.)

Following the momentous development of shells, the last half-billion years or so have seen enormous growth in both the complexity and diversity of life. A summary of major developments is given in Table 25-1 (see Appendix B for more details).

Geological Time

Before the development of radiometric dating in this century (see Chapter 12), scientists knew about the existence of fossils, and could see that some fossils were older than others by the sequence of rock layers. However, they had no way of attaching numbers to any of the changes they observed in the fossil record. Several landmarks that stand out in the process of evolution were used as boundaries in the delineation of past times.

In the nineteenth century, scientists were not aware of bacterial fossils, or even fossils of soft-bodied organisms. To them, fossils seemed to indicate that life suddenly appeared at the beginning of the Cambrian (when fossils of hard-bodied organisms first appeared). The era from the beginning of Earth's existence to 545 million years ago was therefore called the *Proterozoic* ("before life"). Next was the *Paleozoic* ("old life") era from about 545 to 250 million years ago. This era saw a marvelous diversification of life, including the development of fish, amphibians, land plants and animals, and rudimentary forms of reptiles. The third great era (250 to 65 million years ago) was the *Mesozoic* ("middle life"), also known as the age of dinosaurs, when the major vertebrate life forms on Earth were large reptiles. Finally, the *Cenozoic* ("new life") era began with the extinction of the dinosaurs some 65 million years ago and continues to the present day. This is the time when mammals proliferated and began to dominate the Earth. The human species arose at the very end of the Cenozoic.

Throughout this long and intricate process of change, the principle of natural selection was always at work, shaping and molding life forms (Figure 25-5).

Mass Extinctions and the Rate of Evolution

Under normal circumstances, the rate of extinction seems to be such that roughly 10% to 20% of the species at any given time will be extinct in a matter of 5 or

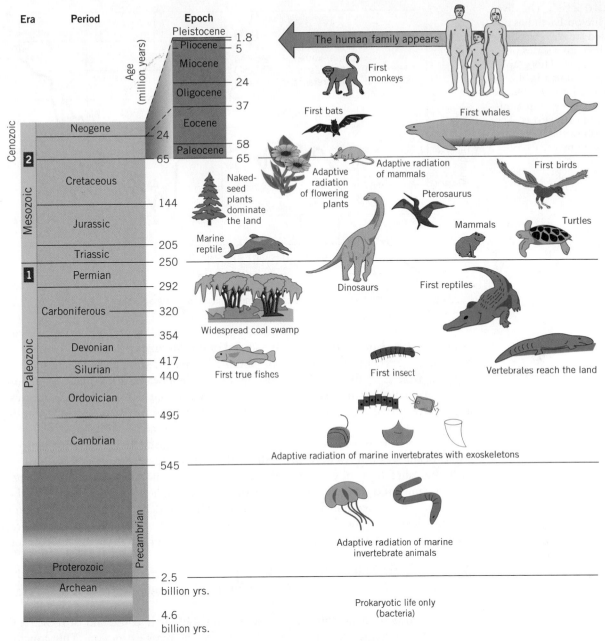

Era   Period   Epoch

Era	Period	Epoch	Age (million years)
Cenozoic	Neogene	Pleistocene	1.8
		Pliocene	5
		Miocene	24
		Oligocene	37
		Eocene	58
		Paleocene	65

Pleistocene, Pliocene, Miocene, Oligocene, Eocene, Paleocene

The human family appears

First monkeys

First bats

First whales

Adaptive radiation of mammals

First birds

Adaptive radiation of flowering plants

Naked-seed plants dominate the land

Pterosaurus

Mammals

Turtles

Marine reptile

Dinosaurs

First reptiles

Widespread coal swamp

First true fishes

First insect

Vertebrates reach the land

Adaptive radiation of marine invertebrates with exoskeletons

Adaptive radiation of marine invertebrate animals

Prokaryotic life only (bacteria)

Neogene — 24

Cretaceous — 144

Jurassic — 205

Triassic — 250

Permian — 292

Carboniferous — 320 — 354

Devonian — 417

Silurian — 440

Ordovician — 495

Cambrian — 545

Proterozoic

Archean

Precambrian

2.5 billion yrs.

4.6 billion yrs.

- **Figure 25-5** The geological time scale with representative living things illustrated.

6 million years. The fossil record shows, however, that not all extinctions are "normal." **Mass extinctions**, rare catastrophic events in the past, have caused large numbers of species to become extinct suddenly (Figure 25-6).

By "large numbers of species," we mean anywhere from 30% to 90% of the species alive at the time. By "suddenly," we mean a time too short to be resolved by standard geological techniques. The extinction may have taken place over a period of a few tens of thousands of years, or over a couple of days.

The best known of these mass extinctions is the one in which the dinosaurs perished some 65 million years ago at the end of the Cretaceous Period, which was at the end of the Mesozoic Era. In that extinction, about two-thirds of all living species disappeared. In some cases, as with ocean plankton, this number may have climbed

• **Figure 25-6** The diversity of life on Earth has not increased steadily, but has gone through a series of sharp changes. This graph of marine animals in the fossil record is indicative of the overall growth in families and of extinctions. The extinction of the dinosaurs is indicated by the event labeled 5.

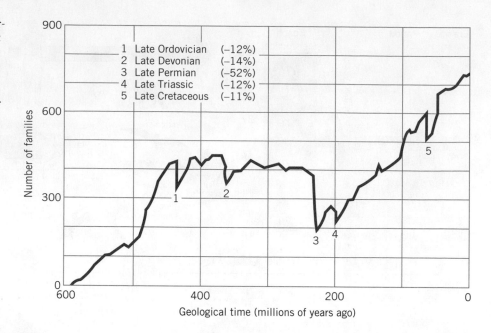

as high as 98%. But the extinction at the end of the Mesozoic was neither the largest nor the most recent mass extinction. About 250 million years ago near the end of the Paleozoic Era, about 80% of existing species disappeared in a single extinction event. A somewhat milder extinction, which wiped out 30% of existing species, appears to have taken place about 11 million years ago. In fact, geologists who study the past history of life in detail distinguish about a dozen mass extinctions.

One of the most interesting explanations for how these mass extinctions could occur was put forward in 1980 by the father-and-son team of Luis Alvarez (a Nobel laureate in physics) and Walter Alvarez (a geologist). Based on evidence they accumulated, they suggested that the impact of a large asteroid killed off the dinosaurs and other life forms. Such an impact would have raised a dust cloud that blocked out sunlight for several months. This catastrophe would have been such a shock to the world ecosystem that it is a wonder anything survived at all.

 Stop and Think! What would happen if an asteroid like the one hypothesized by Luis and Walter Alvarez hit the Earth today?

Most scientists today accept that an asteroid hit the Earth at the end of the Cretaceous, and they agree that it was responsible for the mass extinction. This conclusion was bolstered in 1992, when a crater over 100 miles across was discovered buried under the seafloor near the Yucatan Peninsula in Mexico (Figure 25-7). Less certain is the role that other factors played in these events. The world ecosystem was under a great deal of stress at that time because of rapid changes in climate and the recent creation of mountain chains, both of which were altering habitats.

Mass extinctions illustrate an important point about the history of life on our planet. Evolution is not a smooth, gradual progress through time. There are times when sudden changes (such as those in the mass extinctions) are followed by rapid evolution, as new species develop to take the place of those that disappeared. After the extinction of the dinosaurs, for example, the number of species of mammals increased dramatically. Scientists continue to debate about the rate of evolution. The two extremes in the debate have been the *gradualism* hypothesis, which holds that most change occurs as a result of the accumulation of small

ANIMAL EVOLUTION	MAJOR GEOLOGICAL EVENTS
Appearance of *Homo sapiens* First use of fire Appearance of *Homo erectus*	Worldwide glaciations Linking of North America and South America
Appearance of hominids Appearance of first apes All modern genera of mammals present In seas, bony fish abound Rise of mammals First placental mammals	Opening of Red Sea Formation of Himalayan Mountains Collision of India with Asia Separation of Australia and Antarctica Opening of Norwegian Sea and Baffin Bay
Dinosaurs extinct Modern birds	Formation of Alps Formation of Rocky Mountains
First birds Age of dinosaurs	
Explosive radiation of dinosaurs First dinosaurs First mammals Complex arthropods dominant in seas First beetles	 Opening of Atlantic Ocean
Widespread extinction Appearance of mammal-like reptiles Increase of reptiles and insects Decline of amphibians	 Final assembly of Pangaea
Early reptiles First winged insects Increase of amphibians	 Formation of coal deposits
Amphibians diversify into many forms First land vertebrates—amphibians	
Golden Age of fishes First land invertebrates—land scorpions	
First vertebrates—fishes Increase of marine invertebrates	
Trilobites dominant Explosive evolution of marine life	

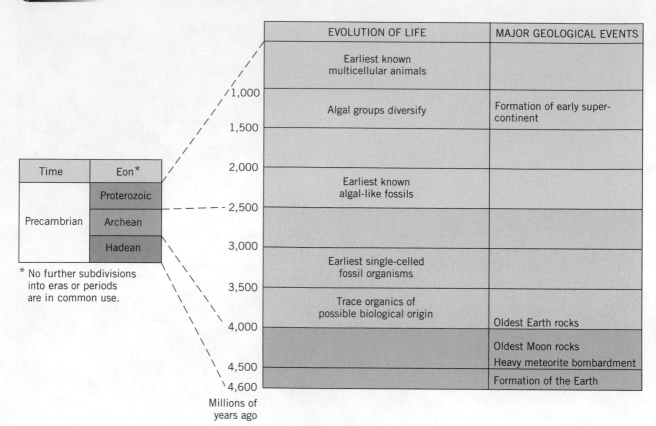

Time	Eon*
Precambrian	Proterozoic
	Archean
	Hadean

* No further subdivisions
into eras or periods
are in common use.

	EVOLUTION OF LIFE	MAJOR GEOLOGICAL EVENTS
1,000	Earliest known multicellular animals	
1,500	Algal groups diversify	Formation of early super-continent
2,000		
2,500	Earliest known algal-like fossils	
3,000		
3,500	Earliest single-celled fossil organisms	
4,000	Trace organics of possible biological origin	Oldest Earth rocks
4,500		Oldest Moon rocks / Heavy meteorite bombardment
4,600		Formation of the Earth

Millions of
years ago

D
Selected Physical Constants and Astronomical Data

Avogadro's number
$6.022 \times 10^{23}/mol$

Charge on electron
$1.602 \times 10^{-19}C$

Electron mass
$m_e = 9.10939 \times 10^{-31}$ kg

Gravitational constant
$G = 6.674 \times 10^{-11}$ N $\cdot$ m^2/kg^2

Planck's constant
$h = 6.62608 \times 10^{-34}$ J $\cdot$ s

Proton mass
$m_p = 1.6726 \times 10^{-27}$ kg
$= 1836.1 \ m_e$

Speed of light in a vacuum
$c = 2.9979 \times 10^8$ m/s

Astronomical unit
AU $= 1.4959789 \times 10^{11}$ meters

Hubble's constant
$H \sim 20$ km/s/Mly

Light-year
ly $= 9.46053 \times 10^{15}$ meters
$= 6.324 \times 10^4$ AU

Mass of Sun
$M_{sun} = 1.989 \times 10^{30}$ kg

Radius of Sun
$R_{sun} = 6.96 \times 10^5$ km

Mass of Moon
$M_{moon} = 7.348 \times 10^{22}$ kg

Radius of Moon
$R_{moon} = 1.738 \times 10^3$ km

E
Properties of the Planets

Planet	Length of Day	Distance from Sun (millions of km)	Length of Year (Earth year)	Average Radius (km)	Radius (Earth radii)	Mass (kg)	Mass (Earth masses)
Mercury	58.65 days	57.9	0.24	2,439	0.38	3.30×10^{23}	0.0562
Venus	243.01 days (retrograde)	108.2	0.615	6,052	0.95	4.87×10^{24}	0.815
Earth	23 h 56 min 4.1 s	149.6	1.000	6,378	1.00	5.974×10^{24}	1.000
Mars	24 h 37 min 22.6 s	227.9	1.881	3,397	0.53	6.42×10^{23}	0.1074
Jupiter	9 h 50.5 min	778.4	11.86	71,492	11.19	1.899×10^{27}	317.9
Saturn	10 h 14 min	1424	29.46	60,268	9.45	5.68×10^{26}	95.1
Uranus	17 h 14 min (retrograde)	2872	84.01	25,559	4.01	8.66×10^{26}	14.56
Neptune	16 h 3 min	4499	164.8	25,269	3.96	1.03×10^{26}	17.24
Pluto	6.39 days (retrograde)	5943	248.6	1,140	0.18	1.1×10^{22}	0.0018

F

The Chemical Elements

Table of Atomic Weights

Elements by Name/Symbol, Atomic Number, and Atomic Weight
(Atomic weights are given to four significant figures for elements below atomic number 104.)

Name	Symbol	Atomic Number	Atomic Weight	Name	Symbol	Atomic Number	Atomic Weight
Actinium	Ac	89	227.0	Flourine	F	9	19.00
Aluminum	Al	13	26.98	Francium	Fr	87	223.0
Americium	Am	95	243.1	Gadolinium	Gd	64	157.2
Antimony	Sb	51	121.8	Gallium	Ga	31	69.72
Argon	Ar	18	39.95	Germanium	Ge	32	72.59
Arsenic	As	33	74.92	Gold	Au	79	197.0
Astatine	At	85	210.0	Hafnium	Hf	72	178.5
Barium	Ba	56	137.3	Hassium	Hs	108	(269)
Berkelium	Bk	97	247.1	Helium	He	2	4.003
Beryllium	Be	4	9.012	Holmium	Ho	67	164.9
Bismuth	Bi	83	209.0	Hydrogen	H	1	1.008
Bohrium	Bh	107	(264)	Indium	In	49	114.8
Boron	B	5	10.81	Iodine	I	53	126.9
Bromine	Br	35	79.90	Iridium	Ir	77	192.2
Cadmium	Cd	48	112.4	Iron	Fe	26	55.85
Calcium	Ca	20	40.08	Krypton	Kr	36	83.80
Californium	Cf	98	252.1	Lanthanum	La	57	138.9
Carbon	C	6	12.01	Lawrencium	Lr	103	260.1
Cerium	Ce	58	140.1	Lead	Pb	82	207.2
Cesium	Cs	55	132.9	Lithium	Li	3	6.941
Chlorine	Cl	17	35.45	Lutetium	Lu	71	175.0
Chromium	Cr	24	52.00	Magnesium	Mg	12	24.30
Cobalt	Co	27	58.93	Manganese	Mn	25	54.94
Copper	Cu	29	63.55	Meitnerium	Mt	109	(268)
Curium	Cm	96	247.1	Mendelevium	Md	101	256.1
Dubnium	Db	105	(262)	Mercury	Hg	80	200.6
Dysprosium	Dy	66	162.5	Molybdenum	Mo	42	95.94
Einsteinium	Es	99	252.1	Neodymium	Nd	60	144.2
Erbium	Er	68	167.3	Neon	Ne	10	20.18
Europium	Eu	63	152.0	Neptunium	Np	93	237.0
Fermium	Fm	100	257.1	Nickel	Ni	28	58.69

Table of Atomic Weights (Continued)

Name	Symbol	Atomic Number	Atomic Weight	Name	Symbol	Atomic Number	Atomic Weight
Niobium	Nb	41	92.91	Silver	Ag	47	107.9
Nitrogen	N	7	14.01	Sodium	Na	11	22.99
Nobelium	No	102	259.1	Strontium	Sr	38	87.62
Osmium	Os	76	190.2	Sulfur	S	16	32.07
Oxygen	O	8	16.00	Tantalum	Ta	73	180.9
Palladium	Pd	46	106.4	Technetium	Tc	43	98.91
Phosphorus	P	15	30.97	Tellurium	Te	52	127.6
Platinum	Pt	78	195.1	Terbium	Tb	65	158.9
Plutonium	Pu	94	239.1	Thallium	Tl	81	204.4
Polonium	Po	84	210.0	Thorium	Th	90	232.0
Potassium	K	19	39.10	Thulium	Tm	69	168.9
Praseodymium	Pr	59	140.9	Tin	Sn	50	118.7
Promethium	Pm	61	144.9	Titanium	Ti	22	47.88
Protactinium	Pa	91	231.0	Tungsten	W	74	183.8
Radium	Ra	88	226.0	Ununbium	Uub	112	(285)
Radon	Rn	86	222.0	Ununnilium	Uun	110	(271)
Rhenium	Re	75	186.2	Unununium	Uuu	111	(272)
Rhodium	Rh	45	102.9	Ununquadium	Uuq	114	(289)
Rubidium	Rb	37	85.47	Uranium	U	92	238.0
Ruthenium	Ru	44	101.1	Vanadium	V	23	50.94
Rutherfordium	Rf	104	(261)	Xenon	Xe	54	131.3
Samarium	Sm	62	150.4	Ytterbium	Yb	70	173.0
Scandium	Sc	21	44.96	Yttrium	Y	39	88.91
Seaborgium	Sg	106	(266)	Zinc	Zn	30	65.39
Selenium	Se	34	78.96	Zirconium	Zr	40	91.22
Silicon	Si	14	28.09				

[a] Names of elements 110–114 are temporary; official names and symbols must be approved by the International Union of Pure and Applied Chemistry.

AAAS (pronounced "triple-A S") See *American Association for the Advancement of Science.*

abiotic Nonliving. (Ch. 19)

absolute magnitude The brightness a star appears to have when it is viewed from a standard distance. (Ch. 14)

absolute zero The temperature, zero kelvins, at which no energy can be extracted from atoms; the coldest attainable temperature, which is equal to $-273.16°C$ or $-459.67°F$. (Ch. 4)

absorption One of three possible responses of an electromagnetic wave encountering matter, in which light energy is converted into some other form, usually heat energy. See also *transmission* and *refraction.* (Ch. 6)

absorption line A dark line in an absorption spectrum that corresponds to the absorbed wavelength of light. (Ch. 8)

absorption spectrum The characteristic set of dark lines used to identify a chemical element or molecule from the photons absorbed by the material's atoms or molecules. (Ch. 8)

AC See *alternating current.*

acceleration The amount of change in velocity divided by the time it takes the change to occur. Acceleration can involve changes of speed, changes in direction, or both. (Ch. 2)

acid Any material that when put into water produces positively charged hydrogen ions (i.e., protons) in the solution; for example, lemon juice and hydrochloric acid. (Ch. 10)

acid rain A phenomenon that occurs when nitrogen and sulfur compounds in the air interact with water to form tiny droplets of nitric and sulfuric acid, which makes raindrops more acidic than normal. (Ch. 19)

acquired immune deficiency syndrome (AIDS) A disease caused by a virus known as the human immunodeficiency virus (HIV), which is transmitted by exchange of bodily fluids, most commonly in sexual contacts and the sharing of needles among drug abusers. (Ch. 24)

adaptation A structure, process, or behavior that helps an organism survive and pass its genes on to the next generation. (Ch. 25)

addition polymerization The formation of a polymer in which the basic building blocks are simply joined end to end; for example, polyethylene. (Ch. 10)

adenosine triphosphate (ATP) An energy-carrying molecule, found in a cell, that contains three phosphate groups, the sugar ribose, and the base adenine. (Ch. 22)

aerobic A process that requires the presence of oxygen; for example, respiration. (Ch. 22)

AIDS See *acquired immune deficiency syndrome.*

air pollution A serious environmental problem, with immediate consequences for urban residents, from the emission of NO_x compounds, sulfur dioxide, and hydrocarbons into the atmosphere. (Ch. 19)

algae Single-celled organisms (or simple multicelled ones) that carry out between 50% and 90% of the Earth's photosynthesis. (Ch. 20)

alkali metals Elements that are highly reactive, such as lithium, sodium, and potassium; listed in the far lefthand column of the periodic table of elements. These elements possess one valence electron. (Ch. 8)

alkaline earth metals Elements that combine with oxygen in a one-to-one ratio and form colorless solid compounds with high melting temperatures. Listed in the second column in the periodic table of elements: beryllium, magnesium, calcium, and others. These elements possess two valence electrons. (Ch. 8)

alkane A family of molecules based on the methane molecule, which burn readily and are used as fuels. (Ch. 10)

alloy The combination of two or more chemical elements in the metallic state; for example, brass (a mixture of copper and zinc) or bronze (an alloy of copper and tin). (Ch. 10)

alpha decay The loss by an atom's nucleus of a large and massive particle composed of two protons and two neutrons. (Ch. 12)

alpha particle A subatomic radioactive particle, made of two protons and two neutrons, used by Ernest Rutherford in a well-known experiment in which the nucleus was discovered. (Ch. 8)

alternating current (AC) A type of electrical current, commonly used in household appliances and cars, in which charges alternate their direction of motion. (Ch. 5)

AM See *amplitude modulation*.

American Association for the Advancement of Science (AAAS) One of the largest scientific societies, representing all branches of the physical, biological, and social sciences. AAAS is a strong force in establishing science policy and promoting science education. (Ch. 1)

amino acid The building block of protein, incorporating a carboxyl group (COOH) at one end, an amino group (NH_2) at the other end, and a side group (which varies from one amino acid to the next). Ch. 21

amino group A group of atoms of nitrogen and hydrogen (NH_2) that forms one end of an amino acid. See *carboxyl group*. (Ch. 21)

amp See *ampere*.

ampere A unit of measurement for the amount of electrical current (number of charges) flowing in a wire or elsewhere per unit of time. (Ch. 5)

amphibians The first vertebrates adapted to live part of their lives on land; modern descendants include frogs, toads, and salamanders. (Ch. 20)

amplifier A device that takes a small current and converts it into a large one to do work. (Ch. 11)

amplitude modulation (AM) A process by which information is transmitted by varying the amplitude of a radio wave signal being transmitted. After transmission, the signal is converted to sound by the radio receiver. (Ch. 6)

amplitude The height of a wave crest above the undisturbed level of the medium. (Ch. 6)

anaerobic A process that can occur in the absence of oxygen; for example, fermentation. (Ch. 22)

angiosperm The class of vascular plants that flower. (Ch. 20)

animals Multicelled organisms that get their energy by eating other organisms; one of five kingdoms in the modern Linnaean classification. (Ch. 20)

annihilation A process that occurs when a particle collides with its antiparticle, completely converting both masses to energy. (Ch. 13)

antibiotic A medicine capable of destroying foreign bacteria in an organism. (Ch. 20)

antimatter Particles that have the same mass as their matter twins, but with an opposite charge, magnetic characteristics, and other properties. (Ch. 13)

apparent magnitude The brightness a star appears to have when it is viewed from the Earth. (Ch. 14)

applied research The type of research performed by scientists with specific and practical goals in mind. This research is often translated into practical systems by large-scale research and development projects. (Ch. 1)

aquifer An underground body of stored water, often a layer of water-saturated rock bounded by impermeable materials. (Ch. 18)

arthropods All invertebrate animals with segmented bodies and jointed limbs. The most successful phylum in the animal kingdom in terms of numbers of species and total mass; includes insects, spiders, and crustacea. (Ch. 20)

artificial intelligence A field of research based on the idea that computers eventually will be able to perform all functions of thought that we normally think of as being distinctly human. (Ch. 11)

artificial selection The process of conscious breeding for specific characteristics in plants and animals. (Ch. 25)

asteroid belt A collection of small rocky planetesimals, located in a circular orbit between Mars and Jupiter, debris of material that never managed to collect into a single planet. (Ch. 15)

asteroids Small rocky objects, concentrated mostly in an asteroid belt between Mars and Jupiter, that circle the Sun like miniature planets. (Ch. 15)

astrobiology The scientific search for the origin and distribution of life in the universe. (Ch. 25)

astronomy The study of objects in the heavens. (Ch. 14)

atmospheric cycle The circulation of gases near the Earth's surface, which includes the short-term variations of weather and the long-term variations of climate. (Ch. 18)

atom Fundamental building blocks for all matter; the smallest representative sample of an element. It consists of a positively charged nucleus surrounded by negatively charged electrons. (Ch. 8)

atomic number The number of protons in the nucleus, which determines the nuclear charge, and therefore the chemical identity of the atom. (Ch. 12)

atomism The hypothesis that for each chemical element there is a corresponding species of indivisible objects called atoms. (Ch. 8)

ATP See *adenosine triphosphate*.

Australopithecus The first hominid, a primate closer to humans than any other; lived approximately 4.5 to 1.5 million years ago, walked erect, and had a brain about the size of that of a modern chimpanzee. (Ch. 25)

autotroph A complex organism that is able to manufacture the essential building blocks of life from simple molecules. (Ch. 20)

axon The longest filament connecting one nerve cell to another, along which nerve signals move. (Ch. 5)

basalt A dense, dark, even-textured volcanic rock forming the oceanic plates; rich in oxides of silicon, magnesium, iron, calcium, and aluminum. (Ch. 17)

base A class of corrosive materials that when put into water produce negatively charged hydroxide ions; usually tastes bitter and feels slippery. (Ch. 10)

base load The steady day-to-day demand in the mass market of electricity. (Ch. 3)

base pair One of four possible bonding combinations of the bases adenine, thymine, guanine, and cytosine on the DNA molecule: AT, TA, GC, and CG. (Ch. 23)

basic research The type of research performed by scientists who are interested simply in finding out how the world works, in knowledge for its own sake. (Ch. 1)

battery A device that converts stored chemical energy into kinetic energy of charged particles (usually electrons) running through an outside wire. (Ch. 5)

beta decay A kind of radioactive decay in which a particle such as the neutron spontaneously transforms into a collection of particles that includes an electron. (Ch. 12)

big bang theory The idea that the universe began at a specific point in time and has been cooling and expanding ever since. (Ch. 15)

binomial nomenclature The two-part scientific name assigned to every organism that begins with the genus name and ends with the species name. (Ch. 20)

bioinformatics revolution The increased use of computers in biological experiments and scientific study. A term often used in reference to the Human Genome Project. (Ch. 23)

biology The branch of science devoted to the study of living systems. (Ch. 20)

biodiversity The number of different species that coexist at a given place. (Ch. 1)

biotic Living. (Ch. 19)

bird Modern descendant of reptiles with an anatomical adaptation to flight and feathers evolved from scales. (Ch. 20)

bit Binary digit: a unit of measurement for information equal to "yes-no" or "on-off." (Ch. 11)

black hole Formed at the death of a very large star, an object so dense, with a mass so concentrated, that nothing—not even light—can escape from its surface. (Ch. 14)

blue-green algae Also known as *cyanobacteria*. Single-celled organisms that are classified as monera, even though they carry on photosynthesis. (Ch. 20)

blueshift The result of the Doppler effect on light waves, when the source of light moves toward the observer: light-wave crests bunch up and have a higher frequency. (Ch. 6)

Bohr atom A model of the atom, developed by Niels Bohr in 1913, in which electrons exist only in allowed energy levels. In these energy levels, the electrons maintain fixed energy for long periods of time, without giving off radiation. (Ch. 8)

boiling A change of state from liquid to gas caused by an increase in temperature or decrease in pressure of the liquid, which speeds up the vibration of individual molecules of the liquid, allowing them to break free and form a gas. (Ch. 10)

bony fish A class of vertebrates that includes salmon, perch, and other fish with bone skeletons. (Ch. 20)

brain The central organ of the human nervous system, which receives signals from sense organs, as well as signals that keep it apprised of the status of internal organs. It sends out signals to keep the body functioning, and serves as the seat for all higher functions, such as thought and speech. (App. A)

Brownian motion A phenomenon that describes the rapid, random movements caused by atomic collisions of very small objects suspended in a liquid. (Ch. 8)

bryophyte The phylum of primitive terrestrial plants, including mosses, that can use photosynthesis, are anchored to the ground by rhizoids, and absorb water directly through aboveground structures. (Ch. 20)

byte In a computer, a group of eight switches storing eight bits of information; the basic information unit of most modern computers. (Ch. 11)

c The speed of light and other electromagnetic radiation; a constant whose value is 300,000 kilometers per second (about 186,000 miles per second), equal to the product of the wavelength and frequency of an electromagnetic wave. (Ch. 6)

calorie A common unit of energy defined as the amount of heat required to raise 1 gram of room-temperature water 1 degree Celsius in temperature. (Ch. 4)

Cambrian explosion The sudden change in life on Earth, well-documented in the fossil record, when hard-bodied organisms first appeared about 545 million years ago. (Ch. 25)

Cambrian period The geological period, beginning about 545 million years ago, during which animals first began to develop shells and skeletons. (Ch. 25)

cancer A type of disease characterized by the uncontrolled growth of cells in the body. (Ch. 24)

carbohydrate A class of modular molecules made from carbon, hydrogen, and oxygen that form the solid structure of living things and play a central role in how living things acquire oxygen. (Ch. 21)

carbon cycle The cycle a carbon molecule may undergo in an ecosystem. For example, it may start in the atmosphere, be taken in by a producer, then a eaten by a consumer. When the consumer dies, it is broken down by a decomposer, at which point the carbon molecule is released back into the atmosphere. (Ch. 19)

carboxyl group A group of atoms of carbon, hydrogen, and oxygen (COOH) that forms one end of an amino acid string. See *amino group*. (Ch. 21)

carnivore Animals that get their energy by eating organisms in the second trophic level. (Ch. 3)

CAT See *computerized axial tomography*.

cell A complex chemical system with the ability to duplicate itself; the fundamental unit of life. (Ch. 22)

cell membrane A structure, formed from bilayers of lipids, that separates the inside of a cell from the outside, or separates one part of a cell from another. (Ch. 22)

cell theory The theory that holds that all living things are made up of cells, the cell is the fundamental unit of life, and all cells arise from previous cells. (Ch. 22)

cell wall A solid framework made from cellulose molecules and other strong polymers, by which plant cells are separated from one another. (Ch. 22)

cellulose A long, stringy polymer that is the main structural element in plants but cannot be digested by humans. (Ch. 21)

Celsius scale A temperature scale that measures 0 and 100 degrees as the freezing and boiling points of water, respectively. (Ch. 4)

Cenozoic Era The fourth era, which began 65 million years ago and continues to the present day, also known as "new life." The time when mammals proliferated and began to dominate Earth. (Ch. 25)

central processing unit (CPU) The part of a computer in which transistors store and manipulate relatively small amounts of information at any one time. (Ch. 11)

Cepheid variable A type of star with a regular behavior of steady brightening and dimming, which is related to the star's luminosity. Cepheid variables are used to calculate distances to many millions of light-years. (Ch. 14)

ceramics A broad class of hard, durable solids, ranging from rocks and minerals to bones. (Ch. 10)

CFCs See *chlorofluorocarbons*.

chain reaction The process in a nuclear reactor in which nuclei undergoing fission produce neutrons that will cause more splitting, resulting in the release of large amounts of energy. (Ch. 12)

change of state Transition between the solid, liquid, and gas states caused by changes in temperature and pressure. The processes involved are freezing and melting (for solids and liquids), boiling and condensation (for liquids and gases), and sublimation (for solids and gases). (Ch. 10)

chaos A field of study modeling systems in nature that can be described in Newtonian terms but whose futures are, for all practical purposes, unpredictable; for example, the turbulent flow of water or the beating of a human heart. (Ch. 2)

chemical bond The attraction that results from the redistribution of electrons between two or more atoms, leading to a more stable configuration—particularly by filling the outer electron shells—and that holds the two atoms together. The principal kinds of chemical bonds are ionic, covalent, and metallic. (Ch. 10)

chemical evolution An area of research concerned with the process by which simple chemical compounds present in Earth's early atmosphere became an organized, reproducing cell. (Ch. 25)

chemical potential energy The type of energy that is stored in the chemical bonds between atoms, such as the energy in flashlight batteries. (Ch. 3)

chemical reaction The process by which atoms or smaller molecules come together to form large molecules, or by which larger molecules are broken down into smaller ones; involves the rearrangement of atoms in elements and compounds, as well as the rearrangement of electrons to form chemical bonds. (Ch. 10)

chlorofluorocarbons (CFCs) A class of stable and generally nonreactive chemicals widely used in refrigerators and air-conditioners until the late 1980s. See *ozone hole*. (Ch. 19)

chlorophyll A molecule, found in the chloroplasts of plant cells, that absorbs energy from sunlight and uses the energy to transform atmospheric carbon dioxide and water into energy-rich sugar molecules such as glucose and oxygen (as a byproduct). (Ch. 22)

chloroplasts The main energy transformation organelles in plant cells; places where the molecules of chlorophyll are found and photosynthesis occurs. (Ch. 22)

cholesterol An essential component of the cell membrane synthesized by the body from saturated fats in the diet; in high levels, can cause fatty deposits that clog arteries. (Ch. 21)

chordate A phylum of animals with a thickened set of nerves down their backs; includes the subphylum vertebrates. (Ch. 20)

chromosomes A long strand of the DNA double helix, with the strand wrapped around a series of protein cores. (Ch. 22)

chromosphere One of the Sun's outer layers, visible for a few minutes as a spectacular halo during a total eclipse of the Sun. (Ch. 14)

circulatory system The system that distributes blood through the body; includes the blood vessels and the heart. (App. A)

class The third broadest classification in the Linnaean classification system; humans are in the class of mammals. (Ch. 20)

classical genetics The laws developed from the observations of Gregor Mendel: (1) traits are passed from parent to offspring by genes, (2) each parent contributes one gene for each trait, and (3) genes are either dominant or recessive. (Ch. 23)

climate The average weather conditions of a place or area over a period of years. (Ch. 18)

cloning The process of engineering a new individual entirely from the genetic material in a cell from another individual. A clone is genetically identical to the cell donor. (Ch. 24)

closed ecosystem An ecosystem through which energy will flow but material will cycle. (Ch. 19)

closed system A type of system in which matter and energy are not freely exchanged with the surroundings; an isolated system. (Ch. 3)

closed universe A universe in which the expansion will someday reverse because the universe holds enough matter to exert a strong enough gravitational force to reverse the motion of receding galaxies. (Ch. 15)

cloud A concentration of tiny water droplets or ice crystals, which form when the air becomes saturated with water. (Ch. 18)

cloudiness A weather variable caused by the formation of clouds as air masses rise and fall and the air is saturated with water. (Ch.18)

cluster A collection of galaxies. (Ch. 15)

COBE See *Cosmic Background Explorer.*

codon The set of three bases on mRNA that determines which of the possible tRNA molecules will attach at that point, and which amino acid will appear in a protein. (Ch. 23)

cold-blooded Animals, such as amphibians and reptiles, that must absorb heat from their environment to maintain body temperature. (Ch. 20)

combustion A rapid combination with oxygen, producing heat and flame (Ch. 10)

comet An object, usually found outside the orbit of Pluto, composed of chunks of materials such as water ice and methane ice embedded with dirt. A comet may fall toward the Sun, if its distant orbit is disturbed, and create a spectacular display in the night sky. (Ch. 16)

compass A needle-shaped magnet designed to point at the poles of the Earth's magnetic field. (Ch. 5)

complexity A new branch of science that studies systems in which many agents act on, and are affected by, other agents. Ecosystems, stock markets, and the human brain are examples of complex systems. (Ch. 20)

composite material A combination of two or more substances in which the strength of one of the constituents is used to offset the weakness of another, resulting in a new material whose strengths are greater than any of its components; for example, plywood and reinforced concrete. (Ch. 11)

compressional wave One of two principal types of seismic waves, in which the molecules in rock move back and forth in the same direction as the wave; a longitudinal wave. (Ch. 17)

compressive strength A material's ability to withstand crushing. (Ch. 11)

computer A machine that stores and manipulates information. (Ch. 11)

computer-assisted drug design An approach to developing new drugs that relies on computers to predict the shapes, and therefore the behavior, of molecules. (Ch. 24)

computerized axial tomography (CAT) A scan that uses high-energy photons to produce a three-dimensional picture of the interior of the body and that uses a computer to quantify the density of each point of the body where the photons make contact. (Ch. 9)

community Organisms that interact to sustain life, including producers, consumers, and decomposers. (Ch. 19)

condensation A change of state from gas to liquid caused by a decrease in temperature or pressure of the gas, which slows down the vibration of individual molecules of the gas, allowing them to form a liquid. (Ch. 10)

condensation polymerization A chemical reaction often used to manufacture plastics and other polymers, and which, in the body, occurs during the formation of a peptide bond. (Ch. 10)

condensation reaction The formation of a polymer in which each new polymer bond releases a water molecule as the ends of the original polymer molecules link up. (Ch. 10)

conduction The movement of heat by collisions between vibrating atoms or molecules; one of three mechanisms by which heat moves. (Ch. 4)

conduction electron An electron in a material that is able to move in an electrical field. (Ch. 11)

conductor A material capable of carrying an electrical current; any material through which electrons can flow freely. (Ch. 11)

cone A light-absorbing cell in the eye, which is sensitive to red, blue, or green light, enabling color vision. Compare to *rod*. (Ch. 6)

conservation law Any statement that says that a quantity in nature does not change. (Ch. 3)

constructive interference A situation in which two waves act together to reinforce or maximize the wave height at the point of intersection. (Ch. 6)

consumers Organisms, such as animals, that sustain life from the carbon-based molecules created by producer organisms in an ecosystem. (Ch. 19)

continental drift A theory that states that the Earth's continents are in motion and are, therefore, not fixed. Continental drift is part of the modern theory of plate tectonics. (Ch. 17)

convection The transfer of heat by the physical motion of masses of fluid. Dense, cooler fluids (liquids and gases) descend in bulk and displace rising warmer fluids, which are less dense. One of three mechanisms by which heat moves. (Ch. 4)

convection cell A region in a fluid in which heat is continuously being transferred by a bulk motion of heated fluid from a heat source to the surface of the fluid, where heat is released. The cooled fluid then sinks and the cycle repeats. (Ch. 4)

convection zone The outer region of the Sun, comprising the upper 200,000 km (about 125,000 mi) where the dominant energy transfer mechanism changes from collision to convection. (Ch. 14)

convergent plate boundary A place where two tectonic plates are coming together. (Ch. 17)

core (*a*) In geology, the heaviest elements of the Earth's mass, primarily iron and nickel, concentrated at the center with a radius of about 3400 km (2000 mi). (*b*) In astronomy, a small region in the center of a star where hydrogen burning is generally confined. (Ch. 14, Ch. 17)

corona One of the Sun's outer layers, visible for a few minutes as a spectacular halo during a total eclipse of the Sun. (Ch. 14)

Cosmic Background Explorer (COBE) An orbiting observatory that measures the presence of microwave radiation present as background noise in every direction of the sky. (Ch. 14)

cosmic microwave background radiation Microwave radiation, characteristic of a body at about 3 K, falling to Earth from all directions. This radiation is evidence for the big bang. (Ch. 15)

cosmic rays Particles (mostly protons) that rain down continuously on the atmosphere of the Earth after being emitted by stars in our galaxy and in others. (Ch. 13)

cosmology The branch of science that is devoted to the study of the structure and history of the entire universe. (Ch. 15)

coulomb (pronounced "*koo*-loam") The unit for measuring the magnitude of an electrical charge. (Ch. 5)

Coulomb's law An empirically derived rule that states that the magnitude of the electrostatic force between any two objects is proportional to the charges of the two objects, and inversely proportional to the square of the distance between them. (Ch. 5)

covalent bond A chemical bond in which neighboring molecules share electrons in a strongly bonded group of at least two atoms. (Ch. 10)

CPU See *central processing unit*.

critical mass The minimum number of uranium-235 atoms needed to sustain a nuclear chain reaction to the point where large amounts of energy can be released. (Ch. 12)

crust A thin layer at the surface of the Earth formed from the lightest elements, ranging in thickness from 10 km (6 mi) in parts of the ocean to 70 km (45 mi) beneath parts of the continents. (Ch. 16)

crystal A group of atoms that occur in a regularly repeating sequence. Crystal structure is described by first determining the size and shape of the repeating boxlike group of atoms and then recording the exact type and position of every atom that appears in the box. (Ch. 10)

current A river of moving water on an ocean's surface, found in each of the ocean basins. (Ch. 18)

cyclone A great rotational pattern in the atmosphere, hundreds of kilometers in diameter, that can draw energy from warm oceanic waters and create low-pressure tropical storms. (Ch. 18)

cyclotron The first of the particle accelerators, for which Ernest Lawrence won the 1939 Nobel prize in physics. (Ch. 13)

cytoplasm The fluid that takes up the spaces between the organelles of a cell. (Ch. 22)

cytoskeleton A series of protein filaments that extend throughout the cell, giving the cell a shape and, in some cases, allowing it to move. (Ch. 22)

dark matter Material that exists in forms that do not interact with electromagnetic radiation and that may constitute 90% of the matter of the universe. (Ch. 15)

DC See *direct current*.

decay chain A series of decays, or radioactive events, ending with a stable isotope. (Ch. 12)

decomposers Organisms, such as bacteria and fungi, that renew the raw materials of life in an ecosystem. (Ch. 19)

deep-ocean trench A surface feature associated with convergent plate boundaries in which no continents are on the leading edge of either of the two converging plates and one plate penetrates deep into the Earth. (Ch. 17)

dendrite One of a thousand projections on each nerve cell in the brain through which nerve signals move; each is connected to different neighboring nerve cells in the brain. (Ch. 5)

deoxyribonucleic acid (DNA) A strand of nucleotides with alternating phosphate and sugar molecules in a long chain, and with base molecules adenine, guanine, cytosine, and thymine at the side. The nucleotide strand bonds with a second nucleotide strand to make a molecule with a ladderlike double helix shape. DNA stores the genetic information in a cell. (Ch. 23)

deoxyribose The five-carbon sugar lacking one oxygen atom in deoxyribonucleic acid (DNA). (Ch. 23)

depolymerization The breakdown of a polymer into short segments. (Ch. 10)

destructive interference A situation in which two waves intersect in a way that decreases or cancels out the wave height at the point of intersection. (Ch. 6)

diatomic The simplest molecules, containing two atoms of the same element, such as the diatomic gases hydrogen (H_2), nitrogen (N_2), and oxygen (O_2). (Ch. 10)

differentiation The process by which heavy, dense materials (such as iron and nickel) sank under the force of gravity toward the molten center of the planet, while lighter, less dense materials floated to the top, resulting in the layered structure of the present-day Earth. (Ch. 16)

diffuse scattering A process by which light waves are absorbed and reemitted in all directions by a medium such as clouds or snow. (Ch. 6)

diffusion The transfer of molecules from regions of high concentration by ordinary random thermal motion. (Ch. 22)

digestive system The parts of the body that are responsible for breaking down food so that its stored energy can be used by cells; includes the stomach, small intestine, liver, pancreas, and gall bladder. (App. A)

diode An electronic device that allows electrical current to flow in only one direction. (Ch. 11)

dipole field The magnetic field that arises from the two poles of a magnet. (Ch. 5)

direct current (DC) A type of electrical current in which the electrons flow in one direction only; for example, in the chemical reaction of a battery. (Ch. 5)

distillation A process by which engineers separate the complex mixture of petroleum's organic chemicals into much purer fractions. (Ch. 10)

divergent plate boundary A spreading zone of crustal formation; a place where neighboring plates move away from each other. (Ch. 17)

Divine Calculator An eighteenth-century idea, proposed by Pierre Simon Laplace, which stated that if the position and velocity of every atom in the universe is known, with infinite computational power, the future position and velocity of every atom in the universe could be predicted. (Ch. 2)

DNA See *deoxyribonucleic acid*.

DNA fingerprinting A procedure by which DNA in human tissue is used to match the tissue to an individual. This technique is becoming increasingly important in the judicial system in the United States. (Ch. 24)

DNA mapping The process of finding the location of genes on chromosomes. (Ch. 23)

DNA sequencing The process of determining, base pair by base pair, the exact order of bases along a specific stretch of a DNA molecule. (Ch. 23)

domain Region in magnetic material where neighboring atoms line up with each other to give a strong magnetic field. (Ch. 11)

dominant A genetic characteristic that always appears, or is expressed. (Ch. 23)

doping The addition of a minor impurity to a semiconductor. (Ch. 11)

Doppler effect The change in frequency or wavelength of a wave detected by an observer because the source of the wave is moving. (Ch. 6)

double-blind clinical trial A procedure for testing the effectiveness of new medical treatments. A group of patients is separated into two sections; half the people will be given the new treatment while the other half will be given a placebo. (Ch. 24)

double bond The type of covalent bond formed when two electrons are shared by two atoms. (Ch. 10)

double helix The twisted double strand of nucleotides that forms the structure of the DNA molecule. (Ch. 23)

ear A sense organ that includes a membrane that vibrates at the arrival of sound waves. (App. A)

earthquake Disturbance caused when stressed rock on Earth suddenly snaps, converting potential energy into released kinetic energy. (Ch. 17)

ecological niche The habitat, functional role(s), requirements for environmental resources, and tolerance ranges within an ecosystem. (Ch. 19)

ecology The branch of science that studies interactions among organisms as well as the interactions of organisms and their environment. (Ch. 19)

ecosystem Interdependent collections of living things; includes the plants and animals that live in a given area together with their physical surroundings. (See *open ecosystem* and *closed ecosystem*.) (Ch. 19)

efficiency The amount of work you get from an engine, divided by the amount of energy you put in; a quantification of the loss of useful energy. (Ch. 4)

El Niño A weather cycle in the Pacific basin that recurs every four to seven years and can cause severe storms and flooding all along the western coast of the Americas, as well as drought from Australia to India. (Ch. 18)

elastic limit The point at which a material stops resisting external forces and begins to deform permanently. (Ch. 11)

elastic potential energy The type of energy that is stored in a flexed muscle, a coiled spring, and a stretched rubber band. (Ch. 3)

electric circuit An unbroken path of material that carries electricity and consists of three parts: a source of energy, a closed path, and a device to use the energy. (Ch. 5)

electrical current A flow of charged particles, measured in amperes. (Ch. 5)

electrical field The force that would be exerted on a positive charge at a position near a charged object. Every charged object is surrounded by an electric field. (Ch. 5)

electric generator A source of energy producing an alternating current in an electric circuit through the use of electromagnetic induction. (Ch. 5)

electric motor A device that operates by supplying current to an electromagnet to make the magnet move and generate mechanical power. Many motors employ permanent magnets and rotating loops of wire inside the poles of this magnet. (Ch. 5)

electrical charge An excess or deficit of electrons on an object. (Ch. 5)

electrical conductivity The ease with which a material allows electrons to flow. The inverse of electrical resistance. (Ch. 11)

electrical conductor Any material capable of carrying electrical current. (Ch. 11)

electrical insulator Material that will not conduct electricity. (Ch. 11)

electrical potential energy The type of energy that is found in a battery or between two wires at different voltages; energy associated with the position of a charge in an electric field. (Ch. 3)

electrical resistance The quantity, measured in ohms, that represents how hard it is to push electrons through a material. High-resistance wires are used when electron energy is to be converted into heat energy. Low-resistance wires are used when energy is to be transmitted from one place to another with minimum loss. (Ch. 5)

electricity A force, more powerful than gravity, that moves objects both toward and away from each other, depending upon the charge. (Ch. 5)

electroweak force A force resulting from the unification of the electromagnetic and weak forces. (Ch. 13)

electromagnet A device that produces a magnetic field from a moving electrical charge. (Ch. 5)

electromagnetic force A term used to refer to the unified nature of electricity and magnetism. (Ch. 5)

electromagnetic induction A process by which a changing magnetic field produces an electrical current in a conductor, even though there is no other source of power available. (Ch. 5)

electromagnetic radiation See *electromagnetic wave*.

electromagnetic spectrum The entire array of waves, varying in frequency and wavelength, but all resulting from an accelerating electrical charge; includes radio waves, microwaves, infrared, visible light, ultraviolet, X-rays, gamma rays, and others. (Ch. 6)

electromagnetic wave A form of radiant energy that reacts with matter by being transmitted, absorbed, or scattered. A self-propagating wave made up of electric and magnetic fields fluctuating together. A wave created when electrical charges accelerate, but requiring no medium for transfer. Electromagnetic radiation. (Ch. 6)

electron Tiny, negatively charged particles that surround a positively charged nucleus of an atom. (Ch. 5)

electron microscope An instrument, introduced in the 1930s, that was a major new advance in microscopes because it used electrons instead of light to illuminate objects and had resolving power up to 100,000 times that of the optical microscope. (Ch. 22)

electron shell A specific energy level in an atom that can be filled with a predetermined number of electrons. (Ch. 8)

electrostatic The type of electrical charge that doesn't move once it has been placed on an object, and the forces exerted by such a charge. (Ch. 5)

electroweak force The force resulting from the unification of the electromagnetic and weak force. (Ch. 13)

element A material made from a single type of atom, which cannot be broken down any further. (Ch. 8)

elementary-particle physics The study of particles that are believed to comprise the basic building blocks of the universe; for example, the particles that make up the nucleus, and particles such as electrons. Also known as high-energy physics. (Ch. 13)

elementary particles Particles that make up the nucleus, together with particles such as the electron; the basic building blocks of the universe. (Ch. 13)

ELF radiation Extremely low-frequency waves associated with the movement of electrons to produce the alternating current in household wires. (Ch. 6)

embryonic stem cell A cell that is totipotent and able to develop into any of the specialized cells that will later appear in the adult organism. (Ch. 24)

emission spectrum The characteristic set of lines used to identify a chemical element or molecule from the total collection of photons emitted during quantum leaps. (Ch. 8)

emitter The region in a transistor that first receives an electrical current. (Ch. 11)

endocrine system A group of glands that secrete hormones that are taken by the bloodstream to produce specific chemical effects; part of the body's control system. See *nervous system*. (App. A)

endoplasmic reticulum One of the cellular organelles that contribute to protein and lipid synthesis. (Ch. 22)

endothermic A chemical reaction in which the final energy of the electrons in the reaction is greater than the initial energy; energy must be supplied to make the reaction proceed. (Ch. 10)

energy The ability to do work; the capacity to exert a force over a distance. A system's energy can be measured in joules or foot-pounds. (Ch. 3)

entropy The thermodynamic quantity that describes the degree of randomness of a system. The greater the disorder or randomness, the higher the statistical probability of the state, and the higher the entropy. (Ch. 4)

environment The nonliving chemical and physical parts of an ecosystem, including the water, soil, and atmosphere. (Ch. 19)

enzyme A molecule that facilitates reactions between two other molecules, but which is not itself altered or taken up in the overall reaction. (Ch. 21)

essential amino acid One of the 8 amino acids that cannot be synthesized by the body and have to be consumed. (Ch. 21)

eukaryote An advanced single-celled organism and all multicelled organisms that are made from cells containing a nucleus. (Ch. 22)

evolution An ongoing process of change. There are various theories of evolution that differ in regard to how fast it proceeds and by what mechanisms. (Ch. 25)

excited state All energy levels of an atom above the ground state. (Ch. 8)

exothermic A chemical reaction in which the final energy of the electrons is less than the initial energy, and therefore energy is given off in some form. (Ch. 10)

experiment The manipulation of some aspect of nature to observe the outcome. (Ch. 1)

experimentalist A scientist who manipulates nature with controlled experiments. (Ch. 1)

extinct Species that have lived on Earth and have died out. Scientists estimate that for every species on the planet today, 999 species have become extinct. (Ch. 25)

extinction The disappearance of a species on Earth (Ch. 25)

extrasolar planet Any planet that exists outside of Earth's solar system. (Ch. 16)

extrusive rock See *volcanic rock*.

eye The most important of the five sense organs through which human beings become aware of their environment. (Ch. 6)

Fahrenheit scale A temperature scale that measures 32 and 212 degrees as the freezing and boiling points of water, respectively. (Ch. 4)

falsifiability A property of the scientific method that states that every theory and law of nature is subject to change, based on new observations. (Ch. 1)

family A grouping of similar genera in the Linnaean classification system; humans are in the family of hominids. (Ch. 20)

fat-soluble vitamin A vitamin that can be stored in the body, including vitamins A, D, E, and K. (Ch. 21)

fault A fracture in a rock along which movement occurs. (Ch. 17)

fermentation An anaerobic cellular process in which pyruvic acids are broken down and the energy is used by the cell to keep glycolysis going. (Ch. 22)

fern Primitive vascular plants that reproduce by producing sperm that must swim through water to fertilize eggs and generate spores. (Ch. 20)

ferromagnetism The property of a few materials in nature, such as iron, cobalt, and nickel metals, in which the individual atomic magnets are arranged in a nonrandom manner, lined up with each other into small magnetic domains to produce a small magnetic field. (Ch. 11)

field The force—magnetic, gravitational, or electrical—that would be felt at a particular point. For example, forces exerted by one object that would be felt by another object in the same region. (Ch. 5)

field researcher A scientist who works in natural settings to observe nature. (Ch. 1)

first law of thermodynamics The law of the conservation of energy. In an isolated system, the total amount of energy, including heat energy, is conserved. (Ch. 3)

first trophic level All plants that produce energy from photosynthesis. (Ch. 3)

fission A reaction that produces energy when heavy radioactive nuclei split apart into fragments that together have less mass than the original isotopes. (Ch. 12)

flat universe A model of the future of the universe in which the expansion slows and comes to a halt after infinite time has passed. (Ch. 15)

fluorescence A phenomenon in which energy contained in ultraviolet wavelengths is absorbed by the atoms in some materials and partially emitted as visible light, or "black light." (Ch. 6)

FM See *frequency modulation.*

food chain, or food web A complete set of pathways by which animals in an ecosystem obtain their energy and raw materials. (Ch. 3)

foot-pound The amount of work done by a force of one pound acting through one foot; the unit of energy in the English system. (Ch. 3)

force A push or pull that, acting alone, causes a change in acceleration of the object on which it acts. (Ch. 2)

fossil Evidence of past life preserved in rocks; notably when atoms in the hard parts of the buried organism are replaced by minerals in the water flowing through the surrounding area. (Ch. 25)

fossil fuel Carbon-rich deposits of ancient life that burn with a hot flame and have been the most important energy source for 150 years. Examples include coal, oil, and natural gas. (Ch. 3)

fossil record A term that refers to all of the fossils that have been found, catalogued, and studied since human beings first began to study them in a systematic way. (Ch. 25)

frames of reference The physical surroundings from which a person observes and measures the world. (Ch. 7)

freezing A change of state from liquid to solid caused by a decrease in temperature or increase in pressure of the liquid, which slows the vibration of individual molecules and forms the solid structure. (Ch. 10)

frequency The number of wave crests that go by a given point every second. A wave completing one cycle (sending one crest by a point every second) has a frequency of one hertz, 1 Hz. (Ch. 6)

frequency modulation (FM) A process by which information is transmitted by varying the frequency of a signal. After being transmitted, the signal may be converted to sound by circuits in a receiver. (Ch. 6)

fungi One of the five kingdoms in the Linnaean classification, organisms that obtain energy by absorbing materials through filaments and reproduce by production of spores. May be single-celled (e.g., yeasts) or multicellular (e.g, mushrooms). (Ch. 20)

fusion A process in which two nuclei come together to form a third, larger nucleus. When this reaction combines light elements to make heavier ones, the mass of the final nucleus may be less than the mass of its constituent parts. The "missing" nuclear mass can be converted into energy. (Ch. 12)

g A constant numerical value for the specific acceleration that all objects experience at the Earth's surface, determined by measuring the actual fall rate of objects in a laboratory. It is equal to 9.8 m/s^2, or 32 feet/s^2. (Ch. 2)

G See *gravitational constant.*

galaxy A large assembly of stars (between millions and hundreds of billions), together with gas, dust, and other materials, that is held together by the forces of mutual gravitational attraction. (Ch. 15)

gametes Sex cells that are formed when a single cell splits into four daughter cells during the process of cell division called meiosis, each gamete processing half the number of chromosomes that normal cells have. (Ch. 22)

gamma radiation A kind of radioactivity involving the emission of energetic electromagnetic radiation from the nucleus of an atom, with no change to the number of protons or neutrons in the atom. (Ch. 12)

gamma ray The highest-energy wave of the electromagnetic spectrum with wavelengths less than the size of an atom, less than one-trillionth of a meter; normally emitted in very high-energy nuclear particle reactions. (Ch. 6)

Gamma Ray Observatory (GRO) An orbiting observatory that detects the highest-energy end of the electromagnetic spectrum, gamma rays. It was one of the first permanent orbiting observatories launched by NASA's Great Observatories Program for monitoring in all parts of the electromagnetic spectrum. (Ch. 14)

gas Any collection of atoms or molecules that expands to take that shape and fill the volume available in its container. (Ch. 10)

gauge particles Particles whose exchange produces the fundamental forces that hold everything together; corresponds to every force between two particles. (Ch. 13)

GCM See *global circulation models.*

gene A unit of biological inheritance, or a section of a long molecule of DNA. One gene carries the information needed to assemble one protein. (Ch. 23)

gene therapy A promising future technology that involves replacing a defective gene with a healthy one. (Ch. 24)

general relativity The second and more complex of two parts of Einstein's theory of relativity, which applies to any reference frames whether or not those frames are accelerating relative to each other. (Ch. 7)

genetic code The correspondence between base-pair sequences and amino acids. The connection, in all living things, between the codons and the amino acid for which they code. (Ch. 23)

genetic disease A hereditary mutation that can cause sickness or death; for example, hemophilia. (Ch. 23)

genetic engineering A technology in which foreign genes are inserted into an organism, or existing genes altered, to modify the function of living things. (Ch. 24)

genetics The study of ways in which biological information is passed from one generation to the next. (Ch. 23)

genome The sum of all information contained in the DNA for any living thing; the sequence of all the bases in all the chromosomes. (Ch. 23)

genus A grouping of similar species in the Linnaean classification system; humans are in the genus *Homo.* (Ch. 20)

glacier A large body of ice that slowly flows down a slope or valley under the influence of gravity; found primarily in Greenland and Antarctica. (Ch. 18)

glass A solid with predictable local environments for most atoms, but no long-range order to the atomic structure. Compared to crystal, glass lacks the repeating unit of atoms. (Ch. 10)

global circulation models (GCM) Complex computer models of the atmosphere that are the best attempts to date to predict long-term climate and to discuss various types of ecological changes such as global warming. (Ch. 18)

global warming A change in average global temperature and in the temperature gradient between equator and poles that could result from the temperature increase owing to the greenhouse effect (Ch. 19)

glucose An important sugar ($C_6H_{12}O_6$) in the energy cycle of living things, figuring prominently in the energy metabolism of every living cell. (Ch. 21)

gluon A massless particle, confined to the interior of particles, that mediates the force holding quarks together. (Ch. 13)

glycogen A glucose polymer that is formed in animals and stored in the liver and muscle tissues. Also called *animal starch.* (Ch. 21)

glycolysis The first step in the extraction of energy from glucose, which takes place in nine separate steps, each of which is governed by a specific enzyme, and which splits each glucose molecule into two smaller molecules called pyruvic acids. (Ch. 22)

gneiss The metamorphic rock formed from slate under extreme temperature and pressure. (Ch. 18)

Golgi apparatus One of the cellular organelles that takes part in the synthesis of molecules (Ch. 22)

gradualism A hypothesis that holds that most evolutionary change occurs as a result of the accumulation of small adaptations. (Ch. 25)

granite A rock that is lower in density than the mantle rock it caps, and which forms much of the continents. (Ch. 17)

gravitational constant (*G*) A universal constant that expresses the exact numerical relation between the masses of two objects and their separation, on the one hand, and the force between them on the other; equal to 6.67×10^{-11} N-m^2/kg^2. (Ch. 2)

gravitational escape One way that a planet's atmosphere can evolve and change. Molecules in the atmosphere heated by the Sun may move sufficiently fast so that appreciable fractions of them can actually escape the gravitational pull of their planet. (Ch. 16)

gravitational potential energy Energy associated with the position of a mass in a gravitational field. The gravitational potential energy of an object on the surface of the Earth equals its weight (the force of gravity exerted by the object) times its height above the ground. (Ch. 3)

graviton The gauge particle of gravity. (Ch. 13)

gravity An attractive force that acts on every object in the universe. (Ch. 2)

great bombardment An event following the initial period of planetary formation in which meteorites showered down on planets, adding matter and heat energy. (Ch. 16)

greenhouse effect A global temperature increase caused by the fact that the Earth's atmospheric gases trap some of the Sun's infrared (heat) energy before it radiates out into space. (Ch. 19)

GRO See *Gamma Ray Observatory*.

ground state. The lowest energy level of an atom. (Ch. 8)

groundwater Fresh water from the surface, which typically percolates into the ground and fills the tiny spaces between grains of sandstone and other porous rock layers. (Ch. 18)

gymnosperm The class of vascular plants that produce seeds without flowers, such as fir trees. (Ch. 20)

gyre A circulation of water at the surface of the ocean, transporting warm water from the equator toward the cooler poles, and cold water from the poles back to the equator to be heated and cycled again. (Ch. 18)

hadron Particles, including the proton and neutron, that are made from quarks and are subject to the strong force. (Ch. 13)

half-life The rate of radioactive decay measured by the time it takes for half of a collection of isotopes to decay into another element. (Ch. 12)

heat (thermal energy) A measure of the quantity of atomic kinetic energy contained in every object. (Ch. 3)

heat conductor An object that allows heat to flow through it, such as metal. (Ch. 4)

heat insulator An object that impedes the flow of heat, such as wood. (Ch. 4)

heat transfer The process by which heat moves from one place to another, through three different mechanisms: conduction, convection, or radiation. (Ch. 4)

helium burning The final energy-producing stage of a star in which the temperature in the interior becomes so hot that the helium begins to undergo nuclear fusion reactions to make carbon. The net reaction is: $^4\text{He} + {}^4\text{He} + {}^4\text{He} \rightarrow {}^{12}\text{C}$. (Ch. 14)

herbivore Animals that get their energy by eating plants of the first trophic level. (Ch. 3)

hertz (Hz) The unit of measurement for the frequency of waves; one wave cycle per second. (Ch. 6)

Hertzsprung-Russell (H-R) diagram A simple graphical technique widely used in astronomy to plot a star's temperature (determined by its spectrum) versus the star's energy output (measured by its energy and brightness). (Ch. 14)

heterotrophs Organisms that must consume the essential building blocks of life from the surrounding environment to survive. (Ch. 20)

hierarchy A system that organizes all species based on shared and differing qualities into categories within a larger framework. (Ch. 20)

high-energy physics See *elementary-particle physics*.

high-grade energy Sources of energy that can be used to produce very high-temperature reservoirs; for example, petroleum and coal. (Ch. 4)

high-level nuclear waste The radioactive materials with long half-lives that remain in the nuclear reactor when uranium-235 has been used to generate energy. (Ch. 12)

high-quality protein Foods that supply amino acids in roughly the same proportion as those in human proteins, such as meat and dairy products. (Ch. 21)

high-temperature reservoir Any hot object from which energy is extracted to do work. Within the cylinder of a gasoline engine is a high-temperature reservoir. (Ch. 4)

HIV See *human immunodeficiency virus*.

hole The absence of an electron; in a silicon crystal, for example, a hole is left behind after the conduction electron is shaken loose. (Ch. 11)

homeostasis A balance among the populations of an ecosystem, resulting from the fact that matter and energy are limited resources that must be shared among all individuals of an ecosystem. (Ch. 19)

hominid The family of the order primate whose members walk erect; includes humans, which are the only hominids that are not extinct. (Ch. 20)

Homo erectus ("man the erect") The species of modern human's genus who first walked erect and learned to use fire; disappeared about 500,000 years ago. (Ch. 25)

Homo habilus ("man the toolmaker") The first member of the genus of modern humans who appeared about 2 million years ago in East Africa; distinguished by a larger brain and stone tools. (Ch. 25)

Homo sapiens The single species that includes all branches of the human race; recognized in fossils as old as 200,000 years. (Ch. 20)

horsepower Unit of power equal to 550 foot-pounds per second in the English system of measurement; commonly used to assess the power of engines and motors. (Ch. 3)

hot spot A dramatic type of volcanism indirectly associated with plate tectonics. Large isolated chimney-like columns of hot rock, or mantle plumes, rising to the surface in certain places of the Earth; for example, Yellowstone National Park, Iceland, and Hawaii. (Ch. 17)

Hubble Space Telescope (HST) An Earth-orbiting reflecting telescope, launched in 1990, with a 2.4-meter mirror designed to give unparalleled resolution in the visible and ultraviolet wavelengths. Manufacturing flaws in the main mirror were corrected by astronauts in late 1993. (Ch. 14)

Hubble's law The law relating the distance to a galaxy, d, and the rate at which it recedes from Earth, V, as measured by the redshift: $V = Hd$, where H is the Hubble constant. (Ch. 15)

Human Genome Project A large-scale scientific project that will result in a complete knowledge of the entire human genome, which includes 46 chromosomes and 3 billion base pairs. (Ch. 23)

human immunodeficiency virus (HIV) A virus that causes the disease AIDS and is transmitted through the exchange of bodily fluids. (Ch. 24)

humidity A measure of the atmosphere's variable water content. (Ch. 18)

hurricane Tropical storms having winds in excess of 120 km/h (75 mi/h) that begin in the Atlantic Ocean off the coast of Africa and affect North America. (Ch. 18)

hybrid An individual whose parents possess different genetic traits. (Ch. 23)

hydrocarbon A chainlike molecule from a chemical compound of carbon and hydrogen, which provides the most efficient fuels for combustion, with only carbon dioxide and water as products. (Ch. 10)

hydrogen bond A bond that may form when polarized hydrogen atoms link to other atoms by a covalent or ionic bond. (Ch. 10)

hydrogen burning A three-step process, generally confined to a small region in the center of a star, in which four protons are converted into a ^{4}He nucleus, two protons, and a photon. (Ch. 14)

hydrogenation The addition of hydrogen atoms into the carbon chains of polyunsaturated products; a process that eliminates the carbon–carbon double bonds. (Ch. 21)

hydrologic cycle The combination of processes by which water moves from repository to repository near the Earth's surface. (Ch. 18)

hydrophilic Attracted to water. (Ch. 21)

hydrophobic Repelled by water. (Ch. 21)

hypothesis A tentative guess about how the world works, based on a summary of experimental or observational results and phrased so that it can be tested by experimentation. (Ch. 1)

Hz See *hertz*.

ice age A period of several million years during which glaciers have repeatedly advanced and retreated, causing radical changes in climate and influencing human evolution. (Ch. 18)

ice cap Layers of ice that form at the north and south polar regions of the Earth. (Ch. 18)

igneous rock The first rock to form on a cooling planet, solidified from hot, molten material; intrusive or extrusive (volcanic). (Ch. 18)

immune system The system that defends an organism against harmful microorganisms by recognizing the geometric shape of molecules of foreign invaders and destroying them without harming the body's cells. (Ch. 23)

in vitro gene therapy A process where the gene is injected into cells outside of the body and then these cells are introduced into the body. (Ch. 24)

in vivo gene therapy A process where genes are injected into cells inside the body. (Ch. 24)

inertia The tendency of a body to remain in uniform motion; the resistance to change. (Ch. 2)

inflation A short period of rapid expansion of the universe, which, according to the grand unified theories, accompanied the "freezing" at 10^{-35} seconds. (Ch. 15)

inflationary theories Those cosmological theories that incorporate the phenomenon of universal inflation. (Ch. 15)

infrared Astronomical Satellite (IRAS) An orbiting observatory launched in 1983 by the United States, United Kingdom, and Netherlands to view infrared radiation in the universe. IRAS is no longer functioning. (Ch. 14)

infrared energy A form of electromagnetic radiation that travels from a source to an object, where it can be absorbed and converted into the kinetic energy of molecules. (Ch. 4)

infrared radiation Wavelengths of electromagnetic radiation that extend from a millimeter to a micron; felt as heat radiation. (Ch. 6)

insulator A material that will not conduct electricity. (Ch. 11)

integrated circuit A microchip made of hundreds or thousands of transistors specially designed to perform a specific function. (Ch. 11)

Interference When waves from two different sources come together at a single point, they interfere with each other. The observed wave amplitude is the sum of the amplitudes of the interfering waves. (Ch. 6)

interglacial period A period that occurs between two major glacier advances during an ice age. (Ch. 18)

intrusive rock Igneous rock that cools and hardens underground. (Ch. 18)

inversely proportional The relationship between two variables such that if the value of one variable increases, the other variable decreases, and vice versa, by a constant proportion. (Ch. 2)

invertebrates Organisms without backbones. (Ch. 20)

ion An atom that has an electrical charge, from either the loss or gain of an electron. (Ch. 8)

ionic bond A chemical bond in which the electrostatic force between two oppositely charged ions holds the atoms in place, often formed as one atom gives up an electron while another receives it, lowering chemical potential energy when atom shells are filled. (Ch. 10)

ionization Stripping away one or more of an atom's electrons to produce an ion. (Ch. 12)

IRAS See *Infrared Astronomical Satellite.*

isolated system A type of system in which matter and energy are not exchanged with the surroundings; a closed system. (Ch. 3)

isomer A molecule that contains the same atoms as another molecule, but has a different structural arrangement. (Ch. 10)

isotopes Atoms whose nuclei have the same number of protons but a different number of neutrons. (Ch. 12)

jet stream A high-altitude stream of fast-moving winds that marks the boundary between the northern polar cold air mass and the warmer air of the temperate zone. (Ch. 18)

joule The amount of work done when you exert a force of one newton through a distance of one meter. (Ch. 3)

Jovian planets Huge worlds also known as "gas giants" located in the outer solar system and made up primarily of frozen liquids and gases such as hydrogen, helium, ammonia, and water, with atmospheres of nitrogen, methane, and other compounds: Jupiter, Saturn, Uranus, Neptune. (Ch. 16)

kilowatt A commonly used measurement of electrical power equal to 1000 watts and corresponding to the expenditure of 1000 joules per second. (Ch. 3)

kinetic energy The type of energy associated with moving objects; the energy of motion. Kinetic energy is equal to the mass of the moving object times the square of that object's velocity, multiplied by $\frac{1}{2}$. (Ch. 3)

kingdom The broadest classification in the Linnaean classification system, corresponding to the coarsest division of living things. (Ch. 20)

Krebs cycle A complex series of chemical cellular reactions in which the products of glycolysis are broken down completely into carbon dioxide and water, releasing some energy to the ATP molecules and storing some in other energy-carrying molecules. (Ch. 22)

Kuiper Belt A region close to our solar system that contains comets that orbit the Sun; a reservoir of new comets. (Ch. 16)

laser An instrument that uses a collection of atoms, energy, and mirrors to emit photons that have wave crests in exact alignment. The instrument name is the acronym for *l*ight *a*mplification by *s*timulated *e*mission of *r*adiation. (Ch. 8)

lava Molten rock that flows from the surface of a volcano. (Ch. 17)

law of conservation of linear momentum A law that states that the quantity of an object's momentum will not change unless an outside force is applied to the object. Therefore, the object's present momentum will be conserved. (Ch. 2)

law of nature An overarching statement of how the universe works, following repeated and rigorous observation and testing of a theory or group of related theories. (Ch. 1)

law of unintended consequences A phenomenon demonstrating the interdependent nature of ecosystems: it is virtually impossible to change one aspect of an ecosystem without affecting something else, often inadvertently. (Ch. 19)

length contraction The phenomenon in relativity in which moving objects appear to be shorter than stationary ones in the direction of motion. (Ch. 7)

lepton A particle (such as the electron, muon, and neutrino) that participates in the weak and electromagnetic, but not the strong, interaction. (Ch. 13)

lichen (pronounced "*lie*-kin") A combination of a fungus and a single-celled organism that can use the Sun's energy through photosynthesis; important to the processes of weathering rock and creating soil. (Ch. 20)

light A form of electromagnetic wave to which the human eye is sensitive. Light travels at a constant speed and needs no medium for transfer. (Ch. 6)

light-year The distance light travels in one year, 10 trillion kilometers (about 6.2 trillion miles). (Ch. 14)

limestone A sedimentary rock formed from the calcium carbonate ($CaCO_3$) skeletons of sea animals, shells, and coral. (Ch. 18)

linear accelerator A device for making high-velocity particles, which relies on a long, straight vacuum tube into which particles are injected to ride an electromagnetic wave down the tube. (Ch. 13)

linear momentum The product of an object's mass times its velocity. (Ch. 2)

Linnaean classification A systematic attempt by Swedish naturalist Carolus Linnaeus to catalogue the diversity of all living things according to their shared characteristics so that each organism is as close as possible to those things it resembles, and as far apart as possible from those it does not. (Ch. 20)

lipid An organic molecule that is insoluble in water. At the molecular level, lipids form the cell membranes that separate living material from its environment. Lipids are also an extremely efficient storage medium for energy; for example, fat in foods, wax in candles, and grease for lubrication. (Ch. 21)

liquid Any collection of atoms or molecules that has no fixed shape but maintains a fixed volume. (Ch. 10)

liquid crystal A recently synthesized substance, used in digital displays, which is formed from very long molecules that may adopt a very ordered arrangement even in the liquid form. (Ch. 10)

load The location in an electric circuit where the useful work is done, such as the filament in a light-bulb or the heating element of a dryer. (Ch. 5)

longitudinal wave A kind of wave in which the motion of the medium is in the same direction as the wave movement; pressure wave or sound wave. (Ch. 6) Also, one of two principal types of seismic waves in which molecules in the rock move back and forth in the same direction as the wave; a compressional wave. (Ch. 17)

Lorentz factor A number, equal to the square root of $[1 - (v/c)^2]$, that appears in relativistic calculations and is an indication of the magnitude of change in time and scale. (Ch. 7)

low-quality protein Foods, such as that from plants, that lack one or more of the amino acids found in human proteins. (Ch. 21)

low-temperature reservoir The ambient atmosphere into which the waste heat generated by an engine is dumped; for example, from a cylinder in a gasoline engine to the atmosphere. (Ch. 4)

Lucy The name given to a nearly complete skeleton of a female *Australopithecus*, found in Ethiopia in 1974. (Ch. 25)

luminosity The total energy produced by a star. (Ch. 14)

lymphatic system An extensive network of capillaries and veins, parallel to the blood system and linked to about 500 lymph nodes in the human body. (App. A)

lysosome One of the cellular organelles that has digestion and breakdown of wastes as its primary function. (Ch. 22)

magma Subsurface molten rock, concentrated in the upper mantle or lower crust, which can breach the surface and harden into new rock. (Ch. 17)

magnet Materials that exert a magnetic field on other objects. Magnetite or "lodestone" is a common natural magnet. (Ch. 5)

magnetic field A collection of lines that map out the direction that compass needles would point in the vicinity of a magnet. (Ch. 5)

magnetic force The force exerted by magnets on each other. (Ch. 5)

magnetic monopole A hypothetical single isolated north or south magnetic pole, existing in theory but not yet located through experimentation. (Ch. 5)

magnetic potential energy The type of energy stored in a magnetic field. (Ch. 3)

magnetism A fundamental force in the universe. (Ch. 5)

main-sequence star A star that derives energy from the fusion reactions of hydrogen burning; found on the Hertzsprung-Russell (H-R) diagram within a bandlike pattern. (Ch. 14)

mammal One of a group of vertebrates made up of individuals that are warm-blooded, have hair, and whose females nurse their young. Human beings are mammals. (Ch. 20)

mantle The thick layer rich in oxygen, silicon, magnesium, and iron that contains most of the Earth's mass; it overlies the metal core of the Earth. (Ch. 16)

mantle convection A force deep within the Earth, driven by internal heat energy, that moves continents and the plates of which they are a part. (Ch. 17)

marble A metamorphic rock that begins as limestone that is subjected to intense pressure and high temperatures.

mass The amount of matter contained in an object, independent of where that object is found. (Ch. 2)

mass extinctions Rare and catastrophic events in the past that have caused large numbers of species to become extinct suddenly. (Ch. 25)

mass number The number of neutrons plus the number of protons, which determines the mass of an isotope. (Ch. 12)

Maxwell's equations Four fundamental laws of electricity and magnetism: (1) Coulomb's law: like charges repel and unlike charges attract; (2) magnetic monopoles do not exist in nature; (3) magnetic phenomena can be produced by electrical effects; and (4) electrical phenomena can be produced by magnetic effects. (Ch. 5)

mechanics The branch of science that deals with the motions of material objects and the forces that act on them; for example, a rolling rock or a thrown ball. (Ch. 2)

meiosis The division process that produces cells with one-half the number of chromosomes in each somatic cell. Each resulting daughter cell has half the normal complement of DNA. See *mitosis*. (Ch. 22)

meltdown The most serious accident that can occur at a nuclear reactor, in which the flow of water to the fuel rods is interrupted and the enormous heat stored in the central part of the reactor causes the fuel rods to melt. (Ch. 12)

melting A change of state from solid to liquid caused by an increase in temperature or decrease in pressure of the solid, which increases the vibration of individual molecules and breaks down the structure of the solid. (Ch. 10)

Mesozoic Era The third era, from 250 to 65 million years ago, known as "middle life," when the dinosaurs existed. (Ch. 25)

messenger RNA (mRNA) The single-stranded molecule that copies the sequence for one gene and carries that DNA information to the region of the cell where proteins are made. (Ch. 23)

metabolism The process by which a cell derives energy from its surroundings. (Ch. 22)

metal An element or combination of elements in which the sharing of a few electrons among all atoms results in more stable electron arrangement; characterized by a shiny luster and ability to conduct electricity. (Ch. 19)

metallic bond A chemical bond in which electrons are redistributed so that they are shared by all the atoms as a whole. (Ch. 10)

metamorphic rock Igneous or sedimentary rock that is buried and transformed by the Earth's intense internal temperature and pressure. (Ch. 18)

meteor A piece of interplanetary debris that hits the Earth's atmosphere and forms a bright streak of light from friction with atmospheric particles: a "shooting star." (Ch. 16)

meteor showers A set of spectacular, regularly occurring events in the night sky, caused by the collision of the Earth with clouds of small debris that travel around the orbits of comets. (Ch. 16)

meteorite The fragment of a meteor that hits the Earth. (Ch. 16)

microchip A complex array of *p*- and *n*-type semiconductors, which may incorporate hundreds or thousands of transistors in one integrated circuit. (Ch. 11)

microwave Electromagnetic waves, with wavelengths ranging from approximately 1 meter to 1 millimeter, which are used extensively for line-of-sight communications and cooking. (Ch. 6)

Mid-Atlantic Ridge The longest mountain range on Earth, which is located in the middle of the Atlantic Ocean. (Ch. 17)

Milankovitch cycles Slow cyclical changes in the Earth's climate due primarily to orbital effects. (Ch. 18)

Milky Way A collection of hundreds of billions stars that forms the galaxy of which the Sun is a part. (Ch. 15)

Miller-Urey experiment A demonstration of chemical evolution, performed in 1953 by Stanley Miller and Harold Urey, which showed that a combination of gases, believed to be present in the early atmosphere, and a series of electrical sparks, simulating the lightning on the early Earth, will produce amino acids, a basic building block of life. (Ch. 25)

mineral In a nutritional context, all chemical elements in food other than carbon, hydrogen, nitrogen, and oxygen. (Ch. 21)

mitochondria Sausage-shaped organelles that are places where molecules derived from glucose react with oxygen to produce the cell's energy. (Ch. 22)

mitosis The process of cell division producing daughter cells with exactly the same number of chromosomes as in the mother cell. See *meiosis*. (Ch. 22)

molecular genetics The study of how the mechanism that passes genetic information from parents to offspring functions on the basis of molecular chemistry. (Ch. 23)

molecule A cluster of atoms that bond together; the basic constituent of many different kinds of material. (Ch. 8)

monera Single-celled organisms without cell nuclei; the most primitive living things in the Linnaean classification of kingdoms. (Ch. 20)

monosaccharide An individual sugar molecule. (Ch. 21)

monounsaturated A type of lipid that forms when one kinked "double bond" forms between two carbon atoms in a molecule. See *unsaturated*. (Ch. 21)

monsoon Any wind system on a continental scale that seasonally reverses its direction because of seasonal variations in relative temperatures over land and sea. (Ch. 18)

Moon The Earth's only satellite, which may have formed when a planet-sized body hit the Earth early in its history. (Ch. 16)

mRNA See *messenger RNA*.

mudstone A sedimentary rock formed from sediments that are much finer-grained than sand. (Ch. 18)

mutation A change in the genetic material of a parent that is inherited by the offspring. (Ch. 23)

N See *newton*.

n-type semiconductor A type of electrical conductor formed from doping, that has a slight excess of mobile negatively charged electrons. (Ch. 11)

nanotechnology A new field of engineering that concentrates on extreme miniaturization and often creates new objects, atom by atom. (Ch. 11)

National Academy of Sciences A nationally recognized association of scientists, elected to membership by their peers to provide professional advice for the government on policy issues ranging from environmental risks and natural resource management, to education and funding for science research. (Ch. 1)

National Institutes of Health A federal agency that provides funding for basic and applied research in medicine and biology. (Ch. 1)

National Science Foundation A federal agency that funds American scientific research and education in all areas of science. (Ch. 1)

natural selection The mechanism by which nature can introduce wide-ranging changes in living things over long periods of time by modifying the gene pool of a species. (Ch. 25)

Neanderthal man A type of human with a large brain who lived until 35,000 years ago in groups with a complex social structure; either a separate species of the genus *Homo* or a subspecies of *Homo sapiens*. (Ch. 25)

nebulae Dust and gas clouds, common throughout the Milky Way galaxy, rich in hydrogen and helium. (Ch. 15)

nebular hypothesis A model that explains the formation of the solar system from a large cloud of gas and dust floating in space 4.5 billion years ago. This cloud collapsed upon itself under the influence of gravity and began to spin faster and faster, eventually forming the planets and the rest of the solar system along a flattened disk of matter surrounding a central star. (Ch. 16)

negative charge An excess of electrons on an object. (Ch. 5)

nervous system One of two control systems in the body that mediate responses to the environment. See *endocrine system*. (App. A)

neurotransmitter A group of molecules, produced in nerve cells, that transfer a nerve signal from one nerve cell to another. (Ch. 5)

neutrino A subatomic particle, emitted in the decay of the neutron, that has no electrical charge, travels at the speed of light, and has no rest mass. (Ch. 11)

neutron A type of subatomic particle, located in the nucleus of the atom that carries no electrical charge but has approximately the same mass as the proton; one of two primary building blocks of the nucleus. See *proton*. (Ch. 8)

neutron star A very dense, very small star, usually with a high rate of rotation and a strong magnetic field; the core remains of a supernova, held up by the degeneracy pressure of neutrons. (Ch. 14)

newton (N) A unit of force defined as the force needed to accelerate a mass of 1 kg by 1 m/s^2, or 1 kilogram-meter-per-second-squared. (Ch. 2)

Newton's law of universal gravitation Between any two objects in the universe there is an attractive force (gravity) that is proportional to the masses of the objects and inversely proportional to the square of the distance between them. In other words, the more massive two objects are, the greater the force between them will be, and the farther apart they are, the less the force will be. (Ch. 2)

Newton's laws of motion Three basic principles, expressed as laws, that govern the motion of everything in the universe, from stars and planets to cannonballs and muscles. The *first law* states that a moving object will continue moving in a straight line at a constant speed, and a stationary object will remain at rest, unless acted on by an unbalanced force. The *second law* states that the acceleration produced on a body by a force is proportional to the magnitude of the force and inversely proportional to the mass of the object. The *third law* states that for every action there is an equal and opposite reaction. (Ch. 2)

noble gases Elements listed in the far righthand column of the periodic table of elements, including helium, argon, and neon, which are odorless, colorless, and slow to react. (Ch. 8)

nonrenewable energy Sources of energy that, once used, are not quickly replaced; for example, petroleum and coal. (Ch. 4)

nonrenewable resources Resources such as coal and petroleum, which are forming at a much slower rate than they are being consumed. (Ch. 3)

nuclear reactor A device that controls fission reactions to produce energy when heavy radioactive nuclei split apart. (Ch. 12)

nucleic acid Molecule originally found in the nucleus of cells that carries and interprets the genetic code; includes DNA and RNA (Ch. 23)

nucleotide Molecule that is the basic element from which all DNA and RNA are built; formed from a sugar, a phosphate group, and one of four bases (adenine, guanine, cytosine, and thymine or uracil). (Ch. 23)

nucleus (1) The very small, compact object at the center of an atom; made up primarily of protons and neutrons. (2) A prominent structure in the interior of a cell that contains the cell's genetic material—the DNA—and controls the cell's chemistry. (Ch. 8, Ch. 18)

observation The act of observing nature without manipulating it. (Ch. 1)

ohm A unit of measurement for the electrical resistance of a wire. (Ch. 5)

oil shale A form of fossil fuel in which petroleum is dispersed through solid rock. (Ch. 3)

omnivore Animals that gain energy from plants and from organisms in other trophic levels. (Ch. 3)

Oort cloud A region beyond the orbit of Pluto that contains billions of comets circling the Sun; the reservoir for new comets. (Ch. 16)

open ecosystem An ecosystem in which materials are free to move in and out. (Ch. 19)

open system A type of system within which an object can exchange matter and energy with its surroundings. (Ch. 3)

open universe A model of the future of the universe in which the expansion will continue forever because the universe lacks enough matter to exert a gravitational force to slow receding galaxies. (Ch. 15)

optical microscope An instrument that uses visible light to present a magnified image from a sample through a lens to an eyepiece. (Ch. 22)

order The fourth broadest classification in the Linnaean classification system; humans are in the order of primates. (Ch. 20)

organelle Any specialized structure in the cell, including the nucleus. (Ch. 22)

organic chemistry The branch of science devoted to the study of carbon-based molecules and their reactions. (Ch. 10)

organic molecules Carbon-based molecules that may or may not be part of a living system. (Ch. 21)

osmosis A special case of molecular movement in which materials such as water are transferred across a membrane while at the same time molecules dissolved in the water are blocked. (Ch. 22)

outgassing Release of gases from nongaseous materials; extrusion of gases from the body of a planet after its formation. (Ch. 16)

oxidation A chemical reaction in which an atom such as oxygen accepts electrons while combining with other elements; for example, rusting of iron metal into iron oxide, or animal respiration. (Ch. 10)

oxides Chemical compounds that contain oxygen, such as most common minerals and ceramics. (Ch. 11)

ozone A molecule made up of three oxygen atoms, instead of the usual two, which absorbs ultraviolet radiation. (Ch. 19)

ozone hole A volume of atmosphere above Antarctica during September through November in which the concentration of the trace gas ozone has declined significantly. (Ch. 19)

ozone layer A region of enhanced ozone (O_3) 20 to 30 miles above the Earth's surface where most of the absorption of the Sun's ultraviolet radiation occurs. (Ch. 19)

p-type semiconductor A type of electrical conductor, formed from doping, that has a slight deficiency of electrons, resulting in mobile positively charged holes. (Ch. 11)

paleomagnetism The field devoted to the study of remnant magnetism in ancient rock, recording the direction of the magnetic poles at some time in the past. (Ch. 17)

Paleozoic Era The second era, lasting from 545 to 250 million years ago, during which time fish, amphibians, land plants and animals, and rudimentary reptiles developed; term meaning "old life." (Ch. 25)

Pangaea A giant continent consisting of North America, South America, Eurasia, and Africa, which existed 200 million years ago. (Ch. 17)

parallel circuit A circuit in which different loads are situated on different wire loops. (Ch. 5)

parsec A unit of measurement equal to about 3.3 light-years, which roughly corresponds to the average distance between nearest-neighbor stars in our galaxy. (Ch. 14)

particle accelerator A machine such as a synchrotron or linear accelerator that produces particles at near light speeds for use in the study of the fundamental structure of matter. (Ch. 13)

Pauli exclusion principle A statement that says no two electrons can occupy the same state at the same time. (Ch. 8)

PCR See *polymerase chain reaction*.

peak load The especially high demand in the mass market of electricity due to special circumstances, such as a heat wave. (Ch. 3)

peer review A system by which the editor of a scientific journal submits manuscripts considered for publication to a panel of knowledgeable scientists who, in confidence, evaluate the manuscript for mistakes, misstatements, or shoddy procedures. Following the review, if the manuscript is to be published, it is returned to the author with a list of modifications and corrections to be completed. (Ch. 1)

pencillin A substance that kills bacteria; the best-known modern antibiotic. (Ch. 20)

Penicillium A common mold that secretes the substance penicillin, an antibiotic. (Ch. 20)

peptide bond A connection between two atoms that remains after hydrogen (H) at one end of an amino acid and the hydroxyl (OH) from the end of another amino acid combine, releasing a water molecule (H_2O). The process is identical to the condensation polymerization reaction. (Ch. 21)

periodic table of the elements An organizational system, first developed by Dmitri Mendeleev in 1869, now listing more than 110 elements by atomic weight (in rows) and chemical properties (in columns). The pattern of elements in the periodic table reflects the arrangement of electrons in their orbits. (Ch. 8)

petroleum Thick black liquid found deep underground, derived from many kinds of transformed molecules of former life forms. (Ch. 10)

phosphate group One phosphorus atom surrounded by four oxygen atoms. (Ch. 21)

phospholipid The class of molecules that form membranes in cells. Lipids have a long, thin structure with a carbon backbone, and a phosphate group at one end of the molecule. One end of these molecules is hydrophilic, one hydrophobic. (Ch. 21)

photoelectric effect A phenomenon that occurs when photons strike one side of a material and cause electrons of that material to be emitted from the opposite side. This effect is observed in modern cameras, CAT scans, and fiber optics. (Ch. 9)

photon A particle-like unit of light, emitted or absorbed by an atom when an electrically charged electron changes state. The form of a single packet of electromagnetic radiation. (Ch. 8)

photosphere The gaseous layers of the Sun's outer part, which emit most of the light we see. (Ch. 14)

photosynthesis The mechanism by which plants convert the energy of sunlight into energy stored in carbohydrates, the chemical energy of virtually all life on Earth: energy + CO_2 + H_2O → carbohydrate + oxygen. (Ch. 22)

photovoltaic cell A semiconductor diode that uses sunlight to produce electrical current. They are also used in hand calculators and in some cameras for power. (Ch. 11)

phylum The second broadest classification in the Linnaean classification system; humans are in the phylum chordata, subphylum vertebrata. (Ch. 20)

Planck's constant (*h***)** A constant named after German physicist Max Planck that is the central constant of quantum physics, equal to 6.63×10^{-34} joule-seconds in SI units. (Ch. 9)

planetesimal Small objects, which range in size from boulders to several miles across, formed from the accretion of solid material during the formation of the planets. (Ch. 16)

plants Multicelled organisms that get their energy directly from the Sun through photosynthesis. One of five kingdoms in the Linnaean classification. (Ch. 20)

plasma A state of matter existing under extremely high temperatures in which electrons are stripped from their atoms during high-energy collisions, forming an electron sea surrounding positive nuclei. (Ch. 10)

plasmid A loop of DNA in which genes are linked; it can be introduced into a cell for DNA replication. (Ch. 24)

plastic Synthetic polymers that are formed primarily from petroleum. They consist of intertwined polymer strands, much like the strands of fiberglass insulation. When heated, these strands slide across each other to adopt new shapes. When cooled, the plastic fiber mass solidifies into whatever shape is available. (Ch. 10)

plate A rigid moving sheet of rock up to 100 km (60 mi) thick, composed of the crust and part of the upper mantle. (See *plate tectonics.*) (Ch. 17)

plate tectonics The model of the dynamic Earth that has emerged from studies of paleomagnetism, rock dating, and much other data. A theory that explains how a few thin, rigid tectonic plates of crustal and upper mantle materials are moved across the Earth's surface by mantle convection. (Ch. 17)

Pluto A rocky body that is located beyond the Jovian planets and is the smallest of all planets in the solar system. (Ch. 16)

polar molecule Atom clusters with a positive and negative end; exerts electrical force on neighboring atoms. Water is a polar molecule. (Ch. 10)

polarization The subtle electron shift from negative to positive that takes place when the electrons of an atom or a molecule are brought near a polar molecule such as water, resulting in a bond caused by the electrical attraction between the negative end of the polar molecule and the positive side of the other molecule. (Ch. 10)

poles The two opposite ends of a magnet, named north and south, that repel a like magnetic pole and attract an unlike magnetic pole. (Ch. 5)

polymer Extremely long and large molecules that are formed from numerous smaller molecules, like links in a chain, with predictable repeating sequences of atoms along the chain. (Ch. 10)

polymerase chain reaction (PCR) A process of copying select strands of DNA so that as much can be created as is needed for research. (Ch. 24)

polymerization A reaction that includes all chemical reactions that form long strands of polymer fibers by linking small molecules. (Ch. 10)

polypeptide A bonded chain of amino acids. See *peptide bond*. (Ch. 21)

polysaccharide A molecule that is the result of many sugar molecules strung together in a chain; for example, starch and cellulose. (Ch. 21)

polyunsaturated A type of lipid that forms when two or more kinked "double bonds" between carbon atoms are in the molecule. See *unsaturated*. (Ch. 21)

positive charge A deficiency of electrons on an object. (Ch. 5)

positron The positively charged antiparticle of the electron. (Ch. 13)

potential energy The energy a system possesses if it is capable of doing work, but is not doing work now. Types of potential energy include magnetic, elastic, electrical, and chemical. Any type of energy waiting to be released; stored energy. (Ch. 3)

power The rate at which work is done or energy is expended. The amount of work done, divided by the time it takes to do it. Power is measured in watts in the metric system, horsepower in the English. (Ch. 3)

power stroke The downward motion of a piston in a gasoline engine, in which the actual work is done and the energy released by combustion is translated into the motion of the car. (Ch. 4)

precession The circular motion of the spinning axis of the Earth in space, which causes the tilt of the Northern Hemisphere to change on a 26,000-year cycle. (Ch. 18)

precipitation A chemical reaction that is the reverse of a solution reaction, producing a solid that separates from very concentrated solutions. (Ch. 10)

prediction A guess about how a particular system will behave, followed by observations to see if the system did behave as expected within a specified range of situations. (Ch. 1)

pressure A force on a surface divided by the area of the surface. (Ch. 18)

prevailing westerly Wind in the temperate zones that blows primarily from west to east, causing weather patterns to move in the same direction. (Ch. 18)

primary structure The simplest of the four stages of the organization of amino acids in a protein molecule. The exact order of amino acids along the protein string. (Ch. 21)

primates An order of mammals that have grasping fingers and toes, eyes at the front of their heads, large brains, and fingernails instead of claws; includes monkeys, apes, and humans. (Ch. 20)

primordial soup A rich broth of amino acids and other molecules thought to have been produced in the early oceans over a period of several hundred million years, recreated by the Miller-Urey process. (Ch. 25)

probability The likelihood that an event will occur or that an object will be in one state or another; how nature is described in the subatomic world. (Ch. 9)

producers Organisms, such as plants, that obtain atoms and energy from physical surroundings to produce carbon-based molecules of life in an ecosystem. (Ch. 19)

prokaryote A type of primitive cell in which the DNA is coiled together, but not separated in the nucleus. Prokaryotes constitute the kingdom monera, including all cells that do not have a nucleus. (Ch. 22)

protease inhibitor A molecule that is designed using new computer visualization techniques to combat HIV as a result of long study of the HIV virus structure and processes. (Ch. 24)

protein An extremely complex molecule, which can consist of thousands of amino acids and millions of atoms formed in a chain structure. Proteins function as enzymes and direct the cell's chemistry. (Ch. 21)

Proterozoic Era The era lasting from the beginning of the Earth's existence to 545 million years ago; a term meaning "before life" (Ch. 25)

protista Single-celled organisms with nuclei, and a few multicelled organisms that have a particularly simple structure. One of five kingdoms in the Linnaean classification. (Ch. 20)

proton One of two primary building blocks of the nucleus; with a positive electrical charge of +1 and a mass 1.672643×10^{-24} g approximately equal to that of the neutron. (Ch. 12)

pseudoscience A kind of inquiry falling in the realm of belief or dogma, which includes subjects that cannot be proved or disproved with a reproducible test. The subjects include creationism, extrasensory perception (ESP), unidentified flying objects, astrology, crystal power, and reincarnation. (Ch. 1)

publication A peer-reviewed paper written by a scientist or a group of scientists to communicate the results of their research to a larger audience. A publication will include the technical details of the methodology, so that the research can be reproduced, and a concise statement of the results and conclusions. (Ch. 1)

pulsar A neutron star in which fast-moving particles speed out along the intense magnetic field lines of the rotating star, giving off electromagnetic radiation that we detect as a series of pulses of radio waves. (Ch. 14)

pumice Frothy volcanic rock rich in silicon from magmas that mix with a significant amount of water or other volatile substance. (Ch. 18)

pumping The process in a laser that adds energy to the system from the outside to return atoms continuously to their excited states so that coherent photons can be produced. (Ch. 8)

punctuated equilibrium A hypothesis that holds that evolutionary changes usually occur in short bursts separated by long periods of stability. (Ch. 25)

purebred Bred from members of a single strain. (Ch. 23)

pyruvic acid Three-carbon molecules in a cell that were formed by glycolysis, splitting a glucose molecule into two smaller molecules. (Ch. 22)

quantized Whenever energy or another property of a system can have only certain definite values, and nothing in between those values, it is said to be quantized. (Ch. 9)

quantum leap A process by which an electron changes its energy state without ever possessing an energy intermediate between the original and the final energy state; also known as a quantum jump. (Ch. 8)

quantum mechanics The branch of science that is devoted to the study of the motion of objects that come in small bundles, or quanta, which applies to the subatomic world. (Ch. 9)

quarks (pronounced "quorks") The truly fundamental building blocks of the hadrons. Particles that have fractional electrical charge and cannot exist alone in nature. (Ch. 13)

quartzite A durable rock in which the original sand grains of sandstone, under high temperature and pressure, recrystallize and fuse into a solid mass. (Ch. 18)

quasar Quasi-stellar radio source. Objects in the universe, where as-yet unknown processes pour vast amounts of energy into space each second from an active center no larger than the solar system; the most distant objects known. (Ch. 15)

quaternary structure The joining of separate protein chains, each with its own secondary and tertiary structures. (Ch. 21)

R&D See *research and development.*

radiation The transfer of heat by electromagnetic radiation. The only one of the three mechanisms of heat transfer that does not require atoms or molecules to facilitate the transfer process. (Ch. 4) Also, the particles emitted during the spontaneous decay of nuclei. (Ch. 12)

radio wave Part of the electromagnetic spectrum that ranges from the longest waves—wavelengths longer than the Earth's diameter—to waves a few meters long. (Ch. 6)

radioactive decay The process of spontaneous change of unstable isotopes. (Ch. 12)

radioactivity The spontaneous release of energy by certain atoms, such as uranium, as these atoms disintegrate. The emission of one or more kinds of radiation from an isotope with unstable nuclei. (Ch. 12)

radiometric dating A technique based on the radioactive half-lives of carbon-14 and other isotopes that is used to determine the age of materials. (Ch. 12)

radon A colorless, odorless inert gas that can cause an indoor pollution problem when it undergoes radioactive decay. (Ch. 12)

receptor A large structure found in the cell membrane and made of proteins folded into a geometrical shape that will bond chemically only to a specific type of molecule. (Ch. 22)

recessive A characteristic that will appear only if no dominant gene is present. (Ch. 23)

recessive gene A gene that is present in offspring and can be passed along to subsequent generations, but may not determine the offspring's physical characteristics. (Ch. 23)

red giant An extremely large star that emits a lot of energy but whose surface is very cool and therefore appears somewhat reddish in the sky; found in the upper righthand corner of the H-R diagram. (Ch. 14)

redshift An increase in the wavelength of radiation received from a receding celestial body as a consequence of the Doppler effect. A shift toward the long-wavelength (red) end of the spectrum. (Ch. 14)

redshifted The result of the Doppler effect on light waves, when the source of light moves away from the observer: light-wave crests are farther apart and have a lower frequency. (Ch. 6)

reduction A chemical reaction in which electrons are transferred from an atom to other elements, resulting in a gain in electrons for the material being reduced; for example, smelting of metal ores, and photosynthesis. (Ch. 10)

reductionism The quest for the ultimate building blocks of the universe. An attempt to reduce the seeming complexity of nature by first looking for an underlying simplicity and then trying to understand how that simplicity gives rise to the observed complexity. (Ch. 13)

reflection A process by which light waves are scattered at the same angle as the original wave; for example, from the surface of a mirror. (Ch. 6)

refraction One of three responses of an electromagnetic wave encountering matter, in which electromagnetic waves slow down and change direction in the matter. See also *absorption* and *transmission*. (Ch. 6)

relativity An idea that the laws of nature are the same in all frames of reference, and that every observer must experience the same natural laws. (Ch. 7)

reproducible A criterion for the results of an experiment. In the scientific method, observations and experiments must be reported in such a way that anyone with the proper equipment can verify the results. (Ch. 1)

reproductive cloning An application of cloning technology that produces a new living being. See *cloning*. (Ch. 24)

reptiles The first animals fully adapted to life on land; includes lizards, turtles, and snakes. (Ch. 20)

research and development (R&D) A kind of research aimed at specific problems, usually performed in government and industry laboratories. (Ch. 1)

reservoirs Locations where a substance is to be found. Earth's water, for example, is found in oceans, rivers, ice caps, and several other reservoirs. (Ch. 18)

residence time The average length of time that any given atom will stay in ocean water before it is removed by some chemical reaction. (Ch. 18)

respiration The process by which animals retrieve energy stored in glucose, in a complex series of cellular chemical reactions, which include breathing in oxygen produced by plants, burning carbohydrates ingested for food, and breathing out carbon dioxide. (Ch. 22)

respiratory system The system that takes oxygen from the air and transfers it to the circulatory system; includes the lungs and the alveoli. (App. A)

restriction enzyme Proteins that have the ability to cut a DNA molecule so that the DNA has several unattached bases at the cut end. (Ch. 24)

ribonucleic acid (RNA) A molecule that consists of one string of nucleotides put together around the sugar ribose, and with the bases adenine, guanine, cytosine, and uracil. RNA plays a crucial role in the synthesis of proteins in the cell. (Ch. 23)

ribose The standard sugar containing five-carbon atoms in ribonucleic acid (RNA). (Ch. 23)

ribosomal RNA (rRNA) A constituent of ribosomes; involved in the synthesis of protein. (Ch. 23)

ribosome One of the cellular organelles that is the site of protein synthesis. (Ch. 22)

RNA See *ribonucleic acid*.

rock cycle An ongoing cycle of internal and external Earth processes by which rock is created, destroyed, and altered. (Ch. 18)

rock formations Bodies of rock that form as a continuous unit, possibly combining many different types of rock. (Ch. 18)

rod One type of light-absorbing cell in the eye providing night vision; sensitive to light and dark. Compare to *cone*. (Ch. 6)

Roentgen Satellite (ROSAT) An X-ray satellite launched in 1990 by the United States, United Kingdom, and Germany as the latest in a series of satellites equipped to detect X-rays. (Ch. 14)

ROSAT See *Roentgen Satellite*.

rRNA See *ribosomal RNA*.

sandstone A sedimentary rock formed mostly from sand-sized grains of quartz (silicon dioxide) and other hard mineral and rock fragments. (Ch. 18)

saturated A fully bonded carbon atom in a lipid. In a straight lipid chain, every carbon atom bonds to two adjacent carbon atoms along the chain and two hydrogen atoms on the sides. (Ch. 21)

scattering A process by which electromagnetic waves may be absorbed and rapidly re-emitted; can be diffuse scattering or reflection. (Ch. 6)

schist Metamorphic rock formed from slate under extreme temperature and pressure. (Ch. 18)

scientific method A continuous process used to collect observations, form and test hypotheses, make predictions, and identify patterns in the physical world. (Ch. 1)

second law of thermodynamics Any one of three equivalent statements: (1) heat will not flow spontaneously from a colder to a hotter body; (2) it is impossible to construct a machine that does nothing but convert heat into useful work; and (3) the entropy of an isolated system always increases. (Ch. 4)

second trophic level All herbivores, including cows, rabbits, and many different kinds of insects, that get their energy by eating plants. (Ch. 3)

secondary structure Shapes taken by the string of amino acids that makes up the primary structure of a protein.

sedimentary rock A type of rock that is formed from layers of sediment produced by the weathering of other rock or by chemical precipitation. (Ch. 18)

seismic tomography A branch of Earth science that enables geophysicists to obtain three-dimensional pictures of the Earth's interior. (Ch. 17)

seismic wave The form through which an earthquake's energy is transmitted, causing the Earth to rise and fall like the surface of the ocean. (Ch. 17)

seismology The study and measurement of vibrations within the Earth, dedicated to deducing our planet's inner structure. (Ch. 17)

semiconductor Materials that conduct electricity but do not conduct it very well. Neither a good conductor nor a perfect insulator; for example, silicon. (Ch. 11)

series circuit An electric circuit in which two or more loads are linked along a single loop of wire. (Ch. 5)

shale A sedimentary rock formed from sediments that are much finer grained than sand. (Ch. 18)

shear strength A material's ability to withstand twisting. (Ch. 11)

shear wave One of two principal types of seismic waves, in which molecules move perpendicular to the direction of the wave motion. A transverse wave. (Ch. 17)

single bond The type of covalent bond formed when only one electron is shared. (Ch. 10)

skeleto-muscular system An internal structure that supports the weight and produces movement of the human body. (App. A)

slate A brittle and hard metamorphic rock, formed from shale or mudstone. (Ch. 18)

smog The brownish stuff of modern urban air pollution that you often see over major cities during the summer, caused by a photochemical reaction. (Ch. 19)

solar system The Sun, the planets and their moons, and all other objects gravitationally bound to the Sun. (Ch. 16)

solar wind A stream of charged particles—mainly ions of hydrogen and electrons—emitted constantly by the Sun into the space around it. (Ch. 14)

solid Any material that possesses a fixed shape and volume, with chemical bonds that are both sufficiently strong and directional to preserve a large-scale external form. (Ch. 10)

solution reaction A chemical reaction in which a solid such as salt or sugar is dissolved in a liquid. (Ch. 10)

somatic stem cell A cell in an adult organism that may be made to develop into other specialized cells. (Ch. 24)

sound wave A longitudinal wave created by a vibrating object and transmitted only through the motion of molecules in a solid, gas, or liquid. The energy of the sound wave is associated with the kinetic energy of those molecules. (Ch. 3)

special relativity The first of two parts of Einstein's theory of relativity that deals with reference frames that do not accelerate. (Ch. 7)

species The basic unit of the Linnaean classification; an interbreeding population of individual organisms. (Ch. 20)

specific heat capacity A measure of the ability of a material to absorb heat energy, defined as the quantity of heat required to raise the temperature of one gram of that material by 1°C. Water displays the largest heat capacity of any common substance. (Ch. 4)

spectroscopy The study of emission and absorption spectra of materials in order to discover the chemical makeup of a material; a standard tool used in almost every branch of science. (Ch. 8)

spectrum The characteristic signal from the total collection of photons emitted by a given atom that can be used to identify the chemical elements in a material; the atomic fingerprint. (Ch. 8)

speed The distance an object travels divided by the time it takes to travel that distance. (Ch. 2)

speed of light *(c)* The velocity at which all electromagnetic waves travel, regardless of their wavelength or frequency; equal to 300,000 kilometers per second (about 186,000 miles per second). (Ch. 6)

spindle fibers A series of fibers that develop after chromosomes have duplicated and the nuclear membrane has dissolved. (Ch. 22)

spreading The widening of the seafloor, as magma comes from deep within the Earth and erupts through fissures on the seafloor. (Ch. 17)

standard model Theories, supported by experimental evidence, that predict the unification of the strong force with the electroweak force. (Ch. 21)

Staphylococcus A common infectious bacteria that can be killed by penicillin and other antibiotics. (Ch. 20)

star Objects such as our Sun that form from giant clouds of interstellar dust and generate energy by nuclear fusion reactions. (Ch. 14)

starch A polysaccharide, with glucose constituents linked together at certain points along the ring. A large family of molecules found in many plants, such as potatoes and corn. (Ch. 21)

states of matter Different modes of organization of atoms or molecules, which result in properties of gases, plasmas, liquids, or solids. (Ch. 10)

static electricity A phenomenon caused by the transfer of electrical charge between objects. Often observed as lightning or as sparks produced when walking across a wool rug on a dry, cold day. (Ch. 5)

steady-state universe A model, no longer believed to be valid, that describes a universe that is constantly expanding and forming new galaxies, but with no trace of a beginning. (Ch. 15)

strength The ability of a solid to resist changes in shape; directly related to chemical bonding. (Ch. 11)

strong force The force responsible for holding the nucleus together; one of the four fundamental forces in nature. This force operates over extremely short distances and between quarks to hold elementary particles together. (Ch. 12)

subduction zone The regions of the Earth where plates converge and old crust returns to the mantle. (Ch. 17)

sublimation The direct transformation of a solid to a gaseous state, without passing through the liquid state. (Ch. 10)

sugar The simplest of the carbohydrates. Common sugars contain five, six, or seven carbon atoms arranged in a ringlike structure. (Ch. 21)

superclusters Large collections of clusters and groups of thousands of galaxies. (Ch. 15)

superconductivity The ability of some materials to exhibit the complete absence of any electrical resistance, usually when cooled to within a few degrees of absolute zero. (Ch. 11)

supernova A stupendous explosion of a star, which increases its brightness hundreds of millions of times in a few days; results from the implosion of the core of a massive star at the end of its life. (Ch. 14)

synchrotron A particle accelerator in which magnetic fields are increased as particles become more energetic, keeping them moving on the same track. (Ch. 13)

system A part of the universe under study and separated from its surroundings by a real or imaginary boundary. (Ch. 3)

taxonomy The science of cataloging living things, describing them, and giving them names. (Ch. 20)

technology The application of the results of science to specific commercial or industrial goals. (Ch. 1)

tectonic plate One of a dozen sheets of moving rock in various sizes forming the surface of the Earth. (Ch. 17)

telescope A device that focuses and concentrates radiation from distant objects; used by astronomers to collect and analyze radio waves, microwaves, light, and other radiation. (Ch. 14)

temperature A quantity that reflects how vigorously atoms are moving and colliding in a material. (Ch. 4)

temperature scales Standard scales that can be used to measure and compare the temperatures of two different objects. (Ch. 4)

tensile strength A material's ability to withstand pulling apart. (Ch. 11)

terminal electron transport The final stage of respiration in which energy is used to produce more ATP molecules. (Ch. 22)

terminal velocity The point at which a dropped object stops accelerating and continues to fall at a constant velocity. (Ch. 2)

terrane A mass of rock as much as several hundred kilometers across, found in most of the western part of the United States, which was once a large island in the Pacific Ocean and carried toward the North American continent by plate activity. (Ch. 17)

terrestrial planets The relatively small, rocky, high-density planets located in the inner solar system nearest the Sun: Mercury, Venus, Earth, the Earth's Moon, and Mars. (Ch. 16)

tertiary structure The complex folding of a protein, caused by the cross-linking of chemical bonds from side groups in the amino acid chain. (Ch. 21)

theories of everything A term that scientists use to refer to theories that unify all of the four forces. (Ch. 13)

theorist A scientist who uses mathematical models and logical inference to make statements about the universe in order to explain its processes and organisms. (Ch. 1)

theory A description of the world that covers a relatively large number of phenomena and has met many observational and experimental tests. A conclusion based upon observations of nature. (Ch. 1)

theory of relativity The idea that the laws of nature are the same in all frames of reference. Einstein divided his theory into two parts—special relativity and general relativity. (Ch. 7)

therapeutic cloning An application of cloning technology that uses cloning in medical procedure to improve human health. See *cloning*. (Ch. 24)

thermal conductivity The ability of a material to transfer heat energy from one molecule to the next by conduction. When thermal conductivity is low, as in wood or fiberglass insulation, the transfer of heat is slowed down. (Ch. 4)

thermal energy The kinetic energy of atoms and molecules; what we normally call heat. (Ch. 3)

thermodynamics The study of the movement of heat; the science of heat, energy, and work. (Ch. 3)

thermometer A device that measures temperature using a temperature scale and a material that expands and contracts with temperature change, such as mercury. (Ch. 4)

time dilation A phenomenon in special relativity in which moving clocks appear to tick more slowly than stationary ones. (Ch. 7)

tornado The most violent weather phenomenon known. A rotating air funnel some tens to hundreds of meters across, descending from storm clouds to the ground, causing intense damage along the path where the funnel touches the ground. (Ch. 18)

totipotent A state that occurs in an early stage of embryonic cell division where each cell retains the ability to express all of its genes; the cell is not yet specialized. (Ch. 24)

trace element A chemical, such as iodine in the thyroid gland and iron in the blood, that is needed in minor amounts by the body. (Ch. 21)

trace gas A gas that constitutes less than one molecule in a million in the Earth's atmosphere; for example, ozone. (Ch. 19)

trade wind Surface winds near the equator of the Atlantic Ocean that blow east to west. (Ch. 18)

transcription A process by which a cell transfers information in DNA to molecules of mRNA. (Ch. 23)

transfer RNA (tRNA) The molecule with special configuration that attracts amino acids at one end, and, at the other end, attaches to a specific codon of mRNA. (Ch. 23)

transform plate boundary The type of boundary between plates that occurs when one plate scrapes past the other, with no new plate material being produced; for example, California's San Andreas Fault. (Ch. 17)

transistor A device that sandwiches *p*- and *n*-type semiconductors in an arrangement that can amplify or redirect an electrical current running through it; a device that played an essential role in the development of modern electronics. (Ch. 11)

transmission One of three responses of an electromagnetic wave encountering matter, in which light energy passes through the matter unaffected. See also *absorption* and *refraction*. (Ch. 6)

transverse wave A kind of wave in which the motion of the wave is perpendicular to the motion of the medium on which the wave moves. (Ch. 6)

triangulation A geometrical method used to measure the distances to the nearest stars up to a few hundred light-years away. The angle of sight to the star is measured at opposite ends of the Earth's orbit and the distances are calculated. (Ch. 14)

tRNA See *transfer RNA.*

trophic level All organisms that get their energy from the same source. (Ch. 3)

tropical storm A severe storm that starts as a low-pressure area over warm ocean water and, while drawing energy from the warm water, grows and rotates in great cyclonic patterns hundreds of kilometers in diameter. (Ch. 18)

tsunami A great wave, which can devastate low-lying coastal areas, occurring when the energy of an earthquake under or near a large body of water is transferred through the water. (Ch. 17)

typhoon A tropical storm that begins in the North Pacific Ocean (Ch. 18)

ultraviolet radiation High-frequency wavelengths, shorter than visible light, ranging from 400 nanometers to 100 nanometers. (Ch. 6)

uncertainty principle The idea quantified by Werner Heisenberg in 1927 that at a quantum scale, the location and velocity of an object can never be known at the same time, because quantum-scale measurement affects the object being measured. Specifically, "the error or uncertainty in the measurement of an object's position, times the error or uncertainty in that object's velocity, must be greater than a constant, *h,* divided by the object's mass." (Ch. 9)

unified field theory The general name for any theory in which fundamental forces are seen as different aspects of the same force. (Ch. 13)

uniform motion The motion of an object if it travels in a straight line at a constant speed. All other motions involve acceleration. (Ch. 2)

unsaturated In a lipid chain, a carbon atom bonded with two carbon atoms and one hydrogen atom, and with one kinked "double bond" with one of the adjacent carbon atoms. See *saturated*. (Ch. 21)

vacuole In plants, a cellular organelle that is responsible for waste storage. (Ch. 22)

valence electron An outer electron of an atom that can be exchanged or shared during chemical bonding. (Ch. 10)

valence The combining power of a given atom, determined by the number of electrons in an atom's outermost orbit. (Ch. 10)

van der Waals force A net attractive bond and weak force resulting from the polarization of electrically neutral atoms or molecules. (Ch. 10)

vascular plant The phylum of plants that have internal "plumbing" capable of carrying fluids from one part of the plant to another. (Ch. 20)

vector A quantity that measures rate and direction. Velocity and speed are examples of vectors because they are measured in units of distance and time. (Ch. 2)

velocity The distance an object travels divided by the time it takes to travel that distance, including the direction of travel. The velocity of a falling object is proportional to the length of time that it has been falling. (Ch. 2)

vertebrate A subphylum of chordates in which the nerves along the back are encased in bone. (Ch. 20)

vesicle The vehicle by which a particle moves around inside a cell; a tiny container formed from the cell membrane, and a particle with its receptor. (Ch. 22)

vestigial organ A bodily feature that serves no useful function at present and is compelling evidence for evolution. (Ch. 25)

virus A short length of RNA or DNA wrapped in a protein coating that fits cell receptors and replicates itself using the cell's machinery. (Ch. 23)

visible light Electromagnetic waves with a wavelength that can be interpreted by nerve receptors in the brain; wavelengths range from 700 nanometers for red light to 400 nanometers for violet light. (Ch. 6)

vitamin One of a host of complex organic molecules that, in small quantities, play an essential role in good health; for example, by mediating the body's chemical reactions. May be fat soluble and stored, or water soluble and not retained by the body. (Ch. 21)

volcanic rock Extrusive igneous rock that solidifies on the surface of the Earth. (Ch. 18)

volcano Places where subsurface molten rock breaks through to the surface of the Earth to form dramatic short-term changes in the landscape. (Ch. 17)

voltage The pressure produced by the energy source in an electric circuit, measured in volts. (Ch. 5)

_w_ particle A massive particle that, along with the _z_ particle, mediates the weak interaction. (Ch. 13)

warm blooded Animals, such as birds and mammals, that have a four-chambered heart and can maintain a constant body temperature in any environment. (Ch. 20)

water-soluble vitamin A vitamin that can dissolve in water and is not retained by the body, including vitamins B and C. (Ch. 21)

watt A unit of measurement that is the expenditure of 1 joule of energy in 1 second. (Ch. 3)

wave A traveling disturbance that carries energy from one place to another without requiring matter to travel across the intervening distance. (Ch. 6)

wave energy The kinetic energy associated with different kinds of waves, such as kinetic energy possessed by large amounts of water in rapid motion, and electromagnetic radiation stored in changing electrical and magnetic fields. (Ch. 3)

wave mechanics Another term for quantum mechanics, indicating the dual (wave and particle) nature of quantum objects. (Ch. 9)

wavelength The distance between adjacent wave crests, the highest points of adjacent waves. (Ch. 6)

weather Daily changes in rainfall, temperature, amount of sunshine, and other variables resulting partly from the general circulation in the atmosphere, and partly from local disturbances and variations. (Ch. 18)

weathering A process in which rock wears away, for example by washing away particles, dissolving rock, or freezing in rock cracks. (Ch. 18)

weight The force of gravity on an object. (Ch. 2)

white dwarf A star that has a very low emission of energy but very high surface temperature; plots on the lower lefthand corner of the H-R diagram. (Ch. 14)

wind A weather variable that is caused by atmospheric convection—a process that redistributes heat. (Ch 18)

wind shear Violent air turbulence created from sudden downdrafts, which can cause an extremely dangerous condition near airports. (Ch. 18)

work The force that is exerted times the distance over which it is exerted; measured in joules in the metric system, in foot-pounds in the English. (Ch. 3)

X-rays High-frequency and high-energy electromagnetic waves that range in wavelength from 100 nanometers to 0.1 nanometer, used in medicine and industry. (Ch. 6)

z particle A massive particle that, along with the *w* particle, mediates the weak interaction. (Ch. 13)

CREDITS

PHOTO CREDITS

Title Page
Michael P. Gadomski/Photo Researchers.

Chapter 1
Page 2: Jules Frazier/PhotoDisc, Inc./Getty Images. Page 3: Charles E. Rotkin/Corbis Images. Page 5: © The British Museum. Page 7 (top): Corbis Digital Stock/ Corbis Images. Page 7 (bottom): PhotoDisc, Inc./Getty Images. Page 9: © Tom Sanders/Photri/Corbis Stock Market. Page 11 (left, center & right): David Tilman. Page 12: Chemical Club Library. Page 15: David G. Houser/Corbis Images. Page 17: The Art Archive/Real Biblioteca de lo Escorial/Dagli Orti. Page 19: Digital Vision. Page 23: Dr. Seth Shostak/Science Photo Library/Photo Researchers.

Chapter 2
Page 30: Roger Ressmeyer/Corbis Images. Page 37: Museo della Scienza, Florence, Italy/Art Resource. Page 38: Uffizi, Florence, Italy/Scala/Art Resource. Page 41: © Estate of Harold Edgerton, courtesy of Palm Press, Inc. Page 44: Department of Defense/Still Media Record Center. Page 46: Stone/Getty Images. Page 47: Mercedes-Benz of North America. Page 48 (bottom): © Lee Snyder/Photo Researchers. Page 48 (top): © 99 Lester Lefkowitz/Corbis Stock Market. Page 50: Milton Heiberg/Photo Researchers. Page 51: © Corbis. Page 56: Roe, D. Malin/AAO/Photo Researchers.

Chapter 3
Page 62: Ryan McVay/PhotoDisc, Inc./Getty Images. Page 63 (bottom): Jerry Ohlinger's Movie Material Store. Page 63 (top): Lowell Georgia/Photo Researchers. Page 65: David Madison/Stone/Getty. Page 66: Bettmann/Corbis Images. Page 68: Francois Gohier/Photo Researchers. Page 71 (bottom, left)): Vladimir Pcholkin/Taxi/Getty Images. Page 71 (right): Dennis Galante/Taxi/Getty Images. Page 71 (top, left): Paul A. Souders/Corbis Images. Page 72: The Granger Collection. Page 75 (left & right): © Leonard Lessing, FBPA/Photo Researchers. Page 76: Dave Jacobs/Stone/ Getty Images.

Chapter 4
Page 86: Corbis Images. Page 87 (top left & right, & bottom): © Fred Charles/Liaison Agency, Inc./Getty Images. Page 90: Courtesy Torka Inc. www.torka.com. Page 92: © Charles Thatcher/Tony Stone Images/New York, Inc. Page 93: Bryan and Cherry Alexander Photography. Page

94: Brenda Tharp/Photo Researchers. Page 96 (center): Photo Researchers. Page 96 (top, right): David E. Meyers/ Stone/Getty Images. Page 96 (bottom, right): B & C Alexander/Photo Researchers.

Chapter 5
Page 112: Pablo Corral Vega/Corbis Images. Page 113: Paul A. Souders/Corbis Images. Page 114 (top): Painting by Benjamin West, c. 1805, Mr. and Mrs. Wharton Sinkler Collection, courtesy Philadelphia Museum of Art. Page 114 (bottom): © Antman/The Image Works. Page 119 (top): Andy Washnik. Page 119 (bottom): D. Blackwill & D. Maratez/Visuals Unlimited. Page 119 (center): John Chumack/Photo Researchers. Page 121: Bettmann/ Corbis. Page 122: Jerry Ohlinger's Movie Material Store. Page 123: © Grantpix/Photo Researchers. Page 126: PhotoDisc, Inc./Getty Images. Page 130: © Arthur Hill/Visuals Unlimited. Page 132: David Job/Stone/ Getty Images. Page 135: Courtesy Smithsonian Institution.

Chapter 6
Page 141: Jutta Klee/Corbis Images. Page 143: Neil Rabinowitz/Corbis Images. Page 145: Nubar Alexanian/ Corbis Images. Page 147: Stephen Dalton/Photo Researchers. Page 148: Education Development Center. Page 149: Liaison Agency, Inc./Getty Images. Page 155: PhotoDisc, Inc./Getty Images. Page 156 (bottom): Adam Jones/Photo Researchers. Page 156 (top) & Page 157: Jack Hollingsworth/PhotoDisc, Inc./Getty Images. Page 161: U.S. Air Force Photo by Staff Sgt. Andy Dunaway, Department of Defense. Page 162: Courtesy Daedalus Enterprises, Inc. Page 163: David Parker/Photo Researchers. Page 165: © Pete Saloutos/Corbis Stock Market.

Chapter 7
Page 172: Martyn Goddard/Corbis Images. Page 174: Topham/The Image Works. Page 182 (left & right) & Page 183 (left & right): © 1989 Ping-Kang Hsiung. Page 187 (right): Imtek Imagineering/Masterfile. Page 187 (left): Courtesy NASA, Richard Ellis (Caltech) and Jean-Paul Kneib (Observatoire Midi-Pyrenees, France).

Chapter 8
Page 193: Royalty-free/Corbis Images. Page 194: Nancy Wolff/Omni-Photo Communications. Page 196: Courtesy Sémus Davis, Department of Physics, Cornell University. Page 197: © AP/Wide World Photos. Page 200: American Institute of Physics. Page 204 (left, center & right): Yoav Levy/Phototake. Page 206: Bausch &

Lomb. Page 209 (left): Alexander Tsiaras/Photo Researchers. Page 209 (right): © Ray Nelson/Phototake.

Chapter 9

Page 217: © AP/Wide World Photos. Page 218: © Mark E. Gibson/Visuals Unlimited. Page 224: American Institute of Physics. Page 226: Larry Nulvehill/Photo Researchers. Page 227: Education Development Center.

Chapter 10

Page 233: Philip James Corwin/Corbis Images. Page 238: Yves Forestier/Corbis Sygma. Page 245: G. Tompkinson/Photo Researchers. Page 247: Lawrence Dutton/Stone/Getty Images. Page 259: Fotopic/Omni-Photo Communications.

Chapter 11

Page 264: Ulf Sjosted/Taxi/Getty Images. Page 265: Andy Sacks/Tony Stone Images/New York, Inc. Page 266: © Gerard Vandystadt/Photo Researchers. Page 267: Corbis Stock Market. Page 268 (top): Bruce Hands/Stone/Getty Images. Page 268 (bottom): Hank de Lespinasse/The Image Bank/Getty Images. Page 270: Dennis MacDonald/Photo Edit. Page 271: Joseph Sohm/Photo Researchers. Page 273 (left): University of Birmingham/Science Photo Library/Photo Researchers. Page 273 (right): G. Davis/Corbis Sygma. Page 276 (top): David Cumming; Eye Ubiquitous/Corbis Images. Page 276 (bottom, left): Courtesy Texas Instruments. Page 276 (bottom, right): Don Mason/Corbis Images. Page 277: © Hank Morgan/Science Source/Photo Researchers. Page 280: © Uniphoto, Inc. Page 283: Grantpix//Index Stock. Page 284: Courtesy Paramount Pictures.

Chapter 12

Page 289: PhotoDisc, Inc. Page 290: © Earl & Nazima Kowall/Corbis Images. Page 295 (top): Tom Raymond/Stone/Getty Images. Page 295 (bottom): Courtesy College Physicians of America. Page 301: SPL/Photo Researchers. Page 302: Patrick Mesner/Liaison Agency, Inc./Getty Images. Page 303: John Reader/Science Photo Library/Photo Researchers. Page 307: © Breck P. Kent/Animals Animals/Earth Scenes. Page 309 (top): Courtesy Princeton University Physics Laboratory. Page 309 (bottom): © AP/Wide World Photos.

Chapter 13

Page 315: Susumu Nishinaga/Photo Researchers. Page 316: James Stachan/Stone/Getty Images. Page 319: Lawrence Berkeley Laboratory. Page 320 (top): CERN/Science Photo Library/Photo Researchers. Page 320 (bottom, left): Courtesy Fermi National Accelerator Laboratory. Page 320 (bottom, right): Bill W. Marsh/Photo Researchers. Page 323 (left): California Institute of Technology. Page 323 (bottom, right): Lawrence Berkeley Laboratory. Page 324.

Chapter 14

Page 334: Sunstar/Photo Researchers. Page 335: Jim Ballard/Stone/Getty Images. Page 336: Roger Ressmeyer/Corbis Images. Page 337 (top): Larry Mulvehill/Photo Researchers. Page 337 (bottom): NASA/Roger Ressmeyer/Corbis Images. Page 338: Corbis Sygma. Page 339 (top):/National Center for Atmospheric Research. Page 340: George Lepp/Stone/Getty Images. Page 342: © AP/Wide World Photos. Page 345: Courtesy Harvard College Observatory. Page 346 & Page 351 (top): Courtesy NASA. Page 351 (bottom): Royal Observatory, Edinburgh.

Chapter 15

Page 358: Charles O'Rear/Corbis Images. Page 359: American Institute of Physics. Page 360 (right): © Photri/Corbis Stock Market. Page 360 (left): Celestial Image Co./Photo Researchers. Page 361: Courtesy NASA. Page 362 (left): California Institute of Technology. Page 367: Courtesy C. Park and J. R. Groth, Princeton University. Page 377: Courtesy NASA.

Chapter 16

Page 382: Richard Cummins/Corbis Images. Page 387 & Page 388 (top): Courtesy NASA. Page 388 (bottom): Private Collection/Bridgeman Art Library/NY. Page 389: Bonestell Space Art. Page 390: Courtesy NASA. Page 392: Van Valte. Page 394: Breck P. Kent/Animals Animals/ Earth Scenes. Page 396: Courtesy NASA/JPL. Page 397: NASA/Science Photo Library/Photo Researchers. Page 398 & Page 399: Courtesy NASA. Page 400: Lowell Observatory. Page 402: © Lynette Cook. Page 404: Paul and Lindamarie Ambrose/Taxi/Getty Images.

Chapter 17

Page 410: Cindy Kassab/Corbis Images. Page 411: David A. Rosenberg/AllStock/Stone/Getty Images. Page 412 (left): © Michael Wickes/The Image Works. Page 412 (right): David Muench/Stone/Getty Images. Page 413: © Krafft/Hoa-Qui/Photo Researchers. Page 414: © Hosaka Maoto/Liaison Agency, Inc./Getty Images. Page 416: Marie Tharp. Page 424: Courtesy NASA. Page 426: Dewitt Jones Prod./AllStock/Stone/Getty Images. Page 432: Paul Morin.

Chapter 18

Page 438: Nancy Ney/Corbis Images. Page 449: National Oceanic and Atmospheric Administration/DLR-FRG/Roger Ressmeyer/Corbis Images. Page 455: P. Degginger/Bruce Coleman, Inc. Page 456 (left): © Francois Gohier/Photo Researchers. Page 456 (right): © Chromosohn/John Sohm/Photo Researchers. Page 458: Tom Bean/DRK Photo. Page 459: Tim McKenna/Corbis Images. Page 460: David Muench/AllStock/Stone/Getty Images. Page 461 (right): © Walker Bros. Creations/Photo Researchers. Page 461 (left): Dr. K. Roy Gill.

Chapter 19
Page 468: David Weintraub/Photo Researchers. Page 469: Jeff Hunter/The Image Bank/Getty Images. Page 473: B.S.P.I./Corbis Images. Page 478: NASA/Goddard Space Center. Page 479 (top) & (bottom): Jim Mendenhall. Page 480 (left & right): Courtesy Westfalishches Amt fur Denkmalpflege. Page 481 (left & right): Environmental Elements Corp. Page 483: Archivo Iconografico S.A./Corbis Images.

Chapter 20
Page 490: James Randklev/Photo Researchers. Page 491 (left): David Maitland/Taxi/Getty Images. Page 491 (top, right): L. West/Photo Researchers. Page 491 (bottom, right): Hans Christian Heap/Taxi/Getty Images. Page 493: Stephen Dalton/Photo Researchers. Page 494: UNEP-Say Boon Foo/The Image Works. Page 498 (top, left, center & right): David M. Phillips/Visuals Unlimited. Page 498 (bottom): Eric Grave/Science Source/Photo Researchers. Page 502: B.G. Thomson/Photo Researchers. Page 504: © Karen McGougan/Bruce Coleman, Inc. Page 508: Murray Wilson/Omni-Photo Communications. Page 510 (top): P. Goetgheluck/The Image Bank/Getty Images. Page 510 (bottom): © Robert Lubeck/Animals Animals/Earth Scenes. Page 513: Joel Glenn/Cole Group/PhotoDisc, Inc./Getty Images.

Chapter 21
Page 518: Jonathan A. Meyers/Photo Researchers. Page 522 (top, left): Nuridsany et Perennou/Photo Researchers. Page 522 (right): Donna Day/Stone/Getty Images. Page 522 (bottom, left): Laurent/Lamy/Photo Researchers. Page 527 (left & right): Courtesy T. A. Steitz, Department of Molecular Biophysics and Biochemistry, Yale University. Page 529: Walter Bibikow/Getty Images. Page 533: James Leynse/SABA. Page 535: PhotoDisc, Inc./Getty Images.

Chapter 22
Page 541 & Page 543: Royalty-Free/Corbis Images. Page 545 (top): Will & Demi McIntyre/Photo Researchers. Page 545 (bottom): David Scharf/Peter Arnold, Inc. Page 548 (top, left): USDA/Public Affairs. Page 548 (top, left): Courtesy University of Texas. Page 548 (top, left): Biophoto Associates/Photo Researchers. Page 548 (top, left): Biophoto Associates/Photo Researchers. Page 548 (top, right): Courtesy Dr. Eliot Weir. Page 548 (top, right): Courtesy Brookhaven National Laboratory. Page 548 (bottom): Courtesy Cell Research Institute, University of Texas, Austin. Page 549 (left): Courtesy Tektoff-Rhone-Merieux, CNR/Photo Researchers. Page 549 (left): Secchi-Lecaque/Roussel-UCLA/CNRI/Photo Researchers. Page 549 (left): David M. Phillips/Visuals Unlimited. Page 549 (right): © Gopal Murti/Phototake. Page 549 (right): Courtesy CNRI/Photo Researchers. Page 549 (right): Secchi-Lecaque/Roussel-UCLA/CNRI/Photo Researchers. Page 553: Vicky Kasala/PhotoDisc, Inc./Getty Images.

Page 554: PhotoDisc, Inc. Page 556: Tim Davis/Photo Researchers. Page 558: Dr. Andrew Bajer. Page 559: David Becker/Stone/Getty Images.

Chapter 23
Page 566: Ken Huang/The Image Bank/Getty Images. Page 570: © Carson Baldwin, Jr./Animals Animals/Earth Scenes. Page 575: Dr. Gopal Murti/Photo Researchers. Page 576: Ken Eward/Photo Researchers. Page 582: CDC/Photo Researchers. Page 583: Photo by Lennart Nilsson. Reproduced with permission, courtesy of Albert Bonniers Forlag AB. Page 585: Marty Katz.

Chapter 24
Page 591: Mauro Fermariello/Photo Researchers. Page 593 (left): Chris Knapton/Science Photo Library/Photo Researchers. Page 593 (right): Dr. R. L. Brinster. Page 595. Philippe Plailly/Photo Researchers. Page 597 (top): © Roslin Institute/Phototake. Page 597 (bottom): M. Baret/Photo Researchers. Page 599: © AP/Wide World Photos. Page 601: © Jessica Boyatt. Page 602 (left & right): Michael Atkinson. Page 607 (left): Richard R. Hansen/Photo Researchers. Page 607 (right): Michael P. Gadmonski/Photo Researchers. Page 609: Louise Lockley/Photo Researchers.

Chapter 25
Page 614: Gary Kufner/Corbis Images. Page 615 (left & right): James L. Amos/Photo Researchers. Page 615 (right): Alfred Pasieka/SPL/Photo Researchers. Page 617: Tom Brakefield/The Image Works. Page 620: Visuals Unlimited. Page 621: Biological Photo Service. Page 623: AFP/Corbis. Page 625 (top left & right: Jeanne White/Photo Researchers. Page 625 (bottom, left): CMCD/PhotoDisc, Inc. Page 626 (left & right): Courtesy Professor Lawrence Cook, University of Manchester. Page 628: From Stephan Jay Gould, Wonderful Life, New York, 1989, W. W. Norton & Company. Page 635: Institute of Human Origins. Page 637: Chris Ochsner/Topeka Capital-Journal/ © AP/WideWorld Photos.

Appendix A
Page 5 (bottom, left): Don Fawcett, K. Saito, K. Hama/Photo Researchers. Page 5 (top, right): Photo by Lennart Nilsson from BEHOLD MAN, p. 178. Reproduced with permission, courtesy of Albert Bonniers Forlag AB.
Page 7 (left, center & right): Photo by Lennart Nilsson from A CHILD IS BORN. Reproduced with permission, courtesy of Albert Bonniers Forlag AB.

ILLUSTRATION CREDITS

Figure 1–4 Courtesy New York Public Library.

Figure 2–2 Data from monograph of Dr. John Snow, 1854, as published in M. Goldstein and I. Goldstein, *How*

We Know: An Exploration of the Scientific Process (New York: Plenum Press), 1978.

Figure 3–5 From *Geography: A Modern Synthesis,* Revised Third Edition by Peter Haggett. © 1983 by Peter Haggett. Reprinted by permission of Addison-Wesley Educational Publishers, Inc.

Figure 3–6 Adapted from "Energy from Fossil Fuels" by William Fulkerson, Roddie R. Judkins, and Manoj K. Sanghvi. © 1990 by Scientific American, Inc. All rights reserved.

Figure 6–12 Adapted from a diagram by E. J. Chaisson.

Figure 15–10 Adapted from a diagram by J. Burns.

Figure 16–1 Reprinted from I. Gass, et al., *Understanding the Earth,* (Cambridge, MA: The MIT Press), 1971, p. 65.

Figure 16–6 Adapted from a NASA diagram.

Figure 17–6 Based on maps prepared by A. M. Ziegler and C. S. Scotese of the University of Chicago's Paleographic Atlas Project.

Figure 19–2 Data from A. M. Ujhara and M. Gough, 1989, "Managing Ash from Municipal Waste Incinerators," in *Resources for the Future,* Center for Risk Management.

Figure 19–8 C. D. Keeling, et al. A three-dimensional model of atmospheric CO_2 transport based on observed winds: 1. Analysis of observational data. *American Geophysical Union Monograph 55,* Figure 16, 1989. Copyright by the American Geophysical Union.

Figure 19–9 John Fowler, *Energy and the Environment,* Second Edition, New York: McGraw Hill, Inc., 1984, p. 82. Reproduced with permission of the McGraw Hill Companies.

Figure 20–4 Adapted from "How Many Species Inhabit the Earth?" by Robert M. May. © 1992 by Scientific American, Inc. All rights reserved.

Figure 23–11 Reprinted with permission after F. S. Collins, *Science,* 262:45, 1993. © 1993 American Association for the Advancement of Science.

Figure 24–4 1992 *Los Alamos Science.* Adapted from *The Washington Post* Science Section, November 15, 1993.

Figure 25–1 Reprinted with permission of Dr. Stanley L. Miller.

Figure 25–5 Reprinted with permission from *Biodiversity.* © 1988 by the National Academy of Sciences. Courtesy of the National Academy Press, Washington, D.C.

Figure 25–6 Reprinted with permission from D. M. Raup and J. J. Sepkoski, Jr., "Mass Extinctions in the Marine Fossil Record," *Science,* 215:1501-2, 1992. © 1992 American Association for the Advancement of Science.

The following figures were reprinted from Harris Benson, *University Physics,* Revised Edition. © 1996 John Wiley & Sons. Reprinted by permission of John Wiley & Sons, Inc.: 2–10, 5–6, 6–4, 13–4, 22-1b.

The following figure was reprinted from George M. Bodner and Harry L. Pardue, *Chemistry: An Experimental Science.* © 1989 John Wiley & Sons. Reprinted by permission of John Wiley & Sons, Inc.: 10–16.

The following figures were reprinted from Daniel Botkin and Edward Keller, *Environmental Science: Earth as a Living Planet.* © 1995 John Wiley & Sons. Reprinted by permission of John Wiley & Sons, Inc.: 3–3, 19–5.

The following figures were reprinted from James E. Brady and John R. Holum, *Chemistry: The Study of Matter and Its Changes,* Second Edition. © 1996 John Wiley & Sons. Reprinted by permission of John Wiley & Sons, Inc.: 4–6, 6–7, 8–10.

The following figure was reprinted from James E. Brady and John R. Holum, *Chemistry: The Study of Matter and Its Changes.* © 1993 John Wiley & Sons. Reprinted by permission of John Wiley & Sons, Inc.: 10–6.

The following figures were reprinted from Gil Brum, Larry McKane, and Gerry Karp, *Biology: Exploring Life,* Second Edition. © 1994 John Wiley & Sons. Reprinted by permission of John Wiley & Sons, Inc.: 8–15, 19–1, 20–2, 20–5, 20–6, 20–7, 20–8, 20–9, 21–3, 21–4, 22–6, 22–10, 23–8, 24–1, 24–3, 25–4, 25–8, A–1, A–3.

The following figures were reprinted from John Cutnell and Kenneth Johnson, *Physics,* Third Edition. © 1995 John Wiley & Sons. Reprinted by permission of John Wiley & Sons, Inc.: 5–2, 5–4, 5–5a, 5–11, 5–14, 8–4, 11–2, 11–8, 11–10.

The following figures were reprinted from John Cutnell and Kenneth Johnson, *Physics,* Second Edition. © 1992 John Wiley & Sons. Reprinted by permission of John Wiley & Sons, Inc.: 5–3, 5–13, 8–6, 9–3a, 9–4, 9–5, 13–1.

The following figure was reprinted from Gerald C. Davison and John M. Neale, *Abnormal Psychology,* Sixth Edition. © 1994 John Wiley & Sons. Reprinted by permission of John Wiley & Sons, Inc.: 5-9.

The following figures were reprinted from H. J. de Blij and Peter O. Muller, *Physical Geography of the Global Environment,* Second Edition. © 1996 John Wiley & Sons. Reprinted by permission of John Wiley & Sons, Inc.: 16–1, 18–2, 18–3.

A

AAAS (American Association for the Advancement of Science), A21

Abiotic, 469, A20

Absolute magnitude, 343, A20

Absolute zero, 88, A20

Absorption lines, 206, A20

Absorption of electromagnetic waves, 155–156, A20

Absorption spectrum, 205, A20

AC, *see* Alternating current

Acceleration:
  defined, 39–40, A20
  effect on pilots and astronauts, 43–44
  experiencing, 43–44
  extreme, 43–44
  and falling object experiments, 40–43
  gravity vs., 185–187
  and Newton's second law of motion, 46–47

Acids, 253–254, A20

Acid-base reactions, 253–254

Acid rain, 480–481, A20

Acquired immune deficiency syndrome (AIDS), 607–610, A20

Adaptation, 626, A20

Addition polymerization, 256, A20

Adenosine triphosphate (ATP), 551, 555, A20

Aerobic, 553, 555–556, A20

Aging, 107, 181

AIDS, *see* Acquired immune deficiency syndrome

Air pollution, 479–481, A20

Algae, 504, A20

Alkali metals, 210, A20

Alkaline earth metals, 210–211, A20

Alkanes, 257–258, A20

Alloys, 238, A20

Alpacas, 513

Alpha decay, 296–297, 299, A20

Alpha particles, 296–297, 299, A20

Alternating current (AC), 135, A20–A21

Alvarez, Luis and Walter, 632

AM, *see* Amplitude modulation

American Association for the Advancement of Science (AAAS), A21

Amino acids:
  defined, A21
  essential, 527–528
  as protein building blocks, 522–523, 537
  role in evolution, 618–620

Amino group, 522, A21

Amperes (amps), 125, A21

Ampere, Andre-Marie, 125

Amphibians, 511, A21

Amplifiers, 278–279, A21

Amplitude, 143, 145, A21

Amplitude modulation (AM), 159–160, A21

Amps, *see* Amperes

AM radio transmission, 159–160

Anaerobic, 554–556, A21

Anatomy, A1–A7

Anderson, Carl, 322–323

Andromeda galaxy, 366

Angiosperms, 506–508, A21

Angular momentum, 50–52

Animals:
  defined, A21
  and Earth's trophic levels, 76–78
  evolution, 629–630, A14–A16
  humans as, 501
  insulation in, 95–97
  invertebrates, 509–510
  overview, 508
  regulating temperature, 97–98
  use of sound, 147–148
  vertebrates, 501
  vestigial organs, 617–618

Animal kingdom, defined, 498

Annihilation, 322, A21

Ants, 490–491

Antacids, 255

Antarctica, 463

Antibiotics, resistance to, 610–611

Antimatter, 322–323, 372–373, A21

Appalachian Mountains, 427–428

Apparent magnitude, 343, A21

Applied research, 21–22, A21

Aquifers, 441, 443, A21

Archaea, 499

Arthropods, 509–510, A21

Artificial intelligence, 284, A21

Artificial selection, 624, A21

Asteroids, 385, 401, A21

Asteroid belt, 385, A21

Astrobiology, 624

Astrology, 17–18

Astronomical unit (AU), A17

Astronomy. *See also* Planets; Stars; Sun
  ancient observers, 30–31
  data and properties list, A17
  defined, 334, A21
  historical background, 35, 36
  measuring distances, 344–345, A17
  night sky, 30–31, 34–35
  overview, 34–37
  role of Copernicus, 35, 36

  role of Kepler, 36–37
  role of Ptolemy, 35, 36
  role of Tycho Brahe, 35–37
  and Stonehenge, 31–32

Atlantic Ocean, 419–420

Atmosphere:
  circulation, 451–452
  evolution of, 395–396
  and global warming, 483–485
  and greenhouse effect, 481–483
  planetary, 395–396
  weather variables, 449–451

Atmospheric cycle, 448–455, A21

Atmospheric pressure, 449–450

Atoms. *See also* Electrons; Nucleus; Quantum mechanics
  artificial, 228
  Bohr model, 200–204
  clusters of, 213
  contribution of ancient Greeks, 193
  Dalton's hypothesis, 193–194
  defined, 114, 198, A21
  and electromagnetic radiation, 202–203
  and electron shells, 211–212
  formation of, 374–375
  and freezings, 374–375
  nucleus vs. electrons, 289–290
  role of nucleus, 289–290
  Rutherford model, 198–199
  speculation over, 195
  structure of, 198–200
  viewing, 213

Atomic bomb, 309–310

Atomic nucleus, *see under* Nucleus

Atomic number, 292, A21

Atomism, 194, A21

ATP, *see* Adenosine triphosphate

Atrial fibrillation, 610

AU (astronomical unit), A17

Aurora borealis, 119, 339, 340

Australopithecus, 633–635, A21

Automobiles:
  electric, 123–124
  starting, 127

Autotroph, A21

Avogadro's number, A17

Axons, 128, 129, A22

B

Bacon, Francis, 415

Bacteria, 499, 505, 610–611

Balancing chemical equations, 250

Bardeen, John, 278

Basalt, 421, 456, A22

Bases, 253–254, A22
Base load, A22
Base pairs, 572, 573–575, A22
Basic research, 21–22, 136, A22
Bats, use of sound by, 147
Batteries:
  defined, 123, A22
  and electric cars, 123–124
  invention of, 123, 196
Beach erosion, 463–464
Becquerel, Antoine Henri, 295
Bednorz, George, 272
Bernoulli, Daniel, 195
Beta decay, 297–299, A22
Big bang theory:
  analogies for, 367–368
  defined, A22
  expanding-balloon analogy, 368
  overview, 365–366
  raisin-bread dough analogy, 367–368
  supporting evidence, 369–370
Binomial nomenclature, A22
Biodiversity, 11–12, A22
Bioinformatics revolution, A22
Biology, 490, A22
Biosphere, 106
Biotic, 469, A22
Birds, 95–96, 512, A22
Bits, 281–282, A22
Black holes, 352, A22
Black smokers, 620
Blood, 13–14, 259
Blue-green algae, A22
Blueshift, 154, A22
Bohr, Niels, 200–201, 204
Bohr atom, 200–204, 207, 211,
  226–229, A22
Boiling, 248, A22
Boiling point, 88
Boltzmann, Ludwig, 104
Bombs, nuclear, 309–310
Bone loss, 388
Bony fish, A22
Border security, 310
Brahe, Tycho, 35–37
Brain:
  and breathing, 561
  computer vs., 284
  defined, A22
  overview, A4–A5
  research on, 323–324
Brattain, Walter, 278
Brown dwarfs, 347
Brownian motion:
  defined, 195, A22
  as evidence of atomic theory, 195
  role of Einstein, 195
  role of Perrin, 195
Bryophytes, 506, A22
Bungee jumping:
  and first law of thermodynamics, 79
  as interchangeability among energy
    forms, 74, 75

Burnell, Jocelyn Bell, 351
Bytes, 282, A22

C

Calories:
  calculating, in diet, 79–80
  defined, 79, 88, A22
  dietary vs. thermal, 88
Cambrian explosion, 629–630, A22
Cambrian period, 629–631, A22
Camels, 513
Cancer, 602–604, A22
Cannon, Annie Jump, 345
Carbohydrates, 529–530, A23
Carbon, 197, 198, 239–240, 292, 519
Carbon-14, 302–303
Carbon cycle, 470, 471, A23
Carbon dating, 302–303
Carboxyl group, 522, A23
Carnivores, 77–78, A23
Cars:
  electric, 123–124
  starting, 127
CAT (Computerized Axial Tomography),
  A24
CAT scan, 226
Cavendish, Henry, 53–54
Cavendish balance, 53–54
c (constant), A22. *See also* Speed of light
Celera Corporation, 585–586
Cells, 543–550
  calculating division, 622–623
  cytoskeleton, 550
  defined, A23
  discovery of, 542
  division by meiosis, 559–561, 575
  division by mitosis, 557–559, 575
  energy in, 551–556
  and evolution, 562
  first cell, 621–622
  and metabolism, 551–556
  nucleus, 547–549
  observing inner workings of, 228
  overview, 541–542
  stem, 25
Cell membranes, 533–534, 545–546,
  A23
Cell theory, A23
Cellulose, 530, A23
Cell walls, 547, A23
Celsius scale, 88, A23
Cenozoic Era, 630, 631, A23
Central processing unit (CPU), 282,
  A23
Cepheid variable stars, 345, 359, A23
Ceramics, A23
CFCs, *see* Chlorofluorocarbons
Chain, Ernst, 505
Chain reactions, 306, A23
Chandrasekar, Subramanian, 338
Chandra X-Ray Observatory, 337–338
Changes of state, 248–249, A23

Chaos theory:
  defined, A23
  Newton's laws vs., 57
"Charge conjugation violation," 329
Charon (moon), 399
Chemical bonds:
  covalent, 238–240
  defined, 234, A23
  and electron shells, 233–235
  ionic, 235–236
  metallic, 236–238
  in organic molecules, 520
  types of, 235–242
Chemical elements:
  atomic number, 292
  and atomic theory, 195
  and big bang theory, 370
  in combination, 195
  defined, 194, 198
  discovering, 196–198
  and electron shells, 211–212
  isotopes of, 292–293
  list of properties, A18–A19
  natural vs. laboratory-produced, 310
  in oceans, 443–444
  in organic molecules, 519
  periodic table, 12–13, 196, 210–212
  residence times in human body, 444
  and stars, 353
Chemical equations, balancing, 249–250
Chemical evolution, 618–624, A23
Chemical potential energy, 70, A23
Chemical reactions, 249–250
  acid-base, 253–254
  balancing chemical equations, 250
  defined, A23
  depolymerization, 256–257
  endothermic, 251
  and energy, 250–251
  exothermic, 251
  overview, 249–250
  oxidation, 251–253
  polymerization, 256–257
  precipitation-solution, 253
  reduction, 252–253
  types of, 251–254
Chernobyl, Ukraine, 307
Chinese room paradox, 285
Chlorine, 478
Chlorofluorocarbons (CFCs), 477–479,
  A23
Chlorophyll, 550, 552, A23
Chloroplasts, 550, A23
Cholera, 32–33
Cholesterol, 532, A23–A24
Chordates, 501, A24
Chromosomes, 557–559, A24
Chromosphere, 339, A24
Circuits:
  parallel, 129
  series, 129
Circulatory system, 13–14, A1, A3, A24
Classes, 496, A24

Classical genetics:
  basic rules, 569–570
  defined, 568, A24
  dominant vs. recessive genes, 568
  qualitative vs. quantitative, 570
Classifying living things, 495–498
Clausius, Rudolf, 104
Climate, 449, 453, A24
Clinical trials, 604
Clocks, light, 177–180
Cloning, 597–599, A24
Closed ecosystems, A24
Closed systems, 78–79, A24
Closed universe, 377, A24
Clotting (of blood), 259
Clouds, 441, 450–451, 482, A24
Cloud chamber, 322–323
Cloudiness, A24
Clusters, 366, A24
COBE, see Cosmic Background Explorer
Codons, 576, A24
Cold-blooded animals, 512, A24
Combustion, 252, A24
Comets, 56, 385, 401–403, A24
Community, A24
Compass, 118–119, A24
Complexity, A24
Composite materials, 268–269, A24
Compressional waves, 431, A24
Compressive strength, 266–267, A24
Computers, 282–283, A24
Computer-assisted drug design, 608–610,
  A24
Computerized Axial Tomography (CAT),
  A24
Condensation, 248, A24
Condensation polymerization, 256, 522,
  A24
Condensation reaction, 256, A24–A25
Conduction, 91–93, A25
Conduction electrons, 270, A25
Conductors, 269–270, A25
Cones, 163, A25
Conservation laws, 78–79, A25
Conservation of energy, 78–81
Constants:
  gravitational constant (G), 52–54
  overview, A17
  speed of light (c), 151, 175, 183, 184
Constructive interference, 149, A25
Consumers, A25
Continental Drift, 415, 419–420, A25.
  See also Plate tectonics
Convection, 93–95, A25
Convection cells, 93, 451, A25
Convection zone, 338, A25
Convergent plate boundaries, 424–426,
  429, A25
Conversions, temperature, 89
Conversion of units, A9–A12
Copernicus, Nicolas, 35, 36
Coral reefs, 459
Core, 338, 350, 391, A25

Corona, solar, 339, A25
Cosmic Background Explorer (COBE),
  370, 377, A25
Cosmic microwave background radiation,
  369–370, A25
Cosmic rays:
  defined, A25
  and discovery of antimatter, 322
  and particle accelerators, 319–321
  as source of elementary particles, 318
Cosmology:
  big bang theory, 365–370
  defined, 359, A25
  role of Edwin Hubble, 359
Coulombs, 116, 125, A25
Coulomb, Caries Augustin de, 115–116
Coulomb's law, 115–116, 136, A25
Covalent bonds, 238–240, A25
CPU, see Central processing unit
Creationism, 107, 637
Cretaceous period, 631, 632
Critical mass, 310, A25
Crust, Earth's, 391, 392, A25
Crystals, 244–246, A25
Curie, Marie Skladowska, 295
Curie, Pierre, 295
Current(s):
  electrical, see Electrical current
  ocean, 441–442, A25
Curtis, Heber D., 358–359
Cyanobacteria, 505, 629
Cyclones, 452, A25
Cyclotron, 319, A25
Cystic fibrosis, 599–600
Cytoplasm, A25
Cytoskeleton, 550, A25

D
Dalton, John, 193–195
Dark matter, 376–377, A26
Darwin, Charles, 624, 627–628
Davy, Sir Humphry, 72, 135
DC, see Direct current
Decay chains, 303–305, A26
Decomposers, A26
Deep ocean trenches, 425–426, A26
Deep time, 462
Democritus, 193, 195
Dendrites, 128, A26
Deoxyribonucleic acid (DNA). See also
  Ribonucleic acid
  in cell nuclei, 547–549
  and cloning, 597–599
  copying via PCR process, 595–597
  defined, A26
  double helix, 572
  as evidence of evolution, 616–617
  and gene therapy, 586
  and genetic engineering, 591–594
  and mutations, 580
  overview, 571–572
  repair mechanisms, 604–606

replication of, 573–575
structure of, 572
and transcription, 575–576
variable number tandem repeat
  sequences in, 594–595
Deoxyribose, A26
Depolymerization, 256–257, A26
Destructive interference, 149, A26
Devil's Tower, Wyoming, 456
Diamonds, 392
Diatomic molecules, A26
Diet:
  calculating calories, 79–80
  food fads, 537–538
  role of proteins, 527–528
Differentiation, 391, A26
Diffuse scattering, 156, A26
Diffusion, A26
Digestive system, A3–A4, A26
Digital cameras, 217
Dimensional analysis, 39
Dinosaurs, 78, 632
Diodes, 275–277, A26
Dipole field, 120, 132, A26
Direct current (DC), 135, A26
Distillation, 258, A26
Divergent plate boundaries, 424, 429, A26
Divine Calculator, 57, 229, A26
DNA, see Deoxyribonucleic acid
DNA fingerprinting, 594–595, A26
DNA mapping, 583–584, A26
DNA sequencing, 584, A26
Dolly (sheep), 597
Dolphins, use of sound by, 148
Domains, 274, A26
Dominant genes, 568, A26
Doping, 275, A26
Doppler, Christian Johann, 153
Doppler effect, 152–154, 362, A26
Doppler radar, 455
Double-blind clinical trials, 604, A27
Double bond, 239, A26
Double helix, 572, A27
Double-slit test, 223–225
Drugs, 528–529, 608–610
Drug-resistant bacteria, 610–611
Dwarf galaxies, 360
Dynamos, 134
Dyson, Freeman, 343
Dyson spheres, 343

E
E. coli, 537, 593
$E = mc^2$, 73, 290
Ears, 146–147, A4, A5, A27
Earth (planet):
  age theories for, 80–81
  atmospheric cycle, 448–455
  atmospheric evolution, 395–396
  characteristics of, 385, A17
  climate changes, 453–454
  defined, 384

Earth (planet): *continued*
  and diamonds, 392
  force of gravity, 392
  formation of, 389–392, 396–387
  hydrologic cycle, 440–448
  ice ages, 445–446
  interdependence of cycles, 463
  interior of, 391, 392
  as magnet, 118
  magnetic field, 417
  mantle convection, 421–422
  origins of life, 394–395
  overview of cycles, 439–440
  and radioactive decay, 80–81
  and radiometric dating, 302–303
  rock cycle, 455–462
  rotation and orbit, 446–447
  sources of heat energy, 440
  trophic levels, 76–78
Earthquakes, 413–414, 430, 432, A27
East African Rift Valley, 424, 427
Ecological communities, 469
Ecological niches, 471, A27
Ecology, 11–12, 468, A27
Ecosystems:
  and acid rain, 480–481
  change in, 472
  characteristics of, 469–472
  defined, A27
  energy flow in, 470
  and greenhouse effect, 481–483
  living organisms, 469–470
  niches in, 471
  nonliving parts, 469
  overview, 468–469
  and ozone layer, 476–479
  recycling of matter, 470
  and solid waste disposal, 474–475
  and unintended consequences, 472–473
Efficiency:
  calculating, 101–102
  of coal-fired electrical generating plant, 102
  defined, 100, A27
Einstein, Albert:
  and Brownian motion, 195
  $E=mc^2$, 73, 290
  general relativity theory predictions, 187–188
  and quantum mechanics, 229
  relativity theories of, 173–175
  and streetcar, 175, 176
Elastic limit, 267, A27
Elastic potential energy, 70, A27
Electrical charge:
  and atomic particles, 116
  in atoms, 114
  and Coulomb's law, 115–116
  defined, 113, A27
  magnetic effects, 130–131, 135–136
  positive vs. negative, 113, 114
  role of Benjamin Franklin, 113–114
  role of Luigi Galvani, 120–123

Electrical conductivity, 269–270, A27
Electrical conductors, 269–270, A27
Electrical current, 125, A27
  alternating, 135
  defined, 122, 127
  direct, 135
  and electromagnets, 130–131
  role of magnetic field, 133–134
Electrical fields, 117, 134, A27
Electrical insulators, 270, A27
Electrical potential energy, 70, A27
Electrical power, *see* Power
Electrical resistance, 125, 127, A27
Electric cars, 123–124
Electric circuits, 124–125
  calculating load, 126
  defined, 124, A27
  energy sources for, 124
  nervous system analogy, 127–129
  water analogy, 125
Electric generators, 134–135, A27
Electricity:
  connections with magnetism, 129–133
  defined, 113, A27
  and economics of solar energy, 81
  magnetism's effects on, 135–136
  role of Luigi Galvani, 120–123
  static, 112–117
Electric motors, 131–132
  defined, A27
  generators vs., 135
Electrolysis, 196
Electromagnets:
  defined, 130, A27
  in electric motors, 131–132
  uses for, 130–132
Electromagnetic force, 135, 326, 328–329, 374, A27
Electromagnetic induction, 133, A27
Electromagnetic radiation, 97, 149. *See also* Electromagnetic waves; Photons
Electromagnetic spectrum:
  defined, A27
  gamma rays, 166–167, 298
  and human eye, 340–341
  illustrated, 158
  infrared radiation, 97, 162–163
  microwaves, 160–162
  overview, 157–158
  radio waves, 158–159
  reflection of, 156
  role of James Clerk Maxwell, 149–150
  scattering of, 156
  transmission of, 154–155
  ultraviolet radiation, 163–164
  visible portion, 151–152, 163, 340–341
  x-rays, 164–166
Electromagnetic waves:
  absorption of, 155–156
  and atoms, 202–203
  defined, 149, A27
  Doppler effect, 152–154

  at extremely low frequencies, 167
  forces within, 116
  as form of wave energy, 73, 151–152
Electromagnetism, *see* Electromagnetic force
Electrons:
  behavior of, 114
  and beta decay, 297–299
  charge of, A17
  defined, 114, 198, A28
  discovery of, 198
  energy levels, 201, 203
  in excited state, 201, 203–205
  mass, A17
  and nucleus, 289–290
  as particles, 227
  and Pauli exclusion principle, 211
  viewing, 218
  and wave-particle duality, 226–227
  as waves, 226–227
Electron microscopes, 545, 548, 549, A27–A28
Electron shells, 211–212, A28
Electrophoresis, 595
Electrostatic charge, A28. *See also* Static electricity
Electroweak force, 329, 371–374, A27, A28
Elements, A28. *See also* Chemical elements
Elementary particles:
  accelerating, 319–321
  antimatter, 322–323, 372–373
  as building blocks of matter, 317
  cosmic rays as source, 318
  defined, A28
  detecting, 319
  and freezings, 374
  hadrons, 321, 322
  leptons, 321, 322
  in nucleus, 318
  overview, 318
  quarks, 324–325
Elementary-particle physics, 317, A28
ELF (extremely low frequency) radiation, 167, A28
Elliptical galaxies, 360
El Niño, 452–453, A27
Embryo, development of, A7
Embryonic stem cells, 598–599
Emission spectrum, 206–207, A28
Emitters, 278, A28
Endocrine system, A5–A6, A28
Endoplasmic reticulum, 550, A28
Endothermic chemical reactions, 251, A28
Energy:
  calculating consumption, 66–67
  in cells, 551–556
  and chemical reactions, 250–251
  conservation of, 78–81
  defined, 65, A28
  and diet, 79–80
  direction of flow, 98–107
  in Earth's interior, 421–422

economics of alternative sources, 81
in ecosystems, 470
and efficiency, 100–102
and force, 63
forms of, 67–74
from fossil fuels, 81–82, 106
interchangeability among forms, 74–78
kinetic, 67–69
and mass, 73, 184–185, 290–291
new sources, 74, 76
from nuclear fission, 305–307
from nuclear fusion, 307–308
potential, 67, 69–70
power vs., 65–66
and radioactive decay, 80–81
solar, 76
and stars, 334–335
wave, 72–73
and wave-particle duality, 222–226
and work, 65
Engines, 100–102
Entropy, 104–105, A28
Environment. *See also* Ecosystems
and acid rain, 480–481
defined, A28
and greenhouse effect, 481–483
indoor radon pollution, 305
and ozone layer, 476–479
physical and chemical, 469
and solid waste disposal, 474–475
Enzymes, 525–527, A28
Epidemics, 582–583
Erosion, 410–412, 463–464
Essential amino acid, A28
Ether, 150–151
Eubacteria, 499
Eucaryea, 499
Eukaryotes, 548, 629, A28
Europa (moon), 398
Evolution, 636
acceptance of, 614
animal, 629–630, A14–A16
biochemical evidence, 562, 616–617
chemical, 618–624
creationism vs., 637
debate over theories of, 614
defined, A28
fossil record as evidence, 615–616
gradualism hypothesis, 632
human, 633–636
plant, 630, A14–A16
punctuated equilibrium, 633
rate of, 630–633
role of Darwin, 624–628
vestigial organs as evidence, 617–618
Excited state, 201, 203, 204, A28
Exons, 579
Exothermic chemical reactions, 251, A28
Exotic species, 486
Experiments, 4–5, A28
Experimentalist, A28
Extinction, 513, 616, A28
Extrasolar planet, A28

Extremely low frequency (ELF) radiation,
see ELF radiation
Extrusive rocks, 456
Eyes, 163, 164, 340, A28

F
Fahrenheit scale, 88, A28
Falsifiability, 9, A28
Families, 496, A28
Faraday, Michael, 133–135
Fats, 531–533
Fat-soluble vitamin, A28
Fault(s), 413, A28
Federal Communications Commission, 159
Fermentation, 553–555, A29
Ferns, 506, A29
Ferromagnetism, 274, A29
Feynman, Richard, 228, 327, 328
Fields, 117, A29. *See also* Electrical fields;
Magnetic fields
Field researcher, A29
First law of motion, 45–46, 112
First law of thermodynamics, 78–81, A29
First trophic level, 77, A29
Fish, 510–511
Fission, nuclear, 305–307, A29
Flat universe, 377, A29
Fleming, Alexander, 505
Flight, 636
Florey, Howard, 505
Fluorescence, 164, 203, A29
FM, *see* Frequency modulation
FM radio transmission, 159–160
Food:
calculating calories, 79–80
dietary fads, 537–538
digestive system, A3–A4
minerals in, 534–536
phyla as, 513–514
proteins in, 527–528
vitamins, 536–537
Food chain, 470, A29
Food web, 470, A29
Foot-pounds (ft-lb), 64, 65, A29
Force. *See also* Gravity
defined, 45, A29
electromagnetism as, 135, 326–329, 374
electroweak force, 329, 371–374
and energy, 63
as exchange of gauge particles, 327–328
and freezings, 371–374
gravity as, 326, 327, 392
nature of, 185–187
and Newton's first law of motion, 45–46
and Newton's second law of motion,
46–47
and Newton's third law of motion,
47–48
strong force, 294, 326, 328–329,
371–374, A43
weak force, 326, 328–329, 374
and work, 63–65

Fossils, 615–616, A29
Fossil fuels:
and acid rain, 480–481
defined, A29
and greenhouse effect, 482
as nonrenewable resource, 81–82,
106
and second law of thermodynamics, 101,
106
Fossil record, 615–616, A29
Frames of reference:
defined, A29
different, 173
overview, 172
and relativity, 173–174, 183–184
and speed of light, 184
Franklin, Benjamin, 113–114
Freezing(s), 248, 371–375, A29
Freezing point, 88
Frequency:
defined, 142, A29
relationship to wavelength and velocity,
143–144
of sound waves, 146
as wave property, 142
Frequency modulation (FM), 159–160,
A29
Frogs, 486
Fungi:
defined, A29
as kingdom, 498
overview, 503–504
plants vs., 506
reproductive strategies, 504
Fusion, nuclear:
defined, A29
as energy source, 307–308
and Sun's energy, 341–342

G
g, A29
Galaxies:
defined, 359, A29
distance measurement, 363–364
dwarf, 360
elliptical, 360
formation of, 378
and Hubble's law, 362–364
Local Group, 366
Milky Way, 358–360
role of Edwin Hubble, 359
spiral, 359–360
types of, 359–360
Galen, 561
Galilei, Galileo, 38–42
Galileo spacecraft, 397–398
Galvani, Luigi, 120–123
Gametes, 559, A29
Gamma radiation, 298, A29
Gamma rays, 166–167, 321, A29–A30
Gamma Ray Observatory (GRO), A30
Garbage, 474–475

Gases:
 and changes of state, 248–249
 defined, A30
 as evidence of atomic theory, 195
 role of Bernoulli, 195
 as state of matter, 243
Gauge particles, 327, A30
GCM, see Global circulation models
Geller, Margaret, 366
General theory of relativity:
 defined, 174, A30
 and gravitational red shift, 188
 and nature of forces, 185–187
 and planetary orbits, 188
 predictions, 187–189
Generators, electric, 134–135
Genes. See also Genetics
 activating, 580–581
 defined, A30
 dominant vs. recessive, 568
 role of Mendel, 567
Gene therapy, 586, 600–602, A30
Genetics, 566–570, 586, A30
Genetic code, 575–585, A30
Genetic diseases, 599–606, A30
Genetic engineering, 591–594, A30
Genome, 583, A30
Genus, 496, A30
Geological time scale, 630–631,
 A13–A16
Geology, see Continental drift; Earth-
 quakes; Plate tectonics; Volcanoes
Gilbert, William, 117–118
Glaciers, 441, 447–448, 463, A30
Glass, 246, A30
Global circulation models (GCM), 454,
 483, A30
Global warming, 483–485, A30
Glucose, 529–530, 553–555, A30
Gluons, 328, A30
Glycogen, A30
Glycolysis, 553, A30
Gneiss, 460, A30
Gold, 197, 445
Golgi apparatus, 550, A30
GRACE (Gravity Recovery and Climate
 Experiment), 433
Gradualism, 632, A30
Granite, 421, 457, A30
Gravitational constant (G), 52–54, A17,
 A30
Gravitational escape, 395, A30
Gravitational potential energy, 69–70, A30
Gravitational pull, Earth's, 433
Gravitational red shift, 188. See also Red-
 shift
Gravitons, 327, A30
Gravity:
 acceleration vs., 185–187
 and atomic particles, 116
 and bones, 388
 defined, 52, A31
 as force, 326, 327, 392

gravitational constant, 52–54
Newton's law of universal gravitation,
 52–53
and potential energy, 69–70
role of Newton, 52–53
and unified field theories, 328–329
and weight, 54–56
Gravity Recovery and Climate Experiment
 (GRACE), 433
Great bombardment, 389, A31
Great Rift Valley, Africa, 424, 427
Greenhouse effect, 481–485, A31
GRO (Gamma Ray Observatory), A30
Ground state, 201, 203, A31
Groundwater, 441, A31
Gymnosperms, 506, 507, A31
Gyres, 441, A31

H
Hadrons, 321, 322, A31
Half-life, 301–302, A31
Halley, Edmond, 56
Halley's Comet, 56, 402
Harvard Smithsonian Center for Astrophysics, 378, 405
Harvey, William, 13–14
Heart:
 anatomy of, A3
 irregular beating of, 610
Heat (thermal energy). See also Heat transfer
 caloric theory, 71
 defined, 70, 88, A31
 direction of flow, 98–107
 early study, 70–71
 and kinetic energy, 70
 measuring, 88
 overview, 70, 88
 role of Benjamin Thompson, 71
 specific heat capacity, 91, A42
 temperature vs., 88
Heat conductors, 92–93, A31
Heat death, 105–106
Heat insulators, 93, A31
Heat transfer:
 by conduction, 91–93
 by convection, 93–95
 defined, 91, A31
 by radiation, 97
Heisenberg, Werner, 219–220
Heisenberg uncertainty principle:
 Divine Calculator vs., 57, 229
 and human brain, 229
 and Newton's laws of motion, 220–221
 overview, 219–220
 and probability, 221–222
Helium, 197, 207
Helium burning, 348, A31
Herbivores, 77, A31
Hertz (Hz), 142, A31
Hertzsprung, Ejnar, 345
Hertzsprung-Russell (H-R) diagram,
 345–349, A31

Heterotrophs, A31
Hierarchy, 495, A31
High-energy physics, 317, A31. See also
 Elementary particles
High-grade energy, 101, A31
High-level nuclear waste, A31
High-quality protein, 527, A31
High-temperature reservoirs, 101, A31
HIV (Human immunodeficiency virus),
 607–610, A32
Holes, 270, 271, 276, A31
Homeostasis, 471, A31
Homes, insulation, 93, 95
Hominids, 501, A31
Homo erectus, 635, A31
Homo habilus, 635, A31
Homo sapiens, 501, 634–636, A31
Hooke, Robert, 542
Horsepower, 67, A31
Hot spots, 429–430, A32
H-R diagram, see Hertzsprung-Russell dia-
 gram
Hubble, Edwin, 359, 363–365, 369
Hubble's constant, 363–365, A17
Hubble's law, 363–365, A32
Hubble Space Telescope, 337, A32
Huchra, John, 366
Human beings:
 aging, 107, 181
 brain, 284, 323–324, A4–A5
 circulatory system, 13–14, A1, A3
 classification of, 501
 digestive system, A3–A4
 ears, 146–147, A4, A5
 effect of extreme acceleration, 43–44
 endocrine system, A5–A6
 evolution of, 633–636
 eyes, 163, 164, 340
 heart, A3
 limits of hearing, 146–147
 lymphatic system, A3
 nervous system, 127–129, A4–A5
 regulating temperature, 98
 reproductive system, A6–A7
 respiratory system, A1, A3
 skeleto-muscular system, A1
 and space exploration, 405–406
Human Genome Project, 583–585, A32
Human immunodeficiency virus, see HIV
Humidity, 450, A32
Hurricanes, 452, A32
Hutton, James, 461–462
Hybrids, 566–567, A32
Hydrocarbons, 257, 259, 479, A32
Hydrogen:
 in living organisms, 519
 role in formation of stars, 341
 as source of Sun's energy, 341–342
Hydrogenation, 532, A32
Hydrogen bomb, 310
Hydrogen bonds, 241, A32
Hydrogen burning, 342, A32
Hydrologic cycle, 440–448, 463, A32

Hydrophilic, 546, A32
Hydrophobic, 546, A32
Hypotheses, 8, A32

I
Ice ages, 445–446, A32
Ice caps, 441, A32
Ice streams, 463
Igneous rocks, 456, A32
Ignition, automobile, 127
Immune system, 581–583, A32
Induction, electromagnetic, 133, A27
Inert gases, 234
Inertia, 46, A32
Inertial Guidance System, 52
Inflation, 373–374, A32
Inflationary theories, 373–374, A32
Information technology, 281–282, 353
Infrared Astronomical Satellite (IRAS), A32
Infrared energy, 97, A32
Infrared radiation, 162–163, A32
Insects, 509–510
Insulation:
    animal, 95–97
    home, 93, 95
Insulators, electrical, 270, A32
Integrated circuits, 280, A32
Interference, 148–149, A32
Interglacial period, A33
Intergovernmental Panel on Climate
    Change (IPCC), 484
Internal magnets, 119–120
Introns, 579
Intrusive rocks, 456–457, A33
Inversely proportional, A33
Invertebrates, 509–510, A33
In vitro gene therapy, A32
In vivo gene therapy, A32
Io (moon), 398
Ions, 198, 235–236, A33
Ionic bonds, 235–236, A33
Ionization, 300, A33
Ionizing radiation, 300
IPCC (Intergovernmental Panel on Cli-
    mate Change), 484
IRAS (Infrared Astronomical Satellite), A32
Islands, as ecosystems, 473
Isolated systems, 78–79, 105, A33
Isomers, 258, A33
Isotopes:
    carbon-14, 302–303
    chart, 292
    complete set, 292–293
    defined, 292, A33
    half-life, 301–302
    and radioactivity, 299

J
Jet stream, 450, A33
Joules, 64, 65, A33
Joule, James Prescott, 64, 72, 79

Jovian planets, 384–385, 387, A33
Junk DNA, 580
Jupiter (planet):
    characteristics of, 385, A17
    defined, 384–385
    formation of, 387
    moons, 398–399
    study of, 397–398

K
Kelvin, Lord, 80–81
Kelvin scale, 88
Kepler, Johannes, 36–37
Kepler satellite, 405
Kilowatts, 66, A33
Kinetic energy. See also Heat; Wave energy
    calculating, 68–69
    defined, 67, A33
    examples of, 68
    and heat, 70
    overview, 67–69
    and waves, 72–73
Kingdoms:
    animals, 498
    defined, 497, A33
    fungi, 498
    monera, 497, 498
    plants, 498
    protista, 498
    reconsideration of, 499
Krebs cycle, 555, A33
Kuiper Belt, 402, A33

L
Lake Victoria, Africa, 472–473
Landfills, 474–475
Laplace, Pierre Simon, 57, 346, 385
Large Magellanic Cloud, 351
Lasers, 207–209, A33
Lava, A33
Laws of motion, see Newton's laws of
    motion
Laws of nature, 9, A33
Laws of thermodynamics:
    first, 78–81
    second, 98–107
Law of conservation of linear momentum,
    A33
Law of unintended consequences,
    472–473, A33
Law of universal gravitation, see Newton's
    law of universal gravitation
Lawrence, Ernest O., 319
Leakey, Richard, 427
Leavitt, Henrietta Swan, 345
Length contraction, 181–182, A33
Leptons, 321–322, 325, A33
Library analogy, 315–317
Lichen, 504, A33
Life, beginnings of, 628–630
Life cycle costing, 260

Life force, 120–122
Light:
    calculating wave frequency, 152
    defined, A33
    gravitational bending, 187–188
    and relativity, 175, 177–180
    speed of, 151, 175, 183
    visible, 151–152, 163, 340–341
Light bulbs, 66
Light clocks, 177–180
Lightning rods, 114, 126
Light-years, 344, A17, A33
Limestone, 458, A34
Linear accelerators, 321, A34
Linear momentum, 49–50, A34
Linnaean classification, 495–498,
    501–502, A34
Linnaeus, Carolus, 495–496
Lipids, 531–534, A34
Liquids, 244, 248–249, A34
Liquid crystals, 247–248, A34
Living organisms:
    characteristics of, 492–494
    classifying, 495–498
    defining, 492
    and Earth's trophic levels, 76–78
    role of Darwin, 624–628
    studying, 490–492
    water in, 441
Llamas, 513
Load, 81, 126, A34
Local Group galaxies, 366
Lockyer, Joseph Norman, 207
Longitudinal waves, 144–145, A34. See
    also Compressional waves
Lorentz factor, 180, 181, 184, A34
Low-quality protein, 527, A34
Low-temperature reservoirs, 101, A34
Lucy, 634, A34
Luminosity, A34
Lymphatic system, A3, A34
Lysosome, 550, A34

M
MacArthur, Robert, 473
MacAyeal, Douglas, 454
Magma, 413, 424, A34
Magnets:
    defined, 117, A34
    internal, 119–120
    in nature, 120
    poles of, 117–119
Magnetic fields, 118–119, 133–134, 274,
    417, A34
Magnetic field reversals, 417
Magnetic force, 117, A34
Magnetic monopoles, 120, 132, 136,
    A34
Magnetic navigation, 119–120
Magnetic potential energy, 70, A34
Magnetic resonance imaging (MRI),
    132–133

Magnetism:
  connections with electricity, 129–133
  defined, A34
  electrical effects from, 133–136
  historical background, 117–118
  overview, 117–120
Main-sequence stars, 345, 347, 348, A34
Mammals, 501, 512–513, A34
Mammoths, 303
Manhattan Project, 310
Manned space exploration, 405–406
Mantle, Earth's, 391–392, A34
Mantle convection, 421–422, A34
Marble, 460–461, A34
Mars (planet):
  characteristics of, 385, A17
  defined, 384
  exploring, 396
  formation of, 386–387, 394
  possibility of life on, 623–624
Mass:
  defined, 46, A34
  distribution in solar system, 384–385
  and energy, 73, 184–185, 290–291
  and Newton's second law, 46–47
  of planets and moons, A17
  relativity of, 183–184
Mass extinctions, 631–633, A34
Mass number, 292, A34
Materials:
  composite, 268–269
  compressive strength, 266–267
  conductors, 269–270
  electrical properties, 269–273
  insulators, 93, 95–97, 270
  magnetic properties, 273–274
  overview, 264–265
  radioactive properties, 300–301
  semiconductors, 270–271
  shear strength, 266, 267
  strengths of, 266–269
  superconductors, 271–272
  tensile strength, 266, 267
  thermal conductivity, 92–93
  types of strength, 266–267
Mathematics, 6–8
Matter. See also Antimatter
  building blocks, 317
  dark, 376–377, A26
  recycling, in ecosystems, 470
  states of, see States of matter
Maxwell, James Clerk, 135–136,
  149–150
Maxwell's equations, 136, 173–175,
  319–320, A35
McPhee, John, 462
Mechanics, 37, A35
Medicine. See also Drugs
  clinical trials, 604
  resistance to antibiotics, 610–611
  role of radioactive materials, 300–301
  use of particle accelerators, 321
  viral epidemics, 582–583

Meiosis, 559–561, 575, A35
Meltdown, 307, A35
Melting, 248, A35
Mendel, Gregor, 566–570
Mendeleev, Dimitri, 12–13, 196, 210
Mercury (planet):
  characteristics of, 385, A17
  defined, 384
  formation of, 386–387, 394
Mesozoic Era, 630–632, A35
Messenger RNA (mRNA), 576, A35
Metabolism, 551–556, A35
Metals:
  chemical bonds, 236–238
  defined, A35
  thermal conductivity, 92–93
Metallic bonds, 236–238, A35
Metamorphic rock, 460–461, A35
Meteors, 389, 403, A35
Meteorites, 403, A35
Meteoroids, 403
Meteor showers, 403, A35
Michelson, Albert A., 151
Microchips, 274–284, A35
Microscopes, 196, 543–545
Microwaves, 160–162, 369–370, A35
Microwave ovens, 161–162
Mid-Atlantic Ridge, 417, 424, A35
Milankovitch, Milutin, 446–448
Milankovitch cycles, 446–448, A35
Milky Way galaxy, 358–360, A35
Miller, Stanley, 618
Miller-Urey experiment, 618, A35
Minerals, 534–536, A35
Mitochondria, 549, 550, A35
Mitosis, 557–559, 575, A35
Molecular genetics, 570–575, A35
Molecules:
  alkanes, 257–258
  atoms in, 194
  as building blocks, 519
  Dalton's hypothesis, 193–194
  defined, 198, A35
  in drugs, 528–529, 608–610
  in living organisms, 503, 505
  organic, 518–521
  polar, 240–241
  role of enzymes, 525–527
  and van der Waals force, 241–242
Momentum, 49–52
  angular, 50–52
  linear, 49–50
Monera, 497, 498, A35
Monosaccharides, 529, A35
Monsoons, A35
Moon(s):
  of Earth, 55–56, 384, 392–394, A17,
    A36
  planetary, 383–385, 398–399
Morley, Edward W., 151
Morowitz, Harold, 513
Moths, use of sound by, 147
Motion, see Newton's laws of motion

Motors, electric, 131–132
Mountains. See also volcanoes
  longevity of, 410–412
  volume lost to erosion, 410–412
Mount St. Helens, Washington state, 413,
  429
Mount Wilson Observatory, California,
  359
MRI, see Magnetic resonance imaging
mRNA, see Messenger RNA
Mudstone, 457–458, A36
Müller, Karl Alex, 272
Multicellular organisms, 503
Muons, 310
Music, 145–147
Mutations, 580, 628, A36

N

Nanotechnology, 213, A36
National Academy of Sciences, 358, A36
National Institutes of Health, A36
National Science Foundation, 23, A36
Natural selection, 624–627, A36
Navigation, magnetic, 119–120
Neanderthal Man, 635–636, A36
Nebulae, 346–347, 358–359, 385–388,
  A36
Nebular hypothesis, 346–347, 385–388,
  A36
Negative charge, 113–115, A36
Neptune (planet):
  characteristics of, 385, A17
  defined, 384–385
  formation of, 387
  study of, 401
Nerve cells, 127–129, 284
Nervous system, 127–129, A4–A5, A36
Neurotransmitters, 129, A36
Neutrinos, 297–298, 341–343, A36
Neutrons:
  and beta decay, 297–298
  defined, 198, A36
  and isotopes, 292
  in nucleus, 291
  variations in number, 292
Neutron stars, 351–352, A36
Newton, Sir Isaac:
  and gravity, 52–53
  laws of motion, 45–48
  overview, 45
  portrait of, 45
Newton-meters (N-m), 64
Newton (N), 47, A36
Newton's law of universal gravitation,
  52–53, A36
Newton's laws of motion:
  defined, A36
  and Einstein's theories of relativity,
    173–175
  first law, 45–46, 112
  Maxwell's equations vs., 173–175
  overview, 45, 48–49

and relativity, 173–175
second law, 46–47
significance of, 48–49
third law, 47–48
and uncertainty principle, 220–221
Night sky, 30–31, 34–35
Nitrogen, in living organisms, 519
Nitrogen oxides, 479
Noble gases, 234, A36
Nonrenewable energy, 101, A36
Nonrenewable resources, 81–82, A36
Northern Lights, 119, 339, 340
N-type semiconductor, 275, A36
Nuclear fission, 305–307, A29
Nuclear fusion:
    defined, A29
    as energy source, 307–308
    and Sun's energy, 341–342
Nuclear radiation, *see* Radiation
Nuclear reactors, 306–307, 311, A37
Nuclear tracers, 300–301
Nuclear waste, 311
Nuclear weapons, 309–310
Nucleic acids, 571, A37. *See also* Deoxy-
    ribonucleic acid
Nucleotides, 571–572, A37
Nucleus:
    atomic, 199–199
    cellular, 547–549
    and decay chain, 303–305
    defined, 114, 198, 199, A37
    and electrons, 289–290
    energy from, 290, 305–310
    exotic elementary particles in, 318
    half-life, 301–302
    neutrons in, 291
    in nuclear fission process, 305–307
    in nuclear fusion process, 307–308
    protons in, 291
    role in magnetism, 132–133
    role of Rutherford, 198–199, 291
    and strong force, 294
Nylon, 248

O

Observation:
    cholera example, 32–33
    defined, A37
    experimentation vs., 5
    scientific importance of, 32–33
    in scientific method, 4–5, 112
Observatories:
    earth-based, 335, 336
    orbiting, 336–338
Occam's razor, 33–34
Oceans:
    chemical cycles of, 443–444
    and continental drift, 416–417
    currents in, 441–442
    and global circulation models, 454, 484
    gold in, 445
    saltiness of, 443–444

    as site of life's origin, 620
    water in, 440–441
Ocean ridges, 416–417
Ocean rises, 417
Octane, 258
Oersted, Hans Christian, 130
OGLE (Optical Gravitational Lensing
    Equipment), 405
Ohms, 125, A37
Oil shale, 82, A37
Olestra, 533
Omnivores, 77, A37
Oort cloud, 402, A37
Open ecosystems, A37
Open systems, 78, A37
Open universe, 377, A37
Optical fibers, 353
Optical Gravitational Lensing Equipment
    (OGLE), 405
Optical microscopes, 544, A37
Orders, 496, A37
Organs, pipe, 145–147
Organelles, 549, 550, A37
Organic chemistry, defined, 239, A37
Organic molecules:
    carbohydrates, 529–530
    characteristics of, 518–520
    chemical notation for, 520–521
    defined, A37
    lipids, 531–534
    proteins, 521–530
    role of Friedrich Wohler, 521
Osmosis, A37
Outgassing, 395, A37
Ovens, microwave, 161–162
Oxidation, 251–253, A37
Oxides, 272, A37
Oxygen, 193, 519
Ozone, 476, A37
Ozone hole, 477–479, A37
Ozone layer:
    decline in concentration of, 477–478
    defined, 476, A37
    discovery of "hole" in, 477–478
    threats to, 479

P

Paleomagnetism, 417, A37
Paleozoic Era, 630–631, A37
Pangea, A37
Parallel circuits, 129, A37
Parsecs, 344, A37
Particles:
    elementary, *see* Elementary particles
    waves vs., 222–226
Particle accelerators, 319–321, 330, A37
Patterns, identifying, 5–6
Pauli exclusion principle, 211, A37
PCR, *see* Polymerase Chain Reaction
Peak load, A38
Peer review, 25, A38
Penicillin, 505, 610, A38

Penicillium, A38
Penzias, Arno, 369–370
Peppered moth, 626, 627
Peptide bonds, 522, A38
Periodic table of the elements, 12–13,
    196, 210–212, A38
Perrin, Jean Baptiste, 195
Perspective, *see* Frames of reference
Pesticides, 606–607
PET, *see* Positron emission tomography
Petroleum, 101, 258–259, A38
Philosopher's stone, 297
Phosphate groups, 551, A38
Phospholipids, 531, 533–534, A38
Photoelectric device, 217
Photoelectric effect, 225, A38
Photons, 202–203, 205, 335, 340, A38
Photosphere, solar, 339, A38
Photosynthesis, 505, 552, A38
Photovoltaic cells, 76, 277–278, A38
Phyla, 496, 508, 509, 513–514, A38
Pipe organs, 145–147
Pitch, musical, 146
Pixels, 282–283
Planck's constant *(h)*, 220, A17, A38
Planets:
    ancient observers, 30–31
    differentiation process, 391
    discovery of new systems, 403–404
    evolution of atmospheres, 395–396
    extrasolar, 284, 403–405
    formation of, 386–387, 389–394
    great bombardment, 389
    Jovian, 384–385, 387
    moons of, 383–385, 398–399
    night sky, 30–31, 34–35
    outer, 384–385, 387, 396–398
    terrestrial, 384, 386–387
Planetary orbits, 188, 383–384
Planetesimals, 386, 389, A38
Plants:
    angiosperms, 506–508
    classifying, 505
    defined, A38
    and Earth's trophic levels, 76–78
    evolution, 630, A14–A16
    ferns, 506
    fungi vs., 506
    gymnosperms, 506, 507
    as kingdom, 498
    measuring growth, 494
    primitive, 506
    vascular, 506–508
Plasma, 243–244, A38
Plasmids, 592–593, A38
Plastics, 246–247, A38
Plates, 420, 424–427, A38. *See also* Plate
    tectonics
Plate tectonics:
    acceptance of theory, 423
    boundaries between plates, 424–427
    competing model, 422–423
    convergent boundaries, 424–426, 429

Plate tectonics: *continued*
defined, A38
divergent boundaries, 424, 429
and earthquakes, 430
initial reaction to, 423
overview, 420–421
transform boundaries, 426–427
and volcanoes, 428–430
Plato, 4
Plutonium, 310
Pluto (planet):
characteristics of, 385, A17
defined, 385, A38
discovery of, 400
moon, 399
Polarization, 240–241, A38–A39
Polar molecules, 240–241, A38
Poles, 117–118, 132, A39. *See also* Dipole field
Pollution:
of air, 479–481
from radon, 305
of water, 32–33
Polymers:
defined, A39
as form of solid state, 246–247
overview, 255
uses for, 256
Polymerase Chain Reaction (PCR), 595–597, A39
Polymerization, 256–257, A39
Polypeptides, 522, A39
Polysaccharides, 529, A39
Polyunsaturated lipids, 532, A39
Positive charge, 113–115, A39
Positrons, 321–323, A39
Positron emission tomography (PET), 323–324
Potassium-argon dating, 303
Potential energy:
calculating, 69–70
defined, 67, A39
examples of, 69–71
overview, 69–70
Power:
calculating amount used, 126
defined, 65, A39
energy vs., 65–66
Powers of ten, A11–A12
Power stroke, 100, 101, A39
Precession, 446, A39
Precipitation, 253, A39
Predictions, 8–9, 57, A39
Pressure, A39
Pressure waves, 145
Prevailing westerlies, 451, A39
Primary structure, 523, 524, A39
Primates, 501, A39
Primordial soup, 619, A39
Principle of relativity, *see* Relativity
Probabilities, 221–222, A39
Probes, ocean-monitoring, 213
Producers, A39

Prokaryotes, 548, 629, A39
Protease inhibitors, 609, A39
Proteins:
amino acids, 522–523
defined, 523, A39
and diet, 527–528
as enzymes, 525–527
estimating number of, 525
high-quality vs. low-quality, 527–528
primary structure, 523, 524
quaternary structure, 525
role in evolution, 618–620
secondary structure, 523–524
structure of, 523–525
synthesis of, 576–580
tertiary structure, 524
Proterozoic Era, 630, 631, A39
Prothrombin, 259
Protista, 498, A39
Protons:
and atomic number, 292
defined, 198, A39–A40
and gamma radiation, 298
mass, A17
role in nucleus, 291, 292
Pseudoscience, 15–17, A40
Ptolemy, Claudius, 35, 36
P-type semiconductor, 275, 280, A37
Publications, 25, A40
Pulsars, 351, 403–404, A40
Pumice, 456, A40
Pumping, 209, A40
Punctuated equilibrium, 633, A40
Purebred, 566, A40
Purebred plants, 566–567
Pyruvic acid, 554–555, A40

Q
Quantized, 217, A40
Quantum dots, 228
Quantum leaps, 203, 205, A40
Quantum mechanics:
defined, A40
overview, 217–218
strangeness of, 228–229
and wave-particle duality, 222–226
Quarks, 324–326, 329, A40
Quartzite, 460, A40
Quasars, 360, A40
Quaternary structure, 525, A40

R
Radar, Doppler, 455
Radiation. *See also* Electromagnetic waves; Radioactivity
cosmic microwave background, 369–370
defined, 97, A40
extremely low frequency, 167
health effects of, 299–300
heat transfer by, 97
ionizing, 300

Radioactive decay, 303–305, A40. *See also* Radioactivity
alpha decay, 296–297, 299
beta decay, 297–299
types of, 295–298
Radioactive tracers, 300–301
Radioactivity, A40
alpha decay, 296–297, 299
beta decay, 297–299
defined, 294, A40
discovery of, 195
as evidence of atomic theory, 195
gamma radiation, 298
half-life, 301–302
and mass as energy, 73
overview, 294–295
role of Marie Curie, 295
role of Rutherford, 296
Radiometric dating:
carbon-14 method, 302–303
defined, A40
of oceanic rocks, 419
potassium-argon methods, 303
uses for, 302–303
Radio telescopes, 335, 337
Radio waves:
AM vs. FM transmission, 159–160
defined, A40
as part of electromagnetic spectrum, 158–159
Radon, 305, A40
R&D, *see* Research and development
Reactions, chemical, 249–250
Receptors, 546–547, 561, A40
Recessive genes, 568, A40
Recycling:
in ecosystems, 470
landfills vs., 474–476
technology of, 475–476
Red giants, 345, 348, 349, A40
Redshift, 362, A41
Redshifted, 154, A41
Reduction:
as chemical reaction, 252–253
defined, A41
oxidation vs., 251–253
Reductionism, 316, A41
Reference frames, *see* Frames of reference
Reflecting telescopes, 335
Reflection, 156, A41
Refraction, 155, A41
Relativity:
defined, A41
and distance, 181–183
and frames of reference, 173–174, 183–184
and length contraction, 181–183
and mass, 183–184
origin of Einstein's work, 173–175
significance of, 180–181
and space travel, 181
special vs. general theories, 174
and speed of light, 175, 183–184

and time dilation, 176–181
  underlying principle, 174
  understanding, 188–189
Reproducible experiments, 26, A41
Reproductive cloning, A41
Reproductive system, A6–A7
Reptiles, 511–512, A41
Research and development (R&D), 22,
  136, A41
Reservoirs:
  energy, 101
  water, 439–443, A41
Residence time, 444, A41
Resistance, electrical, *see* Electrical resistance
Resistant bacteria, 610–611
Respiration, 553, 555–556, 561, 605, A41
Respiratory system, A1, A3, A41
Restriction enzymes, 591, 592, A41
Ribonucleic acid (RNA), 572–573,
  575–579, 620–621, A41
Ribose, A41
Ribosomes, 550, A41
Richter, Charles, 414
Richter scale, 414
Ring of Fire, 429
RNA, *see* Ribonucleic acid
Rocks:
  basalt, 456
  extrusive, 456
  gneiss, 460
  granite, 457
  igneous, 457
  intrusive, 456–457
  limestone, 458
  marble, 460–461
  metamorphic, 460–461
  quartzite, 460
  sandstone, 457
  schist, 460
  sedimentary, 457–459
  shale, 457–458
  slate, 460
  volcanic, 456
Rock cycle, 455–462, A41
Rock formations, A41
Rods, 163, A41
Roentgen Satellite (ROSAT), A41
Rumford, Count, *see* Thompson, Benjamin
Russell, Henry N., 345
Rutherford, Ernest, 198–199, 291, 296
Rutherford model, 198–200

S

Sahelanthropus tchadensis, 633
Salt water, 443–444
San Andreas Fault, 426
Sandstone, 457, A41
Saturated lipids, 531, 532, A41
Saturn (planet):
  characteristics of, 385, A17
  defined, 384–385

formation of, 387
  moon, 399
Scanning tunneling microscope, 196
Scattering, 156, A41
Schist, 460, A41
Schleiden, Matthais, 542
Schopf, William, 621
Schwann, Theodor, 542
Science:
  branches of, 20
  divisions of, 18–20
  funding for, 23–24
  organization of, 18–25
  role of, 2–4
  why study, 3–4
Scientific journals, 25
Scientific meetings, 25
Scientific method:
  creativity in, 10
  defined, A41–A42
  hypotheses in, 8
  observation, 4–5, 112
  overview, 9–11
  predictions in, 8–9
  steps in, 4–11
  testing in, 8–9
  theories in, 8
Scientists, communication among, 24–25
Seafloor spreading, 417, 419–420, 422, 424
Search for Extraterrestrial Intelligence
  (SETI), 22–23
Searle, John, 285
Secondary structure, 523–524, A42
Second law of motion, 46–47
Second law of thermodynamics, 98–107,
  A42
Second trophic level, 77, A42
Security, border, 310
Sedimentary rocks, 457–459, A42
Seismic tomography, 432, A42
Seismic waves, 72, 431–432, A42
Seismology, 431–432, A42. *See also* Earthquakes
Semiconductors:
  defined, A42
  doped, 275
  as type of materials, 270–271
Series circuits, 129, A42
SETI, *see* Search for Extraterrestrial Intelligence
Shale, 457–458, A42
Shapley, Harlow, 358–359
Shear strength, 266, 267, A42
Shear waves, 431, A42
Shockley, William, 278
Siccar Point, Scotland, 461
SIDS (Sudden Infant Death Syndrome), 561
Silicon, doping, 275
Simberloff, Daniel, 473
Single bond, 239, A42
Single-celled organisms, 503, 548
SIRTF (Space Infrared Telescope Facility),
  337

Skeleto-muscular system, A1, A42
Slate, 460, A42
Slinky, 75
Smog, 479, A42
Snow, John, 32–33
Solar energy, 76, 81, 277–278
Solar neutrinos, 341, 342–343
Solar system. *See also* Planets; Stars; Sun
  defined, 383, A42
  distribution of mass, 384–385
  features of, 382–385
  nebular hypothesis of formation,
    385–388
  planetary orbits, 188, 383–384
Solar wind, 339, 340, A42
Solids:
  and changes of state, 248
  crystals, 244–246
  defined, A42
  glass, 246
  polymers, 246–247
  as state of matter, 244–247
  types of, 244–247
Solid waste, 474–476
Solution reactions, 253, A42
Somatic stem cells, 599, A42
Sound waves:
  defined, A42
  Doppler effect, 152–154
  as form of energy, 72
  limits of human hearing, 146–147
  musical, 145–147
  pipe organ calculations, 145–147
  use by animals, 147–148
Space Infrared Telescope Facility (SIRTF),
  337
Spallanzani, Lazzaro, 147
Special theory of relativity, 174, 176–185,
  A42
Species, 495, 496, 499–501, A42
Specific heat capacity, 91, A42
Spectroscopy, 206–207, A42
Spectrum, 205, A42. *See also* Electromagnetic spectrum
Speed, 38–39, A42
Speed of light (c), 151, 175, 183, 184,
  A17, A42
Spindle fibers, 558, A42
Spiral galaxies, 359–360
Spreading, 417, 419–420, 422, 424, A42
Standard candle, 345
Standard model, 329, A43
Staphylococcus, A43
Stapp, John, 44
Starches, 529–530, A43
Stars:
  ancient observers, 30–31
  apparent magnitude, 343
  birth of, 346–347
  brown dwarfs, 347
  Cepheid variables, 345, 359
  and chemical elements, 353
  death of, 347–351

Stars: *continued*
defined, 334, A43
and Dyson sphere hypothesis, 343
as energy emitters, 334–335
formation of, 341
and Hertzsprung-Russell diagram, 345–346
life cycle, 349–351
main-sequence, 345, 349
measuring distances, 344–345
neutron, 351–352
night sky, 30–31, 34–35
red giants, 345, 348, 349
Sun as, 338–340
variety of, 343–345
white dwarfs, 345, 348, 349
States of matter:
changes of, 248
defined, A43
gases, 243
liquids, 244
overview, 242–243
plasma, 243–244
solids, 244–247
Static electricity, 112–117, A43
Steady-state universe, 369, A43
Steam engines, 67
Stem cells, 25, 598–599
embryonic, 598
somatic, 599
Stonehenge:
as astronomical structure, 31–32
conjecture about, 31–34
Strength, 266–269, A43
Strong force, 326
defined, A43
and freezings, 371–374
overview, 294
and unified field theories, 328–329
Subatomic particles, *see* Elementary particles
Subduction zones, 425, 429, A43
Sublimation, 248, A43
Sudden Infant Death Syndrome (SIDS), 561
Sugars, 529, A43
Sun:
calculating solar radiation, 76
chromosphere, 339
convection zone, 338
corona, 339
death of, 349
as energy source, 76–78, 339–340
energy source of, 341–342
and force of gravity, 347–348
and human eye, 340
life cycle, 346–349
mass, A17
photosphere, 339
radius, A17
as star, 338–340
stellar core, 338
structure of, 338–340
and ultraviolet radiation, 164

Superclusters, 366–367, A43
Superconducting supercollider, 330
Superconductivity, 271–272, A43
Supernovas, 350, 353, A43
Swinburne, Algernon, 105–106
Synchrotron, 319, A43
Systems:
defined, 78, A43
increase in disorder, 102–105
isolated, 105

T
Taste receptors, 561
Taxonomy, 495, A43
Technology, 22, A43
Tectonic plates, 420, 424–427, A43. *See also* Plate tectonics
Tel-Aviv University, 378
Telescopes:
defined, 335, A43
earth-based, 335–337
Galileo's, 38
Hubble Space Telescope, 337
Mount Wilson Observatory, 359
orbiting, 336–338
radio, 335, 337
reflecting, 335
schematic diagrams, 336
Temperature:
atmospheric, 449
and changes of state, 248
conversions, 89
defined, 88, A43
and global warming, 483–485
and greenhouse effect, 481–483
heat vs., 88
measuring, 88, 90–91
regulating, 97–98
Temperature scale, A43
Tensile strength, 266, 267, A43
Terminal electron transport, A43
Terminal velocity, A43
Terranes, 427, A43
Terrestrial planets, 384, 386–387, A43
Tertiary structure, 524, A43
Testing (in scientific method), 8–9
Thales (Greek philosopher), 316
Theories, 8, A43–A44
Theories of everything (TOEs), 329, A43
Theorist, A43
Theory of relativity, 174–189, A44
Therapeutic cloning, A44
Thermal conductivity, 92–93, A44
Thermal energy, 70, A44. *See also* Heat
Thermodynamics:
defined, 78, A44
direction of heat flow, 98–99
first law, 78–81
second law, 98–107
Thermometer, 90–91
Thermostats, 130–131
Thinking machines, 285

Third law of motion, 47–48
Thompson, Benjamin, Count Rumford, 71–72
Thompson, William, Lord Kelvin, 80–81
Thomson, Joseph John, 198
Three Mile Island, Pennsylvania, 307
Tidal waves, 414
Tilman, David, 11–12
Time dilation, 176–181, A44
Titan (moon), 399
TOEs, *see* Theories of everything
Tombaugh, Clyde, 400
Tornadoes, 452, A44
Totipotent, 598, A44
Trace elements, A44
Trace gases, 476, A44
Trade winds, 452, A44
Transcription, 575–576, A44
Transfer RNA (tRNA), 576, A44
Transform plate boundaries, 426–427, A44
Transistors, 276, 278–279, A44
Transmission, 154–155, A44
Transverse waves, 144–145, A44
Trash, 474–476
Trees, 507
Triangulation, 345, A44
tRNA, *see* Transfer RNA
Trophic levels, 76–78, 470, A44
Tropical storms, 452, A44
Tsunamis, 414, A44
Turing, Alan, 285
Typhoons, 452, A44

U
Ultraviolet radiation, 163–164, A44
Uncertainty principle:
defined, A44
and human brain, 229
and Newton's laws of motion, 220–221
overview, 219–220
and probability, 221–222
Unified field theories, 328–329, 373, A44
Uniform motion, 45, A45
Unintended consequences, *see* Law of unintended consequences
U.S. Federal Communications Commission, 159
Units of measurement:
ampere, 125
coulomb, 116, 125
foot-pound, 64, 65
hertz, 142
horsepower, 67
joule, 64, 65
light-year, 344
newton-meter, 64
ohm, 125
overview, A8–A12
parsec, 344
volt, 125
watt, 66

Universal gravitation, *see* Newton's law of universal gravitation
Universe. *See also* Solar system
  building blocks, 316–317
  end of, 377–378
  evolution of, 371–375
  expanding, 365–366, 369, 371–375, 378
  and freezings, 371–375
  and inflation theory, 373–374
  as large-scale structure, 366–367
Unsaturated lipids, 532, A45
Upright walking, 427
Uranium, 303–305, 310
Uranus (planet):
  characteristics of, 385, A17
  defined, 384–385
  formation of, 387–388
Urban landfills, 474–475
Urea, 521
Urey, Harold, 618

V
Vacuole, 550, A45
Valence, 234, A45
Valence electrons, 234, 235, A45
Van der Waals forces, 241–242, A45
Van Helmont, Joannes Baptista, 494
Van Leeuwenhoek, Anton, 542
Variable number tandem repeat (VNTR) sequences, 594–595
Vascular plants, 506–508, A45
Vectors, 39, 586, A45
Velocity:
  calculating, of waves, 144
  defined, 38–39, 142, A45
  and falling object experiments, 40–43
  and relativity, 183
  rules for adding multiple velocities together, 183
  and wavelength/frequency, 143–144
  as wave property, 142
Venter, J. Craig, 585
Venus (planet):
  characteristics of, 385, A17
  defined, 384
  formation of, 386–387, 394
Vertebrates, 501, 510–513, A45
Vesicles, 547, 550, A45
Vestigial organs, 617–618, A45
Vicuna, 513
Viral epidemics, 582–583
Viruses, 581, A45. *See also* AIDS

Visible light, 151–152, 163, 340–341, A45
Vitamins, 536–537, A45
VNTR, *see* Variable number tandem repeat sequences
Volcanic rocks, 456, A45
Volcanoes, 413–414, 428–430, A45
Volta, Alessandro, 122, 123, 125, 196
Voltage, 125, 127, A45
Voyager spacecraft, 401

W
Wallace, Alfred Russell, 627
Warm blooded animals, 512, A45
Waste heat, 102, 105
Water:
  chemical cycles in oceans, 443–444
  circulation on Earth, 441–442, 454, 484
  in clouds, 441
  distribution on Earth, 441–442
  in groundwater, 441
  heat transfer by convection, 93–95
  in ice caps and glaciers, 441
  in lakes, 440–441
  in living things, 441
  in oceans, 440–441
  polarity of molecules, 240–241
  in reservoirs, 439–443
  in rivers, 440–441
  shortages of, 443
  in streams, 440–441
Water pollution, 32–33
Water-soluble vitamin, A45
Watts, 66, A45
Watt, James, 66, 67
Waves:
  calculating velocity of, 144
  defined, A45
  electromagnetic, 149–157
  electrons as, 226–227
  energy as, 222–226
  energy transfer by, 141–142
  interference, 148–149
  longitudinal, 144–145
  nature of, 141–149
  particles vs., 222–226
  pressure, 145
  properties of, 142–143
  sound, 145–147
  transverse, 144–145
Wave energy, 72–73, A45. *See also* Electromagnetic radiation; Seismic waves

Wavelength:
  defined, 142, A45
  and frequency/velocity, 143–144
  as wave property, 142
Wave mechanics, A45. *See also* Quantum mechanics
Wave-particle duality, 222–226
Weak force, 326, 328–329, 374. *See also* Electroweak force
Weapons, nuclear, 309–310
Weather:
  atmospheric variables, 449–451
  climate vs., 449, 453, 454
  common patterns and conditions, 452–453
  defined, A45
  Doppler radar as tool, 455
Weathering, A45
Wegener, Alfred, 415, 423
Weight:
  calculating, 54–56
  defined, A45
  relationship to gravity, 54–56
Whales, 148
White dwarfs, 345, 348, 349, A45
William of Occam, 33–34
Wilmut, Ian, 597
Wilson, Edward O., 473
Wilson, Robert W., 369–370
Wind, 451–452, A45
Wind energy, 76
Wind shear, 455, A46
Wohler, Friedrich, 521
Wolszczan, Alexander, 403–404
Work:
  defined, 63–64, A46
  and energy, 65
  and force, 63–65
W particle, 327, A45

X
X-rays, 164–166, A46. *See also* CAT scan
X-ray crystallography, 196

Y
Young-Earth creationism, 637

Z
Z particle, 327, A46